2n[d]

Mr. Cheap's
Boston

Mark Waldstein

Editor
Tami Monahan Forman

Associate Editor
Andy Richardson

Editorial Assistant
Hilary Mead

ADAMS PUBLISHING
Holbrook, Massachusetts

Also in the Mr. Cheap's® Series:

Mr. Cheap's® *Atlanta*
Mr. Cheap's® *Chicago*
Mr. Cheap's® *New York*
Mr. Cheap's® *San Francisco*
Mr. Cheap's® *Seattle*

More cities are still being added—check the travel
section of your favorite bookstore!

ACKNOWLEDGMENTS

When the first edition of this book was published, I did not get a chance to express my gratitude to the man who made it all happen, my longtime friend and playwright *extraordinaire*, Brandon Toropov. And as much as I try, I can never acknowledge enough the help of my small but hardy (and detail-crazed) staff: Tami Monahan Forman, who keeps it all together; Andy Richardson, who now knows Boston better than any other transplant; and Hilary Mead, who has set a standard which interns for years to come can only try to match.

Thanks also to the many friends who offered suggestions of places for Mr. C to check out: John Becker and Mary Christin, Rick Dey, Andreae Downs, Mary Haller and Lynn Heinemann, Bob Katzen and Millie Alpert, Julie & Bruce Menin, Jim Murphy, Bob Perlstein, and Arthur and Andrea Waldstein.

Tami thanks: My dad, Tom Monahan, for a *very* full list of the best cheap eats in Quincy. My husband Preston makes this all possible for me and for that I'm very grateful. Also thanks to Abigail Myers and John Sweeney for help with research and writing and to Susan Beale for a never-ending supply of production wisdom.

Andy thanks: Mom and Dad and Robin and Michael, for both supporting and dealing with me and my wanderings these past several years. Also, thanks to Mark, for being one of relatively few employers who could view such erratic behavior as a job credential. And Tami, the Answer Woman.

Hilary thanks: Alexis, Isabel, Kate, Margaret, Rodney, and Susannah—dear Bostonians! Thanks also to friends further afield, yet always with me. Mark, Tami, and Andy: You revealed the ways of the Cheap with humor and patience. As ever, thanks and love especially to Mum, Dad, and Lindsey.

Published by Adams Media Corporation
260 Center Street, Holbrook, MA 02343

Mr. Cheap's® is a registered trademark of Adams Media Corporation

ISBN: 1-55850-556-3

Printed in Canada

D E F G H I J

Library of Congress Cataloging-in-Publication Data
  Waldstein, Mark.
    Mr. Cheap's Boston / Mark Waldstein ; editor, Tami Monahan Forman ; associate
editor, Andy Richardson ; editorial assistant, Hilary Mead. — 2nd ed.
      p.   cm.
  Includes index.
  ISBN: 1-55850-556-3 (pbk.)
  1. Boston (Mass.)—Guidebooks.   2. Shopping—Massachusetts—Boston—
Guidebooks.   3. Restaurants—Massachusetts—Boston—Guidebooks.   4. Outlet
Stores—Massachusetts—Boston—Guidebooks.
  I. Title.
  F73.18.W35   1995
  917.44'610443—dc20   95-41970
                                                                          CIP

This publication is designed to provide accurate and authoritative information with regard to the subject matter covered. It is sold with the understanding that the publisher is not engaged in rendering
legal, accounting, or other professional advice. If legal advice or other expert assistance is required,
the services of a qualified professional person should be sought.
          — From a *Declaration of Principles* jointly adopted by a Committee of the
          American Bar Association and a Committee of Publishers and Associations.

This book is available at quantity discounts for bulk purchases.
For information, call 1-800-872-5627 (in Massachusetts, 781-767-8100).

Visit our home page: www.adamsmedia.com

CONTENTS

A FEW EXTRA WORDS FROM
MR. CHEAP (NO CHARGE)

Plenty has happened in the three years since I first wrote *Mr. Cheap's Boston*. The book wound up on the bestseller lists in the *Globe* and the *Herald*, as I became a frequent guest on TV and radio shows all over town. *Mr. Cheap's New York* came next (with a rave notice in the *Times*), and was followed by books for other cities from coast to coast. Little did I know, when I started, that I was on a mission!

Meanwhile, in that same time, many low-priced (and thus, low profit margin) stores and restaurants in Boston left the scene. New ones came along to replace them. And, as I got more proficient at seeking out bargain spots with each book, I realized it was time to turn my sights back toward my home turf—the place where it all began.

The result is the vastly improved volume you hold in your hand. The second edition of *Mr. Cheap's Boston* details lots of newcomers and revisits old favorites. It takes you further out into the suburbs, for more bargain-hunting depth. Because the outlet craze has continued to boom, I've included a chapter devoted just to them. And there are all kinds of other refinements, especially in the appendix and index, which should make the book even more useful.

What has not changed, of course, is my definition of "cheap"—or people's love-hate reactions to the word. Y'see, low prices don't necessarily make these stores and restaurants *cheap*. Nor does it make anyone who uses this book a *cheapskate*. I think *thrifty* or *frugal* are better adjectives. A cheap person, in my mind, is someone who has plenty of money to burn, but refuses to touch it; a thrifty person will spend cash-on-hand for something of good value. Most of us fall into the latter category, don't we?

Now, for those of you who came in late, here's a quick recap (it costs less than the full saga) of my credentials. The whole idea for these books arose out of my personal experience, from years of living on the financial edge as a "starving artist." My background is in the theater; as most people know, actors don't make any money even with steady work. I learned to live cheaply out of necessity—and well, you know the rest.

There is, by now, a research technique behind these books, but "cheaping" is hardly an exact science. Prices change all the time. Stores come and go. Restaurants re-do their menus. So you may not find the exact same items that I found during my travels, but these examples will help you make comparisons and track down the source that's right for you.

A few words of caution. "You gets what you pays for," as the old saying goes, and that's generally true. With new merchandise in particular, prices are marked down for a reason. It may be that the item is simply a leftover from last year, and still perfectly good; in other cases, if the price is low, the quality may not be far behind. I have tried to point out, wherever I could, items that are cheap because they are less well made, or because they are irregular, damaged, or secondhand. Maybe you're handy with a hammer, or a needle and thread. Even junk can be worthwhile if you only need it to last for a short time—furniture for a dorm room, for example. Sometimes, the "truly cheap" is all you need.

I fully expect to hear from readers who insist I've left out their favorite diner, or some resale boutique they love. To these fellow bargain hunters, I always say, Mr. C can't be *everywhere*; but I encourage you to pass along the information, and I'll be happy to scout your suggestions out for our next edition. The address is:

Mr. Cheap
c/o Adams Media Corporation
260 Center Street
Holbrook, MA 02343

So, get ready to use the book—but be careful how you use the name! As you see, "cheap" can mean many things. And when you tell your friends that you paid only $45 for your designer outfit, nobody will be laughing. They'll just want to know how you did it.

On to the goodies!

Mark Waldstein
a.k.a. Mr. Cheap

SHOPPING

The hundreds of stores in this section are all places which will save you money in some way. They actually cover a broad spectrum of discount shopping, from the latest designer clothing to thrift shops, new furniture and used, major brands and second-rate imitations. Mr. Cheap wants to cover it all, giving his readers as many options as possible for saving cash.

Whenever possible, Mr. C points out *why* an item is marked down—whether it's discontinued, second-quality (imperfect), or just plain cheap stuff. Thus informed, it is up to you to decide which stores and merchandise are for you.

The prices quoted, again, are based upon items Mr. C found at the time of his research. You shouldn't expect to find the same items, at the same prices, when you shop; these prices are just examples which are similar to what you may find. Even as prices go up overall, you should still find the book completely useful in comparing one place against another.

Many stores which sell several kinds of merchandise have been cross-referenced for you, appearing in each appropriate chapter; but remember to consult "Discount Department Stores" and "Flea Markets and Emporia" for many of the same items which have their own chapters. Similarly, the "General Markets" portion of the "Food Shops" chapter gives you more places to look for individual kinds of foods.

Okay, enough talking—*Go to it!*

PREFACE:
GOING TO THE OUTLETS

New England is outlet mall heaven. Within an hour's drive from Boston, in all directions, are several malls and complexes featuring factory stores; if you're willing to drive a *couple* of hours, you'll find even more gold at the end of the rainbow.

But before we all jump into the car, a few words of advice from Mr. C. Shopping at these places can indeed save you money, but it does not always guarantee unbeatable bargains you would not be able to find anywhere else. Here are some important things to keep in mind:

- You won't clothe your entire family for $9.99.
- Not every item in these stores is sold at discount; many stores offer a mix of clearance *and* regular merchandise.
- Some outlet stores sell goods made specifically for them—close, but not identical, to similar goods found in full-price stores.
- It's helpful to go in *knowing* what you want, and how much it costs elsewhere, so you'll know a bargain when you see it.

Having gotten that off his chest, Mr. C certainly recommends that you visit the outlets. Careful shoppers will come away with some good deals, especially those who are willing to wait until late in the retail season. This makes perfect sense; after all, who *really* wants to think about winter coats in the height of summer?

These represent some of the better-known, more established outlets in the area. Along with vital address and phone info, Mr. C has included a sampling of some of the stores you'll find at each center. For full listings, call the individual mall; they'll be more than happy to send you a brochure.

NORTH OF BOSTON

Freeport Outlets
- Exits 17-21 off I-95, Freeport, ME; (207) 865-1212
- Two and one-half hours from Boston
  Bed & Bath—linens, housewares
  Calvin Klein—clothes
  Coach—leather goods, luggage
  Cole-Haan—shoes
  L.L. Bean Outlet Store—sportswear, sporting goods
  Olga/Warner's—lingerie

Patagonia—outdoor sportswear
Timberland—shoes
Villeroy & Boch—china, crystal

Kittery Outlets
- Rte. 1, Kittery, ME; (800) 746-7441
- One hour from Boston
  Over 120 outlets, including:
  Black & Decker—hardware
  Brooks Brothers—clothes, suits
  Crate & Barrel—housewares
  Dansk Factory Outlet—chinaware

Donna Karan—clothes
J. Crew—clothes
Joan & David—shoes
Maidenform—lingerie
Nine West—shoes
Oneida Silver—silver
OshKosh B'Gosh—kids' clothes
Polo/Ralph Lauren—clothes
Waterford/Wedgwood—china,
crystal

SOUTH OF BOSTON

Cape Cod Factory Outlet Mall
- One Factory Outlet Rd., Sagamore,
  MA; (508) 888-8417
- One hour from Boston
  Bass Outlet—shoes
  American Tourister—luggage
  Bugle Boy Factory Store—clothes
  Petite Sophisticate Outlet—
  women's clothes
  London Fog—outerwear

Howland Place Designer Outlet Mall
- 651 Orchard St., New Bedford,
  MA; (508) 999-4100
- 90 minutes from Boston
  Anne Klein Jewelry—jewelry
  Harvé Benard—clothes
  Jones New York—clothes
  Libbey Glass—glassware
  Moda—mens' clothes

Quality Factory Outlets
- 638 Quequechan St., Fall River,
  MA; (508) 677-4949

Wampanoag Mill Factory Outlet Center
- 420 Quequechan St., Fall River,
  MA; (508) 678-5242

WEST OF BOSTON

Worcester Common Fashion Outlets
- 100 Front St., Worcester, MA;
  (617) 798-2581
- One hour from Boston
  Barney's New York Outlet—clothes
  B B & Beyond—home furnishings
  B.U.M. Equipment—sportswear

North Hampton Factory Outlet Center
- Rte. 1, North Hampton, NH; (603)
  964-9050
- One hour and fifteen minutes from
  Boston
  American Tourister—luggage
  Bass—shoes
  Polly Flinders—childrens' clothes
  Timberland—shoes and sportswear
  Van Heusen—clothes

- One hour from Boston
  Carter's Childrenswear—
  childrens' clothes
  Corning/Revere—china, kitchen-
  ware
  Farberware—cookware
  Levi's—jeans, sportswear
  Saucony—athletic shoes

Tower Outlet Mill
- 657 Quarry St., Fall River, MA;
  (508) 674-4646
- One hour from Boston
  Champion-Hanes—sportswear
  Izod—clothes
  L'eggs/Hanes/Bali/Playtex—lingerie

VF Factory Outlet
- 375 Faunce Corner Rd., North
  Dartmouth, MA; (508) 998-3311
- 90 minutes from Boston
  Healthtex—childrens' clothes
  Jantzen—sportswear
  Lee—denim and casual clothes
  Vanity Fair—lingerie

Donna Karan—clothes
Guess?—clothes
London Fog—outerwear
Media Play—music, books, software
Milton's Clearance Outlet—
clothes
Saks Fifth Avenue Clearing-
house—department store

AUTOMOTIVE SUPPLIES

Alas, there's no real "factory-direct" source for things like motor oil and other basic supplies. The big retail chains are most likely your best shots, especially when the items you need turn up in their weekly or monthly sales. These places include **ADAP/Auto Palace** and **Lappen Discount Auto Parts**, along with the smaller local chains **Foreign Autopart** and **Gem Auto Parts**. Their newspaper ads will alert you to good sales.

For parts themselves, there is another road to take. When someone kindly snaps off your antenna, and your dealer says the replacements are $90 each—most dealers seem to use the same warehouse as the Pentagon—consider a *secondhand* part instead. There are junkyards (er, automotive recycling centers) all over the city, filled with perfectly good parts from hood ornaments to taillights, for all makes of cars. These can cost half, or even less, of the original retail prices. Why, a rebuilt engine, at far less than the cost of a new one, can even be the difference between keeping your current car and throwing it on the junk heap yourself.

Does this mean you have to get your hands dirty? Nope. These shops have done all the picking around for you, organizing their inventory just like any retail store. The best of the bunch (nearly all, these days) are even computerized; they can find out in a jiffy whether they have a particular part. Some shops are even linked to each other, and if the place you're asking doesn't have what you need, they can get it within a few days. A further convenience, no doubt because of zoning laws, is that many yards are clustered together. Good neighborhoods to roam include the area between Union Square, Somerville, and Inman Square, Cambridge; Allston, near the Mass. Pike and along Western Avenue; Massachusetts Avenue and Dorchester Avenue in Dorchester; and Everett Avenue in Chelsea. Here are a few of the bigger yards:

A-M Used Auto Parts
• 1149 Harrison Ave., Boston; (617) 442-4629

This South End shop has a large selection of every kind of part for late-model foreign and domestic cars, including engines, transmissions, radiators, and accessories. They also have access to stock from their second branch, located in Rowley. A-M specializes in Cadillac parts, of which Mr. C's readers may not need many; but they have plenty of supplies for other makes too. Open weekdays 8 A.M. to 5 P.M., Saturdays 8 A.M. to 3 P.M.

Borr's Auto Parts and Sales
• 300 Everett Ave., Chelsea; (617) 889-0091

A huge operation near Everett Stadium, Borr's will even let you wander around the yard and look at its collection of parts. And they have quite a lot. Nearby, **Emerald Auto Parts and Sales** at 177 Everett Ave., Chelsea, telephone (617) 884-6851, also has a large stock of both new and used parts. They'll do the installing, too.

Bucky's Auto Parts
- 330 Webster Ave., Cambridge; (617) 354-2255

Cambridge Auto Parts
- 290 River St., Cambridge; (617) 491-0111

These two yards cut a parts swath through Cambridge, from the river to Inman Square. Both are hooked up to computers, and thus to each other, for a very comprehensive selection of parts. They can tell you right away whether they have what you need, where it is, and how much it will cost. Open weekdays from 7 A.M. to 5 P.M., Saturdays from 7-2.

Some of the other yards in the same area include: **Columbia Auto Parts**, 305 Webster Ave., Cambridge, telephone (617) 547-1800; **Nissenbaum's Auto Parts**, 480 Columbia St., Somerville, (617) 776-0194; **J & A Auto Parts**, 517 Columbia St., Somerville, (617) 628-4691. J & A even offers a delivery service!

Ellis the Rim Man
- 1001 Commonwealth Ave., Brighton; (617) 782-4777

Nothing used here, but this is a particularly big store for accessories to adorn your chariot. Wheel covers, air conditioners, anti-theft devices, roof racks, wiper blades, radar detectors and more are all here, many sold at discount. Ellis also specializes in

---

MR. CHEAP'S PICK
Automotive Supplies

✔ **Auto Junkyards**—When your dealer says that new headlight will cost you $500, check out your local yard instead. They've probably got one for $50.

---

goodies for your jeep, van, or truck. Located near the Boston University campus, it's open from 8 A.M. to 6 P.M. weekdays and 8 A.M. to 5 P.M. Saturdays.

Watertown Used Auto Parts
- 183 Grove St., Watertown; (617) 923-1010

This huge warehouse just off Route 128 specializes in the hard-to-find. They have a tremendous amount of parts in stock, with easy access to late-model stuff. And if they don't have your part close at hand, they'll find it pronto—their locator service links them with 140 other businesses in the area. They also have some new items, particularly radiators, at good prices.

TIRES

Tires can be expensive, especially if you need to replace a whole set. They are a very important investment, of course, for your own safety. The best prices on new tires, from Mr. C's research, are at the large chains (no pun intended there); you'll have to shop around and see who's best for the size and grade of tire you want. Again, check the newspapers (usually in the sports section) for current sales.

Some of the likely places to try for good rates are:

Cambridge Tire Centers
- 290 Albany St., Cambridge; (617) 864-7575
- *And other suburban locations*

Dedham Wholesale Tires
- 5218 Washington St., West Roxbury; (617) 325-6600

Liner Tire
- 144 Boylston St., Brookline; (617) 232-4869

Merchants Tire Company
- 1299 Boylston St., Boston; (617) 267-9200
- *And other suburban locations*

National Tire Warehouse
- 201 Cambridge St., Allston; (617) 783-8212
- 21 Needham St., Newton; (617) 244-1313

- 1675 V.F.W. Pkwy., West Roxbury; (617) 469-2600
- *And other suburban locations*

Sullivan Tire
- 950 Commonwealth Ave., Boston; (617) 731-2200
- *And other suburban locations*

RETREADS

Another money-saver on tires, by the way, is *retreads*. This process puts a brand-new layer of grooves onto a worn-out tire. Many places keep retreads in stock, offering a fairly large selection of tires which cost about half the price of new; they can cost as little as $15 or $25 apiece. Of course, they won't take you as far; they are good for twenty thousand miles or so, about half the life expectancy of new economy-level tires. But, if you're short of cash at the moment, or plan to sell your car soon, this can be a good interim move.

Along with smaller selections at local gas stations, the major retread dealer in Boston is:

Dorchester Tire Service
- 1160 Dorchester Ave., Dorchester; (617) 436-0900

Very good service, friendly guys ("We kill you with kindness"), and tires mounted while-you-wait from their large stock. DTS retreads are guaranteed against defects for the life of the tire, a pledge you won't always find—even on *new* tires. Open weekdays from 7 A.M. to 5 P.M., Saturdays from 7-12 noon.

APPLIANCES

The Appliance Outlet
- 160 Cambridge St., Burlington; (617) 229-1112
- Hingham Plaza, 100 Derby St., Hingham; (617) 749-0033
- 881 Worcester Rd., Natick; (508) 655-8811

When major appliances get bumped around on the delivery truck, scratched, dented, or whatever, they go back to the manufacturer—which cannot legally sell them at full price anymore. So, they sell them off through places like this, at hundreds of dollars below the original price. In some cases, all that's been dented is the box. A note on the front of each appliance will point out exactly where the boo-boos are; you decide if you can live with them. All defects are cosmetic—these appliances work fine and carry the full manufacturer's warranty.

Thus, you may find a Tappan "Pro Design" gas range, normally $1,195, selling here for $920. A Maytag dishwasher, with retail price of $518, was recently seen for $399. And a combination microwave and convection oven, regularly $720, was $554. Merchandise "ranges" from high-end models to the less-expensive department store brands. Obviously, the stock is constantly changing. If you're looking for something specific, stop in often—or ask these nice folks to keep an eye out. All three are located next to Building 19 stores (ooh, a Cheapster's day on the town!). Open seven days.

The Appliance Store

- 1476 River St., Hyde Park; (617) 364-8348

Look carefully for this nondescript warehouse, or you'll miss it. Once inside, though, you'll be amazed at the number of reconditioned appliances on display—and at the prices too.

Mr. C found an Admiral side-by-side refrigerator/freezer, with an ice dispenser built into the door, selling for $559; it carried a one-year warranty, almost unheard-of in the secondhand biz. Most items here come with a 90-day store warranty, which is still about as good as you'll find at any such store.

A few appliances are "scratch & dents," not used, but perhaps scuffed a bit in transit; this can be a great way to save big. Other used machines noted were a Kenmore washer for $170; a Magic Chef electric range for just $130; and a Whirlpool trash compactor for the same price. These were all fairly recent and well-kept; you can also check out older models (some in that *lovely* avocado green) from $99 and up. All repair work is done on the premises. Delivery is available at an extra charge. The store is open from 8 A.M. to 5 P.M. daily, except Sundays.

Ashmont Discount Home Center

- 464 Quincy Ave., Braintree; (617) 848-7350
- 587 Centre St., Brockton; (508) 583-1710
- 4165 Washington St., Roslindale; (617) 327-2080
- 1202 Washington St., Stoughton; (617) 341-1710

Around since 1947, Ashmont carries everything from small appliances to hardware supplies to furniture and bedding. They are keen on beating

---

MR. CHEAP'S PICKS
Appliances

- ✔ **The Appliance Outlet**—A discontinued model, or maybe a scratch here or there, will save you hundreds off a major appliance.

- ✔ **Commonwealth Builders Supply**—Good selection of everything from razors to refrigerators, all at discount.

---

competitors' prices; if you bring in an ad for a particular item, they will match the price.

Meanwhile, their own prices are pretty good to begin with. On sale recently were a Whirlpool large-capacity washer, reduced from $430 to $390; a small Caloric gas range for $250; a Eureka upright vacuum cleaner, with a 9-amp motor, for $89.99; plus toasters, irons, fans, razors, and the like. Open seven days a week.

Black & Decker Service Center

- 12 Market St., Brighton; (617) 782-6264

Official Black & Decker service shops are also good places to look for bargain prices on factory-reconditioned appliances and power tools. It's hardly the grimy workshop you may expect; these pleasant stores have a separate sales area, and several aisles are filled with a full selection of current B & D machines from blenders to drills to lawn mowers. They're sold at 10% to 20% below retail prices, and they all carry the full 1-2 year manufacturer's warranty.

Among the items Mr. C found on these shelves were a coffee bean grinder for $15.99; Dustbusters for $17.99; and a five-speed mixer, with built-in timer, for $90. A ten-inch band saw had $15 knocked off the price just because it came in a "blemished carton." And a 19-inch, rear-bag electric lawn mower was marked down from $250 to $189. Open weekdays from 8 A.M. to 5 P.M.

Broadway Appliance
- 77 Dorchester St., South Boston; (617) 268-7080

Located in Perkins Square, where East meets West (Broadway, that is), Broadway Appliance sells new and used refrigerators, washers and dryers, stoves, etc. Most of the stock is used and has been fixed up on the premises—with a 90-day warranty. During that period they will repair your purchase for free, or replace it, if necessary.

There are at least three or four models of each kind of appliance; most items are only a year or two old, and they look quite good. A Frigidaire side-by-side refrigerator/freezer, with twenty cubic feet of space, which probably retailed for over $1,000 a couple of years ago, was seen here for $300. Other fridges were on sale for $250. Good deals. Open from 8 A.M. to 5 P.M., every day but Sunday.

Commonwealth Builders Supply
- 375 Boylston St., Brookline; (617) 731-1800

An old-fashioned neighborhood store that's hung on in the face of mega-super-chains. Everything here is sold at discount—from small appliances like toaster ovens and boom-boxes to the big-ticket "white goods"—refrigerators and washer-dryers. All items are brand new and fully warrantied.

A Black and Decker iron, normally $30, sells here for $19; a Braun "Flex" rechargeable razor, retailing for $164, is just $90. Save $40 on an Amana microwave oven; a Eureka vacuum cleaner lists for $159, but sells here for $99. Not to mention air conditioners and heaters, televisions, and much more in this large showroom. More recently, they've added European import lines like Asko and Miele; friendly, knowledgeable service, too. Open daily from 10 A.M. to 6 P.M., 'til 5 on Saturdays.

Mystic Appliance
- 135 Cambridge St., Charlestown; (617) 242-9679

This store specializes in reconditioned refrigerators, washers, dryers, and ranges, in all major brands, for as much as half their original cost. Taken from building renovations and trade-ins, Mystic inspects and repairs everything from top to bottom and turns out machines that look like new. Prices generally start in the neighborhood of $150, depending on the age of the machine. Some of these babies are only a year old! All carry a healthy 90-day warranty on parts and labor. Open weekdays from 9 A.M. to 6 P.M., Saturdays from 9-4.

Sozio Major Appliances
- 495 Concord Ave. (Rte. 2), Cambridge; (617) 547-2252
- 61 Squire Rd., Revere; (617) 284-4363
- 999 Worcester Rd. (Rte. 9), Wellesley; (617) 235-8010

Rotary rats in the Fresh Pond area have undoubtedly seen this store while speeding (or crawling) by; it's worth a stop on the commute home. Top-quality appliances by Frigidaire, GE, Maytag, and more are discounted from retail, and the prices just keep getting slashed: Most appliances were marked down from their normal store prices when Mr. C visited.

Mr. C saw a Frigidaire side-by-side fridge and freezer, with an ice maker in the door. Usually $1399 here, it was on sale for $1279. An 800-watt microwave by the same folks was just $189.95. And a washing machine by GE was $420, some $50 under its original Sozio tag. Bargain-hunters will appreciate bagging a Tappan electric range, with oven, for just $300.

Floor models are clearly marked as such, and discounted even more deeply. Everything in this store, out of the box or off the floor, carries the full manufacturers' warranties. In addition to appliances, Sozio also deals in dining room furniture; you can get a medium-sized oak table and four oak chairs for as little as $300. All branches are open seven days, except for Cambridge which is closed on Sundays. Hours vary.

Suburban Appliance Servicenter

- 271 Moody St., Waltham; (617) 893-6694

Don't let the small size of this storefront make you think that Suburban can't compete with the superstores; the rear area has a wonderful, miniwarehouse atmosphere of the sort Mr. C prefers. The selection may be smaller, but there are plenty of good deals on brand name products. A Braun "Multipractic" food processor with a list price of $103.95, for example, was recently seen here for a mere $34.88—including a full one-year manufacturer's warranty. All manner of small appliances are represented here, from microwaves to can openers, in such reliable name brands as Norelco, KitchenAid, and Interplak. No large appliances, though.

As the store name implies, Suburban is also big on repair work. Better still, they sell the accessories that most department stores don't—like clean air filters and unusual-size vacuum cleaner bags. The people working here sure know their business, if they are somewhat lacking in social graces. It's one of those long-time, working-class, neighborhood joints. Long may they reign. Open weekdays from 9 A.M. to 6 P.M., and Saturdays from 9 A.M. to 1 P.M.

Trotman Office Machine Service

- 537 Shawmut Ave., Boston; (617) 424-7143

This shop sells and services fax machines, copiers, computers, calculators, and typewriters. More importantly to devoted Cheapsters, Trotman also sells *reconditioned* units in most of the above. This can be a great way to save big on expensive office equipment. They will try to match you up with just the features you want. All reconditioned machines come with a 90-day warranty, very fair indeed. Open weekdays from 9-5.

BOOKS

Save money at many of these used book stores by bringing them the ones you don't want anymore. They'll give you more for your books if you take store credit rather than cash. It's a good, cheap way to keep your libraries lean, or to try out new authors.

Also, check the "Thrift Shop" listings for more places to find used books. Many have good selections for anywhere from a quarter to a buck.

Annie's Book Stop

- 193 Belmont St., Belmont; (617) 489-3763
- 322 N. Main St., Randolph; (617) 986-4014
- 27 Broadway, Wakefield; (617) 246-3730
- 85 River St., Waltham; (617) 899-4384
- 167 Commonwealth Rd. (Rte. 30 & 27), Wayland; (508) 655-5433
- 681 High St. (Rte. 109), Westwood; (617) 326-8120

- *And other suburban locations*

Annie's Book Stop (or Swap, at some branches) offers plenty for the hungry bookworm to feed on. Used paperbacks sell here at half of their original cover prices; Annie's shelves are lined with everything popular from Harlequin Romances to science fiction series. Novels by the likes of Danielle Steele, Sidney Sheldon, and Tom Clancy are found here in abundance.

In addition, you can trade in your own oldies for store credit (some shops offer cash if you prefer). Here's a typical plot: Mary Higgins Clark's *I'll Be Seeing You* has a cover price of $6.99, which you can pick up here for half-price, or $3.49. When you're finished, you can bring it back and receive $1 credit toward something else. Total outlay: $2.49. Cool.

So, why feel guilty about reading a trashy novel when you've only spent a coupla bucks, and you can always swap it for a classic? Helpful charts fully outline the credits available for various cover prices. As individual franchises, there is some variation from one Annie's to the next: Some do add new, full-price books, while others sell cards and gifts. All are open seven days a week.

Arlington Books
- 212 Massachusetts Ave., Arlington; (617) 643-4473
- 52 J.F.K. St., Cambridge; (617) 441-8211

A couple of doors down from the (discount!) Capitol Theater, Arlington Books is two storefronts' worth of used books of all kinds, including complete-volume sets from estate collections. Many are rare and unusual. They also specialize in textbooks, foreign language books, and rare children's books, many from decades long past. Their newer branch in Harvard Square is a good bet for math, science, and other textbooks, at half-price. Both stores are open Sundays through Wednesdays from 10 A.M. to 6 P.M.; Thursdays 10-9; Fridays 10-4; and closed on Saturdays.

Ave. Victor Hugo Bookshop
- 339 Newbury St., Boston; (617) 266-7746

Fiction fans, *this* is your used book store. That's the specialty here, especially science fiction and mysteries. Most books sell for about half of their cover price, both paperbacks and hardcovers. There are also some new books, many at 10% off; also, reviewers' copies—a great way to get a recent book for one-third to one-half of the cover price.

You can buy, sell, or trade your own books in. AVH has lots of back-issue magazines too, and estate collections and sets. They're open six days from 10 A.M. to 10 P.M.; Sundays from 12 noon to 10. Recently, the store expanded to the second floor of the building; also, see the listing below for their sister store in Cambridge, the Bookcellar Cafe.

Barnes and Noble
- 395 Washington St., Boston; (617) 426-5184
- 660 Beacon St., Boston; (617) 267-8484
- 150 Granite St., Braintree; (617) 380-3655
- 325 Harvard St., Brookline; (617) 566-5562
- Burlington Mall Rd., Burlington; (617) 270-5500
- 170 Boylston St. (Rte. 9), Chestnut Hill; (617) 965-7621
- *And other suburban locations*

One of the country's best-known book discounters, B & N sells all new hardcovers at 20% off the cover price; same discount for paperbacks on the New York Times bestseller list. In addition, some 15-20 "staff recommendations" are marked 30% off.

There is an extensive selection of remainder books, such as Stephen King's *Dolores Claiborne*, right after the release of the movie, marked down from $23.50 to $6.99. And then there are the $1 shelves, with books by Arthur C. Clarke and Erma Bombeck. Now *there's* a combination for ya.

They also host a full slate of author appearances, storytelling, and the like; see the listing under "Entertainment—Readings and Literary Events." In 1995, B & N added the Boston University Bookstore in Kenmore Square into its fold. Store hours vary, but all branches are open seven days, including every evening but Sundays.

B. Dalton Bookseller
- South Shore Plaza, Braintree; (617) 848-9542
- Cambridgeside Galleria, Cambridge; (617) 252-0019
- Liberty Tree Mall, Danvers; (508) 777-4580

- Framingham Mall, Framingham; (508) 872-1264
- Emerald Square Mall, North Attleboro; (508) 699-6988
- Arsenal Marketplace, Watertown; (617) 923-4401

One of the biggies in the bookselling wars, B. Dalton wins the race in its computer section, which encompasses more subjects than many competitors do. Dalton's also discounts current hardcover *New York Times* bestsellers by 25%.

Here's another Mr. C money-saving tip: If you join B. Dalton's "Booksavers Club," you'll get an automatic 10% off every book every day, even if they're already discounted. The club costs $10 per year to join, but for true bookworms, it soon pays for itself. Store hours vary; open seven days a week.

The Bookcellar Cafe

- 1971 Massachusetts Ave., Cambridge; (617) 864-9625

A funky little book shop run by the same folks who brought you the famous Ave. Victor Hugo bookstore on Newbury Street, this Porter Square shop sells both new and used books. New titles, whether hardback or paperback, are all 10% off the retail price, while used books are generally about half of their cover prices.

As befits brainy Cambridge, literature is the specialty here, coupled with more unusual selections like a shelf of "Writers' Lives," or a whole section of poetry books. Plenty of sci-fi, too, and there's a smallish area of kids' and young adult's books. Used magazines and literary journals, too.

Shelves in the adjacent cafe room hold a more random selection of older books. All paperbacks in the cafe are 50¢ (five for $1), and all hardbacks are $1 (six for $5). The organization in this area is loose, to say the least: Mr. C spotted a copy of the Bible next to a Judith Krantz romance! Great food and entertainment in the cafe, too—see the listing under "Entertainment—Readings and Literary Events" for more details.

MR. CHEAP'S PICKS
Books

✔ **Ave. Victor Hugo**—Used paperback paradise, especially for all kinds of fiction.

✔ **Buck a Book**—This fast growing chain snaps up bookstore surplus, and sells most of them for a dollar apiece—honest.

✔ **Harvard Book Store**—Classy overstock tables upstairs, lots of used books downstairs, including textbooks.

✔ **New England Mobile Book Fair**—All new and recent hardcovers at 20% off, along with perhaps the biggest collection of remainders in the area.

Bookmarket

- 1815 Massachusetts Ave., Cambridge; (617) 661-7311

At the other end of Porter Square, a bookstore the size of a football field has moved into the former Sears building. Bright signs everywhere proclaim that books here sell for up to 75% off. Most of these are publishers' overstocks, usually with several copies of each title. When Mr. C visited, paperback fiction was on sale at three for $5, mainly mysteries and romances. Special deals also exist at the other end of the literary scale: Paperback classics were also three for $5, and poetry collections were just $3 each.

Non-fiction includes loads of self-help, sports, and health books. Deepak Chopra's *Ageless Body, Timeless Mind* was $5, down from $15. Hardback cookbooks were as little as $5. Snap up tons of kids' books, too, with hardback storybooks from $1.50, and *Pocahontas* coloring books, normally $7.95, just $2 during its summer of hype. Venture downstairs to the basement for a selection of (mostly older) textbooks, as well as books without jackets as "buy one, get one free" deals. Meanwhile, quantity purchasing allows Bookmarket to discount even hot bestsellers. This enormous store is open Mondays through Saturdays from 10 A.M. to 9 P.M., and Sundays from 12 noon to 6 P.M.

Borders Books and Music

- 300 Boylston St., Chestnut Hill; (617) 630-1120
- 85 Worcester Rd. (Rte. 9), Framingham; (508) 875-2321
- 151 Andover St., Peabody; (508) 538-3003

Chasing Barnes & Noble all around the country with superstores of its own, Borders' newest and glitziest store is in Chestnut Hill's equally glitzy Atrium Mall—about the only place Mr. C can be seen in there. But this chain is wonderful for browsing, and they do offer similar discounts to B & N. *New York Times* hardcover bestsellers are always 30% off; nearly all other hardcovers are 10% off. A dozen or more staff recommendations also get the 30% treatment.

Borders presents a strong slate of authors and musicians, usually in its cafe; see the listing under "Entertainment—Readings and Literary Events" for more info. Open seven days and evenings a week.

Boston AudioBooks

- 80 Arch St., Boston; (617) 338-4234

A cross between a secondhand bookshop and a Videosmith, Boston AudioBooks features that fast-growing segment of the literary biz, books on tape. Their business is mainly rentals, and because the customers are mostly business people on-the-go, the focus is on service, service, service.

But Cheapsters will want to check out the selection of used tapes. Tom Clancy's *Patriot Games*, as read by Martin Sheen, originally sold for $17; here it's been found for $8.50. And who says the classics can't be fun? *A Christmas Carol* comes alive when read by Patrick Stewart (he of the golden voice on *Star Trek*)—and you shouldn't feel like a Scrooge just because you paid $8 instead of $16. The audio book market is still dominated by self-help guides and language tapes, but you'll find a good selection of fiction, non-fiction, and even children's stories. With the money you save, it's almost enough to make paying tolls bearable.

Boston Book Annex

- 906 Beacon St., Boston; (617) 266-1090
- 705 Centre St., Jamaica Plain; (617) 522-2100

Both locations of the Boston Book Annex are terrific for used books. The Boston store is most geared to popular titles; check out the trademark browsing tables outside the front door, with hardcovers for a dollar and paperbacks for 50¢.

Most hardcovers are sold at half the original cover price. There are as many sections here as in any retail bookstore, from history to movies to medicine to humor. In addition to popular fiction and non, Mr. C found a major deal on a "Harvard Classics" literature set—fifty volumes of the greats, all for $200—that's a mere $4 apiece!

The JP branch focuses more on antiquarian and educational textbooks and sets. It even has the impressive look of a law library, complete with rolling wall ladders. Boston is open daily from 10 A.M. to 10 P.M., Sundays from 12 noon to 10; Jamaica Plain, Mondays through Saturdays from 9-5.

Brandeis Bookstall

- 12 Sewall Ave., Brookline; (617) 731-0208

Down a flight of stairs behind the Harvard Street stores in Coolidge Corner, Brandeis Bookstall is a cozy little used bookshop whose proceeds are contributed to the Brandeis University libraries. In general, you'll find most hardcover fiction around $1 to $3; paperback novels go from 50¢ to $2, with a large section at four for a buck. There are also art and travel books; individual sections of French, German, Spanish, Russian, and even Asian books; sheet music collections; lots of Judaica; and sections for senior citizens and children. Each month, one subject—such as law books, or medicine—goes on sale for just $1 per book, any title. And twice a year, *everything* goes into a half-price sale. Open Mondays through Saturdays from 10 A.M. to 5 P.M., Thursdays 'til 9.

Brattle Book Shop
• 9 West St., Boston; (617) 542-0210
One of Boston's most venerable book shops, the Brattle is right out of an old movie—every corner is crammed, with over 250,000 used, rare, and out-of-print books. It's a wonderful place to browse. There's plenty of history, politics, and fiction, but also some harder-to-find subjects like New England and nautical books.

Most hardcovers seem to be priced at $7.50. Titles espied at this bargain rate included Truman Capote's *Answered Prayers* and *The Final Days* by Woodward and Bernstein. Mr. C also found *Harry S. Truman,* by daughter Margaret, in hardcover for $10 *and* in paperback for $4.50.

Brattle's half-off tables, inside and outside the store, yield more amazing bargains. BBS also has old magazines, including a huge selection of "Life" from its heyday decades. They are fun to look at, lining the staircase and suspended from the ceilings. Brattle is open Mondays through Saturdays from 9 A.M. to 5:30 P.M.

Brookline Booksmith
• 279 Harvard St., Brookline; (617) 566-6660
This recently expanded, ever-popular shop in Coolidge Corner primarily sells new books, discounting current in-store bestsellers by 30%. Better yet, they always have several tables of remainders at markdowns of up to 80%. A coffee table bio of Jimi Hendrix, originally $27.50, was seen on sale for $9.98; Calvin Trillin's hilarious *Travels with Alice* was marked down from $18.98 to $3.98.

Booksmith is always fun to

browse (*that's* cheap), and is a particular favorite before or after a movie across the street. They offer a large selection of funky greeting cards too, as well as frequent author appearances; see the listing under "Entertainment—Readings and Literary Events." Open seven days and evenings a week.

Brookline Village Book Store
• 12 Station St., Brookline; (617) 734-3519
This shop recently moved around the corner, more than doubling its size and stock. Most hardcovers go from $4 to $8, a bit high for secondhand, but still well below list prices. Many of these are in excellent condition, and the quality and selection reflect the owner's careful tastes. Along with increased space has come better organization, and less of the cramped, cluttered feel of the original store. Open from 10 A.M. to 6 P.M. Mondays through Saturdays.

Bryn Mawr Book Sale
• 373 Huron Ave., Cambridge; (617) 661-1770
Here's a great place to snap up inexpensive used books, and feel like you're doing a good deed at the same time. That's because all books in this shop are donations, and the proceeds benefit Bryn Mawr College's New England Scholarship Fund.

Books on everything under the sun are crammed into this small shop; there are particularly good selections of novels, biographies, psychology and religious books. For linguists, there's French, German, and Italian fiction. At the time of Mr. C's visit, all mystery and true crime books were on sale: $1 for hardbacks, just a quarter for paperbacks. And take a look at the racks outside: For just 10¢ each, you'll be able to fill your arms with books for a dollar or two. Open Tuesdays through Saturdays from 10 A.M. to 5 P.M. and reduced hours during July and August.

Buck a Book
• 38 Court St., Boston; (617) 367-9419

- 551 Boylston St., Boston; (617) 266-0019
- 636 Beacon St., Boston; (617) 266-7219
- 125 Tremont St., Boston; (617) 357-1919
- 30 J.F.K. St., Cambridge; (617) 492-5500
- 55 Davis Square, Somerville; (617) 776-1919
- *And other suburban locations*

So, just what kinds of books can you get for a dollar? All kinds—this large chain snaps up bookstore returns, over-stocks, hardcovers that don't sell once the paperback comes out, and the like. The selection varies from branch to branch, yet each location rivals any "regular" bookstore's offerings.

Recent novels, *Star Trek* paper-backs, biographies, dictionaries, chil-dren's activity books, and more are all creatively displayed. Some titles push the envelope, but are still cheap: Olivia Goldsmith's novel *Flavor of the Month* was seen shortly after its run on the bestseller lists, for just $4. Other sections feature large-size art and coffee table books, from $3 to $10; and computer software guide-books, like *The WordPerfect Bible*, usually at half the cover price. Greet-ing cards are two for a buck. Plus low-grade videos, cartoons, and self-help programs, from $1.50 to $5; and books on tape for $2 each. Open seven days a week.

Canterbury's Book Shop
- 1675 Massachusetts Ave., Cambridge; (617)864-9396

This sprawling book shop is a perfect place to spend an afternoon brows-ing. The organization here is chaotic or charming, depending on how you look at it: You'll find books on shells next to those on dogs, while the movie section is right near the politi-cal science tomes. Even within a sec-tion, there's quite a range—Mr. C spotted an old, leather-bound copy of Walt Whitman's poetry ($12.50) next to a hardback copy of *The Bonfire of the Vanities* (for $10, down from $20).

There are also kids' books, mostly older storybooks, but the *Choose*

Your Own Adventure series is here for $2 each. It's worth noting, too, that Canterbury's stocks foreign lan-guage books (from $2.50 for a pa-perback). In good weather, you can find extreme bargains on the "50¢ table" outside the shop. Although al-most all books here are secondhand, there is a small selection of new uni-versity press books. These are all 50% off their cover prices; most likely reviewers' copies. Hours are Mondays through Saturdays from 10 A.M. to 6 P.M.

Derby Square Book Store
- 215 Essex St., Salem; (508) 745-8804

The owner boasts that he runs the only discount book store north of Boston; unlikely though that seems, it's extensive enough that you may not need another. Thousands of new books, bought directly from major publishers and selling for 20% below cover prices, tower above overtaxed tables and shelves—defying you to pull one out and risk burying your-self. As Mr. C was rebuilding a pile demolished in just that way, a fellow customer smirked, "Glad that hap-pened to you instead of me." Such are the ordeals of being a die-hard Cheapster.

Structural design aside, these books have at least been arranged with some sense of organization. Re-cent bestsellers by such authors as Michael Crichton and John Grisham can be found here, along with myster-ies by the likes of Sue Grafton and Tony Hillerman and fantasies by Piers Anthony.

While all hardcovers are at least 20% off, a dangerously-overloaded ta-ble in the middle of the store has books marked down to $5.99, and an-other offers a "Buy One, Get One Free" deal. Tempting.

Derby Square is open 9 A.M. to 9 P.M. Mondays through Saturdays and 11 A.M. to 8 P.M. Sundays. While in the area, skip across the street and check out **The Old Book Shop**, at 296 Essex St.; telephone (508) 744-4193. They have a rich selection of older titles. Strong in literary criticism, abridged versions of classics for children, and biographies, many hardbacks are in the $3-$5 range—while easy chairs and classical music set an ideal bookstore mood. It's open 11:30 A.M. to 3:30 P.M. every day but Wednesdays and Sundays.

The English Bookshop
- 22 Rocky Neck Ave., Gloucester; (508) 283-8981

An interesting store operating out of an old house, the English Bookshop would be worth checking out solely for its Artists' Gallery location, where amateur Picassos can be seen capturing the rustic beauty of Gloucester Harbor. But the store itself has an appeal of its own.

Scale the front staircase to the Upper Annex, the front lobby of which always displays books for purchase on the honor system. Older books, like a Dostoyevsky classic, are just 50¢—or three for a dollar. Talk about a place to stock up on summer reading! Then, assuming the rest of the store is open, walk into a room steeped with age for a wide variety of books on religion, languages, and history, at $4-$6 for most hardcovers.

Outside once more, duck past sweet-smelling honeysuckle bushes to the store's lower room, in which crafts and toys complete with old, if not solely English, books for attention. Shakespeare and Chaucer abound as expected, along with other literary titles. Open afternoons only, Mondays through Saturdays. A-yuh, that's New England all right—quirky.

Harvard Book Store
- 1256 Massachusetts Ave., Cambridge; (617) 661-1515

Right across the street from Hahvahd Yahd, HBS gets high marks for its thorough inventory. In addition to current titles at full-price, there are two discount options here—first, a good-sized table of remainders, ranging from bestsellers to literary collections. These, as in many stores, sell for anywhere from 50% to 80% off. The store also picks fifty "notable" new releases for a 20% discount each month.

Downstairs in the basement, though—this is the place to be for any book lover. The used book department has almost as much selection as the main level's regular shelves—or those of any other book store, for that matter. Arts, politics, science, novels—mostly paperbacks, all sold at half the cover price. Used textbooks are 25% off. For students, and any readers on a budget, this is a must. Open daily from 9:30 A.M. to 11 P.M., Sundays from 12-8.

Harvard Coop
- 1400 Massachusetts Ave., Cambridge; (617) 499-2000
- 3 Cambridge Center, Cambridge; (617) 499-3200
- 84 Massachusetts Ave., Cambridge; (617) 499-2000
- 14 Everett St., Cambridge; (617) 499-2000
- 333 Longwood Ave., Brookline; (617) 499-3300

Look for the Harvard Square Coop's book department *behind* the main store, in the Palmer Street building. Following the lead of the big chains, all *New York Times* bestsellers are 25% off, with a 10% reduction for NYT best-selling paperbacks. Furthermore, several long tables of remainders are always stacked with books on just about any subject, at up to 80% off the original prices. Great for browsing. Anne Rice's *Lasher* was glimpsed, not long after its general release, marked down from $25 to just $4.98. Open daily; hours vary by branch.

House of Sarah
- 225 Hampshire St., Cambridge; (617)547-3447

This cozy used bookstore in Inman Square sells books in such excellent condition that you could be forgiven for thinking they were new. Nearly perfect books are available at huge discounts, usually at half off the cover. Periodic sales may reduce prices even more—on Mr. C's visit, all fiction was an extra 25% off. And there are sale racks where books are always half off their regular discount prices.

Americana, Art History, Literature, and Psychology shelves are especially strong. Mr. C found the Prentice Hall Guide to English Literature for $17.50, down from $35. There was a stack of computer guides like "Microsoft Word Made Easy," for $8.50, from $18.95. Don't neglect the upstairs section, where most of the paperbacks are kept. Also upstairs is an entire room of books about "women in religion," a specialty here.

When you've picked out some books, settle into one of the squishy sofas, relax, and read. This welcoming shop is open Mondays through Saturdays from 11 A.M. to 9 P.M.; Sundays from 12 noon to 5 P.M.

Kate's Mystery Books
● 2211 Massachusetts Ave., Cambridge; (617) 491-2660

Not a discount store *per se*, but one of the best mystery book stores around. Now, as you may know, mystery fans go through novels the way Sy Sperling goes through hairpieces. That means they have a lot of useless books on their hands. And they bring 'em into Kate's by the boxful.

If you're a part of this food chain, Kate's is the place for you. Bring in your old mysteries (hardcover or paperback) for credit toward other new or used books. And if you're just looking to buy, check out the several shelves of used paperbacks, mostly priced from $1 to $3. Used hardcovers are mixed in with the new ones, so they take a bit more sleuthing.

Whodunit fans go through books so quickly, in fact, that you can often find current bestsellers only a few months after their publication. And mysteries apparently age like wines—a recent used title may actually cost less than an older one. Great way to support your habit—and save! Open weekdays from 12-7 P.M. (an hour later on Thursdays), Saturdays 11-5, Sundays 12-5.

Magazines by Joseph
● 279 Newbury St., Boston; no phone

Up on the second floor, overlooking posh Newbury Street, this tiny store is crammed with hundreds and hundreds of used magazines. The collection is eclectic, to say the least—a milk crate filled with *Ms.* magazines sits next to one stocked with old Victoria's Secret catalogs. Hmmm. Whatever your passion or pleasure, you'll find back issues of all your favorites.

The bestsellers of the biz, like *Esquire*, *Life*, *Playboy*, and *National Geographic*, are plentiful. But you'll also find lesser-knowns like *The Progressive*. The prices are unbeatable. Expect to pay 35¢ to 50¢ for mass markets like *Glamour* and *Vanity Fair*, a dollar or two for high-brows like *Architectural Digest* and the *Utne Reader*. While away an hour tracking down out-of-prints like *Lear's* and rare back issues. Open seven days a week from 11 A.M. to 7 P.M.

New England Mobile Book Fair
● 82 Needham St., Newton; (617) 964-7440

One of the most amazing bookstores in the Boston area—indeed, anywhere in Mr. C's travels around the country. This is truly a book lover's paradise, the sort you can lose yourself in for hours. Blink as you cruise Newton's discount mile and you'll miss this olive-drab, concrete warehouse; but go inside, and you'll be astounded by acres and acres of shelves.

The store divides into two halves: Current books, arranged by publisher (some by subject), and a separate area of remainders, with as diverse a selection as any other retail store. Titles currently in print are sold at 20% off the cover price, with *New York Times* bestsellers at 30% off. The incredibly well-read staff can help you find, or look up, almost any book you could possibly want.

Remainders offer discounts of up to 80%, with hundreds of titles in every subject: history, literature, children's, travel, cooking, computers. Find David Halberstam's excellent account of the Red Sox-Yankees rivalry in *The Summer of '49*, marked down from $21.95 to $4.98. There are also many collector's edition books, such as the giant, sealed *Art of Walt Disney*—originally $60, here $39.95.

NEMBF has recently expanded its hours. They're open Mondays through Saturdays from 9 A.M. to 5:30 P.M., plus Wednesday and Thursday evenings until 8:30; Sundays, from 12-5.

Pandemonium Books & Games

- 36 J.F.K. St., Cambridge; (617) 547-3721

See the listing under "Toys and Games."

Royal Discount Book Store

- 753 Boylston St., Boston; (617) 375-9299
- 485 Massachusetts Ave., Arlington; (617) 643-4422
- 75 Stockwell Dr., Avon; (508) 587-5868
- 43 Middlesex Tpke., Burlington; (617) 273-1850
- 917 Worcester Rd. (Rte. 9), Natick; (508) 653-0950
- 74 McGrath Hwy., Somerville; (617) 623-6593
- 381 Main St., Wakefield; (617) 245-0519
- 824 Washington St., Weymouth; (617) 331-8288
- 348 Cambridge Rd., Woburn; (617) 932-3760

Everything at this chain is offered at *some* discount. Titles on the *New York Times* bestseller list are sold at 35% off the cover price; 25% off for paperbacks on the list. All other hardcovers are reduced by 15%, paperbacks by 10%. Special tables piled high with overstocks and remainders offer discounts of 50% to 80%.

Mr. C found (but did not pick up) *Lady Boss*, by Jackie Collins, marked down from $21.95 to just $5.98. Robert Ludlum's latest was there. So was Dave Barry's. And on the overstock table, a large-size Bruce Springsteen photo biography was just 98¢, from $10.95. Sorry, Boss.

Royal Discount also has magazines, books on tape, calendars, and gift items, as well as greeting cards at a 30% discount. Open daily.

Starr Book Shop

- 29 Plympton St., Cambridge; (617) 547-6864

As you may have begun to notice, Cambridge is renowned for having one of the highest concentrations of bookstores per square mile in the country. Starr shares space in the narrow, oddly-shaped Harvard Lampoon building, just off Mt. Auburn Street. Don't worry—the store is much more serious about books than its upstairs neighbors.

Most hardcovers are around half of their original prices, unless they are very old or worn. Generally, the quality here is quite good, and the selection is large. Mr. C saw a like-new copy of Norman Mailer's *Tough Guys Don't Dance*, reduced from $16.95 to $8.50. More diverse are the non-fiction subjects, with a lot to browse through in sociology, psychology, law and medicine, history, art and travel. Open Mondays through Wednesdays from 10 A.M. to 6 P.M., Thursdays through Saturdays 'til 9, and Sundays from 12 noon to 6 P.M.

Meanwhile, the other scholarly used bookshops in the area are **McIntyre & Moore Booksellers** at 8 Mt. Auburn Street, Cambridge, (617) 491-0662 and **Pangloss Bookshop** at 65 Mt. Auburn Street, Cambridge, (617) 354-4003.

Waldenbooks

- 2 Center Plaza, Cambridge St., Boston; (617) 523-3044
- Dedham Mall, Dedham; (617) 326-9212
- 1316 Washington St., Hanover; (617) 826-8526
- 1713 Massachusetts Ave., Lexington; (617) 862-7870
- 45 Merrimack St., Lowell; (508) 459-0843
- Meadow Glen Mall, Medford; (617) 391-1558
- 1024 Great Plain Ave., Needham; (617) 444-1150
- Assembly Square Mall, Somerville; (617) 628-4533
- Swampscott Mall, Swampscott; (617) 592-1290
- Walpole Mall, Walpole; (508) 668-3540
- *And other suburban locations*

In addition to discounting its own

weekly in-store picks by 25%, Waldenbooks offers its customers a "Preferred Reader" discount card. Show it at the cash register wherever you buy something in any branch, nationwide. You'll get 10% off your purchase; and, for every $100 you spend during the course of a year, you'll get a $5 credit toward future purchases. This credit can likewise be redeemed at any Waldenbooks store, on anything except newspapers, magazines, and cards. Membership costs $10; sign up in any store. Waldenbooks also displays a good selection of publishers' overstocks and remainder books, at significant discounts. Hours vary with each location.

Waterstone's Booksellers
- 26 Exeter St., Boston; (617) 859-7300

The British are coming! Located in the former Exeter Street Cinema building, this two-level store was among the first landings of this classy chain in The States. They too discount *New York Times* bestsellers, by 30%; in addition, staff recommendations sell for 20% off the cover. Apart from these bargains, everything else sells at full price.

The sales staff is very knowledgeable, and stands ready to place special orders, especially for British editions. The reference, literature and classics sections are especially deep here. And many prominent authors visit Waterstone's for free readings; in recent months, these have included Barbara Kingsolver, Cynthia Heimel, Lani Guinier, and Robert Parker. Open daily 10-10, Sundays 11-7.

WordsWorth Books
- 30 Brattle St., Cambridge; (617) 354- 5201

Perhaps the king of Harvard Square bookshops, the two-story WordsWorth looks out regally over the open plaza at the beginning of Brattle Street. It offers a very complete selection of current books— over 100,000 titles under nearly 100 categories, from Native American studies to linguistics to bestsellers. All are sold at 15% off hardcover prices and 10% off paperbacks.

On the second floor, by the windows, you'll also find further reductions on leftover editions. *New and Selected Essays* by Robert Penn Warren, originally $25, was on sale for $6.25. WordsWorth is open late seven days a week.

CAMERAS

When buying a new camera, it's important to make sure it comes with an American warranty, as opposed to a foreign one. That way, if you have any problems, you won't have to send it to the Far East. Worth asking about.

Apart from big sales in department stores, the best way to save big money on a camera is to buy one secondhand. Well cared-for, a good camera will last longer than a good car; most used models still have several years of snaps left in them. Downtown Crossing is one of the best places to shop, with many stores in the same area.

Bromfield Camera Company
- 10 Bromfield St., Boston; (617) 426-5230

This store has perhaps the largest se-

lection of used cameras around; the display cases are filled with them, and the sales staff is happy to show you one or all. $140 can get you a

Konica TC 35mm camera with semi-automatic features. It originally retailed for around $250. Stepping up just a bit, they had a Canon AE-1—"the most popular camera of the seventies," said the salesman—for $175. These cameras come with lenses, and there are other used lenses to choose from as extras. Add a used leather case for another $10.

Nikons start around $250 and up. At the other end of the range, Mr. C saw a Polaroid "One-Step" for just $25. All cameras here come with a 30-day full warranty; or you can buy a seven-year extended warranty from the store for an additional $50 (an extra bargain—this used to be a *four*-year plan!). Open seven days.

Cambridge Camera Exchange
- 727 Revere Beach Pkwy., Revere; (617) 284-2300

This full-price camera and film developing shop has a good selection of used and discontinued cameras and lenses at reduced prices. Mr. C found an old Nikon "F" camera, with manual exposure and focusing, for $160; also a more recent Minolta 7000, with manual or automatic functions, for $290 with lens. This was an unused, discontinued model; the version that has replaced it sells for around $500 today.

You'll also find used lenses and filters and even a box of outdated film (all varieties, $2 each). The equipment comes with a 30-day full warranty; you can purchase a one-year warranty for $20 extra. Knowledgeable staff, too. Open weekdays only, from 8:15 A.M. to 6 P.M.

Cameras Inc. Stereo and Video
- 474 Massachusetts Ave., Arlington; (617) 648-8111

In business for some forty years, this store has really kept up with the times, adding video and other electronics to their lines of 35mm cameras. Video equipment, in particular, are good deals here; you can save as much as $100 over the prices even at the major chains on 8mm and VHS camcorders, as well as VCRs, televisions, and audio. One reason for the

low prices: They've been here so long, they own their building—hence, lower overhead costs. Yowza.

Prices are competitive on still cameras and accessories, whether you're in the market for pro-grade or point-and-shoots. The store also buys, sells and trades used cameras; because of their unique mixture, you can even trade in a used camera toward a new television, Walkman, or whatever. Used items for sale carry a 30-day parts and labor warranty. Cameras Inc. is open weekdays from 8 A.M. to 6 P.M. (Thursdays 'til 8), and Saturdays from 9 A.M. to 5:30 P.M.

General Photographic Supply Co.
- 71-73 Canal St., Boston; (617) 742-7070

In business since 1946, this large store near North Station has a tremendous selection of new and used photo equipment, mainly in 35mm still cameras. There are always lots of brands to choose from, including Minolta, Canon, and especially Nikon. New cameras are usually priced just above cost; used equipment is even less. A used Nikon 5005, with auto focus, may be around $300. General Photo is very choosy about used cameras; they only sell stock that is in good to excellent condition, and all items have a 30-day warranty.

GPS has used enlargers and tripods; and new supplies, like chemicals, paper, and film, all sold at 30% off list price. They also rent cameras, projectors, and screens, and do their own repair work. Open weekdays 8:30 A.M. to 5:30 P.M., Saturdays from 12-5.

International Camera, Inc.
- 4 Bromfield St., Boston; (617) 423-2968

This seems to be one of the few camera stores that has compact, automatic cameras among its used models. A Nikon "One Touch" 35mm camera, the kind with the sleek body that fits into the palm of your hand, sells for $89. It's a point-and-shoot type. Other SLR's start around $100, with such brands as Pentax, Olympus, and

MR. CHEAP'S PICKS
Cameras

✔ **General Photographic Supply Company**—A big place with good bargains on high-quality used 35mm cameras and darkroom equipment.

✔ **Kenmore Camera**—What are they doing in Cambridge? Selling used cameras of every shape and kind under the (filtered) sun.

✔ **Newtonville Camera**—One of the only places selling used *video* camcorders—a good way to save on an expensive item.

projectors. These may, of course, be older models, which are sold "as is"; more recent ones carry a 30-day warranty. Open from 9 A.M. to 5:30 P.M., Mondays through Saturdays.

Newtonville Camera and Video
- 249 Walnut St., Newton; (617) 965-1240

Perhaps the largest selection of new and used cameras in this area, Newtonville has everything from current models to the old and unusual. This shop is frequented by amateur photographers and professionals, making for a strong selection in the second-hand department. They also have lots of tripods and lenses. Used cameras carry a full 90-day warranty, longer than most other stores offer.

More interesting yet is Newtonville's selection of used video equipment. Camcorders by Sony, JVC, and others are available in the $300 range, a substantial savings over new models, which seldom come in under $600. They have used VCRs too, which carry a 30-day warranty.

As far as Mr. C knows, this is the only major reseller of used video equipment around; though when it comes to saving money, he is *always* happy to be corrected. Open every day but Sunday from 9 A.M. to 6 P.M. ('til 7 on Wednesdays and Fridays).

Perfecta Camera
- 42 Bromfield St., Boston; (617) 542-6928
- 81 Charles St., Boston; (617) 248-1909
- 1054 Beacon St., Brookline; (617) 734-0540
- 309 Walnut St., Newton; (617) 244-4174
- 548 Washington St., Wellesley; (617) 235-0890
- *And other suburban locations*

This chain, primarily known as a good, quick processing lab, also has some good deals on basic cameras and packages. A recent sale offered an Olympus "SuperZoom" 35mm camera with lots of automatic features for $199, some $70 off their regular selling price. Plus slide projectors, lenses, and other accessories.

Minolta. All cameras have a thirty-day warranty, with the option of purchasing a longer warranty plan. Open seven days.

Kenmore Camera
- 50 Church St., Cambridge; (617) 661-6643

"We have *everything*," says Lenny, the owner of Kenmore Camera (which sounds like it should be under the Citgo sign instead of in Harvard Square). He went on to recite a litany that proved his point: 35mm cameras, movie cameras, lenses, tripods, projectors, and even some video camcorders (which don't stick around for long).

Lenny encourages customers to shop around, confident that they'll come back here to make their purchases. You'll find all major brands in the used department: Nikons from $150, Pentaxes from $99, plus Bell and Howell, Minolta, Kodak, Leica. . . .The store also specializes in the exotic and hard-to-find. There are plenty of items under $100. Some cameras start as low as $30, as do some of the movie and slide

The Bromfield Street branch, formerly Stone Camera, adds good used cameras for under $100 and up. Mr. C liked a Ricoh KR-5 manual 35mm camera with a 55mm lens for $90. Even at this low price, you'll get a through-the-lens light meter and focusing system. Used cameras are guaranteed for thirty days, full parts and labor, as other stores do; but their warranty continues at 50% for the *rest of one year*—they'll cover half of any repair work you may need. A unique deal. It's open daily 8:30 A.M. to 5:30 P.M., Saturdays 10-5; other store hours vary.

Ritz Camera Centers

- 659 Boylston St., Boston; (617) 266-8931
- 34 Bromfield St., Boston; (617) 426-7811
- 24 Tremont St., Boston; (617) 367-9045
- 32 Leonard St., Belmont; (617) 484-8545
- 694 Washington St., Brookline; (617) 734-5010
- CambridgeSide Galleria, Cambridge; (617) 577-9252
- Porter Square Center, Cambridge; (617) 354-1311
- 31 Church St., Cambridge; (617) 661-5727
- Atrium Mall, Chestnut Hill; (617) 965-0172
- Arsenal Mall, Watertown; (617) 926-9313
- *And other suburban locations*

Well, Mr. C doesn't usually give much space to chains you probably know about already; but Ritz, long known as a photo developer, has expanded to carry complete lines of current cameras by most major brands. And, thanks to those 500 stores nationwide, prices stay low. One of Canon's latest "Sure Shot" 35mm zoom lens cameras, with a retail price of $485, sells here for $290; and it was recently on sale at $20 off that. Other Canons start as low as $60.

Ritz also has video camcorders by Panasonic, Fuji, and Minolta, starting around $700 (complete with tripod, batteries, and carry bag). Plus binoculars, personal stereos, cellular phones, and accessories for everything. Open seven days a week.

And, if you're traveling southward, Ritz has one of its eleven "Outlet Centers" in Warwick, Rhode Island. Clearance stock is marked at 40% to 80% off retail here; call 1-800-52-FOCUS (36287) for more details.

Sherman's

- 11 Bromfield St., Boston; (617) 482-9610

See the listing under "Electronics."

CARPETING AND RUGS

Able Rug Company

- 20 Franklin St., Allston; (617) 782-5010
- 75 Newbury St., Danvers; (508) 762-0444
- 1176 Washington St. (Rte. 53), Hanover; (617) 695-9569
- 974 Worcester Rd. (Rte. 9), Natick; (508) 655-9393

This giant carpeting store's home base faces the Mass. Pike at the very top of Harvard Avenue. Able sells imported rugs, wall-to-wall and remnants, most at good discounts. You may find a 5' x 8' hand-knotted rug from India, valued at $1,000, on sale for $399; or a 3' x 5' handmade Dhurrie for as little as $39.

Upstairs you'll find more bargains, particularly in remnants of all kinds. One overstock sale on Mr. C's visit was a 4' x 6' bound contemporary rug—beige with two bold diagonal stripes of maroon and turquoise across the middle. It was valued at $458, and reduced to $115. A 6' x 9'

Mr. Cheap's Pick
Carpeting and Rugs

✔ **Ben Elfman Carpet**—Over
the bridge and through
Chelsea, to carpet a house we
go...Tons of bargains on
commercial, residential, and
Orientals.

---

bound rug in grey, with diamond
shapes cut into it, was $89. And a 3'
x 6' Oriental-style rug—actually
made in Belgium, with a country
floral design on 100% wool—was
marked down from $150 to $99.

Able has lots more to see, with frequent sales. They also provide padding and installation. Open seven
days a week.

Ben Elfman Carpet
• 260 Second St., Chelsea;
   (617) 884-8600
As you may have seen on a certain
TV commercial, Mr. C loves Elfman's. Patriarch Ben founded this
wholesaler in 1907; about a dozen
years ago, they began selling to the
public at those same high-volume
prices. Find DuPont "Stainmaster"
for $9.99 a square yard, *installed*;
this would retail for over $20 else-
where. Commercial carpeting starts
as low as $6.99 installed, with a 20-
year guarantee.

Sculptured-texture nylon carpeting is as low as $5.99 per yard, and
6' x 9' bound remnants start at a fantastic $19 in a large variety of col-
ors. Oriental rugs of the same size,
valued at up to $150, sell for just
$39. And, would you believe 2' x 4'
hand-woven Orientals for just
$9.99? Believe it.

As one of the largest distributors
in the region, Elfman's gets sweet
deals from the mills, and prefers to
pass those savings on to keep customers coming in. Every two months or

so, they run a 25% off sale on every
item in the store; twice a year, all Orientals are cut by 40% to 70% to clear
room for new arrivals. And don't
miss "Ben's Basement," where everything is half-price. Elfman's includes
padding and installation in the prices
of all broadloom. Located just north
of the Tobin Bridge, they're open
from 10 A.M. to 9 P.M. on weekdays,
Saturdays 10-6, Sundays 12-5.

C & S Carpet
• 1704 Washington St., Boston;
   (617) 262-9822
Recently moved to the South End, C
& S installs carpets for homes and
major businesses throughout Boston.
Broadlooms start as low as $11.99
per square yard; commercial weaves
can be even less. Remnants sell for
$5 per square yard—period. They
also have imitation Oriental rugs; a
9' x 12' rug sells for $150. Open
from 8 A.M. to 5 P.M., Mondays
through Saturdays, C & S can also
arrange to come to your home and
give a free estimate.

The Carpet Liquidator
• 212 S. Main St., Middleton; (508)
   777-8081
"If you compare apples to apples,
you won't touch our prices," vows
the manager here, and it's tough to
imagine you could improve upon the
selection and prices at this spacious
North Shore warehouse. Employees
criss-cross the building on forklifts,
laden with closeouts, short rolls, and
discontinued colors of broadlooms
from major mills such as Mohawk,
Galaxy, and Image.

Most of the carpeting available is
on the heavy side, and you'll find numerous rolls marked down from $40-
$50 per square yard (ouch!) to
$19.99. Colorful remnants, in wools
and synthetics, are half-off or better
in most cases; one large piece
(enough to fit a couple of rooms) was
reduced from a retail value of $900
down to $399.

You won't get rolled, but extra
charges do apply for delivery and installation. But then, that's standard
for rock-bottom flooring of this kind;

think of it as ordering *a la carte*. Check these guys out from 10 A.M to 8 P.M. Mondays, Thursdays, and Fridays; 'til 6 P.M. Tuesdays and Wednesdays; and to 5 P.M. weekends.

Carpet Mill Outlet Store

- 1602 Concord St., Framingham; (508) 877-8002

If you're planning to carpet a room or a house, check out these folks for an estimate. Their prices may not be much lower than other retail stores, but the same amount of money here gets you higher-quality materials that will ultimately last longer and look better. They will also try to save you money by measuring the yardage as efficiently as possible; a hidden seam here or there may mean less scrap to pay for.

They also have a big selection of unbound remnants, in over one hundred varieties of materials, thickness, and colors. At $5 a yard and up, these can be up to 50% less than retail prices. Open daily from 9 A.M. to 5 P.M., Thursday and Friday evenings 'til 8, and Sundays 1-5.

Carpet Works

- 137 Harvard Ave., Allston; (617) 787-5064

Popular with the student and starving-rock artist types who inhabit this area, this place sells all the home basics from pine futons to broadloom and remnants. You won't find much in the way of fancy stuff here, but if you're looking around for something to cover your floors quickly and cheaply, it's definitely worth a look.

A few doors down, **Boston Paint and Supply** at 151 Harvard Avenue, telephone (617) 254-1060, offers similar stock and prices. Makes this neighborhood a sort of bargain district for home furnishings.

Lechmere Rug Company

- 200 O'Brien Hwy., Cambridge; (617) 876-9700

Lechmere Rugs is a small place that deals directly with several mills, in high volume, to offer discounts on first-quality factory surplus and closeouts. You can find nylon carpeting for under $10 a yard, and wool blends from $21.99 a yard—about half of retail.

A 6' x 9' remnant may go for $60, a bit more if you want one that's bound. Orientals start around $150. Lechmere also offers full service throughout the Boston area and beyond, with padding and installation available; they are open seven days a week, including weeknights until 9.

Wholesale Rug Shak

- 173 Msgr. O'Brien Highway, Cambridge; (617) 576-SHAK (7425)

The owner of this "shak" claims that his prices are lower than any he's seen. . . and he may well be right. This shop buys and cuts rugs straight out of the mill, with no distributors to inflate the prices. All the rugs on sale are new and first quality. There are a few wool weaves, like a 6' x 9' handmade wool Oriental for $219; but synthetic rugs make up the bulk of the stock here. You can get a 9' x 12' piece of heavy synthetic carpeting for just $79, roughly less than half of retail. Commercial carpeting, high-quality low pile, starts at just $4 a yard.

Mr. C saw some famous brand names here: Mohawk, Galaxy, and Aladdin among others. At the high end of the Galaxy range, a thick pile carpeting was $11.95 a yard (normally $26-$27 a yard retail). Berber rugs are $4 to $6 per yard. If you're still in school (or living as if you were!), check out the "student corner," where Mr. C saw an 8' x 10' remnant for a thrifty $20. All rugs carry a warranty of at least a year; the average length of warranty is five years. Open Mondays through Wednesdays from 9:30 A.M. to 6:30 P.M.; Thursdays and Fridays to 9 P.M.; and Saturdays to 6 P.M.

And you probably know about this major chain, weaving its way around the country:

New York Carpet World
- 75 Stockwell Dr. (Rte. 24), Avon; (508) 559-6033
- 599 Worcester Rd. (Rte. 9), Natick; (508) 653-7773
- 333 Providence Hwy. (Rte. 1), Norwood; (617) 769-7191
- 444 Broadway (Rte. 1), Saugus; (617) 231-9850

CDs, RECORDS, AND TAPES

Like used book shops, many of these places allow you to trade in music you no longer want (some, alas, don't accept LPs anymore). You can get cash for the deal, but you'll get more by taking store credit instead. Besides, this is an easy way to check out artists you may not want to try at full price.

CD Spins
- 187 Harvard Ave., Allston; (617) 787-7680
- 324 Newbury St., Boston; (617) 267-5955

The original Allston shop, a tiny walk-down, has split itself in two. Both have lots of good music (on cassettes as well as CDs), and a very liberal return policy. Rock is the main dish at the Allston branch; the downtown branch, near Tower Records, houses their jazz, classical, and folk collection.

You may find the Grateful Dead's double CD set *Without a Net*, on sale for $18.99; a couple of never-opened Genesis discs were each $8.99. New titles are often mixed in with the used ones. And there is a large rack of bargain CDs, priced from just $1 to $6; even there, you'll find such names as Robert Plant and LL Cool J.

Now, here's the best part. All CDs are fully returnable for seven days—even used ones—for full credit (keep that receipt!). So your music shopping is essentially risk-free. A further bargain: If you buy four CDs, you can get a fifth one at half-price.

Cheapo Records
- 645 Massachusetts Ave., Cambridge; (617) 354-4455

Well, this has to be Mr. C's favorite, just from the name alone. Fortunately, there's more to recommend it than that. Cheapo has a huge collection of records and tapes, along with CDs. This long, narrow store, crammed from floor to ceiling on two levels, is a bit tough on claustrophobics—but the music sure makes it worthwhile, especially downstairs.

Here you'll find secondhand LPs and tapes from $1.99 to $5.99, with CDs around $7.99. A special rack of CDs under $5 boasts a wide selection. Cheapo gets high marks for variety; both floors have every kind of music you can think of. Rock, of course (*lots* of oldies), soul, Latin, country—often in great detail. From the South alone there are sections for Dixieland, Cajun and zydeco, blues—and how many places have an entire three-section bin dedicated to "Louisiana Swamp Music"? Or an extensive collection of "'60s Surf" tunes? None too many. They also have over fifty *thousand* 45rpm singles. Wow. Open Mondays through Saturdays from 10 A.M. to 6 P.M. (Thursdays and Fridays 'til 9); and Sundays from 11-5.

Disc Diggers
- 401 Highland Ave., Somerville; (617) 776-7560

This big shop in Davis Square has a fine selection of pop music, jazz, and sounds from all over the world—reggae, soca, soukous, and other happening rhythms. In fact, they claim to have the largest selection in New England; but you won't find any records here. Yes, vinyl die-hards, they've made that dreaded move. Ah well. . .

The selection and prices are terrific, though. Used CDs are about $7.99 on average, with some new ones mixed in at only $9.99. They also have lots of those cute little CD singles for a buck or so. Most cassettes come in around $3.99, with many at lower prices.

Dig in Mondays through Saturdays from 10 A.M. to 9 P.M., Sundays from 12 noon to 7 P.M.

Diskovery
- 113 Brighton Ave., Allston; (617) 787-2640
- 385 Washington St., Brighton; (617) 789-3775

This is a business with an identity crisis: Is it a used book store or record store? Who cares—there are lots of both. Most cassettes and LPs are priced from $2.50 to $4.50; records are the most plentiful (!), mainly in rock 'n roll. Meanwhile, tons of paperbacks are $1 to $2 each. What makes this store more interesting, for those who bring stuff to trade in, is the option of using trade-in credit for either music *or* books. There is even a bit of room for wheeling and dealing. Get creative!

In Your Ear!
- 957 Commonwealth Ave., Boston; (617) 787-9755
- 72A Mt. Auburn St., Cambridge; (617) 491-5035

One of Boston's many great used music stores, IYE has sprouted two locations. Rock 'n roll, both new and old, is ably represented here—from vintage 60s records to tapes by Boston's newest local bands. They have other

---

MR. CHEAP'S PICKS
CDs, Records, and Tapes

✔ **CD Spins**—Dedicated primarily to compact discs, the best way to get good quality used tunes. Very liberal return policy.

✔ **Cheapo Records**—Who else? Mr. C's favorite name in town, and one of his favorite spots for any kind of music.

✔ **Disc Diggers**—Funky shop in Somerville with lots of hip music—especially jazz and world beat—secondhand.

---

kinds of music, but those sections are not extensive.

Records and cassettes are reasonably priced, from $3.99 to $5.99; most compact discs are in the range of $5.99 to $7.99, with some as low as $2.99. Iggy Pop and the B-52s were both seen at $5.99. They also have lots of boxes filled with records and tapes for a buck—even good ol' 8-track tapes (yow) for 50 cents.

In Your Ear! also sells new and used music videos, lots of rock and movie posters, accessories, and even turntables. Open Mondays through Saturdays 'til 8 P.M., Sundays 12-6.

Looney Tunes
- 1106 Boylston St., Boston; (617) 247-2238
- 1001 Massachusetts Ave., Cambridge; (617) 876-5624

Here's another large selection of used albums, tapes, and CDs. The main store is located near the Berklee music school; and so, in addition to lots of rock and pop, Looney Tunes has a healthy offering of classical music at both stores. Most LPs are $2 to $5; cassettes, $3 to $5; CDs, $5 to $10. Check out the bargain section, where records are 99¢, tapes are $1.49, and CDs are just $4.99 or even less.

Not to mention used videos for $2 to $10—hundreds of 'em. Open daily until 9 P.M. in Boston, 'til 11 P.M. in Harvard Square.

Mystery Train Records

- 306 Newbury St., Boston; (617) 536-0216
- 1208 Massachusetts Ave., Cambridge; (617) 497-4024

As you may guess from the name, this place can really give you a case of the blues—secondhand (rock too, of course). These are mainly on tapes and CDs; the original Cambridge store, in particular, is tiny. Vinyl fans will do better at the Boston branch—which also offers used videos for $7 or so.

Most records and cassettes are priced around $3 to $5. Compact discs are about $8 to $9 for most popular groups. And there are lots of rare records, British imports, 1950s lounge music, and the like, starting around $15 to $20. MT also has a good selection of movie soundtracks and Broadway musicals. Open seven days a week, until 7 P.M. in Cambridge, 7:30 in Boston.

Nuggets

- 486 Commonwealth Ave., Boston; (617) 536-0679
- 1354A Beacon St., Brookline; (617) 277-8917

Of Kenmore Square's many used record stores, Nuggets has always been one of the largest. In recent years it has both spawned a branch in Coolidge Corner *and* moved its original location into newer, even more spacious digs.

You can find plenty to choose from in all formats. Rock is their primary seller (including lots of local bands), but there is a good selection of jazz too. Most CDs are in the $7 to $10 range; Eric Clapton's *Crossroads* was seen here for $35—and that's a four-CD set. There are new discs mixed in too, usually $11 or $12. Tons and tons of vinyl is priced from $1.99 and up. Plus music videos, T-shirts, posters, and even old copies of *Rolling Stone* for a buck apiece.

One drawback about Nuggets' cassette section: Every kind of pop music—rock, jazz, soul, etc.—is mixed in together, alphabetically by artist. Most stores don't do that. Nuggets doesn't even do it with records and discs. Oh well.

The Brookline outpost is smaller and more cramped, but draws from the same overall stock as its parent store. It's hidden down an alleyway between Beacon Street and the big parking lot behind the movie theater. Both stores are open every day; downtown, until 10 P.M. each night but Sunday.

Pipeline Records

- 1110 Massachusetts Ave., Cambridge; (617) 661-6369

A relatively recent addition to Harvard Square's already crowded music store scene, Pipeline offers a strong selection in new and used CDs, cassettes, and good old "vynal."

This pipeline sends forth lots of straight-ahead rock (you can hear it even as you approach the store). Most used CDs are $6.99 and $7.99, including titles by Nirvana and Phish. Separate bins offer clearance discs at $3 each, or four for $10. Mr. C snapped up a cassette copy of REM's *Out of Time* for $3.99. And if you just can't live without an LP of Kiss's *Double Platinum*—a classic—they've got it here for $5.99.

Plus a room full of psychotronic and horror films on video, for purchase or rental. Open seven days a week, including most evenings 'til 8 or 9 P.M.

Planet Records

- 536 Commonwealth Ave., Boston; (617) 353-0693

For a small store, this longtime favorite packs a lot in—plenty of records, tapes, and CDs. Like anything in Kenmore Square, rock is king here—but Planet is also strong in soul, jazz, and R & B.

A couple of years ago it looked like they were getting out of vinyl, going mainly with CDs. But that's not proven to be the case. Instead, they expanded the store by one-third;

and, to make the used LPs more attractive, most are hand-labeled with a sound quality rating ("8.5 out of 10"). Great idea.

Most good or new LPs are priced around $4 to $8. Planet also has a good variety of imports, rare LPs and special sets. Singles, including lots of oldies, are 49¢ to $2.99. And then there's the vintage stuff, kitschy albums from the fifties and sixties—it's hilarious just to look at the covers. Many cassettes are $4 and $5, and CDs are usually $7 to $9. Open daily from 10 A.M. to 8 P.M., Fridays and Saturdays 'til 9, Sundays 12-7.

Skippy White's Records

- 538 Massachusetts Ave., Cambridge; (617) 491-3345
- 315 Centre St., Jamaica Plain; (617) 524-4500

This has long been Boston's definitive store for all kinds of black music, from rap and urban pop to reggae, soul, R & B, and lots of gospel. Mr. White, in fact, spins "The Gospel Train" each week on WNRB radio. He knows his stuff.

These stores, the bigger of which is in JP, collectively boast one of the "largest collections of vintage 45s in the Northeast," with some 500,000 in stock dating all the way back to the 1940s.

Used LPs are the best bargains here, though many are well-worn. Prices range from 99¢ to $9.99. New CDs are carried here at full price. Local artists, along with hard-to-find titles and out-of-print discs, are another specialty. Closed Sundays.

Stereo Jack's Records

- 1704 Massachusetts Ave., Cambridge; (617) 497-9447

Yet another of Cambridge's many fine used music shops, Stereo Jack's specializes in jazz, straight-ahead blues, and R & B records, which are still a vital format in this area of music. These are mostly $1 to $4; most used CDs average from $5 to $8. Jack's doesn't seem to concentrate that much on tapes.

There is also a vast bargain bin of records for $1. "Some people come

in and only look there," says Jack. "They always walk away with something." He is more proud, though, of his extensive jazz selection. Open weekdays from 10 A.M. to 8 P.M., Saturdays 10-6, Sundays 12-7.

Strawberries "Underground"

- 38 J.F.K. St., Cambridge; (617) 354-6232

This Harvard Square branch of the local chain is a regular Strawberries on one side, and their overstock clearance outlet on the other. Turn right as you enter the store, and you'll find a small but interesting selection of bargain CDs like the Steve Miller Band's classic *Living in the 20th Century* for $7.99, the average price for these discs. Cassette tapes go for $2.99 and $3.99—again, with groups you're likely to have actually heard of.

In addition, this Strawb's buys and sells used CDs, unusual for a commercial chain. These tend to be priced from $2.99 to $7.99, which was the price spotted for a copy of Nirvana's *In Utero*. They even have some deals on VHS concert videos. Open seven days, including weeknights.

A few doors closer into the square, **Discount Records** is a tiny, longtime fave hangout at 18 J.F.K. St. (telephone 492-4064). They do not in fact sell records anymore, but they always have lots of the latest releases on sale (CDs $11.99, tapes $7.99). Students also get a 15% discount on non-sale music.

Tower Records

- 360 Newbury St., Boston; (617) 247-5900
- 95 Mt. Auburn St., Cambridge; (617) 876-3377

Huh? What's this doing in here, Mr. C? Tower may be big, they may be open 365 days a year and all, but are they cheap? Well, not necessarily for current titles—although they always discount the entire *Billboard* Top 100 by a coupla bucks.

But many shoppers aren't aware that Tower has a vast selection of cutouts—as many as 5,000 titles! These are overstocked titles that won't sell at full price anymore. Many of these cost $2.99 to $4.99 for big-name artists like Stevie Wonder and Prince (sorry P, don't have that symbol-thing on the computer).

Jazz cutouts are located in a separate section; same deal for classical, and for cassette tapes. The tape selection may be smaller, but you can often find good stuff for $3.99. No cutout LPs, though. Both stores are open daily until midnight.

CLOTHING—NEW

Know what you're buying! Clothing, like anything else, is sold at discount for many reasons. Let's go over some terms: **First-quality** means brand-new merchandise that has no flaws. It may be reduced in price as a sales promotion, because it's overstock, or because it's left over from a past season. **Discontinued** is self-explanatory; but again, these items are new and most are perfectly good.

Second-quality ("seconds," "irregulars," "IR") means new clothes that have some slight mistakes in their manufacture or that have been damaged in shipping. Often these blemishes are negligible. A reputable store will call your attention to the problem with a sign, or a piece of masking tape on the damaged spot.

MEN'S AND WOMEN'S WEAR—GENERAL

ABC Retail
- 2 Center Plaza, Cambridge St., Boston; (617) 426-5700
- 31 St. James Ave., Boston; (617) 423-3447
- 145 Bay State Dr., Braintree; (617) 843-0552
- 43 Middlesex Tpke, Burlington; (617) 229-1855
- Marshall Plaza, Framingham; (508) 626-2225,5621
- 400 Lynn Fells Pkwy., Saugus; (617) 233-5566
- 616 Middle St., Weymouth; (617) 331-6220

ABC has a large selection of women's and girls' clothing, first-quality and seconds, in both current and past-season styles. Browning blazers were recently on sale for $25, originally $60; designer T-shirts with gold appliqué were half-price at $19; so were Adolfo jackets at $29. Along with recognizable name brands, ABC carries many lesser-known, but good "everyday" labels. Stretch pants with stirrups and polka dots were reduced from $24 to $8, and a bathing suit sale featured one price—$12—for every item in that department. Open seven days.

Allston Beat Outlet Store
- 72 Brighton Ave., Allston; (617) 254-4420

If you're into funky clothes but balk at trendy high prices, this outlet near B.U. is for you. The loud music and factory-like atmosphere make a fitting backdrop for such clothes. Most of the stock here is new, although Mr. C did see a vintage wool overcoat for just $20, and tweed blazers for $10. On the same visit, all new leather jackets were on sale for 20% off, and a Knucklehead brown jacket, usually $139, was $69 *before* the reduction (end result: $56.20). The most outlandish stuff is also the most pricey: A long silver lamé dress was $79, and a jungle print fake fur bra went for $35. But where else can you get these beauties?

Hip brand names abound: A Stussy sweatshirt was $32 (down from $45) and Dr. Marten jean shorts, usually $75, were reduced to just $19 here. Speaking of the Doc, you can also get his shoes and boots here: Mr. C saw "Air Waiv" model leather lace-ups for $49, instead of the normal $95. The outlet store is open Mondays through Fridays from 11 A.M. to 6 P.M.; Saturdays until 7 P.M.

Burlington Coat Factory
- 705 Granite St., Braintree; (617) 848-3200
- Cloverleaf Marketplace, Speen St. (off Rte. 9), Natick; (508) 651-2526

See the listing under "Discount Department Stores."

Cyrk Factory Outlet
- 2 Pond Rd., Gloucester; (508) 283-5800

A small store with large savings on sportswear (manufactured right across the street), the Cyrk Factory Outlet offers up to a 50% discount on overstock, off-season, and closeout merchandise. Savings are even better on slightly damaged or just imperfect goods, including T-shirts, sweatshirts, and running togs.

On one of several bargain racks, find $3 all-cotton color T-shirts with missed seams or streaks, all minor and clearly marked with masking tape. Doral sweatshirts, 100% cotton and in several colors, are $10, and baseball caps $4, many just because they're not stamped with a company logo, which is much of Cyrk's business.

A June visit found fleece jackets priced at $30, a reduction of 40% (timing is everything). Racks of sports-themed T-shirts, with large soccer or tennis designs, were $5; cotton polo shirts trotted in at $12, and nylon running jackets for a sleek $15. Round out any outfit with a pair of sunglasses from a selection that normally runs $10-$50; here, they're five bucks. Cyrk is open from 9 A.M. to 5:30 P.M. Mondays through Saturdays, and Sundays from noon to 5 P.M.

MR. CHEAP'S PICKS
Men's and Women's Wear—General

✔ **Eddie Bauer Outlet**—"Eddie Bauer." "Outlet." Need we say more?

✔ **Freedberg's**—Not exactly "cheap"; the finest men's suits, factory-direct.

✔ **Frugal Fannie's**—Out in the 'burbs, three gold mines of past-season fashions; ask any woman who's been there.

✔ **Harry the Greek's**—This South End joint is like Filene's Basement, only packed in much tighter. Good place to take the kids for jeans and sneakers.

✔ **The King Size Outlet Store**—If you are "big and tall," you can fill all your clothing needs here, good and cheap.

Dan Howard's Maternity Factory
- 717 Granite St., Braintree; (617) 848-9397
- 34 Cambridge St., Burlington; (617) 272-4003
- 1399 Washington St., Hanover; (617) 826-7750
- 1298-E Worcester Rd. (Rte. 9), Natick; (508) 653-4722
- 120-134 Broadway (Rte. 1), Saugus; (617) 233-5254

Dan Howard manufactures and sells its own line of comfortable, quality maternity wear. Since they don't sell to other retail outlets, the "retail" prices on the tags are more like an estimate of the garments' worth; but the selling prices, thanks to the lack of middlemen, are quite good indeed.

Here, you'll find both career and casual styles, giving moms-to-be plenty of options. DH uses top-quality fabrics, in families of colors (excuse the pun) which allow you to mix and match separates flawlessly. It's all at 25% to 40% less than comparable department and specialty store goods. A stylish two-piece short set, for example, valued at $113, sells here for $79. And a sleeveless rayon dress, listed at $84, goes instead for $59—and was recently on sale for an additional 30% off. Open seven days a week.

Decelle
- Porter Square Shopping Center, Cambridge; (617) 354-7314
- 1690 Massachusetts Ave., Lexington; (617) 861-8554
- 418 Walpole St., Norwood; (617) 769-5533
- 1870 Centre St., West Roxbury; (617) 325-1400

Like its Cambridge branch in the basement of Star Market, Decelle is basically a supermarket for clothing. Men, women, boys and girls can be outfitted from head to toe here. Decelle sells a mixture of irregular items (all marked); clothes from past seasons (on clearance racks); and current fashions, bought by Decelle in large quantities and thus discounted. You'll see some upscale brand names dotted around the store, like the Liz Claiborne cotton skirt (suggested price $58) for just $30 that Mr. C found. For everyday wear, the store is lined with racks of inexpensive separates, like $15 washed silk blouses.

Men's clothes for all seasons are equally affordable. A polyester trench coat was $90 cheaper than its list price of $240, and Ocean Pacific swim trunks, elsewhere $24, were just $10 here. Lots of quality stuff for the kids, too: Mr. C saw infants' Carter's cotton sleepsuits for the tiny price of $8, and Osh Kosh rompers for girls from $15. For under it all, Decelle stocks underwear by folks like Bali, Warner, and Maidenform. Shoes, hosiery, bags, socks, and accessories round out this bargain clothing store. Open Mondays through Saturdays, 9 A.M. to 9 P.M., and Sun-

days 12 noon to 6 P.M.

Eddie Bauer Outlet
- 230 Washington St., Boston; (617) 227-4840

People who know and wear Eddie Bauer clothing swear by it, and so they love this store—where you can buy almost the same popular clothes at savings of 30% to 70% off retail prices. Most of the stock is made up of seconds and irregulars from the factory; but the boo-boos are usually so minuscule as to escape notice.

Find dresses for as little as $19.99 that had originally retailed for anywhere from $42 to $68, or sweaters for $10, and all kinds of other sportswear, outdoor gear, and shoes. Plus luggage, like duffel bags reduced from $40 to $29.50. Open daily from 10 A.M. to 7 P.M., Sundays 12-6.

Filene's Basement
- 426 Washington St., Boston; (617) 542-2011

See the listing under "Discount Department Stores."

Freedberg's Of Boston
- 112 Shawmut Ave., Boston; (617) 357-8600

Not much here is *cheap* in the usual sense—and certainly not in terms of quality. But when you can get men's suits like these at drastically reduced prices, Mr. C says that's newsworthy. Freedberg's makes clothes for the best: Louis of Boston, Saks Fifth Avenue, and the like. Way upstairs at their South End factory, on Saturday mornings from 8 to 12 noon, you can peruse the racks yourself for the current season's fashions at anywhere from 40% to 70% off. More recently, they've expanded these hours to include Thursdays and Fridays from 11 A.M. to 3 P.M.

The styles range from European cuts to conservative Wall Street looks; there are also ties, sweaters, and some women's suits and dresses. Men's suits are the main item, though. These start around $300-$450, which may sound like a lot, but these would easily cost twice as much in trendy stores. Some, in fact, would retail at well over $1,000. Go.

Frugal Fannie's Fashion Warehouse

- 55 New York Ave., Framingham; (508) 872-5800
- 1 General Ave., Reading; (617) 942-2121
- 24 Wilson Way (off Rte. 1), Westwood; (617) 329-8996

Bargain hunters have come to swear by Frugal Fannie's as much as any basement for women's fashions at big discounts. They wait for sale announcements in the mail and jump in the car. These stores are no-frills warehouse style, with common dressing rooms; this, plus limited hours, keeps overhead—and prices—low on vast racks of career and casual wear. The clothing includes both first quality and seconds.

Here you may find an irregular Albert Nipon dress of 100% silk, marked down from $298 to $120; a Jones New York skirt suit reduced from $350 to $170; or a shoulder-padded Liz Claiborne blouse for $17, originally $40.

Gloria Vanderbilt jeans were half-price at $20, and a Stanley Blacker navy blue trenchcoat was marked down to $90, from $220. There are also basement-style bargain tables of jewelry, hosiery, and other accessories.

Adding to the offbeat nature of the store is a waiting area for all the guys who've been dragged along; there is a TV as well as toys for the kids. Looks more like a holding pen. FF is truly geared to the working woman; hours are Fridays from 7-9:30 P.M., Saturdays 8-6, and Sundays 10-6 only.

Gap Outlet

- Corner Mall, 425 Washington St., Boston; (617) 482-1657

In spite of its casual clothing, Mr. C has generally found the Gap's prices anything but casual; at the Gap Outlet, recently moved from Watertown to Downtown Crossing, rates are certainly more reasonable.

You'll find clothes for men, women, and kids, from Gap and its sister brand, Banana Republic. Men's rugby shirts, originally $34, have been seen for $10; khaki walking shorts for $15; denim jackets can be a cool $20.

Women were recently nabbing BR print blazers, reduced from a snooty $148 to a respectable $40; like about half of the stock here, these were irregulars. Other ladies' stuff may include cotton scoop-neck T's reduced from $17 to $4. Lots of socks and underwear, too—a good place to stock up. Open daily.

Harry the Greek's

- 1136 Washington St., Boston; (617) 338-7511

This South End shop—which looks more like an indoor version of selling off the back of a truck—has attained legendary status when it comes to inexpensive basics for the whole family. Don't expect much in the way of amenities; the aisles are narrow and cluttered with boxes and people. But the folks are very nice; and the *deals* . . .

Much of the clothing is seconds and irregulars. As usual, this is hardly noticeable in most of the items. Among the ever-changing stock, you may find such bargains as solid-color T-shirts for $4; Hanes sweatshirts and pants for $7.50 to $8.50; men's "unbranded" sneakers for $12; and white painters' pants for $10. They also carry lots of children's sizes (recent sale: kids' Wrangler jeans, two pairs for $18).

Then there are the shoes—well, mostly sneakers and work boots, plus hiking boots by Timberland and Herman's. These include first-quality at good prices, and seconds at even better. A pair of Asics "Gel" running shoes was marked down to $35. Pick up six pairs of tube socks to go with them for five bucks.

Harry's also mixes in used jeans, unusual for a store like this; pick up a pair of nicely faded Levis for $8-$10 or so. Take cash with you—because Harry "doesn't take checks and he doesn't take American Express" . . . or any other credit cards, for that matter. Open Mondays through Saturdays from 8 A.M. to 5:30 P.M., Fridays until 6.

Hit or Miss Clearance Center

- 91 Franklin St., Boston; (617) 338-1208

Many shoppers aren't aware that this branch of the popular chain has its own bargain basement near Downtown Crossing. Prices on these career clothes for women are automatically reduced every few weeks. You may find a Boston Classics linen skirt, half-price at $20; a two-piece nylon running suit, marked down from $50 to $30; or a silk-type paisley blouse, originally $33, now just $5.

There are some big-name brands, like an Oleg Cassini linen blazer reduced from $90 to $40; or a D'Albert cotton dress in a houndstooth check, same price, from an original $140. As usual, these are mostly seconds and last season's leftovers. Open weekdays from 9 A.M. to 6 P.M., Saturdays 10-5.

The King Size Outlet Store

- Christmas Tree Plaza, Pembroke; (617) 871-4100

Big and tall men often have a hard enough time finding clothes that fit right—never mind the quality. Many turn to the King Size catalog because it's filled with stylish fashions that are well-made. Here on the South Shore, you can shop at the company's outlet, where you'll find leftover and discontinued styles for at least 50% off catalog prices.

Cotton and linen shorts—just in time for summer!—were seen recently at $29.99, a savings of $30 off the original price. Pair them with a cotton sport shirt by Gant, regularly $49.95, here just $19.99. Great selection of jeans, too, priced from $9.99 to $19.99.

If the merchandise still doesn't move fast enough, they just keep marking it down. A wool blend blazer was $175 in the catalog, $79.99 in the store, and then on sale for $19.99. Wow. Mr. C found racks of better-quality blazers, slacks, and such, worth $100 or more, marked $20 to $30. Truly royal treatment. King Size Outlet is open Mondays through Saturdays from 10 A.M. to 6

P.M., Thursdays and Fridays 'til 8 P.M., Sundays and holidays 12-5 P.M.

Loehmann's

- Burlington Village, 43 Middlesex Tpke., Burlington; (617) 272-1300
- 600 Worcester St. (Rte.9), Natick; (508) 655-1750
- Paradise Rd., Swampscott; (617) 599-7000

Loehmann's means low prices on fancy women's clothing and shoes, plain and simple. These folks practically *invented* the designer closeout store year ago in New York; suave Manhattanites still schlep out to Brooklyn for their famous deals.

Mr. C found a rayon pantsuit by Karen Miller, which retails for $190, selling here for just $90; and a Gillian wool coatdress, list price $270, here just $150. Two-ply cashmere sweaters were just $100, but get to the store early if these are advertised, because they sell out *fast*.

Don't miss the better-name designer suits and eveningwear in the now-famous Back Room. Here, a Bill Blass silk plaid dress was slashed from an original $390 to an amazing $60; and a Bob Mackie silk blouse was just $80, less than half-price. Calvin Klein fashions can usually be found here too, like a pure cashmere sweater listed at $750 but reduced to $400.

At the time of Mr. C's visit, Loehmann's was running a special sale, offering a selection of suits at a ridiculously low *two* for $199. These were originally valued at $225 to $300 each, made by designers like Kasper for A.S.L. and Oleg Cassini.

Note also that petites can do very well for themselves here—with plenty of suits, dresses, and pants to choose from. A petite dress by Depeche was seen for $299, almost $400 off the retail price. Open from 8 A.M. to 8 P.M. Mondays through Fridays, from 9:30 A.M. to 7 P.M. on Saturday, and Sunday from 11 A.M. to 6 P.M.

Milan Ltd.
- 36 Waltham St., Lexington; (617) 863-MENS (6367)

The little green awning declares "affordable excellence," and by importing most of its merchandise directly from Italy, Milan seems to achieve it. Neat and unassuming, the store lets wooden desks and a large trunk serve as tables. Yet these display some truly fine-looking men's clothing.

Find a row of suits, from Zegna and Cerruti, for $299, $399, and $450 versus (according to the signs) $900 to $2,000 "at an exclusive Boston men's store." Infer what you will. In any case, handmade 100% silk ties start at $35, not the lowest price around, but certainly reasonable. Casual summer shirts, in bright, busy patterns, are $22-$29 (down from $60-$95), and dress slacks are slashed (try saying that three times fast) from $300 down to $79.

Milan also does custom embroidery, and while its posted hours are 10 A.M. to 5 P.M. Tuesdays through Saturdays, Mr. C has firsthand knowledge that those aren't always to be trusted—so call before you go.

Newton's of Waltham
- 410 Moody St., Waltham; (617) 891-5776

This discounter specializes in sports and casual clothing seconds. They sell whatever they can get, but that may include fleece sweat shorts for $5, baseball caps with major league team insignias for $3.99, and lined Adidas jackets for $25. Printed T-shirts are three for $10. Men's insulated duck boots, in the L.L. Bean style, were recently seen for $35; men's and ladies' Wrangler jeans, irregulars, for $10; Dickie's painter pants for $12, and a six-pair pack of tube socks for $4.99. All sales are final. Open Mondays through Saturdays, 9 A.M. to 5:30 P.M.

Nobody's Perfect
- 151 Endicott St., Danvers; (508) 762-0480
- 327 West St. (Rte. 140), Milford; (508) 634-3824
- 1479 Hancock St., Quincy; (617) 479-5074
- Northgate Shopping Center, Revere; (617) 284-6183

This chain gathers up first-quality overstocks and slight irregulars from several national specialty stores. You can then buy these clothes at 50% to 90% off their original prices. Some of the names you'll find here are The Limited, Capezio, Gap, and Eddie Bauer. Merchandise is mostly second-quality, and some is damaged.

Would you believe ladies' blazers, valued at $60 to $190, selling for $8 to $16? Of course you wouldn't. Well, no one *should* ever have paid that $190 price, but still . . . . How about skirts and leggings for $8, pants for men and women, all at $12, or childrens' knit separates for $3 each?

Get on their mailing list for notification of special warehouse clearance sales. Store hours vary.

North Bay Factory Outlet
- 123 Portland St., Boston; (617) 227-1096

Heaven forbid it should rain or snow in Boston, but if it does, head into this shop and equip yourself. This men's and women's outerwear by well-known designers (especially Forecaster) will take you through three seasons of the year. The outlet store stocks closeouts, irregulars, discontinued models, and some damaged items (marked as such). North Bay works on a "shrinking price" system—every few weeks, the prices get slashed even lower, and you'll like what you see.

Mr. C found a women's Forecaster poly/nylon parka with a (fake) fur collar on sale for $89.95, down from $200. He also saw a wool blend peacoat by the same folks that at $79.95 was almost a hundred bucks below its list price of $175. Misty Harbor rain slickers in primary colors were just $16.95 each. And an elegant, full-length rayon coat by J. Gallery, listed at a frightening $195, was a more reasonable $79.95 here. Not neglecting you, fellas. A London Fog trench coat with a warm zip-out lining was seen for $99.95 here, but $185 elsewhere. North Bay is open weekdays only, from 9:30 A.M. to 5 P.M.

Stork Time Discount Maternity
- 1015 Boylston St. (Rte. 9), Newton; (617) 969-5930

In business since 1945, Stork Time can easily claim to be the longest-established maternity shop in New England. Generations of expectant mothers have, er, flocked here for deals on clothing that is high-style, but won't put a dent in the college fund.

It's a small shop, packed with looks for the office, "after 5," and around the house. Owner Joan Starkman, part of the original family that created the place, says one key to their success is the constant turnover of merchandise. "We get shipments almost on a daily basis," she points out. "Women in the area know they can come in here anytime and find something nice."

That includes smart-looking two-piece tailored suits, the popular Care Wear line of nursing tops, denim jumpers, and even bathing suits, year 'round—all at 20% to 50% off retail prices. The atmosphere is friendly, the service is first-rate, and best of all, you can pull in off the highway and park right at the door. Given the particular nature of these clothes, all sales are final; the store is open Mondays through Saturdays from 10 A.M. to 5 P.M.

Surman's Clothing
- 8 Central Square, Cambridge; (617) 492-7665

"We have one price for everybody—the lowest price," said the gentleman. He clearly meant it; he works to strike a bargain with his customers.

"You like the jacket? Take two, I'll give you twenty dollars off." Surman's is an old-style men's clothier—suits, accessories, and tailoring all under one roof at reasonable prices.

Casual suits start well under $100. During his visit, Mr. C loved a closeout on Pierre Cardin suits which brought the price down from $195 to $80. Dress shirts, slacks, and sportcoats are all here at great prices, along with jeans and corduroys.

Clothes make the man, and service is what makes this store; take your time, try whatever you like. As the salesman said, "Show people a little kindness and they'll come back." Open Mondays through Saturdays, 9 A.M. to 6 P.M.

Urban Outfitters Bargain Basement
- 11 J.F.K. St., Cambridge; (617) 864 0070

Prices at this oh-so-trendy chain are generally too big-city for Mr. C; but the bargain basement at their Harvard Square location is like an inexpensive suburb. Overstock and clearance items from the main selling floors of UO branches across the country find their way down here, at prices guaranteed to be $14.99 or less.

The fixed-price policy was instituted in late '95, as management decided this might attract even more attention than previous discounts, which started at 25% off original tags. Although it seems unlikely you'd turn up a $100 jacket for fifteen bucks, store personnel assert that virtually anything is possible. Open from 10 A.M. to 10 P.M. Mondays through Thursdays, 'til 11 P.M. Fridays and Saturdays, and 11 A.M. to 8 P.M. Sundays.

CHILDREN'S AND JUNIORS' WEAR

Baby Boom
- 1000 Washington St., Braintree; (617) 848-1600

Not that it will make you suddenly want to raise a huge family, but Baby Boom combines darling decor, ebullient employees, and a super selection to make things easier if you are.

Hundreds of brand-name goods vie for attention, all new but discounted according to deals cut with individual manufacturers, often on overstock or closeout merchandise. Dresses from JoLene run $11.99-$14.99, down from $19.99-$24.99. Flowered outfits from Petit Ami, in sizes for preemies all the way to 14-year-olds, are reduced from $31.99 down to $20.99. And Squiggles Playwear for boys and girls sells for $13.99, down from $27.99.

For first-time parents, everything is clearly grouped into sections for three-, six-, and twelve-month-old infants. The staff is always ready to help out. Hours are 10 A.M. to 6 P.M. Mondays through Fridays, 9:30-5 on Saturdays.

Marsha Factory Outlet

• 32 Tioga Way, Marblehead; (617) 631-5511

When you care enough to spend on the very best, Marsha clothing—carefully crafted children's wear, sold at such fine stores as Saks and Bloomingdale's—is the genuine article. And, if you can find their well-hidden outlet store, you'll shave 40% and more off retail prices.

Marsha gets clothes wholesale from companies like OshKosh, modifying them in unique and colorful ways. Some are cut apart into new outfits; most are embroidered with hand-designed images of soccer balls, flowers, trains, and even Sesame Street characters. At this outlet, jeans and lovely dresses are reduced from $62 (for kids' clothes?) to a more reasonable $38. Overalls are

marked down from $74 to $46, and cotton shirts from $55 to $33. Some items cost as little as $11.

Marsha gets new stuff in all the time, and needs it to move as fast as your children. Mr. C's mid-summer visit coincided with a special month-long 50% off sale; there's also a long rack of seconds marked at 75% off, blemished by small spots or imperfect adhesive on decorations. To find this unique shop, take an awkward turn off of Green Street and work your way toward the colorful sign. Open from 10 A.M. to 4 P.M., Mondays through Saturdays.

Priceless . . . Kids

• Hingham Plaza, 100 Derby St., Hingham; (617) 740-4252

This regional discount chain offers mid- to high-quality children's clothing with a unique pricing system: Everything is based on "$10." Some items are a straight ten bucks, some are two for $10, three for $10, and so on. Not everything falls into this scheme (Mr. C did see "Snoopy" T-shirts for $8.99), but most of it does.

A lot of the merchandise is buy-outs from major department stores and catalog companies. Priceless . . . Kids gets clothing and accessories from Sears, Spiegel, J.C. Penney, and others. Canvas sneakers by Jantzen were recently spotted at two pair for $10. Shirts by Arizona Jeans Co. and Bugle Boy were three for $10. Only want two? No problem—just pay 25¢ to 50¢ more per item. Still a bargain. Open seven days.

ACCESSORIES

Boston Sweats Outlet

• 16 Brighton Ave., Allston; (617) 782-0480

The main business here is custom-printed clothing: T-shirts and caps with your team's name on them, silk-screen designs, etc. But they do have display racks with samples, leftovers, and irregulars, which you can grab for a song. "Cheers" T-shirts are $6. Sweat pants and shirts with a variety

of college logos are $10 and under; baseball hats are $5. Open weekdays from 10 A.M. to 6 P.M. or thereabouts.

Kingston Textiles

• 116 Kingston St., Boston; (617) 542-8140

Near South Station, here's another silk-screening shop where you can get all sorts of activewear by Fruit of the Loom, Hanes, and others at below-retail prices. Hanes solid-color sweatshirts and pants are $6.98 and up; and their 50/50 cotton-poly T-shirts are $2.99 in white, and $3.87 in a variety of classic colors. Lee "Superweight" cotton sweatshirts—and boy, are they heavy—go for $14, almost half of what they cost in department stores. Plus tote bags for $5, baseball caps, and more. Needless to say, if there's anything at all you'd like printed on these (at extra cost), KT can do it for ya. Open weekdays only, 8:30 A.M. to 5:30 P.M.

Super Socks

- 10 Winter St., Boston; (617) 482-3750
- 520 Commonwealth Ave., Boston; (617) 247-7092
- 300 Harvard St., Brookline; (617) 739-2456
- 360 Longwood Ave., Brookline; (617) 734-9366

Women love this chain of tiny shops—it's a good place to stock up on stockings, socks, lingerie, and exercise wear. Cotton slouch socks are $2.99 a pair, as are nylon trouser socks; Hi-Performance tights, sold for $8 elsewhere, are $4.99 here. Some of the designs are on the racy side; catch a pair of fishnets here for $5. Exercise body suits are marked down from $15 to $10. There is usually a huge selection of stuff in the $1 bins, too. Hours vary, but most branches are open seven days a week, including evenings.

Swank Factory Store

- 656 Warner Blvd., Taunton; (508) 822-2527

Swank is a distributor for accessories by well-known manufacturers including Anne Klein, Pierre Cardin, Capezio, and Buxton. Leftovers, closeouts, and seconds wind up here in the factory store, usually for 50% off the original retail price.

A huge selection of Anne Klein and Guess jewelry was recently seen at an amazing 70% below retail: Anne Klein watches, listed at $195, were just $49.95. Other items include sterling silver jewelry, belts, briefcases, handbags, and more. Mr. C found a black nylon wheeled carry-on bag, valued at $159.95, for $64.99. Swank is swell for gift ideas, or a personal splurge. Open 8 A.M. to 5 P.M. Mondays through Saturdays; noon to 5 P.M. on Sundays.

TANI The Leather Outlet

- 243 Washington St., Boston; (617) 973-4884

A small storefront in Downtown Crossing, TANI is filled with everything from the tiniest handbag to the most oversized duffel. It's all crammed in higgledy-piggledy, but that adds to the bargain-hunting fun. Leather backpacks, originally $220, sell here for $189. A straw and leather handbag, retail price $41, was seen for $36. Great deals on luggage, too: A wheeled weekender, the sort flight attendants use, was found for $50 off the retail price.

Regular sales lead to even bigger markdowns. At a recent sale, Mr. C found a straw tote bag for $19.90, down from the original $39—just in time for summer beach-going. TANI also carries plenty of organizers and accessories, including Filofax, wallets, checkbook holders, and the rest. Open seven days.

Tavros Outlet Store

- 217 Newbury St., Boston; (617) 536-2999

Even the overhead on trendy Newbury Street doesn't drive prices up when you're buying directly from the manufacturer. Tavros makes its own line of leather goods in Greece, bringing them to a handful of stores here on the East Coast. This branch has been here since 1989, but only recently became an outlet store.

You'll find discounted briefcases, handbags, wallets, and more—all first quality. A black briefcase, with plenty of pockets, was a steal at $175, down from the original price of $218. A Coach-style "saddlebag," with an original retail of $96, was seen for $77. And an overnighter was reduced from $320 to a much lighter $256.

Tavros has a great selection of leather organizers, too, as well as belts and sandals. A small section of second-quality merchandise is marked at 50% to 75% off; there is also some imported silver jewelry at reduced prices. Open seven days.

Vintage, Etc.
- 1796 Massachusetts Ave., Cambridge; (617) 497-1516

In spite of the name, it's the "etc." part that offers unique values here. More than other stores, Vintage specializes in new hosiery bargains: Berkshire opaque tights for $5 in a range of sizes and hot colors, Danskins for $6, Hue socks for $5 and tights for $10.

They also have a selection of the offbeat, such as Voila pantyhose—hand silkscreened in various designs for $12. There are, of course, all kinds of great clothes to "go with" these accessories. Open Mondays through Saturdays, 10 A.M. to 6 P.M.; Sundays, noon to 6 P.M.

BRIDAL WEAR

Bridal Reflections
- 327 Pleasant St., Belmont; (617) 489-5888

First-quality gowns and dresses for brides, their mothers, and their bridesmaids fill this store; all are discounted from 10%-20% from the list prices. The more expensive the retail price, the bigger the discount, of course.

If you're familiar with wedding gowns, you'll know these brand names: Jasmine, Mon Cheri, Eden, and Justine are just some of the designers. Mr. C admired a Victoria satin gown with hand beading and a grand, sweeping train for $616.25 (15% off the list price of $725). Some of these dresses are on display in the store, but you can also order just about any gown you choose from these designers' selections.

Elegant bridesmaids' dresses by Watters and Watters start at about $145, as was a Lizette polyester ankle-length dress. And if you're really serious about getting a bargain, cruise through the sale racks at the front of the store, where you can snap up discontinued bridesmaids' dresses for just $20.

Lots of stuff besides dresses: Headpieces and veils range between $50 for a simple floral barrette to $275 for a custom-made long veil. The store will also dye pumps to match your dress, arrange dried flowers for you, order your wedding invitations, make referrals. . . the owner mused that "brides like to be pampered.

That's what we do." Heavenly! Open Tuesdays through Saturdays; Sundays and Mondays by appointment only.

David's Bridal
- 8 Newbury St., Danvers; (508) 777-8232
- 890 Providence Hwy. (Rte. 1), Dedham; (617) 251-9100

By dealing directly with their own manufacturer, David's is able to price everything in the store 30%-40% below the maker's suggested retail value. Consequently, a walk down their aisles will present wedding gowns reduced from $900 to $499 and from $189 to $155. There's a huge clearance selection of dresses at 50% off for brides and bridesmaids. Lovely flower girl dresses are as low as $99, reduced from $175.

In addition, David's provides a

MR. CHEAP'S PICK
Bridal Wear

✔ **Filene's Basement**—Didya know? Four times a year they have a one-day sale of designer gowns off the rack, $199 each. It's more like a one-hour sale, by the time they're all gone.

large selection of Oleg Cassini wedding gowns (one was reduced from $1,000 down to $566) and bridesmaid dresses, such as a beautiful emerald green grouping marked from $165 down to $130. Other assorted makers are represented too.

The store can fill special orders within four to six weeks; and a variety of accessories are 20% off when bought on the same day as the gown. Open from 10 A.M. to 9 P.M. Mondays through Saturdays, noon to 6 P.M. Sundays.

Filene's Basement
● 426 Washington St., Boston; (617) 542-2011

Four times a year, Filene's Basement in Boston runs a most unusual sale. At these magical moments you can buy designer wedding gowns, valued from $400 to $3,650—discontinueds, irregulars, and floor samples—for the single low price of two hundred bucks.

Word gets around, and this has become as hallowed an event as the nuptials themselves. Brides-to-be, joined by moms or best friends (don't try this alone) start gathering at dawn. The doors open at 8 A.M., and the frenzied rush is on. Everyone grabs whatever they can off the racks, jumping in and out of dresses (no time for fitting rooms), trading with each other until they find the right one. Five hundred gowns are gone in about thirty minutes, and the sale is over.

Is this any way to get married? Perhaps. After going through all that, you'd think twice about a divorce. Meanwhile, you can wind up with a honey of a deal. If this scene is for you, call Filene's to find out the next sale date, or keep an eye on the newspaper ads.

Saugus Shoe Barn
● 31 Osprey Rd., Saugus; (617) 233-1295

See the listing under "Shoes and Sneakers."

Not enough for ya? There are several national chains, on which Mr. C felt no need to waste precious ink—you *know* what they offer. Here are their addresses, though:

Dress Barn
● 100 Powdermill Rd., Acton; (508) 897-1557
● 123-127 Pearl, Braintree; (617) 356-0911
● 732 Belmont St., Brockton; (508) 588-3480
● 25 White St., Cambridge; (617) 497-7067
● 400 Cochituate Rd. (Rte. 30), Framingham; (508) 875-4778
● 1294 Washington St., Hanover; (617) 826-0605
● 400 Lincoln St., Hingham; (617) 749-8962
● 158 W Central St., Natick; (508) 655-6581
● 241 Needham St., Newton; (617) 332-8710
● 111 Lenox St., Norwood; (617) 762-7169
● 300 Andover St., Peabody; (508) 532-6188
● 100 Parkingway St., Quincy; (617) 479-0713
● 37 Memorial Pkwy., Randolph; (617) 963-7061
● Redstone Plaza, Stoneham; (617) 438-1751
● 427 Paradise Rd., Swampscott; (617) 595-6780
● 1092-1094 Lexington, Waltham; (617) 891-9019
● 390 Cambridge Rd., Woburn; (617) 933-8728

Marshalls
● 500 Boylston St., Boston; (617) 262-6066
● Westgate Mall, Brockton; (508) 559-2104
● 34 Cambridge St., Burlington; (617) 272-6362
● 95 Washington St., Canton; (617) 828-9570
● 80 Worcester Rd. (Rte. 9), Framingham; (508) 879-7636

- Lincoln Plaza, Hingham; (617) 749-6162
- Meadow Glen Mall, Medford; (617) 391-1331
- 275 Needham St., Newton; (617) 964-4987
- 1343 Main St., Reading; (617) 944-6150
- 655 Broadway, Saugus; (617) 233-9319
- Red Stone Shopping Center, Stoneham; (617) 438-1520
- 1005 Paradise Rd., Swampscott; (617) 581-5330

- Arsenal Mall, Watertown; (617) 923-1044
- Pleasant Shop Mall, Weymouth; (617) 337-5816

TJ Maxx
- 480 Boston Rd., Billerica; (508) 663-6228
- 300 V.F.W. Pkwy., Dedham; (617) 329-8162
- 770 Cochituate Rd., Framingham; (508) 390-3000
- 750 Fellsway, Medford; (617) 393-0027
- 450 Paradise Rd., Swampscott; (617) 595-4490

CLOTHING—USED

Used clothing is another great way to save lots of money—and don't turn up your nose at the idea. Recycling doesn't just mean bottles and cans. In these recessionary times, people are taking this approach to nearly everything, and it make a lot of sense. There is a wide range of options, from trashy stuff to designer labels. Again, a few terms:

Consignment and resale shops sell clothing they call "gently used"—by one owner who wore the article only a few times and chose to resell it. This merchandise is nearly always of high quality, and it's a great way to save lots of money on a designer piece that looks like new. Mr. C has also found several children's resale shops, which are very popular since most kids outgrow clothes faster than they out-wear them.

Vintage clothing is usually well-worn but may still cost you a bit—since "retro" styles are very popular these days. Nevertheless, there are great bargains for the persistent vintage hound. Finally, **thrift stores** sell used merchandise that has seen a lot of duty, often donated for charity. Quality and selection are strictly grab-bag, but you can sure get a lot of stuff super-cheap.

CONSIGNMENT AND RESALE SHOPS

Allison's Wonderland
- 101M Union St., Newton; (617) 969-3655

Walk down from the street level on this pricey block near the Newton Centre "T" and you'll enter a wonderland all right—a cozy shop filled with women's fashions both elegant and everyday. It's the kind of place where you can find a sexy Versace gown in black suede, originally priced around $2,000, selling for $175. . . or broken-in Gap jeans for $18.

Lots of blouses, blazers, and casual looks; a J. Crew "barn coat" was seen for $40, and a rack of leather jackets from $50 and up. For the office, two-piece suits by Ann Taylor and Jones New York go for around $60. Plus jewelry of all types, and a good selection of handbags by Louis Vuitton, Coach, and Gucci from $40 to $80. All with friendly, personal service. Open from 10 A.M. to 5 P.M., Mondays through Saturdays.

Anne's Glass Slipper
- 7 Cushing Ave., Belmont; (617) 484-7513

This is one glass slipper that fits like a dream. In among the consignment racks you'll probably see a few labels that ring "designer!" bells, like a Victoria's Secret sweater for $6, or a Jones New York cotton blouse for $10. Other clothes are suitable for work (a 2-piece rayon suit was $30) and play (a leather skirt for $20). And snap up consignment store standards, like $5 tank tops.

Glass Slipper has two excellent deals on new accessories. Hanes pantyhose and stockings are all 30% off the retail prices, while new pocketbooks are even more sharply discounted. Mr. C spotted a leather bag made by the folks at Keds; ticketed at a hefty $59, it was just $35.40 with the 40% markdown. Open Tuesdays through Saturdays from 10 A.M. to 5 P.M.

A Change of Pace
- 406 Main St., Melrose; (617) 665-8585

It's women and children first at this cozy little corner store, with impressive bargains on lovely resale clothing. A homey atmosphere lets you relish such joys as $1 clothing racks, marked with signs encouraging you to fill a whole bag for a mere $6.95.

And those clothes may include Gitano T-shirts, Lee khaki shorts, and Anderson-Little plaid shirts for women. Elsewhere, Mr. C found Banana Republic and Guess shorts ($3-$5), Dakota Blue jeans ($2), a slinky black Liz Claiborne dress ($10), and a good selection of jeans (including Gap and Ralph Lauren) as low as $4.

The children's racks offered OshKosh overalls for $5, a two-piece Hush Puppies outfit ($4.50), and an array of Carter's and Fisher-Price clothing for even less. Bridging the mother and child gap is a selection of maternity clothing, such as a Mothercare poly-cotton dress for $8 and lots of blouses for $2.50. Adding dimension to the shop is a bevy of vintage purses, priced from $4-$10. Open 9:30 A.M. to 4:30 P.M. Mondays through Saturdays.

The Bargain Box
- 117 Newbury St., Boston; (617) 536-8580

Given the neighborhood, you'd expect the fancy names on these labels—but not the bargain-basement prices. Would you believe an $800 Alan Bilzerian dress—used maybe once or twice—for $185? Or an Escada floral silk print skirt and blouse, originally priced at $500 and $380, respectively, here just $225 for the set?

More down-to-earth, there are plenty of blouses for $10 to $25, blazers for $25 to $55 and dresses for $18 to $68; as well as evening gowns, shoes, jewelry, and accessories. Many sport popular names such as Liz Claiborne, Adolfo, and others.

The Bargain Box carries no men's clothing, but their "Bargain Tots" department downstairs offers similar deals on children's stuff (see the listing in that section). All purchases benefit the Junior League of Boston, a non-profit women's organization that sponsors volunteer programs around the city. They've operated the store for nearly fifty years. Open Mondays through Saturday from 10 A.M. to 6 P.M., Thursday nights until 8 P.M., and Sundays noon to 5 P.M. These shops are staffed largely by volunteers, so always call ahead to confirm hours.

The Closet
- 175 Newbury St., Boston; (617) 536-1919

Here's another fun place to find designer names cheaply on Newbury Street. A pair of Ellen Tracy slacks, originally $42, was seen here at half that price. Also, a pair of Papagallo shoes for just $16 and an Ann Taylor dress of 100% silk for $59.

There is a limited selection of men's clothing, such as a Giorgio Armani sportcoat for $165—a splurge, yes, but a great deal. Perhaps a Christian Dior dress shirt for $26 to go with it. The Closet is open Mondays from 12-6 P.M., Tuesdays through Saturdays from 10 A.M. to 6, Thursdays 'til 7.

Further up the block, check out **Déja Vu** at 222 Newbury St., telephone (617) 424-9020, for more fancy women's consignments. Open Tuesdays through Saturdays from 10:30 A.M. to 5:30 P.M.

Daisy's Discoveries
- 407 Waverly St., Framingham; (508) 620-1656

Mr. C isn't sure which is the real discovery: this jam-packed little shop, or Daisy herself. She's an outgoing sort who warmly greets everyone who walks in—and winds up being a surrogate mother to many of them by the time they walk out.

Clothing, housewares, jewelry, and decorative bric-a-brac from the 1920s onward fill every square inch of this former railroad building, across from the Framingham train station. Though it has the feel of a thrift shop, all of this merchandise is sold on consignment. You may find some new items, like a batch of Bill Rodgers mesh running shirts for $2.99 each; most of the clothing is used, as was a Neiman-Marcus blazer and blouse set ($20).

Amazingly, Daisy has managed to cram ten rooms full of stuff. Head down to the basement, for instance, and you'll find vintage fashions from the '50s and '60s (very popular with area college students and theater groups). The fanciest of gowns rarely tops $15. Not only can you find hats and gloves to complete the outfit, but back upstairs, you can even add a chartreuse-shaded parlor lamp.

As Daisy herself told Mr. C, "We specialize in the fun, the dumb, the weird, and the unusual." Most unusual of all is the store's guest book; given the town's melting-pot new-

---

MR. CHEAP'S PICKS
Consignment and Resale Shops

- ✔ **The Bargain Box**—Cheap clothes on Newbury Street? Hey, if you want classy secondhand deals, you've gotta go where the money is. Lots here for children, too.

- ✔ **Silk Road Consignerie**— Recently expanded, an ever-changing collection of fancy women's fashions.

- ✔ **Something Extra**—$28 silk dresses and $200 mink coats prove that elegant doesn't have to mean expensive.

- ✔ **The Turnabout Shoppe**— Perhaps the classiest used clothing store you'll ever see.

---

comers—many of whom make this an early stop—she's had customers from as far away as Russia, England, and China. There's lots of children's stuff here too, by the way. Open Tuesdays through Saturdays from 10 A.M. to 5 P.M. (Thursdays to 7); closed Sundays and Mondays.

Encore
- 66 Billings Rd., Quincy; (617) 328-1179

Encore describes itself as a "quality consignment shop," and lives up to this by having the look, feel, and in many cases the merchandise of a retail boutique. Accordingly, the prices are a bit higher than some Cheapsters will want to pay; the labels, however, are top-notch, and everything is in fine condition.

On the designers rack, featuring lots of brand-new clothing (with original tags), gals may find blazers from Leslie Fay, Adolfo, and Ann Taylor for as low as $19.99. On another, a royal blue Christian Dior suit was seen for $49.99, and a pantsuit from Liz Claiborne for $34.99.

Most slacks can be had for $10, and blouses for around $8. Shorts from Guess run $5.99, and a wall of colorful dresses included a beaut from Karin Stevens for $19.99. You're definitely paying for the name (since no-name dresses here are just $9.99), but nowhere near as much as you *could*. Any items looking even a bit worn are drastically reduced in price, and after 30 days, another 20% is taken off.

Encore also features shoes, leather shoulder bags, and some jewelry, as well as two racks of children's clothes. They're open Tuesdays through Saturdays from 10 A.M. to 5 P.M.

Encore
* 251 Newbury St., Boston; (617) 375-1059

When you're looking for upscale clothing, Newbury Street is of course the place to go. Want to save a bundle by going secondhand? Guess what—same advice. Encore offers a great selection of designer duds, including glitzy special occasion wear, at a fraction of the original prices.

Cheapsters will love these fashions by Donna Karan, Escada, Anne Klein, Saks Fifth Avenue, Yves St. Laurent, and more. A woman's suit in off-white wool was $150—a lot less than it originally cost at Neiman Marcus. A Perry Ellis cranberry-colored wool coat—slightly damaged, but definitely fixable—was a mere $50. A silk jacket by Ellen Tracy ($60) would pair well with an Armani skirt ($70). Open Tuesdays through Fridays from 11 A.M. to 6 P.M.; Saturdays and Sundays 12-5 P.M.

Encore Exchange
* Harvard Arcade, 318 Harvard St., Brookline; (617) 566-4544

This Coolidge Corner boutique is filled with incredible bargains for the sophisticated shopper. Some of the designer dresses, furs, jewelry, and accessories are new; more often, "gently used."

A new leather jacket by Andrew Marc, meant to retail for $650, was on the racks for just $250. Most gowns start at $60, with other clothes from $30 and up.

There is also quite a selection of semi-precious and costume jewelry, some one-of-a-kind creations, like a locket made with Swarovski crystal by a California artist—it would sell for $450 on Rodeo Drive, and here it's $150. At the other end of the price spectrum, there are lots of $5 and $10 earrings too. Open Mondays from 12-4 P.M., and Tuesdays through Saturdays from 11:30 A.M. to 4:30 P.M.

Le Bon Marché
* 10 Arrow St., Cambridge; (617) 497-0390

Sharing a little sidestreet space with an antiques dealer, this shop has lots of dressy and dress-down looks for the ladies. So, whether you prefer a Lord & Taylor petite blazer and skirt for $40, or a full-length nightgown in slinky black from Victoria's Secret for $12, or just jeans and a top for less than $20, you'll probably find something here that's just right.

This schizoid approach makes LBM perfect for its Harvard Square locale. Plenty of jewelry and accessories, too. Open daily from 11 A.M. to 7 P.M., Sundays from 1-5 P.M.

Models Resale
* 969 Concord St. (Rte. 126), Framingham; (508) 875-9094

Hidden away in the handsome Old Path Village shopping center near the intersection of Routes 30 and 126, this store is attractive both outside and in—what with its emphasis on eveningwear and smart professional outfits for women. Owner Carolann Gillard has created a consignment shop with a strong reputation for top-quality clothing.

The place is spacious and airy, with attractively furnished fitting rooms. There is plenty of fine clothing to see, from a fancy silk strap dress and shawl by Judith Ann (originally over $1,000, here $160) to a European-style herringbone blazer and skirt by Harvé Benard for $34. Plus shoes in great condition, like a pair of

Nine West boot shoes for $18, and lots of handsome sterling silver and costume jewelry. All in a friendly, relaxed setting. Models Resale is open seven days, including Wednesdays through Fridays until 7 P.M.

Not far away, on the westbound side of Route 9, is another popular women's consigner, **Jodi's Resale Boutique**. The address is 419 Worcester Rd.; telephone (508) 626-0900. Jodi usually has a good supply of the big names on hand, from Dior to DKNY. Closed Sundays and Mondays.

Nancy's Place
• 905 Great Plain Ave., Needham; (617) 444-0367

This cozy little corner shop makes the most of its small space by only displaying clothes for the current season. Though you may find something as fancy as a Louis Ferald suit, once $900 (selling here for $150), or a gauzy Anne Klein cocktail dress reduced from an original $500 to just $120, most of the looks and labels are more casual. Plenty of jeans, and colorful tops and vests, range from $5-$12 or so. Shoes, both dressy and funky, are barely worn. And there's a good selection of jewelry to accent any fashion—from consignment pieces ($10-$15) to creative new sterling silver ($12-$30).

Owner Nancy Weitzman learned the consignment biz by working for someone else first, then opening her own shop about three years ago. She keeps the place bright and fun. Open Tuesdays through Saturdays, usually from 10 A.M. to 6 P.M.

One More Tyme
• 1271 Washington St., Newton; (617) 969-2959

For about 25 years, this tidy, friendly shop has been selling used and consignment women's clothing in excellent condition. There are many designer labels, from Armani and Mondi to Jaeger and more. One visit even turned up a St. John strapless evening gown, retailing for $500, on sale for $195—its original owner purchased it for the one-tyme-only occa-

sion of meeting Princess Di!

The shop also has a selection of belts, jewelry, and handbags. Senior citizens receive a special discount. Open Mondays through Saturdays from 11 A.M. to 4:30 P.M.

Not far away is **Second Appearance** at 801 Washington Street; telephone (617) 527-7655. The quality of these women's items varies more here, but blemishes are clearly pointed out. Mr. C's expert liked a Laura Ashley "sailor suit" in light blue, only $45. Open 10 A.M. to 5 P.M., Mondays through Saturdays.

Repeat Performance
• 448 Massachusetts Ave., Arlington; (617) 641-2824

A wonderful source of (primarily) consigned kids' clothing. For rock-bottom prices, rummage through the $1 bin to find play clothes and everyday basics. At the other end of the scale, look for famous brands, like a Baby Dior infant romper ($5.75) or a size 8 Polly Flinders sailor suit ($15). In between these extremes, Mr. C saw a Mickey Mouse sweatshirt for $4.75, and cotton infants' sleepers from $2.75. Also look for used shoes, like a $5 pair of patent leather flats. This store isn't squeamish: It even sells used training pants ($4 and up) and used socks (50¢ a pair). Well. . .

A separate room features second-hand equipment, like a Fisher Price car seat ($22) or a girls' Columbia bicycle ($25). These are non-returnable. Used toys and books are good bargains: Mr. C saw an Etch-a-Sketch for $8.

New stuff here is more expensive, of course, but sales can bring the prices down substantially. When Mr. C visited, a two-piece longjohn set was $13.56 instead of $16.95. This store focuses on the little ones, but it doesn't ignore Mom. Maternity clothes include bathing suits (from $15), pants ($10 and up) or a Mothercare cotton sundress ($18). Plus a rack of "how-to" parenting books. Open Mondays through Saturdays from 10 A.M. to 5 P.M.

Second Time Around

- 167 Newbury St., Boston; (617) 247-3504
- 8 Eliot St., Cambridge; (617) 491-7185
- 1169 Walnut St., Newton; (617) 964-4481

Well-established and fun to browse, Second Time Around has really branched out. The original Newton store is still "around," though the men's shop down the street is gone. Now, all three offer a mix of men's and women's new and used clothing. A Mary McFadden couture evening gown, with a beaded top, still bore its original price tag of $4,580 (!) but STA's price was $995.

Among the more affordable goodies seen here recently were a pair of J. Crew slacks for $20, long-sleeve cotton blouses for $12, and a two-piece DKNY ensemble for a terrific $168. Men's items included a Brooks Brothers blazer for $98. There are also lots of new accessories, like Zegna neckties, not $120 but a less-constricting $42.

Colored price tags alert you to further reductions of 20% to 50% on slower-moving merchandise. It's all fine stuff. Open seven days, except for the Newton branch which is closed on Sundays.

Silk Road Consignerie

- 1382A Beacon St., Brookline; (617) 739-3399

"Designers charge too much, for what? Their names," says Miki Boni, the artist who created her own shop in response to high prices. She's filled that shop with beautiful clothes, thanks to women who empty their closets of these fancy things.

Giorgio Armani, Escada, Anne Klein, and Valentino are just a few of the names you'll find here, at a fraction of their original costs. In many cases these are salesmen's samples—display pieces they took to major stores for a season and then had no more use for. These, obviously, have never been worn. Ms. Boni is very big on recycling; why should such clothes go to waste? "You can look

better for your career without having to pay a lot."

Indeed, some examples bear this out. A black leather jacket and skirt by Avanti was on sale for $75; Bandolino open-toe dress shoes were $12; a pair of Anne Klein linen slacks were $25. There is also jewelry, including many antique and one-of-a-kind pieces. Open Mondays through Saturdays from 10 A.M. to 6 P.M., Thursdays 'til 7.

Something Extra

- 474 Massachusetts Ave., Arlington; (617) 648-2400

This is the Saks Fifth Avenue of consignment clothes shops. Think of your favorite designer; Something Extra probably has something with his or her label on it. Everything here is on consignment, and it's all for women (lucky them!). Mr. C found an Oleg Cassini poly/rayon suit, a Gillian silk dress, and a long London Fog trench coat, each priced at just $28. Even casual clothes are often famous brands, like Bill Blass jeans ($8) and an Izod madras cotton blazer ($11).

Something Extra specializes in furs, and there are tons of choices in mink, fox, raccoon, beaver, and others. A long black diamond mink coat was $200; black or gray Persian lamb coats with mink collars, just $98. This is also a fantastic place to buy gowns for special occasions: Prom dresses (around $21), even a beaded wedding gown ($150) are among the possibilities.

Everything here is in fabulous condition; some clothes still have their original tags on them. Finish off your outfit with a pair of secondhand pumps or heels, or accessories like $2 leather belts. Open from 10 A.M. to 5 P.M., six days a week.

Treasure Chest

- 124 Pleasant St., Marblehead; (617) 631-8085

"Avast, me hardies! Take half off any price tag dated more than a month ago! Har harrr!" Such is the message buried in this Treasure Chest, whose used clothing selection is as deep as the ocean itself—and a vast percentage of the tags when Mr. C visited were indeed at least a month old.

That policy does not include the better designer clothing at the front of the store, but a $3,000 blue leather jacket and skirt suit by Jean Claude priced at $300 doesn't need further enhancement. Nor does a Gap sweater, with its original $84 tag, selling for $40, or a Neiman Marcus silk jacket and skirt outfit for $28.

Miles of racks feature plenty of those month-old bargains on women's clothes, such as a cotton Bill Blass dress selling for $12, and a variety of Lizwear cotton sweaters for $6-$7. Lots of shoes, too.

There are several racks of men's clothes *way* in the back, including suit jackets from Filene's as low as $12 and pants from Dockers for $8, but this is primarily a women's clothing store. Descriptive tags identify virtually every piece of clothing. Open 10 A.M. to 5 P.M. six days, Sundays 12-5.

The Turnabout Shoppe
• 30 Grove St., Wellesley; (617) 237-4450

A few years ago, Elaine Sugarman needed a little project to help cope with some health problems. Interested in fashion, she decided to open a clothing resale store; not only did it "turn about" her life, but it's turned into one of the finest such places Mr. Cheap has found in any city.

An 1869 woodframe house in downtown Wellesley gives the store extra charm. Wind your way through a series of small rooms on two floors: At the front is the "couture room," filled with dazzling creations by Armani, Donna Karan, Karl Lagerfeld, jewelry by Chanel, and more. Turnabout specializes in upscale names, so the place is not inexpensive; but when you see a $350 Escada suit which originally cost $3,000, it *is* a bargain. And they're very fussy about what they take in, going only for clothes in fine condition.

The same approach is taken with Anne Klein suits, Joseph Abboud sweaters, Perry Ellis overcoats, leather jackets, like-new shoes, and unworn samples too. But, in the words of Elaine's husband (and business partner) Herb Kutzman, "There are no jeans here." Nor anything for men or kids, though that was attempted early on. Hey, when you're a hit with one thing, you stick with it.

How much of a hit? Women actually fly up from New York to spend a day shopping here. Sure, they'll drop some heavy change; but, for a few hundred bucks, they'll come away with an entire "new" wardrobe of eye-catching, unique looks. If you live around here, you can stay ahead of even *these* trendy folks. Open Mondays through Saturdays from 10 A.M. to 6 P.M., and Thursdays until 8.

Unique Repeats
• 395A Harvard St., Brookline; (617) 738-7545

Formerly occupied by Zazu, one of the first consignment shops in the Coolidge Corner area, this successor carries on the tradition with a comparable selection of fine designer names in women's fashions. Changing ownership right around this book's press time, Mr. C can't offer too many details, but Unique Repeats promises to be worth a visit. Open seven days, including Tuesdays and Thursdays until 7 P.M.

Wearevers
• 106 Prospect St., Cambridge; (617) 497-0220
• 1356 Cambridge St., Cambridge; (617) 491-4427

These stores sell both used and new clothing; you'll be able to determine between them because new clothes are labeled with white tags, and used clothes have colored tags. The prices on the tags will be a giveaway, too: As you'd expect, the used clothing is a much bigger bargain. Still, although most new clothes are fairly pricey, some are more affordable, especially the items on sale. An embroidered cotton shirt was on sale for $32 when Mr. C visited, down from $110. But who'd pay the $110 when a few racks away, a perfectly clean, secondhand Pierre Cardin blouse hung for a mere $8?

As you poke through the second-hand clothes, you'll see a lot of familiar labels: Gap chinos for $12, or an Express velour dress for the same price. Nice cotton sweaters were available from just $8, and tank tops were a steal at $5. Mr. C also found some good bargains on used shoes such as Sam & Libby ballet flats for $8. Everything here is in excellent shape, and all clothing is made of natural fibers.

BRIDAL WEAR RESALE SHOPS

Vows Resale Bridal Boutique

- 680 Worcester Rd. (Rte. 9), Framingham; (508) 620-6867
- 132 Adams St., Newton; (617) 332-7870

Husband and wife team Leslie and Rick DeAngelo began this small business three or four years ago in Newton, selling secondhand wedding gowns just as that idea was taking off. They sure got in at the right time; these days, they get enough used and new gowns (usually closeouts) to fill two stores—several hundred in stock.

Upscale silk dresses from designers like Diamond, Bianchi, Galina, and Christos can frequently be found here. All dresses, whether new or used, are initially marked at half their original retail value. Unlike some other bridal stores, Vows specializes only in gowns and headpieces; they don't do alterations themselves (the store gets too busy), but can make arrangements for you with a seamstress. Vows is open in Newton Tuesdays through Fridays from 10 A.M. to 8 P.M. by appointment only; walk-in hours are Saturdays from 10 A.M. to 5 P.M. The Framingham store was just opening at press time; call for their schedule.

Zazu Resale Bridal

- 80 Winchester St., Newton; (617) 527-2555

New England's very first resale bridal store, Zazu has more than a distinctive name—a well-established reputation for quality, price, and service. The store gets secondhand wedding gowns with high-end labels like Christian Dior, Priscilla, Bianchi, and Amsale—designer silk dresses which start around $600 (amazing). Lesser-known brands can be had for as little as $250. All of these are 50% to 75% off the original prices.

Mother-of-the-bride dresses are also secondhand. The only new items in the store are found in the "Alternative" section—fine quality dresses for brides or bridesmaids (get a discount on three or more) in the $150-$200 range. And heck, these can actually be used more than once! How's that for wedding gown value?

On that subject, original owner Anita Belt has also made a mission of saving newlyweds cash by warning them of a little-known ripoff: wedding dress "preservation." Dry cleaners charge a pretty penny to treat and seal up gowns after the wedding, but evidently there is little that can be done to avoid yellowing—apart from sealing and stashing the dress yourself, which works about as well for free.

Zazu now offers all sorts of related bridal services along with its clothes; Anita also cautions that this kind of shopping may require several visits. Dresses come in almost daily—be patient, and you're bound to strike gold within a couple of weeks. Open Tuesdays through Thursdays 11 A.M. to 8 P.M.; Fridays and Saturdays 10 A.M. to 5 P.M.

CHILDREN'S RESALE SHOPS

Bargain Tots
- 117 Newbury St., Boston; (617) 536-8580

If you already know and love the Bargain Box (see the listing above), and you have children, then you'll be wild about Bargain Tots. Downstairs from the grownups' shop, they have an equally good selection of designer label and quality brand children's and maternity clothes.

Is your tot trendy at two? Get a pair of Guess overalls for $15. Purple overalls by OshKosh B'Gosh, with a matching T-shirt, were seen for $12. Teeny turtlenecks (size 18 months), in a variety of colors, were a recent steal at $1 each. At the other end of the spectrum, a blue velvet party dress—brand new!—was a mere $60. Plus accessories like a cloth baby carrier, in very good condition, for $15.

Bargain Tots is also a good place to check out for new and used maternity wear. Moms-to-be may snap up a two-piece knit ensemble for $45. Hours, like the Bargain Box, are Mondays through Saturday from 10:30 A.M. to 5:30 P.M., and Sundays noon to 5 P.M. These shops are staffed largely by volunteers, so always call ahead to confirm hours.

Children's Orchard
- 807 Boylston St. (Rte. 9), Brookline; (617) 277-3006
- 861 Edgell Rd., Framingham; (508) 788-0072
- 2088 Commonwealth Ave., Newton; (617) 244-0030
- 1001 Providence Hwy. (Rte. 1), Norwood; (617) 769-4388
- 15 Scammell St., Quincy; (617) 770-4979
- *And other suburban locations*

Many of Mr. C's young-parent friends consider this chain of resale shops to be among the best. Unlike most such stores, clothing is organized not by type but by size (look for the apple "number" at the top of each rack). Thus, instead of roaming around, you can easily find everything they have for your toddler at that moment. The buyers are very se-lective, only taking in items that are in good condition. Sizes range from infant to size 8.

There are also plenty of other things in the Orchard, including lots of shoes, toys and games, and some furniture. Car seats start as low as $20. Store hours vary.

Kid to Kid
- 14 Brandy Ct., Reading; (617) 944-5835

Any store can sell children's clothing; but not every store gives the appearance of truly welcoming children. Kid to Kid sure does, and its prices show plenty of affection for the tight budget, as well.

The comfy, carpeted corner store feels like a living room, with immaculate used clothes for toddlers to 12-year-olds. Hundreds of girls' dresses, by OshKosh, Bryan, and Nannekins, are under $6, while boys' shirts by Buster Brown and Izod are under $5. Be an MVP with the growing sports fan by bringing home items like Red Sox pajamas ($6.95), tiny Patriots' jackets ($5.95), and Celtics' warm-up outfits ($5). Many of these have never been worn at all. New bonnets were seen here too, reduced from $10 to $6.95. Round out the trip with a Mattel "Speak 'n Say" toy for $5, or Fisher-Price toys as low as $1. Kid to Kid is open Mondays through Saturdays from 10 A.M. to 4 P.M.

The Peanut Gallery
- 45 South Main St., Natick; (508) 655-9440

Owner Joan McMahon has packed this little gallery with tons of new and used clothing, shoes, strollers, and the like. Sizes range from infants to teens (girls size 14, boys size 20), as well as maternity clothes for moms.

New items recently included "Power Ranger" T-shirt-and-short sets on sale for 20% off retail; used goodies offered a girl's (size 10) party dress by Diane von Furstenburg for $10.50. Maternity deals: New Delia McKain jersey knit pants for $8, a

---

MR. CHEAP'S PICKS
Children's Resale Shops

✔ **Kid to Kid**—Colorful and inexpensive clothes and accessories—Mr. C kids you not.

✔ **Wear It Again Kids**—Fancy stuff, all in great condition—they're *very* fussy here.

---

used Lady Roi print long dress, with an ivory blouse, $32. And don't forget to check the 75% off rack, and the 50¢ bin! Open Tuesdays through Saturdays from 10:30 A.M. to 4 P.M.

Wear It Again Kids
• 32 Lincoln St., Newton; (617) 244-7060

A friend of Mr. C's, with two infants on her hands, insisted that this is one of the best children's resale shops around. Indeed, owner Marge Altshuler is well-renowned for her exceedingly fussy tastes, filling her store only with clothing in fine condition, and lots of designer labels. Furthermore, she takes in no synthetics at all; only clothing made with natural fibers like wool and cotton.

Brands found here include the Gap, Polo, Mousefeathers, Blue Moon, and many others. Mr. C even saw a flower-girl dress by Valentino! Sizes here range from infant to boys' and girls' size 12. Nicely faded denim jeans are arranged in bins from 6 to 14; a pair of Calvins was seen for $12. And a pair of black patent leather shoes by 9 West Kids looked like new for $8.

There are also some never-worn items, selling for half of their retail price; used clothes are one-third of their original value. Lots of new hair bows, toys and knick-knacks as well, most for a dollar or two. A classy store. Open Mondays through Saturdays from 10 A.M. to 4 P.M.

VINTAGE SHOPS

Bananas
• 78 Main St., Gloucester; (508) 283-8806

There's a *bunch* of reasons for shopping at Bananas. Its scenic location in downtown Gloucester, and great clothing from the '50s and '60s at throwback prices are among them.

Waltz down memory lane in a beaded pink gown ($12) or a prom dress right out of *Peggy Sue Got Married* ($24); tuxedo jackets sell for $30, with ruffled shirts as low as $12. A striking satin gown in fuchsia was seen for $40, and one in black taffeta (with a belt) for $16. All items sport fully descriptive tags.

Mr. C found a great old-time baseball jacket for $14; a gold nylon men's shirt ($14) may draw accolades in some circles and animosity in others. Well-heeled women's shoes by Martinique and Imperial are $5, and hats, such as a black straw antique, come in as low as $7. Spruce up your outfit with a colorful feather boa for $8, or a silk tie for $3. Plus a wealth of vintage sterling silver jewelry for $10-$16, and leather bags and purses for $4-$6.

Racks of clothes stretch the length of the store, so be prepared to spend some time. Deals like these don't exactly grow on *trees*, y'know. Open from 10 A.M. to 5 P.M. Mondays through Saturdays, and 12-5 on Sundays.

Bertha Cool
• 528 Commonwealth Ave., Boston; (617) 247-4111

One flight above Kenmore Square, Bertha Cool has lots of great stuff to wear down on the street—in Kenmore, Copley, Harvard, or any other place where it's hip to be square.

The clothing is a bit on the pricey

side for used, but it's of great quality and still less than what you'd pay for new. A nicely broken-in pair of Levis is $15; a new pair of men's patent-leather uniform shoes can be found for $40. For women, a long, black sequined dress is $75; other dresses range down to $55 and less. A really sharp-looking leather jacket was also $75.

You'll find vintage jewelry here, too—a man's tie tack, with a horse-head design, is $9; women's ankle bracelets are $14. And don't forget cool sunglasses and hats. The shop is small, but crammed from floor to ceiling. Open Mondays through Saturdays from 11 A.M. to 6 P.M., Sundays 1-5.

Cinderella's Closet
● 370A Chestnut Hill Ave., Brighton; (617) 566-8511

Perhaps the name fits best because Cinderella's fairy godmother made so much out of so little at hand. This small, cozy shop in Cleveland Circle has a limited but lovely selection of nice clothing, such as dresses for $10 to $20 and jeans for $9; plus hats, shoes, funky horn-rimmed sunglasses, and more.

Most of the stock is women's stuff, with a few items for the guys. There are also lots of period looks, like flapper dresses for $75; many of these can be rented as well, especially popular during prom season at nearby Boston College. Open seven days a week, unusual for this kind of store.

Cafe Society
● 131 Cypress St., Brookline; (617) 738-7186

Like so many vintage shops, the woman behind the counter here is the one who owns the store, and finds the great clothing. Cafe Society has fancy retro clothes, like tuxedos for $50, a black chiffon ruffle skirt for $28, and men's brown and white wing-tip shoes for $40. There are lots of hats, fedoras for men and veiled Victorians for women. All sorts of handbags and costume jewelry, too.

In more contemporary styles, there

MR. CHEAP'S PICKS
Vintage Shops

✔ **Bananas**—Hip vintage clothing and no monkey business on pricing make this Gloucester spot worth the trip from anywhere.

✔ **The Garment District**—Perhaps the city's largest retro clothing store; pick a decade and do yourself up. Home of the legendary "Dollar A Pound" department.

✔ **Keezer's**—*The* place to buy used formal wear, along with everything else for men. Great prices, lots to see.

✔ **Oona's Experienced Clothing**—The '60s will never die at this Harvard Square landmark.

---

was a Laura Ashley jumpsuit, in a floral print, for $22, and many dresses from $20 and up. Jeans for men and women were mostly around $15, in nicely broken-in condition. The store is clean and bright, and all the clothing is well-marked and displayed. Open weekdays from 12 noon to 6 P.M., Saturdays 11-6.

Dragonfly
● 1297 Cambridge St., Cambridge; (617) 492-4792

According to its owner, this vintage clothing shop sells "a little bit from each decade," from the Victorian age to the present day. If you'd like to dress as a '20s flapper, a '50s housewife, or a '70s disco dancer, this is the place for you. Many items are helpfully marked with their original decade. Mr. C found a neon green '70s bell-bottom suit for $32; a "Jackie O" style '60s coatdress for $25; a '50s full chiffon skirt for $28.

The shop sells basic clothing as well: Men's wool suit jackets range from $16-$20. Lots of leather here—a bomber jacket with a fake fur collar was $65.

This is also an excellent shop for accessories. Shelves of hats—both plain and elaborate—line one wall. The simpler ones were priced from about $10. Gold or silver lamé pouch evening bags were just $8. Dragonfly also stocks vintage jewelry, along with glasses and chinaware, bedspreads, and tablecloths. Predictably, Dragonfly does brisk business around Halloween, but you'll find affordable, wearable, and fun clothes here for the entire year. All sales are final. Open Mondays through Saturdays from 11 A.M. to 6 P.M.; Sundays from 12 noon to 5 P.M.

The Garment District
• 200 Broadway, Cambridge; (617) 876-5230

Probably the area's best vintage clothing store, this place is huge—*and* they've recently expanded and cleaned up the act. Their clothes are super-cheap as well as fancy: You can find men's Italian suits, or taffeta prom dresses, from $10 to $25. Plus a children's section. They even use a Filene's Basement-type markdown system.

There is usually a big rack of blue jeans for $9.99; long tweed winter coats for as little as $20, especially off-season; skirts from $5 to $20, and much more. And that doesn't even touch the kooky stuff; you won't find a larger collection of Hawaiian shirts ($5 to $10) in town.

Another interesting line is "restyled" clothing by the quirky local designer Eddie Kent. He takes vintage clothes, cutting and sewing them into new creations that blend the present with the past. They are wild. Dresses run from $25 to $50; a pair of black velour hot pants with a rhinestone belt was $28; and a flowered minidress was $26.

More recently, the Garment District has added vintage records to match its clothing. Records from the 1940s to the present sell for $2-$3. The store is open daily until 7 P.M.; parking is extremely limited.

But, before we leave this district, Mr. C must mention the phenomenon known as **Dollar A Pound**. Once a weekend-only event, the first level of this warehouse now opens up each day from 9 A.M. to 2 P.M. (Saturdays and Sundays from 7:45 A.M. to 1 P.M.). They sell off old clothes that would have been made into rags for the shipping industry but may still have some value if you're into the worn look. It all goes for, you guessed it, $1 a pound.

Great Eastern Trading Company
• 49 River St., Cambridge; (617) 354-5279

Here is a vintage shop with lots of fun stuff "from the 20s to the 90s", attractively laid-out and easy to see and try on. The owner clearly takes a lot of care with her merchandise, and has been doing so for over twenty years.

You can find men's sportcoats from $5 to $15, cotton shirts as low as $2.50, Hawaiian shirts for $12, and tuxedo jackets for $25 to $45. Good deals on leather jackets too, as well as lots of used Levis for $18. For women, there is a delightful variety of evening dresses from $10 to $30—lots of sequins and lace. Skirts are $5 to $25, and blouses range from just $3 to $18. There is also fine handcrafted jewelry from around the world, including sterling silver hoop earrings for as little as $1 to $3; plus handbags, hats from various decades, tapestries, lace, and more, from the Victorian era onward. Open daily 11 A.M. to 6:30 P.M., Sundays from 1-5.

Down the street, check out more vintage duds in the basement of **Justin Tyme** at 91 River Street, Cambridge, (617) 491-1088. This small but packed shop features a basement of clothes that lean heavily on the 1960s and 1970s. Open Wednesdays through Fridays from 1 to 7 P.M., Saturdays 11-6, and Sundays "by chance."

Keezer's Harvard Community Exchange

- 140 River St., Cambridge; (617) 547-2455

Across the street from Great Eastern and Justin Tyme is one of the grand-daddies of the clothing resale biz, Keezer's. They've made their name in men's formal wear, but they sell everyday stuff too. Secondhand tuxes are among the best bargains around: Used tuxedo jackets are $40 to $60—most places'll charge you that just to rent a tux for a night. Attention musicians, frequent wedding guests, etc.: Why not own one instead? Add pants for $22.50, and a (new) shirt for $15. Plus bow ties, suspenders, shoes, the works. If you prefer to rent, prices start as low as $40.

Keezer's also has lots of second-hand suits; a Brooks Brothers pin-stripe, for example, was seen for $42.50. Plenty of wool overcoats too (a Burberry coat for $55), along with rainwear and leather bomber jackets. Shoes seen here included a pair of Bally ankle-high brown leather boots for $22.50.

But you don't *have* to go with used clothing: Recently, the store has begun snapping up wholesale deals like Ralph Lauren "Chaps" shirts, selling them for 75% off re-tail prices. New and used chino pants, in all sizes, start from $5. And they do carry new formal wear at great prices—including closeouts at 50% of retail. Keezer's is open Mondays through Saturdays from 10 A.M. to 6 P.M.

Oona's Experienced Clothing

- 1210 Massachusetts Ave., Cambridge; (617) 491-2654

Perhaps the earthiest of Cambridge's vintage clothing stores, Oona's is funky without even trying. The Harvard Square shop winds from room to room, each filled with a different kind of clothing—dresses, men's suits, and their famous $5 leather jackets.

A ton of clothing is mostly $10 and under; sweaters are $5 to $10, men's sportcoats $5, long Indian wrap skirts $4 to $6. Plus genuine fashions from the 1960s and, these days, the 1970s (hmmm). Better quality used leather jackets go for $75 and up; the $5 styles are, well, *really* broken in. Oona's also has lots of handcrafted bead and silver jewelry under $10, plus "Manic Panic" neon hair dyes, and a special selection of wacky stuff for Halloween. Open daily until 7 P.M., Sundays 'til 6.

THRIFT SHOPS

Like commercialized yard sales, thrift shops offer you a crazy hodgepodge of stuff—clothing, housewares, and the ever-popular "bric-a-brac" (what *is* that, anyway?) Remember, the descriptions below are a very loose guide; quality, selection and prices can vary widely over different visits. Any of these places can toss a surprise your way for just a few bucks . . . ya never know.

Amvets Thrift Store

- 80 Brighton Ave., Allston; (617) 562-0720
- 180 Oak St., Brockton; (508) 580-2973

One of the nicest thrifts in the Boston area, Amvets is big, bright, and bulging with very low-priced clothing. Long racks of suits, pants, shirts, sweaters, coats, dresses and more—for women, men and kids—all seem to be priced between $2 and $10. Much of the merchandise is well-worn, but there's enough clothing in good condition to make scouring the racks worth your while.

There is also a good amount of furniture, mostly chairs and tables—as

well as books, TVs and radios, etc.
Amvets is open seven days a week;
every Monday, senior citizens get
25% off purchases of clothing. Hours
are daily from 9 A.M. to 9 P.M., Sundays from 12-6.

Beacon Hill Thrift Shop
• 15 Charles St., Boston; (617)
  742-2323

If you want to find really good donated clothing, you've got to go
where the dough is. This place has a
somewhat limited collection of nice
clothing at terrific prices. Men's
three-piece suits, in good condition,
are $35; however, there may only be
a handful to choose from at any one
time. Add a silk tie for $2. A pair of
ladies' Gap jeans was seen for $8;
several brightly colored dresses for
$15. Plus shoes, antique jewelry,
books and some furniture, and decorative antiques. All purchases benefit
the New England Baptist Hospital
Nurse Scholarship Fund. Open from
11 A.M. to 4 P.M., every day but Thursdays and Sundays.

Beth Israel Hospital Thrift Shop
• 25 Harvard St., Brookline; (617)
  566-7016

Located in Brookline Village, the BI
Thrift Shop has a big selection of
clothing, mostly in good condition.
Men's jackets ranged in price from
$15 to $25; shirts were $4 and up,
and so was a rack of new-looking
women's bathing suits. On Mr. C's
visit, he even noticed a Nipon Boutique dress with the original price tag
of $130 still on it; BI's price was
$20. Of course, those are more rare.

There are also lots of children's
clothes, as well as household items,
books (three for a dollar), and—can
you believe it—8-track tapes! Lots of
used furniture, too. Open from 9:30
A.M. to 5:30 P.M., every day but
Sunday.

Christ Church Thrift Shop
• 17 Farwell Pl., Cambridge; (617)
  492-3335

When Mr. C visited this small shop,
it was hopping with bargain-hungry
Cantabridgians. And it's no wonder:
Although every item here is secondhand, the shop's tony location means
you may find fancy items like the set
of six crystal bowls for just $25 that
caught Mr. C's eye. You'll also see
some famous labels in the clothing
racks, like an Ann Taylor linen
blouse for $6, or a Bill Blass silk
dress for $15. Good quality men's
blazers may be as little as $8; a two-
piece wool suit was $12. Of course,
you can also find thrifty buys on basic clothing. There is a table of kids'
clothes, like $1 "Batman" tank tops.
Shoes (mostly women's) line the
shop's perimeter; a pair of Nine West
patent leather heels was $5. Books
and records, too.

A pricing committee meets every
Monday to weed out anything that
isn't clean and in good repair. All proceeds from the shop benefit the
church. Open from late September to
mid-June only; Tuesdays through
Thursdays 10 A.M. to 4 P.M., and from
10 A.M. to 3 P.M. the first Saturday of
the month.

Discovery Shop of the American Cancer Society
• 300 Washington St., Brookline;
  (617) 277-9499

All of the profits generated by this upscale thrift shop go to the American
Cancer Society's research and service
programs. The store sells mostly
clothing, with some books and children's toys. All of these are gently
used, from fashions that could be
worn to the office, to casualwear fit
for a Sunday picnic; you may even
find good labels mixed in, like a
Laura Ashley dress for $18, or a Gap
blazer for $20. Jeans, starting at $7,
and men's suits, starting at $20, are
also great deals. For extra savings,
check the sale racks. Because donations come in regularly, you do the
same and see lots of new items. This
shop is open from 10 A.M. to 5 P.M.
Mondays through Saturdays, and 10
A.M. to 4 P.M. on Saturdays.

Family Thrift Center
• 2 Hancock St., Quincy; (617)
  471-8387

Looking like the Salvation Army, but
in fact a privately owned retail store,

this immense warehouse acquires used goods from charity organizations and sells them for a song—even offering half-off sales on different items each day. Many selections have been around the block and thus are not for all shoppers, but at these prices...

Racks of all kinds of clothing seem to stretch for miles. Women, find shorts for $1.95-$3.95, including selections from Guess and Gitano; linen pants from Ann Taylor and jeans from Jantzen ($4.95); and charcoal blazers from Brooks Brothers at a stirring $2.95. Mr. C also chanced upon shoes from 9 West, Filene's, and Perry Ellis for under $3.

Men can score jeans as low as $3.95, and chinos (one pair still sporting the original Levi's tags) for $2.95. Colorful Ralph Lauren rugby shirts were also seen at that price, and loads of striped dress shirts are there for under $4. Tons of kids clothing is mostly priced at 95¢ apiece.

Fortunate enough to drop in when all furniture was half-price, Mr. C walked off with a six-sided wooden end table for $12, a floor lamp for $5, and a well-worn leather-cushioned chair for $3.50. And clear plastic grab bags filled with small toys, including good condition Barbies, range from $2.95-$5.95.

A large flea market (open weekends) and a small cafeteria are found under the same high roof as Family Thrift, which is open 9 A.M. to 6 P.M., Tuesdays through Sundays.

Goodwill Bargain Basement

- 1010 Harrison Ave., Boston; (617) 445-1010
- 520 Massachusetts Ave., Cambridge; (617) 868-6330
- 708 Centre St., Jamaica Plain; (617) 983-5354
- 461 Salem St., Medford; (617) 391-7867
- 13 Peabody Square, Peabody; (508) 532-2953
- 179 Parkingway, Quincy; (617) 479-8853
- 230 Elm St., Somerville; (617) 628-3618

MR. CHEAP'S PICKS
Thrift Shops

✔ **Amvets Thrift Shop**—Big, basic selection of clothing in good condition.

✔ **Goodwill Bargain Basement**—Who ever figured a chain store of donated clothing? Not only that, but manufacturers' surplus clothes—yes, new—are mixed in. The South End base store is the best of the bunch.

✔ **Ruth's House**—For North Shore shoppers, this endless warehouse is packed with goods of all kinds at ridiculously low prices.

✔ **Salvation Army Thrift Store**—Like Goodwill, they too have opened a fancy "headquarters" store that borders on the boutique.

- 315 West Broadway, South Boston; (617) 268-7960

Morgan Memorial Goodwill Shops have taken an aggressive approach to thrift shopping for fun and (non-) profit. The South End store, Goodwill's home base, is the largest; but all branches offer a mix of donations and wholesale buyouts from manufacturers. Yes, you can get new clothing and toys at Goodwill!

You will find mostly used clothing, of course—men's suits for $15, ladies' skirts and blouses for $5 and up, children's clothing for $2 to $3. But there may also be racks of new women's blazers for $12, suede skirts for $30, dresses for $25, ski jackets, jogging clothes, and more. The stock turns over quite rapidly and is worth checking out on a regular basis.

The used stuff is more fun for diehard Cheapsters, though. Goodwill runs frequent one-day sales—when all items with blue tags, for example, are an extra 30% off. During one such sale, a whole rack of sweaters went for $1 apiece, and Mr. C snapped up a Henry Grethel all-wool pullover. Plus, comforters and linens, often new; the books, housewares, and appliances are usually worn out but serviceable. All sales are final, but clothing may be returned within seven days for store credit. Open Mondays through Saturdays from 10 A.M. to 6 P.M.

Hadassah Bargain Spot

• 1123 Commonwealth Ave., Brighton; (617) 254-8300

This is one of the larger thrift stores around, two floors of clothes, housewares, furniture, and toys. Clothing prices are quite good; poke through the racks and you may find a two-piece blazer and skirt set by Jones New York for $25 in good condition. Men's jackets are around $20, with lots of dress shirts at $6 to $8. Shoes for all, including kids, run $5 to $20. Plus a selection of linens for the home.

Speaking of which, there is a lot of furniture to see upstairs. There are a few good pieces, but much of it seems a bit overpriced for only fair condition. Mr. C did spot a nice floral print loveseat for $85, several nice dressers at $75, and lots of chairs for $20. Try haggling a bit. They also have sporting goods—bicycles, skis, tennis racquets—old but usable. And, at the counter, several cases of costume jewelry, priced from $1 and up. Open Mondays through Wednesdays from 10 A.M. to 6 P.M.; Thursdays until 8; Fridays 'til 3; and Sundays from 12-6. Closed Saturdays.

Ruth's House

• 14 Stevens St., Haverhill; (508) 521-5575

Sometimes fate and inaccurate maps take you on unexpected turns, which is how Mr. C happened to discover Ruth's cheerfully hand-painted yellow and red signs. Inside, even more surprising, is a 10,000-square foot shopping mall of thrift items, at the kind of rock-bottom prices only possible when everything is obtained inexpensively—in this case, all donated.

An interdenominational store where gospel music rings out from an old cassette deck, Ruth's offers a staggering number of goods for less than a buck. Housewares for 50¢, books for a quarter, and clothes for $1-$2, including racks of women's clothes that would take days to fully explore, although London Fog jackets and Anne Klein blouses did leap out quickly. Decent furniture and appliances, too.

You'll also feel good about yourself, since Ruth's House works with organizations including the Red Cross and Social Services to give money and goods to those in need. A friendly atmosphere, including a living-roomish lounge area near the entrance, is just another surprise at this factory-building store. Give yourself time to stroll 9 A.M. to 4 P.M. Tuesdays through Fridays and 9 A.M. to 2 P.M. Saturdays.

St. Vincent de Paul Thrift Shop

• 1280 Washington St., Boston; (617) 542-0883
• 50 Prospect St., Cambridge; (617) 547-6924
• 4244 Franklin St., Lawrence; (508) 689-2625
• 701 Merrimack St., Lowell; (508) 453-7750
• 11-13 Market Square, Lynn; (617) 598-6606
• 173 Washington St., Plainville; (508) 695-5150
• 18 Canton St., Stoughton; (617) 341-4455

When Mr. C first wrote up this chain, he'd seen only the older, rather dingy Boston and Cambridge branches. Alas, he had yet to discover the main store and distribution center in Stoughton, as big and spotless as a department store; meanwhile, the other branches have recently gotten a facelift.

SVDP receives over ten million pounds (!) of donations annually—clothing, jewelry, housewares, and furniture—both used and new. Furthermore, they have adopted a new "one price fits all" system for clothes: Men's suits, for example—new *or* used—will cost $10. Any women's ensemble is $5. Sweaters are $3, jeans $4...you get the idea.

But don't go thinking these are faded old duds. Many charitable donations come from well-known manufacturers and stores. Recently, a whole rack of brand-new, first-quality Harris Tweed sportcoats sold for $20 each. Overstock linens have come in directly from Bed and Bath. Meanwhile, a batch of secondhand bridal gowns went (quickly) at $10 apiece.

High-quality used furniture may include a five-piece mahogany bedroom ensemble for $1,000, easily worth twice as much new. Other pieces in the "Furniture Outlet" section may need refinishing, but they're steals even if you pay someone to do it. In fact, some branches have hosted classes in this art!

All donations are divided evenly between the seven stores; Stoughton, Boston, Plainville, and Lawrence are the largest. Discounted bulk purchases can also be arranged; ask for a tour of the 70,000-square foot Stoughton warehouse. Open weekdays.

Salvation Army Thrift Store

- 26 West St., Boston; (617) 695-0512
- 328 Massachusetts Ave., Cambridge; (617) 354-9159
- 727 Memorial Dr., Cambridge; (617) 547-9668
- *And other suburban locations*

Like Goodwill, the Salvation Army has taken a step up in the thrift world by adding its boutique-style Downtown Crossing mega-store. At the front there are fancy dresses, leather coats (for $8.99!), and even some new buyouts, like a batch of imported Italian wool women's blazers for just $6 each.

Further in, there are racks and racks of shirts, pants, suits, skirts, and coats, most in fairly good condition. Lots of everything to browse

through, and the prices can't be beat. Jeans for $5. Men's trousers, two pair for $8.99. Three-piece suits, $20. Shoes and boots from $4 to $10 a pair. A ladies' Oscar de la Renta sweater, with a sporty nautical look, was seen for $7.99. Downstairs, check out the "Toddlers" department.

A separate room has furniture, well-used, but not terribly so; easy chairs are $25 to $50. Plus the usual housewares and small appliances. Meanwhile, every Wednesday and Thursday, clearance clothing items are tagged at 50% off; if they're still around, these sell for 50¢ on Friday and Saturday.

Of course, the Army's other outposts continue to sell good ol' super-cheap clothing. Rummage through the racks and tables of jeans for $2, shirts for $1.50, jackets for $5, men's suits for $10, and the like. Some toys and furnishings here, too.

Thrift Shop Of Boston

- 488 Centre St., Jamaica Plain; (617) 522-5676

Quite a large thrift store, with lots of furniture, housewares, and clothing. And lamps, lots of lamps. The general quality of most stuff is on the low end, but it's always worth a look and it's fun to browse. Hours are 10 A.M. to 3:45 P.M., Tuesdays through Saturdays. Proceeds from the store benefit several charities, including Children's Hospital and the New England Home for Little Wanderers.

Transitions

- 484 Harrison Ave., Boston; (617) 423-3657

Opened with much fanfare in the spring of '95, Transitions is run by the noted shelter for the homeless, the Pine Street Inn. Packed with donated clothing and housewares that are not used for its residents, the store has been one of Boston's better thrifts from day one. The names seen here may surprise you: Liz Claiborne, Ralph Lauren, Jones New York, Anne Klein, and others. People give the nicest stuff for a good cause—wouldja believe one million pounds' worth a year?

A men's suit by Geoffrey Beene was recently seen here for $9.99. A pair of girls' jeans from The Limited for $2.99. Dresses go for $4.99 to $7.99. Not to mention stuffed animal toys for 50¢, Afghan blankets for $5 (new ones for $10), books, dishware, and more.

In keeping with its mission, Transitions gives employment opportunities to the shelter's "guests," who seek stability in their lives; hence, the store's name. Profits help the Inn purchase essential goods. In short, buying some cool retro outfit—and saving a ton of money—has never been nobler.

The store's entrance is just off Harrison Ave., at the rear of a large parking lot; look for signs on the side of the building. Open Tuesdays through Saturdays from 10 A.M. to 5:30 P.M.

COSMETICS

A & A Beauty Supply
- 1237 River St., Hyde Park; (617) 361-6606

Near Logan Square, this neighborhood shop is well-stocked with hair products, along with items for nails and skin care. As a wholesale and retail operation, the prices for the general public are quite good.

Shampoos come in huge containers meant for hair salons, but they're just as good—and economical—for big families. Some of these are also generic copies of the brands nobody discounts, like Nexxus and Paul Mitchell. There are lots of ethnic products; save a dollar off the retail price of Dark and Lovely hair color. Plus L'Oreal, Clairol, and more. Or, you can go another route and save 35% to 50% off retail on a selection of quality wigs.

Nail polishes start at just 95¢ apiece; save on Kiss My Face all-natural soaps, as well as hair brushes, curling irons, and the like. Open every day but Sunday, including Fridays 'til 7 P.M.

The Beauty Connection
- 326 Harvard St., Brookline; (617) 734-2114
- 749 Beacon St., Newton; (617) 969-3333

Customers call this "a grownups' candy store," and judging by the level of activity during Mr. C's drop-in, the Beauty Connection satisfies many a sweet tooth. They carry an extensive line of fine cosmetics and fragrances, including men's colognes, all priced at 10% to 25% below retail. Yet, even when it gets hectic in here, the staff takes the time to give plenty of expert service—without heavy sales pressure.

Save 15%, pretty much across the board, on Lancôme, Elizabeth Arden, and Ultima lines. There are tons of hair care products and accessories, many of which are seen for much more at the upscale boutiques in Bloomingdale's and Henri Bendel (the Coolidge Corner branch, which includes a hair salon, has the biggest selection of hair care stuff).

BC carries a vast range of makeup, from several manufacturers. They even offer an instructive, hour-long make-over session in the store for $15; but if you're in a real hurry (or just a good Cheapster), they also do a quick "Mini-makeover" for $8—in other words, a "make me look fantastic for the gala ball tonight" do-up.

Beauty Connection must be doing something right—they've been around for fifteen years. Open Mondays through Saturdays from 9:30 A.M. to 5:30 P.M.

Beauty-Way Cosmetics
- 7 Wethersfield Rd., Natick; (508) 653-3723
- 833 Beacon St., Newton; (617) 527-7172

This pair of suburban shops has a good selection of products for men and women, all well below retail. Fragrances are marked down anywhere from 15% to even 50%; one shelf always has deeply discounted specials, like a 3.5-ounce bottle of Yves St. Laurent's "Opium," reduced from $75 to $60; a 30-ml Pierre Cardin after shave for men was seen for $8.99, from a list price of $12.50.

Cosmetics bargains recently included Givenchy "Prisme Soleil" summer face powder, marked down from $38 to $32; Nailtiques protein, selling for as much as $20 a bottle, goes for $14.99 here. There are gift sets, like a Halston pack of spray cologne and body lotion, listed at $42.50, here $25. Plus Neutrogena hair and skin products, natural bath sponges, hair brushes, travel bags, the works. Both stores are open Mondays through Saturdays from 10 A.M. to 5:30 P.M. (from 9:30 in Natick).

Boston Beauty Supply

- 59 Temple Pl., Boston; (617) 426-0921
- 120 Cambridge St., Burlington; (617) 272-0378
- Liberty Tree Mall, Danvers; (508) 777-4795
- 199 Massachusetts Ave., Lexington; (617) 862-6677
- 92-96 Lafayette St., Salem; (508) 744-7017
- Swampscott Mall, Swampscott; (617) 592-5464
- 1285 Main St., Wakefield; (617) 662-0454

In Downtown Crossing, this second-floor walkup sells professional-grade hair care supplies at discount; the general public is also welcome. Colors, perms, shampoos, sprays; they're all here, in brands such as Clairol, L'Oreal, and Wella. They also carry makeup by Ultima II and Revlon, as well as bath items like Neutrogena's "Rainbath" shower gel, $8.95 for an eight-ounce bottle.

Many items cannot be found in retail stores. L'Oreal hair color, for example, is sold by the bottle for just $2.75. Instead of buying the usual kit,

---

MR. CHEAP'S PICKS
Cosmetics

✔ **The Beauty Connection—** Considered by many to be an "adults' candy store."

✔ **Boston Beauty Supply—** Stock up where the salons buy their stuff. Sure, you can go in, too.

✔ **Perfumania—**This national chain applies the "How do we do it? VOLUME!" approach to designer fragrances at discount for men and women.

---

you can assemble the materials yourself and save.

They also carry several generic copies of expensive name brands; a copy of Paul Mitchell shampoo is just $2.95, about half of the real thing and every bit as good. A 32-ounce generic bottle of peroxide is a low $1.75. Service is friendly and helpful, too. Open weekdays, plus Saturday from 9:30 to 5:30.

Flammia Beauty Supply

- 363 Highland Ave., Somerville; (617) 628-0249

Flammia is not necessarily a discounter, but it does sell beauty products in professional-size large quantities, making for some very good deals. After all, if you shampoo every day, why not buy it a liter at a time? Especially when you can get such a bottle for $3.95, in a variety of brands. You may be spending that much on a smaller size now. The store does not advertise itself to the public, "but we don't turn them away," the clerk noted.

They also carry a generic copies of expensive name brands like Nexxus, for about half the price of the real thing. The recipe is the same! And you'll find everything you'll need for nail sculpturing and hair styling. Open weekdays from 9 A.M. to 6 P.M., 'til 5 on Saturdays.

Perfumania
- CambridgeSide Galleria, Cambridge; (617) 252-3352
- Meadow Glen Mall, Medford; (617) 396-8430

Perfumania is a national chain of 150 stores (and growing); their vast buying power enables them to sell top-name designer perfumes for men and women at cut-rate prices. You can save big on names like Elizabeth Taylor's "Passion" and Cher's "Uninhibited," as well as colognes by Alfred Sung, Paco Rabanne, Ralph Lauren, Paloma Picasso, Halston, and many others. Price tags are color-coded to show you which bottles are selling at 20%, 40%, and 60% off.

Sample as many of these as you like; the staff is extremely knowledgeable and relaxed. The scents are sprayed onto special papers, which are then labeled for you with the respective brand; this way, you don't walk out of the store wearing ten contrasting fragrances.

The store also specializes in boxed gift sets; again, at up to half-off or more. In many cases, you can get a cologne set, with extras like matching lotion or shower gel (or whatever), for the same price as the perfume alone. Some even come pre-wrapped! There are some cosmetic gift sets as well, such as eye shadow color kits. Open daily from 10 A.M. to 9:30 P.M., Sundays 11-7.

Sally Beauty Supply
- 1360 Beacon St., Brookline; (617) 277-0095
- Fresh Pond Mall, 180 Alewife Brook Pkwy., Cambridge; (617) 876-9880
- 1530 V.F.W. Pkwy., West Roxbury; (617) 323-2530
- 423 Washington St., Woburn; (617) 933-4196

This nationwide chain of 1,500 stores is owned by Alberto Culver, the "VO5" folks. So they have plenty of factory-direct products, many of which are for professional use only. This means high quality, large sizes, and good prices.

Thus, you can get a 16-ounce can of hair spray by TRESemme, Alberto's salon brand, for about half-price. Other brands sold at discount include Aussie Moist shampoos, Jheri Redding "Volumizers," Infusium, and Faberge.

Sally also carries those generic hair products made with the same ingredients as expensive name brands. Aura products, which copy the Aveda line, save you about half the cost of those salon exclusives. You'll find generic versions of Paul Mitchell and Sebastian hair products too. Plus nail and skin care items, full lines of ethnic hair products, and discounted professional hair dryers and curling irons. Be sure to check the "Reduced for Quick Sale" and "Cheaper by the Case" sections, too. Open seven days.

DISCOUNT DEPARTMENT STORES

These are some of Mr. C's favorite playgrounds. Keep an open mind about this vast subculture of places that have sprung up to sell anything that has not sold in retail stores. For basic necessities and splurges you'd never make at full-price, they can be lots of fun. And you may be amazed at what hidden, brand-name treasure may await you down the next aisle!

Adventures—A Bargain Store

- 208 Waverly St., Framingham; (508) 875-9798
- 660 Main St., Walpole; (508) 660-3111

With its "Indiana Jones"-type sign out front, this store sets itself up as a wacky sort of place. Mr. C kept looking out for that giant ball to start chasing him up and down the aisles, but he escaped unharmed. Not before scooping up some closeout deals, though, on things like an Orlando Magic NBA sweatshirt for $9.99, an Anchor-Hocking two-quart glass casserole dish for $6.99, and a batch of greeting cards, all sold at 50% off the printed price. Near these, a sign read, "Wrapping Paper $1, Anyone?" They do try to have fun here, giving the place a personal touch.

Adventures really comes off as something like a mini-Building 19. In addition to the clothing and housewares, you'll always find a big selection of toys and games, hardware, car care supplies, low-grade furniture (unfinished solid pine picnic tables, $70, early in the season), canned and packaged foods, gardening stuff, and more. Everything here is new, in a mix of well-known and unknown brands. But if you keep your receipt, you can always get your money back within ten days. Open Mondays through Saturdays from 9-9, Sundays from 12-6.

All For A Dollar

- 95 Summer St., Boston; (617) 426-4008
- Assembly Square Mall, Somerville; (617) 629-0121
- Arsenal Mall, Watertown; (617) 924-4265

This is one of the better-quality dollar stores. Of course, you know the price; the stock includes hardcover books, hair products, snack foods, stationery, sewing and knitting, party supplies, accessories for pets, cooking and cleaning stuff, toys, socks, "Barney" underwear. . . .

It has probably the largest food selection of any of the dollar stores, and has more brand names than most.

You'll find Revlon nail polish, Gerber baby food, Pepperidge Farm and Keebler cookies, Del Monte foods, and more. Open daily.

Big Value Outlet

- 421 New State Hwy. (Rte. 44), Raynham; (508) 824-5117

The BVO (as it is known among locals) buys closeouts, odd-lots, and surplus goods—and sells them off at absurdly low prices. It's a great place to look for all kinds of housewares, cleaning supplies, toys, hardware, and more. Recent finds include a Regal ten-inch frying pan for $7.99, beach chairs for $8.99, Oriental rugs as low as $19.99 (fake, of course), and place mats for a buck. Truly an eclectic mix. Toys are definitely worth checking out here; a Barbie health club, normally $12.99, was seen here for $7.99. In the hardware section Mr. C found Olympic wood stain reduced from $16.99 to $8.99. Big Value Outlet is open Mondays through Saturdays from 9 A.M. to 9 P.M., and Sundays 11 A.M. to 5 P.M.

The Buck Stop

- 449 Massachusetts Ave., Arlington; no phone

In Arlington Center, this was one of the area's first dollar stores. They still have a good supply ranging from basic household items to packaged food to toys and books.

Here Mr. C found packaged cookies, dishwashing liquid, hair spray and accessories, four-packs of those tiny individual cereal boxes, yarn and sewing supplies, and a cassette tape that makes your answering machine sound like Porky Pig. You never know what you'll find, but it's always fun.

Building 19

- 154 Cambridge St., Burlington; (617) 272-1919
- Hingham Plaza, 100 Derby St., Hingham; (617) 749-0019
- 810 The Lynnway, Lynn; (617) 581-1910
- 9/27 Shopping Center (Rte. 9), Natick; (508) 653-1900
- 1450 Providence Hwy. (Rte. 1), Norwood; (617) 769-3700

- Harborlight Mall, 789 Bridge St., Weymouth; (617) 340-6219
- *And other suburban locations*

If Filene's is the traditional bargain basement, Building 19 is the next generation. These folks snap up manufacturers' overstocks, discontinued lines, damaged goods, and irregulars—in clothing, furniture, home decor, hardware, toys, paper supplies, and anything else they can get their hands on. Seconds are clearly marked as such.

So when a ladies' shoe manufacturer goes out of business, B-19 grabs what's left; and first-quality shoes that would have retailed for $45 go on sale for $14.99. You may also see a factory-refurbished espresso maker reduced from $50 to $29; brass table lamps at half-price; mismatched mattress and boxspring sets (as they point out, once the bed is made, who can tell?) marked down from $500 to $289; and $200 Oriental rugs for $79.

Many of the stores also have a "Sample Department," in which they sell designer clothing that has been used only by the salespeople who take it on the road to show to buyers. B-19 sells these at half the retail price. And the stores always have tons of regular clothing for the entire family.

There is a sort of irreverent attitude at Building 19; the idea is that anyone who wants to shop at these prices won't mind the wacky signs, jammed aisles and cement floors. They seem to be correct in this assumption, as the chain keeps growing. All stores are open seven days a week; B-19 now accepts credit cards, another new development.

Burlington Coat Factory

- 705 Granite St., Braintree; (617) 848-3200
- Cloverleaf Marketplace, Speen St. (off Rte. 9), Natick; (508) 651-2526

Not content with being a popular clothing discounter for the entire family, Burlington Coat Factory stores have expanded from within to become something almost like actual department stores. They are quite large, and in each one, you'll not only find discounted clothing for the whole family, but also shoes, jewelry, linens, and infant furnishings.

Most folks know of Burlington for its clothing. They carry big names at good prices; you can find all kinds of coats here—like a Pierre Cardin lambskin bomber jacket, list priced at $300, for just $180, or racks of simulated fur coats for women. But there's more here than meets the elements. Underneath those coats, guys could be wearing a Harvé Benard double-breasted suit of 100% wool, discounted from $400 to $180. For the gals, perhaps a nifty black two-piece Oleg Cassini set, not $270, but $150. A Jones New York turtleneck sweater, reduced from $140 to $90. Size selection is good here, from petite to plus sizes for women, as well as big and tall sizes for men.

Then, there are all the fashions for children, from tots to teens. Boys' Jordache ski jackets were recently seen reduced from $70 to $40; girls will look smart in a dressy red coat by London Fog, marked down from $110 to $80. Both can save ten bucks or so off Levi's jeans, Guess? denim fashions, and others. You can also stock up on basics and accessories here, like ties, hats, and underwear (particularly Burlington hosiery, at $1 to $2 off all styles). There is also a small but serviceable jewelry counter, selling gold chains, bracelets, watches, and the like at permanent discounts of 40% to 50% off retail prices.

Now, let's move on to the specialty stores-within-the-store. **The Capezio Footwear Outlet** extends these savings to all kinds of basic and classy shoes for men, women, and kids; it's not just for dancing anymore. Current styles in dressy shoes and boots are mostly sold at $10 to $20 off list prices; for deeper discounts, though, look over on the long self-service racks, arranged by size. These are mainly closeouts and overstocks, all perfectly good. You may find a pair of red leather pumps by Bandolino, reduced from $72 to $39;

men's dress loafers by Johnston and Murphy, marked down from $165 to $98; plus kids shoes by Sesame Street, Fisher Price, and Hush Puppies.

Baby World sells discounted clothing, furniture, and accessories for newborns and small children. Along with good prices on infant and maternity wear, you can find things like a white crib set, complete with a Simmons mattress and colorful print sheets, reduced from $350 to $205. Also, such diverse items as a Little Tykes plastic table and chairs, for toddler tea parties; Graco strollers, discounted from $140 to $99; a Snugli car seat, reduced from $62 to $36; and clothing not only for newborns, but also for maternity moms.

Luxury Linens does the same deal for home furnishings, many by designers and name brands, at 20% to 50% below retail. Mr. C found things like Ardsley goose down comforters, in full or queen size, reduced from $140 to $90. Laura Ashley flat sheets were discounted from $32 to $12, along with names like Utica, Martex, and Bill Blass. Plus towels by Dundee, bed pillows (including orthopedic styles), shower curtains, decorative baskets, and more—all stacked from floor to ceiling.

Cheapo Depot

- 98 Westgate Dr., Brockton; (508) 588-2044
- 156B Cambridge St., Burlington; (617) 272-9555
- 230 Turnpike St., Canton; (617) 821-1112

When one table here sported a sign proclaiming "Assorted merchandise," Mr. C had to laugh. It's *all* assorted, and you really never know what you'll find. You can bet it will be a bargain, though—usually due to defects or damaged packaging.

Most of these goods are liquidations from department stores, toy shops, and supermarkets, all at deep discounts. Two-drawer filing cabinets with minor scratches were seen for $12-$15; dented cans of Coke were 25¢. An aerobic step-unit, in its original packaging, was $10, minus the

---

MR. CHEAP'S PICKS
Discount Department Stores

- ✔ **Building 19**—The wacky approach to closeout bargains on everything under the sun. Heir to the Filene's throne—as long as it's a "scratch and dent," that is.

- ✔ **Christmas Tree Shops**—This local chain is a must-visit for bargains on housewares, home furnishings, decorative items, and paper goods.

- ✔ **Filene's Basement**—Forget the suburban clones; head down to the original store, where Filene's *made* bargain hunting into entertainment.

- ✔ **Spag's**—Way out west (western Mass., that is), this legendary discount mecca is always worth the trip.

---

workout video which would have kept the price at $30. A selection of clothing included Bugle Boy jeans ($9) and Italian Club cotton plaid skirts ($4), some with a loose thread or two.

All of these flaws are clearly pointed out, often with a touch of humor: A stuffed "Tookie the Talking Toucan" toy was marked, "Doesn't talk." Cheapo Depot offers a 30-day money-back guarantee, no questions asked. Keep your receipt.

In some cases, a different pricing philosophy holds true: Asked how an apparently undamaged full-sized futon and frame set could be had for only $100, a clerk responded, "If we charged more, they'd just sit here, like at all the other stores." Pull into the Depot from 12-8 P.M. Thursdays, 10 A.M. to 8 P.M. Fridays and Saturdays, and 12-5 P.M. Sundays.

Christmas Tree Shops

- 15 Stockwell Dr., Avon; (508) 586-6438
- 28 Broadway, Lynn; (617) 598-0004
- Christmas Tree Plaza, Pembroke; (617) 826-8884
- Old Shrewsbury Village (Rte. 9), Shrewsbury; (508) 842-5945
- *And other suburban locations*

At one time, these stores may have had some relationship to the holiday for which they are named. Today, they have little to do with Christmas and everything to do with bargains. The merchandise consists primarily of housewares: lamps, frames, glassware, dishes, cookware, and gadgets. You can find everything from mini-citronella candles for $2.99 to a metal patio set, including two chairs with cushions, for $169.99. Mr. C found a "Miracle Thaw" defrosting tray—sold on TV for $19.95—for just $6.99. A sixteen-quart Thermos cooler was a recent steal at $12.99.

Christmas Tree Shops are great for bulk purchases, too. Candles, in a range of colors and sizes, are plentiful enough for decorating the largest of weddings. Glasses can be purchased by the dozen. Good deals on baskets and picture frames, too. Like many of the places in this chapter, the inventory at these stores changes daily. Cruise through regularly and you'll be sure to find plenty of great deals. Open daily.

Dad's Liquidation Centers

- 4 Highland Ave., Randolph; (617) 961-5220

Dad's unassuming red exterior belies the world of good quality bargains stuffed inside. Shoes and boots for every member of the family come in a good range of styles and sizes. Mr. C found men's Puma running shoes, listed at $59.95, for $35. A selection of casual clothing complements the shoes. And Dad's got sports gear—adults' and kids' rollerblades were as little as $25; a wool Oakland A's baseball cap was just $7.99. You can even outfit an entire softball team here where "Volume sales are welcome."

The store also stocks a wide range of household goods: Mr. C found Igloo coolers in several sizes (from $20) and a filtered drinking water system for $20. A computer keyboard, retailing for $60, sells for $30, but was on sale for $20 the day Mr. C visited. Kiddies will love Power Ranger duffel bags, and at just $6.99, so will Mom. Snap up a bunch of Disney coloring books for under a dollar each. Every item in this trove is first quality, and Dad's has a 30-day return policy. Open seven days, including weeknights 'til 8.

Filene's Basement

- 426 Washington St., Boston; (617) 542-2011

Undoubtedly the granddaddy of all discount shopping in Boston. Here is where you'll find die-hard bounty hunters diving onto tables piled high with clothing, hurling item after item into the air in the hope that some greater prize lies hidden underneath. Once the treasure has been unearthed, it is clutched tightly, before anyone else even has a chance to consider it, and the search goes on.

For Mr. C's more demure readers, don't worry—not *everyone* is like that here. Just plunge in and find yourself some baah-gains. The stock comes from many quality stores and manufacturers—overstocks, leftovers, irregulars, things from last season. Not everything is super-cheap, but you never know what may turn up. That's why Basement veterans try to cruise through on a regular basis. And of course, every few weeks, prices on unsold items are marked down further. (This is the big difference between the original FB and those watered-down suburban versions.)

Of course, there is more here than just clothing—many shoppers never even venture down to the second level, where similar reductions are taken on housewares, linens, home decorations, children's items, toys, and more. Basement hours are Mondays through Fridays, 9:30 A.M. to 7 P.M., Saturday 9 A.M. to 7 P.M., and

Sundays 11 A.M. to 7 P.M.

Harvard Cooperative Society

- 1400 Massachusetts Ave., Cambridge; (617) 499-2000
- *And other campus locations*

Founded way back when as a money-saving service by-and-for the academic community, the Coop now sells to everyone. However, the original "mission" continues, and all students, faculty, alumni, and employees of Harvard are eligible to become members—as well as those of M.I.T., Wheelock College, the Massachusetts College of Pharmacy, and personnel at the hospitals affiliated with Harvard Medical School.

For an annual fee of $1, members receive a rebate based on their purchases throughout the year. These rebates are based on profitability and vary greatly. The best member's benefit is the special members-only sales, such as a recent one featuring an extra 15% off regular prices on compact discs.

Meanwhile, the Coop sells everything from clothes to TVs to toothpaste, like any department store. They also buy back textbooks (from any school, member or not) for cash on the spot. And the Insignia Shop, on the street level of the main building, is a good place to check for clearance sales of leftover "Harvard" stuff—like a hooded maroon sweatshirt reduced from $30 to $19.99. The Harvard Square Coop is open seven days; hours vary at the other locations.

Jax Liquidation Outlet

- 576 Massachusetts Ave., Cambridge; (617) 492-4435

This recent arrival in Central Square is much like the low-grade clothing and housewares stores you find up and down 14th Street in Manhattan. For certain kinds of basics, especially on a tight budget, this can serve quite well. Most of the goods here are closeouts and salvage from other stores, some of which are name brands: Fruit of the Loom underwear three-packs for $5.99, a set of ten Corelle drinking glasses for $6.99, a

"Lamb Chop's Play Along" lunch box for $4.99. Plus third-world cotton dresses for $14.99, linens and drapes, luggage that'll get you through two or three trips at *least*, and other assorted knick-knacks, all displayed on open tables like the good ol' days at Filene's. Not that there's much comparison beyond that. Open seven days.

Jimmie's Discount Outlet

- 20-22 Bow St., Somerville; (617) 625-5605

This shop near Union Square offers mostly overstocks and buyouts at very cheap prices—if they have something you want. Clothing starts at $3 a piece—for shirts, vests, chino pants, work clothes and uniforms, and sports T's. Some are irregulars and damaged goods.

The store also carries lots of household items, sporting goods, and toys; a new room, in fact, is devoted to toys at wholesale prices. Mr. C found kids' Reebok sneakers ($20), bath towels ($3.99), a three-piece set of microwave bowls ($1.29), a Westclox wall clock ($9), a six-pack of white tube socks ($4.99), and neon sunglasses ($2.99). Plus roller blades for $15 a pair, and a girl's pink tricycle for $22.

Among the more unusual items for this kind of small liquidator: bolts of fabric at $1 per yard, inexpensive luggage, overstock mattresses, and collector's baseball cards at $1 each. Open seven days.

Lechmere

- 88 First St., Cambridge; (617) 491-2000
- *And other suburban locations*

No, it's not the regular store merchandise that attracts Mr. C—though their sale prices are often good. What many shoppers aren't aware of is that Lechmere frequently takes items that have been *returned* and sells them at discount. They are usually gathered on a table in the appropriate department. You may find a Panasonic computer printer for half-price, or a Sony Walkman, or a boom-box tape deck. Some of these had defects and have been repaired, and still come with a limited warranty. Occasionally they have simply been opened and returned unused; the box is damaged, but the item is perfectly good. Open daily.

Mark's Discount Outlet
- 2050 Revere Beach Pkwy., Everett; (617) 381-0669

Set back from the highway by a parking lot that's bigger than the store, Mark's has a crazy but useful array of overstocks and irregulars in housewares, toys, and some clothing.

You'll find socks and T-shirts, including plenty of children's sizes; kids' ballet slippers and tap shoes, too, for $4 to $6 a pair. Plus shampoos and cosmetics, including generic copies of perfumes; packaged candy and gum at half-price; and a large section of hardware and tools. Everything here is 50% to 75% off. Open daily, including Thursdays through Saturdays until 9 P.M.; Mondays and Tuesdays are senior citizen discount days.

$1-$2-$3
- 450 Highland Ave., Salem; (508) 740-2808

Certain stores are blessed with names that simply demand a visit from Mr. C, and he found the $1-$2-$3 store to be worth the trip. Toys, games, jewelry, and small tools are among the overstock, backstock, and (in a few cases) goods in damaged packaging—all of which will bring you change from a Lincoln.

Outside the front of this strip mall store, water guns—just in time for the soaker season—were seen for $1, as were wiffle ball and bat sets and jigsaw puzzles. Inside, you may find assorted low-grade jewelry, with original price tags of $5-$10, for only $2-$3 (probably closer to their true value).

If you dread shelling out supermarket prices for spices, a variety of no-name brands can be had for $1 each. Dog toys are $1-$2—wise purchases when you figure Rufus will shred them to bits inside of a week anyway. Same prices for numerous bathroom

accessories, hardware and tools, etc.

Some items fall outside the range indicated by the store's name, but paying a mere $7 for a Glitter-Hair Barbie (still sporting a $14.99 Kay-Bee sticker) seems pretty reasonable. Open seven days a week, including every evening except Sundays.

Spag's Supply Company
- 193 Boston Tpke. (Rte. 9), Shrewsbury; no phone

Yes, it's a schlep from Boston, but how could Mr. C *possibly* leave a legend like this out and still look himself in the mirror each morning? What began in 1934 as a humble neighborhood hardware store has grown into a multi-million-dollar operation housed in a sprawling complex of several buildings—still presided over by its founder, Anthony Borgatti, the guy in the cowboy hat who does his own TV commercials.

If you've never had the pleasure, brace yourself. This is true bargain-hunter's paradise—but, like all those stories about people who get what they wish for, something's gone a bit haywire. Aisles run diagonally into each other. You'll find weed killer across from food processors, a potentially dangerous juxtaposition. Crowds can be oppressive on weekends. But many folks plunge in anyway, lured by the bargain prices on everything under the sun.

The original store, right on Route 9, and its newer expansion directly behind, are the center of the action. This is where you'll find deals on groceries, hardware, books, toys, luggage, furniture, clothing, and more. Except that you'll also find clothing just up the hill behind the main store, in the "Olde Schoolhouse" building. For that matter, they've got some more furniture in there, too (higher-quality stuff). So much for organization. Power tools, computer software, shoes, and garden sculpture also abound here.

Back down the hill, the smaller "Sport Shoppe" has good prices on gear for every kind of team and individual sport imaginable, from tennis racquets and baseball mitts to tents and fishing rods. And the garden center does the same for, well, gardening.

How do they do it? VOLUME!! Nowhere is that old tag-line more accurate than at Spag's, where they simply do so much business that they can afford to keep the prices low. Mr. C even saw the biggest discount he's ever found on his own humble book (now *that's* cheap).

In order to keep your strength up, refreshments are sold outside the main store and the schoolhouse building. Soda, hot dogs, coffee, and muffins...you'll need it. Spag's is open weekdays from 9 A.M. to 9 P.M., Saturdays from 8-9, and Sundays from 12-5. Also worth noting: They now accept credit cards, a relatively recent addition.

Value Village
- 413 Moody St., Waltham; (617) 899-7771

- 1902 Centre St., West Roxbury; (617) 327-3733

Value Village has an ever-changing variety of clothing, showroom samples, and some furniture, at overstock prices. Mr. C found a wall full of kitchen gadgets, for example, mostly for 99¢ each. Hanes socks for men were $1.99 a pair, and ready-made picture frames were reduced from $40 to $7.99. Plus lots of children's sweatshirts and pants for $2.99 each.

An oak-finish coffee table, meanwhile, was $70; while a dinette table and chairs was $125. Some of the furniture is damaged. There were books for a dollar, sewing supplies, and cheap decorative housewares. And at Christmastime, the place is filled with seasonal stuff. The West Roxbury store also carries lots of sporting goods and camping equipment, much at up to half the original price. Closed Sundays.

WAREHOUSE CLUBS

You hardly need Mr. C to tell you about these giants which have swept the nation. But please take them up on their offer to get a one-day "visitor's pass" and check the store out before you buy in. These megastores are not for all customers. You may not have the kind of storage area to take advantage of grocery deals by the case; there are some stores listed under "General Markets" in the "Food Shops" chapter which offer similar rates on smaller quantities without memberships.

For other kinds of merchandise, the discounts can be terrific, but the *selection* is often limited. Many of their televisions, computers, clothing, furniture, and even jewelry are closeouts; you can only choose from whatever deals they've been able to snap up from manufacturers. If you're looking for the best price on a particular model of refrigerator, they may only have a half-dozen of last year's leftovers. On the other hand, if you only care about the bottom line, this may suit you fine. Again, look before you leap:

BJ's Wholesale Club
- 777 Washington St., Auburn; (508) 832-6500
- 6 Hutchinson Dr., Danvers; (508) 777-0860
- 909 Fellsway, Medford; (617) 396-0691
- North Dartmouth Mall, North Dartmouth; (508) 999-0835
- 901 Technology Center Dr., Stoughton; (617) 341-3300
- 290 Turnpike Rd., Westborough; (508) 898-0008
- 622 Washington St., Weymouth; (617) 335-8500

Costco Wholesale
- 120 Stockwell Dr. (Rte. 24), Avon; (508) 580-3251
- 11 Newbury St. (Rte. 1), Danvers; (508) 777-3936
- 520 Winter St., Waltham; (617) 890-9600

Sam's Club
- 1225 Worcester Rd. (Rte. 9), Natick; (508) 650-9156
- 564 Broadway (Rte. 1), Saugus; (617) 231-8000
- 338 Turnpike Rd. (Rte. 9), Westborough; (508) 836-5555

ELECTRONICS

There are lots of places to save money on appliances and electronics in Boston. Some, unfortunately, are as far below repute as they are below retail. With merchandise that is imported from foreign countries, there is a greater possibility of shady deals, or inferior quality. Mr. C says this not out of any kind of prejudice, but because he wants you to be careful.

One of the best ways to protect yourself, if you have doubts as to *any* store's reliability, is to ask about their guarantee policy; make sure the item you want carries an American warranty. Since some stores deal directly with manufacturers in the Far East, their merchandise many carry a foreign warranty instead. Even for identical products, a foreign warranty can make repairs a hassle—unless you don't mind paying the postage to Japan! Remember, you are perfectly within your rights to inquire about this in the store.

AUDIO AND VIDEO EQUIPMENT

Audio Lab
- 36 J.F.K. St., Cambridge; (617) 864-1144

If you can work your way to the top of The Garage, that silly circular mall in Harvard Square, you'll find Audio Lab. They primarily sell new products, but do repair work as well—and so they have several shelves filled with refurbished items. An Onkyo cassette deck, for example, was seen for a mere $110. Open seven days, weeknights until 8 P.M.

Audio Replay
- 8 Bow St., Cambridge; (617) 492-4604

This tiny shop near Harvard Square does expert stereo and VCR repair and has a full range of components that have been restored to perfect working order. You can always check the board out front (it may be easier than squeezing into the shop), with listings of the many pieces currently for sale.

You'll find all the biggies here: Pioneer, Sony, Toshiba, Technics, Sharp, and more. Mr. C found a JVC dual cassette deck with auto-reverse for $75; a pair of JBL three-way tower speakers for $180; a Yamaha preamp with equalizer for $225; and several CD players for around $80. Lots of turntables, too. All items carry a manufacturer's warranty. Open weekdays from 10 A.M. to 6 P.M., Saturdays 10-4.

Audio/Video Exchange
- 204 Massachusetts Ave., Arlington; (617) 646-4243

Despite its name, this is not a swap meet; it is a consignment dealer for anything and everything in home entertainment. People bring in items they want to sell; the store displays them. Profits are then split between the two.

The quality ranges from basic models to high-end brands. You can find TVs in all sizes, turntables, and even the records to spin on them (hundreds of titles, all $2-$3 apiece). A Sony CD player was seen recently for a mere $59; an Onkyo cassette deck, with automatic music search, for $39. You may even see reel-to-reel tape decks, tower speakers, and other audio buff stuff. Rebuilt VCRs at $60 "are a steal" and a specialty—complete with a 100-day store warranty.

The store's stated goal is to price each item at 25% to 40% of its original retail value. Everything on display is up and running for you to check out. They'll even give you a free estimate on repairs to your own equipment—a service for which many shops charge.

Audio/Video Exchange claims to be the only business in town offering all this under one roof. The hours are kinda funky: Tuesdays through Fridays from 5 to 7:30 P.M., and Saturdays from 11 to 3.

Cambridge SoundWorks Clearance Centers
- 154 California St., Newton; (617) 630-1696
- Worcester Common Fashion Outlets, Worcester; (508) 791-0040
- *And other suburban locations*

Henry Kloss, the engineer who founded the high-end speaker company KLH, started this new lab a few years ago—and has again attracted a lot of attention from hi-fi enthusiasts. More recently, CS has branched out to Cambridge, Burlington, Danvers, Framingham, and other towns—as well as California. At these company stores, you can buy highly rated SoundWorks speakers at factory-direct prices, starting as low as $150 a pair.

MR. CHEAP'S PICKS
Audio and Video
Equipment

✔ **Audio/Video Exchange**—Not a swap shop, but a consignment store with plenty of TVs, VCRs, and more, from the average to the sophisticated.

✔ **Cambridge Soundworks**— Their clearance centers in Newton and Worcester have lots of closeouts on high-quality tape decks, CD players, and speakers at bargain prices.

✔ **Q Audio**—The high end of used stereo components shops.

✔ **Tweeter Outlet Center**— Again, good closeout deals in top-name audio and video.

For greater savings, though, check the discontinued and refurbished stereo components at the two locations noted above. The brands most frequently seen are Pioneer, Sony, and Philips. Mr. C found a Sony five-disc CD changer, reduced from $229 to $189, and a Carver "Pro Logic" receiver, $150 off at $649. There are almost always similar bargains, usually in very limited quantities. The salespeople are very helpful, and will also leave you alone if you prefer. No "hard sell." All stores are open daily from 10 A.M. to 8 P.M. and Sundays from 10-6.

Cameras Inc. Stereo and Video
- 474 Massachusetts Ave., Arlington; (617) 648-8111

See the listing under "Cameras."

Q Audio
- 95 Vassar St., Cambridge; (617) 547-2727

It's a natural—a used audio place on the MIT campus. Q bills itself as "the world's smallest hi-fi shop" but actually has quite a lot of equipment, with plenty of options for the budget (but serious) audiophile. New, used, and "B-stock," or factory blemished items, are all sold at discount.

The brands cover the spectrum, but mostly favor high-end stuff: Paradigm, Marantz, Harman/Kardon, Carver, and the like. Speakers by Klipsch, Polk, and Boston Acoustics were recently selling at 50% off list prices. Plus refurbished turntables, as well as the latest in DAT and satellite TV toys. Among used items, Mr. C noted a Pioneer receiver for $88, an NAD compact disc player for $125, and a Yamaha cassette deck for $99.

Used goods carry an unconditional 14-day money-back guarantee, plus a store warranty of anywhere from 30 days to two years. You can also bring in your own pieces for cash (if they can sell them), trade, or consignment. Open weekdays from 10 A.M. to 7 P.M., Saturdays 10-6, Sundays 12-5.

Radio Shack Outlet Store
- 910 Broadway (Rte. 1), Saugus; (617) 233-2242

You all know Radio Shack. Well, their latest development is to designate one branch in each major city as a combination of regular store and clearance center. Piled up on tables at the rear is a wide range of leftover and slightly damaged merchandise— for those of you who consider this chain as more than a place to get those little adapter thingies. You may find deals on stereo speakers, tape decks for your car, answering machines, and an assortment of cute electronic toys. Open from 10 A.M. to 9 P.M. on weekdays, 9-6 on Saturdays, and 12-5 on Sundays.

Sherman's
- 11 Bromfield St., Boston; (617) 482-9610

On the lower level of this large store near Downtown Crossing, Sherman's displays a wide range of electronics and photo equipment. Televisions and VCRs, cassette decks, receivers and

speakers, boom boxes, Walkmans, and more. A recent sale featured a Denon CD player, originally priced at $300, on sale for $219; and a Panasonic cordless phone marked down from $120 to $88. Some items are factory-refurbished returns; all equipment is guaranteed.

This is also a good place to stock up on blank tape of all kinds; one or two major brands of video cassettes are usually on sale for $2.99 (even high-grade!), and they have many brands of audio cassettes at low prices too. Not to mention bargains on fax machines, refrigerators, air conditioners, and smaller home appliances—irons, rechargeable razors, water filtration devices, and the like— as well as luggage and home furnishings. Be sure to pick up their latest circular at the front of the store for the best deals. Open daily from 9 A.M. to 6 P.M., Sundays from 12-5.

Tweeter Outlet Center
- 874 Commonwealth Ave., Boston; (617) 738-4411

At the rear of Tweeter Etc.'s branch on the Boston University campus is a big room with shelves and shelves of demos, discontinued and refurbished stereo and video equipment, at savings of 20% to 70% (!) off the retail prices.

You may, for example, find a Mitsubishi 50-inch projection TV, listed at $3,800, on sale for a paltry $1,999. Denon receivers start around $300, occasionally $200. And it's not all high-end stuff; How about a Kenwood double cassette deck, marked down from $300 to $180, or a Yamaha CD player with a five-disc carousel at $100 off.

Tweeter offers the original, full manufacturer's warranties on all merchandise. The store is open seven days a week, including weeknights 'til 9 P.M.

Used Sound
- 31 Holland St., Somerville; (617) 625-7707

This Davis Square shop buys, sells, trades, and repairs stereo and video equipment, as well as electric guitars and amps. Cassette decks by Technics and Pioneer were seen in the $65 to $75 range; a Kenwood receiver was also $75, and a Sony CD player was $90. Used VCRs start as low as $95, and turntables from $45.

A special note for collectors of old radios: Used Sound specializes in tubes and has a good stock of these hard-to-find items. All stereo equipment carries a 90-day warranty. Open Mondays through Saturdays.

COMPUTERS

Like any big-ticket item, computers are a tricky purchase. There are ways to save money, but you should be careful in dealing with salespeople; make sure you're getting the features *you* want, and check out the warranty. Most computers, even used ones, work fine; but you do want to be covered. Another note: The computer market is extremely volatile—one of the few in which prices may drop, seemingly overnight. Use the figures quoted here as a general comparison.

Computer Escape
- 83 North Main St., Randolph; (617) 961-5053

Computer Escape deals in new, used, and refurbished PCs and clones, providing repair and service as well. Custom-configured systems are a big part of the business; you can save money by paying for only the features you need.

What Mr. C really wants to tell you about, however, is this store's bargain basement. It is filled with all kinds of old parts: cables, motherboards, cards, etc.—a techie's dream. Computer Escape specializes in hard-to-find components, software, and manuals. Have an old system you don't want to part with? CE can probably fix it or upgrade it. They usually have a decent selection of refurbished notebooks, too. Hours Monday through Friday 10 A.M. to 6 P.M., and Saturdays 10 A.M. to 4 P.M.

Right across the street is **Computer Xchange** at 88 North Main St., Randolph; telephone (617) 963-9313. It's filled to the brim with electronic "junque." The proprietor feels this spelling gives his goodies a classy touch; Mr. C spells it "bargain." Merchandise ranges from Tandys, Ataris, and Commodores to IBMs, Macs, and more—all the old stuff that no one else will carry. You can find a complete IBM system for as little as

$225. A Mac Plus—one of the first Apples ever produced—goes for $175. They carry some new stuff, too—and if you don't see what you want or need, ask. It's probably out back in the storage room. Hours are extremely irregular; call ahead.

The Computer Outlet
- 80 V.F.W. Parkway (Rte. 1A), Revere; (617) 284-0130
- 165 University Ave., Westwood; (800) 817-7060
- 1350 Washington St., Weymouth; (617) 335-5000
- 52 Cummings Park, Woburn; (800) 278-3737

This business (operating through Beach Sales in Revere and Rich's Furniture in Weymouth) specializes in selling off "factory renewed" electronics. You'll find many big names here, such as IBM, Gateway, Texas Instruments, and Digital (no Macs, sorry). These machines were returned and/or defective, and have now been fixed up; they are essentially new, and warrantied (usually for one year); but cannot be sold in full-price stores.

So, you may find an AT&T multimedia 486, with a dual-speed CD-ROM, sound card and speakers, for $799; add a 15-inch Dell monitor for a remarkable $269, and a laser printer by Okidata for $300. The Westwood branch offers the largest selection, including a separate "Note-

MR. CHEAP'S PICKS
Computers

✔ **Solutions Express**—Small Belmont shop that does a big business in both used computers and liquidation bargains.

✔ **Vision Investment Recovery** and **The Computer Outlet**—Two separate businesses both focusing on unused, factory-refurbished computers at prices far below list.

book Room" where Mr. C found a Lexmark 486 (DX2, active-color screen) reduced from a list price of $2,599 to $1,899. And an IBM "ThinkPad 350" for just $899.

Everything carries a ten-day money-back guarantee, on top of the warranties. Store hours vary by location; Westwood is open Thursdays and Fridays from 10 A.M. to 8 P.M. and Saturdays from 10-5 only.

Laptop Superstore
- 28 Batterymarch St., Boston; (617) 330-1666
- 1776 Massachusetts Ave., Cambridge; (617) 491-3454
- 600 Worcester Rd. (Rte. 9), Natick; (508) 650-9800

This chain, with stores in New England and California, offers fine prices on a range of notebooks, laptops, and accessories. In addition, the Cambridge store has a separate area selling factory-refurbished laptops at bargain rates. Any defects have been taken care of by the manufacturers, and now the computers can be resold at discount only.

Mr. C's recent visit yielded a Sharp laptop with an active-color screen for just $1,199; also an AST "Power Exec" for $1,049. Both represented savings of around $500 compared with retail prices.

Consignments may add the occasional NEC or Macintosh models as well. Used machines carry a 30-day store warranty, but extended warranties are available. Open weekdays from 9:30 A.M. to 6 P.M., Saturdays from 10 to 6, Sundays 12-5.

Micro Center
- 727 Memorial Dr., Cambridge; (617) 234-6400

This Ohio-based chain came blazing into town early in '95, transforming the old Stop & Shop (next to the landmark Shell sign) into a gleaming megastore with Pentium-like speed. The place is vast, claiming to stock some 24,000 items, from the tiniest chip to entire IBM and Mac systems.

Each of those worlds gets its own room, in fact; not to mention separate departments for peripherals, books, repairs, and free technical support (that's "help," to ordinary folks). So, what will you find in the way of high-volume prices? Among the deals seen on Mr. C's visit were a WinBook 486 laptop with dual-scan color, on sale for $2,097 (reduced from $2,500); a large supply of Hewlett Packard HP 520 DeskJet printers, factory-reconditioned (with a three-year manufacturer's warranty) for a mere $149 each; and the Apple "Newton" MessagePad 120, with 2mb of memory, for $611 (equal at the time to those low mail-order company prices).

Plus aisle upon aisle of name-brand and budget software and shareware. Accessories, blank diskettes, paper, and assembly-required furniture. Every computer book ever written, apparently. They also tend to have a big selection of manufacturer rebate coupons, and occasional product giveaways, near the registers up front.

The size and scope of the store may be daunting to the less technically-inclined; there is someone posted at the door to help direct you, and most of the sales staff seem to know their bits from their bytes. Micro Center should remain a must-check if you're shopping around for the best price of the moment. Open daily from 10 A.M. to 9 P.M., Saturdays 'til 6, Sundays 12-5.

Schneider Leasing

• 451 D Street, South Boston; (617) 261-6060

As the name implies, this company rents out computer systems of all kinds; when these are returned, you can buy them quite inexpensively. They prefer to work over the phone rather than in person; the salespeople are very helpful and will figure out what you need and what they have to match.

In general, complete systems start around $450 for an IBM-compatible PC. That would get you a 386 unit; 486 systems start closer to $800. Schneider has Macintosh systems too, as well as some notebooks in its ever-changing inventory. All equipment carries a 90-day warranty. Hours are Mondays to Fridays, 8:30 A.M. to 5:30 P.M. only.

Solutions Express

• 169 Belmont St., Belmont; (617) 489-6456

Successor to the now-defunct Progenius, Solutions Express carries on the tradition of top quality used computers and peripherals, along with liquidations on brand-new merchandise. Grab a secondhand 486 system for as little as $650, complete; used goods carry a 30-day store warranty (90 days for monitors).

If you're a bit skittish about rehabbed electronics, manufacturer closeouts offer great deals at slightly higher prices—with a one-year warranty. These may even include Macintosh units mixed in with some of the PCs. More interesting to Mac users: Solutions is the first licensed distributor in all of New England for Macintosh clones: A complete outfit may save you a thousand bucks over the name brand version.

The store also offers software at discount prices, and does expert repairs. The place is tiny, cluttered, and usually frenetic—but have patience, and you're sure to walk away with a super deal. Open Mondays through Saturdays from 9 A.M. to 6 P.M.

Vision Investment Recovery, Inc.

• 12 Linscott Rd., Woburn; (617) 935-5332

With the cool, carpeted refinement of an office itself, Vision fills both a spacious showroom and a large warehouse with deals on new and used computers that must be seen to be believed.

Or you can trust Mr. C, who discovered that the vast majority of this stock is factory-refurbished, and therefore virtually new, but selling for anywhere from 20% to 50% below the original retail price. Recent specials included an AST multimedia desktop system, a Pentium version with similar features, and an Apple Performa system, all easily $300-$500 less than the going department store rates at the same time.

Inkjet printers from Apple go as low as $199, while laser printers can be had for $299. A library of color notebooks, including active-matrix screens, carry a six-month factory warranty; Vision's own refurbished laptops from Toshiba and IBM (as low as $645) offer 90-day warranties. Vision does "a little bit of everything," according to one employee, including networking, configurations, and all types of repairs. Navigate a sea of industrial parks to track them down, from 8:30 A.M. to 5 P.M. weekdays.

And while you're in the area, check out the nearby **Electronic Superstore** at 20 Normac Rd., Woburn; telephone (617) 932-6800. With less in the way of computers but more in the way of accessories, you can pick up salvaged transformers, converters, and the like for $3 from open trays lining the aisles; used keyboards cost as little as $25. Package deals may take you all the way back to a Packard Bell 286 system, without a monitor, for $299 (but you can grab one for $50 more), or a classic old IBM system (with a big 5" floppy drive) for $185 complete. Hours are 10 A.M. to 8 P.M. Mondays through Fridays, 9 A.M to 5 P.M. Saturdays, and 12-5 P.M. Sundays.

Not to mention (but we will) these well-known chains:

Circuit City
- 250 Granite St., Braintree; (617) 356-7700
- 84 Middlesex Tpke., Burlington; (617) 229-1700
- 4 Newbury St. (Rte. 1), Danvers; (508) 777-7100
- 300 V.F.W. Pkwy., Dedham; (617) 329-8282
- 1775 Washington St., Hanover; (617) 829-0025
- 1450 Worcester Rd. (Rte. 9), Natick; (508) 872-0190
- 65 Mystic Ave., Somerville; (617) 623-3400

Computer City
- 341 Cochituate Rd. (Rte. 30), Framingham; (508) 626-2800
- 1160 Broadway (Rte. 1), Saugus; (617) 231-7200

CompUSA
- 205 Market St., Brighton; (617) 783-1900
- 500 Cochituate Rd. (Rte. 30), Framingham; (508) 875-8300
- 335 Washington St., Woburn; (617) 937-0600

FLEA MARKETS

Cary Hill Flea Market
- 220 East Ashland St., Brockton; (508) 583-3100

Located in a building that was once a discount department store, Cary Hill Flea Market carries on the tradition with its own assortment of old records, used appliances, quaint postcards, and other oddities. A recent visit turned up a microwave oven—looked like the first one ever made—for $40, and oversize dorm refrigerators for $85.

Unlike other flea markets, Cary Hill has two features that make it stand out. First of all, the place doubles as an office furniture liquidator. Mr. C found desks, chairs, conference tables, and cubicle partitions. A five-drawer file cabinet, in good condition, was $85. Package prices are available, so give 'em a call if you're looking to outfit a new office.

Second, Cary Hill Flea Market is also home to **Golden Treasures Diamond and Gold Jewelry**. Prices here are about 60% off retail. A sixteen-inch rope chain in 14K gold would be $295 elsewhere; here it's a mere $110. A 24-inch strand of freshwater pearls was a recent steal at $45. Cary Hill Flea Market is open from 9 A.M. to 5 P.M. on Saturdays and Sundays only. There is an admission price of 50¢.

Malden Indoor Flea Market
- 50 Ferry St., Malden; (617) 324-9113

Right at the intersection of Ferry and Route 60, the old Ruderman's Furniture building appears to have been taken over by rats. Packrats, that is—and we all know one or two. The sort of person who just can't throw *anything* away. Some, at least, are willing to sell their collected fortunes, and dozens of such entrepreneurs are tucked into every corner of the building.

Three floors of them, in fact, selling everything imaginable—from antiques to yarn. Some dealers have legitimate goods, while others have simply dredged their basements for junk. In all, it's like the world's biggest yard sale. On any given weekend, you may find a color TV for $75, home perm kits for $3, books at five for a buck, and fresh produce at farm-direct prices—plus children's clothing, decorative brass, small appliances, tools, toys, baseball cards, you name it. In many cases, you can probably name your price, too.

This bizarre bazaar does have a sense of humor; one booth, offering early IBM computers, calls itself "Trailing Edge Technology." Love it. The third floor is taken up with the Antique Co-Op, well-stocked with some nice pieces of older furniture. Some merchants offer layaway plans, and take credit cards.

There's even a snack bar, and as if this weren't exciting enough, state lottery scratch tickets are raffled off every half hour. Admission is 50¢ for adults, and free for kids under 12. It all happens every Saturday and Sunday from 9 A.M. to 5 P.M., year-round.

Mass. Merchandise Mart
• 800 The Lynnway (Rte. 1A), Lynn; (617) 598-5450

Sharing a hangar-like structure with the venerable Building 19, the MMM is a permanent indoor flea market. Independently owned stalls, sharing the rent to cut costs, offer low prices on a world of clothing, housewares, furniture, and assorted goods. Dealers hawk jewelry (solid gold and cheap gold-plated), home and car stereo, shoes, inexpensive foreign-made clothing, linens, and more. Some include warranties and return policies; some are cash-only.

There are even a couple of stores-within-the-store. Krazy Jack's Surplus looks like a mini-version of its next-door neighbor—same closeout rummage tables, same wacky cartoon image of the owner smiling down from the walls. If there's such a thing as a poor man's Building 19, this is it. Nearby, Town and Country Home Furnishings sells brand-new inexpensive furniture—the kind that comes in ensembles like a seven-piece dining table set for $258.

There's a greasy-spoon coffee shop inside as well; out front, C & M Produce sells fresh fruits and vegetables. And, after all those options, if you *still* can't find a deal on what you're looking for, there's now a Wal-Mart next door. Mass. Merchandise is open

---

MR. CHEAP'S PICK
Flea Markets

✔ **Revere Swap-n-Shop Flea Market**—Weekends in the Showcase Cinemas parking lot, plenty of off-the-truck deals on things you actually *want.*

---

year-round, Wednesdays through Sundays from 10 A.M. to 6 P.M. (Thursdays through Saturdays 'til 8).

Revere Swap-n-Shop Flea Market
• Routes 1 & 60 (Squire Rd.), Revere; (617) 289-7100

Taking up a good chunk of the Showcase Cinemas parking lot every weekend from early spring to late fall, this swap meet is the genuine article. Along with lots of okay stuff like knock-off NBA T-shirts for $3 and budget luggage, there are lots of real deals to be found among the dozens of merchants here.

Much of the merchandise consists of good-quality closeouts. One vendor on Mr. C's visit had a good selection of discontinued Nike sneakers for $30 and $40 a pair. Another had irregular jeans from the Gap for $10; the same price at other dealers might yield a pair of work boots, colorful aerobic outfits, or even wristwatches (sure, you *always* find $10 watches at a flea market—but these included a one-year warranty!).

Booth after booth displays useful items like kitchen gadgets and cutlery; fresh produce; secondhand compact discs and Nintendo games; colognes (both real and imitation), cosmetics and Avon products; socks (four pair of Burlington crews for $5); there was even a booth dedicated solely to bras.

Not to mention carts serving up great-smelling sausages, fried dough, slushes, and the like. As long as the weather is warm enough, the Swap-n-Shop operates Saturdays and Sundays from 7 A.M. to 4 P.M., plus any

Monday holidays. Admission is 50¢ for adults, free for kids under 12; and of course, there is plenty of free parking.

FLOWERS AND PLANTS

Calisi's Flowerland
- 289 Walk Hill St., Roslindale; (617) 524-7019

This intersection (with the American Legion Highway) is lush with florists, no doubt because of the many cemeteries nearby. Calisi's is sort of the no-frills shop in the bunch, with less opulent displays than its rivals—but then, that means lower prices.

Fresh roses start as low as $7.50 a dozen (!) for the short-stemmed varieties; these range up to a more standard $30-$40 a dozen for a box of long-stems. The store offers a complete FTD wire service for deliveries. Lovely mixed bouquets, usually $4-$5 around town, go for a mere $2.98 here. Calisi's also has its own small greenhouse, offering potted geraniums for $1.50 in season, and vegetable plants (peppers, eggplant, cucumbers) at $1.98 for a box. Open seven days a week, from 9 A.M. to 6 P.M.

Nearby, you may also want to check out **Lombardi Florist** at 609 American Legion Highway; telephone 524-4455. This is another high-volume, low-price source for flowers and plants. **Blooms and Greens** at 3880 Washington Street, Roslindale, telephone (617) 524-5556, is another cut-price source for cut-rate flowers.

City Farm
- 721 American Legion Hwy., Roslindale; (617) 469-2992

What name could be more appropriate for this urban haven? All you need for creating your own farm, or just a nice window box, is here. By working cash-and-carry, City Farm saves lots of money over most other gardening centers. Better yet, they of-

fer quantity discounts when you buy six or more of any plant. CF also has cut flowers at wholesale prices, including a boxed dozen long-stem roses for $15—and that includes the wrapping and "baby's breath."

Another good deal is on foliage plants for the house. During the summer months, when City Farm can stock large quantities and keep them outside, these decorative large-pot plants are reduced from $35 to just $19.98. And a very helpful feature on all house plants is the color-coding tags, to tell you which plants want lots of light and which ones want to be in the shade. City Farm is open daily from 9 A.M. to 6 P.M., Sundays 'til 5.

Ken's Flower Cafe
- 382 Cambridge St., Burlington; (617) 272-6639
- 158 East Central St., Natick; (508) 655-1909
- 2111 Commonwealth Ave., Newton; (617) 965-5069

Ken's original Newton "cafe" is, in fact, a converted cabin trailer next to a gas station—not as trendy a spot as the name implies, but then, that keeps the overhead costs low. And that means low prices for high quality. No wonder that trailer's been there for twenty years now.

Mixed bouquets start at just $3, with larger ones available for $4.95. Same price for a dozen carnations. A dozen red roses, with 16-inch stems, go for an incredible $9.95; longer stems run you only five dollars more. There are also fancy cut flowers, like irises and tulips, in season; ditto for planting annuals by the flat. And a recent special offered all hanging plants at just $7.95—a great deal.

Deliveries can be arranged (no pun intended); the stores are open seven days a week year-round, including all major holidays. Ken's offers volume discounts, as well as a 20% discount for senior citizens. And there's even a "warranty" of four days on cut flowers, provided you follow their care instructions. How many florists do *that*?

Lambert's Rainbow Fruit

- 820 Crescent St., Brockton; (508) 580-2736
- 77 Morrissey Blvd., Dorchester; (617) 436-2998
- 220 Providence Hwy. (Rte. 1), Westwood; (617) 326-5047

These stores are more like the pot of gold at the end of the rainbow. In addition to all kinds of fresh produce and specialty foods, Lambert's also has an outdoor garden center, selling flowers, plants, and soil, also at competitive prices. Pick a perennial for $1.98 in small pots and $7.99 for larger plants—in season, of course. Annuals were seen for $1.97 a pot. Plus peat moss, potting soil, and all the esssentials. All this, and personal, family-style service. Open seven days.

Marino Lookout Farm

- 89 Pleasant St., Natick; (508) 655-4294

See the listing under "Food Shops."

Ricky's Flower Market

- 283 Washington St., Somerville; (617) 628-7569

Ricky's is right in the heart of Union Square—literally. Whichever direction you travel through that crazy course of roads, you'll be looking right at this open-air stand. It's a family-run business, offering good prices on all kinds of plants and flowers.

The big promotional deal here is a dozen long-stemmed roses for $9.98. But there is also a wide variety of annuals at $1.98 each—petunias, marigolds, violets, begonias, and more. That's also the basic price for herbs and vegetable plants like tomatoes. Hundreds of perennials are $2.89 and up. Interior plants, arriving weekly

---

> ## MR. CHEAP'S PICKS
> ### Flowers and Plants
>
> ✔ **Ricky's Flower Market—** Located in the heart of Somerville's Union Square— literally—is this great place to get your geraniums, with a few gardening tips.
>
> ✔ **Warehouse Flowers**—Cut flowers at cut prices, including one of the lowest prices around on a dozen roses.

---

from Florida, start from $3.98.

Better yet, Ricky also has a "Bargain Basement"—around the side, actually—with tables of pansies and "Tom Thumbs" for a dollar, and a sea of impatiens in pink, purple, red, and white, at $2 each. Taking advantage of rush-hour traffic, the shop is open daily from 8 A.M. to 8 P.M. There are two parking areas on the Washington Street side.

ROSExpress

- 186 South St., Boston; (617) 695-2999

Here's a flower deal that may not seem cheap in price—or in style. That's why it's a bargain. For $29.99, you can buy a dozen long-stemmed (three foot!) roses, boxed and gift wrapped; that's a decent price. But, for an additional $3-$5, you can then have these delivered by a driver dressed to the nines in a full tuxedo. When you figure this all together, it's a way to really impress someone without going into debt.

Part of a nationwide chain, ROSExpress specializes in high-quality gifts and service. Their roses are flown in daily, directly from growers in Central and South America. Over a dozen color varieties are available, from Royalty red to Sterling Silver lavender to Cream Ariana white. You can also order a single red rose ($5), a bud vase with one rose ($8), or a chocolate rose ($3.50 each, $36 a dozen).

The company is pioneering the delivery side of the business in other ways, too. They offer guaranteed delivery, within 24 hours, of a dozen roses anywhere in the country for $49.99; these are shipped in special boxes, lined by hand with styrofoam to keep the flowers fresh. Oh yes, and they even have a "Frequent Flower" credit program. Gotta love it.

Though they do some walk-up business, this is primarily a telephone service; call anytime from 9 A.M. to 6 P.M. Monday through Friday, and from 8 A.M. to 2 P.M. on Saturday.

Warehouse Flowers
- 370 Chestnut Hill Ave., Brighton; (617) 277-0054
- 1 Center St., Burlington; (617) 272-2244
- 68 Chestnut St., Needham; (617) 449-4882

The claim to fame for these shops: One dozen roses for $9.52. Period. Been that way for years. Warehouse features a nice, chilly walk-in where you'll find carnations or irises for $3.99 a dozen, tulips for $5.99 a bunch, orchid corsages for $3.99, and other assortments—or make up your own.

Lily plants and azaleas are $5.99, a variety of flowering plants range from $2.50 to $7, and large floor plants are mostly $14.99. The reason for the low prices is right there in the name: This is a no-frills, high-volume establishment. They make no deliveries, to keep costs below retail florists.

They also extend the warehouse approach to an eclectic mix of cards, posters, artistic gift bags, baskets, and teddy bears. All stores are open Mondays through Saturdays; the Cleveland Circle branch (no pun intended) adds Sundays from 10-5.

Wellington Flower Wholesalers
- 535 Fellsway, Medford; (617) 396-5057

Looking like an oasis in the asphalt jungle, Wellington Flowers has taken root (sorry, couldn't resist) at the busy intersection of Routes 16 and 28. Makes getting in and out *really* fun—but go ahead, it's worth it.

Fancy some roses? Long-stemmed red ones are $14.95 per dozen, or $2 apiece. Colored roses, in several hues, are $19.95 per dozen, and an even thriftier romantic can score a dozen carnations for $5.75.

Flowering hangers in eight-inch pots were the best deal on Mr. C's visit; a huge selection of petunias, geraniums, and fuchsias, among others, were on sale for $5.99, or two for ten bucks. If you prefer flowers of the low-maintenance variety, go for the silk hanging plants ($9.95) instead. Wellington's is open 9 AM to 9 P.M., all year 'round.

FOOD SHOPS

BAKERIES

Bova's Bakery
- 134 Salem St., Boston; (617) 523-5601

Bova's has many varieties of breads and pastries, baked on the premises. Prices are as good as the aroma: Get a loaf of sliced Scali bread for $1.60, or crusty French bread for $1.25; plus Vienna, sourdough, and more. There's plenty of it: In an average night, Bova bakes 2,430 braided rolls and 500 French baguettes, using over 2,000 pounds of flour. It's fantastic stuff. Best of all, the shop is open 24 hours a day! Bravo!

Clear Flour Bread
- 178 Thorndike St., Brookline; (617) 739-0060

The minute you walk in, you'll be floating on air. It smells fabulous in here. Clear Flour is barely a store—more a humble bakery for restaurants and markets—but they are happy to sell to you directly. Baguettes are the best deals here, with prices that have hardly gone up in years. The small ones, well over a foot long, are just $1.25; large ones, which are gigantic, are $2.25—all in French, herb, and sourdough. Round loaves of buckwheat, sourdough, and herb varieties are $2.25. Open from 10 A.M. to 8 P.M., seven days.

Entenmann's Outlet Store

- 105 Providence Hwy. (Rte. 1), Norwood; (617) 769-6635
- 113 Newbury St. (Rte. 1), Peabody; (508) 535-1700

Readers with a sweet tooth will want to take advantage of the chance to get Entenmann's baked goods at tremendous savings—in many cases, over half-off. Their clearance outlet has a large quantity of cakes, cookies, pastries and bread, plus some non-bakery items.

There are three levels of discount on boxed pastry. Fresh goods are sold at bakery-direct prices: French crumb cake, for example, sells at $2.99 in supermarkets and $2.30 here. Market returns, which haven't yet reached their expiration dates, are about half-price: A box of six blueberry muffins was reduced from $2.99 to $1.50. Finally, the markdown section includes goods that can be anywhere from two to eight days old, all priced at $1. Here you may find a box of chocolate chip cookies that had been $2.39. Entenmann's stuff is so good, though, that it doesn't go stale very quickly.

The store also gets products from other area companies at discount, such as Sealtest ice cream and Arnold rye bread. For senior citizens there is a further 10% discount off the total at the register. Open seven days.

Gooche's Bakery

- 4140 Washington St., Roslindale; (617) 325-3928

You'd never guess in a million years that this tiny, wood-frame structure conceals a bakery that supplies upscale food stores with macrobiotic pastries, breads, and pastas—from Cambridge all the way to Alaska. But it's true.

"Gooche" is owner Dominic Candela, a friendly guy who oversees the baking. He cranks out creations like lemon-sesame cookies, carob-walnut brownies, and apple-raisin-cinnamon bread loaves. At a mere $2, the bread is the most expensive of these; the cookies, which are individually packaged, sell at places like Bread & Circus for around $1.50—but you can get 'em here for just 65¢, fresh from the oven. These pastries are made using skim milk, very little oil, and no salt or sugar; they're sweetened with barley malt, and are low in fat. Oh yes, and they're delicious.

Dom's cousin, Bob Mazza, is like a mad scientist of pasta. He's constantly inventing new ways to make pasta, avoiding eggs and using alternative ingredients like rice flour to reduce fat and cholesterol. Inside huge ravioli pockets, he stuffs fillings like garlic, white beans, and escarole (that's all one rav) and sells them for $2.50-$4 a pound. Bob's R & D technique? He tests out his inventions on co-workers first, and if he gets the thumbs-up, they're added to the menu. He's had few failures.

Other varieties include such exotic fare as yam gnocchi and tofu pasta; meat and vegetarian sauces are made here as well. These can get a bit pricey; but considering the freshness and quality, you'll save a bundle here as compared with health food stores.

Having been in business nearly twenty years, Gooche's isn't the best-kept secret in town. Many products sell out by the end of the day, but you can always call ahead and special-order anything on the list. The shop is open every weekday from 9 A.M. to 7 P.M.; since they're closed all weekend, Mondays are clear-out days, when many items are reduced to just a dollar. Go.

Green & Freedman Bakery

- 75 Old Colony Ave., South Boston; (617) 269-4700

Their bread goes to the supermarkets and restaurants all over the city; but if you're near Southie, you can stop in and get some for less. Onion rolls are sort of a specialty of the house, at 35¢ each; a dozen of these aromatic treats costs $4.20 here—about a buck less than in supermarkets. Loaves of rye bread are also lower here. The shop serves sandwiches and soups, as well as pastries; G & F no longer makes its own sweets, but the ones they sell are good! Open from 5:30 A.M. to 7 P.M. seven days a week.

Hoff's Bakery

- 134A Mystic Ave., Medford; (617) 396-8384

Hoff's supplies many of Boston's finest restaurants with pastries, calzones, and specialty items. By going to their bakery, you can buy these directly at considerable savings. Ten-inch cheesecakes, whole or sliced (and reassembled), carrot cakes, Italian rum cakes, mocha tortes, apple crisps, key lime pies, and, of course, Boston cream pies are all made here. Because of Hoff's relationships with area restaurants, they requested that no prices be printed in this book— but they are good. Hoff's also makes large sheet cakes to order, suitable for parties and banquets. Open weekdays from 8 A.M. to 5 P.M., Saturdays 8-12 noon.

Il Fornaio

- 221 Hanover St., Boston; (617) 742-3394

That's "The Baker" to the rest of us (hey, in the North End, *everybody's* Italian). True to its name, this informal eatery also sells fresh-baked breads—at incredibly low prices. Get a loaf of traditional scali bread for $1.50, or something from the ever-changing selection of exotic flavors like pesto, prosciutto, and date-pecan. Yes folks, those are breads, most of which are just $2 for a big, round loaf. And there are usually some good choices in the "day-old" bin, selling at half-price—you may even nab two loaves for $1.39. Open from 8-8 daily.

Kupel's Bake and Bagel

- 421 Harvard St., Brookline; (617) 232-3444

So many restaurants make a proud point of featuring Kupel's bagels. So go to the source, near Coolidge Corner—where you can get a baker's dozen for $4.60, hot from the oven, in about twenty varieties from poppyseed to "Tomato Veggie Onion."

Better yet, peruse their "day-old" rack. This includes bags of eight bagels for 95¢, depending on when you check it. Usually they have the most popular flavors—poppyseed, sesame, pumpernickel. Eight fresh ones would cost you three bucks or so; but when they start out as good as this, yesterday's batch is still terrific. Good pastries, too. Open daily from 6 A.M. to 11 P.M.

Just a few doors down, by the way, is longtime rival **Eagerman's Bakery** at 415 Harvard St.; telephone (617) 566-8771. They also have great bagels, as well as loaves (which Kupel's no longer bakes). They offer a half-dozen day-old bagels for 70¢, and various loaves for around a dollar. As the smaller of the two, they frequently "throw in" an extra bagel or pastry. Open from 7 A.M. to 10 P.M. every day.

Mike's Pastry

- 300 Hanover St., Boston; (617) 742-3050

Mr. C can't even *think* about the North End without sighing at the string of fine Italian bakeries along Hanover Street, the neighborhood's main drag. Mike's is his pick in the area. The store does both wholesale and retail business, and its pastry cases are filled with a colorful palette of cakes and cookies. Why, there are over a dozen varieties of cannoli alone! They also have table service, if you prefer to while an hour away over pastry and an espresso. In the summer, they add homemade ice cream. Mmmm. Open weekdays from 8 A.M. to 9 P.M., weekends 'til 11 P.M.

Neighborhood Restaurant and Bakery

- 25 Bow St., Somerville; (617) 623-9710

This small, extremely popular Union Square restaurant (see the listing under "Restaurants—Somerville") also bakes its own mouth-watering Portuguese sweet bread. It costs $3 a loaf; but early in the day you may even be able to grab one of yesterday's loaves for a buck. Meanwhile, their home-baked white and wheat breads are $1 a loaf fresh—and they're heavenly. Open from 7 A.M. to 10 P.M. daily.

Nissen Bakery Thrift Shop

- 91 Foster St., Brockton; (508) 587-3663

As you've gathered by now, these outlets for major commercial bakeries are terrific places to stock up on essential supplies. As Nissen trucks bring fresh bread to supermarket each morning, they collect whatever was left over from the day before and bring it back to their clearance center. Here, you can get perfectly good loaves, most of which have not yet reached their expiration dates, at half of the supermarket price. Sometimes, if the item is closer to expiration, for even less.

Nissen Thrift carries a few other lines, such as Drake's Cakes. They also have fresh, current merchandise as well; even this is below retail prices. Open Tuesdays through Fridays from 10:30 A.M. to 5 P.M. and Saturdays from 9-4.

Pepperidge Farm Thrift Store

- 87 Blanchard Rd., Cambridge; (617) 661-6361
- Middlesex Mall, Middlesex Tpke., Burlington; (617) 272-5158

More than just a bakery thrift store, this is more like a discount mini-supermarket. Check the tag colors: Red is for fresh items at 25% off retail. Black is just past the expiration date, but still good, at 40% off; and blue means closeouts—though never spoiled—at 50% off.

Loaves of bread and rolls are as low as 99¢; a large chocolate layer cake, reduced from $2.79 to $2.09;

bags of soft-baked cookies, in the gourmet varieties, same price; and of course, good ol' Goldfish. A recent sale offered them at two bags for the price of one ($1.19).

There is also a freezer case, with things like "Le Menu" chicken cordon bleu, reduced from $3.79 to $2.75. The store has weekly specials, and senior citizen discounts on Tuesdays and Wednesdays. And, every few months, a clearance sale reduces these *discount* rates by half. Stock up! Open seven days.

Roma's Bakery

- 201 Somerville Ave., Somerville; (617) 776-0869

Roma's bakes bread for supermarkets all over the area. Buying at the bakery couldn't be simpler; nearly everything is priced at $1.25—large, round soft loaves, sliced scali bread, wholegrain loaves, or a bag of a half-dozen sandwich rolls. You can only save a bit over the stores, but the best part is that after three o'clock you can get the bread straight out of the oven. "So hot it'll burn your hand," says Mr. Roma. This continues until about 9 P.M. daily; Saturdays 'til 5.

Up the avenue toward Union Square is a larger, similar establishment, **La Ronga** Bakery, at 599 Somerville Avenue; telephone (617) 625-8600. They also distribute to area markets, but again, you can get it fresh from the source. A loaf of sliced scali bread is $1.24. They sell day-old bread too, like three baguettes for a dollar; and they also bake up fresh, hot calzones about the size of a football for $2.50, filled with spinach, mushrooms, or broccoli and cheese. Open daily from 7 A.M. to 8 P.M.

Sevan Bakery

- 598 Mt. Auburn St., Watertown; (617) 924-3243

Mr. C loves to roam around this Armenian neighborhood just over the Cambridge line, laced with restaurants and markets. Sevan's specializes in all kinds of baked goods, from baguettes ($1) to something called *zaahtar*—round Syrian bread with a topping of thyme, sesame seeds, sumac, and other spices baked on. $2 gets you a pair of these zesty concoctions. Sevan also has a large case of spinach and feta cheese pies (75¢), baklava made with walnuts or pistachios ($1), and other exotic delicacies.

While you're in the area, check out **Massis Bakery** across and down a bit at 569 Mt. Auburn St., telephone (617) 924-0537; and, walking down Dexter Avenue to the corner of Nichols, **Marash Bakery** at 51 Dexter Ave., (617) 924-0098, has more Middle Eastern baked specialties. Diagonally across from Marash is **Gennaro's Italian Food Center,** 107 Nichols Ave., (617) 924-9550, where you can get great calzones piping hot

from the oven.

Wonder-Hostess Bakery Thrift Store

- 601 Pond St., Braintree; (617) 848-0670
- 647 Andover St., Lawrence; (508) 686-6119
- 429 Eastern Ave., Malden; (617) 324-3800
- 330 Speen St., Natick; (508) 655-2150
- 10 Cape Rd., Taunton; (508) 822-4876
- *And other suburban locations*

Seems kind of funny to make a fuss over Wonder Bread, that most ordinary of loaves. You can get such a loaf here for only 60¢—fresh and direct from the bakery. But there's a lot more here than white.

Hostess Cupcakes and Twinkies are 25¢ a pack; cinnamon crumb cake, fat-free, is reduced from $2.99 to just 99¢. A dozen assorted doughnuts is marked down from $2.49 to the same 99¢. Most of these are reaching their expiration date, but rarely are they past it.

Other brands and products here include Home Pride Butter Top Wheat Bread, 50¢ a loaf; Beefsteak Rye, same price, marked down from $1.69; a box of Uncle Ben's stuffing mix for 99¢. There are also various soup mixes, rice, popcorn, and candies. Open seven days, including weeknights.

CANDY AND NUTS

American Nut and Chocolate Company

- 230 West Broadway, South Boston; (617) 268-0075

Cashews, $3.99 a pound . . . pistachios, $2.99 a pound . . . dry roasted peanuts, half a pound for 99¢. These delicious items are roasted and processed on the premises and sold in a no-frills shop at the front. They also have chocolates and candies, though these are not all made in their factory; get a pound of chocolate-cov-

ered jellies for $1.69, or homemade fudge for $3.99 a pound. Open weekdays from 10 A.M. to 6 P.M. only.

Dairy Fresh Candies

- 57 Salem St., Boston; (617) 742-2639

The store manager remarked, "We enjoy eating what we sell as much as the customer does," and you know if he said otherwise, he'd be lying. A longtime North End landmark for chocoholics, the clientele at Dairy Fresh consists not only of the public, but also chefs from restaurants all over town who bake this chocolate into their dessert creations.

The tiny establishment is literally jammed to the rafters with bargain-priced candy and nuts. At the front counter is an assortment of Peter's chocolate, sold in bulk and not otherwise available for retail sale; it's crudely broken into smaller pieces that can be had for $3.99 a pound. There's also a wide variety of truffles, including amaretto, cherry, and Black Forest, which go for a reasonable $7.99 a pound (approximately 40 of 'em); a box of these are an ideal gift for any occasion, demanded even on the hottest days of the year.

You'll also find pistachios for $3.99 per pound, flavorful Indian cashews for $4.99, and pecans (available year 'round—oh rare!), for $7.99.

Dairy Fresh also boasts a truly inspiring selection of gummi candy, starting from $1.79 a pound (for Swedish fish), making Mr. C feel just like a kid in a...ah, forget it. Open from 9 A.M. to 6 P.M. Mondays through Thursdays, 'til 7 P.M. Fridays and Saturdays. Closed Sundays.

Haviland Candy Shop
- 134 Cambridge St., Cambridge; (617) 498-0500

Ah, to stroll through the sugary, sweet-smelling air of . . . East Cambridge? Land of factories, buses, and sub shops? Yes, this is one factory no one can complain about. From a no-frills front room, they sell gobs and gobs of sweet stuff from Borden, Necco, and their subsidiaries. Long glass counters show you what's currently available, and the shelves above are lined with boxes ready to go. You can't ask for a quarter-pound of this and a half-pound of that; some of the boxes are, well, for the industrial-size sweet tooth.

The bargains vary from week to week. You may find a two-pound bag of caramels for $1.99, or the same size of chocolate peanut clusters for $2.50. And, just like clothing, candy has "irregulars"; these are sold in one-

---

┌─────────────────────────────────┐
│ **MR. CHEAP'S PICK**   │
│ **Candy and Nuts**   │
│ ──────────   │
│ ✔ **Haviland Candy Outlet**—   │
│ Haviland, Borden, and other   │
│ brands are made right here.   │
│ Great prices on boxed   │
│ chocolates, in quantities from │
│ one pound to five.   │
└─────────────────────────────────┘

---

pound boxes for 99¢, and five-pound boxed assortments for just $4.80. What could be irregular about chocolate? It usually has to do with size or shape—never the taste.

There are also sugar-free chocolates, which taste very close to the real thing. For Valentine's Day, they have deals on those little candy hearts with the sayings on them; at Halloween, you'll find discounted bags of name-brand candy bars. Where better to stock up? Of course, this is one of Mr. C's favorite haunts any time of year. Open weekdays only, from 9 A.M. to 4 P.M.

Pearl's Candies
- 371 Worcester Rd. (Rte. 9), Framingham; (508) 875-7772

This tiny shop by the side of the highway (westbound) is packed from floor to ceiling with meticulously packaged sweets and nuts of every kind. A half-pound package of chocolate-covered peanut clusters, for instance, goes for $1.99, while pistachios and Jordan almonds are both $3.99 a pound. There's a vast selection of sugar-free candies, dried fruits (like banana chips, 99¢ for a half-pound), fudge, and jelly beans. During Mr. C's visit, there was even a special on "seconds" of fruit slices: one-pound boxes for $1.69. Hey, who cares if the shapes are a little off? Certainly not your taste buds. Open seven days a week.

Superior Nut Outlet
• 225 Msgr. O'Brien Hwy.,
  Cambridge; (617) 876-3808

Every kind of nut imaginable is processed here and trucked out all over greater Boston. In a tiny office in front of the factory, anyone can walk in and purchase fresh nuts by the bag or jar, at discount. There are usually a few specials, like a twenty-ounce jar of honey-roasted cashews for just $3, *very* cheap indeed. A one-pound bag of mixed filberts, almonds, cashews, Brazil nuts, and pecans was seen for $4. Raw, blanched almonds for baking—whole, sliced or slivered—are about $4 a pound; Spanish peanuts go for $1.75 a pound.

Processed nuts and candies include butter toffee peanuts, $2 a pound; jumbo dried peaches, $4.50 a pound; and all-natural sun-dried raisins, $1.50 a pound. Also, a 3-pound jar of old-fashioned peanut butter for $8.50. Plus gummi bears, bridge mix, and the rest. Open weekdays only, from 8 A.M. to 4:30 P.M.

COFFEE

Beacon Supermarket
• 1028 Beacon St., Brookline; (617)
  232-3286

For years, the single best deal Mr. C has found on fresh coffee beans has been at this old-timey neighborhood market. A wall-full of bins offers dozens of dark roasts, decafs, and flavored beans from just $3.49 to about $5 a pound. Try matching *that*, Starbucks. Open daily.

GENERAL MARKETS

Arlington Food Co-op
• 7A Medford St., Arlington; (617)
  648-FOOD (3663)

Boston Food Co-op
• 449 Cambridge St., Allston; (617)
  787-1416

The Harvest Co-op
• 581 Massachusetts Ave.,
  Cambridge; (617) 661-1580

The idea behind a co-op, of course, is that you become a member, pitch in a few hours regularly behind the register of stocking the shelves, and get big discounts because of the low overhead costs. However, you don't have to be a member to shop at these places. The prices are still quite reasonable, even with the member discounts, and the merchandise is closer to Bread & Circus than Star Market.

For members the savings can be tremendous, though, and the requirements are minimal. At the Arlington Co-op, pay a one-time fee of $25, plus $7.50 per year, and you'll receive a vote in the running of the co-op, as well as a 2% discount off every purchase. The Boston Co-op and the Cambridge Co-op are affiliated, so when you become a member at one, you're a member of both! Their rate is $10 a year which yields you a 2% discount. All three offer deeper discounts if you're willing to invest time. These are generally around 10% for a monthly commitment and 20% for a weekly undertaking.

Much of the food available is organic; all of it is natural, healthy, and good value. Moreover, co-ops offer lots of unusual options, like delicious curried peanut chicken salad by the pound. There are bulk dispensers of everything, including coffee, beans, organic popcorn, sesame seeds, whole wheat macaroni, and instant falafel mix. Buying in bulk is not only cheaper, but also eco-friendly. Bring your own containers or buy them here, and fill up with cereals, rices, grains, herbs, beans, flour, nuts...and on and on. You can get honey and peanut butter (smooth or chunky, with or without salt, organic or conventional . . .) by the pound. Mr. C marveled at the glass canisters of unusual spices and herbs: marshmallow root, lavender flowers, chives, licorice roots, mustard seeds, bee pollen—sold by weight. Bring in your own container to fill with pure water for 19¢ a gallon. And perishable foods, like cheese, fruit, and vitamins, are sold at reduced prices when they get a little past their prime.

The co-op doesn't limit itself to food; it also carries body care products. Huge pumps dispense shampoo and conditioner into your own bottles; again, a real cost-cutter. And there are enough vitamins and homeopathic remedies to cure any malady from candida to kidney problems.

Now, co-ops may not be for everyone. They are in many ways a world unto themselves; these are politically active community organizations. They run several non-food activities, including recycling programs, a clothing exchange, child care, and even free lectures and movies. But again, you can always choose how much or how little you wish to participate. All three are open daily.

Basics Food Warehouse

- 132 Newmarket Square, Boston; (617) 442-1414

This South End enclave of wholesalers, between Mass. Ave. and the Southeast Expressway, deals mainly with restaurants and supermarkets. Tucked away, though, are two adjacent shops offering wholesale prices to anyone who walks in.

Basics can save you dough with large-quantity packaging. You can get Kraft barbecue sauce for $8.99 a gallon, to go with ten pounds of baby spareribs for $19. Add five pounds of frozen French fries for $2.99. Don't worry—not all the meat is meant for armies; some fresh meats are sold by the pound, just like any deli section. Open daily from 6:30 A.M. to 5 P.M., Sundays from 7 A.M. to 1 P.M.

Next door, **Lord Jeff's Beef Place** at 129 Newmarket Square, telephone (617) 445-7000, is similar but a little

---

MR. CHEAP'S PICK
General Markets

✔ **Basics Food Warehouse** and **Lord Jeff's Beef Place**—A pair of wholesale supermarkets which sell to the public.

---

larger. Again, the emphasis is on meats: Five-pound boxes of deli franks or frozen all-beef hamburger patties are each $8.90, while a ten-pound bag of fresh chicken thighs goes for a mere $3.99.

Jeff's offers more overall variety, more like a supermarket. Guzzle a twelve-pack of Coke in cans at $2.99; some of the beer tends to be cheap as well—a Budweiser suitcase for $13.99—but most liquor prices seem average. In the other aisles: Get a carton of 2 dozen eggs for 99¢ (!), a pound of sliced bacon for 69¢, or a five-pound box of Domino sugar for $2.39. Like most warehouses, you may see different items at different times. Both stores can also be your headquarters for soul food—chitterlings, oxtail, smoked neck bones, and goat meat are all here. Lord Jeff holds court from 6:30 A.M. to 5 P.M. every day, except Sundays from 6 A.M. to 1 P.M.

C & C Thrift

- 118 Blackstone St., Boston; (617) 248-0828

Y'know where the Haymarket is held every weekend? Well, there are some actual stores there too, and this basement shop is open all week. C & C sells leftover packaged foods that are near their "Sell by . . ." dates—but are still good if you're going to use them promptly. This store deals mostly in baked goods, such as "Vermont All-Natural Bread" at 89¢ a loaf, reduced from $1.99. You can get two bags of Green-Freedman rolls for a dollar, or boxed apple pies marked down from $2.69 to $1.25. There are also packages of dried pasta, usually $1.50 for a pair of one-pound bags. Lots of cookies, too. Open Mondays to Thursdays from 8 A.M. to 5:30 P.M., Fridays and Saturdays until 7.

J. Pace & Sons

- 42 Cross St., Boston; (617) 227-9673
- 2 Devonshire Pl., Boston; (617) 227-4949

Walk underneath the Central Artery from Faneuil Hall to the North End, and one of the first things you see is Pace's. This packed, bustling market is not a wholesaler but has lots and lots of fresh cheese, bread, and pasta—as well as imported specialty items, like olives and Nutella, that sinfully yummy Italian chocolate-hazelnut sauce. The prices are very reasonable, making this a sort of microcosm of the North End all in one stop. Open from 7-7, Mondays through Saturdays.

A few doors down, you'll find **La Fauci & Sons**, at 46 Cross Street, telephone (617) 523-1158. They offer

great prices on fresh fruits and vegetables, particularly if you're buying in bulk. Open Mondays through Saturdays from 7 A.M. to 5:30 P.M.

Lambert's Rainbow Fruit

- 77 Morrissey Blvd., Dorchester; (617) 436-2998
- 820 Crescent St., Brockton; (508) 580-2736
- 220 Providence Hwy. (Rte. 1), Westwood; (617) 326-5047

These stores are more like the pot of gold at the end of the rainbow. Bins are filled with luscious looking fruit, shiny and healthy, in everything from tiny olives to whole watermelons—depending on the season, of course. Plenty of vegetables, too; not to mention deli meats, dairy products, and baked goods, plus candy and nuts by the pound. Prices are very reasonable indeed, especially for produce of this quality.

Not only that, but Lambert's also has an outdoor garden center, selling flowers, plants, and soil, also at competitive prices. All this, and personal, family-style service. Open seven days.

MEATS

Haymarket's Famous Bargain Basement

- 96A Blackstone St., Boston; (617) 723-5859

Puritan Beef Company

- 90 Blackstone St., Boston; (617) 523-1419

This pair of shops can be found along the same block where the Haymarket takes place each weekend. Only these guys are open all week long. Fresh chicken and beef are the specialties at **Haymarket's Famous**; here, you can get whole chickens for 79¢ a pound. If you can buy in large quantities, you'll save even more. A ten-pound bag of chicken drumsticks is $5.90; or, you can get three pounds of ground beef for $4. The surroundings are no-frills, and so are the burly men behind the counter, but hey, this *is*

the Filene's Basement of meats. It's open Mondays through Saturdays, 8 A.M. to 6 P.M.

Just along the block is **Puritan Beef**—a few steps up, for a change, rather than down. Again, bargain prices, especially in bulk: Turkey wings by the bag, or unsliced bacon. Here's where you can get that pork, such as spareribs for $1.69 a pound; also, strip sirloin for $3.89 a pound. Also a good place for ethnic specialties like goat meat, oxtail, and pig's feet. Open daily from 7 A.M. to 5 P.M., Fridays and Saturdays 6 A.M. to 7 P.M.

Hilltop Marketplace and Butcher Shop

- 210 Union St., Braintree; (617) 848-2899
- 901 Broadway (Rte. 1), Saugus; (617) 231-2300

You know, the Hilltop. The one with the giant cactus and the hour-long wait for a table. Their mega-volume purchasing of meats translates to great prices on their own cuts of beef and chicken, as well as swordfish steaks, ham, and franks. Recent specials (something's on sale each week) have included ground sirloin for $1.49 a pound, spareribs for $1.79 a pound, and lots of meat-packs in family-size quantities for extra savings.

In addition, their stores offer fresh fruits and vegetables, eggs, paper products, and just about everything else you'd find at your local supermarket. Open seven days a week, including weeknights until 9 P.M.

Mayflower Poultry
- 621 Cambridge St., Cambridge; (617) 547-9191

This is the place for poultry lovers with iron stomachs—not because of the food, though. When the shop promises "Fresh Killed Chicken," they mean it. Mayflower raises its birds in New Hampshire, but much of the processing is done on the Cam-

bridge premises. You've never *seen* this much raw poultry in one place before. The prices are definitely right: A recent visit found chicken broilers, roasters, and friers at 99¢ per pound; chicken breasts were just $1.59 a pound ($2.99 boneless). Just 89¢ will get you a pound of chicken legs or thighs; a pound of wings is $1.09. If you're making soup, chicken necks and backs go for a mere 29¢ and 15¢ a pound, respectively.

"Poultry" includes lots of other birds besides chicken: Turkey is $1.09 a pound, or $1.99 a pound for ground turkey. Cornish hen, duck, and even rabbit (well, people do say it tastes like chicken) are also sold here, at slightly higher prices. Of course there are also eggs ($1.47 for a dozen jumbo size). The staff at Mayflower will cut your birds up for free. Talk about factory-direct—it doesn't get any fresher than this, folks. Open Mondays through Saturdays from 7 A.M. to 4:30 P.M. (Fridays until 5 P.M.).

PASTA

Capone Foods
- 14 Bow St., Somerville; (617) 629-2296

Capone Foods supplies the pasta for many fine Boston restaurants—roughly four to five *thousand* pounds every day—pleasing about 15,000 people! This Union Square gem offers fresh and inventive pastas and sauces, combined with first-rate service and reasonable prices.

Some two dozen varieties of fresh pasta are usually available, most priced at $2.50 a pound. Purists will appreciate the egg or spinach pastas, but adventurous types may opt for more exotic flavors like squid ink or red wine. Capone also makes fourteen types of ravioli, from cheese ($3.25 a pound) to the much lauded eggplant ($3.95). Plus five kinds of gnocchi (all at $2.65 a pound) and tortellini, too.

Pick up a pound of marinara for $2.50; amatriciana or putanesca sauce is $3.95 a pound. There's also a selection of international cheeses, gourmet meats, and olives. Capone's even sells do-it-yourself cannoli kits: $10 gets you twenty large (or forty small) cannoli shells, with a filling mix. Just add the demi-tasse and conversation.

A chart in the store shows you how to mix and match pastas and sauces into "good" or "really good" combinations (with this quality, obviously, you can't lose). Note that, because of their wholesale activity, the store is only open to the public Wednesdays through Fridays, from 12-5 P.M.; also Saturdays from 10 A.M. to 5 P.M.

Gooche's Bakery
- 4140 Washington St., Roslindale; (617) 325-3928

MR. CHEAP'S PICKS
Pasta

✔ **Capone Foods**—The numbers say it all: Four thousand pounds of pasta produced every day in 42 varieties, for as little as $2.50 a pound. Outstanding service, too.

✔ **Pasta Del Palato**—A find in Oak Square. Freshly made pastas in a wide variety of exotic flavors, plus homemade sauces. These guys supply some of the best restaurants in town.

See the listing in "Bakeries."

Pasta Del Palato
- 579 Washington St., Brighton; (617) 782-7274

Fresh rolled pasta in Oak Square? Believe it! In this clean, spare kitchen, yards and yards of noodles are spun out in all kinds of innovative flavors. Among the buyers are Rocco's, in the Back Bay, and Uva in Brighton—both of which are known for their fancy cooking, and fancy prices.

Here, for $3, you can get a pound of egg, spinach, or tomato pasta, cut into any of four thicknesses: angel hair, linguine, tagliatelle, and fettucine. For $6 a pound (you can or-

der by the half pound), you get into the more exotic varieties. Lemon, ginger, chipotle, scallion, and roasted garlic are just some of these pungent pastas. Unfortunately, depending on how much of each has been prepared on a given day, your first choices may be gone by the time you get there. PDP sells fresh sauces, too. Open weekdays only, from 9 A.M. to 6 P.M.

Spinelli Ravioli & Pastry Shoppe
- 282 Bennington St., East Boston; (617) 567-1992

Day Square in Eastie is a haven for Italian food lovers. There are several good restaurants and, in a big building across the square, Spinelli's. They make all kinds of pasta right there in the factory and sell it directly to the public. The pasta comes uncooked—shells, fusilli, bow ties, and more—or as prepared dinners.

Ricotta cavatelli is $1.99 a pound, chicken cacciatore is $3.75, and meat tortellini is $4 a pound. You can even get a tray of chicken wings cooked in wine ($3.29) or stuffed peppers ($3 a pound).

Spinelli also serves up hot foods in the store, like ravioli and meatballs ($4.99) or veal parmigiana with spaghetti ($6.25). They specialize in large quantities, for parties of 24 people or more, which you can take away or enjoy in Spinelli's new banquet room. The store is open daily from 8 A.M. to 8 P.M., Sundays from 8-6.

PRODUCE

Allandale Farm
- 259 Allandale Rd., Jamaica Plain; (617) 524-1531

The only honest-to-goodness working farm within Boston city limits. At Allandale you can get the freshest apples (and cider), tomatoes, sweet corn, and whatever else happens to be in season. What's more, you can see the fields these came in

from. Talk about buying factory-direct. Don't you love Boston? Try getting out to the country this easily in New York. Open daily from 10 A.M. to 7 P.M.

A. Russo And Sons
- 560 Pleasant St., Watertown; (617) 923-1500

Outside of Watertown Square, Russo's is about as beautiful a "warehouse" as you're likely to see. The store at the front is modern, architecturally designed in brownstone, and offers near-wholesale prices on all manner of fruits, vegetables, flowers, and plants.

It's tough to delve much into exact prices, since they fluctuate by season. But this is definitely a good place to stock up, especially if you live in the 'burbs and don't want to deal with the hustle and bustle of Haymarket. In fact, it's so handsome and mellow, it's almost *relaxing* to shop there. Open to the public daily from 8 A.M. to 6 P.M., Sundays from 8 to 2.

Baby Nat's Fruitland

• 606 American Legion Hwy., Roslindale; (617) 524-9877

Along with all the flower shops lining this stretch of road, you'll also find this farm stand grown into a full-fledged produce supermarket. Specializing in ethnic favorites, this is the kind of place where you can find yams as well as potatoes, and plantains with the bananas, all at straight-from-the-ground prices.

In addition to fruits and vegetables, though, Baby Nat's also got meat and fish. Fresh cod filets were recently seen here for $3.99 a pound; baby back ribs were $1.99 a pound, and they looked good and meaty. And if you're into soul food, like smoked ham hocks, this is the place to get 'em. Open seven days.

Marino Lookout Farm

• 89 Pleasant St., Natick; (508) 655-4294

Who woulda thunk it? Just a few winding miles south of downtown Natick, you make a turn into what ought to be yet another suburban driveway—and suddenly, you're out in the country. The Marino Lookout Farm is, in fact, one of the oldest continually operated farms in the U.S., established in 1680 (!) and still busy. Today, it sells produce and plants,

both wholesale and retail, along with "pick-your-own" fruits and vegetables; it's also a mini-zoo, with all manner of farm animals creatures you can see up close.

Produce from these fields winds up in eateries all over the Boston area (most notably, Marino's Restaurant in Cambridge). It's all organically grown, and reasonably priced. The tiny shop is packed with a little bit of everything: fruits and vegetables, free-range meats, eggs, hormone-free milk, bulk spices and nuts, and baked goods. Outside the food shop, the nursery sells all kinds of annuals, perennials, herbs, vegetables, and supplies.

In June, you can get in on the act by picking your own strawberries; in September and October, pick apples and raspberries. A central pavilion sells fresh cider and apple pies during the fall as well. Why, you can even pick tomatoes, broccoli, and eggplant in season; call the U-Pick Line at (508) 653-0653 to find out what's available then.

At 115 acres, Marino Lookout Farm is the largest farm close to Boston. Yet everyone here is so open and friendly, you'll *really* think you're in the country. What a getaway. The farm is open daily all year 'round; call them for directions, seasonal hours and activities.

FARMER'S MARKETS

Most towns in the Boston area hold weekly farmer's markets at permanent locations throughout the summer and fall. Like mini-Haymarkets, these are places to buy produce "factory-direct" from the folks who grow it. You'll often find fresh-cut flowers too, as well as prepared foods, like jellies and homemade pies.

To find out this year's exact schedules, call your nearby town hall; or the helpful staff at the Massachusetts Department of Food and Agriculture at (617) 727-3018, extension 175.

Brighton
• Bank of Boston parking lot, 5
  Chestnut Hill Ave., Brighton
Saturdays, 11 A.M. to 6 P.M., mid-July to October.

Brockton
• Brockton Fair Grounds, Brockton
Saturdays, 10 A.M. to 3 P.M., mid-July to mid-October.
• City Hall Plaza, Brockton
Fridays, 8:45 A.M. to 3 P.M., July through October.

Brookline
• Harvard Street parking lot,
  Coolidge Corner, Brookline
Thursdays, 1:30 P.M. to dusk, mid-June through October.

Cambridge
• Norfolk and Bishop Allen Sts.,
  Central Square, Cambridge
Mondays, noon to 6 P.M., mid-May to mid-November.
• Charles Hotel, 5 Bennett St.,
  Cambridge
Sundays, 10 A.M. to 2:30 P.M., mid-June to mid-November.

Charlestown
• Thompson Square, Main and
  Austin Sts., Charlestown
Wednesdays, 2 to 7 P.M., mid-July to mid-October.

Chelsea
• Chelsea Square police station,
  Chelsea
Saturdays, 10 A.M. to 2 P.M., late June to mid-October.

Codman Square
• Washington and Talbot Sts., Boston
Wednesdays, 10 A.M. to 1 P.M., July to October.

Copley Square
• St. James Ave. at Dartmouth St.,
  Boston
Tuesdays and Fridays, 11A.M. to 6 P.M., July through November.

Dudley Square
• 391 Dudley St., Roxbury
Tuesdays, 1 to 4 P.M., July to mid-October.

East Boston
• London Street Mini Park, East
  Boston
Tuesdays, 10 A.M. to 3 P.M., mid-July to October.

Faneuil Hall
• Quincy Market, Boston
Thursdays, 10 A.M. to 6 P.M., August to mid-September.

Framingham
• St. Tarcisius Church parking lot,
  Framingham
Wednesdays, 3 to 6 P.M., and Saturdays 9 A.M. to 12 noon, late June to mid-October.
• Ken's Steak House parking lot,
  Framingham
Thursdays, 12 to 5 P.M., May to mid-October.

Franklin Park
• Zoo entrance, Franklin Park Rd.,
  Dorchester
Sundays, 1 to 4 P.M., July through October.

Fields Corner
• Purity Supreme parking lot, Park
  St., Dorchester
Saturdays, 9 A.M. to 12 noon, July through October.

Government Center
• City Hall Plaza, Boston
Mondays and Wednesdays, 11 A.M. to

6 P.M., July through mid-November.
- Saltonstall Building, 100 Cambridge St., Boston

Thursdays, 11 A.M. to 5 P.M., July to October.

Hyde Park
- Harvard Ave. and Winthrop St., Hyde Park

Thursdays, 12 to 5 P.M., July through October.

Jamaica Plain
- Bank of Boston parking lot, Centre St., Jamaica Plain

Tuesdays, 12 to 6 P.M., mid-July through October.

Lynn
- Blake and Union Sts., Lynn

Thursdays, 11 A.M. to 3 P.M., July through October.

Mattapan
- 525 River St., Mattapan

Thursdays, 12 to 5 P.M., late June to mid-October.

Melrose
- City Hall parking lot, Main St., Melrose

Thursdays, 10 A.M. to 3 P.M., late June to mid-October.

Newton
- Cold Spring Park, Beacon Street (near Walnut Street), Newton

Tuesdays, 1:30 to 6 P.M., mid-July through October.

Quincy
- John Hancock parking lot, Quincy Center

Fridays, 11:30 A.M. to 5 P.M., mid-June through October.

Roslindale
- Taft Court, Roslindale

Saturdays, 9 A.M. to 2 P.M., mid-July through October.

Saugus
- Cliftondale Square, Saugus

Tuesdays, 10 A.M. to 3 P.M., mid-July to mid-October.

Somerville
- Day and Herbert Sts., Davis Square, Somerville

Wednesdays, 12 to 6 P.M., mid-June through October.

South Boston
- 424 West Broadway, South Boston

Fridays, 11 A.M. to 3 P.M., July to October.

Waltham
- Fleet Bank parking lot, Main and Moody Sts., Waltham

Saturdays, 10 A.M. to 3 P.M., mid-June to mid-October.

SEAFOOD

Andy's Seafood Company
- 78 Broadway, Saugus; (617) 233-8880

Not from Route 1—which bombards the nose with its own distinct aromas—but certainly from the parking lot, you'll know this place deals in one thing: seafood. Which is no sinker for the tiny shop, conveniently located, which offers a variety of fresh daily seafood at straight-from-the-dock prices.

Everything is well-displayed, looking almost *eager* to be eaten. Mussels go for 89¢ a pound in season, and Maine steamers sell for $1.99. Under glass, swordfish ($7.99 per pound), haddock ($5.99), and scrod ($4.99)

lay in repose. Smiling plastic fish adorn the walls. Bring your reel Mondays through Fridays from 8:30 A.M. to 5:30 P.M.

Bay State Lobster Company
- 395 Commercial St., Boston; (617) 523-7960

Along the waterfront, this is the supermarket of inexpensive fish. Bay State's stuff is not always local, but the prices are good. All kinds of fresh and frozen seafood can be found here, along with various condiments. Bay State's own cocktail sauce is $2.29 for a one-pound container, and it'll go well on fresh small shrimp at $2.99 a pound. Or get a tub of clam chowder base and some fresh qua-

---

MR. CHEAP'S PICK
Seafood

✔ **East Coast Seafood**—The trip's a bit of an odyssey, but an extensive selection of fresh live lobster (from $4.99 per pound) and other seafood purchased daily from local and national fisherman make this waterfront spot more than worth it.

---

hogs at 69¢ a pound. Bay State's lobsters start around $5 a pound off-season. During the summer they can go under $2. Plus swordfish, perch, and cod. Open 8 A.M. to 6 P.M. Mondays through Thursdays; 7 A.M. to 6 P.M. Friday and Saturdays.

Court House Seafood
• 484 Cambridge St., Cambridge; (617) 876-6716

Just down the street from its East Cambridge namesake, Court House Seafood specializes in whole fish to take home. They generally have low prices on standards and more, like redfish, porgy, and monk fish. If you don't want to do the dirty work, by the way, they will fillet the fish for you. Open from 8 A.M. to 6 P.M., Tuesdays through Saturdays.

A few doors down is the **Court House Seafood Restaurant,** at 498 Cambridge Street; telephone (617) 491-1213. They offer complete seafood dinners for $10 and under, along with homemade clam and fish chowders. Mmmm.

East Coast Seafood
• 175 Alley St., Lynn; (617) 581-5180

This place claims to be the world's largest distributor of fresh live lobster, bought from local fishermen and flown in daily; accordingly, the retail space sports an enormous tank of the creatures on display. There's also a large selection of sole, tuna, and sea scallops (all $6.99 per pound); haddock, halibut, and salmon fillets for $4.99 per pound; and even unusual choices such as octopus for $1.99 per pound.

A blackboard out front displays daily specials, such as fresh salmon ($3.99 a pound on Mr. C's visit). A small takeout menu includes clam chowder, a hearty bargain at $2.49 for a sizable container. Open from 8:30 A.M. to 6:30 P.M. Mondays through Fridays, from 9 A.M. on Saturdays, and Sundays 10-5.

Fresh Pond Seafood
• 355 Fresh Pond Pkwy., Cambridge; (617) 497-9821

Prices fluctuate wildly in the fish biz, but Mr. C has often found excellent deals (and high quality) at this rotaryside shanty on Route 2. These have included things like swordfish and yellowfin tuna steaks around $10 a pound, smoked bluefish for $7.99, and Maryland soft-shell crabs for $2.99 apiece. Open daily from 9 A.M. to 8 P.M.

Morse Fish Company
• 1401 Washington St., Boston; (617) 262-6378

See the listing under "Restaurants—Boston."

Neptune Lobster and Seafood
• 88 Sleeper St., Boston; (617) 426-0961

Cross over that fine old trestle bridge from the Central Artery onto Northern Avenue, and the first stop you'll come to is the tiny but choice Neptune Seafood. Here you can find steamers, all varieties of lobster from "chicks" to culls to jumbos, or just lobster meat. Also scallops and tiny shrimp in bags of one to two hundred. Open daily.

And, further along the waterfront, several more shops make this a great (if obvious) area to do all your seafood shopping. The **Yankee Lobster Company** at 272 Northern Ave., telephone (617) 542-1922, usually has shrimp, crab, and scallops in addition to lobsters; they're open from 5 A.M. (ouch!) to 4 P.M. on weekdays, limited hours on weekends. And **Paul's Lobster Company** at 339 Northern Ave., telephone (617) 482-4234 is another

Mr. C pick, open weekdays from 7 A.M. to 4 P.M., 'til 11 P.M. Saturdays and 9 P.M. Sundays.

FURNITURE AND BEDS

HOME FURNITURE—NEW

Ashmont Discount Home Center
- 464 Quincy Ave., Braintree; (617) 848-7350
- 587 Centre St., Brockton; (508) 583-1710
- 4165 Washington St., Roslindale; (617) 327-2080
- 1202 Washington St., Stoughton; (617) 341-1710

As noted in the "Appliances" chapter, Ashmont sells just about everything for the home. In addition to hardware, housewares, and the like, they sell new furniture very inexpensively. Dinette sets, made from solid wood, start from $129—and can go as low as $99 on sale. Twin mattresses start at $60 per piece, going up to only $399 for a premium queen-size *set* with a 25-year warranty. Plus lots of that inexpensive, assembly-required stuff. Ashmont is open daily from 8 A.M. to 9 P.M., and Sundays from 9-5.

Bedworks Warehouse
- 244 Brighton Ave., Allston; (617) 254-5040

This clearance center sells furniture at discount, but be warned: It still ain't cheap. These are the kind of living room, dining room and bedroom pieces you'd see in an *Architectural Digest* photo spread. So if you're looking to tone up the place with an $1,100 cherry wood dining table, you can get it here for half-price. Or a black metal futon frame, full-size, for $179. Oak and cherry platform beds start from $325, and Bedworks makes its own futons and covers. Plus sofas, armoires, and the like. Most of the pieces are leftovers in perfect condition; some are slightly worn floor models—"one-of-a-kind" bargains. Well, *upscale* bargains.

Open Tuesdays through Saturdays from 10 A.M. to 5:30 P.M. (Thursdays 'til 7:30), and Sundays from 12-4:30.

Bernie & Phyl's Furniture Discounts
- 1 East St. (Msgr. O'Brien Highway), Cambridge; (617) 868-7999
- 2010 Revere Beach Pkwy., Everett; (617) 389-3430
- 320 Moody St., Waltham; (617) 894-6555
- 373 Washington St., Weymouth; (617) 331-4500

Bernie and wife Phyllis claim to have originated a concept in furniture marketing: selling complete room set-ups. Everything in this shop is first-quality, mostly from major brands, bought in bulk and discounted. You can buy enough furniture to equip a bedroom or living room for under $600. This bedroom package includes a full-size Blue Cross mattress (with inner springs; not foam), foundation, and frame; as well as a dresser, chest of drawers, headboard, and mirror. The furniture can be oak or black lacquer (both made by Armstrong), or white Formica finish (made by Ashley). Of course, you can buy these pieces separately, but the package is a better deal. Mattress brands include Sealy and Continental.

The rock-bottom living room combinations are generic brands. A price of $597 includes a three-person sofa, a wing chair, two end tables, a cocktail table and two glass lamps. You get to pick from several fabrics. At the high end of the living room scale, an overstuffed sofa and chair (both made by Klaus) are matched with three oak and glass tables and two lamps, for $997. Bernie & Phyl's carries leather, too, with a large Gaines leather chair just $497. Plus sleep sofas and dinette sets. All items in the store carry a warranty of at least a year, and often longer, depending on the brand. Open seven days, including weeknights until 9.

Bernstein Furniture Company
- 154 Harvard Ave., Allston; (617) 782-7972

One of the several furniture stores along this stretch of Harvard Avenue, Bernstein's has a large selection of beds, sofas, bookcases, lamps, and accessories. The service is friendly and thorough; they will assemble and/or deliver pieces within the Boston area.

You can find a three-piece bed set of mattress, foundation, and frame for as little as $120 (twin size) or $150 (full). Futon frames of 1" heavy pine are $109 in full size, and they have futon mattresses too. There are several styles of lamps, such as a white-lacquered three-lamp tree for $40. Most of the furniture here is made from solid wood. And, if you really poke around, you may find a slightly damaged piece at a further-reduced price.

Similar stores on the block include: **Carpet Works**, at 137 Harvard Avenue, telephone (617) 787-5064; and Boston Paint Supply, 151 Harvard Avenue, (617) 254-1060. Across the river in Cambridge, BPS also runs two branches of **Basics Carpet and Furniture**, offering much the same merchandise and prices. One is in Central Square at 599 Massachusetts Ave., telephone (617) 491-8661; the other is in Porter Square at 1967 Massachusetts Ave., telephone (617) 547-5001. All of these stores are open seven days a week.

Big John's Mattress Factory
- 121 First St., Cambridge; (617) 876-6344

It's all here in one place, folks—the factory is upstairs and the showroom is downstairs, where Big John (who really exists, the salesman said) sells directly to the public. These mattresses, in a variety of sizes and firmness, are of very high quality. Their top-of-the-line model uses *ten layers* of coils and padding; a twin-size set is $449; full-size is $549. At the other end of the spectrum, mattresses start at just $48 twin and $68 full (double those prices for sets). Even these models, though, are sturdy and guaranteed. Most mattresses meet specifications detailed by chiropractors for firm support.

Also interesting are Big John's "New Generation" waterbeds—a truly innovative design that looks just like any normal bed. The mattress is surrounded by a wooden outer shell, which is upholstered like any other mattress; it even takes standard-sized sheets, and needs no heater. These start at $399 for twin and $449 full.

The store offers a 30-day exchange period, immediate delivery, and full warranties. Big John's is open weekdays from 9 A.M. to 9 P.M., Saturdays 9-6, Sundays 12-5.

Bookcase Factory Outlet
- 6 Clearway St., Boston; (617) 247-0885
- 15 North Beacon St., Watertown; (617) 924-7665

Here's a fine source for unfinished furniture at direct-to-you prices. Tri-fold futon frames, in pine or high-quality hardwood, start from $70 to $90, depending on the size; futon mattresses start from $90. A five-drawer birch dresser goes for a reasonable $220, butcher block tables are as low as $70, and they also have desks, TV stands, rocking chairs, the works.

Any item can be stained and finished for you, and delivered (for a fee). Custom designs are welcomed. Open daily from 10:30 A.M. to 6 P.M., Sundays 1-5.

Boston Design Center
- 660 Summer St., South Boston; (617) 737-1867

The Boston Design Center is where licensed interior designers get their furniture, wall coverings, and fancy decorative items. Until recently, they were the only ones permitted to tread

this hallowed ground. That is still primarily true, but now BDC has a
thrice-yearly "Open to the Public"
sale. At these times, some fifteen of
the center's eighty showrooms sell
off samples, floor models, boo-boos,
and the like, at significant discounts.
These are high-end, high-fashion
pieces and include everything you
could imagine in furniture and home
furnishings. Clearance sales are generally held in early fall, around New
Year's, and in mid-spring. Watch the
newspapers for ads, or call.

Boston Interiors! Clearance Centers
- 200 Webster St., Hanover; (617) 871-6416
- 24 Teed Dr., Randolph; (617) 986-7404
- 153 Turnpike St. (Rte. 9), Westboro; (508) 870-0700

Floor models, seconds, and other merchandise left over from this chain of
furniture stores winds up at these
warehouses, to be sold at 20% to
70% off original prices. BI's stock is
contemporary living room, dinette
and bedroom furniture and accessories; you may find a three-piece "Bistro" set—a glass-top table with two
rattan chairs—selling for $150 in-
stead of the original $400.

First-quality Bauhaus sofas, in perfect condition, were on sale for $399
each, reduced from $599. In the sec-
onds area, a writing desk in natural
ash finish, a bit scuffed, but not
enough to notice easily, was reduced
from $400 to just $120. All sales, of
course, are final; the store is only
open Tuesdays-Saturdays from 9:30
to 3:30.

Butcher Block Furniture Factory Outlet
- 383 Boylston St. (Rte. 9), Newton; (617) 928-0910
- 184 Broadway (Rte. 1), Saugus; (617) 233-7300
- *And other suburban locations*

One employee describes this store as
more of a showroom than an outlet,
in that after checking out the models
on display, you pick the color, size,
and style you want—and their fac-

MR. CHEAP'S PICKS
Home Furniture—New

✔ **Big John's Mattress Factory**—They make 'em upstairs and sell 'em downstairs. Good prices on all kinds of bedding, including waterbeds that look (and behave) like boxsprings.

✔ **Domain Warehouse Store**—Hidden off Route 1 in Norwood, incredible deals on slightly damaged but still upscale country looks. Weekends only.

✔ **International Home Outlet**—This one's buried in Framingham; direct importer of European and Scandinavian designs. Just weekends here too.

---

tory will produce the furniture to
your specifications. Everything here
is made from solid oak, enhanced
with a waterproof, maintenance-free
finish, and undeniably beautiful, at
prices that truly are factory direct.

If you've been around the Block
once or twice, you'll find such pieces
as a snazzy stereo cabinet for $385
(with a retail value set at $550); a din-
ing table and chairs, with a golden
finish, reduced from $1,000 to $698;
and mahogany-finished desks as low
as $407 (from $581). Handsome
wine racks can be had for $75, some
25% below retail value.

Hours are 10 A.M. to 6 P.M. Mon-
days through Saturdays ('til 8 P.M.
Thursdays), and noon to 5 P.M. on
Sundays.

Dean's Home Furniture
- 450 Providence Hwy. (Rte. 1), Dedham; (617) 329-4770
- 461 Broad St. (Rte. 1A), Lynn; (617) 595-7113

- 101 Mazzeo Dr. (Rte. 139), Randolph; (617) 963-5993

These stores call themselves the "Home of the Package Deal," and they ain't kidding around. A recent sale included a matching sofa, chair, and cocktail table, plus two end tables with lamps, all for $597. Similar ensembles abound for the bedroom. Dean's offers a free layaway plan, and they're open seven days, including weeknights.

Domain Warehouse Store
- 51 Morgan Dr., Norwood; (617) 769-0383

If you've ever browsed Domain on Newbury Street and just sighed over the stylish designs (with equally stylish prices), make a weekend pilgrimage to their warehouse. Here, they sell off floor models, discontinued lines, damaged goods, and other orphans. The savings are dramatic, to say the least—half-price and better.

Country is the look here, with a few contemporary turns; a plush floral linen sofa which had been in the main store for $1,599 was seen here for $897. Same price for a set of four upholstered dining chairs, originally $1,460. Couches and chairs made up most of the stock when Mr. C visited; plus lamps, pillows, mirrors, and framed art.

Some items are soiled or damaged, but not irreparably so; any flaw is clearly noted on the tag, always a good sign. And, when a leather sofa is reduced from $2,215 to $565, you'll still come out way ahead after any repair costs. Also found in this category were some hand-woven wool scatter rugs with small tears, marked down from $765 to a mere $97. Stitch one up and put it in a room that doesn't get much light.

All sales, of course, are final; delivery is available (for a fee) throughout the Boston area. Watch newspaper ads for occasional tent sales, too. The outlet is only open Thursdays through Saturdays from 10 A.M. to 5 P.M., and Sundays from noon to five; the number above gives recorded directions to this hard-to-find

industrial area, off Route 1, which also includes the **In Warehouse Store** (see below).

Eastern Butcher Block
- 381 Congress St., Boston; (617) 423-2173
- 630 Worcester Rd. (Rte. 9), Framingham; (508) 879-8636

For high-quality hardwood furniture, Eastern Butcher Block offers factory-direct pieces that are still somewhat expensive, even at discount; but these pieces will probably last forever, to be passed down to your children and theirs. In fact, they carry a lifetime factory guarantee.

If you catch one of Eastern's inventory clearance sales, you can save even more—like a 3' x 4' drop-leaf kitchen table, in hard rock maple, for $189. Or contemporary European-style oak chairs for $49 each. All of these prices are well below comparably fancy boutiques. The Framingham store includes a basement clearance center, where Mr. C recently found a terrific maple student's desk reduced from $330 to $199. Factory seconds are not returnable, but they are still covered by the guarantee. Open seven days.

Futon Outlet
- 360 Mystic Ave., Somerville; (617) 776-9429

Hidden in this three-story wooden building, in the shadow of Route 93, is a family business that turns out high-quality futon mattresses at factory-direct prices. You can save $50 or more over department stores, with a variety of sizes and styles to choose from—frames are sold at discount too, though they are not made here.

The basic twin-size futon set goes for $209, including the mattress, trifold pine frame, pillows, covers, and delivery in the Boston area. Frames are also available in birch and maple. There are also bargains on floor models and irregulars, like a queen-size futon mattress for $109, or futon covers at half-price. The folks here are friendly and offer great service; custom orders can be made up and delivered by the next day. Open seven days, including Thursdays through Saturdays until 9 P.M.

Grand Furniture Warehouse

- 1600 V.F.W. Pkwy., West Roxbury; (617) 469-2113
- 134 New Boston St., Woburn; (617) 932-3338
- 40 Millbrook St., Worcester; (508) 757-9400

What's grand about these stores is their size; the merchandise itself is strictly low-to-mid-grade stuff, though certainly at low prices. Grab yourself an entire country-style bedroom ensemble in stained solid pine; it includes a dresser, chest, mirror, headboard, and nightstand, all for $698. A magazine ad, taped up next to it, shows that a competitor sells the same set for $1,199.

Off-brand mattress sets, in a complete variety of quality and firmness levels, are all significantly discounted. Even so, most are warrantied, for as much as 25 years. Most of the couches are foam padded; matching sofa and loveseat sets start around $500. For quick and easy room furnishing on a tight budget, these will do the job.

Grand offers delivery for a fee. Hours vary by location; the West Roxbury store is closed Wednesdays and Thursdays, open other weeknights 'til 9.

Across the highway from that branch, by the way, is a newcomer appropriately called **Parkway Furniture** at 1455 V.F.W. Parkway, telephone (617) 469-6823. They offer higher quality pieces, brought in from America's furniture capital, North Carolina, at discounts of up to 40% below retail. Carpeting, too. They're open Mondays through Fridays 10 A.M. to 9 P.M., Saturdays from 9 A.M. to 6 P.M., and Sundays from noon to 6 P.M.

In Warehouse Store

- 77 Carnegie Row, Norwood; (617) 762-8171

A block from the Domain warehouse (above) is this cavernous space filled with In's unique blend of antiques, antique reproductions, and contemporary furniture. Though many of the items here are the same as those found in their main Natick store, there is more reduced-price stock at this branch.

Even the reproductions at In are often made in Europe out of "original" wood, thus bridging the price gap between true antiques—unaffordable to Mr. C—and modern stuff. Sure, you may think, $495 is a lot to pay for an upholstered rocking chair; but when you consider that a real antique would probably cost over $2,000, it looks better and better. And, considering that it was "list" priced (or market valued, as they say here) at $899, it's a real deal.

There are many similar values in tables, hutches, bookcases, and bed frames. Contemporary couches, in styles that complement these, are available at discounted prices; even so, many can be ordered with a choice of fabrics. In also has occasional clearance sales with even greater bargains. Unlike Domain, this store is open daily from 10 A.M. to 5 P.M. and Sundays from noon to five.

International Home Outlet

- 2 Tripp St., Framingham; (508) 879-9623

Don't be put off by the fact that this store is nearly impossible to find, part of a remote industrial area, and inside a dilapidated old warehouse with boarded-up windows and peeling paint; once you walk inside, it's another world. It's like a Twilight Zone for interior decorators.

Two huge rooms are filled with contemporary European furniture. Suddenly, you're looking at plush leather sofas, rosewood china cabinets elegantly lit from the inside, and classic white Scandinavian modular pieces. All are current lines, available in your choice of finishes and styles; they can be sold at significant discounts because of factory-direct connections and, well, it just don't cost much to run such an out-of-the-way location.

Natuzzi leather from Italy is the standout name on display, with its incredibly soft couches and chairs. One model, a black sleep sofa (there's a tongue-twister), was recently seen for a mere $873; it would be well over a thousand anywhere else. Another sofa, with a retail price of $1,199, was a perfectly good-looking floor model reduced to just $696—nearly half-price. Floor models, of course, are final sales.

The back room features Vestergaard and Scanbirk ensembles from Denmark; spare and functional computer desks, bookcases, and platform beds. There's an amazing variety of configurations and woods, from oak veneer to solid teak to those sleek all-black and all-white looks. A Scanbirk "Bolero" queen bed frame with two built-in nightstands, in a black and birch finish, was seen for $326, about $170 off the list price.

A further cost-cutter for the IH Outlet is its hours. It's open only four days a week—Fridays, Saturdays, and Mondays from 10 A.M. to 5 P.M., and Sundays from 12-5. Do call for directions first!

If you're really doing your house over, the same building includes **The Carpet Bagger**, which offers discounted floor coverings of all kinds. Their address is 5 Tripp St., Framingham; (508) 875-9717.

Woodstuff

- 349 Moody St., Waltham; (617) 646-0370

Owner Don Vogel noticed that his antiques weren't selling as well as they had in pre-recession days. Did he panic? Nope—he adapted. There are hardly any antiques here anymore; instead, you'll find affordable *reproductions* of antique styles. These are solid wood, hand-assembled with screws, not nails, and are available in a variety of designs and finishes.

An extra advantage to this: You can own antiques that could never truly exist. A Shaker-style coffee table, for instance, goes for $59; armoires, which can also open up to reveal an entertainment center, start as low as $179. Be the first on your block to own an "antique" CD rack.

Plus hutches, bookcases, and the rest.

Most intriguing of all, you can custom-order these pieces in any size and configuration—just bring in your specs or a drawing. Open seven days a week from 10 A.M. to 6 P.M., Tuesdays until 9.

Jordan's Furniture

- 100 Stockwell Dr. (off Rte. 24), Avon; (508) 580-4900
- 289 Moody Street, Waltham; (617) 894-6100

There are a few acknowledged giants in the discount furniture game, but you probably don't need Mr. C to tell you about them. After all, even a five-year-old can probably recite the directions to: "In Waltham, take Main Street to Moody Street . . ." You may hate their cloying commercials, but ol' Barry and Elliot do have some good prices on quality furniture. Brand names found here include Bassett, Thomasville, and Highland House. This isn't cheap furniture by any stretch, and even with "underprices" it may be out of some people's budget. Nevertheless, the discounts are good for such high-quality, and Jordan's is a fun place to shop. If you go to the Avon store, don't forget to visit M.O.M. (see the listing under "Entertainment—Movies"). Open seven days a week.

Love's Furniture Warehouse

- 426 Main St. (Rte. 28), Stoneham; (617) 438-9191

For luxurious contemporary furniture and bedding at discount prices, Love's is worth the trip. Their large showroom is filled with bargains; their selection of closeouts, floor samples, and overstocks offers further reductions at really good prices.

Mr. C found oak tables marked down from $519 retail to $399 here; loveseats at $200 below retail; and some slightly damaged bargains, like a glass coffee table reduced from $399 to $199. Go for a complete ensemble, and they'll work out a package deal with you.

Upstairs, an army of recliners in all colors and materials sells for 20% to 35% below retail, except for some clearance models, at 50% off. Nearly everything in the store carries a warranty. Open daily from 10 A.M. to 9 P.M., Saturdays 9 A.M. to 5:30, Sundays noon to 5 P.M.

Mattress Crafters
• 386 Lindeloff Ave. (Rte. 139), Stoughton; (617) 344-2322

Order a custom-made full-size mattress, pay as little as $67, and drive away the same day with your purchase strapped to your car. It may sound unbelievable, but it's true. The factory literally *is* the store here, and you can see for yourself that you're buying direct from the manufacturer; you secure rock-bottom prices by eliminating markups. The company makes seven grades of mattress with a wide price range: The most basic "Borderguard" model costs $67 per piece for a full bed, but even the top of the line "Crown Imperial" mattress is only $197 per full piece.

Every mattress carries a warranty whose length depends on the grade. Premium models carry a 25-year warranty, and it's not pro-rated. Even the least expensive mattresses are warrantied for a full year. Mr. C was amazed to learn that most mattresses can be made to order in one day or less. An additional perk: Free delivery is available within a 25-mile radius with premium sets. This small and specialized factory store is open every day except Sunday.

Mattress Warehouse
• 281 Washington St., Norwell; (617) 659-4961

This independent store has good prices on new furniture for the bedroom, living room, and dining room. It's all first-quality, undamaged, with a good selection of styles. Find sleep sofas by Sealy and Klaus, valued at $799, on sale for as low as $399; dinette sets from $259; plus good prices on living room furniture as well.

In bedding, twin-size platforms start as low as $49; there are also futons and traditional mattress sets on sale. Sealy mattresses in sets start at $57 per piece. Simmons "Maxipedic"

firm beds start at $164 for mattress, box spring, and frame. Open seven days a week, plus Monday, Thursday, and Friday evenings 'til 8.

Maverick Designs
• 1117 Commonwealth Ave., Brighton; (617) 783-0274

The folks at Maverick Designs must never stop working. Their tiny shop in Packard's Corner, near BU, is stuffed with bookcases, CD racks, dressers, desks, stools, futon frames, and much more. They make 'em right here; you can smell the sawdust.

Bookshelves come in all sizes, like a 2' x 6' unit in unfinished pine for $62. Get a 12" x 16" wood-frame mirror for $18, or a wall rack that holds 96 cassette tapes for $17. Curiously, these display racks actually contain used CDs, which you can buy for $2 or $3 each. Larger items include a six-foot tall, 30-inch deep armoire for $199, and a computer desk for $75. Everything is solid and well-made. If you buy something that isn't quite the right fit, you can trade it for a piece that is; and if you need something to fit exact dimensions, they'll custom design it for you. Open seven days.

Mystic Bedding Company
• 81 Mystic Ave., Medford; (617) 396-7878
• 474 Main St. (Rte. 38), Wilmington; (508) 657-7474

Mystic Bedding manufactures its own line of high-quality mattresses, which top the big-name brands for workmanship and durability. The materials used combine a high coil count, heavy-gauge wire, and extra padding to give what the woman in the store called "a Mercedes for the price of a Chevy."

Their "Bostonian Luxury Firm Orthopedic" queen-size mattress and box spring, priced at $550 for the set, is lower in price and better in quality than a comparable Simmons Beautyrest, which can sell for as much as $700 in department stores. The fifteen-year warranty includes free repair or replacement during the first year; after that, repair charges are based on the length of ownership. Mystic offers free delivery in twenty-four hours in the Boston area. Open weekdays from 9 A.M. to 6 P.M., Saturdays until 1 P.M.

Nationwide Warehouse & Storage

- 67 Sprague St., Readville; (617) 364-6630
- 134 New Boston St., Woburn; (617) 932-3338

As the name suggests, Nationwide liquidates furniture and bedding for manufacturers all over the country. The ever-changing stock is mostly in lower- and mid-grade quality—this is the sort of place where you can get a mattress for $18 (twin, on sale). Of course, they have better grades, but even their top-of-the-line pillowtop king mattress is only $149! It comes with a 25-year limited warranty. In furniture, you may find a queen-size canopy bed frame, in "gunmetal" iron, for $148; a competitor's ad was taped to the wall beside it, listing the same bed for $398. Nationwide offers free layaway and is open seven days a week.

Oriental Furniture Warehouse

- 810 Worcester Rd. (Rte. 9), Natick; (508) 651-2100

And now for something completely different—Oriental furniture. This is the real stuff, imported directly from the East; that can mean pricey, even at discounts of 30% to 40%. But if this is your taste, it's well worth the trip.

Six-foot tall shoji screens—you know, with the rice paper and black lattices—are just $89. A black lacquer chest, with ornate figures painted on the front, was reduced from $329 to $229. A ceramic stand for a flower pot, shaped like an elephant with trunk raised, was $119; they also have real bonsai plants ($29), or silk versions of the same.

Downstairs, though, are the real bargains. Their "Oriental Garage Sale" section offers slightly damaged items at further price reductions— like a $350 chair for $99, or four-foot mirrors framed in black or white lacquered wood for $75.

Simply Stated Affordable Furnishings

- 667 Boylston St., Boston; (617) 421-5599

A small storefront directly across from the Boston Public Library, Simply Stated Affordable Furnishings is truth-in-advertising: They discount contemporary furniture, period. A black metal canopy bed, selling for as much as $399 elsewhere, was seen here for $279.95. A metal and glass-top coffee table set, with two matching end tables, was $234.95—a substantial savings off the $499 retail price.

The merchandise here tends to be cheaper by design; most pieces are wood veneer or metal. For that first home or a spare room, however, these may be perfect. Simply Stated has plenty of fun and trendy decorative stuff, too. Lamps, rugs, candlesticks, and other accouterments are plentiful and well-priced. Mr. C particularly liked a black metal easel-back, full-length mirror marked $48.95, half off the list price! Open Mondays through Saturdays from 10 A.M. to 6 P.M., Sundays 12-6 P.M.

Sleep-Rite Factory Outlet

- 1113 Commonwealth Ave., Boston; (617) 782-3830
- 543 Cambridge St., Cambridge; (617) 491-5818
- 225 Worcester Rd. (Rte. 9), Framingham; (508) 879-3072

Sleep-Rite makes twenty different lines of mattresses, plus futons and frames, and sells them factory-direct. Queen-size sets, including mattress, box-spring, frame, and local delivery (free with any set), start from just $319. The same ensemble in department stores can cost hundreds more. All mattresses are also guaranteed for up to twenty years, depending on the type; futons for ten years.

Next door to the Boston shop, they also run **The Linen Closet** at 1111 Commonwealth Ave., telephone (617) 787-0866. This will ably take care of all your pillow, bedspread, and futon cover needs. All stores are open seven days.

Waterbed Warehouse

- 315 The Lynnway (Rte. 1A), Lynn; (617) 581-6900

For traditional-style waterbeds, check WW for prices that are 30% to 60% below retail. Several models cost less than $300 complete, some of which feature bookcase headboards. They are constructed from solid pine or oak, with a variety of finishes available. Custom sizes can be ordered, as well; all sets include frame, pedestal, heater, liner, and all the necessary apparatus. And delivery is available anywhere in the Boston area, or nationwide. WW is open weekdays until 8 P.M., weekends 'til 5.

Workbench Clearance Center

- 1050 Massachusetts Ave., Cambridge; (617) 876-9754

The Central/Harvard Square branch of this popular home furnisher doubles as the clearance center for seconds, slightly-damaged goods, and floor samples. You'll find these downstairs in the basement showroom. Among the recent deals were a plush khaki sofa, with oversized pillows; originally selling for $1,200, it was reduced to $849 because of a tear along the back. So hey, once it's up against a wall, who will notice?

Floor models are usually in better shape, just sat on a bit. Mr. C rather liked a 28-inch glass cocktail table, reduced from $225 to $159. All of these are final sales, and must be paid for at the time of your purchase. The store is open seven days, including Thursdays 'til 9 P.M.

HOME FURNITURE—USED

Belmont Antique Exchange

- 275 Belmont St., Belmont; (617) 484-9839

Despite this store's name, you won't find many true antiques here; look instead for bargains on more recent pieces of used furniture. The stock varies daily, depending on what the owner discovers as she scours yard and estate sales. Mr. C found a 1930's walnut art-deco desk for $140; same price for a modern pine drop-leaf table big enough for four. A child's oak desk was just $50.

Although this shop concentrates on wood furniture, other items here reflect a whimsical sense of humor, like a flowerpot in the shape of a flamingo for $10. When Mr. C visited, all glassware and china was marked 50% off; this made a set of six painted teacups and saucers $15. Although many prices here already seem low, don't feel you have to stick to them. The staff cheerfully admitted that the ticketed prices "mean nothing; bargaining is like a game here." Play the game Mondays through Fridays from 11 A.M. to 6 P.M.; Saturdays from 12-6; Sundays from 1-4.

Consignment Galleries

- 2044 Massachusetts Ave., Cambridge; (617) 354-4408
- 1276 Washington St., Newton; (617) 965-6131

As the name implies, these shops sell estate furniture on behalf of its owners; there are lots of very nice pieces, including antiques, which are at good (and firm) prices, though still not "cheap." However, it's fun to browse, and you may yet find a bargain—especially since items are reduced in price each month they don't sell.

Mr. C saw a mahogany dresser with an attached mirror, slightly scratched, for $295; and an oak chair with a caned seat for $22.50. Check out the basement in the Cambridge store for further markdowns, like lamps for $20, mirrors for $50, and more. Open seven days a week, including Fridays until 7 P.M.

Cort Furniture Clearance Center

- 155 North Beacon St., Brighton; (617) 254-5455

Cort rents home and office furniture to businesses, model homes, and the general public. When these are returned, still in good shape if not sparkling-new, they go into the clearance center at the rear of this large showroom. That's where you can snap up a comfy $325 designer chair for just $89. Or a huge, arc-shaped sectional sofa for $629, marked down from a retail value of $1,100. Plus lamps, dining tables, and more.

On the office side, there are plenty of desks and fancy chairs, such as a 30" x 60" oak desk, marked down from $550 to $179. There is also a "damaged" area, with further reductions on items that have been banged up (flaws are pointed out for you). Here, Mr. C saw a solid cherry dining table, reduced from $875 to $175. Stock changes all the time; most pieces are in fine shape and are good-looking contemporary fashion styles. Open Mondays through Fridays 9 A.M. to 6 P.M., and Sundays 10 A.M. to 6 P.M.

Garage Sales, Inc.

• 1149 Walnut St., Newton; (617) 965-2640

A permanent garage sale? Mr. C's mother would be ecstatic. Steps from the Newton Highlands "T," what is clearly a former gas station has been spruced up and made brighter than it probably ever was. Every square inch—from the office to the service bays, whose doors still open up in warm weather—is packed with used furnishings, collectibles, and good ol' bric-a-brac.

Given its suburban clientele, the merchandise tends to be of high quality. Mr. C found such goodies as a handsome Ethan Allen rocking chair, some twenty years old but in pristine condition, selling for $135. A nearly antique breakfront could grace an entire wall for $265, easily a third of its original cost.

These items are sold on consignment, meaning there may be some squiggle room on the prices. Can't hurt to ask. All sales are "as-is" and final. And, with weekday hours from 11 A.M. to 5:30 P.M., plus Saturdays 11-5 and Sundays 1-4, you don't even have to beat the weekend earlybirds to the bargains.

John's Used Furniture

• 373 West Broadway, South Boston; (617) 269-1238

This little corner shop is so packed with furniture that it spills out onto the sidewalk. The antique pieces are quite nice, if a bit expensive; however, Mr. C did see an art deco dresser for $100, in less-than-pristine condition. Among the more recent used wares, there is a good selection of upholstered chairs from $5 to $50, and coffee tables for $25 to $35. The store has raised its standards, as far as condition is concerned, since Mr. C was here last. Open Mondays through Saturdays from 8 A.M. to 3 P.M.

Organic Furniture Cellar

• 263 Pearl St., Cambridge; (617) 492-5426

You'll have to look carefully for this place, in a large house at the corner of Pearl and Putnam Avenue (between Central Square and the river). It's only open on Saturdays from 10 A.M. to 5 P.M., adding Wednesdays through Saturdays in September; it's closed completely during July and August. Still, bargain hunters have been beating a path to its (rear, basement) door for years.

Once inside, you'll find a surprising selection of antique and "nearly antique" furniture without fancy antique store prices. Mostly, this is because owner Rich Weiner runs a one-man operation with almost no overhead costs. Everything is well displayed and clean, and much of it is in very good condition. Get a big teacher's desk in solid oak for $95; a spruce clothing chest from Sweden, $125; coffee tables from $35 to $75; a cherry headboard for your bed, just $25; plus chairs, lamps, dressers, mirrors, and even the occasional old-time wood-cabinet radio.

Porter Square Furniture

• 95 Elm St., Somerville; (617) 625-9744

Just on the Somerville side of the big Porter Square shopping center, this shop has a nice collection of antiques, used furniture, and also new unfinished pieces, all reasonably priced. They bring in half a dozen truckloads of furniture a week!

Among the used items, Mr. C saw a maple headboard and bed frame for $45, and a drum-style coffee table for $29. Also, lots of lamps, end tables, decorative items, and some carpet remnants, priced "from $5 to $500." New furniture recently included a three-drawer nighttable for $65, and a five-foot tall dining room hutch for $119. They also carry futons and frames; unfinished pine bookcases, too.

The same folks run **Square One Furniture** nearby at 1704 Massachusetts Ave.; telephone (617) 492-5225. You'll find similar stock and prices at both stores.

Putnam Furniture Outlet

- 556 Massachusetts Ave., Cambridge; (617) 354-1742
- 815 Somerville Ave., Cambridge; (617) 354-6172

Like Cort (above), Putnam leases new home and office furniture and sells pieces that come back in order to keep styles current. PFO, however, has more stock; and a lot of it is "everyday"-type furniture, as opposed to fancy designer styles. You can profit nicely by this system; one recent example was a bedroom set—a solid pine headboard, dresser, chest, mirror, and two nightstands—for $900; new, the same ensemble would retail around $2,000. The stock is primarily of high quality, like a large mahogany executive's desk reduced from $1,600 to just $448. There was also one in walnut for $144.

Of course, you can buy individual pieces as well; and if you prefer a new version of anything you see, chances are they can order it for you. Sales pitches are not heavy-pressure. Open seven days in Central Square, closed Sundays in Porter Square.

Used Furniture Outlet

- 108 Ferry St., Malden; (617) 321-7430

Have a close encounter of the furniture kind at the UFO, where two floors of high- and low-end stock are waiting for you to make contact. Mr.

MR. CHEAP'S PICKS
Home Furniture—Used

✔ **Organic Furniture Cellar**— Hard to find, only open on Saturdays, but a collector's collection of really nice furniture—*nearly* antiques.

✔ **Putnam Furniture Outlet**— Save big on living room and bedroom sets with this leased-and-returned furniture.

C's trip turned up a variety of styles and conditions, including good coffee tables and bookshelves as low as $45; venture upstairs for greater bargains, as long as minor scuffs don't concern you.

Many of these are older looks that just haven't come back around yet (perhaps rightfully so). In back, a small selection of reconditioned major appliances included a Whirlpool washing machine, with a 90-day warranty, for $75. Always buying and refinishing merchandise, the UFO opens its doors Mondays through Fridays from 10 A.M. to 7 P.M. (Saturdays until 5), and 12-4 P.M. Sundays.

Whalen Furniture

- 311 Somerville Ave., Somerville; (617) 666-5100

For over thirty-five years, this Union Square shop has been selling used (and some new) furniture. Three large rooms are filled with sofas, kitchen tables, chairs, lamps and bric-a-brac. There are various styles, from classic to hopelessly outdated, mostly in good condition.

Whalen has small appliances, too; not to mention books, records, and old movie stills. Delivery is available for a small fee. All sales are cash or check only. Open from 11 A.M. to 6 P.M., Mondays through Saturdays.

White Elephant Shop Outlet

• Rte. 133, Essex; (508) 768-3329

Antique hunters love to browse the stretch of furniture shops in Essex, a fine day trip from just about anywhere. The White Elephant is a longtime favorite; this nearby branch is their clearance center—if you can imagine such a thing for a place that *already* looks like a yard sale.

At this peeling yellow wood-frame house right on the highway, everything is half-off. Poke around, and you may find a redwood picnic table for $40; an art deco hutch with glass doors, in okay condition, for $250; even a Hammond organ for $50 (yes, it works). Plus all the bric-a-brac your home will ever need.

Adjacent to this building is the "Buck Hut"—evidently the clearance center for the clearance center. Barbecue grills, ice skates, golf clubs, jigsaw puzzles, and a zillion old record albums are, you guessed it, a buck—although, as a sign points out, "Prices are negotiable." Wow. This Cheapster's paradise is open Saturdays from 10 A.M. to 5 P.M., Sundays from 12-5.

OFFICE FURNITURE—NEW AND USED

Ace Office Furniture Liquidators

• 2 Campanelli Industrial Park, Braintree; (617) 848-8550

Take note of what's located in the front room of Ace Office Furniture Liquidators, because that's where you'll find some of their best-looking new and used merchandise to outfit your home or office. But if you're searching for the *real* bargains on furniture that ranges from less-attractive down to merely serviceable, continue through to the immense warehouse in back.

This is where you'll score four-drawer filing cabinets as low as $60, fully functional save for a missing drawer handle here or there. Or, hundreds of styles and colors of desk chairs, most in fine condition and in the $59-$89 range—with some marked "as is" due to a torn cushion or frayed arm-rest and priced to roll at $19.

Ace buys closeouts directly from manufacturers, and complete setups from companies that are downsizing. Savvy deals include leather executive chairs from $250, and desks for as low as $24.99 (a salesman was able to find two truly beaten-up metal ones for that advertised price); the more common price is $90-$150, still a bargain.

Ace Office is always getting in new stock, and they're usually willing to make a deal. They're open Mondays through Fridays from 8:30 A.M. to 5:30 P.M.

Cambridge Office Furniture

• 113 Richdale Ave., Cambridge; (617) 876-6614

Office Furniture Liquidators

• 519 Broadway, Somerville; (617) 625-7060

These two jointly owned stores specialize in used office furniture at discount. Some new pieces and closeouts are available; a barely-sat-in leather executive's chair was seen for $159, reduced from $268; an executive's desk, never used, was on sale for $299, from $500.

The big bargains, though, are downstairs in the Porter Square store and to the rear in the Somerville branch. This stock may be a bit more worn, but there sure is a lot of it— nearly all on sale at better than half-off the original retail price. A Steelcase swivel chair, worth $450 new, was seen recently for $100; a $300 wood-and-tweed guest chair for $89; computer tables for $75 and up; file cabinet after file cabinet for $50 and up. If you're setting up one of those modular offices with free-standing panel walls, you can get used panels here for just $25 per linear foot; new panels can cost as much as $500 apiece.

Many items have no price tags;

salesmen are very knowledgeable about the value of each piece and their own costs. Within that range, they will negotiate a bit in order to make a sale. Cash and carry is the preferred method of business; both stores are open weekdays until 5 P.M.

Capital Office Furnishings, Inc.
• 2 Centennial Dr., Peabody; (508) 532-7220

An office furniture store with Fortune 500 standards, Capital Office Furnishings frowns on most "used" furniture but gobbles up "surplus," which comes their way from offices who refuse it for some reason—don't like the color, have had to tighten their belts, perhaps some nasty take-over....Consequently, Mr. C watched a number of new chairs being pulled out of boxes to be put on display, for some 30% to 50% less than the retail prices.

Browse through laminate furniture with mahogany, oak, and walnut finishes, including desks roughly $100 less than what you'd pay new; heavy duty wooden bookcases as low as $59; and four-drawer vertical file cabinets for $76. Wheel away chairs under $50, or have them delivered for a small fee.

If you don't see what you want, ask, because there's plenty of inventory not on display in this relatively small, yet packed, showroom. Office hours, appropriately, are 8:30 A.M. to 5 P.M. Mondays through Fridays.

Goldstein Office Furniture
• 156 Lincoln St., Brighton; (617) 787-4433

Goldstein's has quite possibly the largest collection of desks, filing cabinets, and chairs you'll ever see in your life. Roam around their cavernous warehouse, where these are stacked two stories high on metal shelving. It feels like everything that was ever discarded from every office in the country has ended up here, and that's pretty much the story.

For over thirty years, these folks have been snapping up used office furniture and reselling it for one-third of its original cost or less. They do stock new furniture at discount as

---

MR. CHEAP'S PICKS
Office Furniture—New and Used

✔ **Ace Office Furniture Liquidators**—Acres of used stuff in all conditions. Great deals on filing cabinets; droves of desk chairs.

✔ **Cambridge Office Furniture/Office Furniture Liquidators**—Two related warehouses, one in Porter Square, one in Somerville. Tons of desks, chairs, file cabinets, you name it.

✔ **Goldstein Office Furniture**—The biggest of the bunch. It's like a small city inside this warehouse. Something for every price range, with enough stock to fill a couple of Hancock towers.

✔ **Office Furniture Bargain Center**—Be a high-powered executive—or look like one for less—behind an imported mahogany desk at 50% to 80% off. Frequent auctions, too.

---

well, but it's the used bargains that Mr. C finds truly amazing. How about a $250 rolling office chair, upholstered with a posture backrest, for $49—or a $525 Steelcase file cabinet, fireproof, with extra-deep drawers, lock and key, for just $149?

And there's so much more. Computer tables and printer stands for $29. Oak office desks for $69. And whatever it is, there are literally hundreds of each. Some items go for as little as five cents on the dollar.

Used sales are final, of course; but if something goes wrong, they will send a repair person out to you. They even offer painting and re-topping services, to match your office or your tastes. It's a good idea to call ahead to make sure they have exactly what you're looking for. Open weekdays only, from 8:30 A.M. to 5 P.M.

New England Office Warehouse

• 399 Moody St., Waltham; (617) 894-1177

Used and discounted new furniture covers the floor of this warehouse. Name brands like Global (primarily), Hon, and Lacasse may be anywhere from 40% to 80% off new retail prices. There are lots of scratch 'n dent pieces, as well as closeouts. But, even though some items are, um, cosmetically challenged, everything is perfectly functional. Friendly service, too. Open weekdays from 9 A.M. to 5 P.M., Saturdays 10-3.

Office Furniture Bargain Center

• 194 Vanderbilt Ave., Norwood; (617) 329-1662

Just off Route 1, amid various industrial buildings, this vast liquidation warehouse offers all kinds of office furniture for at least 50% off. These include used, slightly damaged, and some new (overstock) pieces, with is quite a lot to choose from. Mr. C found a rolltop desk, a bit nicked but otherwise fine, for a handsome $175. A black leather office chair, retailing for $800, was just $249. And a veneer-topped computer desk, with room for PC and printer, was $149, reduced from $308.

If you're furnishing an office, there is a further 10% discount for buying in bulk. They also have backsaver chairs, file cabinets, drafting tables, cutting boards, and even used copiers from $300. Some of the used furniture goes for as little as ten cents on the dollar. Open weekdays only, from 9-5.

Seats

• 1000 Massachusetts Ave., Cambridge; (617) 868-7222

Here's a fun store to visit, if only to test-drive so many different chairs. Seats is a division of Charrette, the art supply stores. Almost everything here is, of course, a seat; all are discounted from the retail price by margins averaging 20%. The basics include folding metal chairs for $18, down from $25, and Cesca cane side chairs for $59 (retail of $75). You can get either a top-of-the-line Telescope director's chair or a retro-trendy vinyl bean bag for $64.

If you've gotta work, you should at least be comfortable. Try one of the many ergonomic office chairs: Mr. C saw a padded Tech 90 seat with an adjustable back and tilt ($191, down from $252). For true luxury, there are also leather chairs and chaise lounges. You'll pay for the privilege, but at least you won't have to pay full retail. Seats also carries the popular Techline brand of desks and work surfaces. Seats is open seven days a week.

Here are some other well-known places whose bedding prices won't keep you up at night:

Mattress Discounters

• 757 Boylston St., Boston; (617) 437-6633
• 872 Commonwealth Ave., Boston; (617) 738-0033
• 485 Granite St., Braintree; (617) 380-0977
• 486 Westgate Dr., Brockton; (508) 584-7005
• 112 Burlington Mall Rd., Burlington; (617) 270-6633

• 194 Alewife Brook Pkwy., Cambridge; (617) 354-0118
• 180 Endicott St., Danvers; (508) 750-6760
• 385 Providence Hwy. (Rte. 1), Dedham; (617) 326-8983
• 140 Worcester Rd. (Rte. 9), Framingham; (508) 620-9771
• 42 Ferry St., Malden; (617) 397-2923
• 45 Worcester Rd. (Rte. 9), Natick; (508) 651-8867

- 180 Needham St., Newton; (617) 527-3692
- 743 Broadway (Rte. 1), Saugus; (617) 231-1116
- *And other suburban locations*

Royal Slumber Shops
- 397 Massachusetts Ave., Arlington; (617) 648-0933
- 361 Boylston St. (Rte. 9), Brookline; (617) 731-2345
- 64 Cambridge St., Burlington; (617) 273-2220

- 251 Worcester Rd. (Rte. 9), Natick; (508) 235-3229
- 68 Highland Ave., Needham; (617) 455-0048
- 980 Providence Hwy. (Rte. 1), Norwood; (617) 762-5268
- 660 Arsenal St., Watertown; (617) 923-6021
- Weymouth Landing, Rte. 53, Weymouth; (617) 337-4901
- *And other suburban locations*

HOME FURNISHINGS

Bed & Bath Outlet Store
- 38 Vanderbilt Ave. (off Rte. 1), Norwood; (617) 769-5895

Not far from Ernie Boch territory, this large clearance center offers significant reductions on closeouts and overstocked merchandise from its chain of stores. Here, you can find such goodies as 100% goose-down comforters for $99 (in all sizes!), cotton-flannel sheets from $8 and up, or Fieldcrest bath towels, originally $10, on closeout at $3.99. Some of the sale items are seconds, but the imperfections are hard to find.

If you can't get to Norwood, Bed & Bath often features unadvertised sales in each department of its regular stores (in Boston, Cambridge, Danvers, Medford, Natick, Needham, Quincy, Woburn, and further suburbs). Two other outlets are located in Sagamore and West Yarmouth. All stores are open seven days.

Ceramic Tile Wholesalers
- 141A Providence Hwy. (Rte. 1), Norwood; (617) 769-6800

Just south of Route 128, this well-stocked shop has lots of good prices on fancy quality tile and bathroom fixtures. A recent sale offered a handsome red granite/marble tile, originally $14.95 per piece, marked down to just $6.99. Green marble was $4.50; other ceramics start as low as $1.79 per square foot. Plus Delft and

terra cotta styles, and floor tiles in stone, wood, and vinyl.

Kitchen and bath fixtures are sold here too, at good prices; occasional floor models are real deals, like a white formica-top vanity sink reduced from $169 to just $99. There always seem to be a few of these to choose from. CTW will design and remodel rooms for you, or sell you the goods—and even let you borrow the tools. Friendly service. Open seven days, including Wednesdays through Fridays until 8 P.M.

Further down Route 1, on the northbound side, **Tile City** is another source to check out. They're at 1560 Providence Hwy., Norwood, next to Building 19; telephone (617) 769-1744. And, on the other side of Route 128, **Boston Tile Company** is another wholesale/retail source at 825 Providence Highway (Rte. 1) in Dedham. Telephone (617) 461-0406.

China Fair
- 1638 Beacon St., Brookline; (617) 566-2220
- 2100 Massachusetts Ave., Cambridge; (617) 864-3050
- 70 Needham St., Newton; (617) 332-1250

China Fair is Mr. C's longtime favorite for glasses, flatware, kitchen accessories, and, well, china. They import most of these items for distribution to fancy stores (all the way up to Tiffany's!); but here, amid jammed, no-frills surroundings, you can shop at the same wholesale prices.

They seem to have just about anything you could want, from complete dinner sets and silverware to glass candy jars, coffee makers and tea kettles, pots and pans, Pyrex cookware for the microwave, and even wicker baskets and bamboo shades.

Crystal wine stems go for around $5 and up, one-third of the price at the above-mentioned ritzy boutique. A three-cup espresso maker was seen for a mere $9.99. A forty-piece dinner set, complete for eight people, was $50. Or, you can buy individual items by the piece. Service is laid-back, but with a smile. Open weekdays and Saturday; closed on Mondays during the summer.

Crate and Barrel Outlet

- 460 Wildwood St., Woburn; (617) 938-8777

You all know and love Crate and Barrel (Mr. C has spoken with enough fellow Cheapsters to be certain of this). Here at their outlet store, relocated from Cambridge, you can save as much as one-half on many lines of china, glassware, cooking utensils, and various household gadgets. Many of these are factory seconds (with tiny, often undistinguishable defects), closeouts and leftovers. Great deals. Open Mondays through Saturdays from 10 A.M. to 5 P.M.

Economy Hardware

- 219 Massachusetts Ave., Boston; (617) 536-4280
- 438 Massachusetts Ave., Cambridge; (617) 864-3300

Remember the hardware stores we all grew up with? The place you'd go to with your dad to get a pipe fitting or a light bulb . . . a dingy, dimly lit place with creaky wooden floors, and aisles with bins and bins of nails . . . . Well, Economy Hardware ain't like that. Oh, they have nails and bulbs, and caulk and window screens; but then there's furniture, boom boxes, coffee makers, VCRs, and more—all cleanly and brightly displayed like a mini-department store.

The prices on many of these are competitive and worth a look. One or two items in each section are usually on sale, too, like $30 off an AT&T cordless phone, or a Goldstar 19-inch color TV for $229. Plus good deals on basic traditional and unfinished furniture.

Among housewares, there are bathroom linens and cooking utensils; kitchen appliances included a West Bend hot-water pot for $14, various irons and toasters, and a microwave casserole dish reduced from $39 to $29. Open seven days a week, including most evenings.

Grossman's Bargain Outlet

- 217 North Beacon St., Brighton; (617) 783-1906
- Rte. 135 at Blanchard St., Framingham; (508) 875-0616
- 260 Eastern Ave., Malden; (617) 324-0774
- 129 Bacon St., Waltham; (617) 894-5100

Though these warehouses sell mostly lumber, electrical supplies, flooring, paints, and the like (at great discount, even from their regular stores), you can also find bargains on many other kinds of items for the home.

Recent specials have included vertical mini-blinds in several sizes, all priced at $4.88; picture frames, in wood, metal, and acrylic, at 50% off retail prices; ceramic-base table lamps for $6.88; ultrasonic humidifiers for $22; a Regina upright vacuum cleaner, valued at $90, for just $48; and a phone with built-in answering machine for $38.73. Also, their "Assortment" section may yield anything up to televisions and VCRs.

Most of these are surplus, returns, and closeouts; some are factory-refurbished. Appliances and lamps are guaranteed to work, or they may be returned. Open seven days a week.

Home Goods

- 254 Grove St., Braintree; (617) 356-3560
- 21 Torrey St., Brockton; (508) 941-6660
- *And other suburban locations*

Household needs of all types are waiting to be filled here, in the reduced price splendor that comes from high-volume purchases, overstock, and some clearance merchandise. Drift along each aisle, moving from cutlery to coffeemakers to carpeting, all at bargain rates as much as 50% below retail.

Looking for fine china? Choose from 50-piece sets by Tienshan for $36-$49, down from list prices of $80-$120. Flatware? Find Farberware sets for $49.99, retailing at up to $100 elsewhere. A 13-piece stainless steel cookware set was recently seen for $89 (reduced from $200) while coffee-makers from Braun and Krups are 30% below retail.

A wide selection of lamps, by names including Tiffany and Stratford, again can be as much as half-off; Mobilite Eurolamps, workable enough for the starving-yet-stylish college student, run $15-$25. Further along, you'll find Laura Ashley bed sheet sets reduced from $129.99 to $74.99, and a large selection of Oriental rugs being cleared out at 50%-75% off. Open 9:30 A.M. to 9:30 P.M. Mondays through Saturdays, 11 A.M. to 6 P.M. Sundays.

Lighting & Lamps Factory Outlet
- 1235 Furnace Brook Pkwy., Quincy; (617) 471-0200

Illuminating the area with closeouts from their own brand as well as other manufacturers, Lighting & Lamps is packed with a broad assortment of lamps of all kinds; most notably, beauties in hand-painted porcelain, and others with hand-sewn silk shades.

Check out a selection of table lamps in brass or porcelain from $15-$25, and if you want something more than the traditional fabric shade (as low as $12.99), try hand-painted silk from $22.99. The friendly one-man staff Mr. C spoke with maintains that these lights are generally 50% below suggested retail prices, while the shades are closer to 30% off, "because they're very labor intensive."

Definitely worth checking out,

though the hours can make this tricky—10 A.M. to 3 P.M. Mondays, 12-4 on Tuesdays, and 10-4 Wednesdays through Saturdays. Closed Sundays.

Light 'N Leisure
- 112 Main St., Kingston; (617) 585-1313
- 380 E. Main St., Milford; (508) 478-5444
- 214 Main St., Reading; (617) 944-5455

Walking into Light 'N Leisure (you know, "the purple building") is sort of like walking into a brilliant cathedral. Lights of all sizes and styles surround you, lining each narrow aisle. In some cases, they literally *ask* you to take them home—sporting overly cheerful "Hello!!! My name is..." signs which outline their um, most shining qualities. Brought in as overstock from about 150 different factories, they're all selling here for 20% to 40% below original retail prices.

Most of the choices are decidely upscale, but there are inexpensive bargains to be had too. A lovely brass candleholder-style chandelier was seen for $119, down from $299; tiny glass "door decorators" were under $5. Scour the aisles for lighting marked down an *additional* 40% to make room for new arrivals. All three stores occasionally have special floor sample sales with up to 70% off scratched or dinged models; all promise a 30-day money-back guarantee.

As their ads tirelessly point out, these stores are hard to miss. Look for them Mondays, Thursdays, and Fridays from 10 A.M. to 9 P.M., other days until 6 P.M., and Sundays from 12-5 P.M.

Newton Electrical Supply Co.
• 44 Mechanic St., Newton; (617) 527-2040

There are lots of bargains on fine-quality lighting fixtures and lamps at this store—if you can find it. Take Elliott Street south from Route 9, and wind your way around to Mechanic Street in Newton Upper Falls.

This full-service store has a large selection of classic and contemporary fixtures. Most prices are nearly half of the list price, which ain't bad. But look around for special deals; there are usually a few in each area. Mr. C saw a Tiffany-style ceiling light with a retail price of $530, on sale for $260; a swing-arm brass floor lamp, originally marked down from $335 to $200, on final sale for $99. And a shiny brass chandelier, listed at $1,050, was reduced to $520.

On a more approachable level, a mauve contemporary table lamp was just $39 (from $96). They also have recessed lighting, mirrors, door chimes, bath fixtures, ventilator fans, and a full range of electrical supplies. Very helpful staff, too. Open weekdays from 8 A.M. to 5 P.M., Wednesdays until 9, and Saturdays from 8-1 during the summer only.

Newton Pottery House
• 1021 Boylston St. (Rte. 9), Newton; (617) 332-8960

A tiny shop by the side of the road—which many Newtonians pass by on their way to Route 128—this is in fact a goldmine for bargains on first-quality china by Dansk, Arabia, Denby, and others, as well as accessories and decorative items for the kitchen and dining room.

Regular prices are all discounted, like a hand-painted china set of 32 pieces (eight full settings), listing for $520; here, it sells for $399. And there are usually plenty of in-store sale items—open stock, discontinued patterns, one-time deals—like a five-piece "Baronesse" setting by the German maker Hutschenreuther. The elegant white china lists at $93.50 per set; NPH normally has it for $70, but it was recently on sale for $46.88. Yup, that's half-price.

Another recent special on Retroneau flatware offered a complete service for eight, along with a four-piece serving set, reduced from an original $467 retail to just $179. Newton Pottery also has enamel teapots, lovely candles and ceramic holders, cotton placemats, cheese boards, and other gifty items. They offer a bridal registry service as well. Open weekdays from 10 A.M. to 5 P.M., Saturdays 'til 5:30.

Pier 1 Imports
• 1351 Beacon St., Brookline; (617) 232-9627
• One Porter Square, Cambridge; (617) 491-7626
• 792 Beacon St., Newton; (617) 233-8500
• 799 Broadway (Rte. 1), Saugus; (617) 233-8500

You know about Pier 1. They get all manner of housewares, clothing, and trinkets made in distant countries, fresh off the boat. As their chain has expanded, some of the stock has gone upscale; but there are still many nice and affordable things for the kitchen, dining room, and around the house.

Handmade iced tea glasses from Mexico, for instance, are $3.99 each; cotton placemats, made in India, are $3.50; basic white china goes for $4 a piece and up; and there are all sizes of picture frames, in wood, metal, and acrylic.

There are always plenty of items on clearance, saving you a bit more. This can be an inexpenive way to give your place a whole new look. Stores are open seven days, including weeknights until 9.

Ralph Pill Electric Supply Co.

- 307 Dorchester Ave., South Boston; (617) 269-8200
- 326 Mystic Ave., Medford; (617) 391-0180
- 219 Washington St., Quincy; (617) 471-7500
- 60 Arsenal St., Watertown; (617) 926-7455

This warehouse-style lighting chain has a lot of pull (sorry!). They are distributors for several decorator brands, which you can buy here with very low markups. These are top-quality fixtures at everyday "sale" prices.

Choose from a wide range of styles, from Colonial to art deco to modern. Some are priced as low as $10, but even in the $30 to $40 range you have lots to look at. They also have things like ceiling fan lights, starting around $60; as well as shades, special bulbs, and more. Open weekdays from 7:30 A.M. to 5 P.M., Saturdays from 8-12 noon.

Reed & Barton Factory Store

- 200 West Britannia St., Taunton; (508) 824-0289

Reed & Barton has been manufacturing silverware in this exact spot in Taunton (a.k.a. the Silver City) since 1824. Which is quite lucky for people in Boston and beyond, because the factory store sells first-quality, seconds, and discontinued items at ridiculously discounted prices. A five-piece setting of sterling silver, which retails for $315, was seen here for $185. Sterling silver serving pieces (say *that* three times fast), were reduced from $85 to just $29.95 per piece.

If sterling is a little rich for your blood, there's always silver plated. A five-piece setting was $50, down from $72.50. R & B also makes your everyday stainless, usually found in 40-piece settings for eight people, or 60-piece sets for twelve. Save as much as $50 a set, and more.

There's something in every price range, with a vast selection of pat-

terns. And Mr. C hasn't even gotten to the seconds and discontinued styles from other manufacturers! Also, though the discounts are not quite as deep, you'll still find substantial savings on things like Disney giftware by Schmid, lead crystal vases, Irish china and crystal gifts, and more. Open Mondays through Saturdays, 10 A.M. to 6 P.M.

Rennie Curtain Outlet

- 42 Adams St., Taunton; (508) 822-9717

A true manufacturer's outlet, you can hear the work going on in the factory as you wander through aisles and around bins filled with curtains, bedspreads, comforters, drapes, sheets, and more. Here, Rennie's sells off its overstocks and slight irregulars at hugely discounted prices.

The selection is good, and you can generally find most of the elements you need to furnish a coordinated room. Mr. C found Lady Pepperell all-cotton bath towels for $4.98 each; any room can be spruced up with pleated fabric window shades, in assorted sizes and colors, for $9.88 each. Twin-size comforters can be as low as $40. Rennie's also carries curtain rods and hardware, plastic bath accessories, wallpaper borders—just about anything you may need.

But there's more! The outlet also sells off fabric remnants from its factory, including designs by Waverly and others. If you're handy with a needle and thread, you can create coordinated accessories to go with those bargain sheets you found. For even bigger savings, stop in on Saturdays from 10 A.M. to 3 P.M. for the weekly "Bargain Basement" sale. Rennie's is open Mondays through Saturdays from 9 A.M. to 5 P.M. (Fridays 'til 6). Seniors get a 20% discount on most items every Monday. Go!

The Tool Shed

- 471 Main St., Waltham; (617) 647-7970

After 14 years of running a similar business in San Francisco, Al Davis (no, not the owner of the Oakland

Raiders) moved east and opened this store specializing in secondhand tools. It's become quite the hangout for area carpenters, plumbers, and *Home Improvement* do-it-yourselfers.

From a Craftsman planer ($380 new, $150 here) to the tiniest of socket wrench attachments (50¢ each), Al's got it all. He rounds up his stock from personal appraisals, much like an estate reseller; there are even some new items, like a recently seen Makita power screwdriver, half-price at $45. And we haven't even gotten to the bargain table yet!

This is where you can find lots of items at one low price, usually $3 or $4; these of course are in less-than-perfect condition, but still have lots of life in them. After all, how pretty do tools need to be? You won't find any hardware supplies here, or garden tools either; what you will find is expert knowledge, both from Al and his regular customers, who like to shoot the breeze. It's an incredibly friendly, small-town atmosphere in the big city. Open Wednesdays through Saturdays only, from 1 to 5 P.M.

Mr. C hasn't forgotten about the big chains. You already know what they have, now you know where they are:

Home Depot
- 60 Stockwell Dr., Avon; (508) 580-0600
- 92 Newbury St. (Rte. 1), Danvers; (508) 774-0400
- 177 Willard St., Quincy; (617) 376-0380
- 75 Mystic Ave., Somerville; (617) 623-0001
- 1213 V.F.W. Pkwy., West Roxbury; (617) 327-5000

HQ
- 205 Carnegie Rd., Norwood; (617)) 255-0922

Lechter's
- 800 Boylston St., Boston; (617) 236-0798
- 65 Dodge St., Beverly; (508) 921-4441
- Westgate Mall, Brockton; (508) 586-9450
- 100 Cambridgeside Pl., Cambridge; (617) 577-0353
- 3850 Mystic Valley Pkwy., Medford; (617) 391-8833
- 623 Broadway (Rte. 1), Saugus; (617) 233-3200
- 133 Middlesex Ave., Somerville; (617) 625-3454
- 450 Paradise Rd., Swampscott; (617) 599-2313

JEWELRY

Afro-Caribbean Arts Etc.
- 248 Elm St., Somerville; (617) 628-5215
See the listing under "Unusual Gifts."

Burlington Coat Factory
- 705 Granite St., Braintree; (617) 848-3200
- Cloverleaf Marketplace, Speen St. (off Rte. 9), Natick; (508) 651-2526
See the listing under "Discount Department Stores."

Cary Hill Flea Market
- 220 East Ashland St., Brockton; (508) 583-3100
See the listing under "Flea Markets and Emporia."

Elements
- 18-20 Union Park St., Boston; (617) 451-9990
See the listing under "Unusual Gifts."

Filene's Basement

- 426 Washington St., Boston; (617) 426-6253
- *And other suburban locations*

Don't forget Filene's for jewelry bargains! Most branches, especially the original downtown basement, offer a good selection of gold, silver, and gemstone pieces at about one-third less than many other department stores. Frequent special sales can reduce these to half of retail. And you get lowest-price protection, as well as a one-year warranty on most items. Sure, it's not as personalized as your local boutique, but if price is your main consideration, consider this option. Open seven days a week.

Freedman Jewelers

- 333 Washington St., Suite 408, Boston; (617) 227-4294

Currently celebrating its 50th anniversary, Freedman's is part of the Jewelers Exchange building in Downtown Crossing. And what better place to get a gold band? Eight floors of jewelers are packed into this single address. Few of them sell to the public; but if you're hunting down a bargain, Freedman's is like finding buried treasure.

They specialize in diamonds, offering highly personalized service. They import their own stones, each one with its own documentation of size and color rating. These are unmounted, allowing you to pick exactly the right one in just about any price range, and put it on your choice of setting. There is also an extensive collection of engagement and wedding bands already made up, along with other kinds of jewelry and watches.

By manufacturing many pieces themselves, Freedman's can price its jewelry well below other stores—some prices are as much as 50% lower and better! This is the kind of place whose regular customers go to the fancy boutiques first, find something they like, then come here to get the same thing for much less. It's a good idea to call ahead and make an appointment, since the folks at Freedman's will sit with you and bring out

---

MR. CHEAP'S PICKS
Jewelry

- ✔ **Cambridge Artists Co-op**— Beautiful, funky creations in Harvard Square, direct from the artists to you.

- ✔ **Elements**—More hand-wrought works of art you can wear, at "bargain basement" prices.

- ✔ **Freedman Jewelers**—For that *special* ring (and other fancy baubles), this shop imports its own diamonds and eliminates the middleman. Highly-attentive, personal service—for over fifty years.

---

as many choices as you want to see. There is virtually no sales pressure, though, as these salespeople know they've got a good thing going. Hours are 9 A.M. to 5 P.M. on weekdays, Thursdays until 7; also Saturdays from 9-4, except in summer.

Jewelry Factory Outlet

- 440 Quincy Ave., Braintree; (617) 843-4001

You may be resigned to spending a pretty piece of change when entering a jewelry store, but the Jewelry Factory Outlet softens the blow with prices that are up to 60% less than most boutiques. "We buy closeouts, keep overhead down, and rely on word-of-mouth advertising," maintains the manager.

Consequently, you can find an 18-inch necklace in 14K gold, stickered at $100, selling here for $39.99; an array of 14K birthstone rings marked down from $79 to $49.99; and diamond anniversary bands as low as $89, about 40% below standard going rates.

Gold earrings range from $16.99 to $24.99, charm bracelets go for $99 (listed at $149), tie bars for $6.99, and a wall of earrings all priced under $4. Pick up Buxton billfolds and ladies wallets for half off, and costume jewelry for a song.

Pleasant and friendly, the Jewelry Factory Outlet was giving an additional 20% off everything when Mr.C visited, and two decades in business speaks well of its reliability. It's open 9 A.M. to 9 P.M. six days, noon to 5 P.M. Sundays.

Pier 1 Imports
- 114 Boylston St., Boston; (617) 542-8874
- 102 Westgate Dr., Brockton; (508) 580-1102
- 1351 Beacon St., Brookline; (617) 232-9627
- One Porter Square, Cambridge; (617) 491-7626
- 701 Providence Hwy., Dedham; (617) 329-9500

- 1278 Washington St., Hanover; (617) 826-3883
- 400 Lincoln St., Hingham; (617) 749-7292
- 792 Beacon St., Newton; (617) 964-5658
- 1591 Hancock St., Quincy; (617) 773-0956
- 799 Broadway (Rte. 1), Saugus; (617) 233-8500
- *And other suburban locations*

Pier 1 always has a bright and colorful selection of handcrafted jewelry from faraway places, generally at very inexpensive prices. Earrings can be as low as $2 to $4, and necklaces around $8 to $12. These range from the exotic to the funky; hammered brass designs, tiny wooden elephants, strung beads, vividly painted ceramics. Many are clearance items, marked down even further. Open seven days a week, including weeknights until 9.

LIQUOR AND BEVERAGES

Like any major city, Boston seems to have a liquor store on every other block. It's virtually impossible to see them all and compare them; many succeed out of convenience rather than price anyway. There are a few which stand out, though. Nearly all are open from 9 A.M. to 11 P.M., Mondays through Saturdays.

Boyle's Buy-Rite Liquors
- 2440 Massachusetts Ave., Cambridge; (617) 354-1000

Always some high-quality wines on special sale.

Brookline Liquor Mart
- 1354 Commonwealth Ave., Allston; (617) 734-7700

Right on the Allston/Brookline border, this store includes a "Bargain Basement" of wines. They also host free wine tastings every Tuesday and Saturday. Ask them to put you on their mailing list.

Gimbel's Discount Liquors
- 1637 Beacon St., Brookline; (617) 566-1672

Small but packed, Gimbel's is a

friendly place where they will help you—but not pressure you—with your choices.

The Ice Box
- 3892 Washington St., Roslindale; (617) 524-6852

Here's a unique concept in the bottled water biz. Any time of day or night, you can stroll up to this ordinary-looking building, put an empty jug under a spout, pop a quarter in, and get a gallon of fresh spring water. That's it. This is about one-third the price of fancy gallons in stores; and besides, it's more fun.

Because this warehouse is not exactly in the nicest area of town, and because the taps run 24 hours a day, the

premises are monitored by security
cameras. The water itself is trucked
in daily from a state-run spring out in
Millis. Meanwhile, you can also get
ice here for your next party: A five-
pound bag is just $1.25. Ask one of
the guys on the loading dock (they're
friendly). The ice part is only open
from May through September, weekdays from 7 A.M. to 5 P.M., Fridays and
Saturdays 'til 6, and Sundays from 7-3.

Mall Discount Liquors
- 202 Alewife Brook Pkwy.,
  Cambridge; (617) 864-7171

Lots of bargain wines in this large
store next to the Stop & Shop in
Fresh Pond.

Reservoir Wines and Spirits
- 1922 Beacon St., Brookline; (617)
  566-5588

A large selection of wines at discount prices, for the student crowd
in Cleveland Circle.

Sav-Mor Discount Liquors
- 15 McGrath Hwy., Somerville;
  (617) 628-6444

A huge, no-frills warehouse with
great monthly specials.

MR. CHEAP'S PICK
Liquor and Beverages

✔ **Brookline Liquor
Mart**—Free weekly wine
tastings, plus their very own
"Bargain Basement."

Upper Falls Discount Liquors
- 150 Needham St., Newton; (617)
  969-9200

Fits right in on Newton's "discount
mile" stretching from Route 9 to
Route 128.

The Wine Press
- 1024 Beacon St., Brookline; (617)
  277-7020
- 143 Providence Hwy. (Rte. 1),
  Norwood; (617) 255-7090

This pair of stores has frequent sales,
offering a big selection of top-rated
wines at several dollars below the
prices of smaller stores. Free wine
tastings are held in the stores, too.
Closed Sundays.

**Of course, most liquor stores have a hard time beating the
big guys on a day-to-day basis. For low prices, the major
chains to check out include:**

Atlas Liquors
- 156 Mystic Ave., Medford; (617)
  395-4400
- 661 Adams St., Quincy; (617)
  472-1573
- 591 Hyde Park Ave., Roslindale;
  (617) 323-8202

Blanchard's Liquors
- 103 Harvard Ave., Allston; (617)
  782-5588
- 741 Centre St., Jamaica Plain;
  (617) 522-9300
- 286 American Legion Hwy.,
  Revere; (617) 289-5888
- 418 Lagrange St., West Roxbury;
  (617) 327-1400

Kappy's Liquors
- 215 Alewife Brook Pkwy.,
  Cambridge; (617) 547-8767
- 120 Liverpool St., East Boston;
  (617) 567-9500
- 746 Main St., Malden; 321-1400
- 325 Bennett Hwy. (Rte. 1),
  Malden; 321-1000
- 10 Revere Beach Pkwy., Medford;
  (617) 395-8888
- 265 Main St., North Reading;
  (508) 664-5555

Martignetti's Liquors
- 64 Cross St., Boston; (617) 227-4343
- 1650 Soldiers Field Rd., Brighton;
  (617) 782-3700
- Parkway Plaza, Chelsea; (617)
  884-3500

MUSICAL INSTRUMENTS

A.A. Rayburn Musical Instruments

- 263 Huntington Ave., Boston; (617) 266-4727

The first sight that greets you upon entering Rayburn's is a wall of autographed photos from giants of the music biz—Sonny Rollins, Henry Mancini, Tom Jones (??), Woody Herman—all thanking and blessing Emilio Lyons. He is also known as the "Sax Doctor," a guru among musicians for keeping their horns in perfect shape.

Rayburn's sells new and used instruments, mainly brass, saxes, and flutes. Many of the used horns are rentals that have been refurbished under this expert care to "like-new" condition: An alto sax that would sell for $650 new may go for $525 used. Trumpets start at $175 and up. They do carry some guitars—electric, acoustic and classical—starting around $125. Trade-ins are accepted; "We wheel and deal," said one salesperson. Hours are 9 A.M. to 5 P.M., Mondays through Saturdays.

Cambridge Music Center

- 4 Hemenway St., Boston; (617) 247-1747
- 1904 Massachusetts Ave., Cambridge; (617) 491-5433

A dealer primarily of used guitars and amps, priced to move. Fender "Squires" start as low as $175 and up; a Japanese-made Ibanez recently went for $100. Used amps tend to be classic tube models from the 1960s and 1970s, as well as new Crate amps, modestly priced.

CMC offers good service, with repairs done on the premises. Used guitars are warrantied for as long as the buyer owns them; chances are, any bugs have already turned up and gotten fixed. Amps, being older, are warrantied for thirty days. Lots of

strings, straps, and accessories; friendly help. Open seven days; the Boston branch is closed Sundays in the summertime.

Central Sales Music Company

- 1702 Massachusetts Ave., Cambridge; (617) 876-0687

Forty years ago, Central Sales began as a family business selling all kinds of used items. Over the years, musical instruments won out as the main line of trade. Here you can find a student guitar for as little as $50, or a full-size Epiphone for $125. Prices include a case, strap, and picks. There are new guitars for sale as well (they're the only authorized Fender dealer in Cambridge), but all other instruments come used only. A repair staff works on site.

Band instruments move well here too. Trumpets start as low as $40 ("or $100 without dents"), saxophones from $250. Used brass and woodwinds carry a 30-day warranty; everything else is covered for one year.

The store offers one other unique guarantee: Within a year of your purchase, you can trade any instrument back in for 75% of its original price in store credit. CSMC is open daily from 10-6.

Daddy's Junky Music Store

- 165 Massachusetts Ave., Boston; (617) 247-0909
- 2234 Massachusetts Ave., Cambridge; (617) 497-1556
- 888 Providence Hwy. (Rte. 1), Dedham; (617) 329-9924
- *And other suburban locations*

With access to inventory from thirteen New England stores, Daddy's has a wide selection of new and used guitars, amps, keyboards, drums, etc. You may find a used Yamaha electric guitar for as little as $80; new models start around $190 (for a Peavey "Predator"). Acoustic guitars start in the same price range. Daddy's is a Gibson dealer, but they have many other brands as well.

There are plenty of used guitars under $200, and lots of amps in the $50 to $100 range. You can also save a bit more by negotiating a package deal; a guitar and amp for as low as $100. All used guitars include a free set-up, a sort of basic examination that normally costs $35.

Used equipment carries a warranty of thirty days on parts, sixty days on labor. Daddy's does a heavy business in trade-ins, using computer stats from their other stores to help determine their offer. Of course, you get more by using it as credit toward a purchase rather than for cash. Open seven days.

Guitar Center
- 750 Commonwealth Ave., Boston; (617) 738-5958

"There are some advantages to being the biggest guitar dealer in the land," boasts the manager at Boston's branch of this California-based chain. Opened with much hoopla in 1994, this vast shop offers standard discounts of 20% to 40% on a variety of guitars (and other instruments) from all major brands.

Better yet, special deals with manufacturers can chop as much as *two-thirds* off the price of a new axe—and Guitar Center gets a pretty regular lineup of these. Recent specials offered a Nady wireless electric guitar, with a list price of $199, marked down to an amazing $49. A Crate "Vintage Club 2100" amp, with two 10-inch speakers, was reduced from $350 to $149. These of course are the heavy promotional deals, but you'll always find something like this in each department.

Speaking of which—since bands do not live by guitars alone—the store also carries keyboards, drums, computers, and recording equipment. Score a Pearl "Export" drum kit, originally list priced at $1,299, marked down to $399; or nab a pair of Sennheiser headphones, not for $129, but just $49.

MR. CHEAP'S PICKS
Musical Instruments

✔ **A.A. Rayburn Music**—A legend in the jazz world, lots of good horns and reed instruments, new and used.

✔ **Daddy's Junky Music Stores**—A vast stock of used guitars and amps for the as-yet-undiscovered rock star.

✔ **Guitar Center**—National chain with incredible deals on new and used guitars, keyboards, drums, and electronics.

GC also does a brisk business in secondhand guitars—there are always plenty of styles to check out. You can trade your old guitar in for credit toward a purchase—even for something brand-new! New purchases are covered by a "Lowest Price" guarantee—for 30 days after you buy an instrument here, Guitar Center will meet any advertised price on the same item. Not only that, but you can even return your purchase within 30 days for a refund or exchange if you're dissatisfied for any reason. They're open weekdays from 10 A.M. to 9 P.M., Saturdays from 10-6, and Sundays from 12-6.

Holland Street Music
- 69 Holland St., Somerville; (617) 776-9699

This Davis Square shop sells lots of used guitars and basses, plus some drum equipment—as well as amps, speakers, microphones, and all the other accessories. Many instruments are for sale on consignment from the original owners, meaning there may be some squiggle room on the prices. In any case (no pun intended), you're sure to get a good deal. Great prices on strings, too; these, of course, are *not* used. Open 11 A.M. to 7 P.M. Mondays through Fridays; 10 A.M. to 6 P.M. Saturdays; noon to 5 P.M. Sundays.

Mr. Music
- 128 Harvard Ave., Allston; (617) 783-1609

Mr. Music has a huge selection of used guitars and basses, primarily Fenders and Gibsons. Japanese-made Fender Stratocasters can be found for as low as $199, and range up to around $650. A Strat "Squire" of black maple was seen for $179. Used and new amps start around $79 and up.

Their prices on new instruments are pretty good too, and may get even better if you're good at haggling a bit. The sales staff here can be alternately brusque or helpful, so be thick-skinned about it. Used guitars are warrantied for 90 days; "If we can't fix it, we'll give you another one." A staff of repair technicians works on the premises. The store also buys used instruments; they sell drum stuff too, as well as strings, accessories, CDs, and tapes. Open weekdays from 10 A.M. to 7 P.M., Saturdays 'til 6.

The Piano Mill
- 311 Needham St., Newton; (617) 928-1237

Cheap grand pianos? Yes, relatively speaking. You can save yourself a grand or so by going used. Piano Mill has a vast selection (the biggest in New England, by their estimation) of "pre-owned" ivories, which are restored to pristine condition on the premises. There are usually dozens of these to look at, in all sizes, shapes, and colors. Some are rental models, others are trade-ins; you may even find some new models that have been cut loose by other dealers. Prices on PM's own new pianos are competitive, too. Open Mondays through Saturdays

from 10 A.M. to 6 P.M.; Sundays noon to 4 P.M.

For similar deals, check out **Boston Organ and Piano** at 104 Boylston Street, Boston, telephone (617) 426-1988; also 677 Worcester Road (Rte. 9), Natick, (617) 332-6650; and 70 Main Street (Rte. 28), Reading, (617) 944-4222.

Sandy's Music
- 896 Massachusetts Ave., Cambridge; (617) 491-2812

This tiny shop between Central and Harvard Squares has a loyal following among the folk music crowd, and it's easy to see why. One wall is lined with all kinds of acoustic and electric guitars, banjos, ukeleles, and violins; the other has racks of folk records and tapes, some used, for as little as $3. Used cases, too, and some amps.

During Mr. C's visit, a man was sitting on a stool in the middle of the shop (not easy amid the clutter) playing a banjo. He turned out to be a customer, not in-store entertainment, of course; and he was raving about the instrument, saying, "I can't believe this is so much better than the one in that other store—and it's a hundred dollars less!" 'Nuff said. Sandy's is open Mondays through Saturdays from 10 A.M. to 6 P.M., Thursdays until 9.

Used Sound
- 31 Holland St., Somerville; (617) 625-7707

In addition to secondhand stereo equipment (see the listing under "Electronics"), Used Sound has guitars and amplifiers starting as low as $90 or so. These include a 90-day warranty. They sometimes get some professional recording equipment in as well. The store is open every day but Sunday, including Thursdays and Fridays until 7 P.M.

PARTY SUPPLIES

The Big Party!

- Liberty Tree Mall, Danvers; (508) 750-8964
- 321 Worcester St. (Rte. 9), Natick; (508) 650-8811
- 100 Granite St., Quincy; (617) 471-1119
- 19 Paradise Rd., Salem; (508) 745-8585
- 880 Broadway (Rte. 1), Saugus; (617) 233-4433
- 100 Boston Tpke. (Rte. 9), Shrewsbury; (508) 767-0477
- 1457 V.F.W. Pkwy., West Roxbury; (617) 323-4344

Taking the superstore approach to party supplies, The Big Party! is certainly as festive as its name implies. These stores are bright and colorful, offering a dazzling array of choices. And while they don't tout any particular percentage-off, high-volume sales allow them to keep prices uniformly low.

Not only will you find all the standard items here, like greeting cards, wrapping paper, and novelty tablecloths; TBP sells party favors and toys, masks, candy, joke books, cook books, helium balloons, and lots more. Along with your basic styles of matching paper plates and napkins, they carry designer looks from Marimekko, Gloria Vanderbilt, and Caspari—gorgeous prints on heavy paper stock. They also have specialty items like wedding cake centerpieces, and take orders for custom-printed invitations.

On top of these competitive prices, senior citizens get a 10% discount on Mondays; teachers get the same on purchases over $25 at any time. Don't forget to check out the clearance tables in the rear of the store, as well. Open seven days, including weeknights until 9.

Brenner's Party Supply Store

- 31 Osprey Rd., Saugus; (617) 231-0555

Brenner's is a full-service store for parties from small to gigantic. Related to two adjacent businesses, Exclusive Millinery and the Saugus Shoe Barn, the trio becomes your complete outfitter for weddings, banquets, and just about any kind of celebration.

From party favors and cake decorating to invitations, banners, and aisle runners, the folks at Brenner's will work with you to help plan just what you'll need. The prices are very reasonable, leading to the long list of regular customers on the North Shore. Open seven days a week, including Thursdays until 9 P.M.

Paperama

- 75 Campanelli Dr., Brockton; (508) 586-3100
- Winn & Cambridge, Burlington; (617) 273-0750
- Independence Way, Danvers; (508) 777-2040
- 1246 Washington St., Hanover; (617) 826-4458
- Natick Towne Mall, Natick; (508) 655-9508
- 1001 Providence Hwy., Norwood; (617) 762-6936
- 169 Parkingway St., Quincy; (617) 472-1496
- 43 Foley St., Somerville; (617) 625-5900
- 1256 Washington St., Weymouth; (617) 337-6823

A recent merger with a New York-area chain makes this longtime discounter bigger and better than ever. They offer permanent discounts like 40% off all paper party goods— plates, napkins, cups, tablecovers— every pattern, every day. You can usually find a similar discount on sports team stuff and even the latest

MR. CHEAP'S PICKS
Party Supplies

✔ **Brenner's Party Supply Store**—Up in Saugus (be sure to call for directions), a place to take care of your every whim. Excellent service; big on weddings.

✔ **Party Needs Warehouse Outlet**—Acres and acres of everything from color-coordinated paper plates to silly kiddie favors.

Disney designs your kids are screaming for (whatever it is this year).

But Paperama goes far beyond party hats. They have low prices on unusual items like disposable cameras (wouldja believe a five-pack for $40?), video greeting cards, arts and crafts kits, silk flowers, croquet sets and other lawn games, pool toys, and lots more. And, senior citizens get a 10% discount every Tuesday. All stores are open seven days a week.

Paper Annex
- 1638 Beacon St., Brookline; (617) 566-2220
- 70 Needham St., Newton; (617) 332-1250

Related to the China Fair stores (see the listing under "Home Furnishings"), Paper Annex has a full line of supplies and decorations for all your party needs. From decorator paper plates at $2.19 a pack, to plastic "Happy Birthday" banners at 79¢ a foot, they have shelves and shelves of the stuff.

Bags of colored tinsel, $1.20;

packs of eight invitations with envelopes, $2; paper American flags for 49¢. Even "prismatic" reflective top hats for $1.59, as well as mylar balloons with cartoon characters on them and even pinatas. Plus several lines of designer supplies by Caspari and others—gorgeous, heavy-duty paper napkins and plates. Open Mondays through Saturdays.

Party Needs Warehouse Outlet
- 411 Waverly Oaks Rd., Waltham; (617) 893-9181

Starting small about twenty years ago, Party Needs has grown to a showroom that covers a quarter of an acre, displaying over 28 *thousand* items from practical to wacky. Why, there are some three hundred different designs of napkins alone, to match any theme or decor. Not to mention plates and cups, streamers, favors, cards and invitations, and all the rest. There's something for any season, holiday, or Disney tie-in.

One aisle features classic "joke shop" toys: Super balls, little rubber dinosaurs, and lots of other party favors for around a dollar or less. All of these are out in open bins; owner Jack O'Connor has a child-friendly attitude. He wants you to play with these things. "Anyone can sell *stuff*," he shrugs. "We sell fun." During good weather, he even puts toys—like giant soap bubble wands—out on the front steps for kids to enjoy.

It's also worth noting that you can purchase items by the case for a discount of between 15% and 25% off, depending on the item. Party Needs is open daily from 9 A.M. to 6 P.M. (Wednesdays through Fridays 'til 9), and Sundays from 12-5 P.M. It's a bit out of the way—look for the sign outside an industrial park, on this stretch of Route 60 near Belmont.

PET SUPPLIES

Commonwealth Pet Center
- 362 Boylston St. (Rte. 9),
  Brookline; (617) 232-0067

This is a fun place just to walk around in—packed with pets and supplies everywhere you look, as you wind around each nook and cranny of the store's layout. The walls and ceilings have been painted with underwater murals; indeed, the whole interior feels like some deep-sea grotto.

One room is, in fact, filled with fish tanks. New tanks come as a complete one-price package with filter, heater, gravel, pH kit and fluorescent light, as well as a gift certificate for fish of $10 to $25, depending on the tank. Further, they offer price breaks whenever you buy fish in multiples of two; the fish are, after all, happier that way. That sums up the style here; service is highly personal for owners and conscientious about the pets. New kittens are discounted in pairs as well.

There are always several unadvertised specials in the store, such as a 50-pound bag of cat litter for $8.99, or an electronic pet feeder (for when you take short trips), marked down from $69.99 to $49.99. Weekly drawings are held for store credit certificates worth up to $100. Commonwealth is open seven days, including weeknights until 8 P.M.

Pet Club
- 486 Westgate Dr., Brockton; (508) 580-1190
- 1600 V.F.W. Parkway, West Roxbury; (617) 327-0444

Wow. These stores claim to have "A Whole Acre of Pets," and that looks about right. Along with clever, open-top glass pens filled with dogs, birds, rabbits, and more—allowing you to reach right in and play—Pet Club takes the high-volume approach to food and accessories. Prices are

about 25%-50% below retail.

The selection, naturally, is vast. Whether you have a hamster or a hippo (*welll. . .*), they've got everything you could possibly need to care for it. Find good prices on dog and cat foods from Iams/Eukanuba, Science Diet, Bil-Jac, and Purina; or, pick up a special, like a 25-pound box of Cadet dog biscuits for only $10.99.

Fin fans may find a 10-gallon aquarium starter kit—everything but the fish—for a mere $14.99. Not to mention bird cages, kitty carry-cases, gerbil runs, and even "ferret condos." There is also a well-stocked book section, all discounted 25% off the cover price.

The staff knows its stuff—mostly young, animal-lover types themselves. Pet Club (which is not a membership club, by the way) is open daily from 9 A.M. to 9 P.M., Sundays from 12-6.

Pet Supplies "Plus"
- 70 Westgate St., Brockton; (508) 584-5400
- 182B Cambridge St., Burlington; (617) 273-0200
- 333 Providence Hwy. (Rte. 1), Norwood; (617) 255-7900
- 1220 V.F.W. Pkwy., West Roxbury; (617) 469-4545

Here's another of the national dis-

Mr. Cheap's Pick
Pet Supplies

✔ **Pet Club**—"An acre of pets"; stock up on basic supplies at discount.

count chains, offering low prices on foods and supplies for dogs, cats, fish, and birds. Like supermarkets, they'll double the value of manufacturers' coupons. And they always have lots of popular items on sale. Recent bargains included a 40-lb. bag of Pro Plan adult dog food, reduced from $24.99 to $19.99; half-price ($22.98) on a scratching-post tripod for cats; and a 29-gallon aquarium, atop an oak-finish cabinet, almost $50 off.

PSP stores are open daily from 9 A.M. to 9 P.M., and Sundays from 12-6 P.M. Further south on Route 1 from the Norwood store, **Pet World** offers good values and very personal service, also worth checking out. They're at 60 Providence Highway., Walpole, telephone (508) 668-4300, with another branch at 1262 Worcester Road (Rte. 9), Natick, (508) 653-9221.

And, a few spots that will keep Spot in kibble until 2020:

Just For Pets Superstore
- 10 Sylvan St., Peabody; (508) 531-7387
- 299 Mishawum Rd., Woburn; (617) 938-7387

Petco
- 119 First St., Cambridge; (617) 868-3474
- 12 Middle St., Plymouth; (508) 746-5688
- 12 Linscott Rd., Woburn; (617) 938-7966

Pet Supply Depot
- 15 Stockwell Dr., Avon; (508) 580-1706
- 820 Providence Hwy. (Rte. 1), Dedham; (617) 320-9700

- 1376 Washington St. (Rte. 53), Hanover; (617) 826-4400
- 395 Worcester Rd. (Rte. 9), Natick; (508) 651-9229
- 682 Broadway (Rte. 1 North), Saugus; (617) 231-2088
- 759 Broadway (Rte. 1 South), Saugus; (617) 231-3331
- 75 Linden St., Waltham; (617) 736-0200
- 545 Washington St., Weymouth; (617) 331-3388
- *And other suburban locations*

Petstuff
- 170 Pearl St., Braintree; (617) 849-6100
- Crossroads Center, Burlington; (617) 270-3545

SEWING AND FABRICS

Fabric Place
- 136 Howard St., Framingham; (508) 872-4888
- Woburn Mall, 300 Mishawum Rd., Woburn; (617) 938-8787

These vast stores, part of a New England chain, have a truly impressive selection of everything relating to sewing and home decor. Head to the rear of the store for their best deals, in the remnant rooms. Here, you'll find tables and bins overflowing with small pieces; one table had fabrics with retail prices of up to $24 per yard selling for just $3.37.

Nearby, the "Seconds" area boasts half a dozen aisles of larger bolts from Waverly, Mill Creek, Kaufmann, Richloom, and lots more. These may have small glitches in the patterns, but there's enough available for you to buy plenty of extra material. And, at 40% to 60% off retail prices—many are $5.98 a yard—you can afford to do so.

There are usually lots of other sale fabrics mixed in throughout the store. Often, you can even find first quality fabrics at similar reductions. Wallpapers are sold here too: In-stock papers are reduced by 30% off retail prices, including designs by Waverly and Laura Ashley. Clearance bins have rolls for as little as $3.98.

Pick up copies of their newsletters and workshop schedules for fashion forecasts and new ideas. Both stores are open six days and evenings a week, plus Sunday afternoons.

The Fabric Showroom

- 319 Washington St., Brighton; (617) 783-4343

Owner Fred Shapiro, whose family has run this company for some 75 years, is justly proud of his store. They have over thirty *thousand* different fabrics, from domestic cottons to imported velvets. "We inspect every roll that comes in here, to make sure they're all first-quality," he points out. "No one else does that."

There's a lot to see. Designer fabrics for reupholstering chairs and making slipcovers for sofas, draperies, or bedspreads. They buy direct from the mills and sell at 30% to 70% off retail. By keeping its prices below even contractors' sources, this store makes designers of *all* its customers. Fabric Showroom will even let you borrow two-foot wide sample swatches to take home and test. "No one else does *that*, either."

Cotton fabrics start around $7.95 per square yard. They have a special rack of fabrics for just $2.99 a yard, or 50% off the last markdown; and a remnants table with more bargains. For further reductions, check out their clearance center, **Freddy Farkel's Fabric Outlet**, at 86 Coolidge Avenue, Watertown; telephone (617) 926-2888. It's open daily; the Fabric Showroom is open every day but Sunday, including Wednesday evenings until 8 P.M.

Sew-Fisticated Discount Fabrics

- Twin City Plaza, 264 Msgr. O'Brien Hwy., Cambridge; (617) 625-7996
- 735 Morrissey Blvd., Dorchester; (617) 825-2949

- *And other suburban locations*

Sew-Fisticated is a complete store for the sewing fan, with fabrics, supplies, and patterns, all at discount. A recent sale, in fact, had several Simplicity and McCall's patterns at 60 percent off. They also run regular "Dollar Day" sales, when remnants of calico, cotton-knit prints and solids, broadcloths, and more are $1 to $1.50 a yard.

Regular store displays always feature items on sale, such as 42-inch wide velvet remnants in solid colors, marked down from $8 to $5.99 a yard. They also have lycra blends and spandex. Service is very friendly and helpful, whether you're a pro or a beginner. Open seven days a week, including evenings 'til 9:30, and Sundays from 12-5.

Sew-Low Fabrics

- 473 Cambridge St., Cambridge; (617) 661-8361

Lots to look at here. Sew-Low features many of the usual fabrics but also has lots of unique materials. Fake fur, as low as $9.99 a yard; velveteen; corduroy, recently on sale for $2.99 a yard; imported Italian tapestries, marked down from $25.99 to $19.99 a yard; plus upholstery and drapery fabrics, yarns and knitting supplies, Simplicity patterns, and more. Friendly, expert advice too. Open weekdays from 9:30 A.M. to 7 P.M.

Winmil Fabrics

- 111 Chauncy St., Boston; (617) 542-1815
- 39 Dodge St. (Rte. 1A), Beverly; (508) 927-3411
- Danvers Plaza (Rte. 1), Danvers; (508) 777-3236

Perhaps the largest of the Downtown Crossing/Chinatown area showrooms, Winmil has a lot to see beyond your basic cottons and synthetics. Metallic lamés at $3.98 a yard, chiffons for $3.19 a yard, sequined lace for $9.98, cotton/lycra in solids and wild patterns for $4.98. Several varieties of crepe du chine were marked down from $6.98 a yard to $2.98; same price for calico. Various wool blends for men's suits were $4.98, and rayon failles $3.98.

Winmil's upholstery department offers yardage for $3.98 to $5.98; lots of designer fabrics and patterns are reduced from $10.98 to $5.98. Plus pillow forms, lace trim, thread (three spools for a dollar) and buttons. Open from 9-6, Mondays through Saturdays; the suburban branches add Sundays from 12-5.

Wandering around this downtown area, you'll find several smaller, long-established fabric stores. These include **Clement Textiles** at 80 Bedford Street, Boston, telephone (617) 542-9511; **New England Textiles** at 50 Essex Street, Boston, (617) 426-1965; and **North End Fabrics** at 31 Harrison Avenue, Boston, (617) 426-2116.

Zimman's Smart Fabrics

- 80 Market St., Lynn; (617) 598-9432

Best guess? That an old Woolworth's once occupied these two floors which now house nothing but rolls of fabrics in all kinds and colors. In any event, the place really does seem to go on forever, and it's packed to the rafters.

Near the door you'll find a variety of home decorating fabric remnants for $4.99 per yard, but that's just a warm-up for what awaits in the basement. There, where all items are on clearance from the main floor upstairs, you may find bolts of gingham, in many colors, at $3.99 per yard; decorator cloth fabrics as low as $2.49 per yard; as well as rayons and cotton knit prints for $2.99 per yard. Among the other choices are a ton of upholstery ($4.99/yard), silky satin ($2.69), and children's novelty prints ($1.99).

It's difficult to conceive of a fabric need that won't be met at Zimman's. Open Mondays through Saturdays from 9:30 A.M. to 5:30 P.M., Thursdays 'til 8:30.

SHOES AND SNEAKERS

The Barn

- 25 Kempton Place, Newton; (617) 332-6300

This sure *is* a big barn of a place, down a little alley off of Washington Street as it runs along the Mass. Pike (watch carefully for the sign as you approach West Newton!). Along with first-quality, current lines at discount, the Barn has a huge selection of closeouts and irregulars (all sales final) at great prices. Parents have taken their entire families here for generations.

Ladies may find Italian leather dress shoes by Vanelli, marked down from $90 to $59. A Nine West boot-shoe, with a strap heel, was recently seen here for $45; the suggested retail was $61, but Mr. C's expert had seen them for even more than that. For men, classic tassel loafers by

Bally were marked down from an astronomical $235 to a more manageable $145. Mr. C was more cozy with Dexter leather walking shoes, reduced from $70 to $54. There are similar savings on athletic shoes, hiking boots, and outdoor footwear for all, from Avia cross-trainers for $34 to Teva sandals below retail (rare).

Both genders get closeout racks of even bigger savings, with some good shoes as low as $20. You take your chances on these final sales, but it's hard to go wrong with leather pumps for $5.

Recently, their second building across the parking lot has been turned into the Kids Barn, specializing in everything children need, top to toe. The Barn is open seven days, including weeknights until 9.

Berkeley Shoes Plus
- 65 Berkeley St., Boston; (617) 542-3424

This little neighborhood shop carries a surprising selection of boots, walking shoes, and other "sensible" footwear. Merchandise from Rockport, Doc Marten, Timberland, Dexter, and Hush Puppies—some of which can be as high in price as in quality—can be found at discounts of $10 to $30 off retail prices. A lot of these are irregulars, and are clearly marked with "IRR," but some are first-quality. The real bargain bonanza is found on the clearance rack—where all shoes are priced at $39. Like any clearance rack, sizes are limited and some shoppers will be luckier than others. Still, it's definitely worth stopping in during any South End jaunt. Open Mondays through Saturdays, 9:30 A.M. to 6 P.M.

Converse Shoe Outlet
- 35 Highland Ave., Malden; (617) 322-1500

The Converse outlet sells its durable brand of basketball, tennis and other athletic shoes at great prices. These include closeouts, but also current styles. In new shoes, the ever-popular "Chuck Taylor All-Stars" high-tops sell here for about ten bucks less than

---

MR. CHEAP'S PICKS
Shoes and Sneakers

✔ **The Barn**—Vast selection of discounted new and overstock shoes and sneakers for men, women, and kids (who now get their own barn).

✔ **Gerry's Shoes**—Designer names at outlet prices. For women only.

✔ **Joan & David Outlet Store**—J & D fans find it well worth the trip to Everett or Worcester.

✔ **L & S Designer Shoes**—Weekends-only warehouse for incredible deals on current lines of top-name women's shoes.

✔ **Reebok Factory Outlet**—Take a trip to Planet Reebok, without paying the full-price fare. **The New Balance Factory Store** does the same for its own popular sneakers.

---

in retail stores. Performance basketball shoes, with retail prices of $80 to $90, sell here for more like $40 to $50. Mr. C snapped up a pair of "Cons" rubber cleats, reduced from $25 to $16.99.

There are also plenty of last year's models, overstocks, and slightly irregular seconds at even better prices. Some are reduced from $90 all the way down to $30. Plus lots of Converse clothing: T-shirts with the famous Converse All-Star patch for $5, sweats, socks, shorts, and more. Unused shoes can be returned within 30 days; they also have a "Frequent Buyer" deal; buy ten pairs, get the next one free. Are you listening, moms? Open seven days, including weeknights 'til 9.

David's Famous Name Shoes

- 75 First St., Cambridge; (617) 354-3730

For over 35 years, David's has been a fixture in East Cambridge, quietly selling Rockport, Timberland, Dexter, and the British Clark's shoes at discount. Anything priced under $100 retail sells here at 15% off; over $100, it's 20% off. Thus, a current Roc-Sports casual, in brown suede, sells for $80 instead of $100.

At the rear of the store are even better bargains—closeouts and irregulars at 30% to 80% off retail. Men may find Nunn Bush leather wing-tips for $30. Other shoes on the racks, in most sizes, start at $19.98. For women the prices are similar, with names like Trotters, Boks, and more. Some of these are in a limited range of sizes only.

David's also has sneakers, and Western boots by Durango, also at discount. Open seven days a week, including Tuesdays and Thursdays until 8.

E.T. Wright Shoe Outlet

- Christmas Tree Plaza, Pembroke; (800) 846-9136

E.T. Wright has been making mens' shoes for over 125 years. That's a lot of shoes. Naturally, they are bound to have some leftovers, irregulars, closeouts, and discontinued styles that they need to get rid of; this outlet is where they do it, resulting in huge bargains. A pair of cordovan wing-tips, so classic your great-grandfather probably wore them (well, not *these* actual ones), normally retail for $250; here, they sell for $139. Not bad.

The outlet also carries some first-quality shoes from other well-known manufacturers. Mr. C was asked not the reveal the names, but you will definitely recognize them. These are discounted, though not as much as the house brand.

There is also a back room with "bargain basement" prices. Here, shoes that were originally $40 to $150 are now priced from $19 to $69. Try not to miss the store's regular warehouse sales, usually in June

and December, when they sell off discontinued styles from their catalog. Most are cancelled because of a change in leather, not style. Open Mondays through Saturdays 10 A.M. to 6 P.M., Thursdays and Fridays 'til 8 P.M., and Sundays from 12-5.

Footwear Marketplace

- 2A Harvard Ave., Allston; (617) 787-9858

This no-frills shop across from the Sports Depot has grown from a weekends-only secret into a daily goldmine. Focusing mostly on casual styles, they have current lines at discount and last year's leftovers at closeout prices. There are also bargains in clothes and accessories.

For top-line sneakers like Reebok, Nike, Fila, and Adidas, there is a good selection of current styles sold at about 30% off retail. A pair of men's Reebok pumps, which would be over $90 downtown, goes for $65 here. Similar deals abound for women and for kids.

At the back of the store the racks are filled with shoes and more sneakers, perfectly good, at prices from $15 to $45 or so. You'll still find brand names like LA Gear, Converse, Nike, and Pierre Cardin. Hardcore Cheapsters will enjoy rummaging through the $10, $5, and $3 (!) bins.

They have basic clothing, too; from slouch socks (three pair for $5) to Harvard sweatshirts ($16 down to $5), tie-dyed women's leggings for $5 and cotton sundresses for $6.95. Some thirty varieties of novelty print T-shirts are all $4.95. Most everything in the store has a good selection of sizes. Open from 10 A.M. to 6 P.M. Mondays through Thursdays; Fridays until 7, Saturdays 9:30-6, and Sundays 12-6.

George's Shoe Store

- 669 Centre St., Jamaica Plain; (617) 524-4866
- 259 Washington St., Somerville; (617) 623-7363

Here are a couple of hole-in-the-wall places to discover. They aren't fancy, but the shoes are—and the prices are amazing. The selections are limited, but you never know what may be hiding on the shelves.

Most of the shoes are for women; brands like Franco Sarto and Phyllis Poland. A pair of black patent leather pumps, retailing for $150, was recently seen here for an amazing $39. Some of the shoes are seconds or irregulars, but most are first-quality closeouts snapped up from other boutiques, like Bonwit Teller.

Most interesting for guys is the exclusive line of shoes by European designer Andre Assous. These are slip-ons of soft leather in a variety of colors. George's imports these directly at considerable savings; they retail for well over $100, but sell here for $29 and up. Both stores are open Mondays through Saturdays from 9:30 A.M. to 5:45 P.M., and Thursdays 'til 7.

Gerry's Shoe Store

- 333 Walnut St., Newtonville; (617) 527-2330
- 8 Wethersfield Rd. (Rte. 9), Natick; (508) 655-6506
- 550 Adams St., Quincy; (617) 328-4554

Gerry's sells fine, first-quality women's shoes at discount. Many of the brands are upscale designers, so the bargains are relative—but they are deals. A pair of dress pumps, decorated with rhinestones, would retail elsewhere for over $200; here, they were seen for $98. Many other shoes are in the $40-$70 range.

Mr. C has been asked not to mention any brand names, but don't worry, you'll know them. If you don't know them, you'll love them. Gerry's is small, with an emphasis on service. Open daily from 9:30 A.M. to 5:30 P.M., plus Sundays 12-5 in Natick and Quincy.

Harry the Greek's

- 1136 Washington St., Boston; (617) 338-7511

See the listing under "Clothing—New."

Hyde Factory Outlet

- 1036 Cambridge St., Cambridge; (617) 547-4397
- 13 Centennial Dr., Peabody; (508) 531-0899

These small shops are packed with athletic shoe bargains. All of these, mostly by Hyde and Saucony, are irregulars, but most of them look just fine to Mr. C. In some cases, only certain sizes are available. Recently, for example, a man with a size nine foot could have stolen bases in a pair of cleats that were a steal themselves at $10.

Other lines are more flexible, and there are many kinds of shoes to see—aerobics, tennis, basketball, running—for men and women. Men's Saucony "V-Grid" running shoes were marked down from $110 to $70. Women's "Jazz 5000," good for daily mileage training, were reduced from $64 to $50.

A special sale wall always features closeouts for $19.88. The Hyde Outlet also has a variety of running clothes and other accessories at slight discounts. The shoes are not guaranteed, and sales are final, except for exchanges in size. Closed Sundays.

Joan & David Outlet Store

- 1935 Revere Beach Pkwy., Everett; (617) 389-8655
- Worcester Common Fashion Outlets, Worcester; (508) 795-0019

Fans of this line of shoes, imported from Italy, are loyal devotees. Most are already frequent visitors to these clearance outlets, where first-quality J & D shoes are sold at up to 30% to 40% off the retail prices charged in their own boutiques. Many of these are recent closeouts and overstock; all are undamaged and unused. For men, there is the companion line, David & Joan's, here too—along with snazzy leather bags and belts. All sales are final; the stores are open seven days a week.

L & S Designer Shoe Warehouse

- 199 Newbury St. (Rte. 1), Danvers; (508) 774-8881

Opened in early 1994, this place took no time to become a favorite among North Shore shoe shoppers (try saying *that* three times fast). The store gets bulk-quantity deals directly from manufacturers, and can thus sell first-quality women's footwear at anywhere from 30% to 50% off retail prices.

Black suede pumps by Jones New York were just one recent value, reduced from a list price of $88 down to $65, in season. Leather Bandolino heels were seen for a remarkable $30, less than half of their $68 retail tag. Similar deals abound on current lines by Evan-Picone, Selby, Easy Spirit, Joan & David, and many others—in a no-frills warehouse setting, with all the boxes out on the selling floor.

L & S also carries some sneakers, slippers, and boots, along with handbags and jewelry, also at direct-to-you rates. Get on their mailing list for flyers about special clearance sales, where prices can be cut in half *again*. The store is only open four days a week: Thursdays from 11 A.M. to 7 P.M., Fridays and Saturdays from 10-6, and Sundays 12-6.

Marion's Shoes

- 30 Commercial St., Braintree; (617) 843-7796

Three rooms of shoes stand around at Marion's, some items previously worn, others factory returns, but all available for as much as half of their original retail prices. Because of relationships with suppliers, Marion's prefers not to publicize any of its brand names, but trust Mr. C—you'll recognize 'em.

Snazzy boots are made for walkin' (out the door) at $29.95, and a table of stylish black-and-silver pumps were recently seen on clearance at $9.95 a pair. Casual shoes run $14-$17, while another table offered a "first pair $21.95, second pair $11.95" deal.

Overhead costs are kept low (Mr. C walked around for 10 minutes before realizing that there actually *was* a clerk in the building), but at prices up to 75% below retail, who needs company? Walk right in, weekdays from 9 A.M. to 9 P.M., 'til 5:30 Saturdays, and 12-5 P.M. Sundays—although calling first is recommended.

Mortt's Shoes

- 1001 Providence Hwy. (Rte. 1), Norwood; (617) 769-4115
- 448 Highland Ave., Salem; (508) 741-3444
- 120 Stafford St., Worcester; (508) 752-9931

Selling a mix of clearance stock and new, first-quality shoes for the entire family, this small local chain holds its own with the bigger stores. Weekends in particular find Mortt's hopping—and not just because you can try on the shoes straight from the racks.

Save 20% to 30% across the board on current lines of shoes from Dexter, Keds, Naturalizer, and even (occasionally) Birkenstock, which is rarely seen at discount anywhere. Women's styles range from the traditional (Selby pumps reduced from $75 to $52) to the trendy (Stegmann wool-fabric clogs, $72 down to $58).

Guys can get a pair of classic wing-tip leather shoes by Dexter, not $90 but $75; not to mention Dingo western boots and Herman "Survivors" leather work boots. Clearance tables often feature various looks all at one price, like $29.90. And, for the kids, how about a deal on Jellies sandals ($7.99!), Nike sneakers, and even ballet and tap dancing shoes. Open seven days a week.

New Balance Factory Store

- 61 North Beacon St., Brighton; (617) 782-0803
- 5 South Union St., Lawrence; (508) 682-8960

The very popular New Balance line of athletic shoes is made right here in New England, folks—and these equally popular stores are filled with rack after rack of seconds and closeouts. The company proudly states that its seconds meet high enough standards to match other makers' best. Indeed, the tiniest of blemishes—you'd do worse to the shoes after wearing them for a week—can land them in the discount pile. There are all kinds of models: running shoes, walking shoes, hiking shoes, basketball, tennis, cross-trainers.

These are at least $20 to $30 below the prices you'd pay in other stores. Ah, but then there are the closeouts. In this section you can find a $90 pair of men's running shoes—in stylish purple, yet—for a mere $19.99. In fact, most of the men's and women's shoes here are $19 and $29. Lots of shoes for kids, too, at $19.99. Remember, though, in the closeouts area, sizes can be very limited. Most shoes can be returned for exchange or store credit.

Athletic clothing and accessories are discounted here, too—running tights, windbreakers, cotton socks, etc. Both stores are open daily from 9:30 A.M. to 7 P.M., Sundays 12-6.

Reebok Factory Outlet
- 300 Technology Center Dr,, Stoughton; (617) 341-2976

The name tells the story. Shoes for men, women, boys, girls, and toddlers come in a range of styles, some from years long past, some from the most recent past season. Not to mention all the related paraphernalia—Reebok shirts, warmup suits (nylon two-piecers, reduced from $90 to $68), caps, water bottles, etc.

Men's "Shaq Attaq II" basketball shoes, originally listed at $100, were on sale for just $40 on a recent visit. Women could find several varieties of cross trainers, reduced by 40%. And for the kiddies, tiny "Weebok" velcro sneakers were $15. Clearance racks at the back of the store hold even deeper discounts: Women's "Aero Step" aerobics shoes were on sale at $50, reduced from the *outlet* price of $56. Some of these are less than recent styles, but they'll do the job. And there are usually special bins of shoes for $19.99 a pair—buy several!

Not *everything* here is Reebok—the outlet also discounts the less sporty, but popular, Rockport brand. A pair of men's leather dress shoes was seen for $20 off the $79 list price. One important caveat: Every item in this store is "cosmetically irregular," even though not all are labeled as such. Still, everything functions perfectly well. Hours are

Mondays through Saturdays from 10 A.M. to 9 P.M.; Sundays 12-6 P.M.

Saugus Shoe Barn
- 31 Osprey Rd., Saugus; (617) 233-1295

The Saugus Shoe Barn offers a vast selection of dress shoes, dyeable shoes (which they can do for you in the store), dance shoes, nurses' shoes, hosiery, handbags, and accessories, all at incredible savings. In order to respect their sources they declined to have prices mentioned here; but big crowds attested to the store's popularity. Open Mondays through Saturdays from 10 A.M. to 5 P.M., Wednesdays and Thursdays until 9.

SSB is part of a three-store, family-run center off of Route 1 South, including **Exclusive Millinery**—makers of bridal headpieces—and **Brenner's Party Supplies**. Together, they make a complete outfitting center for major parties and banquets, or just a place to find just the right shoes for that new dress.

Zapatos
- 98 Union Park St., Boston; (617) 423-2842

Unless you were absent for that day of high school Spanish, you know that *zapatos* is Spanish for *shoes*. Here, it appears to mean "the Filene's Basement of shoes." You will be dazzled by bins and boxes filled with shoes in every style and color imaginable for men, women, and children. Almost all of these are irregulars, and some are damaged; choose carefully, and you'll do fine.

Canvas sneakers, in all colors and sizes, may be just $3 a pair, or two for $5. Racks lining the walls offer shoes that are in better condition. Accordingly, these are more expensive, but still as low as $12. A recent visit found 9 & Co. ivory leather pumps selling for $20. In the men's section, a fancy pair of Alden dress shoes were $75, compared to the retail price of $200. Other brand names seen here include Vittorio Ricci and Mootsie's Tootsies for women, and Nunn Bush, Cole Haan, and Florsheim for men. Mr. C

135

even found in-line skates for $60.

Augmenting this fine footwear are things like printed novelty T-shirts for $4, cotton leggings for $8, and running shorts by Champion, same price. Zapatos is a cash-only operation—but

that cuts costs! Cheap tip: On Wednesdays, every customer who spends $10 or more gets a free gift. This South End shop is open Tuesdays through Saturdays from 9 A.M. to 3:30 P.M.

And of course, everybody loves:

Parade of Shoes
- 395-403 Washington St., Boston; (617) 338-1445
- 171 Newbury St., Boston; (617) 236-1656
- 15 White St., Cambridge; (617) 491-6920
- 699 Providence Hwy., Dedham; (617) 326-9689
- 3850 Mystic Valley Pkwy., Medford; (617) 393-0366
- 210 Needham St., Newton; (617) 244-3312
- Heartland Plaza, Newton; (617) 969-8212
- 134 Nahatan St., Norwood; (617) 769-5561
- 1510-12 Hancock St., Quincy; (617) 472-0953
- Memorial Pkwy., Randolph; (617) 963-4525
- 130 Squire Rd., Revere; (617) 284-3331
- 97 Main St., Stoneham; (617) 438-7915
- 1098 Lexington Ave., Waltham; 9617) 891-6226
- 18 Main St., Weymouth; (617) 337-8437
- 362 Cambridge St., Woburn; (617) 932-3250

Shoe Town
- 34 Cambridge St., Burlington; (617) 272-3401
- 95 Washington St., Canton; (617) 821-1659
- 1400 Worcester Rd. (Rte. 9), Natick; (508) 872-9047
- 615 Broadway (Rte. 1), Saugus; (617) 233-3560

SPORTING GOODS

American Fitness Equipment Company
- Hingham Plaza, 100 Derby St., Hingham; (617) 741-5300

American Fitness manufactures its own line of workout stations and free weights. This is professional-grade machinery, made with heavy gauge steel and handcrafted to be sturdier than the stuff you'd get in department stores. Since they sell direct, it also costs far less than comparable health club-level machines. Basic benches which could retail for as much as $169 are just $90 here; add a simple curling attachment for another $45. You can also have machines custom-designed for your

home. It all carries a one-year warranty for parts and labor.

In addition, they sell secondhand workout gear of all kinds—exercise bicycles, steppers, treadmills, whatever comes into the store. These can come from you as well, in the form of trade-ins for credit on anything you see. It's a friendly, family-run place, with staffers who are very knowledgeable about training. Open Mondays through Saturdays from 10 A.M. to 6 P.M., and Thursdays 'til 8 P.M.

Beacon Street Bicycle
- 842 Beacon St., Boston; (617) 262-2332

This small shop is jam-packed with new bicycles by such makers as Trek,

Univega, and Sterling, at prices of 10% to 40% off. Better yet, Beacon usually has a lot of last year's models on sale at extremely good discounts. These can save you as much as $100 a pop; poke around. They do repairs as well. Open Mondays through Fridays from 10 A.M. to 6 P.M., Saturdays 10-4.

Bicycle Bill
- 253 North Harvard St., Allston; (617) 783-5636

Heading out of Allston toward Harvard Stadium, Bicycle Bill is worth stopping in to see. They have a fairly good-sized selection of racing and mountain bikes, with many leftovers from last year at further discounts. Several of the brands are American-made. Mr. C saw an Iron Horse all-terrain bike for $225, and a Diamond Back city bike, with an alloy frame, at $299. Open seven days a week.

The Bicycle Workshop
- 259 Massachusetts Ave., Cambridge; (617) 876-6555

Near MIT, this store offers low prices on new bikes, with relaxed sales-people and good service. New mountain bikes start from just $199. Bicycle Workshop also has one of the larger selections of used bicycles around; you may find a Raleigh ten-speed racing bike for $110, a Vista ten-speed for $75, or a girls' Huffy ten-speeder for $110. They offer servicing on the premises. Anyone showing a student ID will get an extra 10% discount. Open seven days a week, Thursdays 'til 7.

Bob Smith Sporting Goods
- 9 Spring Lane, Boston; (617) 426-4440

Hidden away in the Financial District, Bob Smith's is, well, hard to hide. It's so big—one of the largest sporting goods stores in the area. They specialize in running, skiing, tennis, fishing, rollerblades, and more.

While these sports are non-competitive, Smith's everyday prices are—lower, in fact, than most department stores. It's not all rock-bottom; their main claim to fame is selection and service. Still, they do get special

---

MR. CHEAP'S PICKS
Sporting Goods

✔ **Bicycle Workshop**—Good prices on new bikes and one of the larger selections of used bikes around.

✔ **Centre Ski and Sports**—Tons of new and used skiing gear in the winter, bicycles and rollerblades in summer. Small-shop service, to boot.

✔ **Hilton's Tent City**—Five floors of super deals on camping and sports gear *should* qualify this place for its own zip code.

✔ **Play It Again Sports**—A consignment store for sports equipment. Find a new or used bargain, or bring in that hockey stick you bought on a whim and never used.

✔ **Sports Replay**—Behind and below the Ski Market near BU, this place sells all kinds of equipment that folks have traded in upstairs. Good for skis, bikes, tennis, and rollerblades.

---

closeout stocks, where you can really save. Reebok sneakers for $29 to $39, Nike clothing, and lots of tennis racquets—as low as $24.95 for a fully-strung Kennex.

And every February they hold their annual "Ground Hog Ski Sale" to clear out their surplus on skis, boots, parkas and accessories by all the big-name makers. Some are reduced 80% to 90% off their original prices, with skis starting at just $20. Keep an eye out for the ad in the sports section. Open Mondays through Fridays from 9 A.M. to 6 P.M.,

Saturdays from 10-5.

Broadway Bicycle School
• 351 Broadway, Cambridge; (617) 868-3392

This is actually a workshop for anyone who wants to learn how to fix bicycles from the ground up. Since there are always projects being worked on, they often have used bikes on sale for $50 to $150. These tend to be older-style bikes, reconditioned with good-quality parts; and you can bring yours back in after one month for a free checkup, just to make sure you haven't gotten a lemon. They usually have deals on some new bikes, too; Mr. C saw a Yokota mountain bike with alloy wheels for $230. Friendly, laid-back place. Closed Mondays.

Centre Ski and Sports
• 1193 Centre St., Newton; (617) 332-0300

From a small, seasonal business, owner Peter Lieberman has built up a year-round neighborhood shop that's as strong on service as it is on prices. He focuses on skiing, of course—downhill, cross-country, and snowboarding—as well as bicycling and rollerblading in summer.

It's a deceptively small place; Peter's got merchandise stashed in basements all over Newton. This allows him to give shoppers more money-saving options than even the big chains. You can, for example, purchase brand-new skis at prices that match any competitor; save a straight 50% off retail on last year's models, many still plastic-wrapped; or pick up a super deal on used skis, with a vast selection in for every age from kids on up.

And here's one Mr. C has never seen before: You can also *lease* a complete setup—skis, boots, bindings, and poles—at a flat rate for the season. This is especially smart for kids, who can trade up to a bigger size anytime. The store gives free adjustments, using a clever gizmo that simulates skiing moves, to get a perfect fit of footgear.

When the warmer weather hits,

CS & S has skates from Rollerblade and Oxygen, a strong but less-expensive line. You can also rent these, or check the limited stock of used blades. And Peter won't let you leave the store until you know everything you need to about the use and care of your skates.

In road and mountain bikes, the store deals mainly in Fuji, whose high-quality bicycles are priced far less than comparable models by Trek and the like. A Fuji "Supreme" 21-speed, with index shifting and a lightweight alloy frame, goes for $279. That includes a lifetime warranty, and your first tune-up here is free.

Plus car racks, clothing, and all the accessories you could possibly need for these activities. The store also accepts trade-ins for credit toward anything they carry. Open seven days a week, including weeknights 'til 7 or 8 P.M.

Earth Bikes
• 35 Huntington Ave., Boston; (617) 267-4733

The main business here is renting bikes to people who want to cycle around Boston. Earth Bikes also sells new bicycles from major brands like Iron Horse and Univega. The big news for Cheapsters, however, is the store's selection of high-end *used* bikes. They will sell off their used rentals, as well as trade-ins from people looking to upgrade to newer models. Either way, you can save big on otherwise expensive models. Stop in and find out. Extra tip from Mr. C: In September, Earth Bikes holds a big sale to sell off the entire fleet of rentals and make way for the new lines. Hours can be erratic; so call ahead.

The Fitness Store
• Lakeport Park, New State Highway (Rte. 44), Lakeville; (508) 947-6211

On your way to a weekend on the Cape, stop into the Fitness Store, which claims to be New England's largest showroom for new and used fitness equipment. Mr. C's not about to argue—this place is huge. About half of the merchandise is secondhand, where the real bargains are found. Check out their stupendous buyback deal: Use new equipment for up to three years, and they'll still buy it back for at least 70% of the original price. Of course you can bring *any* fitness equipment in for credit; it's a great way to trade up to better machines.

A Nordic Track "Pro-Form XC-Skier," $350 new, was recently seen here for $225 used. There's a great selection of weight benches, steppers, bikes and exer-cycles, Reebok Steps ($99 new, $69 here!), treadmills, and more. New machines are also discounted, but as these are high-end brands, the prices may give your wallet a workout.

The Fitness Store is big on service. Instead of ordinary salespeople, they hire personal trainers who can help you figure out what's best for you. They'll teach you how to use your equipment, how to find your heart rate—and why. Open weekdays from 11 A.M. to 7 P.M. (Wednesdays and Thursdays 'til 8), Saturdays from 10-5, and Sundays 12-5. Summer hours vary.

The Golf Club Factory
- 351 Turnpike St. (Rte. 138), Canton; (617) 828-1688
- 203 Worcester Rd. (Rte. 9), Framingham; (508) 875-9300

Knowing that imitation is the sincerest form of flattery, GCF gives duffers the chance to feel like they own the finest clubs made today—without actually shelling out the big green required. These stores buy components from manufacturers the world over, assembling stainless steel and graphite parts into fine, custom-made clubs.

Maybe you've always wanted to own the popular "King Cobra" irons, but didn't want to spend the $500-$600 they can fetch. Here, a "King Snake" set (3-iron through pitching wedge), an exact copy of the major brand, runs you only $248.

Most of the clubs, including a wide variety of putters as low as $19.95, are on display without grips—enabling you to select from

about a dozen options and specify the length. All assembly, as well as repair work, is done in the store. Open from 9 A.M. to 5 P.M., Mondays through Saturdays.

Another chain specializing in component clubs as a way of saving money is **Wayland Golf Shops**, which has branched out from the Wayland Country Club. Visit them there, on Route 27 in Wayland, telephone (508) 358-4775. Also at 54 Middlesex Turnpike, Burlington, (617) 221-0030; and 238 Highland Avenue, Needham, (617) 444-6686.

Golf Day Outlet Store
- 120 Andover St. (Rte. 114), Danvers; (508) 750-4410
- Summer Hill Plaza, 164 Summer St., Kingston; (617) 582-1701
- 135 American Legion Hwy. (Rte. 60), Revere; (617) 284-4653
- 2 Winter St., Weymouth; (617) 331-2600

This national chain specializes in—you guessed it—golf equipment. They carry most major brand names, all at discount. Low prices go even lower during their frequent sales, when you can get accessories like a dozen golf balls for as little as $9.95. A full set of "Lady Wilson" clubs, complete with bag and covers, was recently seen for just $189.

Shoes include brands like Nike, Stylo, and GoreTex, starting around $30; one recent sale added cedar shoe trees for $5 with the purchase of shoes. For serious duffers who like to practice at home, a 7' x 9' net for working on your swing in the backyard is just $49.95. They even have instructional videotapes to improve your game further. Open Mondays through Wednesdays from 10 A.M. to 6 P.M., Thursdays and Fridays 'til 9, and Saturdays 9-5.

Hilton's Tent City
- 272 Friend St., Boston; (617) 227-9242

This North Station spot is *the* place in Boston to camp out if you're looking to save some cash on camping equipment. The store boasts four crowded floors of clothing and gear for every budget and skill level. Nearly all of these are first-quality; occasional irregulars are clearly marked, and are even better bargains.

Tents come from makers like Kelty, Quest, and Sierra Designs. A cozy Eureka! "Crescent 2" tent was seen recently for $79.99, reduced from Hilton's own price of $100; a six-person model was on sale for $295. The whole family could just as easily fit into a CabinTent model Mr. C found—a floor sample, selling "as is" for just $75. To snuggle up inside your tent, you'll need a sleeping bag; look for lightweight Colemans from $30, or a more heavy-duty, expedition-weight Caribou model, listed at $300, available here for $210. Stuff all of your stuff into Eastpak duffel bags, from $14.95.

Hilton's also sells a wide variety of clothing and shoes. A men's Woolrich wool sweater was reduced from $55 to $39. You may find Gore-Tex waterproof anorak jackets under $100—quite rare. A high-tech Helly Hanson windbreaker, with a lifetime guarantee, was $175; if that seems steep, note that the normal price was $215. Speaking of steep, all major brands of hiking boots are sold here.

In the wintertime, Hilton's adds cross-country skis, boots, and poles. Much of the store's gear is available for rental as well. These guys really know their stuff. Every item sold here carries the full manufacturers' warranty; perhaps best of all, Hilton's will match any price tag you bring in. Open seven days a week.

International Bicycle Center

- 89 Brighton Ave., Allston; (617) 783-5804
- 71 Needham St., Newton; (617) 527-0967

This is one of the area's most complete bicycle stores, geared mainly to the pricier brands, such as Cannondale, Trek, and Gary Fisher—though they do carry less-expensive names like Schwinn. It's a high-volume business, so prices are even with, or slightly below, most other dealers.

A particularly good bet here is to

look for leftover models from the previous year; on these, you can find even better savings, like $100 off a Trek mountain bike. International also sells new clothing, shoes, in-line skates, bike racks, and a full line of accessories at discount. Full service repair work is done on the premises. Open seven days a week.

Laughing Alley Bicycle Shop

- 51 Harvard Ave., Allston; (617) 783-5832

Taking up three storefronts' worth of Allston's furniture mile, Laughing Alley carries the upscale bicycle brands like Mongoose, Trek, and Barracuda at competitive prices. A Trek mountain bike with an aluminum frame was marked down from $870 to $750. A similar bike by Miyata, originally $650, was on sale for $530. Several kids' choices as well. The sales staff is very friendly, laid-back, and knowledgeable.

Laughing Alley also carries in-line skates at discount; previous year's models are marked down as much as 25%, reducing a pair of Bauer blades from $230 to $175. They also have clothing, much of which again is clearance stuff at 25% to 85% off. Jerseys from $5, lycra shorts from $12, and more. Open seven days a week.

Natick Outdoor Store

- 38 North Ave., Natick; (508) 653-9400

Some friends of Mr. C who live in Natick—and who do a lot of camping and hiking—recommended this neighborhood store for price and quality. Calling itself "The biggest little sporting goods store in the world," Natick Outdoor does indeed have competitive prices on everything from horseshoe sets to kayaks; no matter how big or small your appetite for the great outdoors, they've got you covered.

Speaking of which, there are also tents and sleeping bags, parkas and raingear, shoes and boots, fishing gear, and just about anything else you can think of. Friendly, expert help, too. Open seven days, including

Thursdays and Fridays until 9.

National Ski & Bike

- 102 Washington St., South
  Attleboro; (508) 761-4500

Walk into National Ski & Bike and
head straight upstairs. That's where
they've put their bargain "basement"
(??), filled with closeouts and discontinued models. A Raleigh mountain
bike with a retail price of $319 was
already a deal at $260; it became a
steal upstairs, where it was reduced
to $219. In-line skates by Roller-
blade, retail $150, were seen for
$119.99 here. During a summer visit,
the place was filled with hundreds of
pairs of ski boots at off-season prices.
A pair by Salomon, $235 retail, were
just $99. It pays to think ahead!

If you're looking for low-priced
sporting equipment, this place is
worth a trip from anywhere. Open
Mondays through Fridays, 10 A.M. to
8 P.M.; Saturdays, 10-6, and Sundays,
12-5.

Play It Again Sports

- 626 Washington St. (Rte. 1),
  Dedham; (617) 320-8114
- 62 East Montvale Ave., Stoneham;
  (617) 438-2399

From humble beginnings in Minneapolis, this has grown into a national
chain of some 400 stores—all buying, selling, and trading new and
used sports equipment. The merchandise gets swapped around between
stores, ensuring a large, balanced selection in every store.

PIAS also gets good deals on new
items that have been discontinued
(but hey, how much can a football
change?). Among these, Mr. C saw
an Alpine Tracker exercise machine,
reduced from $160 retail to a *svelte*
$99.95. A pair of Ultra Wheels in-
line skates were $25 off at $150. And
a Mizuno baseball mitt, worth over
$100, was selling here for $59.

About 60% of the stock consists
of used equipment. Seen recently
were a boy's mountain bike for
$69.95, a pair of K2 downhill skis for
$89.95, billiard cues from $11.95,
and a set of Tommy Armour golf
irons, valued at $1,000, selling for

$399. Plus hockey sticks, basketballs,
baseball bats, shoulder pads for line-
backers of all ages, tennis racquets,
and lots more. Best of all, you can
trade in your old stuff toward anything in the store—even new items.
Open seven days, including Tuesdays
and Thursdays until 9 P.M.

The Ski Warehouse

- 372 Main St., Watertown; (617)
  924-4643

Having moved recently to a new location ("in the basement—like our
prices"), Ski Warehouse sells new,
discounted ski and tennis equipment;
these are mainly closeouts and discontinued items, as much as 50% to
even 70% off of retail prices. Thus, a
tennis racquet that might have listed
for $200 can be found here for
$109—strung and ready to serve.
Owner Hans Track tries to focus on a
few good brands, rather than the selection of a department store; tennis
names include Prince, Head, and
Wilson.

All this, coupled with expert
knowledge and a sense of humor,
makes the store a find. In late summer, they usually hold a "Practically
Giving It Away" ski equipment sale.
Open weekdays from 12-8 P.M., Saturdays from 12-5; summer hours can
be looser, so you may want to call
ahead.

Sports Replay

- 860 Commonwealth Ave., Boston;
  (617) 731-9128

Located in a basement around the corner from the Ski Market, Sports Replay is the clearance store for all the
equipment that people trade in upstairs and at the other Ski Markets.
This varies according to the season
but generally includes bicycles, tennis racquets, and lots of skiing stuff,
all at 30% to 50% below retail.

Used ski equipment includes racks
and racks of boots, like Nordica 997
rear-entry boots, originally $300,
now $189; or Lang front entry boots
for $79, down from $189. Lots of
boots for kids, from $19.95, and
plenty of skis for all. The adult boot
selection includes fantastic closeout

deals on new models by Tecnica, Rossignol, and Nordica.

Bicycles on display during Mr. C's visit included a Mountain Tek, once $250, here $140. Plus safety helmets for $20. Tennis racquets start from about $50; and there are lots of accessories for all sports, from sunglasses to ski socks.

You can buy, trade in, or swap most equipment. Used items are not guaranteed, but Sports Replay does its own servicing and will try to fix anything within a reasonable period of time. Open seven days, including weeknights 'til 8 P.M.

The Thrifty Sport
• 520 Providence Hwy. (Rte. 1), Norwood; (617) 762-6266

If it's exercise equipment you crave, but your bank account is no more bulked up than you are, come see Rich and Mark. This truly no-frills operation sells new and nearly-new treadmills, exercise bicycles, and workout stations; most are commercial-grade name brands.

A Lifecycle 9000 bike, for example—just as you'd see in health clubs—sells for about $2,000 new; a used model was seen here for $700. A brand-new Alpine Tracker, with a list price of $259, was seen for $199, while used Alpine steppers start around $60. And Rich told Mr. C the tragic tale of a man who bought his son a $3,200 Paramount four-station fitness machine, only to see it go untouched; four months old with nary a scratch, it was selling here for $2,000.

Equipment is not warrantied by the store, although everything is checked over, and many new-ish items still carry a transferable manufacturer's plan. Finding the place is as tricky as it is thrifty; it's located at the rear of an undistinguished building on Route 1. Look for the sign on a truck parked out front. Open daily, except on Sundays in summer.

Here are some more chains and superstores to equip you weekend warriors:

Nevada Bob's Discount Golf
• 2 Liberty Sq., Boston; (617) 695-1971
• 1374 Washington St., Hanover; (617) 826-4448
• Lyman, Westborough; (508) 870-0520
• 87 Providence Hwy., Westwood; (617) 461-0750
• 425 Washington St., Woburn; (508) 932-3900

Sports Authority
• 100 Independence Way, Danvers; (508) 774-9400
• Shoppers World (Rte. 9), Framingham; (508) 620-2271
• Worcester Common Fashion Outlets, Worcester; (508) 755-2770

STATIONERY, OFFICE, AND ART SUPPLIES

Pearl Art and Craft Supplies
• 579 Massachusetts Ave., Cambridge; (617) 547-6600

Mr. C thinks of Pearl, one of the country's leading art supply houses, as an artist's department store. They seem to sell everything under the sun, for every kind of craftsperson; whether you want to decorate a blank canvas or a cake, you can get the materials here, all at discount.

Staedtler "Mars Graphic" pens retail for $2.49 each, but sell here for $1.99. A 50-yard roll of Pearl's own tracing paper was $13.08, better than half off the retail price of other brands. In the paints section, you'll see names like Rembrandt, Holbein, and Liquitex; when Mr. C stopped in, a 250ml bottle of Pebeo acrylic paint was reduced from $14 to $8.37. You'll also find clay, gesso, inks, the works.

Look downstairs for ready-made canvases, frames, and the easels to support them. A large Standrite aluminum easel was seen for a low $79. Surround your masterpiece with a gilt frame for $15.35, ten bucks below retail; or, to carry the finished products around, there is a whole portfolio of portfolios, all at discounted prices.

But Pearl appeals to Martha Stewart-types as well. Create a throw pillow with a Bucilla needlepoint kit for $20, or go solo with DMC tapestry wool, a nine-yard skein for 60¢. A seemingly endless supply of beads will let you make all the jewelry you can wear. And big blocks of Fimo clay are under two dollars each.

And, since you're never too old to learn more—or just get started—Pearl also has an extensive collection of art guidebooks and manuals, and some art biographies and travel guides on the shelves, too. All of these are sold at 20% off the cover price. Get the picture? Pearl is open seven days a week, including evenings.

Of course, sometimes you've just got to have fifty-seven cases of paper clips . . .

OfficeMax
- 125 Pearl St., Braintree; (617) 356-5990
- 395 Westgate Dr., Brockton; (508) 583-2990
- 34 Cambridge St., Burlington; (617) 270-4477
- 8-10 Newbury St. (Rte. 1), Danvers; (508) 777-5152
- 820 Providence Hwy. (Rte. 1), Dedham; (617) 329-1667
- 8 Allstate Rd., Dorchester; (617) 445-5152
- 1300 Worcester St., (Rte. 9), Natick; (508) 650-0346
- 1069 Broadway (Rte. 1), Saugus; (617) 233-5763
- 14 McGrath Hwy., Somerville; (617) 625-7516

Staples
- 1249 Boylston St., Boston; (617) 353-1332
- 25 Court St., Boston; (617) 367-1747
- 31 Milk St., Boston; (617) 338-6801

- 757 Gallivan Blvd., Dorchester; (617) 436-0933
- 1660 Soldiers Field Rd., Brighton; (617) 254-3351
- 111 Middlesex Tpke, Burlington; (617) 221-4610
- 160 Alewife Brook Pkwy., Cambridge; (617) 547-2660
- 301 Newbury St., Danvers; (508) 777-9400
- 100 Pennsylvania Ave., Framingham; (508) 370-8500
- 282 Mystic Ave, Medford; (617) 395-8269
- 549 Worcester Rd., Natick; (508) 651-1515
- 210 Needham St., Newton; (617) 630-0682
- 444 Broadway, Saugus; (617) 231-0013
- 1070 Lexington St., Waltham; (617) 647-4846
- 120 Main St., Weymouth; (617) 340-6610
- 335 Washington St., Woburn; (617) 932-4132

TOYS AND GAMES

FuncoLand

- 518 Geneva Ave., Dorchester; (617) 282-4049
- 117 Pearl St., Braintree; (617) 849-1711
- 200 Westgate Dr., Brockton; (508) 559-1710
- 101 Middlesex Tpke., Burlington; (617) 229-8676
- 1298 Worcester Rd. (Rte. 9), Natick; (508) 655-488
- 300 Andover St., Peabody; (508) 532-5511
- 741 Broadway (Rte. 1), Saugus; (617) 233-6652

Can't keep the kids in computer games? It's an expensive little habit, but there *is* a way to beat the system at its own game. The trick is to go with *used* software. Hey, why not— after all, how long would your child let a new game sit in the box anyway?

This national chain, based in Minneapolis, buys and sells games for Nintendo, Sega Genesis, Gameboy, and other formats, as well as the actual systems and accessories. Given their popularity, the stock of titles is enormous—it fills several pages of tiny type in a sort of catalog/flyer, which lists the names and prices that may be available at any branch. Of course, availability changes all the time, so not every title you see listed will be in any one store.

The prices themselves, though below retail, are like those for baseball cards or anything else on the collectibles market; they vary according to each game's popularity, supply, and demand. Mr. C conducted a direct study, comparing the prices of games at random with those at a well-known national toy discounter. In most cases, the savings were good to excellent. *Zelda*, for instance, seen for $30 new in the standard Nintendo format, was also spotted for $8 at FuncoLand. A Sega Genesis version

of *Roger Clemens' Baseball* threw a strike at $44, a savings of $16 off the department store.

You can also save money on used and reconditioned joysticks, power supplies, carrying cases, and other accessories, depending on stock; or, if your system is out-of-date, upgrade it here instead of tossing it out. Everything comes with a 90-day warranty, and you can always try out any games or equipment before purchasing. And you can sell them your old games too, for payment by check or store credit. Again governed by supply and demand, the amount paid out for certain games may be a small fraction of its original price; you'll get more, by the way, if you opt for store credit.

You'll love Funco because of the prices; your kids will love it because it's the modern version of a candy store, complete with several screens available for play. Considering how quickly the novelty wears off on some of these games, the concept of paying less up front—and selling them off at the other end—may be the best way to score a win. Open seven days a week, including weeknights.

The Holt Educational Outlet

- 237 Riverview Ave., Waltham; (617) 647-0396

Talk about buried treasure. The Holt Company markets educational toys, books, and art supplies to schools, children's museums, and the like; but on Thursdays, Fridays, and Saturdays, you can go in there and shop at the same discounted prices.

And remember, "educational" doesn't have to mean "no fun." Save money on Lego building block sets of all sizes; Playmobil cars and trucks; books like the "Curious George," "Madeleine," and the "Anti-

Coloring Book" series; and all kinds of arts and crafts stuff. One special during Mr. C's recent visit was the "Electronic GeoSafari" game, created by National Geographic, on sale at $69.95 from a list price of $100.

The award-winning Brio line of wooden train track sets are all discounted by 20% from the list prices; same for all Crayola products. All "Thomas the Tank Engine" toys are 15% off. In fact, everything in this vast store is at least 10% off; and don't miss the clearance shelves, where items from books to binoculars to tempera paints are all half-price.

You can also save on school desks and chairs, globes, dictionaries, thesauruses—and for that matter, dinosauruses too. The store is open on the days noted above, from 9 A.M. to 5 P.M.

Pandemonium Books & Games

- 36 J.F.K. St., Cambridge; (617) 547-3721

This store is a mecca for fantasy and science-fiction fans—who love a bargain just as much as the rest of us. Pandemonium has all the popular fantasy magazines and games at list prices; more unusual, they have the only *secondhand* game selection Mr. C has found in the area. Poke around, and you'll see recent and older titles, all in good condition—like an "Advanced Dungeons and Dragons 'Dark Sun'" boxed set for $9.95, and an older "Ravenloft" set for $8.95. These go for $25-$30 new. Used

---

MR. CHEAP'S PICK
Toys and Games

✔ **The Holt Educational Outlet**—Wholesaler's discounts to the public on Brio, Crayola, Playmobil, and even Thomas the Tank Engine.

---

game accessories and books are $1.95 and up.

In addition, the store sells new and used books: Hardcovers (with a few exceptions) are sold at 15% off the cover price. New paperbacks are full price—but for better deals, check out the used books which go for as little as 95¢, and seldom more than $2.95. Used hardcover titles are $2.50 and up.

The staff knows its universes, and they encourage browsing. Any customer who spends $25 or more gets a 10% discount; die-hard enthusiasts can join the store's club, in which annual dues of $5 entitle you to a 15% discount on all purchases. And finally, you can sell off your own used games and books. If only D & D could have as many winners! Located in the Garage mall in Harvard Square, Pandemonium is open Mondays through Saturdays from 10 A.M. to 9 P.M.; Sundays from 12-6 P.M.

And when your kids yearn to roam freely across seventeen aisles of the latest action figures and computer games . . .

Kaybee Toy & Hobbie Shop

- 51 Dodge St., Beverly; (508) 922-5616
- 250 Granite St., Braintree; (617) 843-1184
- Burlington Mall, Burlington; (617) 273-3867
- CambridgeSide Galleria, Cambridge; (617) 494-8519
- Liberty Tree Mall, Danvers; (508) 777-9178
- 300 V.F.W. Pkwy., Dedham; (617) 329-4441
- Mystic Valley Pkwy., Medford; (617) 395-0132
- 635 Broadway (Rte. 1), Saugus; (617) 231-5760
- 133 Middlesex Ave., Somerville; (617) 625-9937
- Redstone Plaza, Stoneham; (617) 438-7986

- 90 Boston Providence Hwy. (Rte. 1), Walpole; (508) 668-8169
- 1100 Lexington St., Waltham; (617) 893-2445
- 485 Arsenal St., Watertown; (617) 923-1059

Toys "R" Us

- 105 Campanelli Dr., Brockton; (508) 584-8697
- 160 Alewife Brook Pkwy., Cambridge; (617) 576-8697
- 10 Providence Hwy. (Rte. 1), Dedham; (617) 329-4924

- 14 Allstate Rd., Dorchester; (617) 445-5159
- 1 Worcester Rd. (Rte. 9), Framingham; (508) 872-6242
- 630 Fellsway, Medford; (617) 396-6885
- Northshore Shopping Center, Peabody; (508) 532-0978
- Northgate Shopping Center, Revere; (617) 289-1181
- 366 Cambridge Rd., Woburn; (617) 935-7654

UNUSUAL GIFTS

Afro-Caribbean Arts Etc.

- 248 Elm St., Somerville; (617) 628-5215

This unique Davis Square store dares to make the promise that "Everyone saves. Guaranteed." To this, Mr. C adds the guarantee that these trinkets are sure to be well-appreciated. ACA's owner estimates that 90% of the stock is handmade, so no one is likely to show up with the same gift—that is, unless they've also read this book.

Lots of bright, patterned, and tie-dyed clothing here, like a sundress for $30. Accessorize with a brilliantly colored, woven belt for $12; same price for a straw "Kenya bag." To complete the outfit, add some handsome jewelry: The walls are lined with strands of beads, priced from $6 for hand-painted wooden necklaces. A silver and turquoise necklace was seen on sale for $12, down from $19, and huge sterling silver hoop earrings were just $15.

You can dress up your home just as well. Decorative statues, carvings, and boxes represent many different African cultures. Mr. C noticed a carved wooden box shaped like a turtle ($10) as well as small gourds handpainted to look like tiny people (from $9). Mahogany masks, carved into lifelike expressions, can grace

your walls for as little as $20. Some stuff is solidly practical as well as beautiful, like mahogany bowls for $7 and up. Open every day except Sunday.

Annie's Country Store

- 51 South Main St., Natick; (508) 655-1882

Well, Natick ain't exactly the country, and you won't find any duffers a-settin' around the cracker barrel here. But you can get popcorn or an old-fashioned slush, while perusing all sorts of cute folk crafts. And they do have barrels of penny candy—even if it does cost 3¢ nowadays. Inflation.

Annie and Diane keep the shop filled with an assortment of artsy items; on a recent visit, Mr. C found pins made out of jigsaw puzzle pieces glued on top of each other, for $4; unusually shaped glass jars filled with red, white, and blue layers of jelly beans (President Ronnie would be thrilled), $5; intricate dried flower wreaths for $15; plus teddy bears, country-style pillows and tablecloths, and tiny hand-carved wooden trucks.

There are also lots of gourmet food items, perfect for gift-giving, which feel elegant but will not break the bank. Jars of spicy orange mustard, pepper jelly (!), and such cost as little as $2.50 each—and the folks here will even wrap them in colored tissue paper for you at no extra charge.

Stop in and set a spell. Open every day but Sunday, from 9:30 A.M. 'til whenever—lazily enough, the sign in the window leaves this blank.

Cambridge Artists Cooperative
- 59A Church St., Cambridge; (617) 868-4434

Among the many fine crafts in this beautiful Harvard Square shop are cases of "wearable art"—rings, pins, earrings, necklaces, and other unique jewelry. Each display is by a different artist (some 200 in all), complete with a description of his or her technique. The member artists also run the store, which helps keep costs down.

Sure, you *can* buy jewelry for less, but these prices are excellent for such high quality—and the fact that no one else will ever have a piece that looks exactly like yours. Perhaps you'll pick a pair of brightly colored ceramic fish earrings for $15, graceful sterling silver rings for $35, or large, hammered bronze earrings for $24.

Not to mention wild ceramic housewares, clocks, prints, hand-painted silk ties, and more. The collections are ever-changing, and are just plain fun to browse; there are two floors' worth, plus a third level with a free gallery, which hosts shows about four times a year. The co-op is open daily from 10 A.M. to 6 P.M., Thursdays until 8, and Sundays from 12-5.

Dapy
- Prudential Center, 800 Boylston St., Boston; (617) 236-0482

From Paris to New York's Soho and now Boston, this delightful boutique has made it possible for full-grown adults to play with the silliest of toys (why, complete strangers may even find themselves *talking* to each other!). Dapy specializes in the latest in wacky gadgetry—sort of a high-tech joke shop.

A seemingly harmless hand mirror, for example, starts laughing hysterically when you pick it up and look at your reflection. At $10, it's a

---

MR. CHEAP'S PICKS
Unusual Gifts

- ✔ **Gateway Crafts**—Beautiful and often humorous crafts, made by developmentally disabled artisans.

- ✔ **Gourmet Pottery**—Gorgeous creations, made on the spot. *That's* factory-direct!

- ✔ **Scribble It**—Have your kids' names painted right on these bright and colorful toys, at no extra charge.

---

unique gift—or something to leave around the bathroom for unsuspecting guests. For the same price, you can get a brightly colored ball that manically rolls and lurches around—all by itself.

More sedate, but equally offbeat items include salt and pepper shakers in the shape of the Tower of Pisa (they lean, but don't fall over; $12). Just $3.99 buys a birthday cake candle that plays "Happy Birthday" when you light it—or a set of glow-in-the-dark stars that stick to your bedroom ceiling. More expensive are the lava lamps, "diner" style wall clocks, fish-shaped mailboxes, and other exotic goodies. Don't forget to check the clearance area at the back, where items are reduced by 25%.

And Dapy has those little tin cans that "moo" when you turn them upside down; technology is fine, but some things will never go away. Open seven days and evenings a week, during regular mall hours.

Elements
- 18-20 Union Park St., Boston; (617) 451-9990
- 276 Newbury St., Boston; (617) 437-0319
- 60 School St., Boston; (617) 227-0005

For unique, handcrafted jewelry at prices you can afford, this is a refreshing alternative in some otherwise expensive parts of town. From its South End warehouse, Elements distributes jewelry, ceramics, glassware, clocks, mirrors, and other kinds of eye-catching decorative items. Some are made by the company right there; other pieces are handmade by local artisans. Many can be seen in fancy boutiques and catalogs at much higher prices, like the "cow" shaped coffee mug that was $18 in the Museum of Fine Arts shop, but half that price here.

Starting from that one original store, Elements has become a small chain (sorry, Cheapsters, no pun intended) and a big success story. The Union Park branch is closed in summer; otherwise, all stores are open seven days a week.

Flyrabbit

- 155 Harvard Ave., Allston; (617) 782-1313

Flyrabbit puts a different spin on the funky nostalgia for which this area is well-known. It's devoted to the old-time knick-knacks that kids grew up with during the '50s and '60s, along with more contemporary kitsch. Remember "Magic Rocks," which grew into a colorful display in your fish tank? Flyrabbit's got 'em, the real thing, only $4 a pack. Tiny plastic monsters are a mere fifty cents each. And 3-D postcards, in a range of subjects from raunchy to religious, go for two bucks a pop.

If you're looking for something a bit nicer, there are items by local artists, such as handmade candles ($10); recycled-paper stationery with silk-screened designs of various animals ($8); and sets of strung lights in the shapes of little cars (they're not just for Christmas anymore), $17 for a set of ten. Plus T-shirts, artsy greeting cards for all occasions, and a wild range of underground 'zines and books. Open Tuesdays through Saturdays from 11 A.M. to 7 P.M., and Sundays from noon to 5 P.M.; be sure to wear your patchouli oil.

Gateway Crafts

- 62 Harvard St., Brookline; (617) 734-1577

Gateway Crafts is a combination workshop and store, humming with activity and sparkling with handmade jewelry and ceramics. It's part of a state-funded program for the developmentally disabled, who create these wares and get the satisfaction of seeing them sold (as well as a portion of the profits). The designs are sophisticated, colorful, and often spiced with a sense of humor.

On top of all that, the prices are terrific. Bead necklaces, strung with offbeat shapes, start from just $12; funky collage pins, in iridescent colors, are $7. Put one on your dress or lapel—these eye-catching works could easily have come from a ritzy Soho boutique for twice as much.

Handsome chenille scarves, hand-loomed in the shop (you can watch these folks making them!) are attractively priced from $22. Same price for some rather whimsical wall clocks, and ceramic butter trays in the shapes of animals are $20. Hand-painted T-shirts are $10 to $15, and similarly decorated duffel bags—for the gym, laundry, whatever—are $12. Plus a large selection of terrific cards to go with these gifts, most under a dollar.

Recently, Gateway expanded its space and added an art gallery, showing works by other local artists. It's an amazing place. Open weekdays from 9 A.M. to 4:30 P.M. and Saturdays from 11 A.M. to 3 P.M.

Gourmet Pottery

- 327 Watertown St., Newton; (617) 965-0028

For some fifteen years, ceramic artist Dinny Myerson has been filling this tiny shop with beautiful and functional crafts. You can often catch her spinning her potter's wheel behind the counter. Talk about factory-direct!

The prices are accordingly inexpensive for this kind of high-quality work. Most of these items are around $20 or less. Handsome coffee mugs are $12 each, while larger bowls are

$15 and up. Or, for just $8, you can get an "egg separator": It's a cup with a smiling face carved out of one side, and when you tip it, the white pours out while the yolk stays in. Neat, huh?

There are some larger items; a handmade bowl, decorated with the names of your favorite newlyweds, can be ordered as a wedding gift ($65). Plus hanging planters, table lamps, and some items made by outside artists—photo frames, earrings, funny refrigerator magnets, and colorful glass "sun catchers" for your window.

Dinny herself favors rich blues and purples, along with natural earth tones. It's gorgeous stuff, and fun to buy from the actual artist. They'll also wrap anything up here with multicolored ribbons, and they have greeting cards handmade by local artists. Open daily from 10 A.M. to 5:30 or 6:30 P.M., and Sundays from 12-5, except in summer. Extra hours are added around Christmastime.

The Judaica Warehouse
• 4 Porter St., Stoughton; (617) 341-4460

This tiny little store adjacent to the Stoughton commuter rail station is crammed from floor to ceiling, and wall to wall, with everything in Judaica—all at discount. Seder plates, candlesticks, holiday decorations, *bar/bat mitzah* gifts, and more are all here in abundance. It's quite an experience just to poke around.

The Judaica Warehouse is *the* place to go if you're in the market for Jewish-themed invitations of all kinds. Judy, the owner, does the design personally and works hard to get

you the best stationery at the lowest possible prices. And then she discounts them. *Dayenu!* Hours vary widely, but these include at least one evening per week. Invitation consults are by appointment only.

Scribble It
• 50 Winchester St., Newton; (617) 964-9897

Here's a store packed with fun toys and gifts for children of all ages. Though this isn't a discounter, many items are low-priced; but that's not the real attraction for Mr. C. Everything you see can be colorfully handpainted with your child's name (or anyone's) at no extra charge. Now, *that's unique!*

Pick out a clear-plastic "lunch box," filled with candy and wrapped with a bow, for $10. A large wooden coat rack in the shape of any initial is $25. For just $5, you can get a ceramic piggy bank in the shape of a high-top sneaker. Same price for a set of 64 crayons, in a colorful carry pail, or an oversized plastic hanger (flat, of course, so it can be inscribed).

Scribble It can offer this extra service by having full-time artists on the premises. For an extra fee, more elaborate designs can be added. Most items can be personalized within a few days, but the nice folks here will try to accommodate rush jobs. The store even keeps index cards which track gifts purchased for local kids, so you won't run the risk of duplication; after all, it's hard to return a lunch box with "Brandon" painted on it.

The store is open weekdays from 10 A.M. to 5:30 P.M., and Saturdays from 10-5 ('til 3 in summer).

ENTERTAINMENT

Boston has so much to see and do, and it seems there is more coming along all the time. Lots of entertainment is inexpensive and often free. Movies, concerts, theater, museums, nightclubs . . . you name it, there's a way to experience it on the cheap.

Nearly everything in this section of the book is free, or only a few bucks; in some cases, Mr. C has found activities that are a bit more expensive, but discounted from their full prices. No matter what Jesse Helms says, there is no reason why a limited budget should keep anyone from enjoying the arts.

ARTS AND CULTURAL CENTERS

These centers are great places for a variety of fun and inexpensive activities—whether you're just viewing, or actually participating. Many of the programs and classes are designed for adults, children, or both.

Boston Center for the Arts

- 539 Tremont St., Boston; (617) 426-7700

The BCA comprises several red-brick buildings in the now-fashionable part of the South End. The area has really come on in the last few years, laced with *chic* bistros, antique shops, and hair salons. In summer, the kiosk in front of the BCA serves snacks and beverages, with tables and chairs on the open plaza.

There are three different theater spaces here: The BCA Theater, the Black Box Theater, and the Leland Center. These are of the small and minimalistic variety—thus, well-suited to experimental works. Many of the city's most creative troupes, which cannot afford theaters of their own, rent the place out for productions which may run for a night, a weekend, or a month. Such ensembles have presented everything from Ibsen dramas to the latest gay political themes. Ticket prices are generally in the $10-$15 range, sometimes even less.

To one side is the historic **Cyclorama**, built in the 19th century to house a giant mural-in-the-round commemorating the Civil War. Today, this vast space hosts such prestigious exhibits as the annual Boston Drawing Show (usually in the fall), as well as occasional modern dance performances, and the fund-raising "Artist's Ball" gala each spring. When exhibits are running, gallery hours are weekdays from 9 A.M. to 5 P.M., and weekends from 1-4 P.M.

To the other side of the BCA Theater is the **Mills Gallery** (telephone 426-8835), which shows the work of artists whose studios are in the building upstairs. Painting, sculpture, and video installations have filled this space, which is open Wednesdays through Sundays from 1-4 P.M., as well as Thursday through Saturday evenings from 7-10. The Mills often hosts a free discussion by the artists during each exhibit, as well as your basic wine-and-cheese openings, all of which are open to the public. Check newspaper listings or call the events line (above) to see what's currently happening at this busy place.

Boston Public Library

- Copley Square, Boston; (617) 536-5400

Mr. C *loves* libraries. First of all, you can borrow books, cassettes, records, and videotapes—all free of charge. But the big news at the library is all the other stuff—wonderful free events of all kinds.

The BPL's large Rabb Lecture Hall is the site of free lectures, from "The Boston Sports Scene" to "Images of Violence in Our Society" and "Planning Your Retirement." The Rabb Lecture Hall is also the place to see movies for free, usually on Monday afternoons and evenings. Each month has a theme; recent series have included a tribute to Frank Capra and movies "Made in Massachusetts." The library's senior citizens club, the "Never Too Late Group," also shows weekly films. There are exercise classes, writing workshops, story hours for kids, and book discussion groups. Stop in for a schedule of events.

And, don't forget the BPL for art! In addition to contemporary painting and photography exhibits in its Great

Hall, venture upstairs in the old building for everything from American artists' self-portraits to early baseball
photos to rare manuscripts. Look for
giant murals by John Singer Sargent
on the hallway walls. If you want to
more fully appreciate the building's
art and architecture, take a tour! See
the listing under "Walks and Tours."

Many of the programs offered at
the main BPL are also available at
the numerous branches around the
city. Call or stop into the one nearest
you for more information.

- **North End**, 25 Parmenter St.,
  Boston; (617) 227-8135
- **South End**, 685 Tremont St.,
  Boston; (617) 536-8241
- **West End**, 151 Cambridge St.,
  Boston; (617) 523-3957
- **Brighton**, 40 Academy Hill Rd.,
  Brighton; (617) 782-6032.
- **Faneuil**, 419 Faneuil St., Brighton;
  (617) 782-6705
- **Charlestown**, 179 Main St.,
  Charlestown; (617) 242-1248
- **Adams Street**, 690 Adams St.,
  Dorchester; (617) 436-6900
- **Codman Square**, 690 Washington
  St., Dorchester; (617) 436-8214
- **Fields Corner**, 1520 Dorchester
  Ave., Dorchester; (617) 436-2155.
- **Lower Mills**, 27 Richmond St.,
  Dorchester; (617) 298-7841
- **Mattapan**, 10 Hazelton St.,
  Dorchester; (617) 298-9218
- **Uphams Corner**, 500 Columbia
  Rd., Dorchester; (617) 265-0139
- **East Boston**, 276 Meridian St.,
  East Boston; (617) 569-0271
- **Orient Heights**, 18 Barnes Ave.,
  East Boston; (617) 567-2516
- **Hyde Park**, 35 Harvard Ave.,
  Hyde Park; (617) 361-2524
- **Connolly**, 433 Centre St., Jamaica
  Plain, (617) 522-1960
- **Jamaica Plain**, 12 Sedgwick St.,
  Jamaica Plain; (617) 524-2053
- **Dudley Street**, 65 Warren St.,
  Roxbury; (617) 442-6186
- **Egleston Square**, 2044 Columbus
  Ave., Roxbury; (617) 445-4340
- **Grove Hall**, 5 Crawford St.,
  Roxbury; (617) 427-3337
- **Parker Hill**, 1497 Tremont St.,
  Roxbury; (617) 427-3820

- **South Boston**, 646 East Broadway,
  South Boston; (617) 268-0180
- **Washington Village**, 1226
  Columbia Rd., South Boston; (617)
  269-7239
- **Roslindale**, 4238 Washington St.,
  West Roxbury; (617) 323-2343
- **West Roxbury**, 1961 Centre St.,
  West Roxbury; (617) 325-3147.

Cambridge Center for Adult Education

- 56 Brattle St., Cambridge; (617)
  547-6789

The Cambridge Center for Adult Education offers classes on every con-
ceivable topic, from architecture to
yoga. But you don't have to take a
class to benefit from the educational
riches here. First, CCAE sponsors lectures on a range of seemingly endless
topics. Hear world travelers recount
their experiences in remote lands.
Learn about meditation, the psychology of relationships, and even how to
bargain hunt in major outlets! Admission to most lectures is $2, and $1 for
seniors.

Among its many music programs,
the "Music for a Thursday Evening"
series offers classical, folk, and jazz
concerts each Thursday at 8 P.M. during the spring and fall. These feature
local artists in ensembles and solo.
Tickets are $5 at the door or in ad-
vance. There's also theater, with tickets usually $10 to $12.

Finally, the "Blacksmith House Poetry Series" features poetry and prose
readings by local writers. These take
place on Monday evenings at 8:15
P.M.; admission is $3, and $2 for seniors and students. For more information about all Cambridge Center
events and classes, call for a copy of
the catalog.

Cambridge Multicultural Arts Center

- 41 Second St., Cambridge; (617)
  577-1400

Right near the courthouse in East
Cambridge, CMAC offers a wide variety of visual and performing arts—
dance, theater, music, and art
exhibits. With a dedication to multicultural programming, this can

mean a gospel tribute, a traditional Mexican fiesta, or a modern dance concert. Ticket prices vary, but are rarely more than $12, and many events are free. Gallery hours are from 9 A.M. to 5 P.M. Mondays through Fridays.

The Firehouse Center for the Performing and Visual Arts

• Market Square, Newburyport; (508) 462-7336

This 300-year old firehouse, renovated top to bottom in 1991, is home to one of the North Shore's leading arts centers—boasting a professional theater space, two art galleries, and a restaurant. The Firehouse Center schedules a full calendar of dance, music, comedy, theater, and literary events. Ticket prices range from $8 to $16, with a few free presentations tossed in.

What impresses Mr. C most is the diversity of the offerings. A recent season featured the Bennington Marionettes performing *Sorcerer's Circus*, the North Shore Light Opera presenting Gilbert and Sullivan's *HMS Pinafore*, an evening of sketch comedy with Little City Comedy Company, and a performance by Exit Dance Theater. Did Mr. C mention Italian opera with Connecticut Opera Express, a reading by writer Jan Waldron, lectures by the Newburyport Historical Society, and monthly art exhibits featuring local and regional artists—to name but a few? Whew. Also unusual for a community arts center, activities are available almost daily. At the street level, Ciro's offers fine Italian dining with views of the river.

The French Library and Cultural Center

• 53 Marlborough St., Boston; (617) 266-4351

The French Library offers lectures, films, and language instruction, and cooking classes for the Francophiles among us. Lovers of French film will want to check out the Cine Club, which offers films in French (with English subtitles) every Thursday and Friday at 8 P.M. Classic and current

cinema from the folks who invented the New Wave. Admission is $5, and $4 for members; or get a book of ten for $35. On Wednesday afternoons they offer free video screenings.

Topics from world travel to French cooking are presented in regular lectures at this elegant Back Bay center. Some are given in French, some in English. Most lectures are free to the public, though reservations are recommended; receptions follow the talks. The French Library also sponsors several music series, including a jazz series.

While visiting, don't miss the art gallery with its regular exhibitions of paintings and photography by French and American artists. The library is open Tuesdays from noon to 8 P.M., Wednesdays through Saturdays from 10 A.M. to 5 P.M., and until 8 P.M. on Wednesday and Thursday evenings.

Jamaica Plain Firehouse Multicultural Art Center

• 659 Centre St., Jamaica Plain; (617) 524-3816

Dedicated to Latin American culture, the Firehouse pledges to get "the best artists in Jamaica Plain to show off their stuff"—and we all get to enjoy the results. Art exhibits may focus on a particular culture, or spotlight a single "emerging artist." Admission to the galleries is free; hours are Tuesdays through Fridays, from 11 A.M. to 4 P.M.

Join in the celebration with your ears as well as your eyes. Fall is festival time, when every week offers one or two concerts by the area's rich reserve of talented musicians. The music ranges from salsa to choral jazz; admission is either "pay what you can" or a small fee of $5 or so.

Other events include the annual "Comic Auction," held every November; no, they're not selling Spider-Man posters—this is a full-fledged auction run by comedians! Plus lectures, holiday events, family activities, and classes for children and adults. Most of these require admission or session fees, all very reasonably priced.

Leventhal-Sidman Jewish Community Center

- 333 Nahanton St., Newton; (617) 558-6484

The Leventhal-Sidman JCC is a hub for Boston's Jewish cultural activity. The Starr Gallery mounts regular art exhibitions relating to Jewish history or its cultural heritage; recently, works by contemporary painters looking back at the Holocaust, as well as an exhibit of postage stamps from that era, were on display. The interactive "A Walk Through Jerusalem," took you and your children to the Holy Land. Most of these shows are free; some do charge a small admission fee for non-members.

The center is also home to the **Jewish Theatre of New England**, which performs two professional shows a year, and hosts six other shows by other troupes. In any one season, you may revel to klezmer music, laugh at musical comedy revues, and enjoy thoughtful dramas. Ticket prices vary according to the show; it's usually between $10 and $20 for adults, a few bucks less for students and seniors. Season subscriptions cut costs further.

The Starr Gallery is open Sundays, Mondays and Thursdays from 10 A.M. to 4 P.M., and Fridays from 10 A.M. to 2 P.M. On Tuesday and Wednesday evenings, it's also open from 6 to 9 P.M.

The New Art Center in Newton

- 61 Washington Park, Newton; (617) 964-3424

Recently rechristened (some still know it as the Newton Arts Center), this handsome brownstone former church continues on as a temple to the arts, both viewed and practiced. Classes, taught by talented professionals, take place all year long, for both adults and children. There is a wide range of endeavors—from dance, acting, and comedy to sculpture, yoga, and even "Survival Skills for Artists." Fees vary by course; annual memberships include a 10% discount.

The performance space has also been a venue for everything from

---

MR. CHEAP'S PICKS
Arts and Cultural Centers

✔ **Boston Center for the Arts**—What makes the South End hip. Theaters, art galleries, dance performances, and more.

✔ **Boston Public Library**—There's a lot more here than books! The main branch in Copley Square has movies, lectures, and art exhibits, all free and open to everyone. Many of the outer branches have similar offerings.

---

classical music concerts to children's theater shows to improvisational comedy troupes. In addition, the NAC houses two art galleries, both of which present four shows per year (always running in tandem). Most feature artists from the Boston area; many are curated by local experts as well, who compete for the opportunity.

Gallery admission is usually free, though certain shows may charge a couple of dollars. Hours are generally Wednesdays through Fridays from 11 A.M. to 5 P.M., and weekends from 1-5. Exhibits do not run at all times of the year, so call ahead to confirm the current schedule.

Newton Free Library

- 330 Homer St., Newton; (617) 552-7145

Across the street from its town hall, Newton has a gorgeous new main library, which includes an art gallery and lecture hall. Speakers usually have a book to plug, but these have included such luminaries as Rep. Barney Frank, Pulitzer Prize-winning poet Maxine Kumin, and animator Janet Perlman, an Oscar nominee, showing and discussing her work. Lectures are free and open to all. The

Newton Free Library has an art gallery, with exhibits by local and regional artists.

In addition to these high-brow programs, the library also shows movies on Wednesday evenings at 7. You never know what they'll show (well, you do if you pick up a schedule), from the Marx Brothers to a documentary on Spike Lee to Zeffirelli's *Romeo and Juliet*. They also run a family matinee on the first Saturday of each month. All free.

Other town libraries run free film programs, and many colleges show pop movies in their campus centers, often open to the public for a small fee. Check the ones in your area.

The Strand Theater
- 543 Columbia Rd., Dorchester; (617) 282-8000

In the ethnically diverse, oft-ignored areas of Dorchester and Roxbury, finding quality arts programming can be a challenge. The Strand Theater is a real oasis, presenting music, dance, theater, and community outreach programs. Famous performers who've graced this stage include Dizzy Gillespie, Cab Calloway, and Melba Moore. Renowned troupes have included the Boys Choir of Harlem and Dance Umbrella.

Tickets can go as high as $15 to $20, but there are plenty of lower-priced events as well. And, in keeping with their mission to bring the arts to all, they offer a number of discount opportunities. Call the box office at 282-5230 for more info; the number above gives you a recording of upcoming events.

Zeiterion Theatre
- 684 Purchase St., New Bedford; (508) 994-2900

Opened as a vaudeville theater in the 1920s, the Zeiterion Theatre was soon taken over by that "new" art form—movies. In 1956, in fact, this was the site of the world premiere of *Moby Dick*—Melville's classic is set in New Bedford, after all—with star Gregory Peck in attendance. In the early '80s, the Zeiterion reclaimed its heritage as a venue for affordable, live performances of music, drama, and dance.

The diversity of offerings is impressive. Theater events include Broadway musicals, comedy, and opera; music programs include symphony concerts, folk, and gospel; and dancers from ballet to modern have traipsed across this stage. For all this, tickets can be as low as $8! What's more, Zeiterion has a unique subscription deal: Order tix for as few as *two* shows, and you get a discount on each ticket. The more you order, the bigger the discount. You see only the shows you want, and you don't have to wait in line.

Discounts are also offered for people on income assistance (food stamps, day care vouchers, and so on), senior citizens, and students. Group rates and subscription tix are available to all. And, Mr. C hasn't even *mentioned* the educational programs and community outreach activities. The Z's season runs from October through May. A summer series for young folks runs through July and August, with tickets $5 to $7.50.

ART GALLERIES

Most city dwellers know that browsing through art galleries is one of the truly enlightening and (best of all) free cultural activities around. For no more than the price of an espresso at a nearby cafe—you have to do that, right?—you can while away a fine afternoon or early evening.

Boston's galleries are concentrated into two centers: **Newbury Street**, of course, and the more recent enclave along **South Street**, near South Station. By the way, keep an eye out for **Art Newbury Street**, a Sunday afternoon event happening each spring and fall. The street is closed off to cars, and all the galleries put on their very best. Live music, balloons, face painting for the kiddies, etc.

Some galleries may require you to buzz in, only for security purposes. Don't fear that you're being kept out because of an annual income below that of, say, Ross Perot; go on in! After all, the richer people are, the less they have to care about their appearances—for all the gallery owners know, someone in torn jeans could be an eccentric millionaire. Be sure to sneer at one or two paintings, as though you *could* buy one if it were any good.

In addition to the two main districts, interesting galleries abound throughout the city. Here are a few of Mr. C's favorites:

Alon Gallery
- 1665A Beacon St., Brookline; (617) 232-3388

A small gallery and framing shop in Washington Square, with very impressive exhibits every month by Boston-area artists. Open Tuesdays through Saturdays from 10 to 6 P.M.

Cambridge Art Association
- 25 Lowell St., Cambridge; (617) 876-0246

Exhibitions by CAA members, as well as by members of other groups and individual artists. Painting, sculpture, crafts, jewelry, and more. Open Tuesday through Saturday afternoons.

Chapel Gallery
- 60 Highland St., Newton; (617) 244-4039

Or, more accurately, Boston Sculptors at Chapel Gallery. A co-operative society of some twenty local sculptors present their own works on a regular basis at this church. All are well-respected artists on the New England scene; many are graduates and/or instructors at the Museum School of the MFA. According to co-ordinator Anne McQueen, this is "an alternative venue for art that's not available through Boston's commercial centers." They're noted for their creative use of the large gallery space, often displaying works outdoors as well as in. No wonder the Chapel Gallery has made *The Boston*

Globe's "Ten Best in Visual Arts" roll call. The schedule also includes frequent gallery talks by the artists.

Exhibits usually change on a monthly basis, except in summer, when the gallery takes a hiatus; regular hours are Wednesdays through Sundays from 1 P.M. to 5:30 P.M.

Nearby, the **New Art Center in Newton** has two galleries of its own; see the listing under "Arts Centers."

Chinese Culture Institute
- 276 Tremont St., Boston; (617) 542-4599

This gallery and school next to the Wang Center specializes in folk art by Chinese and American artists. See rustic paintings, calligraphy and more. Open Tuesdays through Fridays, 9:30 A.M. to 5 P.M. On Saturdays, they sleep in 'til 10 A.M.

88 Room
- 107 Brighton Ave., Allston; (617) 562-0840

Upstairs in this "mall" of vintage clothing and funky specialty shops, the 88 Room has month-long exhibits of avant-garde paintings, photography, and installations. Also, periodic sales of "affordable art." Open Thursday and Friday evenings, and Saturday afternoons.

Genovese Gallery
- 535 Albany St., Boston; (617) 426-9738

Art galleries and industrial ware-

MR. CHEAP'S PICKS
Art Galleries

✔ **Mobius**—On the busy Fort Point Channel art scene, this collective charts the cutting edge.

✔ **The Society of Arts and Crafts**—Art that's as *functional* as it is beautiful.

✔ **Zeitgeist Gallery**—This progressive gallery really rocks. Literally.

houses just seem to go together, don't they? Genovese is located in that part of the South End near the expressway, along with auto body shops and flower distributors. Check it out for the latest work by American artists. They now have a gallery "annex" on South Street also. Hours are 10 A.M. to 5:30 P.M., Tuesdays through Fridays.

The Horn Gallery
• Babson College, Wellesley; (617) 239-4570

An art gallery inside a library, and at a business college to boot! The Horn Gallery is located in the entryway of Babson's Horn Library. Half a dozen exhibits go up every year, featuring works by area artists. Lots of photography here, as well as special shows like "The Building of Babson College," and exhibits to celebrate occasions like Black History Month. The gallery is open during the academic year only; hours are Mondays through Fridays, from 12 noon to 4 P.M.

Michael Beauchemin
• 63 Maverick Square, East Boston; (617) 567-0177

Talk about lowering the overhead: This gallery is actually located in the home of Michael Beauchemin. He represents new, young artists in a variety of media, including painting,

sculpture, and photography. His goal is to give underexposed Boston artists the break they need to get to the next level of their artistic career. For you, the bonus is getting a chance to see the future of art, today. Because this is a private home, gallery hours are limited to Saturdays from 11 A.M. to 7 P.M., or by appointment.

Mobius
• 354 Congress St., Fifth Floor, Boston; (617) 542-7416

Down a bit from the Children's Museum, Mobius is a collective of many different kinds of artists: They work in painting, sculpture, graphics, theater, sound, and more. Exhibits here are often environmental installations combining several of these, including performance. There's a lot going on all the time; it's always challenging and offbeat, and sometimes humorous. The gallery is open Tuesdays through Saturdays from noon to 5 P.M., along with evening performance times. Call them for a schedule.

Photographic Resource Center
• 602 Commonwealth Ave., Boston; (617) 353-0700

On the campus of Boston University, this gallery offers month-long exhibits, often on controversial subjects such as AIDS and Vietnam. The gallery does charge admission: $3 general, $2 for students and seniors. Open Tuesdays through Sundays from noon to 5 P.M., and Thursday evenings until 8 P.M. PRC is on an academic schedule, so they close in the summer.

Piano Factory Gallery
• 791 Tremont St., Boston; (617) 437-9365

Converted from an actual piano factory, this large South End building now houses low-cost studios and apartments for artists. Work by different residents is always on display in the gallery, open Fridays from 6 to 9 P.M., Saturdays and Sundays from 2 to 6 P.M.

Richardson-Clarke Gallery
• 38 Newbury St., Boston; (617) 266-3321

In an area saturated with art galleries, Richardson-Clarke stands out because it presents a genre relatively difficult to find in Boston: traditional American and European paintings from the 17th through early 20th centuries. That covers a lot of territory, artistically speaking; the owners like to keep their exhibitions diverse, so there's no telling what you'll see at any given time. Hours vary; call ahead.

Signature & Grohe Glass Gallery
- 24 North Dock Square, Boston; (617) 227-4885

Here in the North End, see ceramic craftwork and glass sculpture from around the world—as far away as London and Japan, and as close as the United States. Many crafts for sale as well. Open seven days a week, including evenings (except Sundays).

The Society of Arts and Crafts
- 175 Newbury St., Boston; (617) 266-1810
- 101 Arch St./34 Summer St., Boston; (617) 345-0033

In existence since 1897, this is still an active society, with its own board of trustees/artists, and membership open to all. Two different locations, in the Back Bay and Downtown Crossing, have exhibition galleries and retail displays, in which you can purchase reasonably priced crafts and small works of art.

But of course, it costs nothing to look, and to marvel at the creativity that abounds in today's local art scene. It always seems to be the most lively stuff. Exhibits, which may run the gamut from glass to quilts, usually run for seven weeks or so; the artists give free talks, too. Pick up a calendar of events when you stop in. Gallery hours at Newbury Street are daily from 10 A.M. to 6 P.M., and Sundays from 12-5; at Arch Street, weekdays only, from 11 A.M. to 7 P.M.

Zeitgeist Gallery
- 312 Broadway, Cambridge; (617) 623-1065

Zeitgeist: a German word referring to current trends of thought or feeling (Mr. C does his research!). The gallery's name is a tip-off to the progressive, and often zany, works on display. Recently, visitors here found "Pictures Worth a Thousand Chords," a collection of visual art works by local rock singers. That should give you an idea of the inclusive and imaginative ethos running this place.

Plenty of solo exhibitions line the schedule, too, featuring sculpture, drawings, and art installations. Why, some of this art even *moves*: A show of locally made animated films was a recent hit. This tiny gallery is located between Central and Inman Squares; admission is free, although the owners admitted they wouldn't turn down a donation. Gallery hours are Wednesdays through Sundays from 2 to 7 P.M.

CHILDREN'S ACTIVITIES

See the "Museums" and "Outdoors" chapters for listings of other activities suitable for children and families.

Arlington Center for the Arts
- 41 Foster St., Arlington; (617) 648-6220

This center offers a wide range of children's activities and shows at some of the best rates around.

Classes are the most frequent programs, ranging in fee from $55 for creative theater to $90 for silk batiking. Sessions run for eight to ten weeks. ACA also sponsors one-day workshops on Saturdays at considerably lower cost. Topics include movement and mask-making. Classes for teens and adults, too; call for a current schedule.

Barnes & Noble Booksellers

- 395 Washington St., Boston; (617) 426-5184
- 470 Southbridge St., Auburn; (508) 832-0855
- 150 Granite St., Braintree; (617) 380-3655
- 325 Harvard St., Brookline; (617) 566-5562
- Burlington Mall Rd., Burlington; (617) 270-5500
- 170 Boylston St.m (Rte. 9), Chestnut Hill; (617) 965-7621

You may already know this fast-growing chain as a great place for discounted books. Much of B & N's success is due to its hosting of book-related events, many of which are intended for younger readers—and all of which are free.

Storytelling sessions include perennial favorites like Maurice Sendak's *Where the Wild Things Are*. Often, these stories are accompanied by appropriate activities to really get kids into the spirit: A recent reading of *Five Live Bongos* led to the making of musical instruments and parading through the store.

Schedules vary by season and by branch, but each store offers several events per month. For a full listing of upcoming events, stop into any branch and pick up a flyer. B & N locations are open seven days a week.

Borders Books and Music

- 300 Boylston St. (Rte. 9), Chestnut Hill; (617) 630-1120
- 85 Worcester Rd. (Rte. 9), Framingham; (508) 875-2321
- 151 Andover St., Peabody; (508) 538-3003

See listing under "Readings and Literary Events."

Boston By Little Feet

- Various locations; Information, (617) 367-2345

This company puts together hour-long walking tours along the Freedom Trail, but adds games and activities to make history fun. It's geared toward ages six through twelve; children must be accompanied by an adult. Boston By Little Feet tours are May through October, on Saturday mornings at 10 and Sunday afternoons at 2. Admission is $5 for all ages.

Boston Children's Theatre

- Tsai Performance Center, 685 Commonwealth Ave., Boston; (617) 424-6634

For nearly fifty years, Boston Children's Theatre has offered "live theatre *for* children *by* children." Along with acting classes, camps, and projects tied in with area schools, BCT provides a full season of productions that kids will love. Classics like *Peter Pan, Hansel and Gretel*, and *The Sound of Music* are all crowd-pleasers. Tickets can cost as little as $3.

Special school-day performances, meant for field trips but open to the general public as well, offer further-reduced ticket prices, and group rates are available. Call for a current schedule.

The Children's Museum

- 300 Congress St., Boston; (617) 426-6500

The granddaddy of the kiddie museums! The very notion of interactive, "please touch" exhibits originated here, and similar institutions have copied its success all around the globe. The secret: Educate children through exciting playtime environments.

Alas, such fun comes at a price. Currently, admission is $7 for adults, $6 for children ages 2-15 and senior citizens, and $2 for children under two (children under one year can slip in free). But don't despair! On Friday nights from 5 to 9 P.M. admission is reduced to just $1 for everyone. Pick up the kids after work and you can all enjoy "Science Playground," "Dress-Up Shop," and the ever-popular "Bubbles" exhibit. Plus all kinds of concerts and special activities. The Children's Museum is open Tuesdays through Sundays from 10 A.M. to 5 P.M., Fridays until 9 P.M. During the summer and most holidays, they add Mondays to the schedule.

The Children's Museum in Dartmouth

- 276 Gulf Rd., South Dartmouth; (508) 993-3361

On two floors of a converted dairy barn, you'll find a world of adventure and discovery tucked away. Interactive exhibits make it fun to learn about nature, science, and art. Favorite exhibits include the Medieval Room, with period clothes and puppets; the Live Animal Room, with turtles, bunnies, ferrets, fish, and parakeets; and the supermarket room with, you guessed it, kid-sized groceries. When kids get tired, they can curl up next to the fireplace in the Teddy Bear Room and read a story. Hours are Tuesdays through Saturdays from 10 A.M. to 5 P.M., and Sundays from 1-5 P.M. Admission is $3.75 for all ages; that's quite affordable, but wait—on the first Friday of every month, the museum is free to all from 5 to 8 P.M. Cool!

The Children's Museum in Easton

- 9 Sullivan Ave., North Easton; (508) 230-3789

Okay, the one in Dartmouth is in a converted dairy barn; this one is in a historic fire station. The Children's Museum in Easton is primarily aimed at children two to eight years old. They'll love sliding down the firepole, playing with dinosaurs at the sand table, play-acting in the performance center, and peering through a giant kaleidoscope. Special events and changing exhibits make the museum new and exciting every time. Admission is $3.50 per person, and children under age two are admitted free. Open Tuesdays through Saturdays 10 A.M. to 5 P.M. and Sundays from 12-5 P.M.

The Discovery Museums

- 177 Main St., Acton; (508) 264-4200

It's two museums in one! **The Children's Discovery Museum** entertains the age one-to-six set with exhibits in the rooms, closets, and corridors of a 100-year-old Victorian

---

> # MR. CHEAP'S PICKS
> ## Children's Activities
>
> ✔ **Boston Children's Theatre**— For almost fifty years, the BCT has delighted kids with classic tales.
>
> ✔ **The Children's Museums**— You know about the one in Boston; but there are also smaller (thus cheaper and less overwhelming) versions in Acton, Dartmouth, and Easton.

---

house. These include "Water Discovery" with a floor to ceiling "bubble hoop"; a room filled with Lego's Duplo building blocks; and the "Rainbow Room," with its giant "Rainbow Wall Puzzle." Puzzles and books are the primary source of fun and learning here.

Older kids will prefer **The Science Discovery Museum**, where hands-on activities teach the fundamentals of science better than any textbook. Exhibits include the "Inventor's Workshop," and the "Electricity Room." Don't miss the "Whisper Dishes" outside: A pair of radar-shaped dishes are spaced 100 feet apart, so perfectly aligned that you can whisper into one and be heard clearly in the other. Of course, Mr. C *knows* how this works; he, um, just doesn't have room to explain it here. . . .

The Discovery Museums sponsor a number of special events, too. These include story hours, demonstrations, nature walks, and plenty of hands-on experiments. Most are free with admission. Either museum costs $5 per person; or, you can visit both in one day for $8. Hours vary by season, so call ahead.

The Freelance Players

- 8 St. John St., Jamaica Plain; (617) 232-1175

The Freelance Players, a multicultural, young people's theater group, produces original musical theater for all audiences. The focus is on theater education and social interaction for the participants; at the end of each session (usually in December and May), the kids perform an original musical they have created themselves. Tickets to these shows are $5. The group is open to budding actors from ages twelve to seventeen. There are also Freelance Troupes for kids eight to twelve. Call the organization for dates and venues.

Museum Of Fine Arts "Drop-In" Workshops

- 465 Huntington Ave., Boston; (617) 267-9300

Introduce your kids to the MFA in an easygoing way with these on-going gallery programs for ages six through twelve. As the name implies, there is no formal registration; just drop in on Tuesdays, Wednesdays, or Thursdays at 3:30 P.M. for a forty-five minute excursion into the world of art. Recent topics include "Splendor of India," a sketching and storytelling workshop. The workshops are free, but admission to the museum is required.

Orpheum Theater

- Foxborough Common, Rte. 140, Foxborough; (509) 543-ARTS (2787)

See the listing under "Movies."

Puppet Showplace Theater

- 32 Station St., Brookline; (617) 731-6400

If your kids love puppet shows (and what kid doesn't?), Brookline Village is the place to go. The Puppet Showplace Theater features adaptations of classic tales like *Cinderella*, *Rumpelstiltskin*, *Sleeping Beauty*, and other stories kids will enjoy, presented by member puppeteers and troupes from around New England—using various styles from masks to marionettes to traditional puppetry, presented by a repertory of different troupes in the region.

Tickets are $6 for everyone. Performances, recommended for ages five and up, are held on Saturdays at 1 P.M. and 3 P.M., with added shows during the summer and school vacation weeks. An occasional program called T.O.T.—"Theater on Thursday"—is especially for pre-schoolers from three to five years of age. Call for a copy of PST's calendar, Puppetplaybill. Oh yes, and Tuesday's Ice Cream Shop next door—a popular *apres-theatre* stop—makes the day complete.

COLLEGE PERFORMING ARTS

Boston is blessed with 17.2 colleges per resident—or something like that. These schools offer a wealth of music, dance, theater, and films which don't require much personal wealth to attend, unlike the colleges themselves. Many events are free to students, of course (don't forget your ID!) but most are also open to the general public, for free or a very small charge. If you want to put culture into your life on a regular basis, this is a great way to do it.

Berklee College of Music

- 136 Massachusetts Ave., Boston; (617) 266-1400

In addition to being one of the city's main venues for major pop concerts, Berklee Performance Center (along with the Berklee Recital Hall next door) hosts shows by faculty and student groups. Many teachers at Berklee are members of prominent local jazz bands or lead their own groups on the club scene; the students they teach sometimes go on to become tomorrow's stars of jazz and rock. Musical styles vary greatly, including gospel, 20th-century American choral music, alternative rock, and acoustic. Concert schedules vary. Recital hall concerts are free and open to the public. Admission at the performance center is often free or may range from $1 to $4, with general seating.

Boston College
• 140 Commonwealth Ave., Chestnut Hill; (617) 552-4800

The Robsham Theater Arts Center hosts music, theatre and dance performances from around town and around the world. Visits by Russian choral groups or the Boston Ballet, as well as plays and dance concerts by student groups, are among the many cultural offerings held here. Admission is modestly priced. The music department also sponsors free concerts and recitals.

Boston Conservatory
• 8 The Fenway, Boston; (617) 536-6340

The lesser-known of the two major conservatories recently marked its 125th anniversary season. At Seully Hall, you can catch piano recitals, modern dance, and even Gilbert and Sullivan. Tickets range up to $12, but many events are free and open to all.

Boston University
• Boston; (617) 353-TSAI (8724)

The well-respected arts program at Boston University attracts high-caliber talent, as both teachers and students. The focal point of performance activity here is the new Tsai Performance Center at 685 Commonwealth Avenue. Other venues include the BU Concert Hall (855 Commonwealth Avenue) and the Huntington Theatre (264 Huntington Avenue). Performing arts groups include the BU Symphony Orchestra (conducted by a member of the Boston Symphony), BU's School of Theater Arts, and the Boston University Chorus. Faculty and student recit-

---

MR. CHEAP'S PICKS
College Performing Arts

✔ **The Berklee School of Music** and **The New England Conservatory**—Two of Boston's famous music schools present an almost daily lineup of student and faculty recitals that are free or just a few bucks. Berklee specializes in jazz and world-beat pop, while NEC has lots of classical ensembles.

✔ **Boston University**—A renowned arts program attracts talented students who frequently present concerts, art exhibits, and theater performances.

---

als add even more options. Ticket prices range from $5 to $10, with plenty of free events, too.

Two other organizations, the BU Chorus and the BU Choral Arts Society, perform at the gothic Marsh Chapel (735 Commonwealth Avenue). The chapel also features free organ concerts on Sunday afternoons.

Brandeis University
• 415 South St., Waltham; (617) 736-4300

The **Spingold Theatre Center** actually contains three different stages of various sizes and shapes; and the quality of the student productions is very high. Most are directed by faculty or major Boston-area directors, and the casts usually feature seriously dedicated and talented MFA students who are not far from Broadway. Elsewhere on campus, the **Slosberg Music Center** offers faculty and student recitals, as well as concerts by such professional groups as the Lydian String Quartet; tickets are generally $5 to $10, though there are a number of free events.

Emerson College

- 69 Brimmer St., Boston; (617) 578-8780

The Brimmer Street Studio has two intimate-sized theaters for student productions as well as local professional troupes who rent the stages for their own works. The college also owns the recently rescued **Majestic Theatre**, across from the Wang Center, and this hall hosts major fall and spring productions by the theater department.

Harvard University

- Harvard Square, Cambridge; (617) 495-8676

It should come as no surprise that Harvard has an extensive calendar of superior arts programming. Harvard has several theaters—the Loeb, of course, which it shares with the American Repertory Theatre; the Agassiz; and the Sanders, which presents lots of commercial concerts. But each of these also offers student productions by both Harvard and Radcliffe groups. In fact, the A.R.T. has its own Institute for Advanced Theatre Training, presenting shows by its apprentice company, many of whom also land smaller roles in the main productions (call the A.R.T. directly for that info at (617) 547-8300). Tickets, when not free, are $4 to $10. Harvard also has dance performances, see the listing in "Dance," for more information.

Longy School of Music

- 1 Follen St., Cambridge; (617) 876-0956

One of the small music schools in the Harvard Square area, Longy presents student and faculty concerts in the Pickman Concert Hall at 27 Garden Street. Hear piano recitals, vocal music, chamber groups using period instruments, and more. Most concerts are free, though some request a $5 donation. All concerts and master classes are open to the public. Call the number above for a recording of all upcoming performances; the schedule is packed.

Massachusetts Institute of Technology

- 77 Massachusetts Ave., Cambridge; (617) 253-2826

Wait a minute, Mr. C, isn't MIT just for high-tech junkies? You may be surprised, but MIT has a wonderful assortment of arts programs, many of which are free. Performance groups are varied, including the Concert Choir (directed by Tanglewood conductor John Oliver), the Symphony Orchestra, MIT Dance Workshop, the Shakesperare Ensemble, and an improv comedy troupe, Roadkill Buffet. MIT is even home to New England's only Balinese gamelan orchestra, the Gamelan Galak Tika. Venues include the MIT Chapel and Kresge Auditorium, which face each other in front of the student center on Massachusetts Avenue, as well as Killian Hall at 160 Memorial Drive. Most concerts are free; theater and dance events range from free up to $9. Don't miss the "Poetry@MIT" series, presenting renowned poets from across the country, free of charge.

New England Conservatory of Music

- 290 Huntington Ave., Boston; (617) 262-1120

Jordan Hall, at 30 Gainsborough Street (diagonally across from Symphony Hall) is one of the city's biggest and best concert halls. Along with major concerts, though, you can go there to hear student ensembles, the NEC Symphony Orchestra, and touring professional groups. There's something doing pretty much every day of the week. Most performances are free.

New School Of Music

- 25 Lowell St., Cambridge; (617) 492-8105

This small, ambitious school offers regular classical concerts by students and faculty. They are generally free and open to the public.

Pine Manor College

- 400 Heath St., Chestnut Hill; (617) 731-7118

Tucked away behind Route 9 near the malls, Pine Manor has a peaceful green campus, lots of free parking, and a lovely concert hall. They boast an active year-round program of classical concerts, theatrical offerings, and lectures, just about all of it for free. While you're on campus, stop by the Hess Gallery, which recently featured an exhibit by children's book illustrator, Ashley Bryan.

Tufts University
- College Ave., Medford; (617) 627-3493

The Arena Theatre presents an ambitious program of drama all year, including both new works and classic plays. These are generally performed by students and directed by the faculty. Tickets range from $4 to $6, with subscriptions available.

University of Massachusetts at Boston
- 100 Morrissey Blvd., Dorchester; (617) 287-5646

Relative to other colleges around Boston, the UMass Harbor Campus is small. Nevertheless, the theater arts department is an ambitious one, staging two major shows each year. Recent productions include *Ghetto*, about the Jewish struggle for survival in Lithuania during World War II, and *Mysteries*, an original work in the form of a medieval pageant. Tickets are generally $5 to $7, with discounts for seniors, students, and groups.

What's more, a student-run group called Campus Players produces shows of its own. These are smaller scale productions, so the admission policy is "by donation." Throw a few dollars in the pot, enjoy an evening of theater. CP also hosts a free open-mike session at the on-campus cafe, Wit's End (in the Wheatley Building) every other Friday, from 2:30 to 5 P.M. These feature mostly play readings and drama, but occasionally include music, dance, or performance art.

COMEDY

Going to a comedy club can be an expensive proposition, between the cover charge and the drinks. Mr. C can't do anything about the price of beer, but don't forget that the larger clubs have shows throughout the week and that the price of admission is lower on, say, a Tuesday night than on Saturday.

The best cost-cutter in the biz remains the "Open Mike" night, when you can get in for a very low cover charge and see up-an-coming "stars of tomorrow." Guaranteed, there'll be plenty of klunkers (does the name Rupert Pupkin ring a bell, De Niro fans?); but the shows are hosted by headliners, so you're sure to get plenty of good laughs no matter what. Many clubs, some of which are listed here, have open mike shows; they tend to be early in the week. Call your favorite venue to see what they offer.

Comedy Connection
- 245 Quincy Market, Faneuil Hall, Boston; (617) 248-9700

One of the longest-established comedy clubs in town, the Comedy Connection moved from the Charles Playhouse to a larger space in Faneuil Hall. With touristy digs, come touristy prices. Once, the top price on weekends was $10. Now, it can be as much as $36! Still, many shows stay in the more reasonable

---

MR. CHEAP'S PICK
Comedy

✔ **Improvisational Center of Boston**—The former Back Alley Theater is home to the long-running ImprovBoston and other comedy troupes. On Thursday nights, admission is free—no joke!

$12 to $15 range. True Cheapsters should come down on Sunday through Thursday nights, when admission is a mere $8.

Improvisational Center of Boston
• 1253 Cambridge St., Cambridge; (617) 576-1253

For something completely different from the clubs, this tiny theater in Inman Square is home to ImprovBoston, one of New England's longest-running improvisational troupes. Tickets are $10 to $12 ($8 to $10 for students and seniors) on Friday, Saturday, and Sunday nights. For the best deal, stop in on Thursday night for Theatresports—comedy as competitive contest—when admission is free!

Improvisation Center of Boston Theater features similarly low-priced tickets for other comedy acts. Recently, "The Lost Scott Show" featured the comedy of Scott Stiffler and tickets were just $8, $5 for students and seniors.

Naked Brunch
• Lyric Stage, 140 Clarendon St., Boston; (617) 859-8163

More prevalent since Mr. C first researched Boston, improvisation is a comedy form that gets audience members into the act. Anyone can shout out suggestions for characters and locales, which the comedians spin out into wacky scenes on the spot. Adding a further twist to the proceedings, Naked Brunch is Boston's only (thus far) gay and lesbian improv troupe. Now *that* makes for some unusual situations.

Admission is just $8 at the door. As of this writing, performances were being held on Fridays at 10:30 P.M. Call ahead though; the Bruncher Mr. C spoke with said they were looking for a new space where they could perform earlier in the evening. The number above will put you directly in touch with the Naked Brunch troupe. If you wish to contact the Lyric itself, call (617) 437-7172.

Nick's Comedy Stop
• 100 Warrenton St., Boston; (617) 482-0930

Nick's is another club that's been dishing out laughs for years. The upstairs comedy room is more like a hall, and in fact it was once a dance ballroom. Frequent national headliners are mixed in with local favorites like D.J. Hazard and Steve Sweeney. Weekend night tickets are $12, which is cheap already, but Monday, Tuesday, Wednesday, and Thursday nights are $8.

DANCE

Unfortunately, there are not many opportunities for inexpensive dance in town. Tickets for most performances start around $12 to $15 and go up from there. Your best bets are mainly at the colleges (see that section), which include both student and faculty shows. Here are a few other options.

Boston Ballet
- The Wang Center, 275 Tremont St., Boston; (617) 695-6950

College students are offered a great opportunity to see one of the world's premier ballets for for just $12! That's a considerable savings off the standard ticket prices of $20 to $50 a pop. Students should come to the theater an hour before the performance—with valid ID, of course—and they'll get the best available seats for $12. Student rush tix are not available on Saturday evenings or Sunday matinee performances.

Dance Umbrella
- Various locations; Information, (617) 492-7578

For fifteen years, this concert series has brought the world's most popular modern dance troupes to Boston. Mark Morris, Mikhail Baryshnikov's White Oak Dance Project, the Bill T. Jones/Arnie Zane Dance Company, Gregory Hines, and many others have been presented under this "umbrella." Tickets, naturally, can leap as high as $40 a pop—though balcony seats are usually a more reasonable $15. Better yet, students and senior citizens get a great deal on rush tickets: half-price when picked up half an hour before the curtain. Groups of ten people or more can also get a 20% discount. Most performances take place at the gloriously renovated Emerson Majestic Theater on Tremont Street in the Theater District. Call the number above for upcoming shows.

Harvard Summer Dance Center
- Harvard University, Cambridge; (617) 495-5535

Maybe you didn't need Mr. C to tell you this, but folks at Harvard are *smart*. Every June and July, the Harvard Summer School organizes a series of dance performances, related lectures, and movies. Almost all of these events are free—and that's pretty rare in the dance world.

MR. CHEAP'S PICK
Dance

✔ **Harvard Summer Dance Center**—A well-respected series of free summer dance concerts!

The series of free performances are called "One Night Stands." These are trysts you're sure to enjoy, with no worries in the morning. Visiting dance companies often follow their performances with an open discussion with the audience. Lectures and panel discussions address issues pertinent to dancers' lives.

The only part of the Dance Center's season that will cost you anything is the faculty performance series. These events showcase better-known faculty members; tickets are $10 and $15, still not bad for this kind of performance.

The New Dance Complex
- 536 Massachusetts Ave., Cambridge; (617) 547-9363

This three-story Central Square building (formerly occupied by Joy of Movement) continues to run the facility as a place to take dance classes, but also features a full schedule of dance performances. Ticket prices are $7 to $10, very reasonable for top-notch dance concerts. Spring and fall are the busy seasons, with two to three performances per month. The striking feature of the New Dance Complex is the diversity of dance styles seen here. Past performances have included modern *pas de deux*, tap ensembles, flamenco, yoga, African dance, martial arts, and even bellydancing. Call for details.

FESTIVALS

Bostonians move outdoors in the summer months, taking full advantage of our allotment of nice weather. Just about every town, large and small, hosts a series of free outdoor concerts, usually in the town park. The *Sunday Boston Globe* generally runs a listing of summer events in early June and the *Globe*'s "Calendar" section on Thursdays is a good source for up-to-the-minute info. Meanwhile, here's a few to check out.

Boston Globe Jazz Festival

- Various locations; Information, (617) 523-4047

Every June, Boston jumps as its major newspaper sponsors a week-long series of jazz concerts. Most shows feature at least two performers or ensembles; it all culminates in a free, all-day jazz-a-thon at the Hatch Shell. This lineup features major names like Al Jarreau, Pat Metheny, and many others, from 12 noon to (617) P.M. Other concerts, generally held in the early evening, take place around the city in places like Copley Square. Most shows are free, with a few exceptions; in some cases, it's a good idea to make advance bookings. Call the information line in May to preview this year's lineup.

Boston Harborfest

- Various waterfront locations; Information, (617) 227-1528

Six fun-packed days in late June and early July mark Independence Day in Boston. Many of these events focus on the history of the city: You can relive the Siege of Louisburg, for example, or tour one of several Navy ships. Bring your kids along—they'll get a kick out of the puppet shows, concerts, and street performers.

All the above-mentioned events are free of cost (of course Mr. C mentioned them first!). Some others charge admission fees; call the information line to receive an up-to-date schedule with prices. The "Chowderfest" is one annual highlight: for $4-

$6, you get to taste and try as many chowders by local restaurants as you wish. Harborfest culminates on the Fourth with an all-out fireworks extravaganza over Boston Harbor. Arrive early; you'll have about 350,000 other folks for company!

Brandeis Summer Music Festival

- Slosberg Recital Hall, 415 South St., Waltham; (617) 736-3331

Faculty and visiting professional ensembles perform frequently throughout the summer, in an acoustically fine concert hall. Many are free to everyone.

Brookline Recreation Department Concerts

- Amory Park, Brookline; (617) 730-2070

Hear local bands play jazz, country, and pop oldies every Wednesday in July. These free concerts are held from 7 P.M. to 9 P.M. Amory Park is located behind the 1100 block of Beacon Street.

Charles Square Summer Music Series

- One Bennett St., Cambridge; (617) 491-5282

From June through September, the courtyard outside the Charles Hotel becomes a concert setting. Jazz, folk, and rock bands from the New England area play on Wednesday through Friday evenings from 6 to 8 P.M. Admission is free.

Composers Conference and Chamber Music Center
- Jewett Arts Center, Wellesley College, Wellesley; (617) 283-2069

A variety of free concerts take place every Wednesday, Thursday, and Saturday at 8 P.M.

Hatch Memorial Shell Concerts
- Charles River Esplanade, Boston; (617) 727-5215

A variety of concerts, including swing, folk, jazz, and country, take place all summer on the Esplanade. Each year, the Boston Pops kick off the season with the Independence Day fireworks concert; they are followed throughout the summer by swing bands, folk and country, international bands, and more. All concerts are free, starting at 8 P.M. most weeknights and 1 P.M. on weekends. Parking is permitted along Storrow Drive near the shell, during concerts only.

Lexington Bicentennial Band
- Hastings Park Bandstand, Lexington; (617) 862-9166

On Thursday evenings at 7:15, weather permitting, this band performs a mix of show tunes, Sousa marches, and assorted light music. Folks bring picnic suppers and relax—it's like a free, mini-Tanglewood.

Newton Arts in the Parks
- Various locations; Information, (617) 552-7130

Summer concerts present major folk and jazz performers in two locations. Tuesday night programs start at 7:15 at the Jackson Homestead, 527 Washington St., Newton. Admission is $4; seniors $2, kids $1. There are also free Sunday concerts starting at 6:15 P.M. on the green at Newton Center.

Oldies Concert Series
- City Hall Plaza, Boston; (671) 338-4636

Sponsored by Oldies 103 FM radio, these concerts take place on several Saturdays from Memorial Day Weekend through mid-August. They bring back such groups as Three Dog Night, Chubby Checker, The Monkees, and many others.

MR. CHEAP'S PICK
Festivals

✔ **Hatch Memorial Shell Concerts**—Free concerts (and movies!) on the Esplanade, all summer long.

Parkman Bandstand Series
- Boston Common; (617) 578-8727

This venerable old bandstand in the middle of Boston Common is the site of free concerts every Friday at 5:30 P.M. through the summer. Light classical, jazz, and old-time popular music can all be heard. These are usually followed at 7:30 by concerts featuring local jazz and pop groups, also free.

Striar JCC Concerts in the Courtyard
- 445 Central St., Stoughton; (617) 341-2016

On Thursday nights throughout the summer, the Striar Jewish Community Center treats you to live outdoor music. Gather at the picnic area beginning at 6 P.M.; a barbecue dinner is available at low cost, or bring your own grub. The concerts themselves start at 6:45. Folk, rock, and country music are featured here, as well as children's concerts, and all of these are free of charge. The JCC also sponsors movies, concerts, and lectures during the year. Some are cheap, some aren't; call for details.

Summer Stage
- Downtown Crossing; Information, (617) 482-2139

A platform set up on Summer Street between Filene's and Jordan Marsh is the sight of a summer's worth of free concerts every Wednesday. The noon-time shows include jazz vocalists, children's theater, tap dance groups, and more.

Waterfront Jazz Series
- Christopher Columbus Waterfront Park, Atlantic Ave., Boston; (617) 635-3911

Free jazz concerts take place in this nifty setting, between Quincy Market and the harbor, on Friday evenings through the summer. Music starts at 6:30 P.M.

MOVIES

Unfortunately, there's not much to be done about the ever-rising prices of first-run Hollywood movies. Some theaters do cut the price a bit on their first shows of the day. But don't despair! There are lots of alternative options for the budget moviegoer.

Brattle Theatre
- 40 Brattle St., Cambridge; (617) 876-6837

The Boston area's mother of all repertory cinemas, the Brattle puts out a massive calendar every two months with dozens of classic films, series of tributes to stars and directors, and occasional premieres. Most dates offer double features, with ticket prices of $6 for the pair. If you only make the last showing, that's $5. You can get a book of six tickets for $30; or better yet, for $50, become a Brattle member and get in for $4 anytime for a year. Members also get two free guest passes and various other goodies.

Brookline Public Library Programs
- 361 Washington St., Brookline; (617) 730-2368

Every Wednesday at 2 and 7:30 P.M., film buff Ted Kingsbury shows classic films upstairs in the main branch of the library in Brookline Village. He's been doing it for years, putting together a different theme each month and introducing the films himself. It's clearly a labor of love, and the choices are terrific—from the well-known to obscure gems. The themes may be tributes to stars or directors, or simply "Romantic Comedies." He runs a similar program on Thursdays, also at 2 and 7:30 P.M. at the **Wellesley Free Library**, 530 Washington St., Wellesley; (617) 235-1610.

On a similar note, films for senior citizens (but hey, anyone can go) are shown every Thursday at the **Coolidge Corner Branch Library**, 31 Pleasant St., Brookline; (617) 730-2380. These can include anything from *An Evening with the Royal Ballet* to *The Way We Were*. Refreshments are at 1 P.M.; movies at 1:30.

Cabot Street Cinema Theatre
- 286 Cabot St., Beverly; (508) 927-3677

This ornate, historic theater shows recent feature films and "art" films for a ticket price of $5—all seats, all times. The Cabot is also well-known in these parts as the home of "Le Grand David and His Spectacular Magic Company." This long-running magic show extravaganza is performed every Sunday at 3 P.M. Tickets are $12 for adults and $8 for children under age eleven.

Coolidge Corner Moviehouse
- 290 Harvard St., Brookline; (617) 734-2500

They no longer show double-features of classic films, but the Coolidge remains one of the city's fine art houses, often showing exclusive runs of foreign films, documentaries, and concert films. Ticket prices have gone up to first-run rates, but you can always go to the first showing of the day for either of their two screens for just $5. There is also a membership program: A $50 annual membership gets you into any showing for just $4.50. If you go to the movies *a lot*, you'll save money. Otherwise, stick with early shows.

Free Friday Flicks at the Hatch Shell

• Charles River Esplanade, Boston; (617) 727-9547

Every summer, from June to August, the City of Boston sponsors a free movie on Friday nights on a big screen in the Hatch Shell. Showtime is 7 P.M., and seating is first-come, first-served. Bring a blanket and some snacks. Past offerings have ranged from *The Wizard of Oz* and *Casablanca* to *The Lion King* and even *The Flintstones*. Yabba-dabba-doo!

Goethe Institut

• 170 Beacon St., Boston; (617) 262-6050

German cinema, naturally. See classics from the silent Expressionists of the 1920s to recent stuff by Percy Adlon, one of the only German directors to make a name in comedy (*Baghdad Cafe*). Films are free, usually shown on Friday and Saturday evenings. They're shown in German, of course, with English subtitles.

Harvard-Epworth Film Series

• 1555 Massachusetts Ave., Cambridge; (617) 354-0837

Catch anything from silent-era comedies to the latest in Japanese cinema in this ongoing series at the Harvard-Epworth Methodist Church. Films are shown on Sunday nights at 8 P.M., October through May. Tickets are $3.

Harvard Film Archive

• Carpenter Center, Harvard University, 24 Quincy St., Cambridge; (617) 495-4700

This most ambitious, long-running series embraces just about every kind of film imaginable: pop features, old-time classics, brand-new documentaries and world cinema. Occasionally, filmmakers will stop by and present their work. Most films are $6 for general admission and $5 for children, students, and seniors. You can also purchase a sea-

---

MR. CHEAP'S PICKS
Movies

✔ **Cameo Theatre**—Tickets $1, all seats, all shows. A bargain that cannot be beat. Similar deals at the Stoughton and Wollaston (Quincy) theaters.

✔ **Capitol Theatre**—Tix at this Arlington palace are all $4—still great—with five screens of recent hits.

---

son passbook of fifteen admissions for $45.

Institute of Contemporary Art

• 955 Boylston St., Boston; (617) 266-5152

The latest in avant-garde and art films by national, international, and Boston filmmakers are screened in the intimate confines of the ICA Theatre. Sometimes these are introduced by the *auteurs* themselves. Admission is generally $5; $4 for students, seniors, and ICA members.

Motion Odyssey Movie: M.O.M.

• Jordan's Furniture, 100 Stockwell Dr., Avon; (508) 580-4900

More like a Disney ride than a movie, M.O.M. has a four-story screen, 48 multi-directional chairs, and an action-packed movie with *you* as part of the adventure. Crazier still, M.O.M. is found in a discount furniture store!

Jordan's has always been known for its offbeat salesmanship. The idea is: "If you give people enough good reasons, they'll come in to buy furniture from *anywhere*." And this ride is a good reason—at least, to come in. The seats move in eight computer-controlled directions, so that you really feel the motion seen in the film. What are the morally uplifting subjects of such a cinematic experience? Dune buggies, roller coasters, elevators, and other thrills 'n chills—the usual.

Admission is $4, and $3 for children under 13. Not that this is intended as a moneymaker; all profits are donated to a different charity each month, from the Red Cross to the AIDS Action Committee. Open daily from 11 A.M. to 8:30 P.M. (Saturdays from 10 A.M.), and Sundays from 12-5 P.M.

Museum of Fine Arts
• 465 Huntington Ave., Boston; (617) 267-9300

The MFA's large, comfortable auditorium, the Remis, has an ambitious schedule of everything from unusual foreign films to rediscovered silent classics to festivals of animation and award-winning TV commercials. Admission is $6.50, and $5.50 for students, senior citizens, and MFA members. You can get a discount if you want to see two movies on the same day: Tickets are $10, $9 for students, seniors, and members. Entrance is from the new West Wing, by the parking lot; you don't have to atmosphere is more casual than you may expect.

Orpheum Theater
• Foxborough Common (Rte. 140), Foxborough; (508) 543-ARTS (2787)

This is Mr. C's favorite part of the Foxborough Regional Center for the Performing Arts. There's a dazzling movie program here; films run the gamut from classics like *Dr. Zhivago*, to Monty Python funnies, to flicks that have just left the big (i.e., full-price) cinemas. On most days, you'll have your pick of at least two shows. And every day, there's a matinee screening of a children's favorite like *Willy Wonka and the Chocolate Factory* or the animated *An American Tail*. Bring your kids, bring your neighbor's kids, borrow some kids—Mr. C cheers these ticket prices. Afternoon shows are $3 (for all ages); evening prices are

$4.50, period.

The Orpheum also presents live theater, including a recently-established "Off-Broadway" professional series. Tix are a bit pricier, though, hovering around $20. But keep an eye out for less expensive performances, like a recent version of *The Emperor's New Clothes* that was only $7.50 at night, and just $5.50 for matinees.

The Screening Room
• 82 State St., Newburyport; (508) 462-FILM (3456)

One of the few art cinemas on the North Shore, the Screening Room is a cozy little place in a converted, air-conditioned storefront. The whole place only seats 99 people, making this more intimate than a megaplex, yet still better than renting a video.

Besides, neither of the above tend to get this many foreign films, documentaries, and animation festivals. Tickets are only $5, and $2.50 for seniors and children; better still, you can get a book of ten for just $35— do the math, folks, that's half the price of most other movie theaters. Get on their mailing list for brochures that include reviews of all upcoming films.

Silent Movies at St. Anne's Church
• 147 Concord Rd., Lincoln; (617) 259-8834

St. Anne's in the Fields Episcopal Church really is "in the fields," a fair drive from Boston; but there's something going on here that's worth the trip. About once a month, the church resurrects the Golden Age of film by screening silent movies—with live piano accompaniment! The program is popular with adults and kids alike, and it's certainly unusual. Where else can you watch Charlie Chaplin, listen to live piano music, and eat ice cream—all at the same time? Admission is $4, and $2 for children. Call for upcoming schedules.

SECOND-RUN DISCOUNT CINEMAS

Second-run movies are the same Hollywood releases that you see in the shopping malls and downtown cinemas, after they've finished their "first runs" in those major venues. Well before they make their way to pay-per-view and videocassettes, they often show up at some of the theaters listed below. Not only do you get one last chance to see recent hits you may have missed—still on the big screen—but the tickets usually cost less than half of those at the big-deal houses.

Cameo Theatre
- 14 Columbian St., Weymouth; (617) 335-2777

This two-screen theater was struggling for awhile—until they lowered ticket prices to $1, all seats, all shows. Now, the place is frequently jammed; get there early if you want a seat on a Friday or Saturday night. Second-run flicks are shown on screens that are half the size of the original theater, but still bigger than the ones at your local 'plex. And nothing beats those ticket prices.

Capitol Theatre
- 204 Massachusetts Ave., Arlington; (617) 648-4340

A grand old moviehouse, regrettably converted into a six-screen complex; but, it is one of the nicer renovations of this sort, with brass rails, comfortable seats, and running lights in the aisles. The developers took care to make each cinema a complete one, so you don't feel like you're sitting in an oddly shaped shoebox. Besides popcorn, the lobby snack bar sells things like frozen yogurt and coffee, and even has tables and chairs. The Capitol shows second-run hits (not that long after their departure from the big houses), with a top price of just $4. Senior citizens pay $3, and before 6 P.M. kids under twelve get in for $2.50. You can also buy books of five tickets for $18.

Cinema Pub Theatre
- 807 Washington St., Stoughton; (617) 344-4566

Combining two great words that go great together, the Cinema Pub easily caught Mr. C's attention. All seats are $1 for all shows, offering movies just a few weeks out of the first-run

houses. Along with old-time prices, the cinema features one big screen and a balcony; how often do you see that anymore?

The place is also decorated with nostalgic movie posters—yet it's air-conditioned, and the modern seats have cup holders, ideal for that $3 pint of Sam Adams you can purchase with your popcorn. Several other beers are offered on tap, a joy for those who recall sneaking beer past the ticket window in their wilder days. Traditional movie snacks are complemented by "pub" fare such as burgers, pizza, and nachos. The prices are more like Fenway than frugal, but hey, how much did it cost to get in?

Occasionally, Cinema Pub also presents community theater performances and comedy shows, with prices usually $10 and under.

Dedham Community Theater
- 578 High St., Dedham; (617) 326-1463

Norwood Cinemas
- 111 Central St., Norwood; (617) 255-0404

These two theaters have a dedicated following, and it's no wonder. First of all, they offer a great ticket price on movies shown before 2 P.M.—a mere $3. After that, regular admission is a reasonable $5, and $3 for children. But, the best deal of all is the discount pass. For $20 you get admission to six films, and a coupon for a free small popcorn. Bonus!

These theaters are well-paired. As a general rule, the Dedham Community Theater shows more of the art house movies, stuff coming out of the Nickelodeon, for example. Mainstream Hollywood meanwhile, is the order of the day in Norwood. Since the discount pass is good at both, you can get your fill of all kinds of fun.

Last Strand Cinema & Drafthouse
- 58 High St., Clinton; (508) 365-5500

Clinton is a bit out of Mr. C's usual geographic territory, but this is so unusual and so cheap, he felt compelled to report on it. A newly renovated historic theater, the Last Strand serves up current movies along with beer, wine, pizza, hot sandwiches, and nachos. Tickets are just $4 ($3.50 for seniors and children). The movies shown here are in that netherworld between first- and second-run: They've been out for a few weeks, but may still be playing in the megaplexes. There is generally one showing on weeknights, two on weekends, and a kiddie matinee on Saturdays and Sundays.

Loring Hall Cinema
- 65 Main St., Hingham; (617) 749-1400

If you're on the South Shore (even if you're not) and love old-time movie palaces, check out the Loring Hall. Go up the narrow stairway to the balcony and grab a seat—this is probably one of the few moviehouses where you can still do that! They show second-run features soon after their main runs, with general admission of $5.50, and $4 for senior citizens. Greal deal already, but come by on Tuesdays, "Bargain Day," when all seats at all times are $3.75.

Somerville Theatre
- 55 Davis Square, Somerville; (617) 625-5700

A great old movie palace in the heart of Davis Square, the large-screen Somerville is one of the few such theaters that still uses its stage for live concerts along with movies. The films are all second-runs, with some foreign films and classics mixed in occasionally. Tickets are a bargain at $2.50.

Wollaston Theatre
- 14 Beale St., Quincy; (617) 773-4600

It's in the National Register of Historic Places, and it's a fair guess that little work has been done on the Wollaston Theatre since it opened in 1926. The ceiling looks sturdy enough, though; and the immense screen *knows* it's a movie screen. Besides, how fussy can you be when you pay just $1 to see a movie? That's the price on any Monday or Tuesday night; other nights, it's a mere $3.

The theatre itself is cavernous, offering far more seating space than is needed on the average night, yet ready to handle the occasional crowd. Attractions lean toward family fare and romantic comedies, with the occasional *Pulp Fiction* tossed in. A fella with a flashlight even came by to ask Mr. C to put his feet down—when was the last time you saw *that* in a movie theater? (Of course, if the floor weren't so sticky from seventy years' worth of soda. . .)

Unlike many discount cinemas, even the snacks are inexpensive: 60¢ for candy, 80¢ for a large soda, and $1 for a large popcorn. These sizes are somewhat smaller than the traditional livestock sizes of today, but a bargain nonetheless. If you go in the summer, dress down; there's no air conditioning, and you'll know it.

MUSEUMS

There are dozens and dozens of museums in the Boston area. The biggest of them are charging up to $6 or $7 admission these days, which can really add up for a family or group. Mr. C wants to bring several to your attention which are free, very inexpensive, or have special free programs once you've paid your regular admission. Remember, to receive student or senior citizen discounts, you must show a valid ID!

Of course, Mr. C firmly believes that *all* museums are bargains. Consider how many treasures you can see, for the price of a movie! If you really enjoy a particular museum, by the way, consider becoming a member. This usually gets you free admission anytime, including perhaps your family, for the price of a couple of visits. It's a money-saver, and it helps out your beloved institution as well.

The Art Complex Museum
• 189 Alden St., Duxbury; (617) 934-6634

Not far from beautiful Duxbury beach, the Art Complex Museum has a wonderful permanent collection of Shaker furniture, European and American prints, American paintings, and Asian art—which includes a traditional teahouse in the museum's Japanese garden. The "Wind in the Pines Hut" is open on Sundays during the summer only, with a public tea ceremony at 2 P.M. on the last Sunday of each month.

The ACM also offers Sunday afternoon concerts of classical, jazz, folk, and contemporary music. In an effort to promote emerging talent, the museum often features rising local musicians. Concerts are at 4 p.m.; call for a schedule. What does one pay for all this art and culture? Nothing! That's right, admission to the Art Complex is free. Open Wednesdays through Sundays from 1 P.M. to 4 P.M.

The Boston College Museum of Art
• Devlin Hall, 140 Commonwealth Ave., Chestnut Hill; (617) 552-8587

This place is pretty impressive for a college art museum. The galleries have movable walls, allowing plenty of flexibility in displaying exhibits. The main gallery is two stories high, suitable for very large works. And the sophisticated security and climate-control systems allow the museum to show off rare and fragile pieces.

BC has been collecting art since the nineteenth century. Its strengths are in Gothic and Baroque tapestries, Italian paintings of the sixteenth and

seventeenth centuries, American landscapes, and Japanese prints. Added to this are traveling exhibits like the recent *Irish Watercolors and Drawings from the National Gallery of Ireland.* And don't miss the "Micro Gallery," an interactive computer system that displays information and images of works in the permanent collection. The museum organizes public lectures, symposia, workshops, film series, and gallery tours. All programs are free of charge. During the academic year, hours are 11 A.M. to 4 P.M. Mondays through Fridays, and noon to 5 P.M. on Saturdays and Sundays. In the summer, BCMA is open 11 A.M. to 3 P.M. Mondays through Fridays.

Cardinal Spellman Philatelic Museum
• 235 Wellesley St., Weston; (617) 894-6735

Stamp collectors will be thrilled silly about the four *million* postal specimens on display here. One of the nation's top philatelic researchers and exhibitors, this museum will introduce you to a hobby which, for many, becomes an obsession. See President Eisenhower's own stamp collection, as well as all kinds of rarities. Admission to the museum is free; hours are from 9 A.M. to 4 P.M. Tuesdays through Thursdays, and 1 to 5 P.M. on Sundays.

Commonwealth Museum
• 270 Morrissey Blvd., Dorchester; (617) 727-9268

The exhibits here focus on various themes related to life and culture in our fair state (er, commonwealth). Recent exhibits include an exploration of the impact of war photography on people at home and an examination of the archeology, technology, and nature of the Quabbin reservoir. Admission is free at all times; hours are 9 A.M. to 5 P.M. Mondays through Fridays, and 9 A.M. to 3 P.M. on Saturdays.

The Computer Museum
- 300 Congress St., Boston; (617) 423-6758

Among its many exhibits, the Computer Museum—next to the Children's Museum on the wharf—features a giant personal computer big enough to walk through. Over 35 hands-on exhibits help you overcome your fear of these machines, or just find out what goes on in there! A recent special exhibit, "The Networked Planet: Traveling the Information Superhighway," included a 30-minute hands-on seminar for Internet beginners. Regular admission is $7 for adults, $5 for students and seniors, and free for kids under five. But on Sundays from 3 P.M. to 5 P.M., admission is half-price for everyone. Hours are 10 A.M. to 6 P.M. daily.

Danforth Museum of Art
- 123 Union Ave., Framingham; (508) 620-0050

Since opening its doors some twenty years ago, the five exhibition galleries of the Danforth have showcased a permanent collection of contemporary works, along with rotating exhibits on loan from artists, collectors, and other museums. A unique children's gallery features plenty of hands-on activities to open youngsters' eyes to the arts.

Danforth presents special events and programs including art film series, concerts, trips to other art museums, workshops, and lectures. School and community groups can request guided, interpretive tours led by trained docents. For all this, admission is only $3, and $2 for senior citizens and students; children under twelve are free. Open Wednesdays through Sundays noon to 5 P.M.

The Davis Museum and Cultural Center
- 106 Central St., Wellesley; (617) 283-2051

This state-of-the-art museum (no pun intended) opened in the fall of 1993—but Wellesley had long been amassing a magnificent art collection of more than 5,000 objects. Highlights include paintings by Monet and Cezanne; drawings by Degas and Matisse; prints by Rembrandt, African sculpture, and pre-Columbian pottery.

What's more, the Davis offers an impressive array of activities. These include video presentations, musical performances, lectures, gallery walks, architectural tours, and open classes. The museum and all its programs are free and open to the public. Hours are Tuesdays through Saturdays from 11 A.M. to 5 P.M. (Wednesdays and Thursdays 'til 8), and Sundays from 1-5 P.M.

DeCordova Museum
- 51 Sandy Pond Rd., Lincoln; (617) 259-8355

A bit out of the way for city folk, the DeCordova is always worth a drive from just about anywhere. The museum itself features several galleries of contemporary art, emphasizing New England artists. The real draw, however, is the adjacent sculpture park. A portion of this rolling 35-acre property is dotted with some forty works that will amuse and delight you. Some are even interactive, perfect for the kiddies to climb on, and visitors can even picnic next to their favorite piece! Museum admission is a hefty $6 ($5 for seniors, students, and children under twelve), but the park is free at all times.

The DeCordova is open Tuesdays through Fridays from 10 A.M. to 5 P.M.; Saturdays and Sundays from 12 P.M. to 5 P.M. The sculpture park is open daylight hours. At the time of this writing, DeCordova was planning to close for six months for renovations, from October 1995 through June of 1996. The sculpture park will remain open during the construction.

Frederick Law Olmsted National Historic Site
- 99 Warren St., Brookline; (617) 566-1689

Visit the home of the architect who designed the Emerald Necklace and New

York City's Central Park. The site is administered by the National Park Service, and its wealth of archival material has made it a focal point for historic landscape interpretation, preservation, and management. Programs include tours of the house, office, and grounds. Park rangers give 40-minute tours every hour on the half-hour, Fridays, Saturdays, and Sundays from 10:30 A.M. to 3:30 P.M. Admission is free.

Fuller Museum of Art

• 455 Oak St., Brockton; (508) 588-6000

Brockton may not be the first place some people think of for the arts, but the Fuller Museum proves that stereotype wrong. The permanent collection is filled with wonderful examples of American arts and crafts, including many works by New England artists. Special exhibits, generally six to eight each year, feature pieces on loan from other museums.

The mission is to make art accessible to the community. To this end, the Fuller Museum sponsors special programs like music, theater, lectures, and literary events. Art classes, for all ages, are also available. FMA is open Tuesdays through Sundays noon to 5 P.M.; admission is by donation.

Gore Place

• 52 Gore St., Waltham; (617) 894-2798

This restored Federalist-era mansion shows you what home furnishings were like during the period from 1780 to 1830. Admission is $4, students and seniors $3, kids five to twelve, $2. Open Tuesdays through Saturdays from 10 A.M. to 5 P.M., and Sundays 2 to 5 P.M. Closed holidays. There are also forty acres of landscaped grounds, open free to all.

Harvard Museums of Cultural and Natural History

• 26 Oxford St., Cambridge; (617) 495-3045

In addition to a wonderful collection of art museums (see below), Harvard also has four cultural and natural history museums. The main museum is the **Museum of**

MR. CHEAP'S PICKS
Museums

✔ **DeCordova Museum**—This fine museum is on the pricey side, but their outdoor sculpture park is always free .

✔ **Museum of Fine Arts**—The venerable MFA stays open on Wednesday evenings with entry by donation; toss in a buck and go.

✔ **Worcester Art Museum**—On equal footing with many of Boston's hallowed institutions, this museum is much less expensive to enjoy. Admission is free on Saturdays if you arrive before noon.

Comparative Zoology, which studies modern animals and great fossils. Displays at the **Peabody Museum of Archaeology and Ethnology** give you a view into different cultures from around the globe. The **Mineralogical Museum** has room upon room filled with the most amazing colors of rocks and minerals. And the **Botanical Museum** is famous for its "Glass Flowers" display, absolutely lifelike plants and flowers of handblown glass.

Admission to the building includes all four museums for $4; students and seniors, $3; children ages three to thirteen, $1. On Saturday mornings from 9 to 11, admission is free to all. Regular hours are 9 A.M. to 4:30 P.M. Mondays through Saturdays, and Sundays from 1 to 4:30 P.M.

Harvard University Art Museums

• Various locations, Cambridge; (617) 495-9400

You already know that Harvard is renowned in the areas of politics, law, medicine, and business. You may not know that it's also the site of three art museums. What's more, you pay one relatively low admission price—$5, $4 for seniors, $3 for students—and you get into all three! Great deal. Anyone under 18 is admitted free.

So, what's to see? The main museum is the **Fogg Art Museum** (32 Quincy St.), specializing in European and American art. Special exhibits include sculpture, drawings, paintings, and prints. Tours are given Mondays through Fridays at 11 A.M. At the same address, the **Busch-Reisinger Museum** concentrates on German and northern European works.

Not far away at 485 Broadway, the **Sackler Art Museum** features classical and Asian collections. A recent special exhibit here called "The Art of the Fan: China, Korea, Japan," featured painted and calligraphic fans and scroll paintings, including examples from the Sung Dynasty. Tours are given Mondays through Fridays at noon. All three museums are open Mondays through Saturdays 10 A.M. to 5 P.M., Sundays 1 to 5 P.M.

Hull Lifesaving Museum
• 1117 Nantasket Ave., Hull; (617) 925-LIFE (5433)

Housed in an actual, restored 1889 U.S. lifesaving station, the Hull Lifesaving Museum lets you experience the drama of a rescue at sea. These techniques are demonstrated on visitors; kids young and old will love swooping along the suspended ropes, just like a real-live action movie.

The admission fee of $3 ($2 seniors, $1.50 students and kids) includes a video presentation and a guided tour of the museum. During the school year, hours are from 12 noon to 5 P.M. on weekends only; in the summer months, the museum is open these same hours on Wednesday through Friday afternoons.

The Jackson Homestead
• 527 Washington St., Newton; (617) 552-7238

Built in 1809—and once a way-station for the Underground Railroad—the Jackson Homestead was renovated into a museum in 1950.

Changing exhibitions, workshops, lectures, and walking tours all show how the city has changed over the years. A special attraction is the "Abolition Room," restored to its look when the Jackson family hid fugitive slaves.

Run by the Newton Historical Society, the home is open on a somewhat limited schedule of 1 to 5 P.M. Mondays through Thursdays and 2 to 5 P.M. on Sundays—but appointments for group tours and research can be made by calling the office between 8:30 A.M. and 5 P.M., Mondays through Thursdays. Regular admission is $2, and $1 for seniors and children.

Institute of Contemporary Art
• 955 Boylston St., Boston; (617) 266-5152

The Institute of Contemporary Art created quite a stir when it showed the Mapplethorpe photo exhibit a few years back. Devoted to the latest in cutting-edge art, ICA features several galleries and a video theater. A recent exhibit, "Familiar Places," featured 20 international artists reflecting on the theme of home in contemporary art. Regular admission is $5.25; students $3.25, children and senior citizens $2.25. Better yet, the museum is free to all on Thursday evenings from 5 P.M. to 9 P.M.

Isabella Stewart Gardner Museum
• 280 The Fenway, Boston; (617) 566-1401

Step inside the Gardner and you've left the city for another world. The rooms are filled with one of the greatest private collections of art, and the central courtyard is a dazzling Mediterranean feast of trees and flowers. Regular admission is $7; students and seniors $5, children twelve to seventeen $3, under twelve free. Also, the museum is $3 to all college students on Wednesdays.

John F. Kennedy Birthplace
• 83 Beals St. Brookline; (617) 566-7937

See the place where our thirty-fifth president was born and spent his early years. This house near Coolidge Corner has just been renovated by the National Park Service. They also offer walking tours of the neighborhood, pointing out the sights Kennedy knew as a youth. Admission is $2; those under 17 are admitted free. The house can only be seen by guided tour, which is given at 10:45 and 11:45 and then on the hour from 1 P.M. to 4 P.M., Wednesdays through Sundays.

Marine Museum at Fall River

- 70 Water St., Fall River; (508) 674-3533

While you're visiting all those Fall River outlets, take some time to check out some of the history of this city by the sea. The Marine Museum has the largest exhibit of artifacts and memorabilia from the H.M.S. *Titanic*, including a 28-foot replica created for the movie *A Night to Remember*. Other exhibits include artifacts from the Fall River Steamship Line of luxury cruise ships. Admission is $3 for adults, $2 for children ages six to fourteen. Hours vary; call ahead.

Mystery buffs know that Fall River was also the home of Lizzie Borden, who may or may not have killed her parents with that axe. At the **Fall River Historical Society**, 451 Rock Street, (508) 679-1071, you can view the evidence from this hundred-year-old riddle and decide for yourself.

Another nearby attraction is the **Fall River Carousel** at Battleship Cove (a tour which Mr. C finds a bit expensive for this book). This beautiful carousel is housed in a Victorian-style pavilion overlooking the harbor. Rides are 50¢ each and multiple ride passes are available. Call (508) 324-4300 for seasonal hours.

MIT Museum

- 265 Massachusetts Ave., Cambridge; (617) 253-4444

Another powerhouse educational institution with a museum of equal caliber. The MIT Museum features demonstrations on holography, strobe light sculptures, and math in three dimensions! Don't miss the "MIT Hall of Hacks," displaying famous pranks for which these clever students are known—including the police car that suddenly appeared one day on top of the MIT dome. Admission is $3, $1 for students, seniors, and children under twelve. Open Tuesdays through Fridays from 9 A.M. to 5 P.M., Saturdays and Sundays noon to 5 P.M.

MIT also has two galleries at 77 Massachusetts Avenue. The **Hart Nautical Gallery** has the exhibit "Ships for Victory: American Shipbuilding's Finest Hour," with photographs and artifacts from World War II era shipbuilding. And, the **Compton Gallery** features a wonderful display exploring the role MIT played in winning World War II. Both of these galleries are free at all times.

Museum of Afro-American History

- 46 Joy St., Boston; (617) 742-1854

The historic African Meeting House on Beacon Hill, just below the State House, is the oldest black church still existing in the country. It offers a black version of the Freedom Trail, highlighting significant spots in the neighborhood. Admission is by a suggested donation of $3, $1.50 for students and seniors. Open daily from 10 A.M. to 4 P.M.

Museum of Fine Arts

- 465 Huntington Ave., Boston; (617) 267-9300

The MFA boasts one of the country's major collections of European, American, and Asian art. Recent special exhibits have included "The Taste for Luxury: English Furniture, Silver, and Ceramics, 1690-1790" and "Poster Mania: the 1890s," including works by French, Swiss, Begian, German, Dutch, and American artists. Add to that the permanent exhibits, and it's too much to see in one day, but there are a few ways to keep the cost of return visits down.

Regular admission is a steep $8; students and seniors, $6; children ages six to seventeen, $3.50. Discounts include $1 off all admissions (50¢ off the children's price) on Thursday and Friday evenings from 5 to 10 P.M. when only the West Wing is open. The entire museum is open on a "pay as you wish" basis from 4 to 10 P.M. on Wednesdays. Free programs with general admission include gallery talks, introductory walks, concerts, lectures, and films. Call extension 300 for a schedule.

Museum of Our National Heritage

- 33 Marrett Rd. (Rte. 2A), Lexington; (617) 861-9638

What better town for a national heritage museum than that watched over by the regal Minuteman statue? Like our country itself, this museum is ever-changing; exhibitions circulate every few months in the six display areas. Some shows have a true historical focus, like "Paul Revere: The Man Behind the Myth." Others are more lighthearted: Recently, visitors could check out "Jeans and Leather Jackets: Street Cool to Urban Chic"! Hey, it's all part of the American culture.

Along with a dozen exhibitions a year, the museum sponsors movies, lectures, and concerts. Once or twice a month, family programs of music, storytelling, or magic will divert the kiddies; these events generally cost $3 per child, and $1 for accompanying grownups. Otherwise, admission to the museum is free, as is the parking. Now, *that* should always be the American way! Whether you're coming by land or by sea, hours are 10 A.M. to 5 P.M. Mondays through Saturdays, and noon to 5 P.M. Sundays.

Museum of the National Center of Afro-American Artists

- 300 Walnut Ave., Roxbury; (617) 442-8614

Wow, this is one of the few museums in Boston with the same admission prices as when Mr. C first wrote this book! That's right, admission is a mere $1.25, 50¢ for students and seniors. The name is a bit of a misnomer: the collection contains paintings, photography and sculpture by black artists from many different countries and cultures. Open only from 1 to 5 P.M., Tuesdays through Sundays. Closed on holidays.

Museum of Transportation

- Larz Anderson Park, 15 Newton St., Brookline; (617) 522-6547

Fun for car buffs of all ages, the Museum of Transportation displays a fascinating collection of antique and classic cars. Recent special exhibits include "Cars of the Stars," with wheels owned by Jack Benny, Gary Cooper, and Elvis Presley, and "An Affair to Remember: America's Century-Long Romance with the Automobile," featuring a 1903 Oldsmobile and a 1929 Packard Roadster. They also host gatherings of vintage car clubs, weekend afternoons on the lawn during the warm months. General admission is $5, and $3 for students, seniors and kids over age three. Open Wednesdays through Sundays, 10 A.M. to 5 P.M.

New Bedford Whaling Museum

- 18 Johnny Cake Hill, New Bedford; (508) 997-0046

New Bedford is another destination with more to offer than outlet shopping. The town has a colorful history as a center for whaling, well-illustrated at this New Bedford Whaling Museum. Climb aboard the *Lagoda*, an 89-foot, half-scale model of an actual whaling vessel; check out harpoons, scrimshaw, captain's logbooks, and a real humpback whale skeleton. Admission is $4.50 for adults, $3.50 for seniors, and $3 for ages six to fourteen. Hours are 9 A.M. to 5 P.M. seven days a week, with hours extended to 8 P.M. on Thursdays.

Across the street, check out the **Seaman's Bethel**. Immortalized in the novel *Moby Dick*, this chapel houses the prow-shaped pulpit from which Melville's character Father Mapple gives his famous sermon. Thirty marble cenotaphs engraved with the names of sailors lost at sea span the whole of New Bedford's marine history, from whalers of the 1800s to commercial fishermen of the 1990s. Open from 10 A.M. to 4 P.M. Mondays through Saturdays, and noon to 4 P.M. on Sundays.

NOAA Fisheries Aquarium

- 166 Water St., Woods Hole; (508) 548-7684

Woods Hole is more than just a place to catch a ferry to Martha's Vineyard; it's also well-known as a hotbed of marine biology. Here at the National Oceanic and Atmospheric Administration Fisheries Aquarium, you can see over 100 different varieties of marine life, most hailing from the waters of the Northwest Atlantic.

Inhabitants include plenty of fish, of course; not to mention crabs, clams, mussels, (none of which are for eating) corals, and anemones. During the summer, there's an outdoor pool of playful seals; try to get there during feeding times at 11 A.M. or 3 P.M., when staffers coax the seals into performing tricks for their supper. Inside, a "hands-on" tank is filled with snails, crabs, and other creepy-crawlies. Kids love it. And parents love the free admission. Hours are daily from 10 A.M. to 4 P.M. in the summer, and the same hours Mondays through Fridays only during the off-season. Admission is free.

Old South Meeting House

- 310 Washington St., Boston; (617) 482-6439

Built in the early 1700s, this building has led a varied life as a church, meeting house, and even a horse stable. It's also the place where those uppity colonists first decided to throw a little tea party. Admission is $2.50, $2 for students and seniors, $1 for children under sixteen. Also the site for many lectures and concerts (see the listing in "Readings and Literary Events").

Paul Revere House

- 19 North Square, Boston; (617) 523-2338

You know, the place where the guy slept when he wasn't out riding. It's also the oldest building in the city of Boston, right in the lively North End. Admission is $2.50, students and seniors $2, children age five to seventeen, $1. The house is open daily from 9:30 A.M. to 5:15 P.M., April 15 through October 31. The rest of the

year it closes an hour earlier, and it's closed on Mondays in January, February, and March.

The Sports Museum of New England

- CambridgeSide Galleria, 100 CambridgeSide Place, Cambridge; (617) 57-SPORT (77678)

Along with exhibits about the local sports legends you'd expect—Ted Williams, Larry Bird, and the rest—the Sports Museum also celebrates the contributions of little-known athletes, including high school football stars, notable college hockey players, and backyard baseball greats. Themes of pride and racial tolerance run throughout. Kids get the hint that sports are a way to succeed in school.

Of course, the exhibits are the real draw. Interactive displays allow you to row in the "Head of the Charles" regatta, simulate a climb up Heartbreak Hill against wheelchair marathoner Bob Hall, and catch a Roger Clemens fastball. Measure yourself up against life-size cutouts of Kevin McHale, Nancy Kerrigan, and Jim Rice. Sight-impaired visitors can compare themselves to bronze castings of the hands of Dick Radatz, Reggie Lewis, Killer Kowalski, and others.

The museum is open Mondays through Saturdays from 10 A.M. to 9:30 P.M., and Sundays from 11 A.M. to 6 P.M. Admission is $6 for adults, $4.50 for seniors and kids under twelve, and free for members and children under four.

The Swatch Museum

- 57 J.F.K. St., Cambridge; (617) 864-9111

If you think all museums are filled with stuffy old artifacts, think again. The Swatch Museum, in Harvard Square's Galleria Mall, is a psychedelic tribute to the watch phenomenon of the '80s (didn't think these would already become period pieces, did ya?). Check out more than 900 Swatches—the largest collection in the world. Some, the museum claims, are worth 450 times their original value. Talk about "time is money!"

These are arranged chronologically (how else?) from 1983 onwards, so you can track the progressive funkiness of the watches. Mr. C was boggled by Keith Haring designs, special Christmas watches, "Stop-Swatches". . .you get the idea.

Watch (no pun intended) for special happenings, like "Design a Swatch" contests for kids. Access to the museum is through the Swatch store on the second floor; although Swatches themselves ain't cheap, the exhibit is free. Open Mondays through Saturdays from 10 A.M. to 8 P.M.; Sundays from 12-5 P.M.

U.S.S. *Constitution* Museum
• Charlestown Navy Yard, Charlestown; (617) 426-1812
"Old Ironsides" is the world's oldest warship still commissioned—though it's hard to imagine her seeing battle at this point. Inside the adjacent museum are exhibits detailing maritime life in the early nineteenth century. Artifacts in the collection include clothing, photographs, paintings, rare coins, and gadgets. The museum theater features a video tour of the ship. Open daily; hours vary by season. Admission is $4; $3 for seniors, $2 for kids age six to sixteen. On weekends, kids under sixteen are admitted free! That makes history both fun *and* cheap.

Worcester Art Museum
• 55 Salisbury St., Worcester; (508) 799-4406
The second largest art museum in New England, the Worcester Art Museum is home to over 30,000 pieces: sculpture from ancient Egypt, medieval frescoes from Europe, and masterpieces of Italian, French, Spanish, Flemish, Dutch, and British paintings from pre-Renaissance to modern times. Exhibits include works by Rembrandt, Goya, Renoir, Monet, Cézanne, and Matisse.

All this in Worcester? Well, there's no reason to be condescending. This museum yields as many wonders as any in the Boston area. Admission is $5 for adults; $3 for seniors, college students, and kids thirteen to eighteen; and children under twelve are free. On Saturdays, if you get here between 10 A.M. and noon, admission is free to all. *That'll* get Mr. C out of bed early.

Aside from the wonderful exhibits, WAM sponsors tours, concerts, family days, lectures, workshops, classes, and films. A recent film festival was titled "All's Fair in Love and War," featuring flicks like *Casablanca, South Pacific*, and *From Here to Eternity*, with tickets priced at $4. Open Tuesdays through Fridays from 11 A.M. to 4 P.M., Saturdays 10-5, and Sundays from 1-5.

MUSIC

CLASSICAL MUSIC

All Newton Music School
• 321 Chestnut St., Newton; (617) 527-4553
This educational center offers a series of free concerts in the Newton area. The "Music All Around Town" series takes place on various dates in the Newton Free Library at 330 Homer St., telephone (617) 552-7145; the Newton Senior Center at 345 Walnut St., (617) 552-7178; and the Yamawaki Art & Cultural Center at

Laselle College, (617) 243-2140). Two or three of these happen each month of the season (September through May); call for a schedule.

The school also sponsors several concert series that are not free, but still reasonably priced. The best deal is the "Boston Composers String Quartet Historical Journey" series, which is held on Saturdays at 9:30 A.M.; tickets are $6. Tix to other events are $10 to $15 each. Subscriptions will save you a few dollars off these prices, too.

Ashmont Hill Chamber Music Series

- All Saints Church, 209 Ashmont St., Dorchester; (617) 436-6370

A semi-regular series of Sunday afternoon concerts featuring small ensembles and choral music. Tickets are around $10, with discounts for students and senior citizens. Subscriptions are available too.

Boston Chamber Music Society

- Various locations; Information, (617) 422-0086

Here's a great way to hear some of the best chamber music in the country. This society has been around for fifteen years, giving concerts which may also feature guest musicians. Their season runs from October to April, with concerts given roughly once a month. Each program is played twice in one weekend, once in Cambridge at Harvard's Sanders Theater, and again at New England Conservatory's Jordan Hall in Boston.

At over $30, the top ticket prices are way above Mr. C's range. But you can also sit in the balcony or at the sides of the lower levels, and pay just $12 or so. Seniors and students get an additional 10% off the ticket price. Call for more details.

Boston Symphony Orchestra

- Symphony Hall, 301 Massachusetts Ave., Boston; (617) 266-2378

Seiji Ozawa conducts the BSO in concerts from September through May. While these are not cheap—tix are $20 to $50—there are two alternatives. **Rush tickets**, $7 each, are set aside for concerts on Tuesday and Thursday evenings at 8, and Friday afternoons at 2. They are sold on the day of performance at the box office only, from 5 P.M. for evening concerts and 9 A.M. for Friday matinees. There is a limited supply, one to a customer, first-come first-served. **Open rehearsals** are another way to hear the BSO inexpensively. There is a separate series of these, usually on Wednesday evenings at 7:30 and

Thursday mornings at 10:30. Each is preceded by a short discussion of the music to be heard, starting an hour before the rehearsal. Tickets are $12, with unreserved seating; these may be purchased in advance.

Community Music Center of Boston

- 34 Warren Ave., Boston; (617) 482-7494

In the South End, the Community Music Center is dedicated to bringing affordable, quality music education to people with limited access to the arts. In keeping with this mission, CMC recitals and faculty performances are free and open to the public. Concerts are generally given on Saturday afternoons or weekday evenings, a few times each month during the academic year. Call for a copy of the schedule.

Federal Reserve Bank of Boston Concerts

- 600 Atlantic Ave., Boston; (617) 973-3453

That very modern building across the street from South Station hosts a regular series of free lunchtime concerts in its auditorium on the ground level. Ensembles from the area's music schools are most often featured; concerts begin at 12:30 on Thursdays.

Isabella Stewart Gardner Museum Concerts

- 280 The Fenway; (617) 566-1401

Two sets of concerts take place in this lavish setting; The Sunday Concert Series, on Sundays at 1:30 P.M., and the Young Artist Showcase, on Saturdays at 1:30 P.M. Both feature soloists or small groups, including the Gardner's own chamber orchestra. The Young Artist series features jazz one Saturday each month. Tickets, which include admission to the museum are $15, $9 for students and seniors, $7 for youths twelve to seventeen, and $4 for members. Regular museum admission is $7; students and seniors $5, children twelve to seventeen $3, and free for members. See the listing under "Museums" for more information.

King's Chapel Concerts

- King's Chapel, Tremont and School Streets, Boston; (617) 227-2155

This stately edifice on the Freedom Trail between Park Street station and Government Center hosts weekday lunch hour concerts every Tuesday at 12:15 P.M., usually solo, duet, or small ensemble recitals. These are mostly classical, but occasionally include jazz or folk artists. A freewill donation is requested. There's also one organ recital each month, also by donation.

Longwood Opera

- Christ Episcopal Church, 1132 Highland Ave., Needham; (617) 455-0960

Longwood Opera offers many opportunities to enjoy opera on a budget. Their season features three operas performed at the church mentioned above, as well as at several other venues around metro Boston. These are complete operas—fully costumed and staged, usually with piano accompaniment—and are performed in English. Tickets are $10, $8 for senior citizens, $5 for students.

The repertoire ranges from contemporary American opera to the classics. These performers are professionals from the Boston area, getting their seasoning after graduation from the area's top conservatories. Many of them go on to larger established companies; see 'em now, before they reach the Met and it costs $60 for nosebleed seats.

But wait, there's more! Every Tuesday in July and August, the Longwood presents free concerts at the Needham location. They do request a $5 donation, but that's still a bargain price. The style changes from week to week; one night it may be classic arias, the next time, Broadway tunes. These concerts begin at 7:30 P.M. and last for about an hour. Call the number above for a schedule of upcoming performances.

Music in the Cathedral

- Cathedral Church of St. Paul, 138 Tremont St., Boston; (617) 482-4826

Need a break downtown on a busy Thursday? Duck into this church for a serene hour of music in a magnificent setting. Concerts are given every Thursday from 12:15 P.M. to 1:15 P.M., with a season running from early October to the end of May. Most often, you'll be listening to organ music; usually, one concert a month features a different type of performance, either instrumental or vocal. All of these are free of charge; freewill donations are encouraged, but not required.

For a similar musical experience, **Trinity Church Organ Recitals** take place on the massive pipe organ at this historic church in Copley Square (corner of Boylston and Clarendon Streets). Musicians from the Boston area, and from as far away as England and Russia, perform each Friday from 12:15 P.M. to 1 P.M. Concerts take place from September through May; admission is by donation. Call (617) 536-0994 for more info.

"Music in the Parlor"

- United Parish Church, 210 Harvard St., Brookline; (617) 277-6860

This grand old church just below Coolidge Corner runs its ongoing concert series on selected Sunday afternoons throughout the year. Concerts have included selections for flute and piano. Tickets are $6; $3 for children, students, and senior citizens. Save by purchasing a six-concert subscription for $30.

Newton Symphony Orchestra

- Aquinas College, 15 Walnut Park, Newton; (617) 965-2555

Bizet, Dvorak, and Prokofiev are just some of the composers whose works the NSO has performed to high acclaim during its 30-year history. The orchestra presents four concerts a year, all on this small college campus just off the Mass. Pike. Tickets to individual concerts are $17 for orchestra seats, but just $13 if you sit in the mezzanine. Dedicated fans, meanwhile, know that a series subscription gives you tickets to all four concerts—plus a lecture before each concert and a reception afterwards—for as little as $50-$65. Sign up early, and the subscription rates are discounted by $4. So what are you waiting for?!

Old West Organ Society
• Old West Church, 131 Cambridge St., Boston; (617) 739-1340

This eminent Beacon Hill church houses one of the city's finest pipe organs, and there is a summer concert series featuring various musicians performing anything from baroque to 20th-century organ music. Concerts are on Tuesday evenings at 8 P.M. Admission is free, though donations are appreciated. During the rest of the year, the Organ Society sponsors three concerts featuring internationally renowned musicians. Tickets to these concerts are $10.

> ## MR. CHEAP'S PICK
> ### Classical Music
>
> ✔ **Symphony Rush Tickets** and **Open Rehearsals**—The BSO doesn't *have* to mean $60 tickets. Show up early and breeze in for $7; or catch one of the regularly-scheduled open rehearsals for only $12, with a bit of behind-the-scenes action into the bargain!

FOLK MUSIC

Boston has long been a stop on the folk circuit. These days, there is a good supply of coffeehouses, open-mike nights, and the singer/songwriters to fill them. A good resource for more information is the Folk Arts Network at (617) 522-3407.

ARTSalem
• 15 Hawthorne Blvd., Salem; (617) 744-6633

Stop into one of the few coffeehouses that actually remains open during the summer, and sip *iced* coffee while listening to some fine music. In fact, this one closes up during the months of December and January. Shows take place every other Saturday night, with doors opening at 7 P.M.; an hour-long "open mike" gets underway at 7:30. Around 9 P.M., the featured act takes the stage. Refreshments are served. Admission is $5 a person, but members get a break at the door and pay only $3.

Brew Moon
• 115 Stuart St., Boston; (617) 523-6467

A popular recent addition to the dining scene in the Theater District, Brew Moon features acoustic guitarist Chad LaMarsh on Monday nights.

There's no cover charge, but you do have to be 21 to get in. The Moon was pretty "new" when Mr. C was researching, so they may have added more entertainment offerings by the time you read this. Stay tuned.

Club Passim
• 47 Palmer St., Cambridge; (617) 492-7679

Once they've progressed from the streetcorners to the clubs, tomorrow's stars hope to make it to Passim. It's one of the best folk rooms in town, with music just about every night of the week. Suzanne Vega, John Gorka, Christine Lavin, and many other stars have played here. Recently, Mary Lou Lord, one-time girlfriend of Kurt Cobain and still-rival of Courtney Love, graced the stage. The cover varies from $6 to $10, depending on the artist; open-mike nights are usually $3. But, since they don't serve alcohol, you can enjoy an evening here very inexpensively. They do serve coffees, teas, and desserts.

Coffeehouse on the Corner

- All Souls Unitarian Universalist Church, 196 Elm St., Braintree; (617) 282-9988

On the first Saturday of each month from September through May, you can sit down to live folk music in an intimate, candle-lit atmosphere. Shows usually present three acts a night, and past performers have included such artists as Ellis Paul and Greg Greenway. Standard coffeehouse refreshments are provided, and ticket prices range from $6 to $10. There are no shows on holidays.

First Friday Coffeehouse

- First Congregational Church, 95 College Ave., Somerville; (617) 625-6485

With a name like First Friday, it's not too hard to figure out when the door to *this* coffeehouse is open. From October to May, on (you guessed it) the first Friday of the month, FFC presents live, local folk music. The first part of each show is the designated "open mike," with anywhere from five to seven acts. This is followed by the featured performer(s) to round the evening out. All tickets are $5, and refreshments are served.

"Live at the Luthiers"

- 99 Moody St., Waltham; (617) 894-4292

For those who are wondering: A luthier is someone who makes stringed instruments. Y'know, lutes. Here at the Luthier's Workshop, that's exactly what they do; but, they also present concerts featuring the results of their craftwork.

The musical styles vary widely, including Celtic, jazz, classical, a "Banjo Bash," and even contra dancing. For a time these concerts were held on a weekly basis, but at the time of this writing they were being scaled back to once a month. Admission is generally $5. In addition, a fiddle club meets on Saturday afternoons for an informal jam session. Call for the latest scoop.

me & thee coffeehouse

- Unitarian Universalist Church, 28 Mugford St., Marblehead; (617) 631-8987

This one wins the award for longevity: me & thee has held monthly folk concerts for over 25 years, making it one of the staples on the coffeehouse circuit. Some of the musicians who've performed here over the years include Pete Seeger, Bill Staines, and Cheryl Wheeler. Lots of regulars in the crowd make for a strong feeling of camaraderie at these Friday evening shows. Admission is $6 to $10.

The Nameless Coffeehouse

- 3 Church St., Cambridge; (617) 864-1630

Where else can you hear half a dozen different acts for a suggested donation of $3? Right in Harvard Square, across from the movie theater, the Nameless has been a folkie institution for years. It's a showcase for rising singers, songwriters, and poets, held at 8 P.M. on Saturday nights, about twice a month or so. The setting is lively and informal, with refreshments available at one end and the evening's performers hawking their tapes at the other. Cambridge at its most soulful.

Speaking of which, you can get all the free folk music you want almost any time the weather's nice in Harvard Square. The warmer months, of course, are particularly rich for these budding Bonnie Raitts. The best-known locations are in front of the Harvard Coop, Au Bon Pain, Grendel's Restaurant, and the corner of Brattle and Eliot Streets. You can while away a whole afternoon or evening by wandering from one to the next, for just a buck in each guitar case. Oh come on, they need it; it's still cheap.

Off the Common Coffeehouse

- First Parish Unitarian Universalist Church, 50 School St., Bridgewater; (508) 697-5425

The Off the Common Coffeehouse is uncommon indeed; it's one of the few church-based java joints that has played host to such major folk artists as Patty Larkin and Cormac McCarthy, along with many local acts. Off the Common runs from October through May, on the first Saturday of each month. Refreshments are served at all shows, in OTC's living room-style atmosphere. Ticket prices are generally $4, though some of those bigger acts will command price of about $8 to $10—still, that's easily half the cost of these same stars at larger clubs.

Strawberry Fair Coffeehouse

• 14 Pond St., Norwell; (617) 878-7878

What's in a name? Well, for this coffeehouse, a huge hint to the motif. The Strawberry Fair Coffeehouse is actually a quaint little restaurant that doubles as a folk music showcase one Sunday evening a month, featuring musicians from the local scene. The restaurant offers soup and sandwiches, as well as the standard coffee-and-pastries fare. More unusual, alcoholic beverages are also served here. Ticket prices range from $5 to $10, which usually depends on the number of acts playing that night.

Toad

• 1912 Massachusetts Ave., Cambridge; (617) 876-5405

"No cover, casual dress." The four magic words. Connected to Christopher's Restaurant in Porter Square,

JAZZ AND BLUES MUSIC

Bay Tower Room

• 60 State St., Boston; (617) 723-1666

High atop Boston Harbor, the Bay Tower Room is known for rather pricey dining. However, you can sit at the bar to hear elegant piano jazz Tuesday through Saturday, with no cover charge. Friday and Saturday nights feature a jazz quartet, and there is a $6 cover charge if you're not dining (don't look for this place among Mr. C's restaurant reviews). Still a deal for such elegance, and no extra charge for that great view.

MR. CHEAP'S PICK
Folk Music

✔ **The Nameless Coffeehouse**— What's in a name? Here in Harvard Square, it's a big lineup of folk performers every Friday and Saturday evening for just a $3 donation. It's a stepping-stone toward the professional circuit.

Toad features an interesting assortment of soon-to-be and semi-famous bands, playing virtually every night of the week. Bands seen here recently include Walking Wounded, the Armadillos, and Division Street. Shows start at 9 P.M.

Underground Coffeehouse

• Arlington Food Co-Op, 7A Medford St., Arlington; (617) 648-3663

Try to time your food shopping trip to this co-operative store (see the listing under "Shopping—Food Shops") to coincide with this monthly concert series. Performances take place on Saturday evenings, and all it costs to attend is $3.

Do dress nicely.

The Cantab Lounge

• 738 Massachusetts Ave., Cambridge; (617) 354-2685

This bar's been here for over 30 years, and by the look of them, so have some of its customers. But there's nothing tired or out-of-date about the music you can hear every night. Thursday, Friday, and Saturday evenings always feature Little Joe Cook and the Thrillers; Joe is best-known within the blues world for his hit, "Peanuts." The cover charge is

$3 on Thursdays, and $5 the other two nights. Sunday and Wednesday nights are usually booked by other bands; Mondays and Tuesdays are "open mike" nights hosted by long-time favorite singer-songwriter Geoff Bartley; they focus on folk and bluegrass, respectively. Best of all, these four nights have no cover charge at all.

Music at the Mall
* The Mall at Chestnut Hill, 199 Boylston St. (Rte. 9) Newton; (617) 965-3037

Every Saturday and Sunday afternoon, the Mall offers free concerts from 2 P.M. to 4 P.M. in the large, airy central space on the main level. Local jazz groups and vocalists are the usual fare; sometimes you can hear a classical ensemble or the cast of one of Boston's musicals. Obviously they're doing it to bring in shoppers, but hey—no one's going to twist your arm if you just want to listen.

Plaza Bar
* Copley Plaza Hotel, Copley Square, Boston; (617) 267-5300

At this famous downtown hotel, you can show good taste for the price of a nice jacket and a few drinks. Well, those may set you back some, but there is no cover charge to hear Arthur Phillips tickle the ivories, Wednesday through Saturday nights.

Regattabar Water Music
* Charles Hotel, One Bennett St., Cambridge; (617) 876-7777

The Regattabar? In the nouveau-ritz Charles Hotel? *That* can't be cheap! Well, no, but you can find a bargain here in Water Music's packed schedule of jazz greats from the national circuit. Players such as McCoy Tyner, Art Blakey, John Scofield, and Pat Metheny have all dazzled in this elegant room. Tickets are anywhere from $8 to $20 per set, with two sets each night; *but*, on Thursday nights you can usually hear two sets for the price of one. Tuesday and Wednesday evenings feature the same deal, but for local artists, so tix tend to stay in the $8-$10 range. Music starts around 8 P.M.

Scullers Jazz Club
* Doubletree Guest Suites Hotel, 400 Soldiers Field Rd., Boston; (617) 562-4111

Jazz *aficionados* have been making this cafe a regular stop for years. Renovated in '95, Scullers now boasts better viewing and acoustics, along with its cozy, candle-lit atmosphere. The club showcases some of the best jazz acts on the national circuit every week from Tuesday through Saturday evenings. Tickets may cost as much as $24, but depending on the show, some tix are more like $6 to $10. Tuesday nights offer only one set (oh, you early-to-bed Boston crowds!), but Wednesdays through Saturdays give you two for your money. Scullers has a full bar; they also offer music/dinner combination deals at prices from $33 to $38 on Friday and Saturday nights.

1359 Jazz Club
* 288B Green St., Cambridge; (617) 547-9320

A few years back, jazz fans bemoaned the closing of Inman Square's wonderfully divey 1369 Jazz Club. Now, the V.F.W. Hall in Central Square attempts to make up for the loss. The goals of the 1359 Jazz Club are twofold: To introduce new audiences to "America's classical music" in a setting that is educational and entertaining, and to provide rehearsal and performance space for lesser-known musicians.

Access is the key (excuse the pun), and the best example of this is live music with no cover charge. To make it profitable for the musicians, though, listeners are requested to make a donation—which goes directly to the band. The 1359 presents bands every Friday and Saturday night, along with a jam session on Wednesdays. All shows begin at 9 P.M.

Top of the Hub
* Prudential Tower, 52nd Floor, Boston; (617) 536-1775

Aah, that fabulous view from high atop the Back Bay. Relax in this cozy, dark lounge, mix in a little free jazz, and you have the makings for a very special evening. A jazz band plays Friday and Saturday nights; Sundays through Thursdays there is a piano player.

Wally's Cafe
- 472 Massachusetts Ave., Boston; (617) 424-1408

For jazz at its grittiest and most traditional, there is only one place—the smoke-filled room at Wally's. Just about every major combo in town has gotten started there. Sets begin around 9 each night and wail until 2 A.M., with no cover charge. The drinks won't run you out of dough, either. There's an open blues jam on Monday nights and Sunday afternoons, and an open jazz jam on Thursday nights.

Willow Jazz Club
- 699 Broadway, Somerville; (617) 623-9874

The other cheap, cool jazz joint in town. The Willow is a must stop on the way up for local as well as national bands; it's tiny and often packed, but the music is worth it. Sets begin at 9 every night except Tuesday, with cover charges from $6 to $14.

MR. CHEAP'S PICK
Jazz and Blues Music

✔ **Wally's Cafe**—For jazz at its rootsiest, this is the place to be. Serious players, a smoke-filled room, and no cover charge. Cool, man.

Wire House
- 20 Park Plaza, Boston; (617) 292-0527

Relatively new to the Boston scene, the Wire House appeals to the information-starved set. Hundreds of international newspapers and magazines are on sale, and TV news is on throughout the day (though when Mr. C stopped in, Donahue was holding forth). This is not just a place for aspiring Woodwards and Bernsteins, though; on Friday and Saturday nights, the Wire House features live acoustic music by local musicians. There's no cover charge. Music starts at 8:30 P.M. and jams 'til 11:30 P.M. Call for a schedule of upcoming acts.

ROCK AND POP MUSIC

There are so many bands in Boston and so many clubs in which to hear them. Here is a hand-picked variety of venues that have live music for free or a low cover charge. Of course the club scene is ever-changing, so check the papers for current prices and policies.

Avalon
- 15 Landsdowne St., Boston; (617) 262-2424

One of Boston's most popular discos, Avalon can always be counted upon for hordes of dancers and high-energy DJs. Mr. C enjoys its inexpensive prices: On Fridays and Saturdays, you can get on the dance floor for free from 9:30 to 10:30 P.M. After that, you'll have to pay $8; the cover is $10 anytime on Thursday nights.

The Brendan Behan Pub
- 378 Centre St., Jamaica Plain; (617) 522-5386

Pale imitations make Mr. C appreciate an authentic Irish pub all the more. From the jovial fellow behind the dark wooden bar to the pint of room-temperature Guinness that takes ten minutes to settle, Behan's is the real thing. Irish countryside photos and concert posters of folks like Mary Black greet the eyes in this cozy spot; "Best Irish Pub" awards from *Boston Magazine* confirm its merit.

Sunday through Wednesday evenings, if you can squeeze yourself in, the pub presents live music with no cover charge. It's not all "The Wild Rover" either: A recent month included rockabilly one night and hip-hop the next. But every Tuesday features a traditional Irish band packing the house. "It's pretty tight, where they set up," admits the manager, which explains why there's no music on weekends. The band would have to play on the ceiling. Open seven days, as late as the law allows—at least.

Burke's

- 808 Huntington Ave., Boston; (617) 232-2191

Famous for its gritty, no-fooling-around atmosphere, Burke's is home to rock and blues bands on Friday and Saturday nights. Cover prices range from $2 to $6. On Wednesday and Thursday nights, stop in for the free blues jam session.

11th Chapter Saloon

- 366A Somerville Ave., Somerville; (617) 628-4300

This narrow bar in Union Square also happens to have great food (see the listing in "Restaurants—Somerville"). And somehow, they fit rock, folk, and blues bands in on Thursdays through Saturdays, with no cover charge. Don't miss their very own 11th Chapter Band on Sunday nights. The atmosphere is dark and funky, with lots of good beers on tap and even more in bottles.

Green Briar Pub

- 304 Washington St., Brighton; (617) 789-4100

There is no shortage of Irish music pubs in Boston. Green Briar is one of the larger, nicer ones. Local Irish rock bands play every Friday and Saturday night, with cover charges around $3. Better yet is Monday night's traditional Irish jam session, with all acoustic instruments and no cover. Music starts after 9 P.M.; toward midnight the kitchen sends out free sandwiches for the players, and you can have one too.

Hard Rock Cafe

- 131 Clarendon St., Boston; (617) 353-1400

How can a restaurant that is now in every city in the world still be a tourist trap? Mr. C isn't sure, but it doesn't seem to matter. Boston's branch does have something that should interest fellow Cheapsters, though: free, live acoustic music on Friday and Saturday nights. "Cavern Club Live" features Boston bands in Hard Rock's hip (if over-hyped) atmosphere. Music starts at 10 P.M.

Irish Embassy Pub

- 234 Friend St., Boston; (617) 742-6618

Acting as goodwill ambassadors to Boston music fans, the folks at the Irish Embassy Pub present live music nearly every night of the week. Styles vary somewhat, but stay within the rock, Irish (naturally), and alternative boundaries. There's no cover charge on weeknights, and weekends usually cost a reasonable $5 (some attractions may go a bit higher). Well-positioned across from the late lamented Boston Garden, it's a popular spot to go after games and other happenings.

Nearby in the North Station area, **The Harp** twangs with good ol' all-American rock 'n roll. There's no cover charge on weeknights, and on weekends it's just $3-$4. The joint starts to jump at 9 P.M.; you must be 21 if you want to join in. They're at 85 Causeway Street; telephone (617) 742-1010.

Joe's American Bar & Grill

- 2087 Washington St., Hanover; (617) 878-1234

Popular with South Shore Cheapsters, Joe's American Bar & Grill features live music five nights a week. Wednesday is blues night, and Sunday offers acoustic guitar. But the heart of the schedule, Thursday through Saturday, is reserved for Top 40 bands. Great for dancing and hanging out with friends. No cover any night of the week.

Johnny D's Uptown Restaurant & Music Club
- 17 Holland St., Somerville; (617) 776-9667

This is an enormously popular venue for all types of music; Mr. C dropped by on a Tuesday night, and the club was humming. On weekends, about the only movement you can make on the packed dance floor is vertical. Originally, Johnny D's produced only country-western shows, but in the '80s the focus changed and by now the club says it has "presented everything from blues to Bulgarian wedding music." They recently received an honor from the Blues Foundation in Memphis, and deservedly so; there's at least one R & B show every week, as well as a regular Sunday night blues jam.

But there's more to life than singing the blues. Monday nights alternate between Cajun dancing night and swing. Other nights may offer rock, folk, or whatever; bands come from all over the U.S. as well as from abroad. Cover charge is $2 to $8; great food, too.

The Kells
- 161 Brighton Ave., Allston; (617) 782-9082

Relatively new to the Allston rock scene, the Kells weighs in with six nights of rock, Irish, and acoustic music. There is a $3 to $4 cover on Fridays and Saturdays, and no cover the rest of the week. On Wednesday nights, the Kells features alternative music "unplugged" (before MTV came along, they called it "acoustic"). Cheap eats here, too.

Kinvara Pub
- 34 Harvard Ave., Allston; (617) 783-9400

One of the many clubs lining the intersection of Harvard and Brighton Avenues, Kinvara serves Irish beers, cheap food (including a traditional Irish breakfast on Sundays) and live music on Thursday, Friday, and Saturday nights. Most bands play Irish traditional and rock, but straight-up rock is mixed in too. Cover is usually around $3 to $4.

MR. CHEAP'S PICKS
Rock and Pop Music

✔ **Johnny D's**—Every kind of music, seven nights a week.

✔ **The Middle East**—There's something for everyone, musically speaking. Lots of bands, lots of genres, not a lot of cash.

✔ **Plough and Stars**—Crowded neighborhood joint that rocks every night; no cover during the week, low cover on the weekend.

Also in the neighborhood, check out **Local 186** at 186 Harvard Ave., (617) 351-2660 and **Harper's Ferry** at 158 Brighton Ave., (617) 254-9743. Both showcase up-and-comers on the Boston rock scene; covers range from $5 to $8.

Limerick's
- 33 Batterymarch St., Boston; (617) 350-7975

In addition to Buffalo wings, turkey melts, and shepherd's pie, Limerick's serves up Irish bands—sometimes rhythm and blues—on Thursday, Friday, and Saturday nights. There is no cover charge. They also have Guinness on tap. For the business suit crowd, mostly.

Linwood Grille
- 69 Kilmarnock St., Boston; (617) 267-8644

Whether you're into rock, blues, or acoustic folk, you'll find it all at the Fenway's Linwood Grille. Live entertainment is offered Wednesdays through Saturdays, and the cover charge is under $5. Some nights, it's free! Add in pub-style cheap eats, and Linwood becomes a great and grungy weekend destination.

Mama Kin

- 36 Lansdowne St., Boston; (617) 536-2100

This popular Lansdowne Street rock club is owned by the gods of the Boston music scene, Aerosmith. Live bands from both the local and national levels play on either of two stages, living up to the club's promise to give plenty of Boston bands a chance to be heard. There is also a theater upstairs, which presents locally produced plays, poetry slams, and even radio broadcasts. Cover charges vary depending on the show, but every Monday you can sit in on the open blues/rock jam session without paying a cover. The jam starts at 10 P.M., and winds up nice and late.

The Marketplace Cafe

- 300 Faneuil Hall, Boston; (617) 227-9660

Now, *here's* a deal! In the North Building at Quincy Market, this three-story restaurant offers free live music every single night of the week. Often, there is something happening on more than one floor at a time. There's no cover charge, and you don't even have to eat at the restaurant to enjoy the tunes (and maybe a dance or two). Nurse a drink along at the bar. Musical styles heard here range from rock to jazz to folk. It's not just for tourists anymore!

The Middle East Restaurant

- 472 Massachusetts Ave., Cambridge; (617) 497-0576

There is no excuse for not being able to find a show that will get you rockin' here. One of the Boston area's most popular music venues, the Middle East has three separate rooms presenting live music. You may catch anything from local rock and acid-jazz groups to a 22-piece circus band, or even a belly dancing performance.

Be sure to take advantage of some of the club's specials: Every Saturday from 3 to 6 P.M., for example, is the Middle East's "Reggae Jam." Cover is a mere $2, mon. Also, on Sundays and Tuesdays, college students can get a dollar off admission with their

school ID. Better yet, shows in the "Bakery" section are free to everyone, seven nights a week. Good cheap food, too; see the listing under "Restaurants—Cambridge."

Just around the corner is **T.T. the Bear's Place** at 10 Brookline St., telephone (617) 492-2327. This is another of Cambridge's longtime favorites for hot local bands, offering music every night of the week (sometimes as many as four groups a night!) at cover prices from $5-$6 and up.

Midway Cafe

- 3496 Washington St., Jamaica Plain; 524-9038

This JP watering hole serves up blues, rock, and R & B every night, with a blues jam on Sundays and a jazz jam on Tuesdays. There is a $2 cover on Friday and Saturday nights; other shows are free, and they serve beer from seven local microbreweries.

Plough and Stars

- 912 Massachusetts Ave., Cambridge; (617) 492-9653

This sounds as though it should be another fine Irish music pub, named as it is after the famous O'Casey play; but in fact, it's good ol' American rock 'n roll spoken here. The owner, who is from Dublin, says flippantly, "There's no such thing as an American bar in Ireland; why should there be an Irish bar in America?" Fortunately for the rest of us, other proprietors disagree. Meanwhile, this is a popular neighborhood hangout, boisterous and crowded at night. Live bands play folk, reggae, blues, and rock every night of the week. There's only a cover charge on Thursday, Friday, Saturday and it's a mere $2. What's more, if you come in before 9 P.M. they don't charge the cover at all! Great beers on tap.

The Rathskeller

- 528 Commonwealth Ave., Boston; (617) 536-2750

It's probably safe to say that the Rat "is" Kenmore Square, as much as anything is. Two floors showcase live bands desperately seeking recording contracts. Downstairs has music every night, and on Friday and Saturday nights there are bands upstairs as well. Covers range from $4 to $7. Shows start at 9 P.M. Good barbecue until 10 P.M., too.

Rhythm & Spice
- 315 Massachusetts Ave., Cambridge; (617) 497-0977

This Jamaican restaurant and bar, a relatively new arrival in the M.I.T. area, cooks up more than terrific jerk chicken and curried conch. Every Friday and Saturday night from 10:30 P.M. to 1 A.M., plus occasional Thursdays, they close up the kitchen and instead serve up live Caribbean dance music. Local bands play every variety of Afropop, from reggae to calypso to soukous. There's a full bar (plenty of Red Stripe beer on hand). Good thing there's a dance floor; this music makes it hard to sit still.

Cover is usually a reasonable $5; or, you can come in before 10 P.M., order dinner, and stay on for no extra charge. The menu is moderately priced (with a few entrees under $10), the food is wonderful, and the service is friendly.

The Tam O'Shanter
- 1648 Beacon St., Brookline; (617) 277-0982

This cozy restaurant and bar is about as hip as Brookline gets—in fact, it's one of the best clubs in the Boston area for local rock and blues bands, seven nights a week. Come in for a hearty meal before the music starts around 9:30 or 10, and you can avoid the cover charge (not to mention the lines that usually wind down the block). The wide open, smoke-free atmosphere makes viewing the bands much more enjoyable than the usual crowded venues. The music is free Sundays through Wednesdays; other nights, the cover ranges between $2-$6. The food leans toward Southern home-style cooking.

The Tam also presents a live classical music brunch on Saturdays from 10:30 A.M. to 3:30 P.M., and a jazz version on Sundays; this is followed by a jazz dinner at 7:30 P.M. There is no cover charge—the music is included with the moderately priced food.

Zanzibar
- One Boylston Place, Boston; (617) 351-7000

At the other end of the dance club alphabet from Avalon, Zanzibar—in the alleyway behind Remington's in the theater district—is one of the veterans of the Boston club scene. Its two floors offer you a choice of dancing on the spacious floor or watching the dancers from above. Admission is $5 Wednesdays through Saturdays.

OUTDOORS

Arnold Arboretum
- 251 The Arborway, Jamaica Plain; (617) 524-1717

One of the area's truly great places to get away to during spring, summer, and, of course, fall. In fact, the Arboretum is open every day of the year, from sunrise to sunset, free of charge. Designed by Frederick Law Olmsted and Charles Greg Sargent, this is more than just a park; it's a living laboratory run by the botanical department of Harvard University. It has over 14,000 trees and shrubs from around the world, all grouped by family and labeled. The fields in between are perfect for picnicking or playing frisbee, and there are long, winding paths for strolling and even careful bicycling. The visitor center includes a gift shop and a video show about the place. To get there without a car, take the Orange Line to Forest Hills, or the "Arborway" bus.

Blue Hills Trailside Museum
- 1904 Canton Ave., Milton; (617) 333-0690

Didja know that the Blue Hills are

one of the five windiest spots in the whole country? This visitor center and museum offers a quick, fun introduction to the beauty and wildlife of the area. Indoor and outdoor areas let you view turtles, snakes, owls, fish, honeybees, otter, deer, wild turkey, and bobcats. It's like a mini zoo! The museum also sponsors plenty of family programs including story times, puppet shows, arts and crafts, and holiday activities. The reservation itself is filled with plenty of hiking trails, beaches, and picnic areas.

The museum is open Wednesdays through Sundays from 10 A.M. to 5 P.M. Admission is $3, $2 for senior citizens, $1.50 for children, and free for members of the Massachusetts Audubon Society. There may be additional fees for some special events.

Boston Common/Public Garden

- Information, Boston Park Rangers, (617) 635-7389

During good weather, take a stroll through the Common during lunch hour and you'll see it teeming with people eating, talking, and watching street performers. Explore it on a weekend and find folks playing on its softball diamond and tennis courts, free to the public. Check out the Civil War Memorial. The Public Garden, laced with colorful flower beds, is home to Boston's famous Swan Boats (see below).

Boston Public Library Courtyard

- Copley Square, Boston; (617) 536-5400

Who would guess that the ultimate city-dweller's getaway is found right in the heart of downtown? Yes folks, if you've never experienced it, the courtyard at the center of the Boston Public Library—where the old building joins the new—is an oasis of tranquility in the midst of the urban jungle.

Enter from either building, and follow the signs; soon, you'll find yourself gazing upon trees, flowers, and a quiet fountain in a reflecting pool. Surrounded on all four sides by the library itself, the walled-in effect is not claustrophobic, but peaceful. You can barely hear the city, even though you're outdoors. Here, people sit in chairs and on benches reading, quietly conversing, or just closing their eyes and listening to the water. It really is quite amazing—even more so because, like all the riches the library offers, it's free of charge. Open during regular library hours, year-round (though you'll find fewer people, and no water, during the winter months).

Boston University Observatory

- 725 Commonwealth Ave., Boston; (617) 353-2630

Wanna see stars? Go up on the roof to BU's tiny but well-equipped observatory. On Wednesday nights at 8:30, in good weather, the telescope is open free to the public, and of course someone from the astronomy department is there to point you in the right direction. Call around 6 P.M. that evening to make sure they'll be open.

Charles River Canoe and Kayak Center

- 2401 Commonwealth Ave., Newton; (617) 965-5110

Out by the unlikely junction of Commonwealth Avenue and Route 128, you can actually find yourself a bit of natural bliss by renting a canoe and paddling for miles along the Charles. With rates as low as $7 an hour, with room for up to three people per boat, it's a great cheap getaway from the city. Pass by lily pad bogs, tiny islands in the stream, or—if you must—glide right under the highway. They'll provide everything you need, including paddles and life jackets. Parking is across the river from the boathouse; walk back over the bridge to the docks. Rates are $7 an hour on weekdays, $8 an hour on weekends. For kayaks, $8/hour weekdays and $9/hour on weekends. Good bargains all. The center is open weekdays 10 A.M. to 8 P.M., weekends and holidays 9 A.M. to 8 P.M.

Community Boating

- Charles River Esplanade, Boston; (617) 523-1038

You've seen all those sailboats dotting the river on a sunny summer's day. Ever thought about trying it yourself? Located behind the Hatch Shell, Community Boating has for many years made the joys of sailing affordable to all. You can join for a month, two months, or the full spring-to-fall season. Membership includes everything you need: instruction, boats and equipment, and use of the boathouse, with a snack bar and showers.

And, believe it or not, rates have actually gone *down* since Mr. C first reviewed them! A 30-day member-ship is just $65—amazing, even if you only go a few times. You can al-ways bring guests along, too. A 75-day membership is $165, and the full season costs $215. Community Boat-ing now offers windsurfing as well.

What's more, they have a junior pro-gram that runs from mid-June through late August, and it costs just $1. Wow. Great, cheap way to keep the kids busy during summer vacation. It's available to kids ages ten to seventeen, who must have parental permission and proof of swimming ability.

Franklin Park Zoo
- Blue Hill Ave. & Columbia Rd., Dorchester; (617) 442-2002

Once a poor man's zoo fallen into ne-glect, Franklin Park had a ton of money poured into it few years back, making it a zoo worth visiting. In ad-dition to its renowned aviary, where hundreds of rare birds flit all around you, the zoo has a brand-new walk-through habitat, the African Tropical Forest. It looks like a spaceship from the outside, but once you go in you'll see all kinds of gorillas, hip-pos, monkeys and snakes all living in full-size replicas of their natural habitats. Further down is that old fa-vorite, the petting zoo, where kids can feed large animals. All of these are included with admission, which is $5.50, $4 for seniors and stu-dents, $3 for kids four to twelve; and free under age four. Everyone is admitted free on Tuesdays, between 9 A.M. to 10 A.M. Open daily from 9 A.M. to 4 P.M., weekends and holi-days 10 A.M. to 5 P.M.

MR. CHEAP'S PICKS
Outdoors

✔ **The Charles River Canoe and Kayak Center**—Need a country getaway without leaving the city? Rent a canoe and while away an hour or two paddling along the Newton stretch of the Charles River. Inexpensive and easy.

✔ **The Franklin Park Zoo**—Kids will love the African Tropical Forest habitat. Parents who bring their troops in during the first hour on Tuesdays will love the free admission.

✔ **Marino Lookout Farm**—Get out to open farmland, just by driving to Natick.

✔ **University Observatories**—Both Boston University and Harvard University offer free weekly observatory nights for stargazers. Look through powerful telescopes at the moon and the stars—weather permitting, of course.

Garden in the Woods
- 180 Hemenway Rd., Framingham; (508) 877-6574

Not far from the suburban sprawl of scenic Route 9, Framingham hides an oasis of truly natural beauty. Owned and operated by the New England Wildflower Society, the Garden in the Woods consists of 45 acres of woodland trails filled with native flowers, ferns, shrubs, and trees. From the first blush of spring through the brilliant colors of fall, the garden is filled with an ever-changing pano-rama of delights.

Guided tours are given at 10 A.M., Tuesdays through Saturdays; self-guided tour booklets are also available. Reservations are required for group tours. The garden is open Tuesdays through Sundays, 9 A.M. to 5 P.M., from April 15 to October 31. Hours are extended during Daylight Savings Time, so call ahead for the current schedule. Admission is $6, $5 for senior citizens, and $3 for children five to fifteen. Better yet, become a member and you can stroll for free as much as you like!

Harbor Island State Park
- Bay State Cruises, Long Wharf, Boston; (617) 723-7800

Residents don't tend to think of the harbor for a day's outing, but it is dotted with beautiful little islands where you can enjoy camping, hiking, and picnicking.

Take a ferry from Long Wharf (next to the Aquarium) to Georges Island, a relaxed, 45-minute ride; the fare is $6.50, and $4.50 for kids. Now, that may sound expensive—but once there, you can take a *free* water taxi to Gallops, Lovells, Grape, Bumpkin, and Peddocks Islands (during summer months only). All of these have picnic areas, fishing and boating piers, guided walks, and restroom facilities. Several also have historic forts to explore, and even camping facilities.

Ferries leave Boston on the hour; boats also run from Hingham, Hull, and Lynn, though not as regularly, so check ahead. For more info, call the Department of Environmental Management at (617) 740-1605, or Friends of the Boston Harbor Islands at (617) 740-4290.

Bay State also offers a $1 "Lunch Cruise" on weekdays from May through October. The trip lasts 30 minutes, departing at 12:15 P.M. Happy landings!

Harvard University Observatory
- 60 Garden St., Cambridge; (617) 495-7461

Another place where you can ascend to the heavens and leave earthly bounds behind. The Harvard-Smithsonian Center for Astrophysics presents a formal 45-minute program on the third Thursday of each month.

There's a lecture and film at 8 P.M. and then telescope viewing at 9 P.M. Get there by 7:45 P.M. since the seats for the lecture are limited. Again, be sure to call ahead if the day's weather is in doubt (in Boston, when isn't it?).

Jamaica Pond Boathouse
- The Jamaicaway, Jamaica Plain; (617) 522-6258

From spring through fall, you can enjoy the beauty of the great outdoors without actually leaving the city. The Jamaica Pond Boathouse rents out rowboats for $6 per hour, and just $3 per hour for senior citizens. Small sailboats are available too, and quite reasonably priced at $10 an hour. If you go out with a few friends and split the cost, this is a true bargain. The boathouse is open daily during the season, from 9 A.M. to 6 P.M.

Lyman Estate Greenhouses
- 185 Lyman St., Waltham; (617) 891-7095

Open to the public by donation, the Lyman Estate Greenhouses are among the oldest in the country. Four greenhouses are filled with grapes, orchids, citrus fruits, and camellias. Many of the Lyman's trees are over one hundred years old—and there are grapevines grown from cuttings actually brought over from England's Hampton Court in 1870! Lyman sells plants, too, and offers advice to fellow green thumbs. The greenhouses are open Mondays through Saturdays from 9:30 A.M. to 3:30 P.M.

The mansion itself, built in the late 1700s by wealthy Boston merchant Theodore Lyman, is also available for tours. These cost $3, available by reservation only.

Marine Park
- Castle Island, South Boston; (617) 727-5290

Not really an island any more, but simply the furthest reach of Southie, Castle Island is an immensely popular destination when the weather's fine. Sea breezes and a two-mile walking path around the manmade Pleasure Bay make this a perfect escape—quick and cheap—on a hot day. As an added attraction, Logan-bound jets come in for a landing right over your head. After your walk, ruin the effort with an ice cream from Sullivan's take-out stand, which operates from March through November.

Looming over the entire scene, atop a low hill, is historic **Fort Independence**. Built in 1851, this imposing stone structure is open for free each year from Memorial Day through Labor Day. Guided tours are given Saturdays and Sundays from noon to 3:30, with "Twilight walks" on Thursdays from 7 P.M. to dusk. Kids will love running around in here, and climbing up to the ramparts, which offer a fantastic view of the harbor.

Marino Lookout Farm
• 89 Pleasant St., South Natick; (508) 655-4294

Just a few winding miles south of downtown Natick, you make a turn into what ought to be yet another suburban driveway—and suddenly, you're out in the country. The Marino Lookout Farm is, in fact, one of the oldest continually operated farms in the U.S., established in 1680 (!) and still busy. Today, it sells produce and plants, both wholesale and retail, along with "pick-your-own" fruits and vegetables; it's also a mini-zoo, with all manner of farm animals creatures you can see up close.

As for the animals, these include deer, sheep, goats, pigs, and even llamas. There are also pens with exotic birds. Crossword puzzle fans can finally see what an emu actually looks like. Take the mile-or-two walking tour over hills, past ponds, and through barns. Have lunch—your own, or something from the shop—at a picnic table or under a tree. There's no charge to walk the grounds; "We want this to be a family place, where people can spend a 'day in the country'," says farm manager Mark Harmon.

On weekends in the fall, they hitch up a tractor and wagon, and give hayrides for a dollar. At any time from June through October, you can also call ahead to arrange for a

guided hayride tour of the farm, stopping to learn about all of the animals, for just $3 a person. It's a great idea for birthday parties.

In June, you can get in on the act by picking your own strawberries; in September and October, pick apples and raspberries. A pavilion sells fresh cider and apple pies, too. Why, you can even pick tomatoes, broccoli, and eggplant in season; call the U-Pick Line at (508) 653-0653 to find out what's available when. The farm is open daily all year 'round; call them for directions, seasonal hours and activities.

Mt. Auburn Cemetery
• 580 Mt. Auburn St., Cambridge; (617) 547-7105

If you're not uneasy about walking among tombstones, Mt. Auburn Cemetery also happens to be an idyllic place to stroll on a sunny day. Fully landscaped with lakes, hills, and huge old trees, there are so many pathways that they actually have street signs. Being a private cemetery, of course, not a public park, they do request "dignified behavior" from visitors; no lying on the grass, picnics, or ball playing. Instead, sign up for a walking tour of famous monuments, or an early morning bird-watching walk; the main house has brochures about Mt. Auburn's programs, for which a donation of $7 is requested ($2 for members). The grounds are open every day of the year, free of charge, from 8 A.M. until 5 P.M., and until 7 P.M. in summer.

New England Aquarium Sea Lions
• Central Wharf, Boston; (617) 973-5200

Admission to the Aquarium is a bit pricey, though well worth it; one thing you can see here for free, however, is the outdoor sea lion pool, during regular Aquarium hours. Watch half a dozen of these shiny, graceful mammals frolic and cavort in the water; if you're lucky, you may catch them at feeding time. It's endlessly fascinating, as the constant crowds prove.

South Bridge Boat House

- 496-502 Main St. (Rte. 62), Concord; (508) 369-9438

Explore the waters, woods, and wild-life of Concord that Thoreau and Emerson made famous. Even if you're not a philosopher or writer, you'll be inspired as you canoe from the boathouse down the Concord, Sudbury or Assabet Rivers. You can even glide under Old North Bridge, site of the Revolutionary War's historic "Shot heard 'round the world."

There are lots of bucolic places to break for a picnic along the waterways. And the prices? Well, they're pretty relaxing, too. Try to go during the week, when it's just $7 an hour for a canoe that fits three; on Saturdays and Sundays the hourly rate is $8.25. Kayaks can be rented for the same prices. The boat house is open from April through October, beginning at 10 A.M. during the week; during the weekends, rentals start at 9 A.M.

Stone Zoo

- 149 Pond St., Stoneham; (617) 438-7459

The big attraction at the Walter D. Stone Zoo is undoubtedly its aviary. The sixty foot-high structure repli-cates a tropical rain forest in both height and climate; it's filled with native plants and some forty species of birds. This alone is worth the price of admission, but you get a whole lot of other animals into the bargain. And that price is pretty low to begin with: $3 for adults, $2 for students and seniors, $1.50 for kids 4-11, and children under four admitted free. Open daily from 10 A.M. to 4 P.M.

The Swan Boats

- Public Garden Lagoon, Boston; (617) 522-1966

For a maritime activity of another sort, there are always those famous Swan Boats. Have you ridden one since your childhood? Y'know, we've had them since 1877; that's a lot of pedaling. Yes, it's one of the only human-powered forms of public transportation, even if you do end up where you started. Rides last about fifteen to twenty minutes, a little haven of quiet and charm in the middle of the city. And such a bargain! Only $1.50 for adults and 95¢ for kids under twelve (hey, this ride makes kids of everyone). The boats run seven days a week, 10 A.M. to 5 P.M., from April to September. Don't forget to bring some bread to feed the ducks.

READINGS AND LITERARY EVENTS

POETRY AND LITERATURE

Boston is a lit'rary kind of town, laced with spots in which one can sip cappuccino and enjoy the spoken word in all its myriad forms. Play readings, storytelling, poetry slams, and sometimes even acoustic music are offered at the venues below, usually for little or no money. Don't forget to check the "Theater" chapter for more examples of dramatic readings.

Agape Poetry

- Community Church of Boston, 565 Boylston St., Boston; (617) 489-0519

Have some thoughts you want to share with the world, or do you just want to sit back and listen to some-one else's observations? If you fit into either of these categories, settle into the intimate atmosphere of Agape's poetry readings. Every Tuesday night from 8 to 10 P.M., you can listen in on original and published works of poetry and short stories, from featured performers and new-comers alike. There is no set admission price, but any donation is accepted.

Barnes & Noble Booksellers

- 395 Washington St., Boston; (617) 426-5184
- 470 Southbridge St., Auburn; (508) 832-0855
- 150 Granite St., Braintree; (617) 380-3655
- 325 Harvard St., Brookline; (617) 566-5562
- Burlington Mall Rd., Burlington; (617) 270-5500
- 170 Boylston St., Chestnut Hill; (617) 965-7621

A great place for discounted books, Barnes and Noble is also a great place for book-related events. Along with the major author-on-the-book-tour-visitations, bringing in such literary luminaries as George Will and "Dilbert" cartoonist Scott Adams, B & N presents lots of lesser-knowns, too, offering readings, lectures, workshops, and children's activities. B & N locations are open seven days a week, usually into the late evening.

The Bookcellar Cafe

- 1971 Massachusetts Ave., Cambridge; (617) 864-9625

Boston magazine has voted the Bookcellar Cafe the best storytelling venue in the city. Clearly, dedication to the spoken word is a high priority here. The Bookcellar hosts storytelling every Tuesday night: The general format is "open telling" at 7 P.M., and then a featured storyteller at 8 P.M. On other nights, poetry readings and acoustic music are part of the scene, too. And theater. And jazz. Plus coffee and pastries. In fact, there aren't too many things the Bookcellar *doesn't* do. Best of all, the entertainment is free. Call for a calendar—it's packed! The store is open from noon to 10 P.M. daily, except Mondays.

The Bookcellar Cafe is also a popular stop for cheap books, affiliated with Boston's **Ave. Victor Hugo**. For more information on both, see the listing in "Shopping—Books."

Borders Books and Music

- 300 Boylston St., Chestnut Hill; (617) 630-1120
- 85 Worcester Rd. (Rte. 9), Framingham; (508) 875-2321
- 151 Andover St. (Rte. 114), Peabody; (508) 538-0089
- *And other suburban locations*

This fast-growing national chain presents a packed schedule of readings, live music, and more. Harry Ellis Dickson, assistant conductor of the Boston Pops, dropped in to read from his book, *Beating Time: A Musician's Memoir.* The stores also sponsor discussion groups, an excellent chance to read new works and meet folks with similar interests.

But wait, there's more! Selling recordings as well as books, Borders hosts regular performances of live music as well. The Chestnut Hill branch, for instance, offers a "Coffee House Series" on Friday nights at 7:30 P.M. in its cafe. Special events have even included an appearance by Bruce Hornsby. MTV meets suburban bookstore chain. Activities vary by branch; to get a full listing of upcoming programs, pick up a copy of their newsletter "FootNote." Borders has lots of kids' events, too, including story times.

Brookline Booksmith

- 279 Harvard St., Brookline; (617) 566-6660

This busy bookstore, one of the area's most popular, hosts author readings and book signings about once or twice a *week*! These include big names: Alice Hoffman, Sue Miller, and Deepak Chopra have all dropped by. That's unusual for an independent; but this is no ordinary neighborhood store. Readings, always free, usually take place in the early evening; space is limited, however, so you may want to pick up tickets in advance or make a reservation by phone.

Murder, she read. . . . Every month, Booksmith sponsors a "Mystery Night," which usually presents a pair of talespinners reading from their latest works. Two reading circles also convene at the bookstore; one focuses on science fiction, the other discusses both contemporary and classic fiction. Again, all of these events are free of charge.

Even little ones can get in on the action, thanks to a regular series of kids' events. Puppet-making, storytelling, and even visits from favorite storybook characters take place throughout the year, with more frequent sessions during summer vacation; and they are (you guessed it!) free.

Grolier Poetry Reading Series
- 26 Plympton St., Cambridge; (617) 547-4648

Performers at the Grolier have at least one thing in common: They've all been published. This certainly sets it apart from many other reading series around town, which tend to mix established authors with up-and-coming types. Here, such well-known authors as Steven Dobbins and Deborah Dix have been known to drop by to read from their works. Readings take place at Adams House (no relation to Mr. C's publisher) in Harvard Square on Tuesday nights from September through May, and every weekend in October. Best of all, these shows are free, though donations are gratefully accepted.

Harvard Book Store Readings
- Boston Public Library, Copley Square, Boston
- Cambridge Public Library, 449 Broadway, Cambridge
- Information, (617) 661-1515

Harvard Book Store runs a series of readings at the BPL and the CPL. These are held weekly, on either Tuesday or Wednesday evening, at 6 P.M. In the past, the series has attracted big names like C. Everett Koop and Garrison Keillor. Readings are followed by a chance to meet the authors and have them sign copies of their books.

Lauriat's Books
- Copley Place, Boston; (617) 262-8858
- 45 Franklin St., Boston; (617) 482-2850

- South Shore Plaza, Braintree; (617) 848-5788
- Shopper's World, Framingham; (508) 879-0303
- The Mall at Chestnut Hill, Newton; (617) 965-1481
- 82 Central St., Wellesley; (617) 235-1846
- *And other suburban locations*

Royal Discount Bookstore
- 753 Boylston St., Boston; (617) 375-9299
- 485 Massachusetts Ave., Arlington; (617) 643-4422
- 43 Middlesex Tpke., Burlington; (617) 273-1850
- 917 Worcester Rd. (Rte. 9), Natick; (508) 653-0950
- 74 McGrath Hwy., Somerville; (617) 623-6593
- 381 Main St., Wakefield; (617) 245-0519
- 824 Washington St., Weymouth; (617) 331-8288
- 348 Cambridge Rd., Woburn; (617) 932-3760

If you want to see the biggest celebrity writers, head to Lauriat's and its offspring, Royal Discount Bookstores. Lauriat's has hosted signings by everyone from politicians Jimmy Carter and Dan Quayle to humorists Dave Barry and Don Imus. Readings, most of which take place at the Arlington branch of the Royal chain, have included Erica Jong, Apollo 13 astronaut James Lovell, and Pulitzer Prize-winner E. Annie Proulx.

Children's events have included visits from the Cat in the Hat, along with regular story hours and craft workshops. For info on upcoming events, call the branch nearest you.

Longfellow National Historic Site
- 105 Brattle St., Cambridge; (617) 876-4491

This large, airy hall is the setting for readings of anything from poetry to Halloween storytelling. These take place on Sunday afternoons or evenings through the summer and early fall. Readings are free and open to the public; some are held out on the lawn. Call for the current schedule.

Stone Soup Poetry

- T.T. the Bear's Place, 10 Brookline St., Cambridge; (617) 227-0845

Stone Soup Poets gather every Monday evening from 8 to 10:30 at this popular club in Central Square. TT's is a raucous rock n' roll bar most other nights, so the atmosphere is more funky than the bookstore cafe settings. Have a beer with your poetry instead of espresso. Admission is $3.

WordsWorth Reading Series

- Brattle Theater, 40 Brattle St., Cambridge; (617) 354-5201

The Brattle Theater, usually home to classic movies, plays host to the WordsWorth Reading Series every Tuesday from September through May. Past authors seen here have included big-name novelists like Martin Amis, Sue Grafton, Pat Conroy, and Margaret Atwood, as well as nonfiction writers like Calvin Trillin and Gloria Steinem.

Tickets are free, but you do need one to get in; these events nearly al-

---

MR. CHEAP'S PICKS
Poetry and Literature

- ✔ **Bookcellar Cafe—** Inexpensive books, yummy food, and a packed schedule of poetry, music, and play readings, all in a cozy and quirky atmosphere.

- ✔ **Brookline Booksmith—** Hobnob with the likes of Ann Beattie, Deepak Chopra and Sue Miller, all for free.

---

ways sell out. WordsWorth requests that you bring a donation of canned food for the Cambridge Food Pantry Network. Tix are available from two weeks prior to the night of each reading, at WordsWorth Books (30 Brattle Street).

LECTURES

Boston is a town that talks! There are plenty of opportunities to hear luminaries pontificate on art, politics, philosophy, religion, and other hot topics. And, in this the cradle of democracy, most are free and open to the public.

Cambridge Forum

- 3 Church St., Cambridge; (617) 495-2727

An ongoing series of discussions on weighty matters, such as "Why Congress Has It Wrong on Welfare Reform: The Empirical Evidence," "The Presidential Nomination Process: Is It Broken? If So, How Do We Fix It?," and "Building Community With Technology." Lectures are held on Wednesdays at 8 P.M. in this Harvard Square church; admission is free to all.

Community Church of Boston

- 565 Boylston St., Boston; (617) 266-6710

This forward-thinking Copley Square church explores a wide variety of fascinating and timely topics. Recent programs included discussions on the letters of the Rosenbergs, the obstruction of peace in the Middle East, and the Contract with America's war on motherhood. These are held on Sunday mornings at 11, and are free and open to all. The season runs September through June.

The Ethical Society of Boston

- Longy School of Music, 1 Follen St., Cambridge; (617) 739-9050

Now celebrating its 40th anniversary, the Ethical Society of Boston holds free lectures on a variety of topics including health care, education, psychology, peace, relationships, and

MR. CHEAP'S PICKS
Lectures

✔ **The Ford Hall Forum** and **Kennedy Library Forums—** Two organizations which present a steady diet of food for thought: lectures and panel discussions featuring prominent authors, experts, and policy makers. The events are free to the public; get on their mailing lists.

economics. Weekly discussions are held on Sunday mornings at 10:30; admission is free and open to all. The society also has monthly book discussion groups that deal with both fiction and non-fiction. Call for a copy of the newsletter. The season runs from September to May.

Ford Hall Forum
• Various locations; Information, (617) 373-5800

For almost a century Ford Hall Forum has made "freedom of speech" a reality. The organization presents well-known speakers on a variety of topics, free and open to the public, so that all may learn from experts about vital matters. Guests range from the beloved, like Red Auerbach, to the controversial, like former PLO spokesperson Hanan Ashrawi. Other recent speakers include Rosalynn Carter, Janet Reno, and U.S. Representative Barney Frank.

Events take place at one of three places: Faneuil Hall, Old South Meeting House (310 Washington Street, Boston), or the Blackman Auditorium (360 Huntington Avenue, at Northeastern University). Lectures take place on Sundays and Thursdays at 7 P.M.; all are followed by a question and answer session. Call to get on their mailing list for schedules.

Kennedy Library Forums
• John F. Kennedy Library, Columbia Point, Boston; (617) 929-4554.

Another impressive series of discussions on important issues, from the "Big Dig: Progress Report" to "Why Americans Hate Politics." Speakers have included Michael Dukakis, former Boston Police Commissioner Francis Roache, *Washington Post* reporter E.J. Dionne, Jr., and public opinion pollster Lou Harris. A reception follows each forum. All events are free and open to the public, but reservations are strongly recommended.

Old South Meeting House
• 310 Washington St., Boston; (617) 482-6439

One of Boston's earliest public gathering places (see the listing under "Museums") continues to serve this purpose with its "Middays at the Meeting House" lecture series. These take place on Thursdays at 12:15 P.M. through the year, and are just $3 ($2.50 for students and seniors). Each month examines a single theme, with different topics from week to week. Subjects have included "Paul Cuffee: A Black Yankee Federalist," "New England Women at Sea in the 19th Century," and "History of Boston's Chinatown." Music also makes up part of the"Middays" series, as in the recent "In Concert: New England Brass." Old South also sponsors several evening lecture series. These are free, and include fun topics like "Boston Diners: Food, American Style" and "Burlesque in Boston." Always call ahead to verify times and locations.

Radcliffe Career Forums
• 77 Brattle St., Cambridge; (617) 495-8631

An 80-year-old institution, Radcliffe Career Services pioneered the concept of career services for women. Today, it offers a wide range of programs and events to help women achieve their career goals. Radcliffe Career Forum lectures cover all kinds of topics, like "Strategies for Salary Negotiations" and "Networking to

Uncover the Hidden Job Market." While preferences are always given to Radcliffe students and alums, all RCS programs are available to the public. Admission is $5; pre-registration by phone is requested.

And, don't miss the Radcliffe Colloquium Series. Every Wednesday at 4 P.M., the Bunting Institute (34 Concord Avenue) presents a talk on a different topic from the areas of art, history, politics, and women's issues. Free and open to the public. Call (617) 495-8212 for more information.

INTERNET ACCESS

Since Mr. C began his work to hunt out bargains in all areas, a new category has presented itself. Cropping up all over the place are "stores" and cafes where the merchandise is access to the information superhighway. Some are very expensive (up to $17.50 *per hour*) and some are bargains. Read on.

Cafe Liberty
- 497B Massachusetts Ave., Cambridge; (617) 492-9900

This funky basement cavern in Central Square—filled with art, newspapers, fantastic coffee drinks, and nibbles—also offers the Internet on its menu. Three workstations are available for public use at a flat rate of $4.50 an hour. IBM and Macintosh formats are both represented. You can also use these for "off-line" word processing and printing; it's like a Kinko's, only fun. Catch a caffeine buzz and go surfing. Open from 8 A.M. on weekdays and 10 A.M. on Saturdays, until 1 A.M. (!) all six nights.

Virtually Wired
- 55 Temple Pl., Boston; (617) 542-5555

In the heart of Downtown Crossing, Virtually Wired offers access to the Internet, including the much-ballyhooed World Wide Web, for a simple donation of $5. In fact, they offer "bus tours" (a VW bus, perhaps?) for the technologically uninitiated. Volunteer instructors will show you how to use the equipment and show you what's available for exploration. All this for five bucks? Believe it. This is a non-profit organization, so of course they won't say no if you're inclined to pay more (and don't be a road-hog, now). At the time of this writing, six computer stations (all donated) were connected to the high-speed phone link. You'll be driving in the fast lane of the Infobahn in no time.

Virtually Wired also offers low-cost classes for the computer-challenged. Two-hour sessions cost $25. Anyone who's priced computer education courses will recognize this as a bargain. Classes include "Introduction to Computers," "Tech Tips," and "Building Web Pages." Virtually Wired is open 11 A.M. to 6 P.M., Mondays through Saturdays.

SPORTS

No, Mr. C can't get you into the Sox game for free—though don't forget that many of the big sports arenas and stadiums do have ticket prices that start around $10. One cheaper alternative is college sports;

there are highly competitive schools throughout Boston, and many have very affordable prices for football, basketball, hockey, and many more. There are often many different sports locations on each campus; the ticket offices, at the phone numbers listed below, can give you all the details.

Boston Red Sox Bleachers

• Fenway Park, 4 Yawkey Way, Boston; (617) 267-1700

No matter how the Sox are doing in the annual pennant race, tickets for their games are always at a premium. Fenway Park, one of the few "original" baseball parks left, is on the small side—and so most games sell out. Ticket prices nudge themselves up a few dollars every season. But you can always save a few bucks by sitting in the outfield bleachers, which cost about half of the box seat prices; this past year, that meant $8, as opposed to $16. Buy them in advance at the box office or right before the game from windows along the back of the stadium, on Landsdowne Street.

When games are sold out, a limited number of standing room tickets are made available at the $8 price; since there are often no-shows, you can sometimes get in cheaply this way and then try to find an empty seat. Be nice about it, though, if the real ticket-holder comes along late!

Boston University

• Information, (617) 353-3838

BU football games, at the very modern Nickerson Field, cost only $10 for adults, and $5 for children. A deal for the diehard is a $25 pass

that gets two people into all five home games. For you sports trivia fans: In another lifetime, this stadium was home to baseball's Boston Braves. BU's hockey team is another perennial contender.

Boston College

• Information, (617) 552-3000

Eagles football has gotten more expensive, thanks to The House that Doug Built, with a top price of $25; and that's if you can even get hold of a pair. But BC hockey is a much more affordable matter. Tix are just $10 for seats and $8 for benches.

Harvard University

• Information, (617) 495-2211

There's more than just studying going on here! Football is the big sport here, and tickets are $10 for seats along the sidelines; $5 if you don't mind the end zone. Prices are a bit higher for games against Dartmouth ($12) and Princeton ($15). And be sure to get your orders in early for the annual Yale game, for which all tix are $25.

Pawtucket Red Sox

• McCoy Stadium, 1 Columbus Ave., Pawtucket, RI; (401) 724-7300

Ahhh, baseball as it was meant to be. Forget about whiny, overpaid major-leaguers. The guys in this league *want* to be in the majors, so they still have the fire that makes sports fun. And, tickets are way cheap. Box seats are $5.50, and $4.50 for kids and seniors. General admission tickets, which you can usually walk up to the window and buy right before the game, are just $4, and $3 for kids and seniors. McCoy Stadium, home of the PawSox, is smaller than Fenway—so there isn't a bad seat in the house. Pawtucket is about an hour's drive from Boston.

MR. CHEAP'S PICK
Sports

✔ **Pawtucket Red Sox**—Real baseball, the way it was meant to be. Tickets are half the price of BoSox bleacher seats.

University of Massachusetts
- Information, (617) 287-7800

The Boston branch of the five-campus UMass system has lots of great sporting events. Tickets to basketball games in the Clark Athletic Center are a mere $2. Hockey is a little bit more expensive at $9. Actually, for *serious* college hoops, trek out to Amherst in the western part of the state. Tickets are a bit more expensive (though still way less than the Celtics) and may be difficult to get, especially as March Madness approaches. Call (413) 545-0810 for ticket information.

THEATER

To save money on professional theater in town, consider a little-known option: **Volunteer ushering**. Many theaters use regular folks to help rip tickets, hand out programs, or guide people to their seats. In exchange for your services, you can watch the show for free. Responsibilities are light: Dress nicely, arrive a bit early to learn the layout of seats, and then go to it. As soon as the show begins, find a seat for yourself and enjoy the show—you're all done. Ushering can even make a fun cheap date—it's a guaranteed conversation starter afterwards! Best of all, you'll save yourself some cash *and* help that theater out at the same time. Call ahead to find out if that show you've been eyeing uses volunteers, and when they have slots available.

If that's not for you, but saving money is still important, here are Boston's leading players for ticket discounts:

ARTS/Mail
- 100 Boylston St., Boston, MA 02116; (617) 423-0372

Become a member of this mail-order organization and you'll receive their monthly newsletter filled with dozens of opportunities to see plays, dance, music, and more, usually at half-price or thereabouts. They've even had Phantom of the Opera and The Nutcracker. If you can schedule your culture in advance (there is generally a choice of dates for each show), you can save money big-time. Write for information.

BOSTIX
- Faneuil Hall Marketplace, Boston; (617) 723-5181
- Copley Square, Dartmouth and Boylston Sts., Boston; (617) 723-5181

These kiosks sell half-price tickets to shows all over the Boston area, including the big shows downtown, whenever empty seats are made available by the individual box offices. In late 1994, BOSTIX opened a second location in Copley Square; each location has the same tickets available. Half-price tickets are sold for that day's performances only; the booth also sells advance tickets at full price, as well as tickets for concerts, museums, and other events. Open Mondays-Saturdays from 10-6, Sundays 11-4. The Faneuil Hall branch is closed Mondays. Cash only.

Now, here is a list of resident theater companies performing in the Boston area at affordable prices:

American Repertory Theatre

- 64 Brattle St., Cambridge; (617) 547-8300

With its Yale-Harvard pedigree and million-dollar-plus budget, the A.R.T. steals much of the theatrical thunder in town with its strong regular ensemble and lavish sets. Name players such as Christopher Lloyd and F. Murray Abraham occasionally strut and fret their hour upon this stage too, along with international directors and major contemporary playwrights. Ticket prices get steep, naturally, but here's an open secret: The A.R.T.'s "Pay What You Can" program.

Each week, fifty tickets are set aside for the upcoming Saturday matinee. They go on sale Monday at 11 A.M. until they are gone; you must buy them in person, two tickets to a customer. And yes, you may literally pay whatever you can afford. A.R.T.'s season runs from November through July.

Beau Jest Moving Theater

- Piano Factory Theater, 791 Tremont St., Boston; (617) 437-0657

Beau Jest calls itself "a center for movement-based theater, dance, and physical comedy." After ten years performing around the country (including the annual "Serious Fun" festival at New York's Lincoln Center), this innovative company has founded its own performance space in the South End. Here, they stage their own creations and welcome visiting theater, cabaret, and dance companies. They generally produce three shows a year; it's always inventive, unusual, and sometimes downright wacky. Because the theater is tiny, it's a good idea to reserve your seats in advance. Ticket prices vary, but the usual rates are $8 general, $5 for students and seniors.

Boston Playwrights Theatre

- 949 Commonwealth Ave., Boston; (617) 353-5443

Boston University is well-respected for its graduate playwrighting program, headed by Nobel laureate Derek Walcott. Virtually hidden on BU's campus, the Boston Playwrights Theatre is home to readings and fully-staged productions of the work done in this program. Tucked down an alley behind the McDonalds, this building houses two fully-equipped, modern theater spaces.

One of the best deals is the "New Stage Series," workshop productions of new plays, followed by a discussion with the playwright, director, and actors. Admission is free. Mainstage productions, ready for a larger (read: paying) audience, are still a bargain at $12 for general admission, $6 for students and seniors.

Filling out its schedule of plays, poetry readings, and lectures, BU also rents this space to other companies, such as the Chekhov Film and Theater Project and even some Equity productions. Tickets are usually $10 or less.

Huntington Theater Company

- 290 Huntington Ave., Boston; (617) 266-0800

One of Boston's premier theaters, the Huntington regularly features well-known actors (not to mention very talented ones you may not know), Tony Award-winning directors, and elaborate costumes and scenery. Their season comprises five shows, ranging from modern dramas and musical comedies to Shakespeare or Gilbert and Sullivan operettas. Some plays are done in conjunction with repertory companies from all over the country.

At 890 seats, the Huntington offers good viewing for a major theater—even from the balcony or back rows. A good thing, because these seats only cost $12. Senior citizens get $5 taken off that price; same deal for students, who can also vie for "rush tickets": Available on Tuesdays and Thursdays only, these tix sell for $10—but they must be bought at the box office on the day of the show.

Mobius

- 354 Congress St., Boston; (617) 542-7416

Boston's longtime, dedicated avant-garde troupe. Run by its artist members, Mobius presents experimental works in theater as well as dance, music, and art installations. They offer a continuous schedule of performance art pieces, usually on weekends. Tickets are $5 to $10. Don't miss the gallery and its wonderful exhibits; see the listing under "Art Galleries" for more information.

New Broadway Theater

- 277 Broadway, Somerville; (617) 625-1300

The latest resident ensemble at the Elizabeth Peabody House/Performance Place, this troupe presents an ambitious season of high-quality plays. These range from classics like Goldoni's *The Servant of Two Masters* to contemporary comedies like *The Kathy and Mo Show.* Tix are usually around $15.

New Repertory Theatre

- 54 Lincoln St., Newton; (617) 332-1646

This highly respected professional ensemble presents a variety of British and American plays from Noel Coward to Sam Shepard. A recent bill of one-act plays included works by Anton Chekov, Peter Shaffer, and Dorothy Parker. Tickets start around $12; subscriptions bring the price down by about one-third. New Rep also has a "Platform Series," staged readings of new plays, with free admission. Discover a future masterpiece!

New Theatre

- First and Second Church, 66 Marlboro St., Boston; (617) 247-7388

In spite of the name, this is one of Boston's oldest established companies dedicated to the development of original plays (*that's* the "new" part). These works are all by Massachu-

---

MR. CHEAP'S PICKS
Theater

✔ **ARTS/Mail** and **BOSTIX**— ARTS/Boston makes two options available for those who want theater, music, and dance on a budget. Buy day-of-performance tickets at half-price at the BOSTIX booths at Faneuil Hall or Copley Square; or, join ARTS/Mail (for free!) and get similar deals in advance.

---

setts-based writers, several of whom have gone on to wider acclaim. This is where you can see their diamonds-in-the-rough, in both simple readings and full productions.

Each January, in fact, brings the annual "NEWorks" festival, which presents a whole batch of workshop productions over a two-week period. You can buy tix to individual plays, or a special discounted pass that's good for the whole shabang. NT also offers acting classes, including a serious two-year conservatory program, which presents classic plays throughout the season. Tickets are usually around $10 for individual productions, and less for conservatory shows.

Nora Theatre Company

- Harvard Union, Quincy St., Cambridge; (617) 491-2026

Another professional company in residence on the Harvard campus, Nora presents an ambitious season of contemporary plays. Tickets are $15 on Thursdays and Sundays, and $18 on Fridays and Saturdays. Discounts are available for students and seniors. Recent shows included Terence McNally's *A Perfect Ganesh*, not long after its New York premiere.

Open Door Theatre

- Jamaica Pond Park, Jamaica Plain; (617) 522-2398

Each summer in the "Kettlebowl," a natural amphitheatre perfectly formal in the ground, the Open Door company offers outdoor theatre under the stars. Run with assistance from the Boston Parks Department, ODT offers Shakespeare, Tennessee Williams, and sometimes new works. Tickets are $10, and there is always a free night for Jamaica Plain residents.

Pilgrim Theatre
- Various locations; Information, (617) 964-8918

The official name is the Pilgrim Theatre Research and Performance Collaborative—a mouthful which indicates their emphasis on the experimental. Indeed, Pilgrim is one of Boston's most respected *avante-garde* theatrical troupes. Innovative and challenging original works have included *A Tempest*, adapted from Shakespeare, and *Oedipus: An Archeological Improvisation for Two Actors, Musicians, and Others*. Another recent piece was called *Letters*, based on the book *Letters from Sarajevo*.

Pilgrim Theatre performs in venues all over town, and ticket prices vary accordingly. Still, they generally stay in the range of $8 to $12. They are committed to keeping prices low enough for everyone. In addition, they offer "pay what you can" evenings and some free performances; call to find out about upcoming plays and places.

Regent Theatre Arts Center
- 7 Medford St., Arlington; (617) 648-6001

Until recently a second-run moviehouse, the Regent now mixes its movies with live theatrical shows. Flicks are still a bargain, with tickets just $2.50 to $4. Live shows are pricier, naturally, but still quite reasonable: Musical events are usually $14 to $16 ($9 to $11 for senior citizens and students). Non-musicals are $10 to $12 ($8 to $10 seniors and students).

Shows are performed by various local troupes. Call for upcoming events.

Theater in the Open
- Maudslay State Park, Pine Hill Rd., Newburyport; (508) 465-2572

Myths and fairy tales, both familiar and not, are the order of the day at this family-oriented outdoor theater. Their re-telling of classic stories will delight audiences of all ages. Ticket prices will delight you most of all: just $5. And, here's a tip from Mr. C: opening day performances are free to the public. One show runs per season for approximately three weeks, with showtimes usually on Saturday and Sunday afternoons.

In addition to the regular line-up, Theater in the Open sponsors two annual events: "The Rites of Spring" in May and "Maudslay is Haunted" in October. Admission to each is $3.

Turtle Lane Playhouse
- 283 Melrose St., Newton; (617) 244-0169

Each summer for over a decade, Turtle Lane has presented high-quality local productions of popular musicals like *Fiddler on the Roof* and *Little Shop of Horrors*. A recent fave was *Something's Afoot*, a cabaret-style Agatha Christie spoof. Tickets are $16 to $18, with subscriptions available for greater savings. In addition, tickets are $10 for students on Fridays and for seniors on Thursdays.

Wheelock Family Theatre
- 180 The Riverway, Boston; (617) 734-4760

Family theater here doesn't necessarily mean children's theater; WFT is dedicated to affordable plays that are appropriate for all ages. This can include classic musicals and even dramas, presented by a professional troupe in a large, comfortable auditorium on the Wheelock College campus. Tickets are around $9-$10.

WALKS AND TOURS

This section is designed as much for "tourists in their own home town" as for out-of-town visitors. There's a lot to see out there!

Art & Architecture Tours at the Boston Public Library

- Main Branch, Copley Square, Boston; (617) 536-5400

You already know that the library is filled with all kinds of interesting freebies. But how many have you actually seen? Volunteer guides will take you on a free hour-long tour of the BPL's magnificent collection of sculptures, paintings, murals, and frescoes.

The original building, designed by architect Charles Follen McKim in 1895, was intended as a "Palace for the People." In 1972, the library expanded with an addition by Philip Johnson. On the art side, there are sculptures by Daniel Chester French; murals by John Singer Sargent; paintings by John Singleton Copley and Winslow Homer; and frescoes by Joseph Lindon Smith and Elmer Garnsey. Tours are given on Mondays at 2:30 P.M., Tuesdays and Wednesdays at 6:30 P.M., and Thursdays and Saturdays at 11 A.M. They start from the Dartmouth Street lobby of the old McKim building, the doors facing Copley Square. For special appointments, call extension 216 at the number above.

Atlantic Coast Brewery Tours

- 50 Terminal St., Boston; (617) 242-6464

Mr. C's got to say one thing about the folks at Atlantic Coast: They sure are proud of their beer! This Charlestown brewery is home to Tremont Ale, a brew advertised as "an honest alternative to mass-produced beers." Take their free tour, and see for yourself how pure barley, hard water, and English hops come together to create the golden liquid so many rave about. In

fact, you'll get a chance to sample a bit and make your own critique. As noted above, it's all totally free. Just call 'em up to arrange an appointment.

Boston Beer Museum

- 30 Germania St., Jamaica Plain; (617) 522-3400

Also known as the Samuel Adams Brewery, this is another place to see how one of America's best beers is made. This is an actual factory with a tour that explains the history of Samuel Adams (both the patriot *and* the beer), brewing, the German Beer Purity Law, and more. Best of all, they give free samples. Tours are given every Thursday and Friday at 2 P.M. and on Saturdays at noon, 1 P.M., and 2 P.M. A donation of $1 is requested, and proceeds benefit the Boys & Girls Clubs of Boston.

Boston Park Ranger Tours

- Various locations; Information, (617) 522-2639

During the warmer months, the Boston Parks Department offers several free walking tours every week in many areas of the city. From the Public Garden to Jamaica Pond, from bird-watching to architecture, these jaunts may show you a side of Boston that you've never seen before. All events are free; call for schedules.

Bunker Hill Pavilion

- 55 Constitution Rd., Charlestown; (617) 241-2575

All right, everyone knows the Battle of Bunker Hill actually happened on Breed's Hill (don't you?). We also know which hill got the credit, as evidenced by the Bunker Hill Pavilion. There's more here than a stone monument; the multi-media extravaganza, "Whites of their Eyes," is presented in a theater-in-the-round with fourteen screens and a professional actor playing Paul Revere. It's all designed to make you feel like you're actually there, waiting to shoot until....well, you know. Admission is $2. The pavilion is open seven days a week from 9:30 A.M. to 4 P.M.; it stays open until 5 P.M. from June through August.

About ten minutes away by foot, follow this with a visit to the actual **Bunker Hill Monument**. Though certainly not high-tech, the monument does offer dioramas depicting the famous battle and a 294-step climb to the top. Great view of the harbor too! Admission is free; hours are 9 A.M. to 5 P.M. daily. Call (617) 242-5641 for information.

Cambridge Historical Society
- Various locations, Information, (617) 547-4252

Every spring, CHS offers 90-minute walking tours through many different neighborhoods of this large city, including the working-class streets of East Cambridge, the snooty estates of Brattle Street, and the patrician homes of North Cambridge. Most tours are $3, and they take place rain or shine.

Charlestown Navy Yard Tours
- Visitor Center, Charlestown Navy Yard; (617) 242-5601

Take a free 45-minute tour of the docks, the rope walk, and the several historic ships moored here, all sponsored by the National Park Service. The visitor center is located next to the U.S.S. *Constitution*. Tours are given Wednesdays through Sundays at 11 A.M. and 1 P.M., mid-June through early September. You can also walk around—and even onto— the ships on your own.

Christian Science Center "Mapparium"
- 175 Huntington Ave., Boston; (617) 450-3790

The publication building of the Christian Science Monitor happens to house one of Boston's unique treasures, something they call the "Mapparium." It's a giant-sized globe of the Earth—which you see from the inside. Walking along a bridgeway through this huge glass bubble, you can look above and below at the nations of the world, rendered in bright handpainted colors. Of course, it's impossible to change something like this, so you'll see the world as it was in 1935, when this was built. The way borders are changing these days, though, it'll probably be correct again before long.

The Mapparium is also known for the wild acoustics of its round glass walls. Stand at one end and whisper to someone at the other; they'll hear you perfectly. Admission is free; hours are from 9:30 to 4 P.M. Mondays through Fridays, and noon to 4 P.M. on Saturdays. The Christian Science Mother Church, next door, makes for a fascinating architectural tour as well.

Commonwealth Brewery Tours
- 138 Portland St., Boston; (617) 523-8383

If you've ever wondered how beer is made, you can see for yourself in the basement vats of the Commonwealth Brewing Company. Free tours are given daily at noon and 4 P.M. Of course, this is a restaurant, so it's not *entirely* free; how can you pass up trying this fine home brew, once you've learned so much about it?

Cranberry World
- Ocean Spray Cranberries, 225 Water St., Plymouth; (508) 747-2350

If you're heading to the Cape this summer, take a detour and visit Plymouth's *other* attraction, Cranberry World. This fun, free tour includes anything and everything you could ever want to know about that humble little fruit. You'll see antique and modern harvesting tools, a scale model cranberry farm, and, of course, a real outdoor cranberry bog. In the spring the bog is covered in light pink flowers; by the end of the summer the more familiar red berries appear.

At the end of the tour, of course, you can sample eight different Ocean Spray cranberry concoctions. Daily cooking demonstrations provide another opportunity for free goodies. CW is only open from May 1 to November 30. Hours are 9:30 A.M. to 5 P.M. daily, including weekends and holidays. Call for a schedule of free summer concerts on the boardwalk, too.

Faneuil Hall

• Government Center, Boston

Dating from 1742, Faneuil Hall became the "Cradle of Liberty" when our forefathers began to debate British taxation policies. The hall continues to be the site of political debates. It was here too that Michael Dukakis (remember him?) declared his candidacy for president in 1988. Meanwhile, you can just stroll in and explore one of our nation's most important meeting places. National Park Service Rangers are on hand to answer questions and give a quick history lesson. The hall is open all year and there's no "tax" on admission. Take the stairs or an elevator from the shops on the ground floor.

Fenway Park Tours

• 4 Yawkey Way, Boston; (617) 236-6666

*Take me out to the ball game....*Since its construction in 1912, Fenway Park has become as indelible a part of America's pastime as it has of the Boston landscape. Tour the park inside and out, and learn even more about one of the oldest ballparks in the country. You can walk around the field (but not on the precious grass!), sit in the dugout, and touch the famous Green Monster (hmm, sounds kinky). Tickets for the 40-minute tour cost $5 for adults, $4 for seniors, and $2.50 for kids under 15. Tours are available Mondays through Fridays, from 10 A.M. to 1 P.M. on the hour. Reservations are recommended; group rates are available.

The Freedom Trail

• Boston Common Visitor Center, Boston; (617) 242-5642

Everybody knows the Freedom Trail—that red line painted down the middle of the sidewalk downtown. But have you ever actually *walked* it? It's probably the fastest history lesson

---

MR. CHEAP'S PICKS
Walks and Tours

✔ **Historic Neighborhoods Tours**—This educational non-profit organization will show you nooks and crannies all over town, for five bucks.

✔ **Mapparium**—Walk through the center of a giant glass globe with the nations of the world (circa 1935) painted in bright colors. Also popular for its bizarre acoustics.

✔ **The State House**—See political fireworks up close, free of charge.

---

you've ever seen, and you'll get exercise too. Nearly three miles of walking brings you to a dozen colonial landmarks—some you'll know, some you may not. And, unless you go into some of them, like the Paul Revere House and the Constitution Museum (which charge small fees), it won't cost you a cent. Pick up a map at the beginning of the trail, the Boston Common Visitor Center on Tremont Street, and off you go. From May through October the National Park Service will take you on a free 90-minute guided tour, starting from the Visitor Center at the intersection of Devonshire and State Streets, near City Hall.

Ask about maps for the **Black Heritage Trail**, the **Women's Heritage Trail**, and the **Harborwalk**, too.

Harvard University Walking Tours

• 1350 Massachusetts Ave., Cambridge; (617) 495-1573

You can't really pahk yer cah in Hahvahd Yahd, but you can walk through this oasis tucked away beside the bustling square. Find out what all the buildings are and what their historical significance is. Free, 45-minute tours are given Mondays through Saturdays at 10 A.M., 11:15 A.M., 1:15 P.M., and 3:15 P.M.; and on Sundays at 1:30 and 3 P.M. Tours meet at the Harvard Information Center in Harvard Square.

Historic Neighborhoods Tours
• 99 Bedford St., Boston; (617) 426-1885

There's no excuse for not learning more about the rich history of Boston—not when Historic Neighborhoods, a non-profit educational organization, conducts 90-minute walking tours for just $5. Explore Beacon Hill, Chinatown, the North End, and the waterfront, with trained guides fleshing out all the significant stuff, as well as fascinating tidbits. Also, kids of all ages will love the "Make Way for Ducklings" tour through Beacon Hill, which re-creates the famous children's story. Reservations are required; six people are needed to guarantee a tour. Ask about group rates.

John Hancock Observatory
• 200 Clarendon St., Boston; (617) 572-6420

New England's tallest building affords a spectacular view of our fair city and the many hills and dales beyond. Admission is $3.75 for adults, $2.75 for senior citizens and children; small price to pay for such an awesome sight. You can stay up there as long as you want. Hours are Mondays through Saturdays from 9 A.M. to 11 P.M., and Sundays from 10 A.M. to 11 P.M., though they can vary in the winter.

Longfellow National Historic Site
• 105 Brattle St., Cambridge; (617) 876-4491

You read the poems in school—now, see where Henry Wadsworth Longfellow wrote the book! This handsome, enormous yellow house, built in 1759, is where ol' Hank lived and wrote from 1837 to 1882. The National Park Service now runs the site, which you can only see on their guided tours.

Hour-long tours take place six times a day. Adults pay a mere $2; anyone under 17 is admitted free. After you admire the house, you can take a stroll around the surrounding park. And Harvard Square is a short ten-minute walk down lovely Brattle Street, where many other period buildings co-exist with modern (tasteful) commercialism. The Longfellow house is open to the public from May through October only. Hours are from 10 A.M. to 4:30 P.M., Wednesdays through Sundays.

Mass Bay Brewing Company
• 306 Northern Ave., Boston; (617) 455-1935

In the pioneering early days of micro-breweries (about ten minutes ago), most were found in the relative wilderness of the Pacific Northwest. More recently, they've been popping up all over the place, including several in Boston. The Mass Bay Brewing Company, brewers of the Harpoon line of suds, offers an hour-long tour of its factory. See the craft of beer-making up close, ask questions, and—best of all—wind up the tour with free samples! Tours are given on Friday and Saturday at 1 P.M. at no charge.

Can't make those times? MBBC also offers the "Harpoon 5:30 Club." Any Tuesday, Wednesday, or Thursday, you and 15 to 80 of your nearest and dearest can enjoy a free tour and tasting in a fun, post-work environment from 5:30 P.M. to 7 P.M. Call in advance for reservations. Annual special events include an Octoberfest, a St. Patrick's Day Party, and various benefits. Call to get a copy of "Harpoon News" for more details.

Prudential Center Skywalk
• 800 Boylston St., Boston; (617) 236-3318

Okay, so it's not as tall as the Hancock. When you're this far up, what's ten more floors? And besides, this one has a view on all four sides, while the Hancock only has three. And it's a view that will knock your socks off. At the time of this writing, the Pru Skywalk was closed for renovations, slated to re-open in fall 1995. Admission prices were uncertain, but figure at least $2.75 for adults and $1.75 for children and seniors. Hours are from 10 A.M. to 10 P.M. on Monday through Saturday, and Sundays from noon to 10 P.M.

The State House
- Beacon Hill, Boston; (617) 727-3676

Ever been inside the State House? Designed by the famous architect Charles Bulfinch, it's a building as full of history as of modern-day importance. They offer 40-minute tours every weekday from 10 A.M. to 3:30 P.M., free of charge. See the governor's "corner office," the Senate and House of Representatives chambers, and perhaps a glimpse of your senator or rep. It's a great opportunity to observe the wacky game of politics up close.

Victorian Society in America
- Various locations; Information, (617) 267-6338

The New England Chapter of this nationwide organization offers inexpensive walking tours of all parts of the city, from the top of Beacon Hill to the lower falls of Dorchester and Milton. Led by expert historians, these tours focus on the social and industrial aspects of a city in development.

(Did you know that the above-mentioned lower falls area was once known as "Chocolate Village," because of the candy factories there?) Tours are usually on Sunday afternoons in the fall and spring and cost $7; $5 for VSA members.

Wang Center for the Performing Arts Tours
- 270 Tremont St., Boston; (617) 482-9393

The Wang Center is home to the ever-popular Boston Ballet; it also stages Broadway musicals (*Phantom, Miss Saigon*), as well as giant-screen movies and other performances. Unfortunately, top seat prices here are well out of Mr. C's territory. But wait! You can go *backstage* at the Wang at a price that's much more manageable.

The tour will let you walk in the footsteps of Pavarotti and Baryshnikov, and examine the theater's ornate interior up-close. There's a special focus on the 75-year history of the Wang Center (*née* the Metropolitan), and its past as a vaudeville and movie theater. Tours are given on Tuesdays and Thursdays at 10 A.M. and 12 noon, as well as the first Saturday of each month at 10 A.M. The hour-long tour costs $4 for adults, $3 for students, and $2 for seniors and kids.

RESTAURANTS

For the dining chapters of the book (which many Cheapsters consider to be its main course), Mr. C decided not to dig in alphabetically—but rather by geographical area. After all, when you're hungry, you want to eat *now*—no matter how appetizing some place halfway across town may sound. The city has been divided into broad sections, so that you can just pick up the book and find the cheap choices in your area. Or, the area where you're going to be. Use this section with the "Entertainment" chapters to plan out a whole day or night on the town!

All of the restaurants in this book are places where you can eat dinner for under $10 per person (or, in many cases, less), not including tax and tip. Lunch prices, of course, can be even lower. Even so, all of these eateries serve filling meals of "real" food, not phony fast food junk.

That $10 limit also does not include alcohol, which is going to be expensive just about anywhere. In fact, many of these places can afford to serve good, cheap food *because* they make their money on the drinks. If you're really tight on cash, you can always nurse one beer or an over-priced soda, eat well, and still come out ahead on the deal. And check out Mr. Cheap's special "Tip-Free" list for establishments where you can safely save an extra buck or two in that department. Enjoy!

TIP-FREE RESTAURANTS

Yes, the truly budget-conscious can even save an extra buck or two by frequenting some of these restaurants. Mr. C is not suggesting that you sneak out and stiff your waiter; these are places which are self-service or take-out establishments. Here's to 'em.

ARLINGTON/BELMONT
  Cafe Fiorella
  Italian Food Shoppe

BOSTON
  ALLSTON/BRIGHTON
  Ali Baba Restaurant
  Angora Coffee Shop
  Big Burrito
  Bill & Don's Cafe
  Cafe Troy
  Jim's Deli and Restaurant
  Riley's Roast Beef
  BACK BAY/BEACON HILL
  Baldini's
  Cafe de Paris
  Joe and Nemo
  Paramount Restaurant & Deli
  The Ultimate Bagel Company
  Venice Cafe
  DORCHESTER/ROXBURY
  Ma Dixon's Restaurant
  DOWNTOWN/WATERFRONT
  Baldini's
  Blossoms
  Fuddruckers
  New York Deli & Grill
  Sultan's Kitchen
  EAST BOSTON
  Riley's Roast Beef
  FENWAY/KENMORE SQUARE
  Baldini's
  Kenmore Cafe
  Moby Dick of Boston
  SOUTH BOSTON
  Ethel and Andy's Sandwich Shop
  SOUTH END
  Morse Fish Company

BROOKLINE
  Imperial Restaurant
  King Tut Coffee Shop
  Mr. Sushi

  Pugsley's
  Rami's

CAMBRIDGE
  Bartley's Burger Cottage
  Boca Grande
  Cafe Liberty
  Caffe Marino
  Cambridge Deli and Grill
  Fresco's Cafe and Grille
  Izzy's Restaurant and Sub Shop
  Jake & Earl's Dixie B-B-Q
  Joanie's Kitchen
  Manhattan Sammy's Delicatessen
  Moody's Falafal Palace
  Picante Mexican Grill
  Sapporo Ramen
  The Skewers
  Tasty Sandwich Shop
  The Ultimate Bagel Company

NEWTON
  Concept Cafe
  The Italian Express
  La Rotisserie
  Sandwich Works
  The Ultimate Bagel Company

SOMERVILLE
  Mike's Restaurant
  O'Sullivan's Pub
  Picante Mexican Grill

WALTHAM/WATERTOWN
  Bagel Depot
  Demo's Restaurant

NORTH SUBURBS
  Italian Express
  Kelly's Roast Beef

SOUTH SUBURBS
  Tony's Clam Shop

WEST SUBURBS
  Comella's
  Nick's Ice Cream

ARLINGTON / BELMONT

Andros Diner
- 628 Trapelo Rd., Belmont; (617) 484-7322

Tucked away in the quiet, leafy area known as Waverly Oaks on the Belmont/Waltham line, this diner is considered by many to serve up some of the best Greek food in Boston. Mr. C particularly likes their *mousaka*, about as tasty as any he's had. It's a huge slab of layered ground lamb and beef, eggplant, and baked custard topping—not to mention rice, warm pita bread, and a fresh salad with Andros' own house dressing (pick up a bottle on your way out)—all for an amazing $5.50. Just *try* to finish.

Andros also specializes in seafood, with most entrees at $7-$9. Broiled bluefish, for example, gives you a pair of tender filets, with homemade soup, vegetables, rice, and bread, for $7.50. And if the baked stuffed shrimp and scallop casserole ($9.25) is on the specials menu, grab it.

Of course, Andros has all the other traditional Greek and American fare, like gyros, souvlaki, and deli sandwiches. Try to leave some room for a heavenly slice of baklava ($1.35) for dessert. The diner also serves up huge breakfasts, and does a brisk take-out business (especially with the nearby McLean Hospital crowd). Open from 6 A.M. to about 8 or 9 P.M. Mondays through Saturdays, and Sundays from 7 A.M. to 1:30 P.M.

Arlington Restaurant and Diner
- 138 Massachusetts Ave., Arlington; (617) 646-9266

Just over the border from the republic of Cambridge, here's a bustling little Greek diner where the waitresses ask, "What would youse like?" Of course, they bring it out quickly—and it's all good stuff.

Everything looks good here. For breakfast try one of the many interesting omelettes, like the "Popeye," filled with spinach and mushrooms, or "Eggs Muckonos," with feta cheese and tomatoes. These range from $2.95 to $4.50, and they are humongous. They come with home fries and toast, natch.

For lunch the "Happy Waitress Special" ($3.95) is an open-face grilled cheese sandwich with bacon, tomato, and French fries, slaw, and pickles. On Fridays, try a cup of homemade clam chowder ($1.75). And, along with Greek and Italian dinners, Mr. C liked "Chicken a la Arlington Diner" ($8.95) which consists of chicken breasts, broccoli, and ziti sauteed in white wine, garlic, and butter. Pretty fancy for a diner, but the cozy place pulls it off. Don't forget to check out the homemade baklava and other desserts, either. Open daily.

Cafe Fiorella
- 263 Belmont St., Belmont; (617) 489-1361
- *Tip-free*

Unrelated to a place of the same name in Harvard Square, this small, cute eatery is beloved among Belmontians for the wondrous aromas which emanate from its wood-burning brick oven. Freshly tossed pizzas come in an endless variety of sizes and configurations, but they all share one ingredient—that thin, crunchy crust. Pies start from just $1.95 for an individual-size basic, pretty much an appetizer; but, topped with things like chicken and pesto, spinach and ricotta cheese, or artichoke hearts, even these can be filling for under $5. Or, step up to medium and large sizes, none of which tops $10.95.

217

MR. CHEAP'S PICKS
Belmont

✔ **Andros Diner**—One of the best diners in all of Boston.

✔ **Rustica**—Fancy Italian food, fancy atmosphere, not fancy prices.

Over a dozen kinds of fresh-baked calzones are $4.95 across the board (ever had a tuna melt calzone? *Hmmm. . .*). Homemade fettucine Alfredo, mixed with chicken and broccoli, is a hearty helping for a lean $6.95, and all pasta dishes are served with hot garlic bread. Plus homemade soups, salads, subs, and the like, to eat-in or to go. All in a cozy storefront that does its best to resemble a Florentine cafe, with the traditional red-checked tablecloths. There aren't nearly enough of those tables, though; Fiorella can pack 'em in at peak times. It's worth a wait. Open six days a week from 11 A.M. to 10 P.M., and closed on Sundays.

Rustica
• 30 Leonard St., Belmont; (617) 489-6333

Okay, not everyone will consider this restaurant—new in '95—to be inexpensive. But for this kind of Euro-fancy food and stylish atmosphere, the prices at Rustica can't be beat.

Nor can the quality of the cooking, ranging from panini sandwiches to grilled chicken and other nouvelle Tuscan treats. After all, have you ever even heard of sweet potato ravioli? Would you believe that such a delicacy, in a sage cream sauce yet, could be had for $7.95? Thought not.

Pizzas come topped with such ingredients as spinach, ricotta, gorgonzola, and onions—that's one pie, folks—for as little as $6.95 (individual) or $11.95 (the splittable 16-incher). You can build a whole meal out of the incredibly fresh salads, homemade soups and vegetable appetizers. Entrees include treats like grilled chicken breast in a sauce of tomato, puréed almonds, and chili pepper ($5.95). There is also a "Rusti-Kids" menu, making the place a hit with families.

Desserts, decidedly yummy, are not such bargains. Apart from cannoli, most of the cakes and pies go for $3.95 a slice, which—along with a cappuccino—can double your bill in no time. Ah, but what a way to go.

The walls are richly done out in Mediterranean colors, and festooned with gorgeous Maiolica ceramics. The atmosphere is boisterous. Rustica is open for lunch, Saturday brunch, and early dinner ('til 9 or 10), every day but Sunday.

For more traditional, basic fare, mention must also be made of the Italian Food Shoppe across the street at 6 Channing Road (telephone 484-9037). It's just your basic spaghetti and sub shop, but with homemade food and a dinner deal that can't be beat: "Pasta Dinner for Two," with meatballs, sausage, eggplant, and chicken—a ton of food for $12.99. Same thing for one person is $5.99. Not cheap enough for ya? Go on Monday nights, and the same deals cost a buck less. Yowza. Open from 8 A.M. to 9 P.M. daily.

BOSTON

ALLSTON / BRIGHTON

Ali Baba Restaurant

- 514 Cambridge St., Allston; (617) 254-4540
- *Tip-free*

The food here is touted as all-natural, and it's good. The atmosphere is fast-food but clean; you eat from styrofoam plates, but each table has a couple of fresh roses for decor.

Chicken and beef, in kebabs or shawarma style, are $3.75 for sandwiches (with lettuce, tomato and tahini sauce) or $5.29 for platters (with rice or fries, hummus, salad and pita bread. Falafel, hummus and baba ganoush sandwiches are $3.25 each, as is the Greek salad. For anyone not acquainted with Middle Eastern cuisine, Ali Baba offers free tastes of selected items.

Perhaps the best bargains are the rotisseried chicken dinners; the chicken plate ($5.49) consists of tender, fresh pieces of chicken pulled off the bones and placed on a bed of rice pilaf. It comes with salad, hummus, garlic sauce, and pita bread. You can also get a whole rotisseried chicken, with garlic sauce and bread, for $6.95, or a half-chicken for $3.95. That's one cheap dinner. Ali Baba is open daily until midnight.

Angora Coffee Shop

- 1020A Commonwealth Ave., Boston; (617) 232-1757
- *Tip-free*

This BU favorite mixes Middle Eastern food with a variety of salads, sandwiches, soups, and individual pizzas for an eclectic and inexpensive menu. Much of the food is homemade, with ample portions.

Soups change daily, with such choices as clam chowder and cream curried chicken. Get soup and a half-sandwich for $4.25; these include brie, corned beef, and smoked turkey. Same deal for soup and quiche. Salads start at $2.45; artichoke and spinach ($3.95) is a winner, with mushrooms, scallions, hard-boiled egg, and croutons tossed in.

A real treat are the Boboli pizzas—eight-inch pies covered with chunks of chicken and broccoli, beef and mushroom, or many other combinations, most around $4.50. They are filling and delicious.

The Mediterranean portion of the menu offers hummus, baba ganoush, tabouli and more, each served on pita bread for $3.75; for hearty appetites, you won't go wrong with the combination platter, which adds a Greek salad to the above, all for just $5.75.

Not to mention bagels from Kupel's, desserts from Rosie's Bakery, and Mrs. Miller's Muffins. Or follow a Greek specialty with a piece of homemade baklava. Lots of gourmet coffees, teas, juices, cappuccino, and espresso to go along with these, too. Open 'til midnight daily.

Arbuckle's

- 1249 Commonwealth Ave., Allston; (617) 782-9508

Burgers, burgers, burgers—that's pretty much the story at this college hangout. Oh, but what burgers—twenty-two different kinds! The basic model, served with lettuce, tomato, and crisp, curly French fries, is $5.95. At the top of the line, just a dollar more, the choices are Mexican, with jalapeño peppers, salsa and a spicy cheese; or the "Boston College," with turkey, lettuce, tomato, bacon and cheese. And Mr. C loves the "Brunch Burger"—topped with bacon and a fried egg. All of these are ten-ounce patties of fresh meat; even bigger than the half-pounders at most other reputable establishments.

There are other eats, but Mr. C always says "Go with the house specialty." Arbuckle's has a long, dark

---

MR. CHEAP'S PICKS
Allston

✔ **Henry's Diner**—Classic
stainless-steel beauty.

✔ **Rama Thai**—Yes it's in a
shopping center, but it's pretty
inside, with prices lower than
most other Thais.

✔ **Sai Gon**—Out-of-the-way,
hole-in-the-wall,
out-of-this-world.

---

wood bar, and a sports decor (which
means plenty of TVs). The list of beers
includes Bass Ale on tap, bottles of Corona and Dos Equis, and those big
cans of Foster's Lager. House wines,
coffee drinks, and creative cocktails
with cutesy names complete the experience—a lively joint with a casual atmosphere. The kitchen is open 'til
midnight seven days.

Armadillo Cafe
● 1314 Commonwealth Ave.,
Allston; (617) 232-4242
Opened in late '92 on the premises of
the late, lamented Play It Again
Sam's, the Armadillo quickly made
lots of new friends among the BU students and assorted yuppies in the
area. They've done a wonderful job
brightening the place up (large vertical windows open up to create an *al
fresco* feeling, even in Allston). Both
sides of the former bar now serve as
dining rooms decorated in bold
Southwestern colors (the whole exterior facade is now bright yellow),
while the downstairs space doubles
as a party room on weekends.

The food, meanwhile, is smartly
done Tex-Mex. Mr. C tucked into
chicken *mole*, a boneless double-
breast in an unsweetened chocolate
sauce, served up with rice and beans
for $7.95. His dining companion,
meanwhile, was overwhelmed with

an order of vegetarian fajitas (same
price)—a heaping platter of veggies
on a bed of rice, topped with melted
cheese, and served with soft tortillas
like a Mexican *moo shi*.

For an unusual starter, try a bowl
of tortilla soup ($4.75), a shellfish
stew with a bit of crunch. Burritos, tacos, and the whole enchilada round
out the south-of-the-border section of
the menu, which also offers a half-
rack of ribs for $6.95; sirloin tips
with fries and baked beans for $8.50;
fried catfish ($7.50); and half-pound
hamburgers ($5.50), all augmented
by a full bar with several good brews
on tap. Open daily for lunch and dinner, plus an all-you-can-eat Sunday
brunch for $7.95 (including a mi-
mosa or "Bloody Maria"!).

Arthur's Seafood and Deli
● 204 Harvard Ave., Allston; (617)
734-8343
Good seafood cheap—that's Arthur's,
just off Commonwealth Avenue. The
place may be lean on atmosphere—
your basic coffee shop look—but the
fish is fresh, you get a lot, and the
choices are extensive.

The place is open daily; lunch is
the best deal here. Arthur's offers a
full slate of daily specials, giving you
an entree with one side dish for as little as $3.95. The regular menu has a
lot more choices, like the fried seafood platter ($5.90), a full plate of
scallops, shrimp, clams and schrod.
Each of these is available as an entree of its own for $5.95 with French
fries and cole slaw.

On the broiled side, starting at $5,
you can get mackerel, bluefish, trout
or smelts—along with two side
dishes. Choose from fries, baked potato, salad, rice pilaf, or the day's
cooked vegetable. Quite a deal. Haddock and sole plates are $5.50; sword-
fish, salmon and halibut are $7.95.
Dinner versions get a bit fancier, with
titles like "Haddock a la Grec"
($7.50), baked in a tomato sauce.
Chicken seafood saute ($9.95) pushes
the tab up, but it's a lovely mix of
chicken, swordfish, shrimp, and scallops in a mushroom and white wine

sauce. Again, you get two side dishes. Meat entrees at lunch and dinner include various shishkebabs, souvlaki, gyros, and loukaniko (Greek sausage). These are all fine; but, when in Rome, as the saying goes . . . .

Big Burrito

- 160 Brighton Ave., Allston; (617) 562-0440
- *Tip-free*

A recent arrival at the busy Harvard Avenue intersection, Big Burrito gets the prize for truth in advertising. Their specialty is just that: A huge soft tortilla, overstuffed with black beans, cheese, lettuce, salsa, and your choice of fillings. Most varieties, from barbecued chicken to Texas chili, are $4.50 each. Ask them to throw some guacamole in there for another half-buck.

The rest of the simple menu covers other Tex-Mex fare, from tacos ($1.95-$2.50) to quesadillas ($3.50) and smoked ribs (a half-rack is just $7.95, with rice and baked beans). Catering to current trends, BB uses natural ingredients wherever possible, including fat-free sour cream and lean ground beef. After ordering from the counter, you can settle into one of many large tables in the spacious, open room. It's brightly decorated in Southwestern colors. All in all, this is one of the cleanest, healthiest dining spots in a neighborhood which prides itself on grunge. Open from 11:30 A.M. to 11 P.M. daily.

Bill & Don's Cafe

- 386 Western Ave., Brighton; (617) 254-9752
- *Tip-free*

Located in a shopping center next to a Caldor, Bill & Don's Cafe is your basic cafeteria—a great place for a quick meal during errands.

Breakfast, first of all, is served all day. But if you get there from 6 to 10 in the morning, you can snag one of the specials—like two eggs, bacon or sausage, home fries, toast, and coffee for $2.59. Later on the guys offer sandwiches, salads, and pizza. But dinners (well, they're only open until

4) are the real deals. How about sirloin tips or stir-fry chicken, each with rice or French fries, for just $3.99? Or spaghetti and meatballs for $3.50, chicken parmigiana with spaghetti for $4.50, and fish and chips for $4.75 . . . ?

Ambience is minimal at Bill & Don's—formica tables with the seats attached. But the service is friendly, and the regulars who keep stopping in attest to the quality of the food. Open from 8 A.M. daily.

Bluestone Bistro

- 1799 Commonwealth Ave., Brighton; (617) 254-8309
- 663 Main St., Waltham; (617) 891-3339

There is an easygoing class about the Bluestone, which manages to be chic without trying too hard. The look of the place, dark marble walls and tables, is actually just painted on. Rhythm and blues give a little beat to the casual atmosphere.

And the food is first-rate, a triumph of cuisine over cash. Pizzas, pastas, and calzones comprise the menu—but these are the kind you'd expect to find on Beacon Hill, not in Brighton. For $7.25, two people can split a pizza with a thick, hot, chewy crust and Bluestone's own sauce. Then, for 75¢ each, add on a variety of toppings, from andouille sausage or artichoke hearts to bay shrimp, blackened chicken, pine nuts, smoked turkey, sun-dried tomatoes, and many more. Calzones, $5.95, contain five cheeses and your choice of fillings, like chicken with pesto.

The pastas are wonderful too, served with sourdough bread. Try the tagliatelli with chicken tenderloin, with artichoke hearts in a roasted red pepper cream sauce ($10.50), or "Checkerboard Ravioli," featuring spinach and black pepper pasta stuffed with a spinach-ricotta filling in a tomato basil sauce ($8.95).

Appetizers are inventive, from a California Cobb salad with bacon and fresh trout ($5.95) to "Prairie Fire" ($4.75), spicy, warm beans with blue corn chips for dipping. It's all

MR. CHEAP'S PICKS
Brighton

✔ **Bluestone Bistro**—Posh pizza for the well-heeled student crowd. Not that expensive, since you split it. Great pastas, too.

✔ **Corrib Pub**—Typical Irish pub, nothing fancy, but a ton of food for under $10.

good, and popular; on weekends especially, get there early before tables—and many of the pasta dishes—run out. Makes a cool date without breaking the bank. Open daily.

Cafe Brazil
- 421 Cambridge St., Allston; (617) 789-5980

Cafe Brazil is a fun, funky, and friendly little place that has been serving up great South American food for several years now. The prices have gone up a bit over the years, with some dinners over Mr. C's limit of $10; but the portions are so generous that you'll probably take some home for leftovers anyway.

Brazilian cuisine is well-seasoned, but not spicy. Dishes of chicken, beef, and fish are flavored with things like cassava root, okra, onions, and garlic. Almost everything is served with rice and black beans. For a good introduction, Mr. C recommends the "Brazil 2001" platter ($9.95)—grilled pieces of chicken, beef, and *linguica* (non-spicy pork sausage) served over a bed of rice and sauteed cabbage. It also includes slices of fried banana and *feijao tropeiro* (a kind of stuffing made from black beans, cassava meal, bacon, sausage, eggs, garlic and onion).

There are several beef, seafood, and chicken dishes, all from $8.95 to $12.95. Also, there is a vegetarian plate ($8.95) with fresh sauteed veggies, mandioca (cassava fried up like potatoes), fried banana, rice, and beans.

A cheaper way to try these out is to go at lunchtime (11:30 to 4), when exactly the same menu is offered. The portions are still generous, and the prices are about $3 lower per dish.

At night, however, you get the romantic addition of live music, except on Mondays. The lights are low as a guitarist strums and sings the relaxing sound of bossa nova. Makes for a nice date. Open seven days.

Cafe Troy
- 181A Harvard Ave., Allston; (617) 782-6455
- *Tip-free*

How can such a large menu come out of such a tiny place? Located a couple of steps down from the avenue, this um, *intimate* shop boasts one counter, plus four stools at a window. It's so small, you have to go outside just to change your mind. (Ba-da-*bing*.) Yet they serve breakfast, lunch, and dinner (mostly for take-out, of course). Grab an egg, cheese, and ham sandwich on your way to the "T"—just $1.58, on a bagel. Ten different salads ($2.35-$4) span the globe, from Greek to Caesar to Oriental chicken. Individual-sized Boboli pizzas ($4.25) offer a similar range of toppings. Pita sandwiches ($3-$4) favor the Middle East.

Daily specials can be real deals: On the day Mr. C visited, they were offering chicken lasagna with soup or a salad, all for $4.45. Plus gourmet coffees, pastries, fruit "smoothies," and other healthy stuff. Open daily, from 7 A.M. to 8 P.M.

Corrib Pub
- 396 Market St., Brighton; (617) 254-2880
- 201 Harvard St., Brookline; (617) 232-8787
- 2030 Centre St., West Roxbury; 469-4177

The Corrib has been a local landmark for many years, and it is easy to see why. The atmosphere is relaxed, with a mix of locals and younger folks; the dark wood surroundings are pleasant. There are lots of great Irish and local beers on tap, friendly service and generously portioned food.

Both lunch and dinner are served. At dinner, Mr. C ordered grilled swordfish steak ($7.95), expecting perhaps a small center cut. What he netted instead was a huge, thick hunk of fish with a fine grilled taste. But that's not all. Each dinner entree comes with a good, fresh salad (or soup), potato or rice, and a side vegetable. Other dinners include chicken Maryland ($6.95) sauteed in orange juice, pineapple, and banana; topping the menu (at $7.95) is New York sirloin—a twelve-ounce center cut.

Homemade beef stew ($1.95 for a cup, $3.25 for a bowl) is a hearty one indeed. Burgers are large and fresh, starting at $3.60; they come with great, crisp French fries, as well as lettuce, tomato, and pickles. Sandwiches ($3.25 to $4.25) include hot pastrami, sliced chicken, and grilled barbecued roast beef. Lunch specials may offer scallops or prime rib, each $5.95, served from 11 A.M. to 4 P.M. Wednesdays through Saturdays. Closed Sundays.

Green Briar Restaurant and Pub
• 304-306 Washington St., Brighton; (617) 789-4100

The Green Briar has become a major part of Boston's strong Irish community. The food here, like so many pubs, is terrific; the bar, with its wide selection of Irish beers (including Murphy's Stout and Woodpecker Cider), is neatly partitioned from the restaurant area.

Lunch is quite reasonably priced, and though many dinner entrees go well above ten dollars, there are still plenty of cheaper options. The best bargains of all are found on Monday through Wednesday evenings, when a two-for-one special is offered at just $10.95. Patrons have a choice of four or five dishes, such as barbecued baby back ribs, teriyaki beef, or broiled schrod.

There are lots of appetizers, from fried zucchini and mushrooms ($3.95) to individual pizzas ($4.95)

with your choice of toppings. Burgers start at just $3.95 for a thick half-pounder on a bulkie roll with lettuce, tomato, pickle, and steak fries. Other luncheon and dinner specials are offered every weekday, plus an all-you-can-eat Sunday brunch from 10:30 to 2:30 for a reasonable $6.95.

This is a good time to mention that the Green Briar is home to a weekly open jam session on traditional Irish instruments. A good crowd gathers each Monday to bow the fiddle, or just listen in, from about 9 P.M. on. Unlike bands at many Irish bars, this music is not amplified, just simple and spellbinding. Late in the evening, the pub even brings out complimentary sandwiches for all. It makes for one of Mr. C's favorite entertainment options.

Live music can also be heard at the Green Briar on Thursday, Friday, and Saturday nights from 9 P.M. to 1 A.M., featuring many of Boston's best Irish bands. The cover charge is $2-$5. Be sure to pick up a copy of "The Local" here, a free monthly magazine devoted to Irish music and the Boston pub scene. Open for dinner 'til 10 P.M. Mondays through Saturdays.

Henry's Diner
• 270 Western Ave., Allston; (617) 783-5844

People who are serious about diners hold one rule uppermost: A true diner must be in the shape of a railroad car, preferably in shining silver metal. Mr. C is such a person, and Henry's is such a place. The joint has been operating, under a succession of names, for over forty years on the same spot. Its current owners have jazzed it up with some kitschy neon, hip music, and a "universal symbol" sign out front—a huge railroad crossing marker with a chef's hat on it. No words necessary; diner below.

Daily specials offer deals like roast stuffed pork, with potato and a vegetable, for $4.95. In fact, nearly *everything* seems to cost $4.95: Marinated sirloin tips, grilled, barbecued, or Southern fried chicken, marinated sirloin tips, meatloaf...you get the idea. Some items are even lower, like a heaping plate of mac and cheese for $3.95.

Desserts feature a range of home-made bread puddings and pies. Henry's is also a fun spot for breakfast or weekend brunch, with big, thick slabs of French toast and eggs any way you like 'em. Even a request for eggs done without the yolks, for a no-cholesterol diet, failed to raise an eyebrow.

Being a true diner, of course, seating is limited. They've packed a good number of counter stools and booths in, but at peak times you may have to wait. It's worth it. Open from 6 A.M. daily.

Jim's Deli and Restaurant

- 371 Washington St., Brighton; (617) 787-2626
- *Tip-free*

Here's an interesting combination—a Greek-style cafeteria in an Irish neighborhood. It works. Nothing fancy here, just your basic deli and grill; grab a tray, tell the man what you want and pay for it at the end. There are plenty of tables, and the restaurant is pleasant and clean.

What's good here? The dinner plates will give you a lot for your money. There are always blackboard specials, like baked haddock ($5.25), chicken parmagiana ($4.25) or an open-face roast beef dinner ($4.95). These come with your choice of mashed or baked potato and rice or cooked vegetables. Whatever you choose, your plate will be heaped with food.

Jim's has several seafood dinners, and the fish is quite good: the baked haddock, for example, was plump and moist, a good-sized serving. Plus salmon croquettes ($4.55), a true diner food if ever there was one, sirloin tips, gyros, and Greek sausages.

Jim's is also a nice breakfast spot. The $1.99 special offers two eggs any style, with home fries, toast, and coffee—with free refills. The quality of the food is fine, and the portions are large. The folks behind the counter are friendly and pressure-free. If the place isn't busy, they may even bring your food out to your table. What more could anyone ask of a cafeteria? Open daily.

Pars Café

- 559 Washington St., Brighton; (617) 783-4900

When this family-run Oak Square venue opened a few years ago, it was both unusual and inexpensive—serving up Iranian cuisine, slightly different from other Middle Eastern food ("Pars" being a variation on Persia). Little on the menu went over $9, and lunch specials started from just $3.

With increased success, alas, comes decreased cheapness. Most entrees have gone up a dollar or two; but this is still wonderful food, with portions that make it a good value. Shish kabobs are the trademark items; if $8.95 seems like a lot for one skewer of marinated chicken, wait 'til you see it—giant cubes of tender, juicy meat, topped with a grilled tomato, on a mountain of light Basmati rice. Some combination plates are better values; "Kabob-i-Pars" offers one skewer of beef filet and one of ground beef for $9.95. And the weekday lunch deals are still priced from $3-$6.

Of course, you can always get pita sandwich versions of same, in the $5-$6 range; not to mention delectable appetizers and soups. Warm pita bread, feta cheese, and greens come to the table as soon as you do. But it's the house specialties in which Pars really distinguishes itself. Fragrant stews, which vary daily, are laced with flavors and spices not found in your average falafel joint. Mr. C went nuts over *fesenjan*, a unique chicken stew made with nuts (fried walnuts, that is) and pomegranate sauce, sweet and tasty. At $9.50, it's at the top of his price range, but there was enough to take some home.

Liquor is not served; coffee and tea are good and strong. The latter is served from a giant ornamental urn, which lends a touch of class to the handsome, serene atmosphere. It's a much more elegant meal than you'd

224

expect in this humble neighborhood, and at these prices. Open for lunch and dinner daily.

Pho Pasteur

- 137 Brighton Ave., Allston; (617) 783-2340

Pho Pasteur holds down one end of the Brighton Avenue/Harvard Avenue intersection in Allston, while V. Majestic (below) reigns a block away at the opposite end. Together they make the neighborhood rich with inexpensive Vietnamese seafood.

At Pho Pasteur, the special style of cooking is "caramel," in which the food is sauteed in a way that brings its natural sugars to the outside for a slightly sweet taste. Caramel shrimp ($8) gives you a good portion served over steamed rice. There are also caramel fish and pork.

But for a treat, stick with the Vietnamese special dinners. For non-fish eaters, there is chicken lemon grass ($7), roasted in honey and marinated in this tasty spice. Rolling beef ($7) is thinly sliced beef marinated in a rich and slightly spicy sauce and wrapped in grape leaves. Or try an assortment of Vietnamese vegetables sauteed over rice ($5.50). Saigon soup ($3.50) contains fish, shrimp, and pineapple. Seaweed soup ($2) is better than it may sound, with your choice of shrimp, scallops, fish, pork, beef, or chicken.

Pho Pasteur offers several special luncheon deals, smaller portions of their main dishes at lower prices. Open from 11 A.M. to 10:30 P.M. Mondays through Saturdays, 'til 10 P.M. on Sundays.

Pig 'n Whistle Diner

- 226 North Beacon St., Brighton; (617) 254-8058

Yet another true diner shines in Allston-Brighton. The Pig 'n Whistle is a cozy little place in the classic diner-car shape, paneled in stainless steel and looking like it's been around forever. Inside, the folks are friendly, the lighting is warm, and the food is basic diner fare.

Daily specials are the best bargains. For $4.50, how about a plate of sliced roast lamb in brown gravy, along with real mashed potatoes and a cooked vegetable . . . or, for $5.50, baked stuffed schrod with the trimmings. A huge bowl of homemade beef stew is $3.90.

Lunch specials include such choices as a grilled ham steak sandwich ($4.95), which comes with a small drink, soup or potatoes, and a vegetable.

You can, of course, get sandwiches and burgers, omelettes, and other breakfast specials, salads, and desserts. Oh, and the coffee is great, too. Open from 5 A.M. to 7:30 P.M. Mondays through Saturdays.

Our House

- 1277 Commonwealth Ave., Allston; (617) 782-3228

Students in the Allston area have known about Our House for years—a truly casual place to party or relax. It's made to look like an upscale basement rec room, with a bar, big plush couches in front of TVs, and a pool table in the back.

The "rec" area is rimmed by tables with white linen tablecloths, there is a separate "cafe" room, and the menu—though packed with burgers and sandwiches—also includes specials like the one Mr. C's friend ordered. On this plate, seven shrimp were lined up on seven wedges of pear, each wrapped in a basil leaf. These were served over rice pilaf, all topped by a caramel glaze sauce. It was a beauty to behold, as well as to eat. The dinner included a salad with fresh vegetables, and a basket of garlic bread (with real minced garlic), all for $8.95.

Yet this is a place where a hand-lettered sign tells you the "Shot of the Week" (Woo Woos for $3!) and the beers, mostly Buds and Millers, are in bottles only.

There are still a dozen different burgers, large and juicy, ranging from $3.75 to $4.50; Canadian, Texas, Italian, Teriyaki, and, of course, Yuppie. Best of all, the big appetizer menu is available until 1:30 A.M.—Buffalo wings for $3.25, five varieties of skins from $3.50 to $4.75, and "loaded fries" ($3.75)—a big basket of spuds with melted cheddar and bacon bits. Friendly service, too. Hours are 4 P.M. to 2 A.M. Mondays through Fridays; open at 11 A.M. on weekends.

Rama Thai

- 181 Brighton Ave., Allston; (617) 783-2434

Rama Thai is a lovely find amidst the rock-and-roll clubs and funky junk shops of Allston. Even more unlikely, it resides in a shopping center next to Dunkin' Donuts, and Osco Drug. But once you step inside, the decor is light and clean and the atmosphere is peaceful. The extensive menu is cheaper than many comparable Thai restaurants in town.

Start with appetizers like Thai rolls ($3.50), a plateful of tiny fried rolls with ground chicken, carrots, and bean thread, served with a sweet dipping sauce. A good order for the table. There are also interesting soups, such as Tom Yum Goong ($2.25), shrimp in a sweet-and-sour broth with mushrooms, scallions, and the popular Thai spices coriander and lemon grass.

The house specialties and seafood dishes are the pricier items on the menu, though you'll get plenty to eat with Thai Ocean ($9.35), a mixture of shrimp, scallops, squid, fish filet, broccoli, carrots, onions, and baby corn. Duck Choo Chee ($8.30) is a good deal—boneless roasted duck sauteed with vegetables in a curry sauce.

The "Chef's Specialties" offer tofu ($5.40), pork ($5.65), chicken or beef ($5.95), or shrimp ($6.65), with your choice of preparations such as basil leaf, ginger, sweet and sour, spicy bamboo shoot, or one of four different curry sauces.

For the true bargains, however, Mr. C recommends the many rice and noodle dishes. There is Pad Thai, of course ($5.25); also a vegetarian version for the same price, or; add shrimp for a bit more ($5.95). Rad Nah ($5.25) consists of heavier pan-fried egg noodles with broccoli and your choice of meat (or tofu) in a black bean sauce.

Rama Thai offers a luncheon menu from 11:30 A.M. to 2:30 P.M., with many of these dishes at even lower prices. Most items are around $5, and may be ordered to take out. You'll get plenty, and it's well worth repeat visits to try the many unusual tastes. Open daily.

Riley's Roast Beef

- 140 Brighton Ave., Allston; (617) 254-9592
- 259 Bennington St., East Boston; (617) 567-9282
- *Tip-free*

Any Bostonian probably knows the Riley's sign—"Roast Beef 'Til 3 A.M."—as a local landmark. Mr. C. has always wanted to go in at 2:59 and order a peanut butter and jelly sandwich, just to see if a burly night cook would shout, "Roast beef! Ya gotta order roast beef! Can't ya read the sign??" The Allston location is cleaner than it once was, well-lit, and even decorated with plants for a cozier feel. It's really a fast-food joint, not what this book is meant to cover; but the food is pretty good, and there is more variety here than you'll find in any McChain.

Roast beef, of course, is the specialty of the house. It comes thin-sliced and hot on an onion roll in four sizes: junior ($1.75) to deluxe ($5.19). All include cheese and barbecue sauce. It makes for a yummy, if messy, handful. You can add a medium order of fries and a soda for about a dollar more.

The place also serves up charbroiled burgers for 69¢ (definitely fast-food-ish), fried clams with French fries and onion rings ($3.99), minestrone ($1.69), and—wouldja believe—daily dinner specials, such as chicken pot pie ($3.99), which comes with corn bread and your choice of two side vegetables.

Riley's even cooks breakfast, from 7 to 11 A.M., with omelettes from $2.29 or three eggs and bacon for $2.89 with toast, home fries, and coffee. And they have home-baked muffins for 69¢—blueberry, corn, and bran. Riley's East Boston location, in Day Square, is a bit more of a take-out stand than a sit-down eatery but offers most of the same foods. Open from 11 A.M. to 3 A.M. daily.

Sai Gon
- 431 Cambridge St., Allston; (617) 254-3373

Well off the beaten path of Allston's Vietnamese restaurant area, this cozy hole-in-the-wall was known as Express Cuisine when *Mr. Cheap's Boston* first came out. Now owned by different members of the same family, it's even more popular, thanks to super food, a wider menu than most such places, and ridiculously low prices—including weekday lunch specials from a mere $3!

You must start off with the obligatory spring rolls—though it's no chore. $1.95 gets you a pair of big, crispy-fried rolls and a tangy dipping sauce. Or, choose from over half a dozen tasty soups and stews, like "Sour Fisherman Soup" ($2.95), a hot-and-sour broth with fish, shrimp and pineapple.

The rest of the menu features several dishes each of chicken, shellfish, beef, pork, and tofu entrees. Mr. C recommends chicken with ginger and onion ($5.75), fried with a bit of zing; and lemon grass tofu ($4.75). Only a few seafood dishes top $6, like "Seafood Delight" ($6.45), with plenty of shrimp, squid, scallops, and fish balls prepared in oyster sauce.

The specialty of the house, *banh xeo*, is a crisp "pancake" rolled up with chicken, shrimp, bean sprouts, scallions (and, seemingly, whatever else the chef can find)—all for $4.95. It's quite a trick if you can eat this with chopsticks.

No liquor is served (you may bring your own, of course). The place has only nine tables; try to get there early for dinner, especially on weekends, as no reservations are taken. Service is friendly, and the mood is quiet and relaxed. Open every day but Sunday, from 11:30 A.M. to 10 P.M.

The Sports Depot
- 353 Cambridge St., Allston; (617) 783-2300

What gives this place its character—is it the authentic brownstone train station of its origin? The autographed murals of Boston sports heroes? Or the nearly fifty TV sets scattered around the place, even in the bathrooms, so you never miss a second of the half-dozen games being shown at any one time?

Surely, it's all of these—not to mention the food, which could fill a stadium itself. Giant burgers and sandwiches, all around $6; complete chicken and steak dinners, with vegetables and fresh salads, at $10 to $11; individual pizzas for $4.95; fajita dinners for $9.95 . . . all with the basic intention of stuffing you silly. Big desserts, too.

Sunday through Thursday, the Depot offers two dinners for $12.95; choose from a BBQ half-chicken, lemon pepper schrod, shrimp Alfredo, teriyaki steak tips, and several others. Salad and coffee are included. Great deal.

There are, of course, several bars of varying sizes around the cavernous room; but for an extra thrill, sit out in the enclosed patio that faces the train tracks. When ol' Casey Jones thunders by, you can practically reach out and touch the cars. Oh, and don't worry—there are TVs here as well. Open from 11:30 A.M. to 12:30 A.M. seven days.

Sunset Grill
- 130 Brighton Ave., Allston; (617) 254-1331

Consistently voted one of the city's best beer joints by every survey in creation, the Sunset does indeed offer an astounding selection of some 400 different brews—over 75 of which are on tap. As you might guess, this includes some pretty far-fetched varieties, from France's Jade Farmhouse organic beer to Old Crustacian Barley Ale from Oregon. Not all of these are cheap, of course; but there are plenty of special deals from week to week. And, as a friend of Mr. C's raves, they also have beer—literally—by the yard, in special armlength glasses.

Given the brisk booze business, you *can* expect reasonable prices on meals. The menu is nearly as varied as the beer list; you can go all night on apps, like homemade chili ($3.25) or a half-rack of barbecued ribs ($5.95). Or, go for a full meal, like "North End Tortellini" ($9.95) with chicken and mushrooms. A halfpound "Hawaii Five-O" burger comes topped with pineapple, mozzarella, and grilled ham for $5.50, one of a dozen such creations.

There are all kinds of salads and sandwiches, too, from a "Shrimp and Tuna Barge" to a classic "Fluffernutter." Basil pesto chicken on a baguette is $6.50, served with curly fries. Larger, more serious entrees—steaks, seafood, fajitas—rise above Mr. C's $10 limit, but are certainly filling.

It all happens in a lively, bustling atmosphere, neon brewery signs blazing through the dim lighting; the walls are covered from floor to ceiling with beer-related paraphernalia, the music cooks, and the place is usually crowded. Food is served until 1 A.M. nightly, making the Sunset a popular stop after the clubs.

V. Majestic Restaurant

- 164 Brighton Ave., Allston; (617) 782-6088

Part of the cluster of very good Vietnamese restaurants in Allston, V. Majestic offers excellent food at low prices. The surroundings are humble, but you won't mind once the food comes out.

Seafood dishes come sauteed in ginger or "caramelized," the preparation that brings out the natural sugars of the food. Mr. C loved the caramel fish ($6.55), delicate pieces of salmon in this slightly sweet sauce, garnished with chunks of cooked pineapple. It comes with a heap of steamed rice and a simple salad. For a variety of seafood, try the "Sea of Vietnam," a combo platter of scallops, shrimp, squid, and vegetables

sauteed with rice. The small portion is $5.50, but large is a real bargain at $6.75.

Other great deals are the soups, many of which again feature fish. Crabmeat soup is just $3 for a large bowl of crab, shrimp, tomato, onion, and vermicelli noodles. Of course, there are also meat dishes. Glowing beef ($4.55) is thinly sliced meat baked in special spices, served with vermicelli. Chicken lemon grass (small $4.55, large $6.95) is a tasty, mildly spiced dish flavored with a touch of honey. It comes with rice and salad.

Most entrees here range from $5 to $7, with good portions. The service is quick and attentive. V. Majestic is authentic Vietnamese food in a friendly, home-kitchen atmosphere. Closed Tuesdays.

Wing It

- 1153 Commonwealth Ave., Brighton; (617) 783-BIRD (2473)
- 1732 Centre St., West Roxbury; (617) 469-WING (9464)

The name says it all. Chicken wings have risen to a new height (sorry!) in this tiny barbecue palace. The emphasis here is on take-out, although there are a few tables and stools. Since they look well-worn by the student crowd that frequents the place, you may prefer to eat at home.

The food, meanwhile, is good stuff. The wings can be cooked six different ways. Buffalo and barbecue come in several grades of spiciness, from mild to "suicide." Honey hot and teriyaki explain themselves; then you have "teridactil," a unique blend of soy sauce and barbecue, and finally the most unusual of all—garlic and Parmesan. These last two are both interesting and worth a try.

A small order, for one person, is $4.15; for two, $8.25; for three, $12.10. Extra large, for up to six nibblers, is $17.35, and you can also order party platters of tremendous sizes.

But man does not live by wings alone, and neither does this establishment: the flip side here is baby back spare ribs. A good and fun sampler here is the "Real Meal Deal," which gives you a half rack of ribs and five wings; you can mix and match the styles for each. It includes one side dish, all for $12.55. The "mega" size doubles the whole deal for $20.95.

Probably the best bargain around, though, takes place at the Brighton location every Wednesday night from 6 P.M. to 9 P.M. Yes folks, it's the all-you-can-eat hot Buffalo wing buffet. For $5.20 you can chow down as much as your tongue can take. (This event must be the reason for the large sink in the middle of the room.) Try it if you dare! Open weeknights until midnight, Fridays 'til 1:30 A.M., and Saturdays 'til 2:30 A.M.

BACK BAY / BEACON HILL

Antonio's Cucina Italiana
- 288 Cambridge St., Boston; (617) 367-3310

Located on the "Back of the Hill," savvy Bostonians refer to this as going to the North End without actually going *into* the North End. In other words, you can actually park nearby. The atmosphere is surprisingly elegant—quiet music, linen tablecloths and napkins, and courteous service.

The food is first-rate, a mix of basics and fancier creations. A plate of fettucine Alfredo, for instance, is $6.95; same price for a more unusual gnocchi in pesto sauce. Steak pizzaola is a reasonable $10.95, as is grilled swordfish. All manner of veal and chicken dishes fall in the $7.95 to $9.95 range, with good portions. Wines and beers are available.

Antonio's serves up smaller versions of many entrees as weekday lunch specials: chicken cutlet with ziti for $4.95, linguine and a meatball for $3.95. Mangia. Open Mondays through Fridays from 11 A.M. to 10 P.M. and weekends from 11 A.M. to 10:30 P.M.

Cafe de Paris
- 19 Arlington St., Boston; (617) 247-7121
- *Tip-free*

How 'bout it—a Back Bay eatery that doesn't try to bilk you for all you've got! This attractive coffee shop serves up soups, salads, sandwiches, quiches—and, of course, pastries—in a setting that is both relaxed and elegant, facing the Public Garden.

Most menu items come in a choice of sizes. Turkey sandwiches are $2.50 for a small and $5.20 for a large. Quiche Lorraine makes a more refined lunch or dinner choice, and is reasonably priced at $2.95 small, $4.25 large. Plenty of salad offerings, from traditional to tabouleh, many around two bucks. Stop in and grab a quick bite for breakfast, too. Muffins are a good bet for 90¢, and the coffee is wonderful.

Bistro-style tables and fresh flower centerpieces give a feeling of refinement without being stuffy. The cafe is open seven days for breakfast, lunch, and dinner, closing up around 9 P.M. (11 P.M. on Saturdays and 7 P.M. Sundays).

Cafe Jaffa
- 48 Gloucester St., Boston; (617) 536-0230

A spacious, attractive restaurant, pleasantly mellow, right in the heart of trendy Back Bay—and affordable, too? Can it be possible? Yup. Eating at Cafe Jaffa is like finding a relaxing oasis in the city, of the sort more often associated with expense accounts. With its natural wood floors, exposed-brick walls decorated with contemporary canvases of Mediterranean scenes, and fresh flowers on each table, the place *feels* like it should be more expensive.

And yet, most entrees are in the $7-$8 range, even for a pair of grilled lamb chops or a shish kabob plate. All come on a bed of rice pilaf, with salad and warm pita bread. Mr. C worked on a mountain of chicken schwarma, tender and smokey, as

MR. CHEAP'S PICKS
Back Bay

✔ **Cafe Jaffa**—Fancy digs in the heart of trendy Back Bay, but it looks more expensive than it is.

✔ **Parish Cafe and Bar**—Can't afford the Four Seasons? Their chef makes a sandwich here. So do chefs from *chi-chi* restaurants all over town.

✔ **Pour House Restaurant**— The name says it all—lotsa beers, and food that won't break the bank.

long as he could—and still ended up taking half of it home.

For lighter appetites, sandwich versions of all these are available in the $4-$5 range. So are combinations like falafel and hummus, along with various salads (be sure to try the tahini dressing) and even burgers and steak tips. In keeping with its name, Jaffa's short list of alcoholic beverages includes Israeli wines; there are also fine-looking desserts and strong Turkish coffee for after the meal. Open for lunch and dinner ('til 10 or 11 P.M.) Mondays through Saturdays, and from 1 to 10 P.M. on Sundays.

Harvard Gardens
- 316 Cambridge St., Boston; (617) 523-2727

This Beacon Hill eatery has been around for more than six decades. It's a comfortable neighborhood restaurant and bar, as typical of the "back of the hill" as that *other* hangout (you know, the one where everybody knows your name) defines the front side.

You can actually match any shape of pasta with any sauce—that's 78 possible combinations! Apple-smoked chicken in cream sauce, atop a bed of penne ($8.95), gets Mr. C's

vote. Pizzas are equally creative. One pie commemorates a nearby landmark, recently departed: the "Phillips Drug Pizza" ($8 for the small size), topped with barbecued chicken and scallions. What the connection is, who knows.

Being a pub, Italian food is hardly the only cuisine available here. Char-broiled burgers are $4.95 naked, about a buck more gussied up with stuff like bacon or guacamole. There are also some fancy sandwiches, like Norwegian smoked salmon on a bagel ($6.25) or grilled veggies on focaccia ($5.95). All of these are served with fries. A full bar, of course, complements just about anything from finger food to fine dining. Harvard Gardens is open for lunch, dinner, and Sunday brunch, closing nightly at 11 P.M.

Joe and Nemo
- 45 Bowdoin St., Boston; (617) 742-5242
- *Tip-free*

"Joe and Nemo, the Hot Dog Kings" is the full title—and they do seem to hold the hot dog title in this town. Founders Joe Merlino and Anthony "Nemo" Colligero no longer run the show, but then, the original 5¢ red hots ain't around anymore either. Today, behind the State House, sits the sole remaining outpost of a chain that once stretched from Scollay Square to Revere Beach.

What also remains are the steamed Pearl all-beef franks, in the crunchy natural-casing, for $1.40. For a quarter more, you can top your dog with chili or cheese. J & N also grills all-beef, quarter-pound hamburgers ($1.60), to which you can again add various condiments. In fact, a burger with chili and cheese—at a whopping $2—is the king of the menu.

There's something to be said for specialization; the franks are still terrific. For that true old-time experience, enjoy one while standing at a counter along the wall; there are no seats here. This is fast-food from before the phrase was invented. Open weekdays only, from 10 A.M. to 4:30 P.M.

King & I
- 145 Charles St., Boston; (617) 227-3320

Yes! You can get a lot of food for a smallish price on Charles Street, and this semi-miracle has customers flocking to King & I. The food here is pretty healthy: No MSG is used, and tofu or vegetables can be substituted into any dish you like. The king's award-winning pad Thai ($7.25) is a must; or, start off with that other Thai favorite, spicy skewers of satay beef, pork, or chicken, each $4.25.

Mr. C's "Rama Garden" chicken dish had big chunks of meat in a yummy peanut sauce, with fresh squash, carrots, mushrooms, and even pineapple tucked underneath, all for $9.95. Other recommended main dishes include yellow chicken curry and ginger pork with vegetables, both $9.95.

Yes, these prices touch Mr. C's upper limit, but remember where you are and what you're getting for your money. Vegetarian dishes are a bit less, and excellent: Fried tofu with vegetables is a sure bet at $8.95. If you're in the area around lunchtime, you'll have even more reason to praise King & I's good value—lunch specials are priced around $5.50. Open for lunch every day except Sunday; dinner is served nightly.

Paramount Restaurant & Deli
- 44 Charles St., Boston; (617) 523-8832
- *Tip-free*

Of course, *this* joint is on Charles Street also, somehow. Maybe you've blown a bit too much on a silver-plated chafing dish for your cat, and you're feeling a bit hungry yourself; but you'd never spend that much on your own meal. Step into the Paramount and have a roast chicken dinner for $4.95, or a cheeseburger from the grill for $1.95.

Yes, it's your basic cafeteria, somehow mixed in with the nobs. Grab a tray and tell the man what you want. Maybe baked macaroni and cheese ($3.25) or a huge bowl of beef stew ($3.55). Mr. C tried the chicken soup ($1.85), a large bowl of thick stock with bits of chicken, carrots, and rice. Beef over rice or noodles ($4.75) is a hearty meal, as is the veal cutlet sandwich ($2.75); breakfast is served all day, like two eggs and bacon for $3.25.

The Paramount serves beer and wine and, unlike many greasy spoons, stays open in the evenings. Filling, heartwarming, and cheap.

Parish Cafe and Bar
- 361 Boylston St., Boston; (617) 247-4777

Are you a Cheapster who dreams of dining at *chi-chi* restaurants like Biba's and the Four Seasons in Boston, Rialto in Cambridge, or the Oyster Bar on Martha's Vineyard? The Parish Cafe is your fancy-meal ticket. Here, you can enjoy scrumptious sandwiches "designed" by chefs from these and other upscale eateries. To be sure, the prices are not as low as Mr. C normally prefers, especially for sandwiches. But, considering the location (just steps from Newbury Street), the quality, and the hearty sizes, he is willing to make an exception.

After all, who could resist "Salamander's Spicy Grilled Eggplant" ($7.95), grilled eggplant on focaccia bread with roasted red peppers and red onion, laced with a yogurt and feta cheese spread. Or "The Rialto," made with paper-thin proscuitto, fresh mozzarella, and basil garlic oil, served on grilled white bread for $9.95. No wonder the Parish was voted the "Best Sandwich Restaurant" by *Boston* magazine. Most sandwiches are served with a salad, and you won't walk away hungry. Desserts are pricey, but worth it. Full bar, too. For a well-deserved splurge that won't make you mortgage the house, give the Parish Cafe and Bar a try. Open from 11:30 A.M. to 1:30 A.M., daily.

Phoenicia
- 240 Cambridge St., Boston; (617) 523-4606

Phoenicia, on the back of Beacon Hill, serves delicious Middle Eastern

---

MR. CHEAP'S PICKS
Beacon Hill

✔ **Antonio's Cucina Italiana**—
Like going into the North End,
without as much parking
hassle.

✔ **Joe and Nemo**—The hot dog
legend lives, right behind the
State House.

---

food in a pleasant cafe atmosphere.
The wooden walls are a fresh white,
with dark brown furniture and green
linen—in short, nicer surroundings
than you usually get with this kind of
food.

Be sure to start off with the fat-
toush salad ($3.75/$4.50); even the
small size is enormous. Greens and
vegetables are mixed with mint, pars-
ley, garlic, and bits of toasted pita
bread for a refreshing appetizer. The
falafel is unusual—flatter and fried
up crispier than most, while the inside remains moist. Just right.

Entrees give you more of the familiar choices, generally ranging
from $6 to $9. Among the more interesting are the broccoli-noodle casse-
role ($6.95), baked with mushrooms
and Swiss and Parmesan cheeses. For
a real bargain, order one of the
eleven combination plates ($7 to
$9.25), with various trios of grilled
chicken, spinach pie, falafel, kafta,
lamb kebabs and more, all served
over rice pilaf. You get a basket of
pita bread with your meal, too. Have
a cup of Turkish coffee (95¢) and baklava ($1.25) for dessert. Hours are
11 A.M. to 11 P.M. Mondays through
Saturdays, 'til 10 pm on Sundays.

Pour House Restaurant
• 907 Boylston St., Boston; (617)
236-1767
People have found the Pour House
out—it used to be a divey, unassuming sort of place to get a big meal

cheap. More recently, it's been discovered by students, yuppies, and
regular folks. So now, despite its two
levels, you can have a tough time
finding a booth, even on a weeknight.

Nevertheless, the joint remains a
rowdy, funky place. Diner food is big
here, like the grilled meatloaf sandwich on white bread, served with
mashed potatoes, gravy and vegetables for $4.95. Burgers are also popu-
lar, starting at just $2.95 for the basic
fresh quarter-pounder. Best deal is
the "Pour Boy," with two patties, bacon, cheese, and sauteed onions for
$3.95. All come with fries and, for
some reason, potato chips.

Mexican food makes up the flip
side of the menu. As an appetizer, the
Mexican pizza ($3.95) is a *huge* flour
tortilla with enchilada sauce, cheddar
cheese, onions, black olives, and
jalapenos. Seven-pepper chili ($2.25
a cup) heats your mouth up slowly.
And among the main dishes, the giant burrito ($5.75) is another big
flour tortilla, filled with cheese and
your choice of beef, chicken, or veggies and covered with enchilada
sauce.

There are plenty of good beers to
wash all this down, of course. In addition to all the booths, there are long,
long bars both upstairs and down.
Oh, and if you can make it to dessert,
how about New York cheesecake
with strawberries for just $2.25?
Won't find it too often at that price.
The Pour House is still a bargain after all these years. Hours are from 7
A.M. to 2 A.M., seven days.

Steve's Authentic Greek Cuisine
• 316 Newbury St., Boston; (617)
267-1817
Dining cheap on Newbury Street?
It's true. If you don't need all those
pretentious cafes with prices to
match, Steve's is the place in this
neighborhood. Most dinner platters
are in the $6-to-$8 range, including
gyros, souvlaki, moussaka, falafel,
and various shish kebabs. Each
comes as a packed plate with plenty
of meat, plus a Greek salad, rice, and
pita bread.

Sandwich versions of the same go from $3.50 to $5 and still give you a lot to work on. There are also many appetizers, both hot and cold. Taramosalata ($3.75) is a caviar salad with potato and spices blended in; for $5.50 you can get a sampler plate combining this with stuffed grape leaves, hummus, eggplant, vegetables, spinach pie, and pita bread.

Desserts include the obligatory baklava, as well as galactobouriko (each around $1.50)—filo dough filled with a sweet custard. Mmmm.

Great for the budget Newbury Street shopper—stop in to refuel after cruising the secondhand clothing stores mentioned elsewhere in this book! 7:30 A.M. to 11 P.M. Mondays through Saturdays, 10 A.M. to 10 P.M. on Sundays.

The Ultimate Bagel Company

- 335 Newbury St., Boston; (617) 247-1010
- 1310 Massachusetts Ave., Cambridge; (617) 497-9180
- 118 Needham St., Newton; (617) 964-8990
- *Tip-free*

If this isn't the ultimate treatment a bagel can get, it sure comes close. After all, *dah-ling*, have you ever tried bluefish paté on an oat raisin bagel? You can have it here, for all of $2.29. Add an espresso, and you're in bagel heaven.

There are enough snazzy sandwiches to make this a frequent pit stop. Basic options, all between $2-$4, include vegetarian, ham, and the like. But hey, get with it—go for a smoked duck and Jarlsberg cheese, with cranberry relish, all for $4.99. Choose your bagel, and be prepared for a handful. These get rather exotic themselves, with such flavors as cinnamon glazed ("They're fantastic," raved a woman in line next

to Mr. C, as she ordered a half-dozen).

Charmingly done up in mauve and dark wood, with padded chairs, the interior is just as fancy. Needless to say, the place is a hit with the yuppies and office worker types, especially around the lunch rush. So trendy, yet so cheap! Open daily.

Venice Cafe

- 204 Cambridge St., Boston; (617) 227-2094
- *Tip-free*

This fine little eatery on the back of Beacon Hill specializes in take-out and delivered food, most notably pastas and pizzas—but not your average kinds. These folks have gotten creative. How about Hawaiian pizza, with ham, prosciutto, and pineapple? Or pesto pizza, self-explanatory; and the ultimate in nouveau pizza, the "Yuppie." This comes with spinach, broccoli, and artichokes. All in all, nearly thirty toppings to choose from, most of which lean toward the unusual. The small pie starts at $5.95, the large $8.50.

On the pasta side, *all* dishes are $8.50. While this may not sound super cheap, you get a lot of pasta for your dough, along with hot garlic bread. And, if you eat in or pick up, all meals are a striking $5.25 from 11 A.M. to 2 P.M., and $6.60 from 2 to 10 P.M. Choose from chicken agostino, which features a lemony cream sauce and broccoli; sauteed ground beef with garlic, red wine, eggplant and tomatoes served over linguine; and eleven other varieties. They are dee-lish.

Venice also serves calzones ($5.50 to $6.25), which come with homemade tomato basil sauce on the side, deli-style sandwiches, burgers, soups, and salads. The restaurant stays open until 1 A.M. weeknights and 2 A.M. Fridays and Saturdays.

CHINATOWN

Buddha's Delight

● 5 Beach St., Boston; (617) 451-2395

One of the real finds in Chinatown, Buddha's Delight features "Vegetarian Specialties from the Orient." Here that seems to translate into "Vietnamese tofu," but read on: This is in no way a limited dining experience. The big secret of Buddha's Delight is the fact that someone has found a way to give tofu some taste; and, more importantly, texture. Try the barbecued tofu and vermicelli ($4.50), and you will think you're eating—yes, chewing on—sliced meat from a pork chop. It comes atop a huge bed of white vermicelli noodles, with a crunchy and delicious spring roll (also vegetarian).

The other substance found throughout the menu is gluten, a wheat product that is used to simulate seafood and chicken. Not all the substitutions are perfect imposters; "roast pork" comes close, while "chicken" slices are a bit less successful. But the point is that they *are* tasty, and you'll never feel as if you're munching on some sponge from the kitchen.

Among appetizers, there are the terrific spring rolls (two for $2.75) mentioned above; Vietnamese gluten and bean cakes ($3.50), which look a bit like deep-fried muffins, with cooked peanuts on top; and the unusual Vietnamese pizza ($4), which actually looks more like a crispy omelette filled with "pork" tofu and vegetables. Noodle soups, most about $4, come in huge, deep bowls—try the steamed noodle with fried tofu and coconut milk.

For dessert, try one of the two-dozen or so blended fruit milk shakes, each about $2. "Pineapple milk with condensed milk shake" and "Pickled lemon with soda" are just a couple of the many exotic choices. The restaurant itself is clean and comfortable, and the atmosphere was festive, with a packed house early on a Saturday evening. No surprise; a recent *Boston* magazine reader's poll named it "Best Vegetarian Restaurant." This is, after all, a place in which two people can eat like kings for a bill that may still come in under $20. Even if only one is a vegetarian. Open 11 A.M. to 10 P.M., seven days.

Dong Khanh Restaurant

● 83 Harrison Ave., Boston; (617) 426-9410

Dong Khanh is a popular spot for lunch, as evidenced by the throngs of people enjoying heaping bowls of *pho*. For the uninitiated, that's any kind of hearty Vietnamese noodle soup. If you're thinking "Soup? That's not very filling," think again. These soups are hard to finish, stocked with things like beef, chicken, vegetables, and *lots* of noodles. All of these vast stews are priced under $5, and they really are meals in themselves. The menu also includes rice, vermicelli, and fried noodle dishes. Just about all of these fall in the $4 to $7 range. Chow down! Open from 9:30 A.M. to 10:30 P.M. Mondays through Fridays, 9:30 A.M. to 11 A.M. on weekends.

Eldo Tea House

● 57 Beach St., Boston; (617) 338-2128

This tiny, unadorned room has a huge and varied menu that crosses the borders of several continents. After all, in what other Chinese restaurant can you order "Spam Ham and Egg Macaroni in Soup"? Many of the more interesting dishes here are combinations of Chinese and American items, as well as cooking styles from elsewhere in the Orient.

Almost everything is very inexpensive, and you can have a great meal—probably a healthy one, too—even for around $5. Lots of the bargain dishes are the unusual soups in big, deep bowls, like watercress and pork for two ($3.75) or sliced beef with noodles ($3.25). The house special soup is stocked with shrimp, squid, broccoli, noodles, and a piece of fried pork in the center. At $3.75, it's a meal all by itself.

Chinese spaghetti is another example of the cross-breeding here: Try it topped with sliced beef in tomato sauce ($3.95); or with baked seafood ($4.95), which includes scallops, squid and shrimp.

There is, of course, plenty of more traditional Cantonese cooking. Most seafood dishes are priced between $6 to $9; beef and chicken dishes are all around $6. Preparations range from sweet and sour to satay to curry, which brings us back to the offbeat nature of the menu. There is a whole slew of entrees from Hong Kong and Singapore, which tend toward the spicy—like *laksa*, served in a large soup bowl with noodles and chicken, pork, beef, or shrimp ($3.95 each). The spices are tangy but not the kind that will set your mouth on fire.

By the way, you get your choice of noodle in many of these soups: pick from egg noodles, fat rice noodles, or rice vermicelli. This is definitely the kind of place where you will want to experiment with repeat visits—and at these prices, you can afford to do so. Open every day, from 8 A.M. to midnight.

Peking Cuisine Restaurant
- 10 Tyler St., Boston; (617) 542-5857

Peking Cuisine's owners proudly exhibit a photograph of the day Larry Bird dined at their restaurant. Clearly, the ex-Celtic knows what he's doing on the court *and* at the table. Peking Cuisine is one of Chinatown's few Mandarin restaurants, offering such authentic fare as braised pig feet and broiled eel.

Whether Larry tried these exotic items, Mr. C has no idea. He himself gravitated to some of the more standard dishes on the vast menu (238 items!) like various *moo shu* entrees for $6.75. Branching out a bit, fresh squid with curry sauce is $8.50, and an awe-inspiring sizzling platter of shrimp, beef, chicken and veggies is $9.75. The health craze has even touched Chinatown: Peking Cuisine now offers a "Revolution Diet" selec-

---

MR. CHEAP'S PICKS
Chinatown

✔ **Buddha's Delight**—This popular spot keeps prices low by serving no meat.

✔ **Eldo Tea House**—At the other end of Beach Street, this ultra-simple kitchen can fill you up for around five bucks.

---

tion of dishes without oil, salt, sugar, or starch ($6.50 and up).

The food here, to Mr. C's taste, has a lightness often lacking at Chinese restaurants. There's really no end to the pleasant food surprises here—this cooking would be good even at prices higher than these. Open seven days.

People's Cafeteria
- 21-23 Edinboro St., Boston; (617) 482-7328

Mr. C wishes he knew the Chinese expression for "a dive," because that would aptly describe the atmosphere of this restaurant. Remember, though, that such unassuming places often serve the most authentic food; the crowds of local families cheerfully munching away offer proof enough.

Mr. C began with Peking ravioli, six huge fried crescents, juicy on the inside, for $3.95. The menu is heavy on the classics, such as chicken with cashew nuts ($6.95); only a bit more for most beef specials, like a beef and vegetable stir fry for $7.50. And of course there are the ubiquitous fried rice, chow mein, and lo mein dishes, all $4 to $5.

Discerning diners, however, will also spot more unusual offerings, like beef with bitter melon for $7.50, and a handful of sea conch dishes, each $8.95. If you're the adventurous type, the staff at People's Cafeteria are famous for their "insider" suggestions;

be sure to ask. Speaking of staff, Mr. C is sorry to point out that, despite the name, this place isn't really a cafeteria—you will have to leave a tip. Well, that's OK, because this menu will leave you with plenty of change in your purse. Open seven days.

DORCHESTER / ROXBURY

Galvin's Harp & Bard

• 1099 Dorchester Ave., Dorchester; (617) 265-2893

Good Irish pubs briefly make you forget there's a world beyond their walls. Dark and wooded as a forest, this longtime favorite has a wide menu of tasty meals—plus daily specials that come in under $4.95. These may include marinated steak tips over rice pilaf, chicken parmigiana with pasta, and baked schrod with potato and vegetables. Sit at a table, or at the huge, U-shaped bar, and enjoy.

A dozen different sandwiches, and juicy half-pound burgers, run $4.25-$4.75, served with French fries or cole slaw. Meat and seafood entrees claw their way onto your plate at prices ranging from $8.95 (for baked haddock, or two jumbo pork chops served with homemade applesauce) to $11.95, for an immense order of prime rib.

Most chicken entrees, such as teriyaki and marsala, are $7.95; and all dinners come with your choice of soup or a salad, plus veggies. It's almost enough to make any Cheapster burst into song—but don't do that on Thursdays and Saturdays, or you'll upstage the DJ. Open seven days.

Ma Dixon's Restaurant

• 478 Blue Hill Ave., Roxbury; (617) 445-4285
• *Tip-free*

This simple place is so famous in its neighborhood, the whole square—at the intersection of Blue Hill Avenue and Washington Street—is named after it. Now, the Grove Hall area of Roxbury may not be comfortable for everyone; but the square is clean, and the folks inside Ma's are friendly as can be.

Meanwhile, Southern food doesn't get much more authentic in Boston than this. Grab a tray, walk along the counter, and watch them load up a plate with a ton of homemade food for about five bucks. That's the price for just about every choice on the limited menu, from chicken (fried, baked, barbecued, or "smothered") to Salisbury steak to genuine oxtail. Barbecued ribs are nice and meaty, and the meat falls right off the bone.

Add two vegetables on the side (mashed potatoes, string beans, collard greens), plus cornbread, all included, and you'll see why this is a deal worth seeking out. The decor is minimal, but a few plants and table lamps make a nice effort. And everybody smiles. Open seven days, until 6 P.M. only.

Maryam's Famous Cuisine

• 310 Bowdoin St., Dorchester; (617) 825-9226

"Home cooking for the way things used to be," proclaim the signs. Mr. C, dining *incognito*, was treated like a king by a very friendly waiter; sweet soul music and the bright red-and-white-checked decor made him forget that this is one of Dorchester's dicier areas.

Specializing in Caribbean cuisine, Maryam's offers immense meals in sizes inexplicably labeled "small." An attempt to order the medium size was met with a doubtful look, while "large" pretty much requires you to have an entourage. Mr. C's "small" order turned out to be a heaping platter of curried chicken, rice, beans, and plantains, plus a second plate piled with broccoli and carrots—all for $4.95 (!) Add $2 for each size increase. Substitute a salad for the vegetables, or macaroni and cheese for the rice if you're so inclined; *do not* miss the plantains, which are absolutely succulent.

Other curried selections include beef, goat, and oxtail, or combos of them all, at the same prices. Jamaican "jerk" chicken—boneless, grilled with hot and sweet spices—weighs in at $6.95-$10.95.

Lunch deals are even more incredible. A kosher frank plate, which for some reason also comes with two chicken fingers, two wings, and fries, costs $3.50. Breakfast offers two eggs, toast, coffee, bacon, and home fries for $3.95. And, for the adventurous of spirit when it comes to beverages, Maryam's whips up its own ginger beer, carrot juice, and other concoctions (from $1.25).

Far and away the bright spot on the street, Maryam's is open from 8 A.M. to 9:30 P.M. weekdays, from 9 A.M. Saturdays, and from 10 A.M. to 9 P.M. Sundays.

Pho Hoa
- 1356 Dorchester Ave., Dorchester; (617) 287-9746

Vietnamese food can be quite an unusual experience for first-timers—especially those who, for instance, prefer their meat with all the fat trimmed off. That's what makes Pho Hoa one of the best of the Dot Ave. Viets; the broad menu of this national chain caters to every taste, including the tender-tummied novice.

Mr. C, who's been touting this cuisine for years as being cheap and satisfying, charged in with an order of *pho tai, gau, sach*; the popular noodle soup came in a huge bowl, flavored by coriander and onions, with slabs of lightly cooked eye round steak, fat brisket, and tripe. The feast was delicious, although not everyone will care for the brisket and tripe. A more Western choice order would be from the menu sections labeled "For the beginner" (tender, leaner cuts of beef) and "A little bit of fat" (much less than the other dishes); or one of the many rice plates ($4.50-$5.25).

Soups come in two sizes, best described as large ($3.85) and extremely large ($4.35), and are served with a small plate of bean sprouts to mix in, plus a fresh lemon drink. Do

---

MR. CHEAP'S PICKS
Dorchester

- ✔ **Maryam's Famous Cuisine**— What? You've never heard of it? If you venture into this not-so-hot neighborhood, you'll never forget their hot Caribbean food.

- ✔ **Pho Hoa**—Delicious noodle soups for practically nothing.

---

start with an order of spring rolls ($1 each), and try one of several different homemade puddings ($1.55-$2) for dessert. Open 9 A.M. to 10 P.M., seven days.

Quan Ngu Binh
- 1052 Dorchester Ave., Dorchester; (617) 282-BINH (2464)

At Quan Ngu Binh, by contrast; Mr. C had no idea what he ordered even *after* he'd eaten it. The meal was delicious, to be sure, but your humble author might have been in real trouble if a friendly waitress hadn't offered to help out.

Initially ordering a plate of pork and shrimp in steamed rice cakes, Mr. C was treated to a sample coated in some rather unusual puck-shaped "rice" which his stomach quailed at. He quickly switched to the waitress's suggestion of grilled beef wrapped in virtually the same thing, which was somehow lighter, served over noodles and sprouts. "Most Americans prefer it," she smiled, sympathetically. Mr. C agreed, and at $5 with a cool lemon drink included, it was indeed the right choice.

A black-and-white checked floor helps create a casual, deli-style feel, as does gentle, albeit unintelligible, music. Every entree in the house is priced under $6; pork, shrimp, beef, chicken, or mixed vegetables, most served with steamed rice or rolled up in thin rice paper. Novices may find Quan Ngu Binh a bit too authentic, but those seeking culi-

nary adventure will find this place a treat. Open 9 A.M. to 9 P.M., seven days a week.

DOWNTOWN / WATERFRONT

Baldini's
- 71 Summer St., Boston; (617) 695-1559
- 304 Stuart St., Boston; (617) 338-0095
- 551 Boylston St., Boston; (617) 262-2555
- 532 Commonwealth Ave., Boston; (617) 267-6269
- 5 Stockwell Dr., Avon; (508) 588-0077
- *Tip-free*

Taking the fast-food approach to Italian cuisine, Baldini's does a good (and clearly popular) job with red-sauce basics.

A plate of pasta in marinara sauce goes for a mere $2.95; adding meatballs or sausage brings the price to $4.43 (no, that's not a typo). A pepperoni and cheese calzone is $3.24 (see?); a slab of lasagna is $4.95. Plus pizzas, sandwiches, and salads.

All in a hip, self-service setting. You won't feel like you're in the North End, but if you can't get there, try one of these spots, from Downtown Crossing to Kenmore Square. Hours vary; open daily.

Blossoms
- 99 High St., Boston; (617) 423-1911
- *Tip-free*

Or, a caterer grows in Boston. Blossoms prepares fine food for many of its Financial District neighbors, and more recently, they've opened up a lovely cafe in the lobby of the Keystone Building. Because their large kitchen is constantly cooking for corporate clients, they can afford to charge low prices here, making this a classy lunch stop if your office is not fortunate enough to get their food already.

The menu ranges from basic deli fare to exotic creations like spinach-feta cheese-mushroom crepes

($4.50), pepper crusted lemon grilled chicken ($4.75), and good ol' New York sirloin ($5.50). Plus homemade soups, pasta salads, mini-pizzas (shrimp scampi and tomatoes, $4.25!) as well as freshly baked pastries, gourmet coffees, and fruit juices.

It's all in a bright, airy room with high ceilings; floor-to-ceiling windows for watching well-heeled worker bees; and potted plants and trees, y'know, blossoming. It's also worth the walk after a morning of big-game bargain hunting at Filene's. Open weekdays only, from 7 A.M. to 4 P.M. (full lunches stop at 3).

The Blue Diner
- 150 Kneeland St., Boston; (617) 338-4639

It looks blue collar, like an old-time holdout amidst modern high-rises. But the Blue Diner puts a trendy spin on classic All-American fare, serving up "comfort food" like flapjacks, meatloaf, crab cakes, and turkey pot pie.

"Dash for the Hash" puts yer basic corned beef hash *inside* a three-egg omelette, topped with cheese, for $6.95 with toast. Homemade chili, served with salad and cornbread, is $8.50; a half-rack of ribs is $7.95, with baked beans, collard greens, and more cornbread. To these are added fajitas, gumbo, Buffalo wings, pastas. . .you get the idea.

Plus their own blend of strong coffee, and homemade desserts, all in a funked-up diner setting with about ten booths and a counter. Open daily for breakfast, lunch, and dinner, the Blue Diner stays open 24 hours on weekends. Ah, if only more of Boston would be so daring.

Boston Sail Loft
- 80 Atlantic Ave., Boston; (617) 227-7280

- 1 Memorial Drive, Cambridge; (617) 225-2222

For an inexpensive meal that will seem like a big night out on the town, catch some fish at the Sail Loft. Located right on the waterfront, it offers a view of the harbor (very romantic at night). In warm weather you may be able to get a table out on the deck and pretend you own one of the yachts moored below.

Meanwhile, the food is terrific and moderately priced. For fresh fish, such as bluefish, mako shark, and more, check the blackboard specials. Regular dinners include a huge platter of fish and chips ($10.95), fried shrimp for the same price, and fried boneless breast of chicken in a honey-mustard sauce ($8.95). These come with French fries and French bread, tartar sauce, and cole slaw.

Burgers are big and juicy, starting at $5.50. For a dollar more, though, try a havarti cheese burger or the Sail Loft burger, topped with Genoa salami, mozzarella, peppers, and mushrooms. A bowl of fresh clam chowder is $3.75; or have a cup with half a sandwich for $6.95.

Compared with most of the other joints in this popular neighborhood, the Sail Loft lets you dine like a captain—and may even give you a head-start on saving up for a boat.

Sail Loft also has a second branch near Kendall Square. Same great food, but alas, no view! Open daily 'til 10 P.M., Wednesdays through Saturdays until 11 P.M.

Fajitas & 'Ritas

- 25 West St., Boston; (617) 426-1222
- 48 Boylston St., Brookline; (617) 566-1222

A novel approach to Mexican food: Mix and match your ingredients by circling exactly what you want—and how much of each item—on an order form. For example, a single chicken fajita plate is $8.10; additional orders will be $7.38 if you're going to share. There are also beef, shrimp, and vegetable fajitas. They all come to your table in a piping hot skillet,

with guacamole, *pico de gallo* sauce, and tortillas.

Nachos are the other staple here, and they offer even more choices, allowing you to "build" your own nacho plate with such toppings as beans, chili, chicken, extra cheese, etc. The concept extends to the "'Ritas" as well—circle on the rocks or frozen, twelve-ounce or liter, regular or strawberry. Plenty of good beers on the list, too, including Pacifico, Tecate, Sierra Nevada and Lone Star; sangria too.

The atmosphere is part of the show at F & R; it's rollicking during the evenings, with the added fun of crayons and white paper table coverings so you can doodle while you eat. Past masterpieces are usually on display. Open 11:30 A.M. to 9 P.M. daily (Saturdays they sleep in 'til noon).

Fuddruckers

- 137 Stuart St., Boston; (617) 723-3833
- *Tip-free*

Boston's sole representative of this national chain, Fuddruckers is a popular pit-stop for theater district tourists and downtown office workers alike. Big on burgers, these are not your paper-thin McChain variety. Choose a half-pounder or third-of-a-pounder (you can see platters of fresh red patties waiting in the refrigerator cases), and add Swiss, bacon, or mushrooms; prices range from $4-$6. Everything is cooked to order. Once you pick up your creation, head to the toppings bar for unlimited amounts of lettuce, tomato slices, jalapeño peppers, the works.

There are a few other choices, like chicken breast sandwiches ($4-$5) and hefty hot dogs ($3.75, covered with chili and cheese). Plus specials for the kiddies, who just love the bright, noisy, rambunctious atmosphere of the place. Sodas, 99¢, include free do-it-yourself refills. For the grownups, a few bottled beers are also offered.

Fuddruckers is located in the atrium of the State Transportation Building, facing the Wang Center and

MR. CHEAP'S PICKS
Downtown

✔ **Blossoms**—A catering company opens its doors to anyone seeking creative cuisine cheap.

✔ **The Blue Diner**—Trendy spin on classic comfort food.

✔ **Le Café at Maison Robert**—Not the chic, super-expensive restaurant upstairs, but the (relatively) affordable *prix-fixe* menu downstairs. Ahhh.

✔ **Sweetwater Cafe**—In the Boylston Place alley of the Theater District, this place serves up Tex-Mex food at surprisingly good prices.

Nick's Comedy Stop. It's open for lunch and dinner seven days a week.

India Samraat
- 51A Massachusetts Ave., Boston; (617) 247-0718

A coupla blocks in from the Charles, India Samraat features huge portions of wonderfully authentic Indian specialties at prices that definitely cater to the area's vast student population. Several lunch specials come in under $5. These all begin with crunchy, spiced *papadam* bread, and include basmati rice, cabbage, and onion chutney. Choose from treats like *saag paneer* (spinach cooked with homemade cheese in a curry sauce, $4.50), chicken curry ($4.75), and *malai kofta* (fried vegetable balls in cream sauce, also $4.75). Mr. C enjoyed a special entree, chicken simmered with vegetables and herbs. Very spicy, but not burn-your-mouth hot.

Dinner entrees are equally cheap and delicious. Enjoy chicken tandoori ($8.25), lamb curry ($7.95), or mixed vegetable curry ($6.95). Dinners

again are served with basmati rice and onion chutney. Curry dishes can be prepared mild or hot; don't be afraid to specify. India Samraat is open from 12 noon to 11 P.M. daily.

Jimbo's Fish Shanty
- 245 Northern Ave., Boston; (617) 542-5600
- 405 Franklin St., Braintree; (617) 848-0300

What better place to snarf down seafood than Boston's waterfront? And what better way, says Mr. C, than at Jimbo's, a casual spot that sports an extensive menu and a lovely view— of Jimmy's Harborside, its parent restaurant. Home of fine dining for 70 years, Jimmy's prices make Jimbo's look even better.

The joint has garnered a following all its own. Wooden walls and tables make for a comfortable atmosphere, enhanced by all the "shanty" requirements: an immense swordfish glowering down from one wall, a ship's wheel hung from another, and netting everywhere. Choose an appetizer from a dozen selections, including mussels, fresh steamed or baked and stuffed, for $5.95; or try a meal-in-itself salad, including spinach with fried bay scallops, for all of $6.95.

Sauteed dinner entrees include calamari and schrod (each $8.95), and four tasty shrimp selections for $11-$12. Fried seafood, though, can be had for as little as $5.95—show up before 6 P.M. to order smaller portions at smaller prices. You won't be disappointed with the self-proclaimed "Jimbo's Classic" of scallops, swordfish, and shrimp *en brochette* served with rice and coleslaw, all for $10.95; or one of the daily specials, like lemon-pepper swordfish, $8.95. Open for lunch and dinner 'til 9:30 P.M. Mondays through Thursdays, and 10 P.M. weekends.

Kingston Deli and Grill
- 83 Summer St., Boston; (617) 338-8572

This large, clean cafeteria is a great place to escape the hustle and bustle of shoppers and business people racing around Downtown Crossing. It has two dining rooms and a large menu of breakfasts, sandwiches, and hot meals. Nothing is over $5.

For breakfast, two eggs and bacon with home fries and toast are $2.45. Omelettes are mostly $2.85. Sandwiches may be pouches, clubs and combos (all $3 to $5), like the Black Russian—turkey, ham, salami, Swiss, lettuce, tomato, onion, cole slaw, and Russian dressing, all for $4.25.

Hot platters include chicken kebabs or steak tips over rice, with salad, each $4.95. Also in the same price range are roast beef, chicken, or turkey, with mashed potatoes and a vegetable. Check the billboard for daily soups and specials, too. Hours are 6 A.M. to 4 P.M. Mondays through Fridays.

Le Café at Maison Robert
- 45 School St., Boston; (617) 227-3371

You walk up to this French restaurant in the historic old City Hall building, and you're thinking, "Come on, Mr. C, we can't *possibly* afford this!" Well, Le Café at Maison Robert is no greasy spoon, but this basement bistro does offer a three-course *prix-fixe* dinner, with reduced portions from the same menu found in the main restaurant upstairs. It's gourmet food at down-to-earth rates.

At each of two price levels, the daily menu offers a choice of appetizers, main courses, and desserts. You might start with a lobster bisque, then move on to poached fillet of sole on a bed of fennel in saffron butter, and finish with hazelnut tea cakes, all for $17. On their regular menu, the poached fillet of sole *alone* is $12!

Big spenders can go for the $23 tier, putting together such combinations as *escargots* baked in garlic, followed by roast lobster in-the-shell with lemon butter, ending with a selection of French pastries.

All of which makes Le Café a top Mr. C pick for that special night out on the town. The cafe may not be as impressive as the formal rooms upstairs, but is still very elegant indeed. Beautiful paintings adorn exposed-brick walls, and fresh flowers grace each table. It's really more romantic down here anyway. Dinner is served from 6 P.M. to 9:30 P.M., Mondays through Saturdays. Reservations are preferred.

Max's Deli Café
- 151 Milk St., Boston; (617) 330-9790

Downtown office worker-bees know that Max's is a must when the noon whistle blows. The menu features fancy, filling dishes for a few bucks each. Hot entrees include shrimp primavera or tortellini with pesto and sun-dried tomatoes (each $6.95), and eggplant parmesan with a Caesar salad ($5.45). All of these are served with focaccia bread.

Lighter appetites and wallets may opt for one of Max's specialty sandwiches for $4.95. You certainly won't sacrifice taste. Try the honey-tarragon chicken salad, prosciutto and provolone, or egg frittata with Italian cold cuts (yes, that's a sandwich). These all come on your choice of bread, including focaccia and baguettes. Max's also has a fine selection of salads and soups. And don't miss desserts. Chocolate truffle, cream cheese brownie, hmmmm. Open from 6 A.M. to 3 P.M., Mondays through Fridays.

New York Deli & Grill
- 11 Temple Pl., Boston; (617) 426-2350
- *Tip-free*

Here's another hidden-jewel lunch spot, convenient for office types as well as Downtown Crossing shoppers seeking fortification. A tiny hole-in-the-wall joint, the New York Deli & Grill serves up all the usual lunchtime grub—but they do an unusually good job of it. When they call it "home-style cooking," dese guys ain't messin' around, y'know? Along with the basics, NY Deli features a few noteworthy offerings like the "Turkey Terrific," with stuffing, cranberry sauce, and mayo for $3.95. Mr. C's companion, meanwhile, raved about their vegetable soup. A far cry from bland, canned mush, this con-

---

MR. CHEAP'S PICKS
The Waterfront

✔ **Jimbo's Fish Shanty**—By the sea, by the sea, by the beautiful sea—and much less expensive than its famous next-door neighbor.

✔ **No Name Restaurant**—Inexpensive seafood, straight from the Boston fish pier.

---

coction floated big pieces of zucchini, carrots, potato, and celery, fresh and flavorful. All this at $1.50 for a BIG cup, or $1.95 a bowl.

Daily specials offer more substantial meals, like meatloaf with mashed potatoes and veggies ($4.50) or beef kabobs with rice and salad ($5.50). Good place to stop in on the way to work, too; the breakfast menu includes omelettes, griddle cakes, and the usual assortment of eggs, pastries, and such. Open 6:30 A.M. to 5 P.M., Mondays through Saturdays.

No Name Restaurant
• 15 Boston Fish Pier, Boston; (617) 423-2705

To legions of seafood fans, nothing says "fresh-from-the-sea" like the No Name. Located smack-dab in the center of Boston's Fish Pier, off the waterfront's Northern Avenue, this restaurant is tucked in among several seafood wholesalers and loading docks—as it has been since 1917.

The place is as no-frills in appearance and style as it is unnamed. But the kitchen rolls out a wealth of broiled and fried selections ranging from schrod and sole (both $7.95) to scallops and a seafood plate (good portions for a reasonable $9.95 each).

Daily specials, when Mr. C docked, included boiled lobster—with a side order of fried shrimp *and* scallops—all for $15.95, and a broiled shrimp sauté for $9.95. It's

tough to skip the seafood chowder, only $1.35 a cup and $2.75 for a brimming bowl. Homemade pies, as if you'll have room, vary daily and are just $1.75 a slice. No wonder this is a popular stop on the tour bus circuit; *this* is Boston. The No Name is open from 11 A.M. to 10 P.M. seven days a week.

The Old Spaghetti Factory
• 44 Pittsburgh St., Boston; (617)737-8757

Here's a rare combination: good value along the waterfront tourist trail. For quality *and* quantity, the Old Spaghetti Factory ranks up there with the best of 'em. It's a big, boisterous, family-oriented restaurant, and feeding the kids here won't gouge a hole in their college fund. The menu, of course, consists of pasta dishes—from spaghetti with mushroom sauce to ravioli to fettucine Alfredo. All the entrees are well under $10, with most in the $6 to $7 price range. The best deals by far are located under the "complete meal" selection; each choice includes salad, fresh baked bread, coffee, tea or milk, plus a spumoni dessert. Basic beers, wines, and cocktails are also available.

The decor in the restaurant is a story in itself. The booths are actually made from the head- and foot-boards of brass and wrought-iron beds. Tiffany-style, fringed fabric lampshades hang close overhead and give a soft light to the otherwise dark dining room; you may *almost* miss the cable car sitting in the middle of the room, which offers additional seating in an even more unlikely setting.

It's open Mondays through Thursdays, from 11:30 A.M. to 2 P.M. for lunch, and 5 P.M. to 10 P.M. for dinner (Fridays 'til 11 P.M.). Weekend hours are from noon to 11 P.M. Saturdays, and from noon to 10 P.M. Sundays.

Rainbow Rollers Cafe
• 7 Liberty Sq., Boston; (617) 227-6900

Sister restaurant to its popular Downtown Crossing predecessor Blazing Salads, the Rainbow Rollers Cafe, now in the Financial District, is a good lunchtime choice for office workers in the area. The food is cheap indeed, and very healthy.

Yes, there are lots of salads and vegetarian delights on the menu, but don't shy away, carnivores! There are plenty of good ol' meat items as well. Common ground for those culinary mixed marriages. The general flavor is Middle Eastern; even burgers are served in pita bread. A quarter-pound of chopped sirloin, with various toppings, these go for $3.25 to $3.50.

Also find several chicken sandwiches, such as the Calypso ($5.25), a sauteed boneless breast with rice pilaf, cauliflower, broccoli, and cheese packed in. Most entrees come with salad and tabouli. The atmosphere is bustling. Place your order, wait in line to pick it up, and then fight your way to a seat. Or have it delivered for free, in the Financial District. Open from 11 A.M. to 9 P.M. Mondays through Fridays.

Remington's

- 124 Boylston St., Boston; (617) 574-9676

This venerable theater district restaurant is one of the few places in the area where you can have a full dinner or late night snack that isn't overpriced or over-trendy. It's a casual, comfortable place with dining rooms on two levels, and since they serve food until midnight, it's good for before or after the show.

Start off with appetizers, like nachos with cheese and chili ($4.50), marinated chicken wings ($4.95), and a platter of cheese, fresh fruit, and French bread ($4.50). There are lots of soups and salads to choose from, such as a crock of French onion soup bubbling with cheese ($2.95). "The Basic Burger" is $5, but for just 50¢ more you can add cheddar, American, or Swiss cheese and hot sauteed mushrooms or bacon. A hefty corned beef on dark rye ($4.75) and crabmeat salad in a pita pocket ($5.50) are among the other highlights. All of the above come with fries, potato salad, or macaroni salad.

Moving up the scale to entrees, there are many inexpensive choices. Several dinners go for $6.95 to $7.95, including steak tips, broiled schrod, fish and chips, and Hawaiian chicken. Each comes with salad and fries or rice and makes for a full meal.

The building that houses Remington's was originally a bank. Downstairs you can eat inside the giant vault. It's nice to know, however, that even amidst chic nightclubs and touristy restaurants, this is one place where you won't have to break the bank for dinner. The kitchen is open until midnight daily.

Serendipity 3

- 120 South Market Bldg., Quincy Market, Boston; (617) 523-2339

Walking through the Faneuil Hall Marketplace one day, Mr. C chanced upon a most unusual thing: A restaurant in this touristy destination offering reasonably priced food, a free happy hour buffet, free acoustic music on Fridays, and a Sunday jazz brunch. Joy!

Sit down over fish and chips or a char-broiled chicken salad platter, either of which goes for a reasonable (in these parts) $8.95. Less expensive yet are several sandwich options, from a good burger and fries ($5.95) to the "American in Paris," chicken marsala topped with sauteed mushrooms on a baguette ($6.95).

Of course, if you *really* want cheap, stop in weekdays from 5 to 8 P.M. for the free happy hour buffet. More than just cheese and crackers, Serendipity 3 features hot appetizers like chicken wings and Peking ravioli. Friday night's buffet is the biggest, and may even include tacos or roast beef sandwiches. It's also the night when local acoustic musicians perform from 9 P.M. to 1 A.M.—definitely one of Mr. C's favorite downtown deals. And the Sunday jazz brunch, from 10:30 A.M. to 2:30 P.M., pairs up live, no-cover music with moderately priced food choices. Open every day for breakfast, lunch, and dinner, serving until 11 P.M., but dessert is available until 11:30 P.M.

(an hour later for each on Friday and Saturday nights).

Sultan's Kitchen
• 72 Broad St., Boston; (617) 338-8509
• *Tip-free*

Founded by a chef from Turkey, Sultan's Kitchen claims to be the only Turkish restaurant in Boston. It's also one of the great spots in the Financial District—and it's jam-packed at lunchtime.

Fight your way in if you can. The food here is fresh, made with all-natural ingredients, and it's delicious. Order and pay for your food; then look for a table nearby, or in the upstairs room, which is pleasantly decorated—though more like a country home than Constantinople.

Anyway, the food is yummy. Soups, at $2.85 for a large twelve-ounce bowl with pita bread, include egg lemon with chicken, a hearty stew; curried lentil; and, on the cold side, cacik (yogurt, cucumber, mint and garlic) and gazpacho.

There are all kinds of salads, from taramosalata (fish roe with olive oil and lemon juice) to well-known Middle Eastern fare such as falafel, tabouli, and grape leaves. All cost around $5 a plate. The meze plate ($6.25) is a great combination of all these vegetarian dishes, with bread. There are soup/salad combinations available for $5.75.

Shish kebabs come in sandwich or dinner form, charcoal-grilled and tasty. Choose from lamb, chicken, kafta (ground lamb mixed with spices), beef, or swordfish. The sandwiches, about $5, come with salad; dinners (around $7) include salad, rice pilaf, and feta cheese.

Baklava, rice pudding, and other desserts are all under $2. In addition to coffees, teas, and fruit juices, beer and wines are available. Sultan's Kitchen is only open Monday to Friday, from 11 A.M. to 5 P.M.

Sweetwater Cafe
• 3 Boylston Place, Boston; (617) 357-7027

The alleyway between Boylston Street and the CityPlace Atrium, in Boston's theater district, is lined with bars and discos. Sweetwater Cafe, next to Zanzibar, is a rambunctious bar with great Tex-Mex food at very reasonable prices, considering the area.

A huge appetizer of chicken wings is $4.95; same price for a pair of soft tacos, filled with beef or chicken with refried beans and rice. Burgers are half-pounders of fresh meat in various styles—Buffalo, barbecue, jalapeno—all in the $5-$6 range. A dinner of chicken fajitas is just $6.50, lower than most other places; and burritos are large at $4.95. Don't miss the chili either, just $1.95 for a cup.

The atmosphere is loud and funky, and the decor is done all in natural Western wood, like a Texas roadside grill. Elvis looks out over the proceedings, as do a shark and some gators. The jukebox bounces from Aretha to Stevie Ray to Sinatra. Pints of Bass, Sam Adams, and more are on tap. Sweetwater is open Tuesdays through Saturdays from 11 A.M. to 2 A.M.

Trattoria Il Panino
• 297 Franklin St., Boston; (617) 338-1000
• 11 Parmenter St., Boston; (617) 720-1336
• 1001 Massachusetts Ave., Cambridge; (617) 547-5818

See the listing under "North End."

Water View Restaurant
• 150 Northern Ave., Boston; (617) 357-8121

Extending out over the harbor, the Water View is done up in the style of a houseboat, with a casual lounge to the left and a narrow dining area along the right. Each boasts the eponymous view, made even more enjoyable by a reasonably priced menu. Only one dinner entree exceeds $10, that being a twin boiled lobster meal for $15.95. Can't fault that, either.

Enjoy a broiled seafood platter of shrimp, scallops, schrod, swordfish, and clams, all for $8.95—served with a tossed salad, potato, and vegetable. Same price for sea scallops, or haddock marinated in vegetables. Fried entrees range from $6.95 (for calamari) to $8.95 (for shrimp), and chicken and beef kebabs are $8.95, served over rice, again with a salad.

Most appetizers are under $5,

and all lunch entrees come in under $7. Now, *this* is a catch! The Water View is open seven days for lunch and dinner.

EAST BOSTON

Jeveli's Restaurant
- 387 Chelsea St., East Boston; (617) 567-9539

"Boston's Oldest Italian Restaurant," states the menu. Jeveli's is indeed a big old family-style dining room, very casual, with ample portions of Italian food. They give you quite a lot to choose from. While most of the dinner entrees are in the $7-$10 range, you'll come away stuffed.

Chicken marsala is a house specialty, served with a big, fresh salad and spaghetti for $8.50. Eggplant parmigiana is $7.75. Again, you get a lot. Seafood choices include baked stuffed shrimp with salad and spaghetti for $9.75, mussels marinara with linguine ($7.25), lobster pie ($10.95), and deep-fried squid ($7.75). The fish is fresh and light.

Pasta dishes are mostly in the $6 to $7 range, like baked manicotti ($6.50) and fettucine Alfredo ($6.95); going up to spaghetti with shrimp sauce ($8.75). There are, of course, daily specials along with everything else—a recent one included shrimp, chicken, and broccoli over ziti for $9.95. Jeveli's also has a pub side, with a "lighter fare" menu. It's a big, sprawling place with meals to match. Open daily 11 A.M. to midnight.

La Famiglia
- 19 Bennington St., East Boston; (617) 567-1060
- 112 Salem St., Boston; (617) 367-6711
- 1032 Beacon St., Brookline; (617) 232-5253

See the listing under "North End."

Riley's Roast Beef
- 259 Bennington St., East Boston; (617) 567-9282
- 140 Brighton Ave., Allston; (617) 254-9592

See the listing under "Allston."

Santarpio's
- 111 Chelsea St., East Boston; (617) 567-9871

After battling your way through the Callahan Tunnel (unless you already live on the other side), you basically can't get into East Boston without encountering Santarpio's, its huge old building looming majestically to the right of the toll plaza. Low on atmosphere and heavy on smoke, this place attracts regulars who recognize great pizza when they taste it.

Rather than burying their pies in cheese, as so many pizzerias do, Santarpio's focuses on a zesty tomato sauce, and combines it with a crisp yet doughy crust to make pizza the way it oughtta be made. The one-size-serves-all 14-incher is just $5.50 plain and as low as $7 for two toppings. Great here, and great at home the next day, too.

The restaurant is also popular for its barbecue skewers, cooked up in "Lefty's Field" in the bar area just inside the front door. This accounts for the place's smoky appeal. Single skewers are $2.25 for pork sausage and $3.25 for lamb; a sizable combo is $5.50, all served with a hefty cherry pepper and some fine Italian bread.

MR. CHEAP'S PICKS
East Boston

✔ **Santarpio's**—Worth a drive through the tunnel (if you're not already there) for some of the best pizza anywhere.

Featuring a lengthy bar with a separate dining area, Santarpio's is open from noon to 12:30 A.M. seven days a week. Any nerve-jangling excursion to Logan would be improved considerably by stopping in here.

FENWAY / KENMORE SQUARE

Crossroads Ale House

- 495 Beacon St., Boston; (617) 262-7371

Crossroads, near Kenmore Square, is a local watering hole that also serves up a varied menu of sandwiches and dinners. There are several good beers on tap, including Bass, Guinness, and New Castle Brown Ale, as well as Woodpecker Cider. The clientele is a mix of students and professionals, and the atmosphere is divey but comfortable.

Create your own pizzas, starting from $4.50 for one person and $7.50 for two. Toppings, include bacon, pepperoni, meatballs, sausage, and more. The appetizer combination platter gives you buffalo wings, potato skins, chicken or buffalo fingers, and mozzarella sticks for $6.25. The chalkboard always lists a half-dozen daily specials, such as a pork chop dinner ($5.95) or a mixed grill offering with steak tips and chicken fingers ($6.25), served over rice with vegetables. There are various hot sandwiches, such as barbecued beef ($4.95), all of which include your choice of soup, onion rings or hand-cut French fries. Burgers, $4.95, are nice and big, made from fresh beef; for an extra 50¢ each you can top them with bacon, cheese, chili, or other items.

The decor is a "crossroads" of Irish pub and college frat house; the crowd can get a bit rowdy at times. Still, the joint is a neighborhood institution, and the food is pretty good. Open daily.

Deli Haus

- 476 Commonwealth Ave., Boston; (617) 247-9712

Deli Haus has been a longtime hangout for the student and artist crowds who "live" in Kenmore Square. It boasts a large and varied menu and is one of the few restaurants in Boston that stay open until 2 in the morning—a good place for a bite after leaving one of the nearby clubs.

Appetizers include ethnic specialties like meat or potato knishes (three for $5.75) and homemade soups. Breakfast is not such a bargain, unless you can handle the "Beat the Haus" special: three eggs, five strips of bacon, German fries, and three slices of toast for $5.25. Your arteries will love you for it.

There is a tremendous selection of sandwiches, both hot and cold: Basic varieties range from egg salad ($3.50) to hot corned beef or roast brisket ($4.95). Or try Romanian pastrami, or imported sardines (a full tin!). Check out the "Velvet Elvis" sandwich ($3.95), with grilled peanut butter and bananas on white bread, just like the King would have it. In the hot category, the barbecued beef sandwich ($5.95) is thinly sliced beef dripping with a tangy sauce on a bulkie roll, served with plenty of French fries.

Dinners have similar prices, making better deals. Marinated steak tips are served with rice pilaf, and a choice of a small salad or veggie of the day, for $6.95. Or try a charbroiled half-chicken, with cranberry sauce, salad, and fries, for $6.25. Drinks include beer and wine.

The fill-you-up approach extends to the desserts, offering an array of giant ice cream sundaes such as the "Thursdae"—scoops of Dutch chocolate and Turkish coffee ice cream topped with coffee syrup, sliced bananas, toasted nuts, whipped cream and a cherry for $4.25. New York-style egg creams, too. Open daily.

Dixie Kitchen

- 182 Massachusetts Ave., Boston; (617) 536-3068

246

Near the Berklee College of Music, the Dixie Kitchen serves up the cuisine that's music too: Cajun. Neon instruments beckon from the front windows, and zydeco music whoops it up on the speakers.

The portions are large and the prices are small—Mr. C's kind of place. Start off with a huge bowl of gumbo; at $3.95, it's big enough for two to share. It's a thick, spicy stock filled with crab and shrimp, or chicken and sausage, and served with a plate of white rice to mix in.

Other appetizers include homemade Texas chili, baked oysters in a shrimp and garlic sauce, extra-spicy zydeco wings, and deep-fried alligator tail (yes, really!). You may then want to move on to the hearty "Po' Boy" sandwiches—fried catfish, shrimp, oysters or chicken on a French bread roll with a sharp remoulade sauce. These are all $5 to $6.

But then you'd miss out on the *real* Cajun delicacies. Jambalaya is a heaping plate of fried rice with smoked sausage, shrimp, and chicken mixed in, served with a dense, warm hunk of jalapeno corn bread—all for $7.95. Catfish Marguery ($8.95) is pan-cooked in a sauce of shrimp, mushrooms, parmesan cheese, and garlic. "Dixie Ribs" arrived hanging out over the edge of the plate—half a dozen meaty slabs in a tangy, not-hot barbecue sauce, sitting on a bed of rice, with cooked corn and beans on the side—all for $8.50. Plenty to share or take home.

Desserts are homemade—pecan, apple, and sweet potato pies, and a zippy bread pudding served with either whiskey or lemon sauce. Be sure to have a cup of "Cafe du Monde" with it; that's the name of the French Quarter spot famous for its strong coffee and "beignets," hot fried doughnuts. Open from 11 A.M. to 10 P.M., Sundays through Thursdays, until 11 P.M. on Fridays and Saturdays.

Hsin Hsin Chinese Noodle Restaurant

- 25 Massachusetts Ave., Boston; (617) 536-9852

Near Kenmore Square, this place seems to belong in the heart of Chinatown. Hsin Hsin is a small, simple noodle house where you can get a lot of basic dishes for very reasonable prices.

The place has only about ten tables. The atmosphere is attractive, clean and casual, and so is the menu; noodles and soups, that's about it. The soups include egg drop, wonton, or hot and sour, each about $1.75. Among appetizers, again the basics: Peking ravioli ($4.50), spring rolls ($2.95), scallion pancakes ($3.50), all yummy. The main dishes divide into about five offerings each of soup noodles, fried noodles, chow foon, lo mein, and fried rice. All are around $5-$6. The portions are very generous, so you'll have plenty of leftovers.

Mr. C loved the egg drop soup, which was delicious and a bit salty, with mushrooms and scallions floating in it. Beef chow foon with pepper and onions consisted mostly of the wide rice noodles; not enough beef mixed in. Try the house special fried noodles ($7.95), crispy noodles with chicken, shrimp, beef, and vegetables. Cold sesame noodles are also tasty, with that slightly spicy, nutty sauce.

The service is friendly and attentive; in an area known for burgers and beers, Hsin Hsin's concentration on Chinese staples is a pleasant surprise. Open from 11:30 A.M. to 11 P.M., daily.

India Quality

- 536 Commonwealth Ave., Boston; (617) 267-4499

This longtime fave in Kenmore Square is consistently good, if basic. The small quarters have recently been renovated and the walls whitewashed, for a brighter atmosphere than earlier days. The food, meanwhile, remains the attraction.

Along with a full menu of all the traditional items, a handful of special

MR. CHEAP'S PICKS
Fenway / Kenmore Square

✔ **Dixie Kitchen**—Great down-home cookin'.

✔ **Hsin Hsin Noodle Restaurant**—Simple, no-frills noodle house. One of the better Chinese places outside of Chinatown.

✔ **Kenmore Cafe**—Flash! Fast-food chain replaced by honest cooking, cafeteria-style; with an emphasis on Middle Eastern.

dishes are made up daily. Creamy chicken coconut curry, mashed eggplant with peppers and onions in yogurt sauce, and other choices are usually $5.95 at lunch, and $10.95 at dinner. Most other meat entrees are in the $8-$10 range; these prices have nudged upward with IQ's popularity, but the quality is indeed strong. And there are about twenty lunch specials starting from just $4.50 complete with rice, bread, and tea. Open for lunch every day but Sunday, and for dinner daily from 5-10:30 P.M.

Kenmore Cafe
- 539 Commonwealth Ave., Boston; (617) 536-4444
- *Tip-free*

A welcome addition to Kenmore Square—replacing a fast-food chicken place—is Kenmore Cafe. Its menu is infinitely more varied, interesting, and best of all, homemade.

Starting with breakfast at 6 every morning, the cafe offers three "Kenmore on the Run" quick specials for $2.75, such as scrambled eggs with bacon and cheese rolled up in pita bread. Steak and eggs are just $4.95, with home fries and toast.

Elsewhere the menu favors Middle Eastern fare, with falafel sandwiches for $3.50, or "The Nile" ($5.50)—a plate of char-broiled spicy lamb and beef, served with rice, hummus, fatoosh, and a house sauce. But there are plenty of American items too; Mr. C enjoyed the daily special, marinated grilled chicken ($4.95) with salad and a heap of very tasty rice pilaf.

Then there are deli sandwiches, burgers, and sixteen-inch pizzas with your choice of up to five toppings, for $8.50. The food is delicious; and good news for the Square—it's served until 1 A.M. every night.

Mal's New York Style Delicatessen
- 708 Commonwealth Ave., Boston; (617) 536-8676

Mal's is a longtime fixture on the Boston University campus, a place where both students and professionals are lunchtime regulars. It's a bustling little place packed with tables (there are a couple just outside the door, if the weather is nice); call your order out at the counter, find a table if you can, and pick up the food.

Mal himself is usually cranking the orders out, a model of efficiency after all these years who still manages a smile amidst the din. He also makes a lot of the food himself. "I got chicken soup today," he answers a patron. "I got corn chowder, I got beef barley, I got . . ." They're all scrumptious.

Burgers are a big deal here, with several different varieties starting at $2.35 for a plain quarter pounder. For $3.60 there are six-ounce salsa and teriyaki burgers, and the half-pound "Jughead" tops the list at $3.95. All are made with fresh meat and come on an onion roll with lettuce, tomato, and a pickle. They're drippy, messy, and wonderful. There are no French fries here (!); go for the homemade potato salad instead.

Mal's opens up early for breakfast, and you can really stuff yourself with the Country Breakfast ($3.75)—two eggs, pancakes, bacon, ham or sausage, toast, home fries and coffee. Hours are 6 A.M. to 6 P.M., daily.

Moby Dick of Boston

- 269 Huntington Ave., Boston;
  (617) 236-5511
- *Tip-free*

The name of this restaurant is a red
herring. The cuisine at this simple eatery in the Symphony area is Per-
sian—hardly Olde New England.
Moby Dick essentially limits the
menu to kebabs—chicken, beef,
lamb, seafood or vegetarian. Each of
these is available as a sandwich or a
full platter. You can get several large
chunks of meat and veggies, deli-
ciously barbecued and stuffed into an
enormous fresh wheat bread pita with
tomatoes, lettuce, onions and minty
sauce, all for about $3-$5. One of
these can fuel you for an entire afternoon. Or, opt for a platter and get a
bigger portion, with salad and fresh
bread on the side, coming in at $4.75
to $6.95.

Specials are slightly more expensive. Try a swordfish kebab, served
with basmati rice, grilled tomatoes, a
salad, and fresh bread, all for $7.95.
Lots of people here seem like regulars; if you're in this neighborhood
often, chances are you'll become one
too. Open seven days a week from 11
A.M. to 11 P.M.

Our House East

- 52 Gainsborough St., Boston;
  (617) 236-1890

Our House East is more like a sports
bar than its cozy Allston sibling. Area
students and professionals know it as
one of the few restaurants in the area
that is both affordable *and* attractive.
The dining tables are natural blond
wood, in a carpeted room adorned
with polished brass. A separate bar
area features wide-screen TV for
sports events, with plenty of beers on
tap in large mugs.

The large menu seems at first
glance to consist almost entirely of
appetizers. From French onion soup
($2.50) to more unusual items such
as Buffalo shrimp ($5.95) and bone-
less Buffalo wings ($4.25), the apps
alone offer quite a range. There are
six different kinds of potato skins,
each around $5 a plate, filled with

cheese, chili, tomato sauce, sirloin
tips, and more.

But don't worry, there are plenty
of sandwiches and dinners. Nine different burgers are all $4 to $5; these
are charbroiled half-pounders and
come with chips, cole slaw, and
pickles. Bigger still is the "Our
House Burger" ($6.95), which
packs—ready for this?—twelve
ounces. Good luck. On the dinner
side, choose from a rotisseried half-
chicken ($5.95), barbecued ribs
($8.95), chicken marsala ($7.25)
and several others. The portions are
substantial and nicely prepared.

Our House East also serves a big
Sunday brunch from 12 P.M. to 3 P.M.,
where $4.95 gets you one of several
cooked egg dishes along with a bagel
and pastry buffet. Hours are 4 P.M. to
2 A.M. weekdays and 11 A.M. to 2 A.M.
on weekends.

Sorrento's Italian Gourmet

- 86 Peterborough St., Boston; (617)
  424-7070

Part of the hip renaissance in the Fenway, Sorento's is a warm, cozy upscale pasta and pizza spot. Its prices
nudge up against Mr. C's limits, but
you get good, hearty portions of delicious food.

Baked in a brick oven, the pizzas
and calzones smell fabulous the minute you walk in. Pizzas start at $7.70
for a basic cheese; the large size is
$9.90. Toppings are 90¢ each, with
all the yuppie faves. Special pies include melanzana, with fried eggplant,
tomato sauce, and romano and mozzarella cheeses. Napoli, their version
of the works, has mushrooms, roasted
pepper, prosciutto, and chicken pesto.

Out of nearly twenty different
pasta dishes, most fall in the $9 to
$11 range. These include rigatoni
with broccoli and chicken, linguine
carbonara, pasta primavera, or
Chicken a l'Abruzzi—chicken breast
pate sauteed in olive oil with spinach.
It's served with a basil cream sauce,
over a bed of capellini, all for $10.95.

The atmosphere is casual and
pleasant, with a black-and-white tile
floor, natural wood chairs, and an

open kitchen. Could just as easily be Soho. Open from 11 A.M. to midnight, seven days.

Stars Ocean Chinese Seafood

- 70-72 Kilmarnock St., Boston; (617) 236-0384

Stars Ocean is a simple, unpretentious Chinese food restaurant in an out-of-the-way location: the Fenway. While it might have been lost in the sauce in Chinatown, here it stands out for good food, a large menu, and low prices.

For starters, Mr. C (guided by a newspaper clipping in the window) tried the Shanghai spring rolls (two for $2.75). Indeed, these were freshly made, served up hot and crisp, with a filling of cabbage and shrimp that was slightly tangy to the tongue. The menu specializes in Cantonese and Mandarin. Peking sesame chicken ($7.95), West Lake beef ($8.95)—beef and scallops with vegetables in sauce—and pork fried with lemon grass ($6.95) are all quite large and the sauces are tasty.

As the restaurant's name suggests, seafood is the specialty. There are over a dozen different choices for shrimp alone, such as Lake Tung Ting ($8.95), marinated shrimp and vegetables sauteed in a white wine sauce. At the high end, "Dragon and Phoenix" ($9.95) combines chicken and lobster meat with vegetables and scallions in a spicy tomato sauce.

Stars Ocean serves generous lunch specials, most for $4.95, with such choices as fried shrimp and chicken teriyaki, roast pork egg foo yung, or spring roll and boneless garlic

chicken. Each plate comes with soup, chicken wings, a fried wonton and pork fried rice. Try to finish all that in one sitting. Stars Ocean is the kind of place every neighborhood should have—a basic, good-quality local Chinese restaurant. Hours are 11:30 A.M. to 10:30 P.M., Mondays through Saturdays, and Sundays from 1 P.M.

Thorntons Fenway Grille

- 100 Peterborough St., Boston; (617) 421-0104

Just a couple of blocks away from Fenway Park, this corner restaurant serves up some home runs of its own. Thorntons offers classics with—or without—a twist. You can get a plain hamburger or grilled chicken sandwich ($4.95 and $5.45 respectively), but Mr. C recommends more exciting versions such as the Cajun "Melt Down" burger, spiced and topped with cheese, salsa, and hot peppers ($6.25). Pea pods, mushrooms, mozzarella, and teriyaki top the "Chinatown" chicken sandwich ($5.95). There are plenty of vegetarian options, like "the Fens," a pita stuffed with avocado and other veggies ($5.45).

Enormous salads are another specialty here. A small Caesar salad goes for just $2.75. Entrees include a half-rack of pork ribs ($7.95) or fish and chips ($8.95). Thorntons' popular brunch is served every day (yeah!), with Belgian waffles topped with whipped cream and strawberries for $4.95. And you thought all you could get around here was "peanuts and Cracker Jack..." Open for breakfast, lunch, and dinner, seven days a week.

JAMAICA PLAIN

Acapulco Restaurant

- 464 Centre St., Jamaica Plain; (617) 524-4328

Originally a local hole-in-the-wall, the Acapulco has grown into a successful Mexican eatery that will fill you up with fine home cooking for little *dinero*. The restaurant has expanded and renovated itself into a

clean, cozy dining room.

The menu offers various combinations of the basics: tacos, burritos, enchiladas. Get any two on a plate with beans and rice for $5.95, or any three for $7.35. Be sure to try one of the platters featuring *mole* chocolate sauce, a traditional cooking sauce that is not sweet but very tasty.

There are many other plates to choose from, and just about all of them are priced around $6 to $9. Go for the chalupa ($6.50), a flour tortilla with ground beef and pork; or one of the seafood entries, such as fried shrimp in onions, garlic, peppers, tomatoes, and white wine, served with rice and beans ($8.50). Wash it all down with a bottle of Tecate, or, for something a little different, a glass of mango juice.

The Acapulco is open until 11 P.M. seven days.

Centre St. Cafe
- 597 Centre St., Jamaica Plain; (617) 524-9217

This is a place to discover, tucked into a little storefront near Pond Street. Taking Jamaica Plain's blend of cultures to heart with a nouvelle cuisine approach, Centre St. Cafe serves up huge, tasty platters from 5 P.M. to 10 P.M. each night.

Start off with a zippy, tomatoey gazpacho ($1.90 a cup), fresh guacamole and chips ($4.25) or a Caesar salad ($3.95). Drinks include a homemade cranberry cooler (non-alcoholic; there is no liquor served) and gingerade, made fresh and tangy with lemon juice.

The menu always includes a quesadilla of the day (*brie*?), as well as daily pasta and fish specials. The rest of the choices, all priced around $5.95 to $7.95, include a yummy Pad Thai and the "South American Stir Fry," rice cooked up spicy in chili butter with black beans, onions, broccoli, and carrots. With many of these dishes you may add your choice of tofu ($1 extra), chicken ($2), or shrimp ($4).

Take some of the meal home and save room for dessert, which includes such doozies as chocolate mousse brownie pie ($2.75). Mr. C also advises you to arrive early, because after 7:30 or so it's hard to get one of the eight tables and you'll have to wait outside—or place an order to take out. Centre St. also serves up a big brunch from 9 A.M. to 3 P.M. on weekends; most selections run $4.95 to $6.95.

Coffee Cantata
- 605 Centre St., Jamaica Plain; (617) 522-2223

A few doors away, Coffee Cantata offers far more than coffee and pastries—surprising for a place this small. Wrap-around windows give the place an airy feel, though, making this a great place to sit at a marbletop table with a cuppa java and watch the world go by.

On a summer stop-in, Mr. C sipped an iced mocha, its cool whipped cream spruced with chunky chocolate shavings, for $2.50; he accompanied this with a sandwich of smoked ham on focaccia bread with cheese, roasted red pepper, romaine, tomato, and a side of chips, all for $3.45. There are vegetarian versions, too. Several small pizzas, also on focaccia, feature toppings like tomato, artichoke hearts, red pepper, mozzarella, and herbs for $5.25.

Dinner is served after 6:30 P.M. Thursdays through Saturdays only, but this leans toward the pricey side. Under glass at the counter are the Cantata's own desserts, most in the $2.50 range, including a yummy apple crisp torte. Muffins and slices of cranberry banana bread are a buck each. Hours are 7:30 A.M. to 7 P.M. Mondays through Wednesdays, 'til 9 P.M. Thursdays and Fridays; 8:30 A.M. to 10 P.M. Saturdays, and 9-3 on Sundays.

Doyle's
- 3484 Washington St., Jamaica Plain; (617) 524-2345

"The Largest Selection of Draft Beers in New England," "Since 1882, Boston's Best Neighborhood Bar" . . . . You'll come across a lot of superlatives at F.J. Doyle & Co.—on the menu, in advertisements, and in conversation. Fact is, it's all true.

Doyle's is a legendary watering hole; the only one, the story goes, to stay open throughout the Prohibition and survive to this day. Mayors, governors, and prominent city officials have been spotted there. It was James Michael Curley himself who, in 1933, declared the bar "officially" re-

---

MR. CHEAP'S PICKS
Jamaica Plain

✔ **Centre St. Cafe**—The perfect
  representation of the melting
  pot that is JP. A little Thai, a
  little South American, a little
  Creole; call it "nouvelle world
  beat."

✔ **Doyle's**—What's left to be
  said about this Boston
  institution? Great burgers, and
  dozens of beers from around
  the world. Drink with the pols.

---

opened. "The Kennedys of Massachusetts" filmed scenes there. It's,
y'know, historic.

It's also got great, cheap food. The
burgers are immense half-pounders
starting from $3.25; the Pot Belly, a
dollar more, adds cheese, bacon,
mushrooms, and peppers. A humongous side of fries or onion rings is
$2.95. Doyle's also serves its own
pizzas (small $4.95, large $5.95),
with a variety of toppings at 75¢
each. These are available until 11:30
every night.

Moving on to the full dinners, bargains all: Barbecued steak tips are
$5.95, as is veal parmigiana with spa-
ghetti. And there are a dozen or so
daily specials, such as stuffed
chicken breast ($5.95), or prime rib
($9.95). Most dinners come with
your choice of two sides: fries, rice,
salad, or vegetables.

But now to those beers. On Mr.
C's visit, he counted twenty-eight
choices—and that's just on tap!
Twenty-one more were available in
bottles. The options range from plain
old Schlitz ($1.50 a bottle) to some-
thing called Chimay Grand Reserve—
a 25-ounce bottle which goes for
$8.95. Needless to say, Mr. C did not
sample that one. In between were all
the varieties of J.P.'s own Sam

Adams; Fuller's and Young's from
Britain; and many more, including
non-alcoholic beers. The list is up-
dated from time to time.

So, have a seat next to Kevin
White's signed photo, check out the
huge old clocks and the wooden tele-
phone booth, and knock back a few.
What a way to get a history lesson.
Open from 9 A.M. to 2 A.M. Mondays
through Saturdays, and from 3 P.M. on
Sundays.

El Oriental De Cuba
- 416 Centre St., Jamaica Plain;
  (617) 524-6464

At El Oriental, a small corner place
with simple tables down one side and
a long counter and grill down the
other, you'll be gloriously reminded
that a sandwich can be far more than
a bite on the run.

The Cuban special consists of
pork, ham, and cheese, grilled on a
sub roll with all the veggie fixings
and a zesty sauce. This is the authentic Havana style, and four bucks is a
small price to pay. Side orders, like
rice, beans, or "mofongo"—a delicacy of mashed green plantains with
pork rinds and garlic sauce—are
$1.50 each.

Variety plates, featuring crispy
chicken, pork chops, and steak, run
$7-$9 and are served with rice,
beans, and plantains or fries. The
day's special of chicken and oxtail
over rice was $7.35 on Mr. C's visit.

Soups, including chicken, beef
tripe, and a hearty Cuban vegetable,
are meals in themselves and priced
accordingly, at $3-$5 for sizable
smalls and $1 more for lavish larges.
Order breakfast until 11 A.M., like a
platter of eggs with Spanish *chorizo*
sausage and French (?) bread for
$3.50. Open from 8 A.M. to 10 P.M.,
seven days a week.

Tacos El Charro
- 349 Centre St., Jamaica Plain;
  (617) 522-2578

Here's the kind of place you'd find if
you were actually *in* Mexico looking
for an informal kitchen that just
served up good home cooking. It's a
very different experience from most

of the other "Tex-Mex" restaurants in Boston.

A TV plays Spanish programs in the corner. The walls are decorated with a few pieces of Mexican folk art, but this is not a place for atmosphere—just great food. It is clear immediately that each dish has been prepared to order—not stamped out on an assembly line. And the service is relaxed and friendly.

Mr. C particularly enjoyed the sopes ($3.95), fried dough shaped into a cup to hold a tasty mixture of beans and ground beef, with lettuce and cheese on top. Tacos ($1.60 each) come filled with beef, chicken, beef tongue, goat meat, or pork with pineapple (surprise—this is spicy!). Combine any two with rice, beans, and salad for $5.95.

The fajitas are delicious. Chicken ($5.95) and beef ($7.95) are entrees in themselves, or great for splitting. By the way, the salsa (mild or hot) and guacamole are homemade, chunky, and first-rate.

For something a little different, try the "Plato Montanero"—($7.95), a stew of beans, pork, and beef served over rice. Avocado and plantains are added on the side. For dessert, vanilla flan ($2.50) is the obvious choice.

Tacos el Charro does not have a liquor license, so don't expect to wash this meal down with a margarita. Fortunately, there are several other delicious options, including a non-alcoholic sangria ($1.50). Best bet, though, is the virgin pina colada, made sweet with chunks of real pineapple. A tall glass is $2. They'll also whip up a fruit milkshake, also $2, that can go with the meal or be a dessert. Open seven days.

NORTH END

Artú
- 6 Prince St., Boston; (617) 742-4336

Cozy Artú's front windows display several delicacies of the day before you even go in. Once inside, you'll find a surprising depth to a restaurant that appears small from the street—matched by a menu that manages to be both simple and exotic.

A local merchant had recommended the place to Mr. C as a good value, and it's easy to see why. A dozen pasta dishes beckon, notably fusilli sauteed with chicken and mustard greens, and homemade maccheroni with pancetta, onions, and fresh tomato (each $8.50). Eggplant parmigiana is just $5.95. Even roasted leg of lamb, which can get pricey, checks in at $9.95—and that includes peppers, marinated eggplant, and potatoes.

For the same great cooking on a tighter budget yet, sandwiches of roast lamb, pork, chicken, and others all range from $4-$5. Several salads come in under $4, and an extensive wine list assures proper refreshment. Arrive between 10 A.M. and 4 P.M. and order from a lunch menu where all pasta dishes are under $7 and all sandwiches are under $5. Admirably, the prices flourish in an atmosphere of elegance which might seem to demand much more of an investment, but doesn't. Open 'til 11 P.M. seven days.

La Famiglia
- 112 Salem St., Boston; (617) 367-6711
- 19 Bennington St., East Boston; (617) 567-1060

La Famiglia is a wonderful homestyle kitchen featuring "Roman cooking at its best." The best thing about it is the value, because the portions here are enormous. Chances are you'll have leftovers to take with you.

The food is delicious. Pasta dishes, cooked to order in the open kitchen, range from your basic garlic and oil ziti ($4.95) to mussels marinara with linguine ($6.95) Chicken entrees range from $6.95 to $8.95, including a version made with a ham,

---

MR. CHEAP'S PICKS
North End

✔ **La Famiglia**—Lines out the door tell the story. Gigantic portions at easy prices, with leftovers guaranteed. Mangia!

✔ **Spuntini**—Tiny kitchen and a few tables. Huge platters of food.

---

pea, and mushroom cream sauce. Veal dishes offer similar choices—the prices go over ten dollars, but again, you get a *lot*.

Best of all are the house specials, easily big enough for two people to share. Try the La Famiglia Special ($16.95)—veal and chicken pieces with mushrooms and onions in a creamy pesto sauce, served over tricolor cheese tortellini. Mmmmmm. Daily lunch specials, $3.95, may offer risotto primavera, or chicken sauteed with artichokes in wine sauce. Friendly staff, too. Open from 11 A.M. to 9:30 P.M. weekdays, Saturdays from 4 P.M. and Sundays from noon.

Spuntini
- 141 Salem St., Boston; (617) 523-3025

An early 1995 addition to the North End restaurant scene, Spuntini combines a casual charm with prices that should help it gain a fast following. Cozy and comfortable even on a hot summer's day, the corner storefront of seven tables is attractively done up in shades of mauve and pink. Start off with an inexpensive appetizer, like marinated olive salad for $2.50—then move on to one of several sandwiches, including four different chicken variations for no more than $4.50 each.

The blackboard on the wall sports daily specials; on Mr. C's visit, these included half a dozen pasta dishes

(all $6.95) like linguine with sun-dried tomatoes, lemon, and spinach. These are served on crater-sized plates certain to stuff you silly; they're big enough for two people to share. Or, splurge for seafood with a special such as the unusual steak pizzaiola ($11.95). What's so unusual about that? It's a grilled *tuna* steak. Mmmmm. Open from 11 A.M. six days a week (Sundays from 3 P.M.), this friendly, family-run establishment welcomes you beneath its slow-turning fan until 10 P.M. daily.

Trattoria Il Panino
- 11 Parmenter St., Boston; (617) 720-1336
- 297 Franklin St., Boston; (617) 338-1000
- 1001 Massachusetts Ave., Cambridge; (617) 547-5818

With its roots in the North End, Il Panino now boasts three locations serving up great fresh pasta dishes quickly and inexpensively.

Mr. C visited the North End hideaway, where lunch specials are $4.95 in the street-level room, which doubles as a sub shop. Don't be fooled. Each weekday there are two specials to choose from, such as tortellini Alfredo, a hefty slice of lasagna, or penne with mushrooms and broccoli in cream sauce. Seafood specials regularly fall on Fridays and Saturdays, such as mussels over linguine. Fresh bread comes with these.

After 3 P.M. the menu expands to over two dozen pasta dishes, all ranging from $6.95 to $9.95. Linguine with clams, ziti with three cheeses, tortellini with pesto, and more. There are also fra diavolo dishes—lobster, clams, calamari, or mussels—as well as chicken, gnocchi, eggplant parmigiana, and more.

For dinner, the trattoria downstairs is a warmer, cozy setting that feels like old Italy—wooden tables nestled against white stucco walls. Il Panino serves beer and wine, and much of its food is made fresh daily on the premises. Hours vary.

ROSLINDALE / WEST ROXBURY

Cafe Le Royal
- 1856 Centre St., West Roxbury;
  (617) 323-3233

Wow—what a find. You could easily pass this small place by; from the outside, it looks like an average bakery with a few tables. But closer examination reveals a creative lunch and dinner menu, taking you from the Hub straight to the Continent.

Afternoons feature such light fare as cheese tortellini salad with artichoke hearts ($4.95), as well as sandwiches—but not just any old sandwiches. How 'bout hot veal with pesto, on a fresh baguette, all for $4.50? Mmmm.

At dinner, things get even more ambitious. Start off with an appetizer of *paté de campagne* ($3), again with a baguette; or perhaps a "Salade Savoyarde" ($4.50), with gruyére cheese, ham, walnuts, and Dijon vinaigrette over fresh greens. Entrees range from the traditional steak *au poivre* for $9.95 to a platter of puff pastry filled with shellfish and mushrooms in a white wine sauce (same price).

Mr. C chose grilled salmon, topped in a tangy tarragon hollandaise sauce, with colorful *al dente* vegetables on the side. It was a sizeable portion of tasty fish for $8.95, grilled just right, not too dry. Needless to say, as this is a bakery cafe, desserts (with cappuccino, of course) are divine and not overpriced.

So, it may not look like you'd get the royal treatment in such a small place, but the atmosphere is clean and bright, the service is friendly, and the food is a real surprise. Open daily from 8 A.M. to 9 P.M., closing at 4 on Sundays.

Corrib Pub
- 2030 Centre St., West Roxbury;
  469-4177
- 396 Market St., Brighton; (617)
  254-2880
- 201 Harvard St., Brookline; (617)
  232-8787

See the listing under "Brighton."

Pleasant Cafe & Restaurant
- 4515 Washington St., Roslindale;
  (617) 323-2111

Don't be fooled by the neon "pizza" sign and humble facade of the Pleasant Cafe, just outside of Forest Hills; this is no sub shop. Inside, it's a huge, folksy, family restaurant with a menu that's big on Italian food—and just plain big.

They do, of course, have pizzas, made to your specifications on a nice, thin, crisp crust. These start at $6.75 and go up, depending on the toppings you choose. There are also sandwiches, like burgers for $3.25 or a veal cutlet sandwich for $5.25.

Dinners include seafood, prime rib and other meats; all of these entrees range from $6 to $10, and most come with scali bread and pasta or vegetables. Chicken cacciatore ($6.95) is a vast plate with chunks of chicken breast, fresh half-mushrooms, peppers, and onions swimming in tomato sauce. It comes with spaghetti or ziti on the side, cooked just right. Broiled swordfish is one of the half-dozen daily specials added in on the blackboard—just $8.50. Or try entrees of lasagna and meatballs ($6.95), pork chops ($7.95), or veal parmigiana ($8.95). All wonderful.

The portions are enormous. Even as they bring your dinner from the

---

MR. CHEAP'S PICKS
Roslindale / West Roxbury

✔ **Cafe Le Royal**—Surprisingly fancy food served up in a West Roxbury bakery.

✔ **Pleasant Cafe**—So much more than a pizzeria; Italian dinners served in a sprawling restaurant/bar for the old folks and young alike.

kitchen, the friendly waitresses tell you not to worry—the doggie bag is ready and waiting. The bar area is lively and boisterous, usually with a ball game on the tube; this room has lots of dining booths, but there are two other large rooms as well if you want (a bit) less noise.

SOUTH BOSTON

Amrhein's Restaurant

- 80 West Broadway, South Boston; (617) 268-6189

This area of Southie isn't really that far from downtown, yet it feels like another world—a simpler time and place. Amrhein's Restaurant is a big part of that. Operating since 1890, this Austrian pub in an Irish neighborhood has kept its old-world atmosphere. Its heritage embraces famous and near-famous politicians; they also claim to have Boston's very first beer pump.

The food, meanwhile, will keep you full for another hundred years—especially if you go for the specials. Mr. C requested roast pork tenderloin; a mound of slices in brown gravy, served with cooked vegetables and two warm rolls and butter, all for $5.45. There was enough for leftovers. Other early specials include chicken *and* veal parmigiana, with spaghetti, for $6.95; and a big chicken pot pie for $6.45.

Mondays through Wednesdays from 4 to 10 P.M., there are better bargains yet, with two-for-one specials such as chicken marsala and linguine, baked stuffed scallops with vegetables, and the house specialty, wiener schnitzel over noodles. Choose any two dinners for just $13.95!

Ethel and Andy's Sandwich Shop

- 134 K St., South Boston; (617) 268-3027
- *Tip-free*

This tiny corner deli, well off the beaten path, has thrived for 25 years by offering a good variety of take-out items at absurdly low prices. Check

Wing It

- 1732 Centre St., West Roxbury; (617) 469-WING (9464)
- 1153 Commonwealth Ave., Brighton; (617) 783-BIRD (2473)

See the listing under "Brighton."

the hand-written menu mounted on the wall outside, and then step into a place so small you'll have to go outside to change your mind. (Ba-da-bing!)

Ethel and Andy serve up hot and cold sandwiches; juicy cheeseburgers run $3.70 with fries and a soda. A special of "Yankee Pot Roast," with potato, vegetables, and a roll checks in at a mere $4.25, and Mr. C just *had* to save room for a luxurious strawberry frappe ($2.25), thick and hearty enough to humble the average straw.

E & A opens at the unbelievable hour of 4:30 A.M. Mondays through Saturdays, serving until 5 P.M. on weekdays and 11 A.M. Saturdays. Breakfast sandwiches will open your eyes at $2-$3, and a full breakfast of two eggs, home fries, toast, and coffee is an easy two bucks. Get up early, or be like Mr. C and just stay up 'til they open.

Loaf & Ladle

- 483 East Broadway, South Boston; (617) 268-7006

Irish chic arrives in Southie! Loaf & Ladle is a bright, airy sandwich shop that would look just as fitting in Cambridge. Sit at the counter, or at the natural wood tables, and have a traditional Irish breakfast of two eggs, Irish sausage, bacon, black and white pudding, home fries, and grilled tomato—along with Irish whole wheat bread and tea or coffee—all for $6.25.

For lunch, turkey, tuna, cheeseburger, or ham and cheese clubs are each $3.95, served with French fries. All soups and chowders are homemade, such as a brimming bowl of

beef stew for $3.50. There are always
several daily lunch specials, though,
such as barbecued steak tips for
$5.95 or chicken curry, served over
rice, for $4.95. They're hot and deli-
cious. Any order can be made for
take-out, too. Dinner is not served;
they close at 4 P.M. every day.

L' Street Diner
• 108 L St., South Boston; (617)
  268-1155

Perhaps one of Southie's best-known
secrets, this cozy eatery is everything
a family diner should be—humble
and relaxed, friendly, and with large
portions of homemade food. The
place is all red-checked tablecloths,
black-and-white tiled walls, and hanging plants; it's not large, but they get
a lot of tables in somehow.

Food is served all day. Breakfast
starts at 5:30 A.M. on weekdays; rus-
tle up two eggs, bacon or sausage,
home fries, toast, and coffee, all for
$2.50—until 8 A.M., that is. Not that
the regular prices will set you back
much more. At lunch, a world of
sandwiches comes in under $5 each,
from Reubens to lemon-pepper
chicken. Burgers start from $3.75,
with lettuce, tomato, and thick
French fries.

Dinner gets even better. Classic
blue-plates are beautifully done; Mr.
C was crazy for turkey pot pie

SOUTH END

Anchovies
• 443 Columbus Ave., Boston; (617)
  266-5088

Boston magazine granted Anchovies
its "Best Kept Secret" award. Well,
word seems to be getting out that this
small, funky restaurant serves up a
variety of pasta dishes at incredibly
low prices. Compare it with Gia-
como's next door, which is way
above Mr. C's budget, and you'll see
that the yup-and-coming South End
is for everybody.

Most of the menu here is mix 'n
match: Pick a pasta, pick a sauce, and
you've got a meal. Pasta choices in-

($4.95), made with large pieces of
white meat and fresh vegetables, with
a flaky homemade crust baked over
the top. Heaven. Steak tips *or* turkey
tips are $5.95; two grilled pork
chops, with potato and a vegetable,
are $7.95. Daily soups include things
like chicken tortellini and turkey
chili. And this doesn't even get to the
fantastic brick-oven pizzas and
calzones!

Basic beers and wines are available. Everything can be ordered for
take-out; there is a separate entrance
on the side for pizzas. Open daily until 9 or 10 P.M.

clude ziti, bows, and linguine. Those
with a light appetite, or a thin wallet,
can top these with meat sauce for
$5.95. Heartier sauces include meat-
balls or mussels in garlic herb butter
(either choice over pasta for $7.25).
Other Italian specialties include lasagna and eggplant parmigiana, each
$7.95. Anchovies makes up fresh
pizza pies as well. Open 5 P.M. to 2
A.M. seven days a week; the kitchen
closes at 1 A.M.

Bob the Chef's
• 604 Columbus Ave., Boston; (617)
  536-6204

"Soul Cuisine at Its Finest," boasts

MR. CHEAP'S PICKS
South End

✔ **Bob the Chef's**—Authentic soul food; huge meals under $10 that stick to your own ribs for a long time.

✔ **Charlie's Sandwich Shoppe**—This friendly, neighborhood place is worth a trip from anywhere for scrumptious, inventive breakfast and lunch dishes.

✔ **Tim's Bar and Grill**—The locals don't want you to know about this one! Brave your way through the bar to the tables at the back, where you'll find huge burgers, ribs, steaks, and seafood.

the menu, and Mr. C finds it hard to disagree. Bob the Chef's is located deep in the heart of the south—South End, that is. But not in the yuppified, trendy area; this is the older, grittier part of the neighborhood, and the joint has the authentic feel of a Southern kitchen. You can sit on a stool at the long counter, or walk past the grill—where someone may be carving meat off of a leg bone—and settle into a booth.

This is heavy, down-home food done up properly, according to a friend of Mr. C's. "You have to have the ribs," he advised; and, being originally from Baton Rouge, he clearly knew what he was talking about. Bar-B-Qued Spareribs were a half-dozen or so meaty pork ribs in a sweet sauce, cooked so tender that the meat practically fell off. The dinner costs $10, but that includes two side dishes plus a plate of warm, fresh corn bread.

Each of the dinners, ranging from $7 to $10, offers the same deal. The side dishes include collard greens,

(very) sweet potatoes, black-eye peas, fresh-cut corn, rice and gravy, mashed turnips, and other Dixie delicacies. All told, you get a very big meal.

For the truly adventurous, try the "Soul Chitterlings" ($10). Our Louisiana expert describes these as "all the parts of a pig that you wouldn't want to eat," somehow cooked into a popular, traditional specialty. Pan-fried porgy, "The Soul Fish," sells at market prices; but you can also have it in a sandwich version for $4.50. In fact, most of the dinner items can be had as sandwiches; from smothered steak and onions ($6) to fried chicken ($3.50). Add a side dish for $1.75 and you have a very cheap meal indeed.

Desserts are homemade and they all look great, if you can fit one in after this kind of meal. Still, try to aim for the pecan pie, $2 for a good-sized slice; sweet potato pie is $1.75. Service is nice and fast, by the way. Open daily 11 A.M. to 10 P.M.

Charlie's Sandwich Shoppe
- 329 Columbus Ave., Boston; (617) 536-7669

A fixture since 1927, Charlie's ties the new and old South End together, serving up hearty portions of surprisingly innovative breakfast foods. Mr. C thought he'd died and gone to heaven, so throughly did he enjoy the "Cape Cod French Toast" ($4.90), thick slices of French toast smothered in hot cranberry compote. Mmmmm. Griddle cakes can come baked with cranberries, blueberries, bananas, strawberries, or smothered in hot apple compote (most, also $4.90).

Everything here is super-fresh (Mr. C watched a delivery of strawberries come in), and cooked to order. Sit at the counter to get a bird's-eye view of eggs being poached, dropped, scrambled, fried, and omeletted. Those omelettes, by the way, are on the pricey side—$5.75 to $7.35—*but* they're served with home fries, toast, and a salad. Start your day at Charlie's, and you can definitely skip lunch.

Or, have it here. It's not called Charlie's *Sandwich* Shoppe for nothing. Wrap your hands around a jumbo hot dog for $2.50 (make it a chili dog for an extra buck), or a hot sausage and egg sandwich for $3.75. Entrees include chicken cutlets with mashed potatoes and gravy for $6.45, served with homemade cornbread.

Charlie's is a neighborhood joint, top to bottom. Walls are plastered with pictures and memorabilia. You may share one of the three tables with strangers, or sit at the counter. Mr. C's only complaint: They get you on beverages ($1.15 for eight ounces of OJ!). That aside, this place is perfect. Open Mondays through Fridays from 6 A.M. to 2:30 P.M., Saturdays from 7:30 A.M. to 1 P.M.

Geoffrey's Cafe Bar

- 578 Tremont St., Boston; (617) 266-1122

Although this part of the South End is on the "coming" side of up-and-coming, Geoffrey's fills its menu with elegant, well-prepared dishes that won't empty your wallet. How often can you order beef bourguignon with roasted garlic potatoes, and be billed a mere $9.95? Or shrimp and smoked salmon, with homemade mango chutney and fettucine in cream sauce for $11.95? Yowza.

Less expensive choices include unusual sandwiches and salads, like grilled Brazilian steak on toasted rye with black bean salsa for $7.50; same price for grilled eggplant with roasted peppers, caramelized onions, pesto, and mozzarella on pita bread. Lunchtime prices are generally the same, although traditional deli-style sandwiches are added in the afternoon for $4.95 to $5.95.

Geoffrey's also serves breakfast. Specialties include challah French toast with fresh berries, and vegetarian eggs Benedict with spinach and tomato (each $6.95). Best of all (Mr. C is a confirmed night-owl), breakfast is served daily until 3 P.M.—and on weekends until 4 P.M.! Geoffrey's is open seven days until 10 P.M.

Mass Cafe

- 605 Massachusetts Ave., Boston; (617) 262-7704

The name makes it sound like your average neighborhood hangout, and you will find burgers and such on the menu; but the Mass Cafe is actually an Ethiopian restaurant. So yes, you *could* order one of the American dishes, but Mr. C always suggests going with the strengths of the house.

These entrees include *zegenie* (beef cubes in a hot, fairly spicy stew, $6.50); *tsebhi derho* (chicken simmered in a spicy red sauce, also $6.50); and *alitcha beghie* (chunks of lamb mildly cooked in an onion and garlic sauce, $7.50). All of these are served with the traditional soft *injera* bread (which you use to scoop up the stews) and fresh vegetables. Even those menu items marked as spicy won't burn your tongue. Hours are 10 A.M. to 9 P.M., Mondays through Saturdays.

Morse Fish Company

- 1401 Washington St., Boston; (617) 262-6378
- *Tip-free*

Sometimes, the best place to find a good, cheap fish dinner is at a fish *market*. Such is the case at Morse Fish. Here, dinners range from as little as $2.95 for a catch of fish cakes to $13.50 for a gigantic seafood platter. Dinners are served with cole slaw and tartar sauce, and a choice of French fries, rice, or onion rings. Can't decide which fish is for you? No problem—try a combination platter. Or, pick a few side orders together, like fish cakes (50¢ each), clam strips ($3.95, medium order), and even chicken wings ($3.50, medium). *Chicken wings?*

Morse is mainly a take-out joint, though there are a few tables. Order your meal at the counter and grab a seat. The ambiance, such as it is, comes mainly from the cases full of fresh fish, also available at good prices. Mr. C saw steamers for $2.99 a pound and mussels for $1.25 per pound. Open 9 A.M. to 6 P.M. Mondays through Saturdays, until 7 P.M. on Fridays.

Tim's Bar & Grill
- 329 Columbus Ave., Boston; (617) 247-7894

Formerly Tim's Tavern, this tiny nook in the South End has been known to locals for years as a funky neighborhood bar that serves up great, cheap barbecue, with a bit of seafood thrown in. The front of the joint is a divey bar with plenty of smoke, chatter, and good tunes. Walk through to the back and you'll find a cluster of formica tables, a waitress or two, and the kitchen.

The food, meanwhile, is incredible—and among the cheapest in town. Starting with the burgers, which are billed as "eight ounces or better," you will indeed have fun wrapping your hands around one. Order it loaded—with lettuce, tomato, onions, and mayonnaise. Even with all that the regular burger is $2.50; a cheeseburger is $2.75. Believe it!

Crispy French fries or onion rings are a dollar extra.

For dinner, how about a good-sized rack of barbecued baby back ribs for $6.95, with rice, rings, or fries—and *that's* the half-rack! A whole rack, at $10.95, will feed an army. Marinated steak tips ($4.95) or lamb skewers ($5.95) come with the same choice of side dish.

In fact, one of the priciest items on the menu is the "X-Large Sirloin Steak, cut to order," at a whopping $9—with a salad and rice or fries. And $7.95 will get you seafood specials like boiled lobster or baked stuffed shrimp.

Beers at Tim's are strictly basic, like the food. There are no taps, and probably the fanciest bottle is Heineken. But hey, this is unpretentious dining—at its best. Hours are 11 A.M. to 1 A.M., Mondays through Saturdays.

BROOKLINE

Angkor Wat
- 404 Harvard St., Brookline; (617) 232-2424

Owned by the folks who run Chinatown's all-vegetarian favorite, Buddha's Delight, this recent arrival outside of Coolidge Corner focuses on the full range of Cambodian and Asian cuisine. The results are just as wonderful.

Like its sibling, AW offers lots of vegetarian fare, including "meat" dishes in which wheat gluten and tofu play pretend. But you can also get the real thing, along with seafood, soups, noodles, and much more. In fact, the huge menu actually boasts a table of contents, divided into two dozen categories.

Fried dumplings, $3.95, are a unique variation on Peking ravioli. Filled with pork and onion and loosely wrapped, they are fresh and yummy. Nearly twenty traditional Viet soups, all $4.50, will stuff you

silly. Mr. C enjoyed a tasty vermicelli platter—a bowl of thin, delicate noodles, piled on with bean sprouts, scallions, greens, a chopped peanut sauce, and grilled beef—also $4.50.

Shrimp and pork specialties, along with some of the veggie entrees, come in a bit higher ($6-$8); these are still amazing prices. But with so many choices under six bucks, plus a pleasant atmosphere and courteous service, Angkor Wat feels like a princely meal for us paupers. Open noon to 10 P.M. seven days (Friday and Saturday nights 'til 11 P.M.).

Corrib Pub
- 201 Harvard St., Brookline; (617) 232-8787
- 396 Market St., Brighton; (617) 254-2880
- 2030 Centre St., West Roxbury; 469-4177

See the listing under "Brighton."

"Dinner at the Mitton House"

- Newbury College, 129 Fisher Ave., Brookline; (617) 730-7037

Here's an unusual opportunity for a truly special meal. At Newbury College's culinary arts school, tucked way up in the fancy hills of Brookline near Chestnut Hill, students learn gourmet cooking techniques which will land them in many of the area's finer restaurants. For a fraction of what those places charge, you can dine here—in a private mansion, no less.

The setting is the George Mitton House, the nineteenth-century home of the founder of Jordan Marsh. Lunches and dinners are served on weekdays through the school year, with entrees such as lobster thermidor, medallions of veal "princess," and cuisines from around the world. Meals are complete, from appetizer through dessert, for one price; and everything is superbly made to order in their kitchens, including the delicate *garde manger* sculptures carved from fruits and vegetables.

Reservations must be made and paid for in advance; dinners cost $20 complete, lunches $10, and you can charge over the phone. With a capacity of only thirty-five to forty people, the tables get booked up well in advance. No alcohol is served, but you may bring your own wine. The service is excellent. Lunch is served Mondays through Thursdays, and Saturdays, at noon; dinner is served Mondays through Thursdays at 6 P.M.

Fajitas & 'Ritas

- 48 Boylston St., Brookline; (617) 566-1222
- 25 West St., Boston; (617) 426-1222

See the listing under "Boston."

Family Restaurant

- 1634 Beacon St., Brookline; (617) 277-4466

True to its name, the Family Restaurant is a friendly mom 'n pop Greek diner, with tons of great food. The atmosphere is cozy, with plants in the windows; there are plenty of tables and a counter.

Greek specialties, of course, are the thing to have here. Mr. C ordered the moussaka dinner and was treated to a mountainous slab of ground beef, eggplant, cheese, and tomato sauce, with rice on the side, all for $6.85. It was too much to finish. Beef or chicken shish kebabs are each $8.25 for a full dinner which includes rice, cooked vegetables, a salad, and rice pudding for dessert.

Seafood is nice and cheap, with a broiled swordfish dinner among the daily specials for $6.95. Plus the usual burgers and gyros. And the Family is a popular spot for breakfast, with two eggs and bacon or sausage for a mere $3.35, served with home fries, toast, and coffee.

The folks at the Family Restaurant use cholesterol-free oils and maintain a commitment to healthy cooking. 'Course, this ain't exactly health food to begin with—it's a home-style filler-up! Open Mondays through Saturdays 7 A.M. to 9 P.M., Sundays from 8 A.M. to 2 P.M.

Imperial Restaurant

- 238 Harvard St., Brookline; (617) 731-3322
- *Tip-free*

Just below Coolidge Corner, the Imperial looks like just another pizza and sub shop. However, in addition to great Italian pizza (crispy thin-crust and Sicilian), calzones, and sandwiches, they serve up hot plates of wonderful, fresh pasta for only a few bucks.

It's simply the basics here: spaghetti, ziti, ravioli, and manicotti, smothered in marinara sauce, and also lasagna. You get a huge, filling plate along with great-smelling, warm Italian bread. The pasta dishes all start at $3.25, whether you order spaghetti, ziti, or cheese-filled ravioli. Add sausage for 50¢ more; or a pair of meatballs the size of tennis balls for a dollar. The manicotti plate is $4, and lasagna tops the menu at $4.50 for a heaping slab.

Nightly specials, from 5 P.M. until midnight, offer more delicious bargains. It's really a bit of the North End in Brookline.

MR. CHEAP'S PICKS
Brookline

✔ **Angkor Wat**—Cambodian and Vietnamese cuisine, good and cheap.

✔ **"Dinner at the Mitton House"**—Fancy gourmet meals in Mr. C's book? Yes, when it's a chef's training school in a hilltop mansion.

✔ **KJ's Deli**—Latest in a long line of eateries from the Jaffe family.

King Tut Coffee Shop
- 7 Station St., Brookline; (617) 277-0066
- *Tip-free*

King Tut is part of the influx of Middle Eastern shops around Boston, and a very good one indeed. This place takes a great deal of care with the quality of the food and the service. It's strictly a take-out shop, located across the street from the Brookline Village T station, and so there is also a selection of hot drinks and pastries, both American and Mediterranean.

But the specialties are things like falafel or hummus and tabouli sandwiches (each $3.40), big and delicious; finger-sized stuffed grape leaves (35¢ each); warm, thick spinach pies ($1.50); and couscous salad ($4.95 a pound), crammed with diced peppers, scallions, carrots, and raisins for a taste that starts out slightly sweet, then kicks in with a bit of spice.

This tiny storefront is only open Mondays through Fridays and usually closes around 6 P.M., though you may find the door still open even later. "If the lights are on, come on in," said the friendly man behind the counter.

KJ's Deli
- 335 Harvard St., Brookline; (617) 738-DELI (3354)

In a neighborhood known for delicatessens, KJ's is a real standout. Run by Ken Jaffe (of Pick-A-Chick fame), this recent arrival is the latest version of a dining dynasty in Coolidge Corner.

The food here is not kosher, but KJ's has all the old-world specialties—kishke, matzo ball soup, cheese blintzes, and the rest. Homemade potato knishes ($3.95 as an appetizer) are surprisingly light and delicate. Mr. C also loved the potato pancakes (a.k.a. latkes), served up hot and delicious for $5.75 with sour cream *and* apple sauce.

Sandwiches are, literally and figuratively, a big deal here. Try one of the "Coolidge Corner Combos," huge creations served with cole slaw and French fries. These whimsically-named handfuls include "Jane's Hungry Horror" (turkey, roast beef, Swiss cheese, and horseradish sauce on rye, $7.95) and "Reuben's Reuben" (a hearty rendition of the classic, $6.95). A little pricey, but you can easily split one of these, or take a half home for later. Each comes with cole slaw, but for 50¢ more you can get those terrific French fries or potato salad. Burgers, soups, and salads are other staples; and, given his family's tradition, Ken still serves up one of the best chicken dinners around. KJ's Deli is open Sundays through Thursdays 7 A.M. to 11:30 P.M., and Fridays and Saturdays 7 A.M. to 12:30 P.M.

Matt Garrett's
- 299 Harvard St., Brookline; (617) 738-5635

The venerable Matt Garrett's is a popular lunch, dinner, and late-evening meeting place. Its menu is one of those "everything under the sun" types—Mexican, Italian, Jewish, Chinese . . . you name it.

The vast list of appetizers includes heaping helpings of Buffalo wings ($4.45/$5.95) and a vegetarian platter of fresh-cut veggies, pita bread, hummus, and herbed cheese ($6.95). "Fingers and Rings for Two," at $7.95, is a huge order served in an edible tortilla bowl. These are not the cheapest prices, but you get a lot!

A sampling of the culinary choices at Matt Garrett's: Mexican pizza ($3.95/$5.95) with spicy beef, olives, and Monterey jack; stir-fry chicken Oriental ($9.95); teriyaki steak tips ($9.95); pasta primavera ($7.95); also, half-pound burgers with fries, from $5.45, and even five kinds of yuppie-topped pizzas ($7-$8). Portions are large, and most entrees come with sides of rice or potato (the fries are excellent), some with salads.

Garrett's also has weekday luncheon specials for $5.25, with choices like schrod, stir-fry, or pasta. And best of all are the early-bird dinner specials, when full meals are just $6.95. Grab them Mondays-Fridays from 3:30 to 5:30. Sunday brunch is a big deal here, too.

Matt Garrett's also has big desserts and sweet specialty drinks from the bar. The atmosphere is lively, and this is one of the few places that serves food until 1 A.M. every day. It's pretty much *the* late-night place in Brookline.

Mr. Sushi

- 696 Washington St., Brookline; (617) 731-1122
- *Tip-free*

This popular delicacy can be hard to find at moderate prices; Mr. Cheap, meet Mr. Sushi. This Washington Square spot, just below Beacon Street, has carved up the competition for several years now. That's primarily because this is a take-out only operation—and although Mr. C usually prefers to write about full restaurants, a rarity like this is worth noting.

Prices for sushi platters are easily a dollar or two lower than comparable dinners at sit-down eateries. Three-piece nigiri orders start under three bucks, in two dozen varieties; same for six-piece maki entrees. Yellowtail tuna maki, for example, is just $3.75, nice and fresh. Go for the Maki Combo, a mix of tekka (tuna), California, and Boston maki (two varieties made with imitation crab meat)—eighteen pieces, all for $9.95.

Mr. S makes sashimi too; a 24-piece combo for $21.95 is hard to beat. You'll certainly pay more at any other sushi joint worth its seaweed. They also do larger party platters. And lunch deals, just $5-$6, are fantastic. Call your order in and pick it up pronto, or have it delivered free in Brookline, Brighton, and Allston; plus Chestnut Hill and Newton in the evenings. Open from 12 noon to 2:30 P.M. for lunch, 5-10:30 P.M. for dinner, and closed on Mondays.

Niko's Restaurant

- 187A Harvard St., Brookline; (617) 277-2999

Tucked cozily into a row of stores a couple of blocks below Coolidge Corner, Niko's Restaurant is a one of the best Greek restaurants around. White linen cloths adorn the neat rows of tables, with a vase of fresh daisies on each one. Lively music of the Greek Isles plays in the background. The place has a light and pleasing look to it.

The Mediterranean specialties are delicious, full dinners with prices mostly in the $5-$8 range. Appetizers include such exotic-sounding items as taramosalata, a dish made from roe, and tza tziki, a cucumber dip with yogurt and garlic. Try the avgolemono ($2.65), egg lemon soup.

Among entrees, Mr. C ordered the moussaka ($5.50), a hearty square of ground beef on layers of cooked eggplant and potato, with a fluffy cheese custard baked on top. The price includes rice pilaf, made with tomato sauce, and a salad.

Zouzoukakia (just fun to say, isn't it?) is a dish of homemade meatballs simmered in a tomato and wine sauce. They come with the same sides for just $4.95, making it a very inexpensive dinner indeed.

Desserts, all $1.45, include baklava, rice pudding, and daily specials; but Mr. C didn't have enough room left to try them! Another time.

Niko's also serves breakfast until 11:30 A.M., seven days a week. Go for those great dinners, though, in an attractive and relaxing atmosphere. Niko's is an inexpensive bit of casual elegance.

Pugsley's
- 41 Harvard St., Brookline; (617) 739-9845
- *Tip-free*

This tiny storefront doesn't look like it serves up freshly prepared seafood, salads, and sandwiches, but it does. An order of fish and chips ($4.50) gives you two large, thick pieces of fish, handcut fries, and tasty cole slaw; there are also fried haddock, clams, and scallops.

Roast beef and roast turkey are cooked in the store and hand-carved for big sandwiches, each around $4. Homemade soups include turkey noodle and clam chowder, $1.50 for a cup, $2.50 for a bowl. Pasta salad ($3.25) is made with rigatoni, fresh tomatoes, and basil.

Breakfast is also popular here. Have two eggs, home fries, toast, and bacon, ham or sausage for $2.75; French toast or pancakes with bacon for $2.95. Pugsley's is an early bird's place, only open Monday through Friday from 7 A.M. to 5 P.M. and Saturday from 9 A.M. to 3 P.M.

Rami's
- 324 Harvard St., Brookline; (617) 738-3577
- *Tip-free*

There is no shortage of falafel in Coolidge Corner. Rami's is the newer kid on the block, looking like a Middle Eastern fast-food shop. The basic falafel sandwich ($3.95), gives you eight of these babies packed into a pita bread pocket with tahini sauce and your choice of vegetables (lettuce, purple cabbage, tomato, cucumber, pickles, etc.). For 50¢ more, you may add a dollop of hummus or baba ganoush. There is also a homemade "sizzling hot sauce" available, but be sure to ask for it.

Other dinners include grilled chicken ($4.95), cooked in spices and topped with minced onions and tahini sauce, with salad. Shawarma, usually made with lamb, is here a turkey-based meat dish in which thin shavings are sliced from a rotating block of seasoned, slowly-cooked meat. Another specialty here is the boreka—a hand-sized puffed pastry pie filled with chopped meat, spinach, or potato. The dough is crisp and flaky, topped with sesame seeds, making for a light snack item (it takes a couple to fill you up). These are all about $2 each. There is even an apple boreka, topped with powdered sugar, which can be a dessert.

A special tip from Mr. C: This is a kosher restaurant, which also means they close around 2 on Friday afternoon and stay closed on Saturday. Sometimes this results in special deals on fresh items they can't keep. It's worth checking out if you're in the area on a Friday afternoon.

CAMBRIDGE

Asmara Ethiopian Restaurant
- 739 Massachusetts Ave., Cambridge; (617) 864-7447

Of Boston's several Ethiopian restaurants, Asmara in Central Square seems to be the least expensive. The food is wholesome and hearty, with all dinner prices under $9.

You'll probably notice there is no silverware on the tables. Ethiopian food is meant to be eaten with your hands, but you can have utensils if you prefer. Most orders come with injera bread, which is more like an open crepe. The waiter doles your food out onto the pancake, and you dig in—tear a piece of bread and use it to scoop up the food.

Many of the dishes are like thick stews, in either mild or spicy sauces.

Alicha fitfit, for example, is diced beef with bits of carrot, rice, and potato; Asmara tibbs has beef sauteed with onions, green chilies, and butter. In fact, herbed butter flavors a lot of these dishes.

There are also chicken, lamb, and vegetarian entrees, many with a Middle Eastern style to them. The food is delicious. Be sure to have a cup of Asmara tea with it. Open seven days.

Bartley's Burger Cottage

- 1246 Massachusetts Ave., Cambridge; (617) 354-6559
- *Tip-free*

Ma Bartley probably does more with a hamburger, and for less money, than anyone you've ever met. The menu shows no less than forty-nine different creations, all made from seven ounces of beef, ground fresh daily. Most are priced from $4.50 to $5, from the Bagel Burger to the Reuben Burger to the Texas Barbeque Burger. Then there is the gourmet section, ranging up to the "Macho Burger" ($7.50), a fourteen-ounce monstrosity served with fries, rings, and cole slaw. You can even design your own monster, with ingredients like guacamole, sprouts, green chili, tabouli, and more.

There are chicken-and-vegetable dinners, all-vegetarian platters (and "garden burgers"), sandwiches, and salads. But as Mr. C always says, if it's a burger place, go with the burgers.

The surroundings are somewhat cramped, and you may be seated at the long, long central table with perfect strangers, but hey—Ma says they're okay. Open from 11 A.M. to 10 P.M. Mondays through Saturdays.

Boca Grande

- 1728 Massachusetts Ave., Cambridge; (617) 354-7400
- 149 First St., Cambridge; (617) 354-5550
- *Tip-free*

Boca Grande is a Mex-food chain that doesn't feel like a chain; it certainly puts Taco Bell to shame. This is real food, fresh and delicious.

The atmosphere is hip, with an open kitchen, lots of plants, and walls painted in bright southwestern colors of clay and turquoise. The food is made to your order, with all fresh ingredients. You can have a full meal, like the half-chicken with warm tortillas and salsa for $3.95, or the Mexican plate, with your choice of beef, chicken, or spicy pork ("carnitas") plus beans, rice, and salsa for $3.75.

Or put a meal together from tacos, burritos, guacamole, chips, quesadilla, and more. The burritos grandes, by the way, are gigantic for just $3.50. Regular specials include a black bean tostada with chicken, beef, or vegetarian for $2.25; or eggplant taquitos, with guacamole, jalapenos, onions, and cilantro, at $2.95 for six.

The Mass. Ave. spot, open daily, has tables by the window; the branch near the Cambridgeside Galleria, closed Sundays, has a separate room upstairs, which is a quiet and cozy way to dine.

Border Cafe

- 32 Church St., Cambridge; (617) 864-6100
- 819 Broadway, Saugus; (617) 233-5308

The Border Cafe has been for several years one of the most popular dining spots in Harvard Square, and it's easy to see why from the moment you step inside. The atmosphere is like a party that's always in full swing. The bright decor features old beer advertisements, looking like all of Tijuana compressed into one room. Stepping up into the bar area, you pass an old-fashioned bathtub that may once have swilled gin. Waiters and waitresses, accustomed to the crowds, zip past you with trays held high over their heads.

The menu is large, specializing in Mexican, Southwestern, and Cajun cuisine; and there is a great variety of meat, fish, and vegetarian dishes to choose from, many of which are at very reasonable prices.

Dinners, more than appetizers and the drinks, are the real bargain here.

MR. CHEAP'S PICKS
Harvard Square

✔ **Bartley's Burger Cottage**—Forty-nine different kinds of burgers—count 'em. Your classic student hangout.

✔ **Fraser's on the Avenue**—Elegant bistro, fancy food, moderately priced.

✔ **Soleil**—Cool cuisines from all the hottest parts of the world.

Most are well under Mr. C's $10 limit and are served with fixings on the side to make for a full meal. A platter of soft tacos is just $4.75; chicken enchiladas are $4.95. Many dinners come with yellow rice and black beans; you can also add a side of chunky guacamole for another buck.

Some items blend Tex-Mex with nouvelle. Chicken Laredo ($5.95) gives you a breast of mesquite-broiled chicken served on a bed of cooked spinach—in a sauce made from smoked chili peppers, butter, and spices, served with the rice and beans. Then there is the Cajun side of the border. Catfish Mardi Gras ($7.25) is a couple of deep-fried filets cooked in a tomatoey Creole sauce and topped with shaved pecans. Jambalaya rice comes with it.

The possibilities are nearly endless. If you don't mind the boisterous surroundings, and are prepared to wait for a table, this is as close to a fiesta as you'll find this far north. Open late nightly.

Boston Sail Loft
- 1 Memorial Drive, Cambridge; (617) 225-2222
- 80 Atlantic Ave., Boston; (617) 227-7280

See the listing under "Boston."

Cafe Liberty
- 497B Massachusetts Ave., Cambridge; (617) 492-9900
- *Tip-free*

Sounds like some sort of flag-waving eatery, all hot dogs and apple pie, right? *Not*. Located in a Central Square basement, this cool cafe mixes eye-popping espresso drinks, sandwiches and pastries, books, art—and the Internet. Opened in early '95 by three young techno-restaurateurs, the name reflects their belief in freedom of access to the Info Superhighway; this on-ramp isn't *quite* free, but it's relatively inexpensive. See the listing under "Entertainment—Readings and Literary Events" for more details.

Along with the 'Net, various coffees and teas are brewed up. Exotic coffee drinks go for around $3—like most coffee bars—but you get a deep ceramic mug filled right up to the top, and each concoction is made with two espresso shots. That is, unless you order "Black Death"—six shots of espresso, period. What a way to go. There are also non-caf choices like Chai tea and steamed cider. The limited but tasty food menu offers turkey or veggie sandwiches for $3.75; homemade soups ($3.25) in sourdough bread bowls; individual pizzas ($3); plus fresh cakes and muffins.

It's all found in an attractive, artsy setting. Large murals and backlit ceiling panels reflect mystical influences from Eastern and Western traditions. Sit at Euro-modern tables, or sink into a futon couch, and read the day's papers. The computer area, known as "The Cave," has *papier-maché* walls which make it look like just that—complete with Native American drawings "carved" in. Another area, in a nod to the low-tech past, features a selection of books for your reading pleasure, as well as a vintage Royal manual typewriter.

And there's more! Live entertainment takes place on Monday evenings with no cover charge—an eclectic mix of open-mike music, poetry, and plays. The place is hopping most every night, especially with all

the other nightclubs in the area; day-
times are mellow and relaxed. Open
daily from 10 A.M. all the way to 1
A.M. Oh yes, and you can reach them
on the World Wide Web at
http://www.cafeliberty.com. Surf's up!

Cafe Troyka

- 1154 Massachusetts Ave.,
  Cambridge; (617) 864-7476

New York may have the Russian Tea
Room, in all its splendor; but here in
cosmopolitan Harvard Square, Cafe
Troyka gives you all that old world
charm in a subdued—and much more
affordable—setting. The food is delicious and quite different from so
many other restaurants.

In fact, the menu is fun to just
pore over, filled with all kinds of
items large and small. You can order
a full-sized entree or put several
smaller dishes together into a Chek-
ovian pu-pu platter. Either way you
can stay under $10 per person (no
wine or beer is served, but patrons
are welcome to bring their own).

Among the appetizer-type dishes,
Mr. C enjoyed mushroom-barley
soup ($2.85), a large bowl with
whole fresh mushrooms in a clear,
tasty broth with a dollop of sour
cream at the bottom. *Piroshki* ($2.65)
are crisp, flaky individual pies filled
with meat, potato, or eggs and
scallions.

There are larger dishes, such as
pelmeni, or Russian dumplings
($6.85), filled with meat or potato.
Bigger still is the meat potato pie
($8.95), which combines layers of all
of these; and the stuffed pepper or
stuffed cabbage dinners ($9.65),
which include a vegetable-tomato
sauce and a side of black beans.
There are also *blini*, Russian pancakes, topped with jam, lox, or cav-
iar; and of course, hot or cold
borscht. Desserts such as chocolate
waffle torte and margarita cake (no,
not the drink—layers of meringue,
custard, and nuts) looked wonderful,
but Mr. C and his guest had so much
fun trying the various dinner items
that they had no room left. Another
visit.

The atmosphere is cozy and intimate; each table has its own Orient
Express brass lamp ("Paris—Istan-
bul"), and the walls are covered with
framed photographs of famous Russian figures from Dostoevsky to
Nabokov to Diaghilev. Not that any
of them have eaten at the Troyka, but
they would certainly have enjoyed it.
It's open daily 11:30 A.M. to 10:30
P.M., Fridays and Saturdays 'til 11 P.M.

Caffe Marino

- 2465 Massachusetts Ave.,
  Cambridge; (617) 868-5454
- *Tip-free*

Why pay upscale prices at Marino's
Restaurant when you can get the
same food on the same premises for
much less? Recently moved here
from Harvard Square, Caffe Marino
features cafeteria-style service, which
means that you can survey all your
options before deciding. This is not
as easy as it sounds; everything looks
so tempting. And it's fresh too, since
Marino's has its own farm in Natick
from which it obtains organic vegetables and chemical-free meats (see the
listing under "Entertainment—Outdoors").

The menu here changes daily. On
a lunch visit, Mr. C enjoyed a large
wedge of frittata studded with vegetables for just $3. Bruschetta loaded
with fresh tomatoes was $2.25 a
slice. And $4.95 buys a heaping plate
of linguine prepared with olive oil
and garlic. There's also a salad bar,
stocked with that organic produce.
Meat lovers can opt for hot specialties like chicken picante ($7.95); all
hot dishes come with pasta, risotto,
or vegetables. For a lighter lunch, try
sandwiches on focaccia bread for as
little as $2.50.

Afterwards, Mr. C was tempted by
six flavors of Italian ice cream ($1.95
a dish) and a chocolatey roll cake
($1.75 a slice). Espresso and cappuc-
cino drinks are also served. The
Caffe is open from 8 A.M. to 9 P.M.
Sundays through Thursdays; Fridays
and Saturdays to 10 P.M.

MR. CHEAP'S PICKS
Kendall Square

✔ **Davio's Riviera Cafe**—Happy hour deals on their outdoor patio along the Charles.

✔ **Miracle of Science**—The miracle is such trendy food at such low prices. Good luck getting in.

✔ **Sazarac Grove**—Creatively casual food, great beers, and a free pool table make this a cool hangout.

Cambridge Deli and Grill

- 90 River St., Cambridge; (617) 868-6740
- *Tip-free*

Here's a great little spot tucked away just outside of Central Square. Don't blink or you'll miss it; and you'll be sorry, if you like barbecue.

You can take out or eat at one of the half-dozen tables. Mr. C loved the Texas-style ribs ($6.95), six meaty bones with lots of tangy sauce sitting atop a plate of fresh salad, shoestring fries, a slab of garlic bread, and a couple of crispy onion rings for good measure. A big, fun meal, complete with moist towelettes.

Chicken plates are available fried, barbecued, or Cajun-style. There are seafood dinners as well, like fish and chips for $4.99 and a fried shrimp plate with fries, cole slaw, and potato salad for $7.25. It's a big menu for a small place. Hours are 11 A.M. to 8 P.M. Mondays through Saturdays. Grab it.

Charlie's Kitchen

- 10 Eliot St., Cambridge; (617) 492-9646

Charlie's Kitchen is one of those places that seems completely wrong for its surroundings; it's the opposite of almost every other restaurant in Harvard Square. Nestled among chic boutiques, across from the Charles Hotel, Charlie's is strictly a townie joint, where the long bar—with sports blaring on the TV—takes at least equal prominence with the dining booths. But don't be put off by its appearance; the guys are friendly and the waitress will call you "hon."

The menu sticks to basics, with food that sticks to your ribs. Just about everything on the menu, from chicken to beef to pork chops, is in the $5 to $7 price range. Burgers, of course, are a mainstay here; the patties are the pre-formed kind, but they're cooked on a flame grill. Add a bottle of Sam Adams and you can't go wrong.

Another good thing to know is that you can eat here late. Well, late is a relative term; until midnight, anyway. It's strictly greasy spoon, but clean; and sometimes, after pushing your way through the crowds that have inexplicably gathered around some streetcorner mime, a joint like Charlie's can be just the sort of antidote you need in Le Square. Open daily.

Christopher's

- 1920 Massachusetts Ave., Cambridge; (617) 876-9180

This popular Porter Square restaurant/bar features a lots of international beers, all-natural food (much of it homemade) and a cozy atmosphere with a large fireplace. The only drawback is parking, which can be impossible in this area. There is a huge shopping center across the street, but—even though the shops are closed at night—you may get towed or ticketed there. Mr. C has warned you.

The menu ranges from politically correct Cantabrigian fare to a world tour. "Chuck's Veggie Peace Burgah" ($4.95) is a vegetarian patty of mushrooms, brown rice, oats, cheese, chilies, egg whites, and other healthy things, all on a whole wheat bun. Part of the price goes to the "1% For Peace" fund.

Spanning the globe, Christopher's has Yucatan chicken wings ($4.95) marinated in citrus juice and mildly spicy; pasta dinners like whole wheat linguine with broccoli ($7.95); stir-fried vegetables in ginger and garlic ($6.95); and great (yes, beef) burgers. These are large, fresh patties of ground sirloin served on whole-wheat buns, with French fries that are thin and crispy. Choose from Cajun, "Surfer" (sprouts and guacamole, dude), or even Boursin.The beer list is extensive, with brands like Courage, Guinness, and Cambridge's own Tall Tale Pale Ale on draft. Bottles add forty more brews, from Aass (Norway) to Xingu Black (Brazil). Woodpecker Cider, too. Nice to hang out with in front of that fireplace on a cold winter night. Open seven days 'til midnight.

Corner Restaurant
- 2366 Massachusetts Ave., Cambridge; (617) 661-5655

Hungry diners looking for authentic Greek food routinely vie for this tiny restaurant's twelve tables. The menu is short and specialized, all good bets. Start off with stuffed grape leaves ($2.95). Spanikopita, a spinach and feta pie in phyllo pastry, is $2.75. The gyros here are delicious, piled with spiced chicken, roast lamb, or a ground lamb and beef mixture, with veggies and cucumber yogurt sauce ($3.75).

More unusual is a platter of broiled butterfly shrimp for $6.95; specialties like moussaka ($6.25) are equally good. Barbecued shish kebabs come in around $7. All the meat at Corner is marinated for at least 24 hours before it is cooked, which accounts for the rich flavor.

This is a no-frills corner of the world; the decor is plain, the place settings merely functional. But it's all eclipsed by the food, which will transport you from North Cambridge to Athens in a heartbeat. Open seven days.

Davio's Riviera Café
- Royal Sonesta Hotel; 5 Cambridge Pkwy., Cambridge; (617) 661-4810

What's this? Mr. C spotted at the Royal Sonesta? Sounds like a scandal. Yet, although Davio's regular menu is just what you'd expect—elegant food at high prices—the cafe does offer a great deal at happy hour. Every weekday from 5-6 P.M., if you buy one appetizer, you get a second one free. And we ain't talking chicken fingers here: Appetizers may include roast eggplant soup ($4.50), homemade veal sausage, or a grilled pizza topped with goat cheese, olives, and eggplant (each $7.95).

This is New England, so of course there are fantastic seafood dishes. A squid, orange, and arugala salad ($8.95) is certainly uncommon, though; shrimp bruschetta ($7.95) and phyllo pastry filled with lobster and oysters ($9.95) are among the other choices. Enjoy your appetizers on the patio overlooking the Charles River, with the Esplanade across the way. On Thursday nights from 6-10 P.M., Davio's hosts a live reggae band. Swanky, huh? Just remember: Mr. C can find a bargain almost *anywhere!*

El Greco
- 251-255 Cambridge St., Cambridge; (617) 492-7232

True to its name, this is your traditional Greek-American diner, located near the courthouse in East Cambridge. It's busiest during the day, when locals stop in for lunch and chatter; beer and wine are available.

Dinner entrees are mostly around $6 and under, served with potatoes and vegetables. Many come with pita bread, but this is not pulled from some plastic bag: El Greco makes its own homemade bread. Hot from the oven, it's thick, chewy, and yummy. Wrap it around souvlaki ($4.75), large chunks of beef in a creamy garlic sauce. It's delightfully messy and big enough to take some home for later.

Check the chalkboard for wonderful daily specials. Homemade egg-lemon-chicken soup is an unusual and tasty concoction, for $2.50. "Greek-Style Fish" ($4.95) gives you flaky pieces of white fish, served over slices of cooked potato and baked in a tomato and herb sauce. It's light and delicious. Meatloaf ($5.25) is also homemade; a customer was heard to tell the hostess it was the best in town.

El Greco opens for breakfast from 6:30 A.M. (they sleep until 11 A.M. on Sundays), with some of the lowest prices around. Two eggs with home fries, toast, and bacon, ham, or sausage are just $1.75. Pancakes are $1.50. Of course, you can just get an order of pita bread. Mmmmm.

El Rancho

- 1126 Cambridge St., Cambridge; (617) 868-2309

Located just outside of Inman Square, El Rancho is one of the few places in Boston where you can get "comidas tipicas" of El Salvador. This tiny storefront kitchen offers Mexican food as well, and it's all carefully prepared and flavorful, with sizeable portions.

Among the more interesting specialties is "Chicken el Sol" ($6.50), in which corn tortilla chips are neatly arranged around the rim of the plate, like a Mayan painting of the sun. A generous portion of rice is laid over this, then another layer of chips, and finally a layer of diced chicken in a tangy tomato sauce. Absolutely delicious. Most interesting among the Salvadoran cuisine are pupusas, soft corn tortillas filled with vegetables and pork or cheese, all fried up brown and moist. A platter of three

with beans and a spicy cole slaw goes for a mere $4.50.

With many of the meals you can add a side order of guacamole for 95¢. Also, there are bottles of hot sauce on the tables for those with spicier appetites. The service is friendly, if a bit slow, and the folks will be happy to explain the delicacies for you. Open Tuesdays through Saturdays from 11 A.M. to 8 P.M. Muy bueno.

Fraser's on the Avenue

- 1680 Massachusetts Ave., Cambridge; (617) 441-5566

This creative bistro is a great place to enjoy fresh Mediterranean food. The restaurant is small and bustling (i.e., you will be able to admire your neighbor's food as readily as your own), but the atmosphere is stylish. The care taken with the cooking shows up in nice touches like chopped hard-boiled eggs sprinkled over a bowl of gazpacho ($4.50).

Fraser's works on a "dinner tapas" theme: Dishes can be considered either small entrees or generous appetizers, depending on your appetite. But one or two orders per person can be enough, especially if you share a delicious bread basket of focaccia, sourdough rolls, and grilled pizza dough, all for $3.50.

Mr. C sampled a tasty grilled pizza topped with chicken, sharp cheese, and pesto for $7. These (relatively) low prices extend even to elegant dishes like grilled bluefish in grape leaves ($8) or duck Tangier with apricots and tabouleh ($9). There are always a few dinner specials (these *are* full-size), but they mostly run to about $14; the truly economical can request half-orders.

Fraser's also serves a weekend brunch. They open at 11:30 A.M. on weekdays, half an hour earlier on weekends; food is served until midnight Sundays through Tuesdays, and 'til 1 A.M. the rest of the week.

Fresco's Cafe and Grille

- 134 Massachusetts Ave., Cambridge; (617) 491-8866
- *Tip-free*

Along the M.I.T. stretch of Mass. Ave., Fresco's is a spiffy cafe with a wide variety of basics at great prices. From breakfast (the house special is two eggs, home fries, and toast for $1.49) through lunch and dinner (the place closes at 9 P.M.), there are all kinds of meals to choose from.

Fish and chips are only $3.95; and at $4.95, the swordfish kebab dinner is a steal. Plenty of charcoal-grilled chunks of fish over rice with a tomato sauce, and salad. Moving (not far) up the scale, you can even get a barbecued half-chicken dinner for $5.25, with a salad and rice or crispy French fries. Plus fried scallops, gyros, veal cutlets with spaghetti, pizzas with all kinds of meat and vegetarian toppings, and salads.

In short, this is the kind of place Mr. C loves: Prices are low, the place is clean and bright, and you can keep going back without having the same kind of food twice. Open Mondays through Fridays from 7 A.M. to 9 P.M., Saturdays 9 A.M. to 4 P.M.

Grendel's Restaurant and Bar

• 89 Winthrop St., Cambridge; (617) 491-1160

A longtime Harvard Square favorite, Grendel's is known for its innovative food, awesome salad bar, and good selection of vegetarian dishes. Everything on Grendel's salad bar looks so healthy and tasty that you'll pile your plate perilously high. It's $3.95 for a small salad or $6.95 for a large; order a main dish with the salad bar, and these prices are reduced by a buck each.

Appetizers include chicken or *chorizo* (sausage) quesadillas, each $5.95. Continuing your tour of the world's kitchens, try the Greek lamb and beef moussaka, a Middle Eastern chicken shish kebab, or a calamari and pasta dish, each just $6.95. Vegetarians are treated very well here: Choose from eggplant Parmesan ($6.95), *alu chole* from India (a stew of curried chick peas, tomatoes, and potatoes, $5.95) or one of many other options.

Grendel's displays creativity even in its sandwiches and lighter fare. You can get a baguette stuffed with turkey, Havarti cheese and pesto sauce (bet you've never heard *that* one before) for $4.75. And a most unusual fresh strawberry omelette intrigued Mr. C ($5.50). Finish up with delights like mocha cake or peach pie (both $3.25). On a sunny day, you can eat *al fresco* and soak up the unique atmosphere of the Square. The Den is open from 11 A.M. to 11 P.M. Sundays through Thursdays; Fridays and Saturdays, until midnight.

Indian Globe

• 474 Massachusetts Ave., Cambridge; (617) 868-1866

Located in the heart of Central Square, Indian Globe is one of the top choices in a crowded field. Service is very quick and attentive, and the prices are about a dollar less per entree than most similar restaurants.

Chicken dominates the menu, from the basic tandoori style ($7.50) to chicken tikka masala ($8.45), boneless pieces of white meat grilled in spices and served in a creamy tomato sauce. There are also plenty of lamb and seafood entrees, such as good ol' lamb curry ($7.65), made to your preference of spiciness. There are no beef items on the menu.

There are plenty of vegetarian choices, though. For a real bargain, you can order the house vegetarian special: Chana masala (chick peas in tomato sauce) and mutter paneer (cooked peas and cheese) with papadam and poori bread, raita (whipped yogurt with cucumber, potato, and tomato), rice, tea or coffee, and dessert, all for $9.50. There's also a lamb and chicken version for $10.25.

Speaking of bargains, Indian Globe serves up daily luncheon plates from the main menu, most of which are $3.95 or so. And for the hefty appetite, there is an all-you-can-eat buffet for $5.95, served from 12-3 P.M. daily. Hours are 11:30 A.M. to 10 P.M. daily.

271

Iruña

- 56 J.F.K. St., Cambridge; (617) 868-5633

A friend of Mr. C's stops in here "whenever I want to treat myself" and orders up a *paella* laced with fish, clams, sausage, and chicken ($10.95) that's just too big to finish. Iruña, as you may guess, is a Spanish restaurant that is hidden down an alleyway across from the Janus Cinema. This makes it quintessential Harvard Square: a place for those "in-the-know," with good, inexpensive food and a foreign accent.

A couple of rooms in this winding house, plus a patio in the back, offer an almost romantically secluded atmosphere—even if the decor is rather plain. Service is gracious enough to make you think you really *are* somewhere in Spain. Appetizers range from *gazpacho* ($2) to marinated artichoke hearts ($2.75); other entrees include pork tenderloin *estofado* (stew) for $8.95, and sirloin a la Baronesa—prepared in a butter, lemon, and garlic sauce for $12. All entrees include soup and a salad—good value indeed. Beer and wine are available. Iruña serves lunch and dinner, every day but Sunday.

Izzy's Restaurant and Sub Shop

- 169 Harvard St., Cambridge; (617) 661-3910
- *Tip-free*

Doesn't sound like it, but this place serves up "Comidas Criollas"—native Puerto Rican dinners.When you walk into this homey, out-of-the-way neighborhood joint, the menu over the counter is bewildering—over a hundred choices. Yes, there are subs, some of which are unusual (fajita subs); you'll also see items that aren't found at too many other places. Looking for some plantain ($1.50), that sweet, deep-fried banana? Have a taste for tripe soup ($2.75 a cup)? They're done to perfection here.

Meanwhile, you can get a full dinner for around five bucks. Combination plates start off with black or red beans, rice, and salad, to which you may add fried ribs (for $5.75); a pair of pork chops ($6); chicken or beef fajitas ($5.25); and more. Or put it all together with the hearty "Montanero Plate" ($7): rice, beans, salad, steak, fried pork, fried egg, and plantain. Wash your meal down with one of the many interesting choices in the refrigerator case, like a non-alcoholic malt beverage or a bottle of pineapple soda.

There are ten tables or so, many decorated under their glass tops with postcards of Puerto Rico, for further atmosphere. The place fills up at the dinner hour, and so Izzy's also does a substantial take-out business. Either way, it's an experience. Closed Sundays.

Jake & Earl's Dixie B-B-Q

- 1273 Cambridge St., Cambridge; (617) 491-RIBS (7427)
- *Tip-free*

This Inman Square hole-in-the-wall is simply the other side of the kitchen—and a cheap alternative—to the pricey East Coast Grill next door. Both are popular spots, noted even in *People* magazine as one of the ten-best barbecue restaurants in the country. They pack a ton of atmosphere in a tiny space: The walls are lined with license plates, old-fashioned advertising signs, a bust of Elvis. There are about five stools along two walls, and that's it. The place is really best suited for take-out.

What's good here? You guessed it: Ribs! "Memphis Dry Rub Ribs" ($8) are a house specialty—a half-dozen pork ribs coated in spices and slow-cooked to a smoky, not spicy, taste. They're served over a slice of white bread—*that's* down home. All plates come with cole slaw, some zingy pork and beans, and a hunk o' watermelon.

The limited menu also offers a pulled pork sandwich plate ($4.25), marinated pork so tender that it's easily "pulled" off the bones and stuffed into a nice, messy sandwich; there's even a "Burnt Ends" version for those who like their meat *really* well done.

Mr. C also likes the Jamaican "jerk" chicken ($7.50); try it with some banana guava ketchup. If you're brave, bottles of "Inner Beauty Real Hot Sauce" stand waiting to enhance your enjoyment. It must take a special kind of glass to contain this fiery condiment. Yow!

Joanie's Kitchen

- 313 Massachusetts Ave., Cambridge; (617) 491-1988
- *Tip-free*

Formerly known as Mom's Kitchen, this little coffee shop has been passed down to chefs Joanie and Rosemarie, who've spruced up both the dowdy decor and the menu. Now, you can find sandwiches like "Cranberry Chutney Delight," a turkey sandwich with zing, for $4.95 (or $3.35 for a half), among the two dozen options.

Everything is made on the premises, and it all shows a personal touch. Oh sure, you can get basic sandwiches and salads. A cup of soup and half a sandwich will only set you back $4.95. But a bowl of, say, *gazpacho* (only $2.35) may surprise the unwary—made with ingredients like diced jalapeño peppers.

Breakfasts stay on the more traditional side. $3.95 will get you two eggs, corned beef hash, toast, home fries, and coffee. And there's a whole wall of freshly baked apple strudel, plump muffins for 95¢ (maple oat, double chocolate chip...), and more.

With it all, you're sure to get a smile from the friendly proprietors. Order at the far end of the counter, and find a table. The joint feels strictly blue-collar; but, located just millimeters from the M.I.T. campus, the conversation overheard is as likely to be about thermodynamics as about the Sox. The hours are a holdover from Mom's: The place is only open from 6 A.M. to 3 P.M. on weekdays, Saturdays from 8 A.M. to 2 P.M. And weekends disappear entirely during summer.

John Harvard's Brew House

- 33 Dunster St., Cambridge; (617) 868-4341

Who says you can't get into Har-vard? This basement restaurant advertises "honest food, real beer," and that's exactly what you get. It's a favorite lunch haunt for businesspeople in the Square; daily lunch "express specials" are $5-$6, speedily delivered. Mr. C sampled a grilled pesto chicken sandwich on focaccia with roast peppers and artichoke hearts. Lots of burgers, too; more interesting is a blackened catfish sandwich for $6.25. Entrees, mostly $8-$9, range from a vegetable *paella* to chicken pot pie. The handsome, dark wood decor features roomy booths which encourage hanging out.

Deciding what to eat is tough; picking a beer is even more challenging. As the name implies, John Harvard's does its own brewing on the premises. There are several varieties of ale; the malty flavor of Dublin stout; and more patriotic American lagers. Not for nothing was this place voted the "Best Microbrewery in Boston" by *Boston* magazine. John Harvard's also offers live entertainment on Mondays from 9 P.M. to midnight, and Tuesdays from 10 P.M. to 12:30 A.M., with no cover charge. The restaurant itself is open for lunch and dinner daily.

Manhattan Sammy's Delicatessen

- One Kendall Square, Cambridge; (617) 252-3347
- *Tip-free*

A little slice of the Big Apple right in Technology Central. Come here when you have a craving for a nice big knish (potato, beef, or turkey) or a bowl of homemade matzo ball soup. But be sure to save room for the centerpiece of any meal at Sammy's—deli sandwiches, which come in two sizes: "large" and "overstuffed." The names don't lie; Mr. C's chin hit the table right alongside his pastrami sandwich. Packed with spicy, lean meat shipped in from New York, it was a meal in itself for only $5.75 (with a nice, big pickle). Chopped liver ($3.75) is also a good bet.

Full dinners include roast brisket ($8.50) or meatloaf ($5.50), served

273

with two side dishes. These are quite wonderful in themselves, like real noodle kugel or potato pancakes. Skip the meat and nosh on a big order of three pancakes with fresh fruit for $6.

Of course, Sammy's is a great place to have breakfast, with a list as long as your arm of three-egg omelettes (from $3.20 plain to $6.50 with lox). Good bagels, too. Sammy's is popular with transplanted New Yorkers, local businessmen, M.I.T. profs, and anyone else who enjoys real deli food. Open during the week from 6 A.M. to 11 P.M. and on weekends from 8 A.M. to 2 A.M. (!)

Marcella's
• 1808 Massachusetts Ave., Cambridge; (617) 547-5000

If you're looking for a place that serves *nouvelle cuisine* without the trendy prices, Marcella's is the answer. Or, to look at it another way, it's a *very* fancy take-out sandwich shop with a dozen white linen-topped tables at the back.

Yes, the sandwiches are priced from $6 to $8, but think of what you get: roast beef with smoked mozzarella, sun-dried tomatoes, and Marcella's own house dressing. Chicken salad made with apples and raisins. And others, all served on fresh, crusty baguettes.

For dinner, the cuisine is Italian, but not the standard red-sauce-and-pasta of the south. Mr. C and his dining companion chose to make a creative, inexpensive meal by sharing a few items, starting with prosciutto and melon ($5), a sparkling combination of sweet and salty. The specialty of the house is the "Pollo Platter" ($7), a rotisseried, juicy half-chicken atop a garnish of tomatoes and cucumbers, with a side dish of oven-roasted potatoes—with plenty of everything. On the side was an order of Tuscan-style garlic bread, several long crusts for $2.

The owners told Mr. C they believe there should *always* be a bottle of wine on the table; selected choices are always available under $10. After-

wards, splurge with an espresso, iced cappuccino, orzata (almond-flavored soda), and something from the bakery—cannoli, cakes, and pastries. With all this, plus fresh flowers on each table, Marcella's is a good bet for a casually romantic dinner spot. Open 7 A.M. to midnight daily.

Mary Chung Restaurant
• 464 Massachusetts Ave., Cambridge; (617) 864-1991

Mr. C wants to let you know that this longtime favorite has reopened in Central Square. It was popular before, and it's popular again. Specializing in Szechuan cooking, the restaurant has an extensive menu (over thirty chicken dishes alone) of exquisitely prepared food at very reasonable prices. Even the seafood entrees all come in under $10. Beer and wine is available.

Luncheon specials are even better values, all under $5. And on weekends from 11:30 A.M. to 2:30 P.M., Mary Chung's serves up a *dim sum* brunch that can't be beat. Open daily for lunch and dinner.

Middle East Restaurant and Cafe
• 472 Massachusetts Ave., Cambridge; (617) 354-8238

How does one begin to describe the vast, venerable Middle East? It's a bit of a Moroccan pleasure palace in the heart of Central Square, sprawling around a busy corner, offering delicious food and adventurous music in various chambers. The main restaurant, a few doors down from the corner of Brookline Street, has the charm of *Casablanca*—large plants everywhere, intimate booths and tables. And, non-smokers be warned: The air is heavy with people enjoying the freedom that is Cambridge.

Connected, by a hallway to the music lounge, is another dining room known as the bakery (with its own door on Mass. Ave.). You can indeed nibble a piece of homemade baklava and sip herbal tea; but the same full menu is available here as in the other room. There is also an extensive list of international beers, including Anchor Steam, Pilsner Urquell, Xingu, and New Castle Brown Ale.

The food itself is terrific, elaborate preparations of smooth stews, kebabs, and exotic bean dishes. Mr. C loved the *msa'ah* ($7.75), a hefty serving of baked eggplant, sauteed onions, tomatoes, and chick peas, served over rice pilaf. Charcoal-grilled kebab entrees, all priced from $8.75 to $9.75, include scallop, swordfish, and shrimp skewers along with the standard beef, lamb, and chicken.

Lunch is an even better bargain at the Middle East, with entrees ranging from $3.50 to $5.75, and generous portions. There are exotic salads and homemade soups as well. Live music is offered nightly, some with no cover charge; see the listing under "Entertainment—Music" for details. Kitchen hours are 11 A.M. to 1 A.M. seven days.

Miracle of Science

- 321 Massachusetts Ave., Cambridge; (617) 868-2866

Everyone assumes the theme of this bar has to do with its proximity to M.I.T., but there's no relation. The real miracle here is that this trendy place, with its hip futuristic decor, serves such terrific food so cheaply.

Big half-pound burgers are $4.75, as is the grilled chicken sandwich; there are several Mexican appetizers as well. The true standouts, though, are the skewer plates—thick, juicy shish kebabs, creatively prepared. Try citrus thyme shrimp with chutney, or pomeroy beef and horseradish sauce. Each plate comes with tortillas, black beans, succotash, and mint cole slaw—nouvelle chic in a bar. One-skewer plates are just $3.75, and two skewers are $7.50. Big desserts, too.

Lots of great domestic and imported beers are available; what's not available most nights, unfortunately, is table space. The place is pretty small and extremely popular, so get there early if you plan to eat. Open for lunch and dinner, seven days.

Moody's Falafal Palace

- 25 Central Square, Cambridge; (617) 864-0827
- *Tip-free*

Moody's is perhaps one of the best of the area's many Middle Eastern eateries. Located right in the square, this tiny kitchen really puts out a ton of great, cheap food. The sandwiches—grape leaves, kebabs, and of course, "falafal"—are giant, and all priced from $2.50 to $2.75. A cup of lentil soup, just 99¢, is light and tummy-warming, with bits of corn and peas mixed in.

The dinners are hearty too—the falafal plate, with salad, is just $2.75. Chicken or beef kebabs, served over rice pilaf, are each $3.95, as are moussaka, kafta, kibby, or grape leaves, with rice or salad. Nearing the top of the line are shawarma and rice ($5), and grilled fish kebabs with rice ($5.25).

There are just a few stools by the window in this humble place, which is clean and bright—and open until midnight, seven days a week.

Nick's Beef and Beer House

- 1688 Massachusetts Ave., Cambridge; (617) 491-9882

This restaurant likes to brag about its "miracle prices," and regular Cheapsters know it has earned those bragging rights. Where else in an urban metropolis can you find a decent, "king size" hamburger for $1.10? Even the McChains can't compete with that! Add cheese for a quarter. Make it a double burger—just $3.15. Getting the idea? Nick's is not a place for snobs; the restaurant is good and divey, and the Formica tables have seen better days. But don't misjudge the place—this food really is good.

The best choices here are the simplest ones, but the menu does extend beyond beef and beer. A big bowl of homemade bean soup is $1.55, a baked half-chicken is just $3.50. A feta cheese omelette is $2.99, including fries and a salad. A dish of scallops is one of the most expensive things on the menu—all of $4.95!

Wow. . . Mr. C *city*. Open for lunch and dinner, seven days, serving until 11:30 P.M.

Picante Mexican Grill
- 217 Elm St., Somerville; (617) 628-6394
- 735 Massachusetts Ave., Cambridge; (617) 576-6394

See the listing under "Somerville."

The Plough and Stars
- 912 Massachusetts Ave., Cambridge; (617) 441-3455

This popular watering hole in Central Square is well known for live music and Guinness Stout. Less widely publicized is its kitchen, which serves up surprisingly creative lunches on weekdays (and brunches on weekends).

A board of four or five specials changes daily. Mr. C dined on grilled tuna with a banana, pineapple, lime, and tequila relish (!), while a friend chose a hearty sausage and seafood gumbo served over rice. All lunch entrees are priced at $6; there are a couple of soups and salads in the $3-$5 range. Great stuff.

Poppa & Goose
- 69 First St., Cambridge; (617) 497-6772

"Poppa" and "Goose" are the pair of M.I.T. grads who founded this East Cambridge restaurant. Expensive education and all, they now serve up elegant Asian food to a crowd of loyal and appreciative diners. The food fairly drips with authenticity; many dishes are contributed by the waiters, international students from local colleges.

Don't be dismayed that most specials are rather costly. You can fashion a delicious, inexpensive meal from the salads, side dishes, and some of the entrees. Vietnamese spring rolls are wonderful, and only $3.95 a pair. Or start with a prawn soup, with vegetables and lemon grass flavoring, same price. Noodles are a specialty here: A heaping plate of pad Thai, mixed with shrimp and vegetables, is $7.50.

Main dishes come in huge portions. Mr. C liked "Jade and Ruby Chicken"—*two* grilled chicken breasts, one made with coconut and cilantro sauce, the other with Indian curry, all for $9.95. "Heaven on Earth" is a vegetarian dish which matches seven different vegetables with five Asian sauces like teriyaki and black bean-ginger ($7.50). No liquor is served; instead, quench your thirst with a fresh fruit shake ($3).

Please note Poppa & Goose's eccentric hours: Lunch is served Mondays through Fridays from 11:30 A.M. to 2:30 P.M. and Saturdays from 12 noon to 3 P.M., while dinner is limited to Tuesdays through Thursdays from 5 to 9 P.M. and Fridays through Sundays from 5 to 10 P.M.

S & S Restaurant
- 1334 Cambridge St., Cambridge; (617) 354-0260

Rumor has it this Inman Square hangout was around before the Pilgrims arrived. The S & S is still one of the toughest tables in town for weekend brunch; even though the place sprawls with several large rooms, it's frequently crowded with smiling diners.

Half-pound hamburgers come with a variety of toppings, plus fries and cole slaw. Mr. C chowed down on a "Continental," made with sauteed mushrooms and Swiss cheese, which (like all burgers) is $5.95. Chicken breast sandwiches are served on toasted focaccia bread nowadays. These too are $5.95, as is a croissant filled with smoked turkey, tuna, or roast beef.

Lunch and dinner entrees come from land and sea; they include a ten-ounce sirloin steak ($8.95), broiled salmon ($9.95), and barbecued chicken ($8.95). All are accompanied by two side dishes of your choice. Lunch specials on Mr. C's visit included grilled vegetarian pizza or fettucini carbonara, both $4.95. Finish off with desserts like triple chocolate truffle cake, mud pie, or fruit tart (all $2.50).

Breakfast-all-day fans will love the anytime brunch food, like huge omelettes, pancakes with sausage, and the obligatory bagels and lox.

The S & S opens at 7 A.M. Mondays through Saturdays (Sundays at 8); they serve until 11 P.M. Sundays through Tuesdays, 'til midnight the rest of the week. But remember, if you want those bagels with your Sunday *Globe*, show up early.

Sapporo Ramen
- 1815 Massachusetts Ave., Cambridge; (617) 876-4805
- *Tip-free*

An upscale noodle shop hidden inside the Porter Exchange building—upstairs from the *chic* but high-priced Cottonwood Cafe—Sapporo Ramen dishes up enormous bowls of delicious Japanese noodles. Servings come in containers as big as mixing bowls; unless you're ravenous, it's a safe bet to share an order with a friend, or bring your leftovers home for tomorrow's lunch. Sapporo Ramen offers three types of noodle sauces—soy sauce flavor, soy bean, or "clear"—and it is these which determine the price. Most noodle dishes come in all three varieties.

Mr. C sampled his noodles with fresh vegetables and tofu ($7.25). The veggies and tofu came in huge chunks; the noodles were thin and the soy sauce flavorful. Other noodle dishes, $6-$8, feature pork slices, seaweed, vegetables, and fish cakes. Add a side dish, like fried dumplings (six for $4.25), and you'll be full and happy. You can watch the cooks prepare your dish; then settle down for a while—Mr. C dares you to finish a bowl of noodles all by your lonesome!

This same area, on the second floor, boasts half a dozen other Asian fast-food shops, each specializing in different styles, including sushi. Mr. C recommends **Cafe Mami** (telephone 547-9130), **Kotobukiya** (354-6914), and **Ittyo** (354-5944). Most of these serve until about 8-9 P.M.; Sundays 'til 6 or so.

Sazarac Grove
- One Kendall Square, Cambridge; (617) 577-7850

A recent addition to the bustling food scene at Kendall Square, Sazarac combines two of Mr. C's favorite qualities: It's trendy *and* inexpensive.

The artsy decor features a Southwestern clay red and mustard yellow motif, in a winding series of dining rooms and lounge areas. One of the smaller rooms has a pool table, available for anyone's use. It's all way hip.

There's also an outdoor patio on the square's brick courtyard, when the weather is nice. Microbrews on tap include Seattle's Red Hook, and Oregon Nut Brown Ale. The menu was still being worked out at press time, but early response assures Mr. C that this place will be a hit—with prices that are a buck or two lower than other restaurants and brewpubs in the complex. The fare is casual but creative; sandwiches like ham and Fontina cheese, with grilled onions and maple mustard ($5.25), served with tabouleh chickpea salad, plus equally distinctive pizzas and salads. Open daily for lunch and dinner until 1 A.M. (food 'til 11 P.M.)

The Skewers
- 92 Mt. Auburn St., Cambridge; (617) 491-3079
- *Tip-free*

Across from the Garage Mall in Harvard Square, this basement spot is a fixture for good Middle Eastern food cheap; this is odd, since according to an article on the wall, the owners are from India. No matter.

The falafel is fresh and made with whole chick peas mixed into the filling, for a bit of crunch. You can get it in a pita sandwich for $2.95, including lettuce, tomato, cucumber, peppers, onions, and sauce. The dinner plate version is $4.95. Shish kebabs of lamb, chicken, or beef, are $3.75 for sandwiches and $5.75 for dinners.

The baked half-chicken dinner is marinated with raisins and mushrooms, and cooked until the meat falls off the bones. It's served with rice pilaf, Greek salad, and bread, all for $6.25. Another big value is the maza combination plate for two ($13), with shawarma, beef kebabs, hummus, baba ganoush, falafel, rice and salad. It's filling and healthy, with a vegetarian version for slightly less.

For dessert, Mr. C overheard someone saying that the baklava ($1.25) was the best he had ever tasted. Interestingly, the restaurant gives you a choice of table service or do-it-yourself counter service, allowing you to save an extra dollar or two. The table area at the back is nice and mellow, a rare commodity in this locale. Open 11 A.M. to 11 P.M. daily.

Soleil
- 18 Eliot St., Cambridge; (617) 876-7018

Opened in the spring of '95, Soleil is a creative addition to the ever-burgeoning Harvard Square restaurant scene. "Peasant foods from sunny lands" is the motto here, and that covers a lot of territory. Cuisines represented include Mediterranean, Mexican, Indian, Italian, and more— a handful of dishes from each.

This allows you to mix 'n match. Start with a plate of crunchy bruschetta ($2.95), and move on to a spicy "Caribbean Pepperpot" of vegetables, grilled chicken and rice ($6.95), or *feijoada*, a Brazilian stew of smoked pork and sausage. Not to mention curries, quesadillas, crepes, pastas. . .

The payoff question is: Can one kitchen make so many specialties well? Well, yes. Mr. C hasn't tried 'em all, but he and a companion sampled a bunch, without a loser among them. Judging by the lively crowd, this is the consensus of opinion. Everything is tasty and fresh, lovingly presented; portions, while not overwhelming, aren't skimpy either. Most entrees are in the $5-$8 range, so you can make several visits and work your way through the menu.

Soleil has squeezed the entire tropics into a narrow, artsy cafe, its stucco walls painted a warm terra cotta red. At the front, a service bar "hut" makes up fruit smoothies and herbal teas (no alcohol). Desserts are equally varied, but at $4 and up, they're not so cheap. Still, with its mellow jazz and cozy banquette tables, this is a fine stop after a film at the Brattle. Open for lunch and din-

ner six days, Fridays and Saturdays 'til midnight; closed Sundays.

Tasty Sandwich Shop
- 2A J.F.K. St., Cambridge; (617) 354-9016
- *Tip-free*

You know "The Tasty," established in 1916 (so it says in the window); it's that tiny corner counter facing Out Of Town News. Unlike so much of the Hah-vahd area, this joint ain't fancy and it sure ain't high-priced. There is only room for about a dozen people looking for a quick burger or a cup o' coffee. And it's open all night.

It does help if you love grease. Most food comes off the griddle, like cheeseburgers for a mere $2.25. It's a thin patty, so Mr. C recommends the double version ($3.50). Grilled cheese and bacon sandwiches are $3; deluxe sandwiches sport local names like the "Brattle Club"—not a secret society, but a sandwich of two burger patties, a fried egg, lettuce, and tomato on a bun, with French fries—all for $5.

Plus soups, omelettes, and French toast. And what better way to top it all off than with a good ol' Boston frappe? These are $2.75. The Tasty is a great little window on the square— and possibly on another place in time.

Third and Charles Bar and Grill
- 202 East Third St., East Cambridge; (617) 547-9310

This hidden gem of a Mexican restaurant is close to, but not in the thick of, the yuppified area that has arisen around the CambridgeSide Galleria. It's in the older, residential part of East Cambridge, so the atmosphere is a neighborhood bar with friendly service.

The well-stocked bar has plenty of Mexican beers and big frozen margaritas on hand. For appetizers, along with the usual, you can get a generous quesadilla ($5.25) filled with your choice of steak and green chili, chicken, or even spinach and broccoli (don't forget, we *are* still in the Republic of Cambridge here).

The menu "dares" you to ask for

your meal hot—or *very* hot. Mr. C likes the enchiladas—soft corn tortillas rolled with beef, chicken or "Florentine" (spinach and cheese) fillings, then topped with a zingy sauce and melted cheese. Dinner entrees include fajitas for only $5.95; "T & C Pollo," same price, is a boneless breast of chicken sauteed with mushrooms and bacon in a sour cream sauce, and served on a bed of rice.

There are a few items from this side of the Tex-Mex border, such as barbecued baby back ribs (each $5.95); but the real house specialties are clearly those south of the border. Mr. C suggests you get your posse on over there and rustle up some grub for yourself. Hours are Mondays

through Saturdays from 11 A.M. to 5 P.M., Sundays from noon.

Trattoria Il Panino
- 1001 Massachusetts Ave., Cambridge; (617) 547-5818
- 11 Parmenter St., Boston; (617) 720-1336
- 297 Franklin St., Boston; (617) 338-1000

See the listing under "Boston."

The Ultimate Bagel Company
- 1310 Massachusetts Ave., Cambridge; (617) 876-0777
- 335 Newbury St., Boston; (617) 247-1010
- 118 Needham St., Newton; (617) 964-8990

See the listing under "Boston."

NEWTON

The Biltmore Cafe
- 1205 Chestnut St., Newton; (617) 964-9179

Not many people seem to know of this fun, divey restaurant/bar, outside of the office crowd that frequents the place for lunch. You'd scarcely expect to find such a joint in an affluent 'burb like Newton, but the Biltmore has actually been here since 1920. The place is a hip landmark.

Elvis memorabilia lines the walls, windows, and every available nook; the jukebox is similarly retro. The pressed-tin ceiling is authentic. Two rooms are set up with basic wooden booths and tables, but the overall feeling is friendly and relaxed. The waitresses are all like Mom, ready to bring you a platter of fried scallops ($7.95, with crispy French fries and a salad) or a tuna salad plate ($3.50).

The burgers, thin and greasy, won't get any prizes from health-food fanatics, but this just ain't that kinda place. They sure are delicious, starting at a mere $2.25 for your basic. Add a plate of "Memphis Fries," slightly zingy, for another $1.75, or a

cup of homemade chili for $2.75. It's downright hard to blow the budget here, even with a brewski or two.

The Biltmore is just open on weekdays, closing up shop at 10 P.M.; food is served from 11 A.M. to 7 P.M. only.

Buff's Pub
- 317 Washington St., Newton; (617) 332-9134

Quietly nestled into a block of sterile Newton Corner office buildings, this tiny watering hole effortlessly bridges the gap between the Boston College co-eds and yuppie professionals who live in the area. "We do not serve shots," notes a sign over the bar, adding, "We do not accept credit cards." Buff's maintains a neighborhood feel, and an intense following. Just try getting in on a balmy evening; there's invariably a line out the door, even on weeknights. A ball game is usually on the tube. And the entire place is smoke-free.

Oh yes, then there's the food. A thick burger and fries sets you back a mere $4.75; a half-dozen entrees are nearly all priced at $6.95—sirloin

MR. CHEAP'S PICKS
Newton

✔ **Buff's Pub**—A tiny bar in Newton Corner, thought to have the best wings around.

✔ **Concept Cafe**—This catering kitchen sells its fancy cooking to the public.

✔ **Dunn-Gaherin's Pub**—Hard to pronounce and harder to find—no wonder the surprising menu is so inexpensive.

✔ **Le Grand Café**—Cheap eats in the Chestnut Hill Mall? This is no food court!

---

tips, teriyaki tips, barbecued boneless chicken breast, and the like. A plate of barbecued ribs is just six bucks. Plus a handful of daily specials, like fried crab cakes, around the same price; all dinners include cooked vegetables, and rice or fries.

Appetizers, at $4-$6, obviously are not such bargains, although portions are generous. Spicy wings are a longtime fave; chili-filled potato skins are a good value too. Wash 'em down with Bass, Sam Adams, or Guinness on tap.

Buff's opens for lunch at 11 A.M. and serves food until 10 or 11 P.M., closing a bit later. If you arrive before dark, you should be able to get a booth. If not, it's worth a wait.

Callahan's Steak and Seafood
- 100 Needham St., Newton; (617) 527-3112

Well-established and unpretentious, Callahan's serves up huge platters of good food in its folksy dining room or chummier sports bar. The selective menu offers up a handful each of meat and fish dinners, starting with big burgers from just $4.35. A

chopped sirloin plate goes up to $7.95, while filet mignon tops out at a still-reasonable $13.95. With all dinners, don't forget, you also get bread, salad, and rice or potato—a good deal.

Mr. C sampled a daily special of grilled salmon ($9.95) and got a hefty slab o' fish, plus the above-mentioned goodies. It was juicy, tasty, and a struggle to finish. That's the way it is here; like so many good pubs, income from the bar makes for extremely affordable food.

Located along a popular discount shopping stretch (next to one of Mr. C's absolute faves, the New England Mobile Book Fair), Callahan's is actually busier at lunch than at dinner. Thus, dinnertime is quiet, and you can be assured of getting seated quickly. 'Course, lunches move briskly too, especially when a New York strip steak goes for just $6.75 (!) with a salad or potato. Callahan's is open 11 A.M. to 11 P.M., seven days.

Concept Cafe
- 859 Washington St., Newton; (617) 964-8322
- *Tip-free*

Fabulous food at low prices—what a concept! This is a storefront location for a company that has been in the catering business for years; their large kitchen takes care of both the catering and the cafe, which means the public has access to Concept's creative, delicious cooking at low cost.

Starting the day off, there are fresh-baked muffins and unusual scones, like orange-poppyseed and lemon-ginger. Plus egg breakfasts, gourmet coffees of course, and a non-caffeine alternative—hot *vanilla*.

Lunch and (early) dinner bring terrific, enormous sandwiches and salads. Daily hot specials may offer such creations as Oriental beef pie or honey pot roast, usually around $5; or such standards as a half-chicken dinner for $6.50, with two side dishes (baked beans, mashed potatoes, stuffing, cole slaw, or a garden salad). You can also pick up pre-arranged chicken or lasagna dinners that in-

clude salad, sides, and dessert for up
to four people. Speaking of dessert:
Don't pass up the yummy homemade
goodies like chocolate-peanut butter
cookies, and cheesecake topped with
fruit. The latter is a mere $1.75 a
slice—such a deal!

The cafe itself is cozy and bright,
small but not cramped. During warm
weather, there are a couple of tables
outside. Owners Diane and Sharon
not only serve with a smile, but they
probably made your meal themselves—and they're happy to chat
about their recipes, too. There's a concept for ya. Open Mondays through
Fridays from 6 A.M. to 7 P.M., and Saturdays 'til 2:30 P.M.

Dunn-Gaherin's Pub

- 344 Elliot St., Newton; (617)
  527-6271

This out-of-the-way place is worth
finding (but forget it if you don't
have a car). It's in Newton Upper
Falls, south of Route 9, near the antique shops and one of the area's
pricier dining rooms, the Mill Falls.
Go to DG's; it's great food cheap,
and much more fun.

Huge burgers start at just $2.50,
with several toppings to choose from.
Great fries and rings, too. Sirloin steak
tips ($6.50) are another good choice,
and the chicken wings are speecy-
spicy hot. The menu goes well beyond
pub fare, though. Mr. C's companion
chose a daily special of charbroiled
swordfish tips ($6.50), which were de-
licious—plenty of them, on a bed of
rice pilaf. There are always several
such specials to choose from, some of
which are *far* from pub food as can
be—like the veggie melt sandwich in
pita bread ($3.95).

Run by a husband-and-wife team,
the atmosphere at Dunn-Gaherin's is
easygoing, with an odd mix of Americana decor amidst the Irish pub setting. The bar room, at the front of the
restaurant, is nice and cozy; the perfect place to relax over a pint of Guinness or a black and tan, especially
with the burning fireplace in wintertime. Open for lunch and dinner,
every day but Sunday.

George's on Washington Street

- 825 Washington St., Newton; (617)
  965-6628

George's is a warm and cozy neighborhood pub for the suburbs, a fine
place to stop in for a full meal or just
a drink and some munchies. It's also
a popular spot for watching a football
game on a Sunday afternoon with the
guys. Turn-of-the-century pictures of
the area adorn the walls, as do a pair
of television sets over the bar.

But this is a full restaurant with a
varied menu, where you can just as
easily come in for breakfast (served
all day) or lunch. For fun and cholesterol, try "Egg Skins" ($4.95)—deep-
fried potato skins filled with
scrambled eggs, cheddar cheese,
diced tomatoes, and scallions.

Salads are generous; soups, like
beef burgundy, are homemade. Sandwiches are big and tasty, all around
$4.75; build your own if you wish.
Burgers are thick, handmade patties
ranging from the basic ($5.50) to
chili-topped ($6.50) or the Virginia,
with ham and cheese ($6.25). All
come with thick steak fries. The
grilled reuben, as well as several vari-
ations of hot chicken breast sandwiches, are about $6.

The dinner menu has a little of
everything. A half-pound steak is
$9.95, served (like all dinners) with a
vegetable and rice or potato. There
are meaty pork ribs in barbecue sauce
($8.50) and barbecued chicken
($7.95), pastas, and seafood dishes.
Fresh, grilled rainbow trout in a
lemon-butter sauce is a very affordable $6.95.

George's has Bass Ale and other
good beers on tap, along with house
wines. Like everything else here, the
range is limited to a worthwhile selection of choices. Open 'til midnight
seven days.

The Italian Express

- 2-4 Hartford St., Newton; (617)
  332-6210
- 600 W. Cummings Park, Woburn;
  (617) 933-5156
- *Tip-free*

When Mr. C's book first came out,

this Newton cafe was a French-style place called "Oh La La." Though it appears relatively unchanged, the cuisine has moved further down the continent. It's still a fine stop for a quick eat-in or take-out meal. (Its Woburn sibling does the same for the office-park crowd.)

The traditional, southern Italian food is homemade and hearty. Just $4.25 gets you a big slab of tender spinach lasagna, slathered in tomato sauce, with a hunk of crusty bread. Same price for a hot chicken parm sandwich, made with fresh, breaded chicken breast. They "roll their own" calzone too, with various fillings. Can't decide? Go for the combo plate—eggplant, meatballs, and sausage, topped with sauce, served with pasta, bread, and a cannoli for dessert, all for $7.95. 'Course, in true European fashion, you'll have to take a nap afterwards.

Those cannoli, by the way, are also made on the premises; half of the Express is a bakery, serving up breads, pastries, and cappuccino. This side of the store has a pleasant ice cream parlor look to it, including bookshelves lined with paperbacks to leaf through while you sit 'n sip (these seem to have survived intact from the previous incarnation). If the weather's nice, you can also sit outside on the brick patio. Open weekdays from 7:30 A.M. to 7:30 P.M.; Saturdays 7:30-6; Sundays 8:30-3. Woburn hours are 7:30 to 3:30, weekdays only.

La Rotisserie
- Chestnut Hill Shopping Center (Rte. 9), Chestnut Hill; (617) 731-5335
- *Tip-free*

Tucked in next to the Star Market, La Rotisserie is a long, narrow shop geared to take-out, though they do have several tables along one wall. You can get a whole barbecued chicken, rotisseried in their gingery sauce, for $7.50, or a lemon Cornish hen for around $6.50. There is even crispy duck *a l'orange*, a bit pricier at $7.95 per pound.

Lunch and dinner plates come with two side orders; choose from real mashed potatoes, long-grain rice, squash, zucchini in tomato sauce, and others. The plates range from $4.50 to $6, including a half-chicken, barbecued ribs, a breast and rib combo, etc. Sandwich versions of these are all between $4 to $5. There are also homemade soups, salads, and pastas—not to mention their "famous" homemade gravy, available by the quart.

Lunch is available 11 A.M. to 3 P.M. Mondays through Saturdays, with dinner served until 9 P.M. Sunday hours are 12 noon to 8 P.M.

Le Grand Café
- The Mall at Chestnut Hill (Rte. 9), Chestnut Hill; (617) 244-3100

Good food in a mall? Well, this is Chestnut Hill, *dahling*, and LGC is a real find. Sure, it's not as cheap as your average food court, but this is creative, high-quality food at reasonable prices—in a restaurant with a delightful European bistro atmosphere.

Start off with one of several homemade soups, different each day; Mr. C loved his "Tuscan White Bean"—vegetables and pasta in a peppery tomato bisque. A hearty cup is $2.50. Perhaps you'll prefer a pear-and-walnut salad ($6.50), dressed with a citrus vinaigrette. Sandwiches are unique: "Roberta's Roasted Chicken Sandwich" ($7.50) may sound expensive, but it's piled high with juicy, rotisseried meat, cranberry relish, and cornbread-pecan stuffing. It's like all of Thanksgiving on a baguette. Others range from $5-$7, such as a grilled sandwich of avocado, sprouts, cheddar, and tomato for $5.50.

Dinner prices are higher, in the $10-$12 range, but they certainly are unusual. The menu changes seasonally, with such creations as "Crispy Corn Polenta with Vegetable Ragout" of asparagus, portobello mushrooms, and fennel ($10.95). Beers and fine wines are available.

Plus a dazzling array of breads, croissants (of course), fancy desserts (not so cheap), and coffees. Great

grabs if you're not going to sit and
eat. It's all in a bustling but elegant
setting that will transport you straight
to *les halles de Paris*—especially on
Thursday and Friday evenings, when
live jazz guitar is added to the mix.
Breakfasts are served in the morning,
and take-out all day. Makes a fine
stop after an early movie down the
street, too. Open from 9 A.M. to 9:30
P.M. daily.

Sabra
* 45 Union St., Newton; (617)
  964-9275

The spelling "Newton Centre" should
tell you already that this is not the
sort of neighborhood in which Mr. C
often hangs out. Yet, among the
snooty shops across from the Green
Line station, this Middle Eastern restaurant combines inexpensive cuisine
with refined surroundings.

The menu is a pedigree of Israeli,
Lebanese, Greek, and Armenian
dishes; unlike their homelands, these
all co-exist quite peacefully. Try a
bowl of lamb curry soup ($3.25) to
lead off with a bit of spice. The
"Mazah Plate" ($13.95) is a sort of
Mediterranean pu-pu platter for two,
with Armenian salad, baba ganoush,
hummus, falafel, spanakopita (spinach cheese pie), and meatless grape
leaves.

Many dinners are priced under
$10, all served with rice pilaf and a
big salad. Mr. C enjoyed the goulash
($8.95), chunks of beef cooked with
carrots and string beans. Vegetarian
dishes are even lower: You may find
unusual specials, like "Pumpkin Kib-
bee," a mixture of bulgar wheat,
mashed pumpkin, and onions, fried
into cakes and served over rice.

But the true bargains are the sandwich versions of the entrees. For just
$4.95, the chicken kebab sandwich is
a two-hands-on affair of tasty, hot
chicken in tahini sauce, stuffed into a
pita pocket with chopped vegetables.
Be warned, though, these are messy—
and fun.

Finish your dinner with one of several liqueur-coffee drinks: Sabra (of
course), Sambuca, Kahlua, and more.

The atmosphere is relaxed and invit-
ing, with exposed brick walls and potted plants everywhere. There is also a
cozy, full bar in a separate room. All
this, and friendly service, makes
Sabra a nice choice for an inexpensive date that definitely won't feel
"cheap." Open 'til 10 P.M. daily.

Sandwich Works
* 827 Beacon St., Newton; (617)
  332-6777
* 1284 Washington St., Newton;
  (617) 244-1211
* Route 9 & Lyman St.,
  Westborough; (508) 870-1766
* 10 Mt. Vernon St., Winchester;
  (508) 729-1857
* *Tip-free*

These tasty little shops are like a
cross between fast-food and a local
deli. The service is over-the-counter
and quick, with tables in a pleasant,
if basic, eating area. All yer basic hot
and cold sandwiches are here, from
grilled cheese ($1.95) to BLT ($2.75)
to roast beef ($3.75). You get your
choice of breads and rolls, and side
orders of cole slaw or "Red Bliss" potato salad are an extra 60¢ each.

What Mr. C really enjoys here are
the special grilled sandwiches, like
the "West Newton" ($3.85)—ham,
turkey, Swiss, and cream cheese
stuffed into dark rye, hot and juicy.
Or try the garden pocket ($3.65)—
broccoli, squash, zucchini, peppers,
and carrots marinated in a special
dressing with cheese, served in Syr-
ian bread. Plus daily specials, soups,
quiches, and more.

Daily newspapers are on sale, making this a nice place to hang out and
relax. SW also makes note of their de-
cision to use healthy, lighter cooking
oils and recyclable materials. That's
always to be applauded! Hours vary
at different locations.

Stromboli's
* 187 North St., Newton; (617)
  630-0002
* 37 Beach St., Manchester; (508)
  526-7774
* 12 Green St., Woburn; (617)
  935-0070

Tired of the big gourmet pizza

chains? (Uno who they are...) This family-run local landmark is every bit as good—better, in Mr. C's opinion. Not that you'd ever suspect fancy food from the outside; the Newton restaurant, in particular, looks like a stucco-covered, roadside sub shop. Wrong.

Fifteen varieties of pizza range from $5.95 for the small basic to $12.95 for the large-size "Garlic Glazed Chicken." Other toppings include shrimp, goat cheese, toasted sesame seeds, artichoke hearts—some thirty in all. The brick-ovened crust is thin and crunchy, the ingredients fresh, and the atmosphere is attractive and cozy. Two people can share even a small pizza, adding salads or soup, and come away satisfied for well under ten bucks each.

Fancy pasta dinners are also made on the premises. Most are priced from $7-$10, a bit higher than in the past; but portions are good and the quality easily matches that of fine (read: expensive) Italian restaurants. The newer menu boasts such cutesy creations as "Chicken Calabrese The Way It Should Be" ($9.25), served with pasta on the side. Beer and good wines are available.

Lunches are more reasonably priced, served from 11-3; pizzas for one are just $3.95, pastas $5-$6. And seniors (60+) get early-bird specials on weekdays and all day Sundays. Stromboli's cooks from 11 A.M. to 10 P.M. daily, Sundays from noon.

The Ultimate Bagel Company
- 118 Needham St., Newton; (617) 964-8990
- 335 Newbury St., Boston; (617) 247-1010
- 1310 Massachusetts Ave., Cambridge; (617) 876-0777

See the listing under "Boston."

SOMERVILLE

Dolly's Late Night Restaurant
- 382 Highland Ave., Somerville; (617) 628-0888

Attention night owls! Near Davis Square, this place lives up to its name, opening every night at 11 P.M. and serving food until 4 A.M. on weekdays, 5 A.M. on weekends. It's very popular with the Tufts crowd; this, plus a certain lack of competition, can make Dolly's a tough table late at night.

The menu is a sort of twist on classic greasy-spoon. Have a grilled cheese and tomato sandwich for $2.25, or a hamburger with bacon, lettuce, and tomato for $3.65. The chicken-salad sandwich ($4.75), when it's on the daily blackboard, is made with giant hunks of chicken breast piled high on a bed of lettuce in a bulkie roll and served with fries. Use both hands.

You can also get a huge Western omelette ($5.25), chicken fingers ($3.95), French toast ($2.55), or a tossed salad ($3.25). Then it gets weirder, with a vast assortment of combinations like sirloin steak and eggs for $5.99. Even Mr. C, a confirmed night person, finds that a bit much for the hour. Still, when you have that craving for a chocolate milkshake in the middle of the night, Dolly's is the place to go.

11th Chapter Saloon
- 336A Union Square, Somerville; (617) 628-4300

In these troubled economic times, most folks know what the term "Chapter 11" means. Well, laying low at the 11th Chapter Saloon is a fine way to help anyone out of a fiscal crisis. This small but elegant-looking bar has great food and beers—requiring little in the way of liquid assets.

From the red brick walls to the dark wooden bar, ceiling fans, and green-shaded lamps, this could be an insider's hangout on Wall Street. Tight quarters put the kitchen right behind the bar—a flame grill that regularly flares up to add a little drama, and great smells, to the atmosphere. Burgers are thick half-pounders served on a bulkie roll with cheese, lettuce, tomato, and fries for $4.50. They serve lunch here too, when you can get combination specials like a half-sandwich and soup for $3, or some chili and a small salad for $3.25.

The real bargains here, though, are the entrees, served until 11 P.M. Steak tips ($6) and pork chops ($6.50) are thick and juicy cuts of meat, flame-grilled in a lip-smacking marinade, served with fries, plus lettuce and carrot sticks. A blackboard of daily specials may add grilled striped marlin for $6.25.

The fine selection of beers includes Anchor Steam, Foster's Lager, and New Amsterdam Ale. On Thursdays through Saturdays, the 11th Chapter presents local bands; the bookings lean toward rhythm and blues. Space is scarce, yeah, but...hey, there's no cover charge. See? Life is good, even if you *are* bankrupt. Open daily.

Johnny D's Uptown Restaurant & Music Club

- 17 Holland St., Somerville; (617) 776-2004

It's been over a quarter-century since Johnny DeLellis founded this Davis Square delight, but the food and ambiance are totally up-to-date. The restaurant cooks with only natural and organic foods and filtered water, just as it cooks with hot live blues bands most nights of the week (see the listing under "Entertainment—Music").

Even if you don't give a hoot about health, the food is just plain terrific. Start with a tomato and feta cheese salad, with a baguette, for $3.95. Individual cheese pizzas are $5.50—a buck or two more with various toppings.

Entrees include both the meaty and meat-free: Try "Chicken Lind-say," a chicken breast with a wine, tomato, and mushroom sauce, served over rice for $8.95. Meanwhile, tofu with ginger and vegetables on a bed of noodles is $6.95. And JD's has great pasta dishes, like penne in an unusual tomato sauce laced with fennel and olives ($7.95).

On Saturdays and Sundays, you can enjoy the famous brunch spread of blintzes, omelettes, fruit, and pancakes that were recently lauded as the "Best of Boston" by *Boston* magazine. The $5.99 "Brunch Combo" lets you pick and choose from these and other options. Open for breakfast, lunch, and dinner, seven days a week; the kitchen stops serving dinner at 9:30 P.M., though lighter fare is usually available until 11 P.M.

Mike's Restaurant

- 9 Davis Square, Somerville; (617) 628-2379
- *Tip-free*

From outside this prominent corner location in the heart of Davis Square, Mike's looks like your average pizza and sub shop—but when was the last time you saw a shrimp scampi pizza?

This place has a whole lot to offer beyond the basics, which are terrific to begin with. Everything's homemade, including fresh sauce and pizza dough made up daily. The prices make it easy to try 'em all, like just $6.45 for a hefty plate of fettucine Alfredo with garlic bread. Or try the lobster ravioli, and the veggie lasagna.

Veal, chicken, and shellfish dinners, around $8-$10, come in all the traditional Italian styles—cacciatore, marsala, parmagiana—with pasta, salad, and bread. As for the wide variety of pizzas, Monday is the time to go: Buy any large pie, and get a second large one for free (plus $2 for toppings).

Mike's has an impressive selection of beverages to wash all this down: imported drinks like orzata, the almond soda commonly found in Europe, plus pitchers of beer and over a hundred special brews in bottles. With its bright orange formica ta-

MR. CHEAP'S PICKS
Somerville

✔ **Dolly's Late Night Restaurant**—A greasy spoon that doesn't even *open* until 11:00 at night.

✔ **Neighborhood Restaurant**—Tiny spot brimming with Portuguese cooking. Brunches will stuff you silly.

✔ **O'Sullivan's Pub**—Cozy bar with perhaps the biggest, cheapest burger Mr. C has ever had.

✔ **Sound Bites**—Seattle-style coffeehouse comes to Somerville.

bles, menu signs lining the walls, and hostesses calling your name over the microphone to pick up your order, Mike's is not exactly big on ambiance; just the portions. Which would you choose? Open until midnight, seven days a week.

Mt. Vernon Restaurant

• 14 Broadway, Somerville; (617) 666-3830

On one side, Mt. Vernon is one of those longtime family-style establishments where people order baked "padaydas" with their steaks or "New England Boiled Dinners." On the other side, it's a lively, casual pub with a separate menu and the Sox on the tube.

Along with two-for-one dinners in the restaurant, the pub offers good bargains. Here, you can have fish and chips for $5.95, macaroni and cheese for $2.95, or a broiled chicken dinner for $6.95. Dinners include salad, potatoes, vegetables, and bread. Sometimes, both sides share the daily specials, such as chicken parmigiana with pasta for $5.95.

Whichever side you're on, you'll get plenty of food, with quick service. The place is just outside of Sullivan Square in Charlestown; getting there by car can be tricky, thanks to Route 93 and the bus station, but once you make it, they have plenty of parking in the back. Open 11 A.M. to 11 P.M. daily.

Neighborhood Restaurant and Bakery

• 25 Bow St., Somerville; (617) 628-2151

Somerville's Union Square has several Portuguese family-style restaurants, several of which are reasonably priced; this is Mr. C's favorite. It's small and crowded, made even more so by the huge, home-cooked platters of food.

Let's start with breakfast, served from 7 A.M. to 3 P.M. It may not *seem* cheap; three eggs and toast are $4.39. But these come with fresh fruit, home fries, coffee, and NRB's fabulous homemade Portuguese sweet bread. The real bargains are on the weekends, with brunch deals like Belgian waffles with homemade syrup, eggs, bacon, linguica sausage, corn bread, sweet bread, fruit, juice, *and* coffee—all for $5.95.

Lunches and dinners, again, are enormous. "Portuguese-style fillets" is a plate of haddock, scallops, and shrimp, for $8.95; for even bigger appetites, go for their paella ($13.95)—chunks of fish, shrimp, sausage, and vegetables in a mountain of yellow rice. A friend of Mr. C's does this so often that the waiters have a doggie bag ready to go. There's enough for two meals.

More moderately priced choices on the lengthy menu include Portuguese-style pork chops ($8), and mussels in tomato sauce ($7). Be sure to ask about the homemade soup of the day ($1.75 a cup), and save room for a dessert flan ($1.25). You can also buy loaves of fresh-baked walnut bread for just a dollar apiece; day-old loaves, if any, are 75¢ each. Open for breakfast, lunch, and dinner Mondays through Saturdays, until 10 P.M. Sundays, they close at 3 P.M.

The Oasis Grille
- 255 Washington St., Somerville; (617)666-5122

This Union Square establishment turns out healthy interpretations of classic Armenian and Middle Eastern dishes. Everything here is grilled with strong and unusual seasonings, such as ground sumac (sounds dangerous, but it isn't).

Start off with an appetizer of sautéed spinach ($3.95), or a large and garden-fresh Greek salad with feta and olives ($4.35). Sandwiches are substantial and outstanding. For $4-$5, you can get broiled chicken, lamb, beef or *losh* (ground sirloin) chunks, rolled into a huge pita with lettuce, tomatoes, onions—and pickled turnips for an extra punch. Vegetarian choices are just as delicious, including a grilled falafel burger or a *labne* sandwich of yogurt, olives, lettuce and tomatoes (both $3.95).

Entrees include all kinds of shish kebabs ($7-$8); *lahmajune*, a thin meaty "pizza" ($6.75); or a tasty stew of string beans, tomatoes and onions ($6.95). But it's the extra touches that win raves from Mr. C. First of all, with any entree, you get warm pita bread *with* hummus (free!). And pay attention to the stuff around the plate—the rice pilaf is the real Armenian kind, but prepared in an Asian rice cooker, making it soft and flavorful.

Only one caveat about this restaurant: It has no air conditioning, so it's no "oasis" in the summer—but this food is worth a little sweat. Open Mondays through Thursdays from 11 A.M. to 9 P.M.; Fridays and Saturdays until 10.

O'Sullivan's Pub
- 282 Beacon St., Somerville; (617) 491-9638

If you look in the dictionary under "dive," you'll probably find a picture of O'Sullivan's Pub next to it. However, dives sometimes hide great food, and if you like burgers, check out this neighborhood spot. It's not as dark and smoky as some, and the grill behind the bar yields one of the best burger deals in town.

The entire menu of burgers and sandwiches fits on one board; Mr. C decided to splurge for the deluxe burger. This consisted of a half-pound of fresh meat, nice and plump, on a big bulkie roll, with lettuce, tomato, mayonnaise, a slice of cheese, a strip of bacon, a slice of ham, and potato chips. How much? Get ready—$3.50. A pint of Bass Ale completed the picture beautifully.

Guinness and other Irish brews are on tap, which fit in with the Ireland travel posters and the dart boards on the walls. The gentleman behind the bar was very friendly, and for that matter, the customers seemed accepting of outsiders too. It's like a Somerville "Cheers." Open 'til midnight seven days.

Picante Mexican Grill
- 217 Elm St., Somerville; (617) 628-6394
- 735 Massachusetts Ave., Cambridge; (617) 576-6394
- *Tip-free*

It's Mexican food for yuppies. The atmosphere at Picante is bright and fun, while the menu is short and simple. Have a taco, cheese quesadilla, or flauta (soft corn tortilla filled with chicken and fried), served with rice, black beans, and salad, for $4.95. Choose any two items for $6.50. An order of nachos is also $4.95, and you can avail yourself of the salsa bar, with various spicy sauces for dipping.

Burritos are a good bet, filled with cheese, rice, beans, and a mild sauce; they range from $4-$6, with your choice of chicken, steak, or (for veggie fans) char-grilled squash and mushrooms. Taco salads ($4.95) are also huge, served in an edible crisp corn tortilla bowl. It's packed with lettuce, carrot sticks, and other vegetables, guacamole, sour cream, black beans, cheese, and sauteed chicken or steak.

There is no liquor license (and no smoking allowed anywhere), but the interesting drinks include a tasty non-alcoholic sangria ($2) and "agua de pina" ($1.50), a tall, sweet cup of pineapple juice with chunks of fruit in it. Very refreshing. And if you have room for dessert, there's home-made flan for $3. Open daily.

The Rosebud Diner

- 381 Summer St., Somerville; (617) 666-6015

This diner is in the true railroad car style, with a handsome black lacquer exterior, parked a block from Davis Square. It's been around since 1941, with a few periods of dormancy—some of which were imposed after run-ins with local officials—but that too is in the past. Refurbished in the spring of 1995, the Rosebud once again serves up good ol' diner food to throngs of customers. Get here early; there are only half a dozen booths plus a long counter, and when Mr. C visited in the middle of the afternoon, the place was full up.

Appetizers include such standards as clam chowder ($3.50) and nachos ($5.25), and less-common offerings like fried zucchini strips ($3.25). Sandwiches all come with cole slaw or French fries. Double-decker BLTs are $4.50, while a fried crab sandwich is $6.95. Half-pounder burgers, served with fries, start at $4 for the basic, up to $5.25 for a "Blue Boy" topped with bleu cheese.

Main dishes include a ten-ounce sirloin steak for just $8.95, or marinated chicken breast, a mere $4.95. But the Rosebud doesn't stop at classic comfort foods; specialties like swordfish in balsamic vinaigrette ($8.95) or fettucini primavera ($6.95) add a nice twist. Sure, the prices may have inched up a bit since the 1940s, when a full turkey dinner was 50¢— but the Rosebud Diner is still affordable and fun. Open from 7 A.M. to 11 P.M., seven days a week.

Rudy's Cafe

- 248 Holland St., Somerville; (617) 623-9201

Rudy's Cafe is a lot like the trendy Tex-Mex restaurants downtown, but in a neighborhood setting—with prices to match. The place seems to have a "mascot" of a big, colorful parrot (stuffed, painted, neon). They also have a full-sized motorcycle parked above the door. The atmosphere is bustling and fun.

The large menu has most entrees priced in the $5-to-$8 range. And these ain't exactly snack items. "El Grande" is a large tortilla dish, filled with beef ($6.50) or chicken ($6.75) along with beans, cheese, lettuce, and tomatoes. It's topped with sauce, cheese, sour cream, and guacamole. Should put a dent in most appetites. The true bargains, though, are Rudy's combination plates: Combo #3, for example, consists of a guacamole taco, an enchilada verde (very spicy), and a small bean and cheese burrito— with rice, sour cream, and guac on the side—for $6.95.

Plus burgers and sandwiches from about $5. More substantial entrees include pollo al carbon ($8.50), a spicy grilled breast of marinated chicken; and baby back ribs ($9.95 half, $12.95 full rack). The bar is stocked with a wide assortment of American and international beers, including Negro Modelo and Pacifico Claro—not to mention creative tequila concoctions. Open daily.

Sound Bites

- 708 Broadway, Somerville; (617) 623-8338

One of the earlier entries into Boston's coffeehouse craze, this Ball Square shop does the latté-and-scone scene one better. Sound Bites—love the name—adds a full breakfast and lunch menu, with creative touches and low prices.

Starting at 6:30 A.M. on weekdays, the kitchen whips up treats like thick "raisin custard" French toast ($4.69, with home fries). Heartier appetites should try the "2+2+2"—that's eggs, pancakes, bacon, and toast, two of each—all for $4.29. Somerville/Cambridge earthy types will appreciate the vegan, spinach version of eggs Benedict, known here as "Green, Eggs, No Ham" (anyone who grew up with Dr. Seuss will get that sound bite).

Plus lowfat muffins, Kupel's bagels, granola, and terrific coffee served in those wide, deep bowl-cups. Lunch switches over to an American-Mediterranean menu, with falafel, kebabs, grilled cheese sandwiches, burgers, salads, and more vegan options. Just about all are in the $3-$5 range, lovingly done (and devoured).

Service in this cozy storefront can be erratic at times, but everybody stays friendly enough—and it's certainly worth a wait. Sound Bites opens up at 8 A.M. on weekends for brunch; they close up at 4 P.M. Saturdays through Mondays, and 11 P.M. Tuesdays through Fridays.

WALTHAM / WATERTOWN

Arsenal Diner

- 356 Arsenal St., Watertown; (617) 926-8371

This friendly little place, down a bit from the Arsenal Mall, caters mostly to working folks—but, of course, anyone is welcome. Like so many good diners, the menu is Greek-American, the food is homemade, and the prices are great. The atmosphere is light and airy, with large windows and walls painted in a Mediterranean blue.

Mr. C started off with a cup of egg-lemon soup ($1.45), which really turned out to be a chicken and rice soup with a tangy, creamy stock. Mmmm. He followed it with a plump half-chicken, rotisserie-barbecued, served with rice pilaf and cooked broccoli and carrots. Plenty of good eats for just $3.95. Other platters, all around $4.50, include hot open-faced turkey, fish and chips, and spinach pie. A plate of barbecued steak tips is $5.25.

Breakfast at the Arsenal is *really* cheap. Three eggs and ham, bacon, or sausage costs $3.80; corned beef hash and eggs are just $4.50. Of course, all of these include home fries, toast, and a bottomless cup of coffee. They also make pancakes—plain, fruit, and chocolate chip. Open from 6 A.M. to 3 P.M. Mondays through Saturdays ('til 9 P.M. Thursdays and Fridays). On Sundays, they only serve breakfast, from 8 A.M. to 2 P.M.

Bagel Depot

- 879 Main St., Waltham; (617) 893-4445
- 339 Washington St., Stoughton; (617) 341-5665
- *Tip-free*

So, you've been trying to get the kids to eat spinach for years, with no luck. Try it in a bagel! Spinach is just one of many unusual varieties at this popular bakery and deli. Other flavors include sunflower, blueberry, and their famous cinnamon-apple. You can get a baker's dozen in any combination for a decent $4.98.

But man does not live by bread alone, even with one of BD's various spreads (veggie cream cheese on that spinach bagel, $1.69, is heavenly). A turkey sandwich on a bulkie roll ($4.99) is very big here in all senses of the word. Add a cup of soup and you've got a wholesome meal. And, unlike other such shops, Bagel Depot offers almost as much in the way of pastries as a full bakery. Sweets include gigantic gourmet muffins (cappuccino—mmm), only 99¢ apiece; plus cinnamon rolls and freshly baked rugelah in flavors like apricot and chocolate.

Perhaps most unusual about the Bagel Depot are its hours. The Waltham store opens every evening at 9:30 (!) closing at 3:30 P.M. the next day, and 2 P.M. on Sundays. Big appeal for the Brandeis crowd. The Stoughton branch keeps (slightly) more normal hours, from 6 A.M. to 6

MR. CHEAP'S PICKS
Waltham / Watertown

✔ **Demo's Restaurant**—
Gigantic shish kebab plates,
family-style dining. Just *try* to
get a table.

✔ **Iguana Cantina**—Fun,
party-like restaurant and bar,
with terrific food.

✔ **Verona Restaurant**—
Heaping portions of basic
Italian cooking.

P.M. weekdays, 6 A.M. to 3:30 P.M. Saturdays, and 'til 2 P.M. Sundays.

Demo's Restaurant
- 64 Mt. Auburn St., Watertown;
  (617) 924-9660
- *Tip-free*

At this longtime Greek favorite just outside of Watertown Square, full meals come in well under $10. "Our Specialty, Shish Kebab," the menu says proudly; and for $7.60 you can get two gigantic skewers of beef, chicken, baked lamb, or a combination—flame-grilled and served on a heaping bed of rice with tomato sauce. The price includes an equally large plate of Greek salad and pita bread. If your stomach is smaller and you don't want a doggie bag, get the "open sandwich" version—one large kebab, salad, rice, and bread for just $4.05. It's still a filling meal, and amazingly cheap.

Another favorite of Mr. C is the beef stew, a tasty bowl with large, tender chunks of meat in a tomato stock, served with rice or French fries and a salad for $3.65. The Greek sausage plate ($4.75) or the veal cutlet ($4.05) are also wonderful. There is also a full bar, house drafts for $1.25, and Greek wines.

Demo's is a good deal, and it shows. The atmosphere is bustling and friendly, with lots of families. The system is a hybrid: Stand in line to place your order and pay, find a table, and the counter staff brings the food over. (How do they always manage to *find* you? Amazing.) You may have to share part of a long table at peak times. Sure, it's no frills here, but at these prices, who's complaining? Open Mondays through Saturdays 11 A.M. to 9:30 P.M., Sundays from noon.

Iguana Cantina
- 313 Moody St., Waltham; (617)
  891-3039
- 577 Washington St., Stoughton;
  (617) 297-7660

From the giant mechanical iguana who greets you ("Enjoy our cantina. . .") as you enter, this place is wacky and fun. Mexican food is the specialty at this suburban pair, with creative, modern touches. Start with a cup of "Tortilla Soup" ($1.50), of chicken broth, vegetables, and crushed chips. Then try the "New Mexican Rice Casserole" ($7.95), made with andouille sausage, shrimp, chicken, veggies, cheeses, avocado. . .sort of a *paella* from this side of the Atlantic.

Of course, they also have tacos, enchiladas, and quesadillas; in fact, you can mix and match any two (with rice and beans) for $6.50, or any three for $8.50. Great fajitas, too, as well as Tex-Mex burgers and sandwiches. Beers include Corona, Harpoon, and other fine brews. Both branches offer weekly specials, like all-you-can-eat wings for $4.50, or a happy-hour taco bar for $2 a person. The place also attracts families, with "Kids Nite" discounts on Tuesdays and Sundays. Both places are open daily for lunch and dinner.

New Yorker Diner
- 39 Mt. Auburn St., Watertown;
  (617) 924-9772

For some reason, Watertown is blessed with a whole railroad's worth of good ol' friendly diners. The New Yorker is a longtime favorite; nothing fancy, just the basics. They do use scali bread for the French toast, though—a nice touch—for $3.75; it's

$5 with bacon or corned beef hash. Burgers and sandwiches are good-sized; a bacon cheeseburger is $3.80. There are daily specials, too, like a ham plate for $4.95.

The New Yorker, taking its name seriously, is especially kind to night owls like Mr. C. Breakfast is served all day, although the day ends at 2 P.M. An "early bird" breakfast special actually runs until 11 A.M., with two eggs, toast, home fries, and coffee, plus ham, bacon, sausage, or hash, for $3.25. Best of all, the diner is open on Wednesday through Saturday nights *starting* at 11 P.M., serving 'til 4 A.M.

Around the corner, you'll find similar food and hours at **Pat's Diner**, 11 North Beacon St., telephone (617) 924-9872; and further up Mt. Auburn toward Cambridge, the true dining-car-shaped **Town Diner** at 627 Mt. Auburn St., (617) 924-9789. Fill up that coffee again, miss, willya?

Verona Restaurant

- 18 Mt. Auburn St., Watertown; (617) 926-0010

The Verona is a humble local establishment with a loyal following and great value. Just because one cannot afford high prices, Mr. C says, one should not have to give up variety! So this is the kind of restaurant he loves—one could dine here every night for a month and not have the same meal twice.

Starting with pasta, choices already bombard you. Pick spaghetti, shells, or ziti, and top it with homemade meat sauce for $7.50; with meat sauce and sausage or meatballs for $8.75; white clam sauce for $8.95; and more. Or have these with homemade fettucine for a dollar extra. Moving on to other dishes, baked lasagna ($8.95) is a mountainous slab with fresh sauce poured over the top. The Italian combo plate is equally generous: A veal cutlet, ravioli, meatballs, shells, and sausage, all for $10.25.

With most entrees you get a side order of pasta and cooked vegetables; but the menu itself goes well beyond Neapolitan fare. Try the homemade lobster meat cutlets, with a crabmeat sauce ($9.75); all seafood is brought in fresh daily.

The Verona offers several interesting desserts, including "Creme Brulee à la Ritz" ($3.50), a sweet custard topped with caramel sauce. The restaurant, recently remodeled, has a family atmosphere; the menu is printed on the placemats, and most of the tables are booths. Closed Mondays.

Vietfoods Restaurant

- 627 Main St., Waltham; (617) 894-9783

More and more people are finding out about this suburban secret, as evidenced by its recent move to larger quarters across from Waltham City Hall; even so, the prices seem too good to be true. This cozy, family-run establishment is what the "new" Waltham scene is all about; inexpensive, authentic, ethnic dining.

Spring roll appetizers (vegetarian and non-veg) are $2 a plate, served with spicy and mild sauces. From there, move on to entrees like "Meatless House Noodles" ($4.25), laced with carrots, scallions, onions, tofu, and bean sprouts. Mr. C opted for a flavorful lemon grass chicken ($6.75). In fact, the most expensive dish on the menu is the "Crispy Hen" at $8.50; yes, this is a whole game hen—stuffed with pork, mushrooms, onions, scallions and rice sticks—then sewn tight, steamed, and deep fried. Now, *that's* different.

Portions are generous; most entrees can be easily shared. The service here is friendly, if a bit slow—but the food makes it well worth the wait. Open for lunch and dinner, every day but Mondays.

Why Not

- 106 Main St., Watertown; (617) 923-9219

This cute little place just outside of the square takes a creative approach to breakfast and lunch. Mornings offer plates like the "222," two each of eggs, pancakes, and bacon, all for

$3.50. Homemade muffins are only 85¢ apiece, in scrumptious blueberry, corn, apple, and banana. Why, you can even get a single large egg, any way you want it, with home fries and toast for a mere $1.50. When was the last time you got a whole meal for a buck-fifty?

Lunches range from various burgers ($2.75-$3.50 and named, for some reason, after historic New Englanders) to vegetarian roll-up sandwiches. Mr. C loved his "Chicken Veggie" ($4.15), juicy slices of white meat with lettuce, broccoli, tomato, ranch dressing, and melted cheese, all rolled into a pita. Almost nothing on this vast menu tops five dollars, except perhaps some seasonal specials—like "Tomato Surprise" ($5.75), a "tuliped" whole tomato filled with tuna, chicken, or egg salad, served with cottage cheese on a bed of lettuce. Of course, such healthy fare leaves plenty of room for a slice of homemade coconut cream pie ($1.95) afterwards . . .

Open from 6 A.M. every day but Sunday, Why Not serves only until 3 P.M. on weekdays, and 12 noon on Saturdays. The place does a brisk business at peak times, making take-out a good option if you're in a hurry.

OUTER SUBURBS

NORTH SUBURBS

Chadwick's
- 903 Waltham St., Lexington; (617) 861-1166

If you don't mind the feeling that you're crashing somebody's birthday party, you'll have no problem enjoying a meal at Chadwick's. Defining itself as an ice cream parlor with food, this popular spot on the Lexington-Waltham line is an *homage* to the turn of the century, from its suspenders-and-straw-hat-clad employees and red brick walls to the ragtime music bouncing over the sound system.

And, although the prices aren't quite such a throwback, they sure are reasonable. Thick, juicy burgers range in price from $2.75 to $4.20, while club sandwiches served with steak fries max out at $5.25. Mr. C was impressed with a deal of clam chowder, a garden salad, and half a turkey sandwich for $4.90.

Most diners here are families, no doubt attracted as much by the "Kiddies" menu (a burger or hot dog and fries, $2.50) as by the famous desserts. Some two dozen flavors of ice cream are made in-house. Six different sundaes are priced at $3.25; an immense banana split is $4.50. A side counter area also serves ice cream for take-out.

Incidentally, you probably *will* be crashing not one but several birthday parties, since Chadwick's offers a free sundae to such honorees (of any age). A drum roll, a startling holler of "Ladeeez and gentlemen!," and a chorus of the traditional song are sure to ring out at least once during your visit. This cheerful place is open seven days a week from 11 A.M. to 10 P.M., and until 11 P.M. on Fridays and Saturdays.

Kelly's Roast Beef
- 410 Revere Beach Blvd., Revere; (617) 284-9129
- *Tip-free*

In the distance, a crowd of people ambles along Revere Beach, converging purposefully upon a corner location. Some sort of waterfront revival meeting? No, it's just a typical evening outside Kelly's, *the* stop along this stretch of historic honky-tonk.

The building with the jolly, blade-wielding butcher astride the roof only does take-out, but there are plenty of tables under a pavilion just across the street. Work your way through the eager crowd to the windows, and you'll find those famous roast beef sandwiches in two sizes, small ($3.25) and large ($4.59)—more accurately described as "hefty" and "immobilizing." There's no pretension here: just a big pile of beef on a bun, warm, juicy, and delicious.

Add some terrific steak fries, available in three sizes. Mr. C unwittingly passed on the small ($1.25) in favor of the medium ($2.50); hoooo-boy. Potato farmers broke their backs gathering that order. Fortunately, there were enough seagulls around to help finish up.

Other artery-clogging goodies include fish and chips for $5.50, and cheeseburgers for $1.95. All of the foods here are made with fresh ingredients, never frozen or made up in advance; and it's obvious that nothing around here lasts long enough to get old. Afterwards—if you have room—stroll further up the strip to Kelly's Kremes for something sweet, like a "Banana Bucket," the perfect finale. Kelly's is open for lunch and dinner every day of the year except Thanksgiving and Christmas.

New Bridge Cafe
- 650 Washington Ave., Chelsea; (617) 884-0134

Distinguished by a pretty plum-colored awning that seems out of place in a residential section of Chelsea, the New Bridge Cafe must also overcome a rather narrow interior. Duck in the door and slip past the long bar, where you will find tables jammed into two different dining areas. Fortunately, the meals are plenty large enough; the cafe further makes up for its size by serving

SOUTH SUBURBS

Bagel Depot
- 339 Washington St., Stoughton; (617) 341-5665
- 879 Main St., Waltham; (617) 893-4445

See the listing under "Waltham/ Watertown."

┌─────────────────────────────────┐
│   │
│   **MR. CHEAP'S PICKS**   │
│   **North Suburbs**   │
│   ─────────────   │
│   │
│ ✔ **New Bridge Cafe**—A tiny   │
│   place in Chelsea that serves │
│   up huge portions of bar food.│
│   │
└─────────────────────────────────┘

up steak tips which some reviewers have called Boston's best.

A nice, big order of bread almost beat Mr. C to the table, always a good sign. Despite a tempting special of the day (baked scallops, $7.95), he just had to go for those sirloin steak tips, marinated in the restaurant's own barbecue sauce and served with a choice of salad, rice, fries, or pasta, all for a striking $6.95. The order was immense and delicious. Pork tips, lamb tips, and country-style ribs, all around $7, are also great deals; get a combination of any two for $7.65.

The remainder of the menu includes a number of pasta dishes ($4.75-$6.95) and sandwiches ($4.95, with big, curly steak fries, gnarled like tree branches), but it's crazy to look past the tip dinners; add a salad for $1.50 to feel better about yourself.

There is, of course, a full bar to go with the food. New Bridge's lounge-type decor appears not to have changed since the 1970s, but no one seems to mind. Talk about overcoming a Napoleonic complex—this tiny place sure gives you a lot. The kitchen is open until 10:45 P.M. every night, Sundays 'til 10 P.M.

DeeDee's Lounge
- 297 Newport Ave., Quincy; (617) 328-5938

Mr. C often remarks that bar food tends to be inexpensive; DeeDee's not only manages that in spades, but it also cooks up far more than your average variety of pub lunch choices. Throw in its convenient location—so close to the Wollaston "T" station that you could have a beer between trains—and you'll see why it's a local favorite.

Mondays through Thursdays, burgers, hot dogs, and personal-size pizzas are all $1 each, all day long. On weekends, these pizzas run $3-$4, and burgers $2.50. Catch a sporting event on one of five televisions, have a pint of Guinness, and order some 50¢ fries.

Lunch specials, served between 11 A.M. and 2 P.M., offer heartier fare. For $4.95, try baked macaroni and cheese with ham; fettucine Alfredo with turkey; or a "Fisherman's Platter" of fried scallops and shrimp. Soups like minestrone ($1.25/cup, $2.50/bowl) and thick clam chowder ($2.75) are good bets, too. The decor could best be described as incongruous, but the atmosphere is generally amiable. The kitchen closes at 10:30 P.M. daily.

Finian's
- 910 Washington St., Dedham; (617) 329-0097
- 1657 Hancock St., Quincy; (617) 770-2592

Is there a greater thrill than sitting down to a meal you can't finish—only to have *free* dessert and coffee forced upon you? It happens at this pair of friendly establishments.

Sink into a comfy booth in the spacious bar, done up in dark wood, and take your time ordering. First scan the blackboard specials, such as vegetarian fajitas ($4.50), a turkey dinner ($7.50), or Cajun catfish ($8.50). Super-specials, available Mondays and Tuesdays, include prime rib ($9.95) and barbecued beef ribs ($7.95). All entrees come with your choice of potato, plus soup or an enormous salad.

Mr. C conjured up a hearty London broil in mushroom gravy, $7.95, one of several options "from the stockyard." Chicken selections run $7-$8, while seafood entrees are around $8-$12. Speaking of fowl, be an early bird and visit between 3 and 5 P.M. to get that free coffee and dessert deal. And in Quincy, cap off your day with a movie at the nearby cinema; any food purchase gets you a half-price ticket to that evening's show.

Finian's, whose kitchen closes at 10 P.M. five days and 11 P.M. Friday and Saturday, is popular with both the locals and, in Dedham, guests of the adjacent Holiday Inn. This branch offers an all-you-can-eat Sunday brunch, which costs $5.95 before 10 A.M. and $7.95 thereafter. That's no blarney.

Also in Dedham, the **Halfway Cafe** at 174 Washington St., telephone (617) 326-3336, is yer great American sports bar. Memorabilia completely obscures the walls; the newspaper-style menu unfolds to reveal a broad selection of sandwiches, grilled entrees, and pastas, mostly in the $5-$7 range. Open from 11 A.M. six days (noon on Sundays) until 11 P.M. nightly.

Iguana Cantina
- 577 Washington St., Stoughton; (617) 297-7660
- 313 Moody St., Waltham; (617) 891-3039

See the listing under "Waltham/ Watertown."

Olympian Diner
- 38 Hancock St., Braintree; (617) 843-9026

Blue-plate specials of the gods? Well, Mr. C thinks so. This is nothing but your classic, stainless-steel, caboose-style diner, serving up heaping portions of worldly food.

At breakfast, one egg with Portuguese sausage, home fries, and toast all comes to a whopping $2.65. Homemade corned beef hash and two eggs, same sides, is $3.35. Lunch moves up to varying daily specials, like a terrific shepherd's pie ($4.25, with a vegetable), fish and chips (same price), or broiled rainbow trout ($5.10). Bottled beers and chablis are available.

The basics, like burgers, sandwiches, and salad plates, are all covered too. And Olympian's chowder ($1.55 a cup) has been named the area's best in several annual competitions. All this, and super-friendly service, makes a seat here tough to find during the breakfast and lunch rush. Open weekdays only, from 6 A.M. to 7 P.M.

S and S Beale St. Diner
- 17 Beale St., Quincy; (617) 479-1806

Having recently undergone a change in management, the Beale St. Diner has also expanded its menu. Two U-shaped counters give one room that classic coffee-shop charm, while plenty of tables give the other section a casual restaurant feel.

Order yourself a gargantuan waffle and a cuppa joe for just $1.95; throw some blueberries on top for 75¢ more. A further buck got Mr. C four strips of bacon that started the day off right. A morning special offered two poached eggs with Canadian bacon on an English muffin, served with baked beans, juice, and coffee—all for a mere $3.50.

Barbecue is the specialty at lunchtime. Blue-plates go for $4.95, whether you prefer a half-chicken or roast turkey. Sirloin tips are $5.95, pork ribs $6.95. All come with a choice of two sides: Quincy baked beans, real mashed potatoes, rice pilaf, fries, and others. And every day offers a different pasta meal for $3.95.

Beale St. is also a fine place to bring the kiddies; a menu designed for them offers a burger, chicken fingers, or a foot-long hot dog (each $2.99) served with fries, a drink, and dessert. The waitstaff is friendly and, at least on Mr. C's visit, remarkably tall. The entire menu is available from 6 A.M. to 3 P.M. Mondays through Saturdays, and from 8 A.M. Sundays.

Tony's Clam Shop
- 861 Quincy Shore Dr., Quincy; (617) 773-5090
- *Tip-free*

It just wouldn't be the shore without a place to gorge yourself on fried clams, and Wollaston Beach doesn't disappoint. Tony's Clam Shop, with over thirty years of history behind it, is

---

MR. CHEAP'S PICKS
South Suburbs

✔ **S & S Beale St. Diner**—Classic diner in Quincy, with an impressive lunch menu and breakfast all day.

✔ **Town Spa**—Huge barn of a place in Stoughton turns out what may be the best thin-crust pizza on the planet.

Mr. C's choice along this stretch. It faces the beach with a front wall that's all windows, offering views of the Boston skyline along with the water. And its food, just as yummy as the nearby Clam Box, is a bit lower-priced.

Sure, you can order burgers, steak tips, and even Middle Eastern specialties here, but why would you? Enjoy a clam strip plate with generous and tasty helpings of clams, fries, and cole slaw ($7.40), and add a full ear of corn—not one of those tiny pieces common to such joints—for an additional $1.50. Servings by the box run $6-$7 for the "small" portions of clams, scallops, and shrimp; rest assured, this will be plenty for one person.

Specials may include marinated, broiled swordfish tips for $8.95. Homemade clam chowder is $2.95 for a large bowl. Order food for take-out, perch yourself (no pun intended) on the seawall, and watch the joggers and dog-walkers parade by. If the weather's not cooperative, there is indoor seating. Tony's hours are 10:30 A.M. to midnight, seven days a week, from April through October only.

Town Spa
- 1119 Washington St., Stoughton; (617) 344-2030

No, it's not a health club. Many folks consider this the best pizza on the South Shore—and some would even say all of Boston. Mr. C, who's sampled a few slices in his time, wouldn't argue.

Starting in 1955, when it was housed at the Stoughton train depot, Town Spa has moved and grown into a huge operation. Two vast dining rooms, fitted out with booths and large-screen televisions (for various ball games, natch) can barely accommodate the crowds; at peak times, you can wait up to half an hour for a table—yet, nobody leaves. A downstairs bar and lounge helps with the overflow.

Must be the pies, most priced under $5; these are all one size, just enough for two people to share (or one hearty appetite). You can have 'em topped with linguica sausage, bacon, pineapple, fresh minced garlic, or about a dozen others. Not only that, but—as Mr. C's pal in the area pointed out proudly—you can request these thin-crusted beauties "well-done" for extra crunch.

Homemade Italian specialties are again basic, but wonderful, with nightly specials like a plate of lasagna for a mere $3.95. Plus sandwiches, burgers, and plenty of finger foods to go with a brewski and the Sox. Pizzas and sandwiches are served until midnight every day; there is a separate take-out kitchen at one side of the spacious new digs, if you just can't wait.

Of course, some would say the pizza at the **Lynwood Cafe**, relatively close by, is every bit as good. The menu at this divey watering hole is simple; none of your sundried-to-matoes-with-a-dash-of-pesto *here*. Individual-sized pies are made to order, for about five bucks. They come out of the oven steaming hot; plan to wait about 25 minutes, or be like Mr. C and call in your order ahead of time. The Lynwood is at 320 Center St., Randolph, telephone (617) 963-9894. Serving nightly until midnight.

WEST SUBURBS

Comella's

- 245 Washington St. (Rte. 16), Wellesley; (617) 431-2359
- *Tip-free*

Comella's will stuff you until you can't move. Everything is homemade and hearty, with nothing fancy; shells "and gravy" (that's red sauce to the uninitiated), veal parmigiana, cheese lasagna. Mr. C tried a "Parmigiana Sampler" for $5.99—several large pieces of both chicken and eggplant, served over pasta, drowning in tomato sauce. Couldn't finish. The lasagna is out of this world. And they even make fat-free pastas, as if anyone comes here to diet. By the way, the restaurant in Charlestown and the Burlington Mall version have closed.

Ebenezer's

- 417 Waverly St. (Rte. 135), Framingham; (508) 626-2220

Neatly housed in the (still working) Framingham train depot, Ebenezer's is a huge restaurant and bar with a lot

going on. Several large rooms are filled with tables and booths, all busily decorated with vintage train signs and memorabilia. If you like this stuff, you may have a hard time keeping your eyes from darting all over.

Speaking of darts, there is a separate bar in a loft area upstairs. On Thursday evenings from 9:30 P.M., live bands play there with no cover charge. But, back to the food: It's good, standard pub fare, with big "Bah-Hum" burgers from $4.95, "All-U-Can-Eat" fajitas from $7.95 (including seafood!), steak tips ($8.95), and tons of appetizers. Food is served until midnight, a bit later on Saturdays. Lots of fine brews, too; it's a boisterous, fun place. Open daily for lunch and dinner.

50's Diner

- 5 Commercial Circle, Dedham; (617) 326-1955

You may not be fooled as to what decade you're actually in here, but

LODGING

Always on the lookout for a bargain, Mr. C has tried to wade through the tricky waters of the hotel biz to find rooms where you can stay for well under $100 a night. In fact, some offer rooms for under $50 a night. These waters are tricky because hotel rates ebb and flow with the seasons. And don't forget that taxes are always going to be added on top of any quoted price. Here, then, are the results of this not-necessarily-scientific survey.

Two important tips: First of all, you should always, *always* ask about discounts. No hotel room ever has only one price. Take advantage of any discounts you can—including corporate, AAA, military personnel, American Association of Retired Persons, and others. Furthermore, if you're going to be in town long enough, ask about weekly rates.

Finally, if you can at all, be sure to make reservations—and make them *early*.

HOTELS AND MOTELS

Days Inn
- 1234 Soldiers Field Rd., Brighton, MA 02135; (617) 254-1234

Daystop
- 1800 Soldiers Field Rd., Brighton, MA 02135; (617) 254-0200
- Reservations for both: (800) 325-2525

In recent years, a pair of older motels became franchises of this well-known national budget chain. Both offer terrific values with basic amenities, and great location for just about anything in Boston, Cambridge, or Newton.

Days Inn is the larger and nicer of the two, just a mile from Harvard Square (you can see the college spires from front windows). Its 113 rooms offer color TV with free Showtime movies and air conditioning, plus an outdoor swimming pool. The lobby restaurant, Enzo on the Charles, is attractive and moderately priced; it presents live jazz every night, and at Sunday brunch. Rates in summer are $99 for a single, $109 for a double; prices drop significantly in late fall and winter.

A mile or so further from downtown, Daystop is more like your basic roadside motel. It has the same basics in each of its 55 rooms, which tend to be smaller here. There is no pool, and no fancy restaurant (just a bar/lounge). But then, they've got a newly spiffied up IHOP next door, one of the few restaurants in all of Boston that's open 24 hours! Daystop's rates are lower than its sibling, more like $79 to $89 at the height of summer, $59/$69 in the off-season.

Both motels also offer 10% discounts for AAA and AARP members. Both have free parking, and are situated across the highway (if you can get across) from a wooded, water-front park with walking and bike trails, picnic areas, and in summer, the outdoor Publick Theatre. Meanwhile, that same highway can get you downtown in ten minutes flat.

Susse Chalet
- 800 Morrissey Blvd., Boston, MA 02122; (617) 287-9100
- 900 Morrissey Blvd., Boston, MA 02122; (617) 287-9200
- 211 Concord Tpke. (Rte. 2), Cambridge, MA 02140; (617) 661-7800
- 160 Boylston St. (Rte. 9), Chestnut Hill, MA 02167; (617) 527-9000
- 385 Winter St., Waltham, MA 02154; (617) 890-2800
- *And other suburban locations*
- Toll-free reservations: (800) 5-CHALET (242538)

This Northeastern motel chain offers comfortable, basic rooms at very affordable prices. These vary by location, but some are actually as low as $50 a night for one person! Up to four people can share rooms for a similarly remarkable $80 or so, making this popular with families on the road.

Most branches offer a free continental breakfast, free parking, free local phone calls, faxing, cable TV, outdoor swimming pools, and other features. Some even have free shuttle buses to local shopping areas, and public transport stations.

MR. CHEAP'S PICKS
Hotels and Motels

✔ **Susse Chalet**—Very affordable local chain, with locations all around Boston.

Terrace Motor Lodge

- 1650 Commonwealth Ave., Boston, MA 02135; (617) 566-6260

Recently taken over as a Best Western franchise and completely renovated, this motel is a surprising find—tucked away in a residential neighborhood, just about halfway between Boston University and Boston College. Rates start around $80 for one person, $90 for two, during the summer season; winter rates come down $10 or so after October. Also,

10% AAA discounts are always offered.

Kitchenettes, outfitted with stainless steel countertops and stoves, are available at the same prices. All rooms have a refrigerator and a color TV; there's a complimentary continental breakfast in the lobby, and free off-street parking—though the Terrace is also located on the "B" branch of the Green Line trolley, making downtown convenient even if you don't have a car.

ALTERNATIVE LODGING

All New Windsor House Bed and Breakfast

- 283 Windsor St., Cambridge, MA 02139; (617) 354-7916

Heidi Lyons is an entrepreneurial Renaissance woman. Not only does she run Cambridge's popular "Weare-vers" clothing stores, but she also owns this cozy bed and breakfast nearby. Located in a residential area roughly ten minutes' walk from three Squares—Kendall, Central, and Inman—this is a great base from which to explore Cambridge.

Rates for each of the two rooms, with a shared bath, range from $50 to $80 a night, varying by room and by season. Both children and pets are welcome here (and that's unusual, as any traveling pet owners know). Rooms have air conditioners and radios; downstairs, a common area with a TV, wood-burning stove, and patio adds to the homey appeal.

Beacon Inn

- 1087 and 1750 Beacon St., Brookline, MA 02146; (617) 566-0088

Brookline offers not one, not two, but *four* guest houses along this historic stretch of Beacon Street (see also the establishments below). This pair of brownstones, one near the Boston line and one near Cleveland Circle, have been beautifully restored and kept up, with lots of nice Victorian touches. They offer cozy rooms at $79 for one person in season, and $89 for two. Out-of-season rates are about ten dollars lower.

Some of the rooms are located up the winding "servants" stairs in these converted, turn-of-the-century homes; all rooms include a continental breakfast of coffee, juice, fruit, and homemade pastries, available in the lobby. Both houses are right on the "C" branch of the Green Line, but parking is available as well, at a reasonable $5 charge. (Overnight street parking is not allowed in Brookline, and tickets are three times higher!)

Beacon St. Guest House

- 1047 Beacon St., Brookline, MA 02146; (617) 232-0292 or (800) 872-7211

Brookline Manor Guest House

- 32 Centre St., Brookline, MA 02146; (617) 232-0003 or (800) 535-5325

These townhouses have been operating as inns for about thirty years now. Both offer rooms with private or shared baths, a quiet atmosphere, and great locations in residential areas on the Green Line. Not as fancy as the Beacon Inns (above), these rooms are nevertheless comfortable and convenient.

Prices vary, but in-season rooms start as low as $59 a night for a one-person room with a private bath. Two people can stay for $69, with one or two beds. Off-season rates, as well as rooms with shared bathrooms, knock about $10 off those prices.

These are all charmingly furnished, some with high ceilings, bay windows, and even a (non-working) fireplace in a couple of rooms. All this at about half the price of the far less charismatic Holiday Inn nearby. The Brookline Manor is right in Coolidge Corner, while its counterpart is closer to Kenmore Square. Limited parking is available.

Bed & Breakfast Agency of Boston

- 47 Commercial Wharf, Boston; (617) 720-3540 or (800) 248-9262 (CITY-BNB)

Not actually a place to stay but a reservation service, Bed & Breakfast Agency of Boston connects weary travelers with host homes across the city, many in historic locations such as the waterfront, Back Bay, and Beacon Hill. Many are located in stately townhouses and 19th-century buildings, with brick walls and heavy wooden beams. Single rates run as low as $65 a night, doubles as low as $70, with tax included.

These prices include continental breakfast, plus a homey touch you just won't find at a motel. Extra perks include a 15% dinner discount at Boston's Bay Tower Room—although given his budget, Mr. C's still not likely to be at the next table—and trolley tour discounts. Additionally,

winter specials (offered from November through February), allow guests to stay three nights for the price of two.

Ultimately, diversity of lodgings is key to this agency; sometimes your night is as simple as a private room in somebody's home. Air conditioning and color TVs are common, and fully equipped kitchenettes are available. The roster is ever-changing, so call the agency and see what's available; they'll describe each setting in detail, and make all the arrangements for you.

Boston International Youth Hostel

- 12 Hemenway St., Boston, MA 02115; (617) 536-9455

Boston's only American Youth Hostel branch combines a convenient downtown location with those great hosteling prices; members stay for $16 a night (plus a $2 fee to rent a pillow and linens). Non-members will pay $19, although they're out of luck in the summer months, when the place is too busy to accept them. The hostel sleeps 200, with three to five beds in each room. Sling your pack onto a bunk and make use of two kitchens, a lounge with a color TV, and the companionship of fellow adventurers from the world over.

A former hotel just a short distance from the Hynes Convention Center/ICA "T" station on the Green Line, the hostel even organizes regular trips to baseball games, Quincy Market, and Harvard Square. Call the office for more information at (617) 536-1027.

American Youth Hostel memberships cost $25 a year, always worth it if you want to do a lot of traveling on the cheap. Call (617) 731-6692 for general membership information.

The College Club

- 44 Commonwealth Ave., Boston, MA 02116; (617) 536-9510

Founded decades ago as the nation's first private society for female college graduates, the College Club continues to thrive (even though co-eds are commonplace now) as a networking group for women in the professional world. Meanwhile, their fashionable digs in the Back Bay maintain inexpensive rooms which are open to anyone—of either gender.

Nine rooms are available to visitors, in two sizes (the rooms, not the visitors). The larger rooms, with a king or twin beds and a private bath, are $75 per night for one person, and $95 for couples; smaller singles go for just $50 a night, with a shared bathroom along the hall.

All of these are great deals for this location, especially considering that you get a continental breakfast and a heckuva lot more Olde Boston charm than you'd find at any large hotel. Windows look out on the tree-lined Comm. Ave. mall. Both the Public Garden and the Esplanade are about a block away, as are the trendy shops and art galleries of Newbury Street. What a find!

Of course, with so few rooms, vacancies can be scarce on short notice. Be as smart as any *cum laude* grad, and call ahead.

Not far away, the **Newbury Guest House** is another Back Bay B & B, with a few rooms as low as $70-$85 a night for one person, and $95 for two. This large brownstone has 32 rooms, all with private baths. It's quite elegant for the price, still lower than downtown hotels. The address is 261 Newbury St., Boston, MA 02116; telephone (617) 437-7666.

The Farrington Inn

- 23 Farrington Ave., Allston, MA 02134; (617) 787-1860

Many years ago, Bob Terwilliger and his wife started what they thought would be a humble little B & B. They're now up to 80 rooms in three different buildings, offering the most flexibility at hostel-ish prices Mr. C has ever found.

With so many different spaces, one person can get a private room around $50 a night—in season—or bunk in with fellow visitors and pay closer to $30. Groups can rent an apartment and wind up paying about $20 a person. Some rooms are dorm-

---

MR. CHEAP'S PICKS
Alternative Lodging

- ✔ **Beacon Inn**—Two attractive and cozy Victorian guest houses in Brookline.

- ✔ **The College Club**—Private club has opened its rooms to the public, right in the heart of the Back Bay.

- ✔ **The Farrington Inn**—Friendly, family-run rooms in Allston that can even beat hostel prices. Good for families and groups.

---

style; some have private bathrooms; some have kitchenettes. There's a bit of everything, and with some advance notice, they can accommodate just about anyone.

All prices include free parking (!), unlimited local phone calls (!!), and a continental breakfast featuring "fantastic muffins." Plus the friendliest, most helpful service you could possibly want. It's all near BU, right on the "B" branch of the Green Line, too. This little-known sidestreet can be tricky, though, so ask for exact directions.

Irish Embassy Hostel

- 232 Friend St., Boston, MA 02114; (617) 973-4841

If the last thing you want to deal with after a day or two of sightseeing is a night out, this place has the answer: It brings the entertainment to you. The Irish Embassy Pub (see the listing under "Entertainment—Music") has opened up a 48-bed hostel upstairs, and has been filling the place ever since.

And why not? The charge is just $15 a night, no membership is required, and there's no fee for linens. (This hostelry is not affiliated with the AYH network.) Live bands at the atmospheric pub, playing four nights a week, are free to all guests. There's even one private room available, also $15 per person, although naturally it's difficult to get. Otherwise, you'll be in a six-to-eight-bed room, where many of your companions will likely be Irish, among the world's friendliest folks (manager Orlaith Noonan lends credence to the notion).

The hostel is air-conditioned throughout, with a kitchen, laundry facilities, and a TV room. If you are interested in painting the town red, you're a few minutes' walk from Quincy Market, the North End, and Beacon Hill.

RESTAURANT APPENDIX

AMERICAN

Arbuckle's
Bagel Depot
Bartley's Burger Cottage
Biltmore Cafe
Buff's Pub
Cafe Troy
Callahan's Steak and Seafood
Chadwick's
Charlie's Kitchen
Concept Cafe
Crossroads Ale House
Dee Dee's Lounge
Ebenezer's
11th Chapter Saloon
Finian's
Fuddruckers

George's on Washington Street
Halfway Cafe
Joe and Nemo
John Harvard's Brew House
Kelly's Roast Beef
Miracle of Science
Mt. Vernon Restaurant
New Bridge Cafe
Nick's Beef and Beer House
Nick's Ice Cream
Remington's
Riley's Roast Beef
The Sports Depot
Thorntons Fenway Grille
Tim's Bar & Grill
Wing It

ASIAN

Angkor Wat
King & I
Mr. Sushi
Pho Hoa
Pho Pasteur
Poppa & Goose

Quan Ngu Binh
Rama Thai
Sai Gon
Sapporo Ramen
V. Majestic

CAFETERIAS

Bill & Don's Cafe
Cafe de Paris
Jim's Deli and Restaurant
Kingston Deli and Grill
Mal's New York Style Delicatessen
Manhattan Sammy's Delicatessen

Max's Deli Café
New York Deli & Grill
Paramount Restaurant & Deli
Sandwich Works
The Ultimate Bagel Company

CARIBBEAN/SOUTH AMERICAN

Cafe Brazil
El Oriental De Cuba
El Rancho

Izzy's Restaurant and Sub Shop
Maryam's Famous Cuisine

CHINESE

Buddha's Delight
Dong Khanh Restaurant
Eldo Tea House
Hsin Hsin Chinese Noodle Restaurant

Mary Chung Restaurant
Peking Cuisine
People's Cafeteria
Stars Ocean Chinese Seafood

COFFEEHOUSES

Cafe Liberty
Coffee Cantata

Sound Bites

DELIS

Deli Haus
KJ's Deli
Mal's New York Style Delicatessen
Manhattan Sammy's Delicatessen

Max's Deli Café
New York Deli & Grill
S & S Restaurant
Why Not

DINERS

Andros Diner
Arlington Restaurant and Diner
Arsenal Diner
Blue Diner
Charlie's Sandwich Shoppe
Dolly's Late Night Restaurant
Ethel and Andy's Sandwich Shop
Family Restaurant
50's Diner
Henry's Diner
Joanie's Kitchen

L' Street Diner
New Yorker Diner
Olympian Diner
Pat's Diner
Pig 'n Whistle Diner
Popover's Restaurant
The Rosebud Diner
S and S Beale St. Diner
Tasty Sandwich Shop
Town Diner

EUROPEAN

Amrhein's Restaurant
Cafe Le Royal
Cafe Troyka
Iruña

Le Grand Café
Loaf & Ladle
Neighborhood Restaurant and
  Bakery

EVERYTHING

Centre St. Cafe
Christopher's
Geoffrey's Cafe Bar
George's on Washington Street
Grendel's Restaurant and Bar
Harvard Gardens
Johnny D's Uptown Restaurant &
  Music Club
Matt Garrett's

Our House
Our House East
The Plough and Stars
Pour House Restaurant
S & S Restaurant
Sazarac Grove
Soleil
Sunset Grill

INDIAN

Indian Globe
Indian Samraat

India Quality

IRISH/PUBS

Corrib Pub
Crossroads Ale House
Doyle's
Dunn-Gaherin's Pub
Finian's

Galvin's Harp & Bard
Green Briar Restaurant and Pub
Mt. Vernon Restaurant
O'Sullivan's Pub
The Sports Depot

ITALIAN

Anchovies
Antonio's Cucina Italiana
Artú
Baldini's
Cafe Fiorella
Caffe Marino
Comella's
Imperial Restaurant
The Italian Express
Italian Food Shoppe
Jeveli's Restaurant

La Famiglia
Marcella's
Mike's Restaurant
The Old Spaghetti Factory
Pleasant Cafe & Restaurant
Rustica
Sorrento's Italian Gourmet
Spuntini
Trattoria Il Panino
Verona Restaurant

MEDITERRANEAN

Ali Baba Restaurant
Andros Diner
Angora Coffee Shop
Asmara Ethiopian Restaurant
Cafe Jaffa
Corner Restaurant
Demo's Restaurant
El Greco
Family Restaurant
Fraser's on the Avenue
Fresco's Cafe and Grille
Kenmore Cafe
King Tut Coffee Shop
Mass Cafe

Middle East Restaurant and Cafe
Moby Dick of Boston
Moody's Falafal Palace
Niko's Restaurant
The Oasis Grille
Pars Café
Phoenicia
Rainbow Rollers Cafe
Rami's
Sabra
The Skewers
Steve's Authentic Greek Cuisine
Sultan's Kitchen

MEXICAN

Acapulco Restaurant
Armadillo Cafe
Big Burrito
Boca Grande
Border Cafe
El Rancho
Fajitas & 'Ritas

Iguana Cantina
Picante Mexican Grill
Pour House Restaurant
Rudy's Cafe
Sweetwater Cafe
Tacos El Charro
Third and Charles Bar and Grill

PIZZA

Angora Coffee Shop
Baldini's
Bluestone Bistro
Cafe Fiorella
Imperial Restaurant
Lynwood Cafe
Mike's Restaurant
Pleasant Cafe & Restaurant

Rustica
Santarpio's
Sazarac Grove
Sorrento's Italian Gourmet
Stromboli's
Town Spa
Venice Cafe

SEAFOOD

Andros Diner
Angkor Wat
Arthur's Seafood

Boston Sail Loft
Callahan's Steak and Seafood
Dixie Kitchen

SEAFOOD (continued)

Jimbo's Fish Shanty
Morse Fish Company
No Name Restaurant

Pugsley's
Tony's Clam Shop
Water View Restaurant

SOUTHERN/TEX-MEX

Armadillo Cafe
Bob the Chef's
Border Cafe
Cambridge Deli and Grill
Dixie Kitchen
Iguana Cantina
Jake & Earl's Dixie B-B-Q
La Rotisserie

Ma Dixon's Resaurant
Pour House Restaurant
Rudy's Cafe
Sweetwater Cafe
Third and Charles Bar and Grill
Tim's Bar & Grill
Wing It

UPSCALE

Blossoms
Davio's Riviera Café
"Dinner at the Mitton House"
Fraser's on the Avenue
Le Café at Maison Robert
Marcella's
Parish Cafe and Bar

Phoenicia
Poppa & Goose
Rustica
Sazarac Grove
Serendipity 3
Soleil
Vicki Lee Boyajian

INDEX

309

What? Mr. C left you out?
Missed your favorite cheap spot?

Mr. Cheap® tries to be everywhere, but hey—it's a big city. If you've got a bargain-priced shop, restaurant, hotel, or entertainment activity (or if there's one you just enjoy), send it in for the next edition of *Mr. Cheap's® Boston*!

CHAPTER HEADING: _____

NAME OF BUSINESS/ORGANIZATION:

_____

ADDRESS: _____

_____

PHONE: _____

WHAT'S GREAT ABOUT IT: _____

_____

_____

_____

_____

YOUR NAME: _____

ADDRESS: _____

_____

Clip this page out and send it to:

Mr. Cheap®
c/o Adams Media Corporation
260 Center Street
Holbrook, MA 02343

Thanks, fellow Cheapsters!

Mr.C

Other Mr. Cheap's titles available

Mr. Cheap's Atlanta
1-55850-292-0, $9.95

Mr. Cheap's Chicago
1-55850-291-2, $9.95

Mr. Cheap's New York
1-55850-256-4, $9.95

Mr. Cheap's San Francisco
1-55850-388-9, $8.95

Mr. Cheap's Seattle
1-55850-445-1, $9.95

Mr. Cheap's Washington DC
1-55850-415-X, 9.95

Available Wherever Books Are Sold

If you cannot find these titles at your favorite retail outlet, you may order them directly from the publisher. BY PHONE: Call 1-800-872-5627 (in Massachusetts 781-767-8100). We accept Visa, Mastercard, and American Express. $4.95 will be added to your total order for shipping and handling. BY MAIL: Write out the full titles of the books you'd like to order and send payment, including $4.95 for shipping and handling, to: Adams Media Corporation, 260 Center Street, Holbrook, MA 02343. 30-day money-back guarantee.